COWBOY
ACTION SHOOTING
GEAR · GUNS · TACTICS

Kevin Michalowski

©2005 KP Books

Published by

kp books
An Imprint of F+W Publications

700 East State Street • Iola, WI 54990-0001
715-445-2214 • 888-457-2873

Our toll-free number to place an order or obtain
a free catalog is (800) 258-0929.

All rights reserved. No portion of this publication may be reproduced
or transmitted in any form or by any means, electronic or mechanical,
including photocopy, recording, or any information storage and retrieval system,
without permission in writing from the publisher, except by a reviewer who may quote
brief passages in a critical article or review to be printed in a magazine or newspaper,
or electronically transmitted on radio, television, or the Internet.

Library of Congress Catalog Number: 2004098431

ISBN: 0-89689-140-2

Designed by Patsy Howell
Edited by Kevin Michalowski

Printed in the United States of America

Contents

Acknowledgments 4

Introduction 5

Chapter 1
No Time Like the Present: Getting Started is Easy 6
by M.D. Johnson

Chapter 2
Dressing the Part 14
by Michael J. Guli and Sharon Moore

Chapter 3
Let's Talk Leather 22
by M.D. Johnson

Chapter 4
Call it Custom and the Sky's the Limit 30
by M.D. Johnson

Chapter 5
The Cutting Edge of Cowboy Shooting 38
by M.D. Johnson

Chapter 6
What'll it be Pilgrim? Black Powder or Smokeless? 44
by John Taffin

Chapter 7
Reloading for Cowboy Action Shooting 52
by John Taffin

Chapter 8
The First Shoot: A New Club Takes Shape 62
by Doc Bonecutter

Catalog Listings 67

SASS-Affiliated Clubs 267

Acknowledgments

This book would never have happened without the incredible paradox
that is the Single Action Shooting Society. I say paradox
because I consider SASS a group of forward-thinking historians
and the movement SASS created has spawned a
brand new business arena in all things old-fashioned.
The national group and the individual clubs all went
out of their way to help others learn about their sport.

The writers, gun companies and ammunition manufacturers
also deserve some credit in the creation of this book.
Thanks to all those who submitted information in a timely manner.

Finally, F+W Publications' book designer Patsy Howell
went above and beyond all expectations to make this book
better than the rest of us ever imagined it could be.
Her initiative and motivation ensured
that this project would rise above the ordinary.

Introduction

In the film *Little Big Man* Dustin Hoffman's character says of his days spent
with the Cheyenne, "I wasn't playin' Indian; I was LIVING Indian."
That sums up the joy of cowboy action shooting.
The romantic notion of the Wild West has a pull many Americans
will never escape. There is something about the lifestyle,
the ideals and the sights, sounds and smells of the Old West
that keeps the dusty cowtowns alive in our memory.
As a cowboy action shooter, you don't just get to play cowboy
you get to—however briefly—live it, from your hat to your boots.

Our intention with this book is to guide you into the sport.
Ours is not the last word; far from it. Consider this book
to be St. Louis on your journey west. In St. Louis
you learned all about what you would need on your trip.
You picked up some supplies, got some sage advice from those
who had been there before and you headed out.
Along the way, you made adjustments to your rig,
learned the finer points and established
your own style in a wide-open frontier.

So there ya got it. Start here. Listen to those who know.
Do some shopping and get ready to join ranks of those
who are not just playin' cowboy, they are livin' it.

Good shooting,

Kev

Kevin Michalowski
editor

Photo courtesy Rockford Regulators

Photo courtesy Coyote Valley Regulators

Photo courtesy Coyote Valley Regulators

Photo courtesy Illinois River City Regulators and Chillicothe Sportsmen's Club

Chapter 1

No Time Like the Present

Getting Started is Easy

By M.D. Johnson

Let's be honest here. At one time or another while watching *High Plains Drifter*, *The Shoot-out at the O.K. Corral*, or your 100th episode of *Gunsmoke*, the thought ran through your mind that it would be, well, kind of neat to be the mysterious stranger, Wyatt Earp, or Marshall Dillon, now wouldn't it? Revolvers blazing. Round after round cycling through that old reliable lever-action. A shotgun blast – BLAM! – in a back alley that takes down another evil villain.

Exciting, eh? Well, you didn't have to live in the mid-1800s in order to experience first-hand the thrill of the quick draw, the smell of burnt powder and the dust of

SASS members often set up at trade and sports shows. This is a great place to meet people and talk about joining a club. Seasoned shooters will be able to tell you all you need to know about getting started.

The Gun Digest® Book of Cowboy Action Shooting

the Old West, thanks to the Single Action Shooting Society (SASS). But what you may not know at this point is how you get started along that dusty trail that is cowboy action shooting (CAS) and the CAS lifestyle. Who can be involved? Where do I get my guns? What guns do I need? Do I need to be a terrific shot in order to compete? Can my wife and family come along? Great questions, and thanks in large part to a fine, upstand'n gentleman named Johnny Colt, we're going to show you just how you – and your family, of course – can get started in one of the fastest-growing shooting sports in the United States and around the world.

When he's not wearing spurs and his six-shooters, Johnny Colt goes by the name of John Semm. Today, he and his ladyfriend, Susan – a.k.a. Kitty Colt – live in northwestern Oregon, where he's owned and operated his Shooter's Service Center for the past 15 years. In addition to supplying exceptional gunsmithing services to the local shooting public, Semm also – surprise! – runs SASS Mercantile #76, at which he provides period clothing and accessories, as well as a long line of firearms and ammunition to the Pacific Northwest's ever-growing contingent of cowboy action shooters.

A tall man who looks every bit the respected sheriff or "Only shoot 'em if they need shoot'n" gunfighter, Semm – henceforth known as Johnny Colt, or simply, Colt – is certainly no slouch in terms of his own shooting accomplishments since becoming a SASS member back in the early 1990s.

"I've been the two-time Northwest regional champion, and have been the Oregon state champion. I've been Summer Range champion, and won in excess of 150 major matches in my career. I'm one of the top shooters here in the Pacific Northwest, and usually finish high in the Winter Range and End of Trail matches, the End of Trail being the world championship," said Colt, who also serves as the territorial governor, or liaison between SASS and the local organization, for his home club, the Oregon Cowboys.

His lady counterpart, Kitty, more than holds her own when it comes to the competitive shooting portion of the Wild West experience, with more than one Northwest Regional Ladies Championships to her credit. With shooting skills like that, it's not surprising that Johnny Colt came a'courting!

But back to getting started. If all this shooting and dressing the part has got you interested in cowboy action shooting, the first thing Colt suggests you do is to check out the SASS Web site at www.sassnet.com. Prospective new members can complete and submit their application online, or you can simply do it the old-fashioned way by calling 1-877-411-SASS, and asking the kind individual on the other end to send you the necessary paperwork via the United States Postal Service.

When you send your membership information into the SASS directors, you're going to be asked to supply an alias. Yes, I said an alias, or by definition, an assumed name. This will be your SASS name, the handle by which you will forever be known among your cowboy action shooting brothers and sisters. Your alias can be a fictional western character like Desert Slim or Tequila Rose. Or it can relate to an old-time profession such as Barkeep Billy or Dance Hall Doris. Firearms, too, lend themselves to aliases like my good friend's

To the winner goes the spoils. You won't win a buckle like this on your first trip to a big shooting match, but you will have a whole lot of fun.

moniker, Lefty Winchester, or even Semm's Johnny Colt.

Regardless of its origin, your alias is unique to you. It describes you and the western image you hope to portray in but a word or two. So give your new handle some thought.

But why an alias? Why not just go by your given name?

"The alias allows you to live part of the persona of the Old West," says Colt. "Many of the people who came to the West did so from the East. Some were bank robbers and the like, and many didn't want to bring their backgrounds West, thus the reason behind many of the aliases that were used back then. With SASS, we're just trying to relive the Old West and trying to get that flavor. Everyone has an alias in the organization."

Still, there's another reason why each SASS member participates under an alias.

"An alias," says Colt, "puts everyone on the same level. This is fantasy. It's make-believe, but the emphasis is always, always on safety. You could have some famous person, maybe some actor, and they'd have a persona or an alias, and if you look down the roster of names at any event, you'd never know that this was some celebrity. It puts everyone at ease and helps folks on a level playing field, so to speak. We're all friends. We're all shooting companions. And it puts everyone on the same level."

This level playing field, Colt stresses, certainly does include the ladies. "Thirty-five percent of the members are women," he claims. "It's the largest percentage of female participants in any of the shooting sports that I know of. A lot of women, even if they're not shooters, participate.

All right. So you've decided on an alias, submitted your paperwork, and in return, received all of your information from SASS headquarters. Congratulations, pardner! You're a full-fledged member! But wait. Isn't there the little issue of firearms? And what if you're not of the same caliber – no pun intended – as a Matt Dillon or Annie Oakley when it comes to marksmanship and gun smarts? Too, there's the competition. Second-guessing yourself now as to how you'll hold up in the shooting contests? Well, hold on there.

"What's really nice about this sport is this," assures Colt. "If you're a competitive person, that competition is there for you. If you want to come out and dress up and live the Old West, that's there. If you just have some friends and you want to compete amongst yourselves, that's there, too. We don't discourage participation in any form. We want you to come out and enjoy yourself.

"But it also is a shooting sport and a shooting competition. We give out prizes and awards and ribbons. One of the things that's done at some of the major matches is that the awards are given out according to place, but the prizes are given out by a drawing. Rather, someone may win a

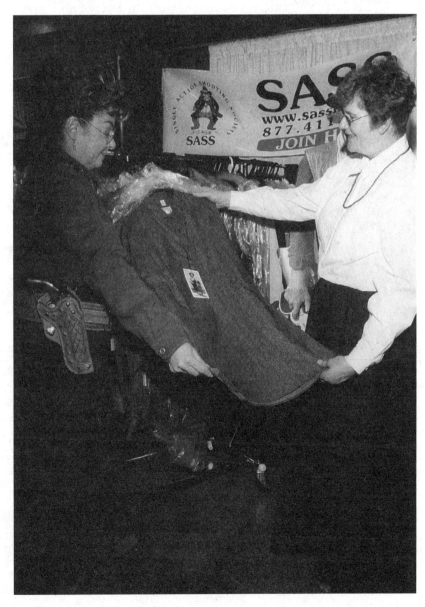

Choosing your outfit is just part of the fun when you join SASS. The clothing requirements are not as restrictive as you might think.

Sharps rifle worth $2,000, and they may have come in dead last. This encourages people, no matter what their shooting skill, and provides something for everyone."

So there's the competition aspect, but what about the educational elements? Well, Colt addresses that point using his home club, Portland's Tri-County Gun Club, as a first-rate example.

"We (Tri-County Gun Club) start with a safety orientation class," says Colt. "You go through the orientation class to become a shooter, if you've decided to become a shooter. If you haven't decided, then we encourage you to come out and watch some of our matches. We'll introduce you to the match director, and we'll put you with someone who can explain what's going on. Or you can wander from stage to stage and ask questions. If you go up to anyone at a Cowboy Match and ask a question, I can guarantee that these folks will go out of their way to answer that to the best of their ability. They'll make you feel comfortable there, too."

Getting Started – The Equipment

With your membership, you'll receive a current copy of the SASS Shooters Handbook. Here, you're going to find information pertaining to the various shooting events, as well as the rules and regulations that keep these events safe, enjoyable, and aligned with the western theme that is cowboy action shooting.

Within the pages of the Handbook, you'll find the specifics dealing with the various types of firearms which are and aren't permitted by SASS rules. Details such as calibers, barrel lengths, modifications, sights, accessories, and other things are discussed for each of the firearms used in competition – rifles, pistols, and

(left) Once you're all duded up all you need are some guns and you can compete. (right) Just pinning on a tin star doesn't make you a sheriff. But joining SASS does get you a badge with your own number.

shotguns. Understandably, these rules are in place in order to ensure Colt's aforementioned level playing field, and to make certain that no shooter holds an unfair advantage over another based solely on equipment alone.

Firearms

"You're going to need a handgun, a pistol-caliber rifle, and a shotgun," says Colt. "You can share equipment. In fact, we have several couples who share equipment. So if you had those firearms, we'd place you in the posse – the group of shooters – so that you could comfortably and easily share those firearms."

The SASS Handbook discusses the following firearms:

Handguns – Single-action revolvers of .32 caliber or larger. Various categories recognize handgun variations to include blackpowder, blackpowder cartridge, and conversion guns. Pistol ammunition must have a muzzle velocity less than 1,000 feet per second (fps). Examples include the Colt New Frontier, the Ruger Blackhawk, and the Ruger Single Six.

Rifles – Lever-or slide- (pump) action rifles or carbines manufactured between 1860 and 1899 – or a period reproduction thereof – with a tubular magazine and exposed hammer. Rifle must be a centerfire firearm of a pistol caliber, .25-20 or larger. Sights to include iron (open) sights or tang-mounted peep sights, and barrels to be a minimum of 16 inches. Popular rifles include Marlins, Winchester Models '92 and '94, and Henrys. Muzzle velocity for rifle ammunition is limited to 1,400 fps.

Shotguns – Side-by-side or single-shots, with or without exposed hammers, are permitted, as are tube-fed pump or lever-action (exposed hammers only) shotguns in 20- to 10-gauge. Shotguns must be typical of the period from approximately 1860 through 1899. The tried-and-true Winchester Model '97 is perhaps the most commonly seen; however, doubles such as the Stoeger Coach Gun are also popular. Shotgun ammunition is limited to standard-velocity rounds shooting #4 lead – no steel or coated – shot only.

Understandably, one of the questions you newcomers are going to have regarding firearms concerns the prices, not only of one firearm but of three or perhaps even four. Fortunately, there are ways to make these firearm purchases much less traumatic. One, as Colt suggests, is to share firearms with members of your posse as you yourself purchase your own guns one by one, thus spreading the expenditure out over a period of time. Secondly, and while new is certainly nice, it isn't the only option available to you, the gun buyer.

"You can shop at gun shows," says Colt, "and you can look for used firearms. You should be able to find something like a used Ruger Blackhawk in the $250 area. You would need two of those. You can get yourself, say, a Marlin lever-action rifle, and you can get something like that in the $250

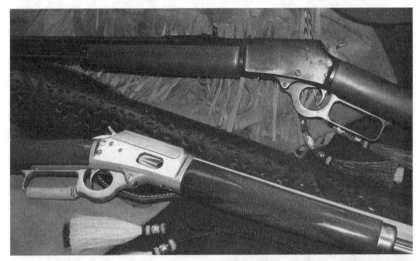

(top) Either of these rifles will work fine. Both are chambered for handgun calibers and are equipped with traditional sights. (bottom) A revolver for use in SASS must be a single-action with fixed sights. Nothing complicated here.

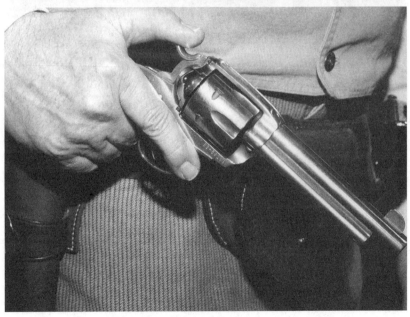

(top) Your leather can be fancy or plain. Either way, get tough functional gear that will put up with wear and tear. (bottom) A simple side-by-side double makes a great cowboy gun. There are plenty to choose from.

to $300 range. If you went up to $375, that would get you a brand new rifle. As for the double barrel shotguns, something like the Stoeger Coach Guns, you can get those brand new for right around $300."

"So if you budget and shop wisely," he continues, "it's not too expensive. There is a cost there, of course. You can also come out to the matches. There's always someone upgrading, and there's always used equipment coming on the market."

Dressing The Part

For many SASS members, the attraction is as much in the 'dressing up' as it is in the shooting events. At matches from the East Coast to the Pacific Northwest, you'll see it all in terms of clothing – dusters, sombreros, vests, chaps, suspenders, spurs, lassos, bullwhips, corsets, petticoats, and bloomers. There are sunbonnets on the ladies, and big brass belt buckles on guys and gals alike. Bandoleers, holsters – you name it, and it's bound to be on display at any cowboy action shooting outing. And while to some all this "getting gussied up" might seem a bit extreme, it is, as Colt mentions, all a very important part of creating the western aura – that born-again persona – that lies at the heart of the SASS lifestyle.

But like firearms, the need for all this new-old finery might at first seem intimidating, particularly to the newcomer. Even the SASS Handbook, what with its ruling – "All shooters must be in costume, and we encourage invited guests and family also to be costumed" – may come across a bit hard-handed; however, rest assured, you with the Levis and the Molly Hatchet t-shirt. As Colt explains, there are some reasonably easy ways to outfit yourself in Old West garb without, that is, robbing the bank.

"Chances are," says Colt, "that you can go through your closet and find something to get started with, clothing-wise. If you had a round brimmed hat. If you had a denim shirt. We'd let you slide with a pair of Levis. Most people get some sort of lace-up boot…a logger-type boot. We have people that wear these things."

He goes on. "When you start attending the larger matches, that's when you start acquiring your outfit. There are always people there selling clothes. At our club, for instance, once or twice a year, we'll have a swap meet where people will bring out their used clothes – clothing that's still very serviceable. It may not fit or whatever, so this type of gear is always cycling around. You can pick up a shirt for $5 or $10.

In our newsletter, we have a section for people who are looking to sell equipment – holsters and guns and clothing, stuff like that. Usually at a reduced price. More economical. People will usually bring stuff out to a match, too, and you can get good prices there."

Fun For The Family

Throughout the whole of Colt's explanation concerning the "how to get started" basics of cowboy action shooting, two common denominators constantly shine through – the organization's emphasis on safety, and their strong desire to promote and maintain SASS as a strongly family-oriented group of firearms and outdoor enthusiasts.

"Our main emphasis is safety," says Colt. "That's the main reason why I started this safety orientation part in our Tri-County Gun Club. I wanted to make sure that the people understand the rules and regulations of cowboy action shooting, and that they were going to be safe with their firearms."

"We've had people come out to our club," he continues, "who have never fired their gun before. They've just taken it out of the box for the very first time. We really have to help these people along. We want to get them started the safe way. And the right way."

And as for the family involvement? Colt puts it very simply, yet very directly.

"The family atmosphere is really pushed at SASS events," says Colt. "We try to push that all of the events involve the family. There's no exclusion. We encourage families to bring the kids out. We provide safety equipment so that the kids may participate. Now, the kids have to be over 12 to shoot and they have to be a SASS member, but we want them to come out. We encourage them to bring their friends. A lot of people bring their relatives because it's like a big celebration. There are food vendors, clothing ventures. There's something for everyone, and I think these events help to pull the family together."

List of required items:

- Two single-action revolvers, .32 caliber or larger.
- One period-specific shotgun, 20-, 12- or 10-gauge. Double barrel shotguns may not have automatic ejectors.
- One period-specific rifle. The rifle must be made in a pistol caliber of .25-20 or larger and must be either a lever-action or a slide-action with an exposed hammer.

Revolvers must be carried in holsters and competitors must be dressed in appropriate period-style dress.

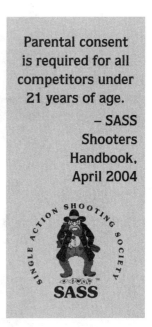

Parental consent is required for all competitors under 21 years of age.
– SASS Shooters Handbook, April 2004

Photo courtesy River Junction Shootist Society

Photo courtesy Okeechobee Marshals

Photo courtesy Dry Gulch Desperados

Photo courtesy Rocky Branch Rangers

Photo courtesy Dry Gulch Desperados

Dressing the Part

Chapter 2

Dressing the Part

By Michael J. Guli and Sharon Moore

So you've got a great alias and a new gun cart full of treasures – you're ready to attend your first SASS shoot, right? Almost, pardner! One of the unique aspects of cowboy action shooting is the fun requirement that all participants be in costume, not only on the firing line, but also for all match events, award ceremonies, dinners, and dances. This encourages the Old West atmosphere that SASS is keeping alive.

Don't let the costuming aspect of this sport keep you awake at night. Depending on your interest level, planning your outfit can be an instant or all-consuming affair. We have found that many shooters just getting into this sport prefer to dress "off the rack" for their first few events, as they start to develop their own style and persona. Feel free to explore several different looks – after all, you probably don't wear the exact same thing every day in real life, do you? What you wear on the firing line will need to withstand the wear

Photo courtesy Illinois River City Regulators and Chillicothe Sportsman's Club

> The best way to develop a costume is to first decide on a character or profession you wish to portray.
> – SASS Shooters Handbook, April 2004

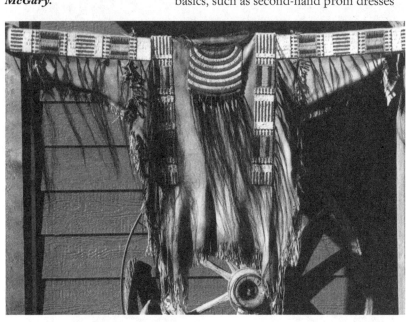

Hand-beaded, brain-tanned leather replica of Short Bull's war shirt made for sculptor Dave McGary.

and tear of the job, while the outfit you select for the banquet will more likely be your "Sunday best."

It's not required that you spend many hours and dollars preparing just the right look. We admire the folks who go so far as to be sure that the underwear they are wearing is historically correct, and even their pocket change – they give us all something to work towards, but the majority of shooters spend far more attention and money on their guns than on their clothes!

Starting simply is never wrong. There are scores of companies that offer great, historically correct or just historically-inspired clothing and accessories. A scan through the *Cowboy Chronicle* or other western publications will give you lots of options. At main shoots across the country, you will find dozens of eager-to-help vendors with rack upon rack of ready-made clothing. There are also quite a few who will build you a one-of-a-kind piece to help you create that unique outfit that others will envy. Modern western-wear stores can help with some pieces and parts, but you will need to be selective and keep in mind a few pointers. For example, jeans with zippers and belt loops hadn't been invented yet in the 1800s. However, if you are trying to build a costume reminiscent of the B-Western movie era, you can get away with such things. Thrift stores can supply great basics, such as second-hand prom dresses that can be transformed into elegant Victorian ball gowns or flashy dance hall girl outfits. A general rule of thumb: The more historically accurate you want your outfit to be, the more likely you'll have to have it custom-made, to ensure the use of correct materials, proper fit, and the implementation of historic construction techniques. The joy of SASS is that there is room for all in this sport, both the "costume" participant, and the "museum-quality" re-enactor.

When planning your Old West outfit, you may find it helpful to study people who lived in that time and place. As westward expansion took place, there developed many new and different archetypes, born out of necessity and a need for freedom and individuality. All of these types had a unique way of expressing themselves through the clothing they wore. They were the people of the West, and they knew how to dress the part.

In the following paragraphs, several archetypes will be discussed, starting with the American Old West, and moving into the Silver Screen, "B-Western" genre. These are just a few brief descriptions of the many different characters that lived in this exciting time, and are based on research from books, museums, diaries, and portraits of the era. Entire books can and have been written on these archetypes, and we encourage you to delve in and take advantage of the many resources available in libraries and online when researching your attire. We will attempt to give "in general" advice, always staying aware that there were as many different styles of dress as there were individuals.

Historical Old West Archetypes

Native American Man – Native Americans were as diverse in dress as Europeans, but in general, the men wore buckskin leggings with a breechclout, low moccasins (sometimes with a leg wrap), and a fringed buckskin shirt. They did not wear pants until much later. If you are interested in the dress of a specific tribe, check your library or go online where you can find a wealth of information. We do make one strong suggestion – to better imitate the natural brain-tanned leather that the Native Americans would have used, be sure that the leather you choose is suede or rough-side out.

Native American Woman – While there were many variations in this category, Native American women often wore either a two- or three-skin fringed deerskin dress made of brain-tanned leather, decorated with their own tribe's particular style and color of beadwork. Sometimes the dress was belted, and worn with high lace-up moccasins, or low moccasins and leggings. Their hair was typically worn long, either loose or braided.

Vaquero – The Vaqueros were dashing horsemen descended from the knights of Spain, and were the first American cowboys. Their distinctive style would have included a short-waisted (often leather) jacket decorated with fancy stitching, scallops and silver conchos, and long fitted pants that buttoned fully up the outside of the leg. Important accessories would be a finger-woven sash, frilly white shirt, long white silk drawers, and a smart Vaquero-style hat.

Spanish Lady – A charming daytime outfit worn by Spanish ladies was made up of a calf-length skirt with a short-sleeved, scoop-necked white blouse. She could complete her look with black low-heeled slippers or moccasins, a tack belt or finger-woven sash, and a rebozo, the long, rectangular shawl, which she wore around her shoulders and with which she sometimes covered her head. However, if she had the means, she might also dress in the latest styles from back East.

Mountain Man – Much of our cowboy clothing influence can be credited to the Mountain Man. His attire was often a combination of European styles and adaptations of the clothing of the Native Americans with whom he interacted. Fringed buckskin shirts, coats and pants, wide leather or beaded belts, loose-fitted cloth shirts, moccasins and a wide-brimmed hat or wool cap complemented his attire. Animal fur hats would typically be worn only in winter for warmth. Again, please use rough-side-out leather.

Top: Hand-made deerskin Native American dress. (bottom) Michael J. Guli as a Mountain Man.

Military – There are many types of military styles that would be appropriate for SASS events. We will not attempt to cover this category, as there is an abundance of resources at libraries, museums, and online to cover this diverse category. If this is your passion, you will enjoy doing your homework on this topic.

Scout – A scout was usually an independent sort of man, often of Native American heritage or a former trapper who knew the land and its people well. As such, he would have the luxury of combining many styles of clothing influenced by his own background and history. For example, he might combine Native American leggings and breech clout or buckskin pants with a cloth shirt and military vest. Some of his accoutrements might include beaded leather pouches and medicine bags along with his cavalry binoculars and holster. Create a one-of-a-kind look if this character is someone you wish to represent.

Cowboy/Farmer/Ranch hand – When a fellow worked for a living on the tough prairies of the West, his garb would show it. Cloth pants with buttons for suspenders (called braces), a collarless shirt, work vest, and neckerchief are the basics you shouldn't be without, and pick your hat with special care. The modern cowboy hat with curled edges just wasn't around yet. Invest in a good quality fur felt hat that won't melt in the rain (plastic covers weren't needed!), and shape it to your own style, after studying the originals. Your hat could tell a lot

about you back then – your profession and where you lived, for example.

Pioneer/Rancher's wife – This can be a nice, simple starting point for ladies just getting into SASS. A basic calico dress or long skirt with high-necked blouse will give you an easy, comfortable outfit. When you are ready to get more authentic, pay closer attention to the fabrics and fit, use buttons instead of zippers, and add the correct accessories such as an apron, petticoats, sun bonnet, low-heeled lace-up boots and of course, a back-supporting, comfortable corset!

Historical Saloon Girl – Remember that not every girl working in the saloon and wearing feathers also worked upstairs! Some of these ladies served drinks, danced for pay, sang or played piano, and never supplemented their income with other entertainments. Of course they wore corsets, but they usually covered them up with a fitted jacket or sleeveless bodice, and often a shorter skirt. Add some feathers and fluff, gloves and fun stockings, and top it off with some pretty jewelry and a pretty smile!

Ranch Owner/Townsman/Lawman/Dandy – You will find many nice selections of clothing for this category from the vendors at SASS events. We would encourage you, however, to avoid the "cookie-cutter" look. Not every man wore a black frock coat – there were grays, browns, plaids, and stripes, as well. Look at the black and white old photos, and select a unique shirt, pants, and vest. Get a good quality hat, and have it suit your character. Don't forget accessories such as gloves, spats, pocket watch, walking stick and necktie, too!

Townswoman – The banker's wife, the milliner, the seamstress, the parson's wife – almost every woman would benefit from developing at least one "town" outfit.

Left: Michael J. Guli as an 1875 Scout. (right) Sharon Moore as an 1875 Townswoman in Bustled Walking Dress.

There is a flattering silhouette for every figure in the Victorian era. A high-necked, long-sleeved blouse paired with a nicely-fitted jacket and long skirt will give you a good look that you can accessorize to your heart's desire. Add a stylish hat, lace jabot at the neck, brooch and jewelry, and don't forget your gloves, reticule (Victorian purse), and parasol, of course! The options are endless, and this ensemble outfit can be very versatile to give you more than one look from your purchase.

Wild West Shows – There were many touring shows in the late 1800s and early 1900s, and the costumes worn had their own creative style. For men, this often meant a fancy fringed, beaded buckskin coat, cloth or buckskin pants, high boots, beaded gauntlet gloves, and a large-brimmed hat. For the ladies, take a leather or sturdy fabric calf-length skirt or split riding skirt, add fringe, beads, or studs, top with a fitted jacket for late 1800s or wide-sleeved blouse with bolero vest for turn-of-the-century, and you have the makings of a distinctive look. Ladies' accessories could include a wide-brimmed hat, large neckerchief, gauntlets or cuffs, wide leather cowgirl belt, and gaiters to cover your boots. The attire of these performers influenced a "buckskin revival" in fashion at this time, and if you ever have the privilege of studying original pieces in museums, you will indeed have found a treasure!

B-Western/Silver Screen

This is a great category, with lots of the old movies available now on DVD for home research. Pop the corn, make some sketches, and get creative!

Hero – Pick your favorite, and then do your best to be true to the character. Shane, The Lone Ranger, Roy Rogers, Gene Autry, a sheriff – these all make wonderful role models for kids and grownups alike. Pay attention to the low-slung holsters, striped pants and shirts, piping, lots of fringe, and lace-up fronts. Belt loops and zippers are welcome here!

Sidekick – Study what it is that set apart your character, from headwear to footwear, and don't forget to rehearse their accent and way of speaking. Goofy and hokey is OK for this role.

Bad Guy – Black shirt or vest, day-old stubble, mean scowl, and attitude are what will set this look apart!

B-Western Cowgirl – Dale Evans, here we come! Get out your fringe, little hats, and short skirts if you like, or go with the more practical style of split riding skirt with matching piped blouse. Another look would be the plaid shirt, round-toed cowboy boots, and old-style jeans that have high-water, big cuffs on the bottom. And don't forget the Hollywood Annie Oakley look with pigtails and fringe everywhere!

B-Western Homesteader – Short sleeves and zippers are fine here, and forget the corset! Take a gingham or calico long

Al Huffman is a perfect Buffalo Bill.

prairie dress, add bias-tape trim, a torpedo bra, and wear your hair down or pulled up on the sides into 1940s rolls with a few ribbons. Attention to detail is what will make or break this outfit – you must make it tackily distinctive from a true attempt at a Victorian day dress.

B-Western Saloon Girl – This is a fun category where some SASS ladies "let it (almost) all hang out!" You can create your own Hollywood look easily by shortening a second-hand prom gown and hooking up the side, and adding gloves, boa, hair feathers, and garters. Sequins and makeup are quite acceptable with this look, and be sure to complete your getup with the right sassy attitude!

B-Western Indian Princess – What comes to mind? Of course, either a stark-white, elaborately fringed and beaded buckskin dress, or else that little mini-skirted look, for the all-too-willing and of course beautiful young thing of an Indian maiden. Forget the history books – add a headband and feather, high-laceup moccasins, and don't worry about the smooth side of the leather showing. Even fake leather with fat fringe will do for this category. Paint your face and have fun!

Once you have selected your character, remember that a little research goes a long way. However, keep in mind that Hollywood is Hollywood, and is rarely historically correct, and sculptors and painters of the past sometimes took "artistic license" with their representations, too. Photographs and diaries can often provide marvelous information when building an outfit. Try to find what it is about the person in the photograph you are studying

Left: Michael J. Guli in action as a Desperado. (right) An early 1900s Cowgirl outfit.

20   Dressing the Part

that "makes" their look. Accessories? The hang of their clothes? The style of their hat can be a very important clue. How about the way they wear their hair? These details are very often neglected, but all fun things to consider when dressing your part.

The level of authenticity you wish to attain will play a large part in developing your costume. An average cowboy or B-Western outfit will probably take less effort to build than say, a beaded, brain-tanned Native American getup or an 1876 Military uniform. And hand-in-hand, the size of your budget is usually a factor in how authentic you can be. Some folks out there can create their own costumes from scratch, but many have to rely on the availability and skill of others. Most importantly, the idea is to have a good time with this aspect of SASS, and not to get caught up in a cut-throat competitive attitude. We all have to start somewhere, so put on your duds, whatever they are, and just continue to enhance or add to your outfit as your knowledge, desire, and budget allow.

Michael J. Guli (Mad Mountain Mike, SASS Life Member #4385) and Sharon Moore (Miss Tabitha, SASS #26972) own and operate River Crossing, Inc., a company that specializes in historic presentations and period clothing, and have 41 years of combined experience in research and re-enactment. Mike's work has been featured in museums, movies, galleries and shops across the country, Europe and Japan, while Sharon has focused on historic dance and fashion. Their partnership enables them to cover many eras and topics, ranging from the Revolutionary War to modern day. Mike & Sharon enjoy presenting history in an entertaining, as well as, educational style.

River Crossing develops new programs each year, and has the flexibility to create an outfit or presentation tailored for your specific needs. For booking information, to answer questions about your outfit, or to create a custom garment for you, please visit their Web site at www.rivercrossinginc.com, call at 970-221-2992 or 970-482-1850, or e-mail at rivercrossing@lycos.com.

> Shooters must remain in costume at all match events: dinners, award ceremonies, dances, etceteras.
> – SASS Shooters Handbook, April 2004

Photo courtesy Rocky Branch Rangers

Photo courtesy Kanawha Valley Regulators

Photo courtesy Windy Gap Regulators

Photo courtesy River Junction Shootist Society

Photo courtesy Okeechobee Marshals

Photo courtesy Windy Gap Regulators

Photo courtesy Windy Gap Regulators

22   Let's Talk Leather

Chapter 3

Let's Talk Leather

By M.D. Johnson

A revolver without a holster is – well, it's like a hotdog without a bun. Translation? Well, that revolver without a holster is just plain out of place. Out of its place might be more like it. Guns belong in holsters. There's no better place to put them.

The holsters that carried the guns of the famous – and the infamous – were often themselves as well known as the men and women who wielded the weapons. Initials, insignia, and brands all adorned these stitched pieces of cowhide. Silver studs and buckles for those with a little bit of folding money, and sand-worn leather for those without. Regardless of your status, however, the facts – then and now – remained the same – if you had a six-shooter, you had a holster.

Dan Brown is a man who understands the value and importance of a holster. Together with his wife and partner, Shelley, Brown owns and operates Ted Blocker

This gunbelt is ready for action. The revolver here is actually the shooter's second gun, his first is hidden behind the cartridge pouch on the left. This simple rig is all that you need, but you might want more.

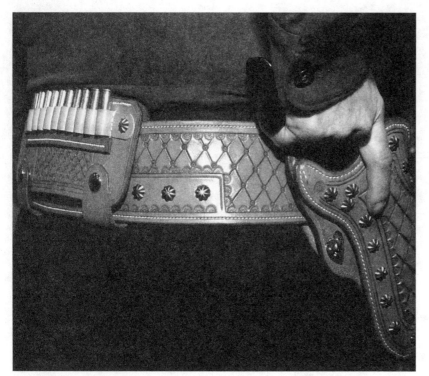

Notice how high the cartridges ride in these loops. That makes reloading just a bit faster. It's little touches like these that help SASS cowboys compete. Real cowboys would have pushed those rounds down deep to insure they never fell out by accident.

Holsters, Inc., in Tigard, Oregon, a company he purchased back in '99.

Brown began working with leather, and holsters in particular, in 1980 when he started as an employee of then 103-year-old George Lawrence Company in Portland. Eventually, said Brown, the company sold and moved out of state. Not wanting to change directions all too radically, this leatherman started his own company, where he created custom leather items, including holsters and belts. One day, Ted Blocker came a'calling, and Brown found himself an employee of the well-established Pacific Northwest holster maker. "Then in 1999," said Brown, "I got an offer that I just couldn't refuse, and ended up buying the company from Ted."

Today, and together with Shelley, who sets up and organizes the company's presence at a number of sportsman's shows along the West Coast, Brown designs and builds holsters, belts, and accessories for cops and cowboys alike. "Shelley and I really enjoy the cowboy action shooting," said Brown, with an obvious note of enthusiasm in his voice.

So it was with this background, both with leather *and* in the Cowboy Way, in mind that we at *The Gun Digest Book of Cowboy Action Shooting* took Brown away from his stitching, molding, and, yes, his Colt replicas and Model '97s, and asked him to sit a spell and talk about one of the things that he knows best – holsters.

Digest: Dan, explain the basic reason behind the existence of a holster.

Brown: A holster's purpose is to facilitate safe carry and accessibility of the gun. Other than that, you can't say a whole lot about it. Function and how they work is a whole 'nother ballgame, but the basic purpose of a holster is to carry your gun in a safe and accessible manner.

Digest: Where does a prospective cowboy shooter start in his or her researching a holster choice?

Brown: When you talk cowboy action shooting, you're talking period holsters. This would be Slim Jims, Double Loops, or variations of that. Or the B-movie style holsters. The old gunfighter styles. But there are people who like the B-movie style holsters, and that's fine, but those aren't great holsters for the competitive cowboy action shooter. And then you have to break that down, too. There's the competitive shooter, and then there's the fun shooter who's competitive. Which one do you want to be?

Digest: Is there a first step in the actual selection of a holster?

Brown: The first thing I tell people is to think long and hard about how much money they want to spend. I've seen it happen over and over. People will rush out and buy two holsters and a belt, just so they can start shooting. Our bottom line model is an Elmer Keith style, single-thick, for $62. Then you can buy a single-thick belt for $75.

What we do as holster people is try to explain to folks the options, and explain to them that they have to decide what (shooting) level they want to go in at. And the look that they want. In holsters, we have basic packages, but when it comes right down to it, your holster is only limited, as my son always said, by your imagination and your wallet. You just need to make sure that your holsters are well-made and going to hold up to the amount that you're doing. When you go out on the weekend and run 100 rounds through your revolvers, you're doing a lot of drawing and holstering. You need a good, stout product.

Digest: For the new buyer, is there one primary variable or characteristic he or she needs to be aware of?

Brown: The main thing you want to look for in a cowboy shooting holster is that the top lip is rolled out so your cylinder doesn't hang up. Depending on the style you're going to shoot – Gunfighter, Duelist, or Traditional – and then you have to decide whether you're going to shoot strong side or cross-draw.

Digest: That said, which particular models do you use, and why?

Brown: I use a combination of holsters myself. I use our Judgment Day and the Vindicator. I use the Judgment Day on the right side just because I like the style better. The Vindicator has the trigger guard area removed, so you can grab the frame and the front of the trigger guard with your left hand and place it in your right hand to shoot Traditional without having to change your grip.

Digest: What about the ladies, Dan? Does there exist a "ladies" holster and belt rig?

Brown: We make the Heartbreaker for the ladies. It's more lady-specific. My wife and Lusty Lill probably get the credit for that. What we found is that by dropping the holsters just a little bit, and putting in a metal shank, we're able to bend the (gun) grip out away from their body. This changes the angle of the draw a little bit. Given ladies' hips and their anatomy, this angle can be an asset. It makes it much easier to draw.

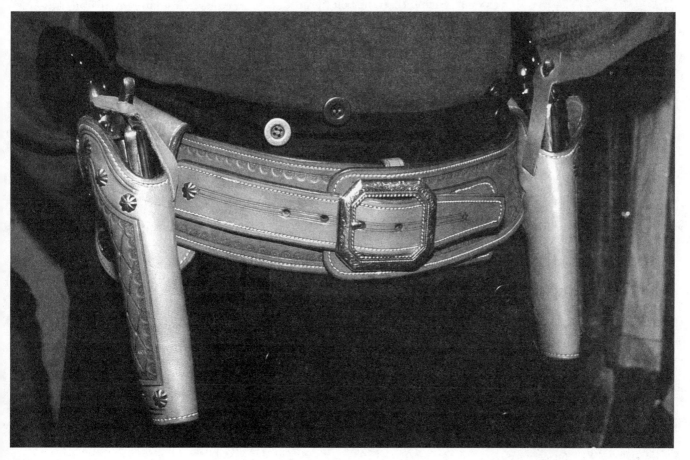

Wide and strong is the order of the day for a good double gun rig. A wimpy belt will fail quickly. Buy the best leather you can afford. Your guns deserve it.

Digest: A holster without a belt is like a six-gun without a holster. What are folks looking for in a gun belt?

Brown: Our belts are contoured, and we find that works real well for ladies and for guys. What that does is, if you have any hip at all, it eliminates the gap in the back of the belt. The belt then lays flatter on you. We have a tension device on our holsters where we actually run screws in underneath the belt, so once the holster is in position, we can cinch it down. It won't slide around on you. If you have your belt positioned right, your gun's going to come out smooth and the holster won't follow it.

Digest: Are holsters and belts a mix-and-match proposition; that is, should you buy a holster here and a belt there?

Brown: I've seen folks buy their holster here and their belt there, but for me, that's not the best way to go. I think they ought to be matched. But that's personal preference. If the belt fits and the belt loop's tight on the holster and they don't flop around on you, well…

Digest: Is there a mistake you see commonly made by folks shopping for their first leather rig?

Brown: One of the mistakes that people make when they're buying a rig is they buy it as if they were going to wear it down on their hips. Like you see in the westerns. But in cowboy action shooting, and in reality, you're wearing your holster a little bit higher. I'm a little short-bodied, and wearing a holster down on my hips – what that does is force me to draw clear up into my armpit to get my gun out of the holster.

By making a notch out of the front of the holster and dropping the holster two inches, I can just about draw the gun without breaking my elbow. Just using my wrist.

Digest: There are so many different makes and models of holsters and belts, even in terms of those made with the cowboy action shooter in mind. How can a buyer expose himself or herself to the biggest selection?

Brown: Find a state or regional match, or go to the convention if you're a SASS member. Or go to End of Trail. Any of the big shoots will have a number of holster makers there. Talk to the competitors. Ask them what they're using. You can walk around to the various makers and touch and feel, and actually see what the other shooters are wearing. I recommend that to everyone.

I went through three different sets of holsters before I came up with a combination I liked. I'm fortunate 'cause I have the luxury of being able to do that, but that's over a six-year period. But I've had a lot of people come to me at shows and say 'this is what we bought 'cause we had to have a holster right now.' And they're finding out that that holster just isn't doing the job.

Digest: Does the type of leather used to make the holster and belt really make a difference?

Brown: We use all oak-tanned leather. We buy all ours from the United States. And that's something that you want to look at when you're buying a holster. You don't want something that doesn't

All the trappings. This pile of gear is complete right down to the Old West spectacles. When it comes to good leather, you can never have stuff that's too good or too tough.

have any body to it. I call it body or temper. We have a process when we're molding our leather that actually hardens the leather a little bit, and that's what I'm talking about. If you get a real soft holster and you lean against something while you're shooting – a wall or a hay bale or a rail – and you mash that holster down, it's just harder to holster your gun. Those are seconds lost. You want a good, firm leather with a little temper to it.

Digest: In terms of hardware – buckles, studs, rivets, silver hearts, and such. Do they have a purpose?

Brown: Ninety-nine percent of the hardware is personal preference. It's whatever works, and helps the shooters be whomever they're trying to portray. For the most part, you can use any kind of buckle as long as it's not stamped out. You don't want it falling apart. I think we carry 10 or 12 different buckles that people can select from. If you're going for authenticity, you might want a clip-corner buckle like on the Ranahan or the 1875.

As for the spots –The silver studs often seen on holsters – there's not much to do with function. It's more ornamentation than anything else. It used to be that some of the hardware was functional, but for the most part, it's just strictly there for looks.

Digest: In many of the Spaghetti Westerns, the actors often made a big show of tying their holsters down. Are holster tie-downs a common thing among the cowboy shooters?

Brown: We include them with most of our holsters – a leg tie-down and hammer thong. We – my wife and I – don't use them when we're cowboy shooting. If the holster fits the gun right, it's usually not a problem. We always put them on the holsters, though.

As for hammer thongs and straps, we make both. The Duke has a simple thong, but the Model 1920 has the safety strap; however, the strap isn't acceptable in cowboy action shooting. Snaps and straps are out. It's a Period issue. They (SASS) just don't want 'em visible.

Digest: Bullet loops or ammo pouches on the belt? Both, or neither?

Brown: Bullet loops aren't a necessity, and again, a lot of it's for show. We're getting more and more people who don't really care if they have 'em

You may not need a whip, but why not? This is all about fun and if you can have fun with a whip... (bottom) This fancy pair of revolvers is resting in an equally fine double rig. Fill the cartridge loops and you'll be ready to shoot.

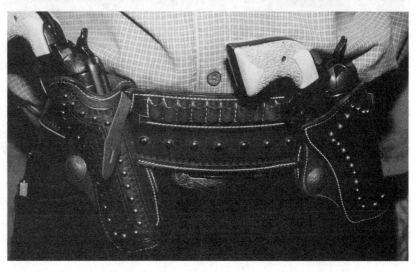

The Gun Digest® Book of Cowboy Action Shooting

(loops) or not. For cowboy shooting, there's not a lot of (pistol) reloading, and a lot of people will reload out of a pouch on their belt. Of those that do have the loops, about half of 'em will turn the belt around backwards so the loops are in the front. They'll put the holsters on the opposite way, with the buckle to the rear.

As for the shotshell slide loops, we've changed those to where you can put it over your buckle between your holsters in front and wear it that way. A lot of people wear the shotgun belt, either with the single loops or the double pouches. A lot of the people who shoot the side-by-sides like the double pouches 'cause it's easier to grab two rounds that way. I always wear a shotgun belt, but I just leave spaces in mine. If I'm shooting my Model '97 and have a scenario where I know how many rounds I'm going to shoot, I'll put up to three rounds together and then skip three. It's all practice and technique.

I don't do a lot of either, but I still have a lot of fun when I go out to shoot.

Digest: What about maintenance?

Brown: With good leather, you shouldn't have to do a lot to it. But you definitely want to keep it clean. The worst things on leather are moisture and extreme heat.

Basically, I tell people to wipe their holsters down. If you have a little saddle soap, you can use that. Don't get it wet to do it; just use a damp cloth, and then wipe it off. Over the years, you might have to add a little light coat of neatsfoot oil. But good leather, if you're reasonably mindful of not getting it sopping wet or throwing it in the sun, you shouldn't have a lot of trouble with it.

The spots, they're nickel, and they shouldn't need a lot of maintenance. Again, you don't want to leave your rig sopping wet if you're out shooting in the snow or the rain.

Check out the shooting star motif near the buckle. It's the little touches that make great leather really excellent. Well-made leather is worth the price.

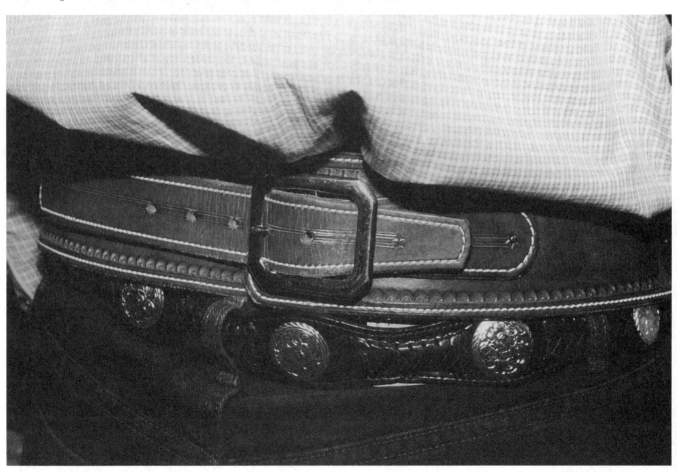

Rules and regulations pertaining to holsters and belts

As with any equipment-oriented aspect of cowboy action shooting, you should consult the current issue of the SASS Shooters Handbook for complete details. And if in doubt, don't hesitate to pick up the telephone and call SASS headquarters. What follows, however, are the basic rules and regulations as they pertain to holsters, belts, and associated gear –

- All handguns must be carried in a safe holster capable of retaining the firearm throughout a normal range of motion.
- Main-match holsters must be located one on each side of the belly button and separated by at least the width of two fists.
- Holsters may not depart from the vertical by more than 30 degrees when worn.
- Ammunition required for reloads during the course of any stage must be carried on the shooter's person in a bandoleer, belt, pouch, or pocket. Rifle and pistol ammunition may not be carried in a shotgun loop. **No ammunition may be carried in the mouth, ears, nose, cleavage, or any other bodily orifice.**
- Bandoleers, cartridge belts, and pouches must be of traditional design, e.g. bandoleers must be loose and not secured in any way to prevent movement. Modern drop pouches, combat-style shotgun loops, wrist or forearm bandoleers, and such are not allowed. Pouches shall have a flap and must carry their contents loose, with no special provisions to organize the contents for rapid retrieval. Leather belt slide ammo loops are acceptable.
- Cartridge loops must not have a metal or plastic liner.
- Shotgun ammo loops may not accommodate more than two rounds per loop, and rifle/pistol ammo loops shall accommodate only one round per loop.
- Ammo belts must be worn around the waist, and at or below the belly button.
- Shotgun ammo loops must conform to the shooter's contour, i.e. not tilt out from the belt.
- Cartridge loops mounted on a firearm's stock or forearm are not allowed.

Contact information:
Dan Brown
c/o Ted Blocker Holsters, Inc.
9438 SW Tigard St.
Tigard, OR 97223
503-670-7972
800-650-9742
www.tedblocker.com
info@tedblocker.com

That open area in the front will help keep the sight from snagging and tearing up your fine holster. Notice also the fine tooling and adornment on this holster. Who wouldn't love to wear something like this?

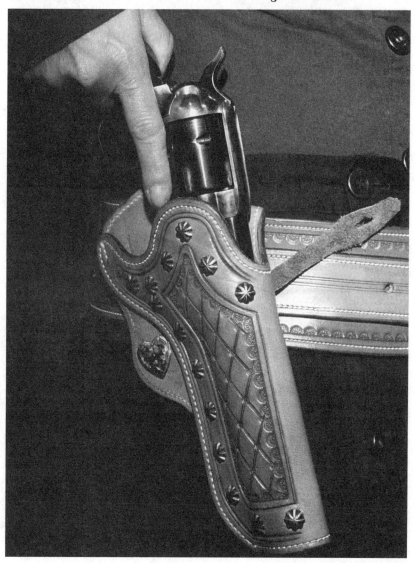

Photo courtesy Rockford Regulators

Photo courtesy Rockford Regulators

Photo courtesy Homesteaders Shooting Club

Photo courtesy River Junction Shootist Society

Photo courtesy Windy Gap Regulators

Call it Custom and the Sky's The Limit

Chapter 4

Call it Custom and the Sky's the Limit

By M.D. Johnson

Okay, admit it. Regardless of whether your handle is Calamity June or Carpetbagg'n Slim, you find it next to impossible to leave well enough alone. What I'm talking about is this – Anytime you buy something, the first thing you do when you get it home is start changing it. No, it doesn't matter if the thing – whatever it was – was perfectly fine to begin with. It's just in your genes, this feeling that you just have to make some type of modification. You have to do something to make that new-found object yours, be it a pickup truck, motorcycle, chainsaw…or firearm.

That's right. Firearms are some of the most often modified and customized things

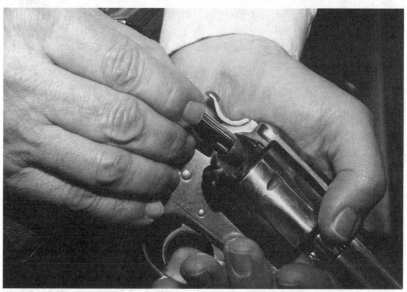

While you can't really go crazy with custom work, little things like polished cylinders will really improve your performance.

(top) Custom grips must fall within the SASS rules. They can be stippled, but things like skateboard tape are definitely out. Also, anything that might be considered a "target style" grip will be escorted from the range. (bottom) Leather wraps are fine on leverguns, but make sure the action still works when you close it up.

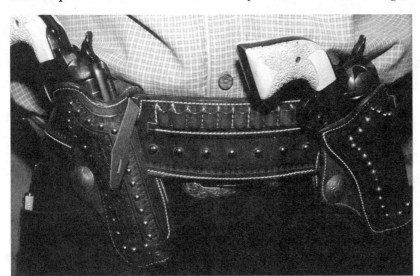

we shooting enthusiasts own. From adding a simple sling to a full-blown radical makeover involving dozens of parts, milling machines, chrome, steel, welders, and even a hammer or two, transforming our firearms from an ordinary, off-the-shelf piece to something that not only performs more efficiently, but virtually shouts out *This Is Me!* well, that's the way it is.

Perhaps not surprisingly, cowboy action shooters are not immune to this need for firearms change. Certainly, many of the modifications and customizations that will be discussed here are done so for a purely functional purpose. After all, and while the emphasis of the events are indeed camaraderie, enjoyment, and relaxation, it does feel quite good to walk away from a match with your handle gracing the number one position in the results listings, doesn't it? Still, there are a goodly number of changes you can make to your firearm, be it rifle, six-shooter, or scattergun, that do serve to fancy up that particular piece. In other words, a little bit of engraving and a little bit of color can go a long way to turning that Plain Jane into a Fancy Dan, and in short order, I might add.

Whoa there, pardner! Before you go to changing that old Model '97 pump-gun into something that looks better suited for Buck Rogers than it does a sanctioned cowboy action shooting event, there are some rules and regulations as to what can and cannot be done to any firearm in way of modifications. Your SASS Shooters Handbook contains a list of guidelines, and additional information can be obtained by contacting the folks back at SASS headquarters; however, here's an abbreviated list meant to get you started –

- Firearms of all approved types should be maintained in as original exterior condition as possible. The firearm must look as though it was manufactured in the late 1800s.

- No visible external modifications other than non-rubber grips, recoil pads on shotguns, and leather wrappings (rifle levers) are allowed.

- Contemporary rubber grips, modern target grips, and grip tapes are not allowed. Replacement grips of wood, ivory, pearl, stag horn, bone, and the like are acceptable so long as they are not so severely customized as to constitute a target grip. That is, they must be of an original shape and scale.

- Minor exterior modifications and cosmetic engravings are acceptable so long as the overall outward appearance of the firearm is not altered. Cosmetic embellishment such as engraving is permitted to the extent it does not create a competitive advantage.

- Modifying the stock length to fit you or changing a barrel to a different legal length is acceptable.

- Colored sights and sight inserts are not allowed. Sight outlines or inserts must be blackened or removed.

- Trigger shoes, compensating ports, counterweights, bull barrels, and all other such modifications are prohibited.

And the reasons behind the firearms restrictions, if you hadn't guessed already, are actually two-fold. First, SASS feels it's extremely important that everyone, regardless of skill level, talent, and ability, be on the same playing field in terms of the equipment they can or cannot use. Secondly, and just as important to the whole of the cowboy action shooting atmosphere is the notion that everybody and everything, firearms included, look and give the impression of being *period*; that is, might have been seen, worn, used, or displayed during the late 1800s. After all, that's what it's all about, isn't it?

But despite the list of firearms restrictions, there's still quite a bit an hombre can do either to speed up or spruce up – or both – his or her favorite shooting iron. Some, engraving your alias on the back strap olikef your Ruger Blackhawk, cost a little. Others – engraving the entire gun *and* having it gold-plated – will cost a lot. But whether your budget is tight or wide-open, there are things that can be done when it comes time to customize your shooting rigs.

Revolvers

We'll begin our discussion of custom rigs for cowboy action shooting with revolvers, but it's important to remember one common thread as we go through this chapter. It's elemental, but a common denominator nonetheless, and it's this – The extent to which you customize your firearm, be it revolver, rifle, or shotgun, depends entirely upon a combination of personal taste, functionality, and pocketbook. That is, what you perceive

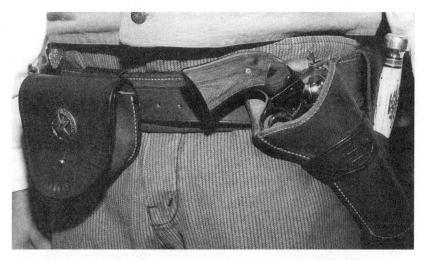

(top) These checkered grips are fine, but any more modification might be more than the rules allow. Remember the Spirit of the Game. (bottom) Externally, it's still a good, old-fashioned Single Action Army. Internally, better springs and a slicked-up action will mean faster and straighter shooting.

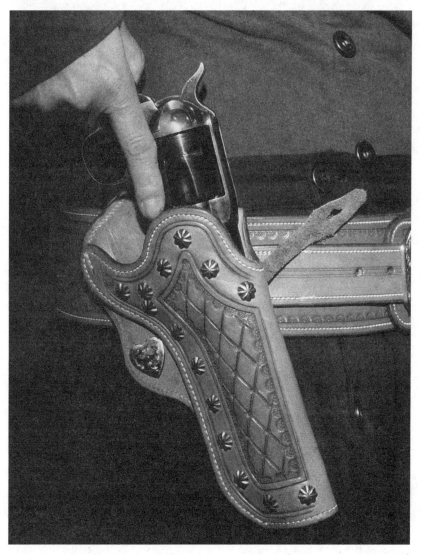

The Gun Digest® Book of Cowboy Action Shooting

> Originals and reproductions of firearms manufactured during the early 1800's, including Colts, Winchesters, Remingtons, Smith & Wessons, Marlins, Sharps, and Henrys, are allowed in SASS competitions, so long as they are in safe shooting condition.
>
> – SASS Shooters Handbook, April 2004

to look good, what works best for you in terms of those modifications, and, finally, what you can afford. It's that simple.

With that then, revolvers, according to Johnny Colt, a.k.a. Johnny Semm, whom you met in an earlier chapter, the two most popular pistol cartridges are the .38 Special/.357, and the .45 Colt. In most instances and for simplicity's sake, shooters will often carry both revolvers *and* rifles in the same caliber. And that just makes sense. There's no trading ammunition back and forth, and there's no chance of having .38 Special rounds when what you really need is .45 Colt ammunition, and vice versa. That said, SASS does recognize and permit pistols of the aforementioned .32 caliber and larger, so it then really boils down to – what do you want to shoot?

But back to customization and modification. Here, Johnny Colt was kind enough to answer a handful of some of the more commonly heard-tell questions concerning the changes often seen made to a cowboy's six-shooter.

M.D.: In a nutshell, Johnny, what can be done to a six-shooter?

Colt: You can do anything you want to the inside of the firearm, and that might be a trigger job or an action job. You can also do some minor sight alterations. You can change the grips as long as they're a natural (non-manmade) material. There are some grips that look like bone or ivory, and they're acceptable as long as they look real. You can change the finish on the firearm. You can reblue it, you can nickel-plate it, or you can even gold-plate it.

M.D.: Engraving seems to be a popular change with the cowboy six-shooters. What about engraving?

Colt: There are things you can and can't do. For instance, you can't go in and simply checker or stipple (Stipples are small pockmarks or indentations in the metal which serve to improve or enhance grip) the back strap of the grip frame. If the stippling is in the background of an engraving, however, that's something else. I'd say that around 40 percent of the shooters do something like this. Usually what folks will do is have their alias engraved down the back strap of the grip frame. As for cost, engraving that back strap will run $25 to $50, depending on who does the work.

M.D.: For the shooter on a budget but still looking for some function-related modifications for his, say, Ruger Single Six. What's available?

Colt: An action job where we polish, smooth, adjust, and change, if necessary, the internal workings of the firearm will run around $85. There are some sight alterations. We can serrate the front of the front sight, or alter the angle of the front sight. We can also widen and deepen the rear sight. Both of these modifications contribute to better and faster target acquisition.

Roughly with handguns and customization, you can figure on the initial price of the gun, plus a third. That's the basic rule of thumb for modifications.

M.D.: If, then, money is no object, how can these modifications change and become more enhanced?

Colt: Certainly you can get into exotic grips. If you want real ivory or stag grips, you can pay as much as $250 to $500 for the grips alone.

You can opt for an in-depth action job. We'd go in and re-time the gun, meaning that the gun locks up tight and the cylinder is aligned perfectly with the barrel every time it rotates. We can re-cut the headspace between the cylinder and the barrel. We can re-cut the forcing cone. All of this can cost upwards of $850, and that's not including the engraving, finishing, or new grips.

It's just like building that dream car or reworking that old Corvette that's sitting in the garage. You just keep adding chrome and competition equipment to it. Basically, though, after an action job, everything else is just glitz.

34 Call it Custom and the Sky's The Limit

M.D.: So far, Johnny, we've talked about customizing the guns themselves. What about handloading, or customizing your ammunition? Is this permitted?

Colt: Yes, handloading is allowed. There's no set minimum velocity factor – NOTE: There are maximum allowed velocities – but it's recommended that your ammunition velocity be over 650 feet-per-second to ensure that your ammunition is capable of knocking over the steel plate targets.

Since this sport involves shooting as quickly and as accurately as possible, most of us shoot reduced loads in order to take advantage of the reduced recoil.

Rifles

Like the revolvers, the rifles used by today's cowboy action shooters are also commonly modified. Some, understandably, are simply for aesthetics; however, other customizations such as action jobs, chroming, and lever wraps do serve a functional purpose.

M.D.: Johnny, what are the most common rifles you're seeing in the matches today?

Colt: The Marlin Cowboy is the most popular. The next two would be the *Yellow Boy*, or the Winchester 1866 and the Model 1873. Going down from there, you'd have the Winchester Model 1892s, and finally, the Model 1894s.

M.D.: What are most shooters doing in terms of customizing their rifles?

Colt: The most common thing to do is an action job. This involves polishing, smoothing, adjusting, the internal workings and changing the internal springs in the firearm. The action jobs I do will run around $125. All the bearing surfaces are polished to a high gloss. (This polishing reduces friction, and friction is the hated enemy of anyone trying to get something metallic to work or cycle really, really fast.)

The action is really the main thing, and really that's all that needs to be done to the gun. There are some other things that can be done to make the firearm more user-friendly, but it all goes back to the custom car example. It's all the little things designed to make that car go faster.

At this point, Colt shows me a Marlin *Cowboy* that has had some obvious, though perfectly acceptable modifications. He explains –

A simple buttplate, some checkering and minor engraving won't violate the rules or the Spirit of the Game. These rifles are good to go.

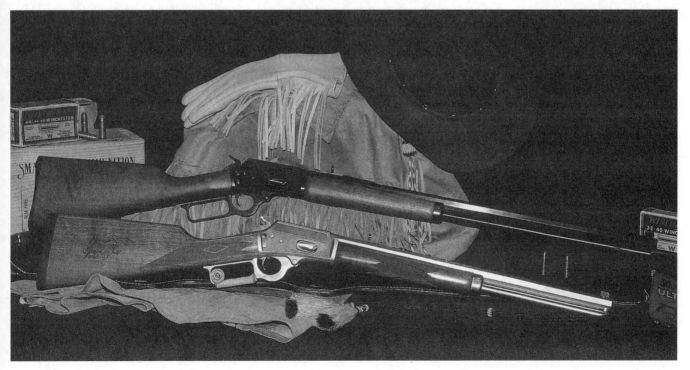

Colt: The length of this particular rifle barrel has been cut from 24 inches to 18-1/2 inches. Underneath, which you can't see, the gun has been lightened. That is, underneath the magazine tube, this gun has been cut. What this does, as is the case with this firearm, is it balances the gun. It's perfectly balanced.

The more weight you have in a gun, it's harder to get it started swinging, and then it takes more energy to stop it. By having a lighter gun, it's faster to move and easier to stop. Also, we often shoot in and out of windows, doorways, and stuff like that, and a shorter gun is just easier to get in and out of those obstacles.

Too, shortening the barrel when using these types of pistol cartridges actually gives you higher velocities. This pistol caliber ammunition has fast-burning powder, and it only takes about 12 inches of barrel to achieve its maximum velocity.

M.D.: Let's stay with this Marlin *Cowboy*. It has what looks like a nickel finish. Explain that.

Colt: This particular Marlin has an industrial brushed hard-chrome finish. It falls within the rules because they did have nickel-plated firearms back in those days, and they did have nickel-plated rifles. This, then, looks like nickel, but it's actually brushed hard-chrome.

Chrome also aids in the life expectancy of the firearm. A lot of these guns, especially the originals, but even the replicas, were never meant to be fired as often as we fire them in these matches. With chroming, all the internal parts of this particular rifle have been polished, chromed, and polished again. This inside of the barrel isn't chrome, but the inside of the magazine tube is. The magazine tubes in lever-action rifles can be a real problem because powder residue and gases can work their way down the tube, and create an environment where rust can form on the inside of the tube. This hard chrome helps to eliminate that.

M.D.: And sights, Johnny. Anything folks are doing with their rifle sights, and yet still staying within the SASS guidelines?

Colt: You have to use all natural materials for the front sight blades, or you can use an ivory or brass bead. As for the rear sights, these are your standard rear sights. You can have the barrel-mounted iron sights, or you can have a tang-mounted peep sight. And there are quite a few shooters who are using the peep sights.

Shotguns

Surprisingly, and while it might not seem as such, there are quite a few modifications that the cowboy action shooters can make to their competition scatterguns. Visually? Well, there's not a whole lot you can do to pretty up a homely old side-by-side; however, there's plenty that can be done to smooth up the operation and re-arming of that blunderbuss.

M.D.: What are you seeing, Johnny, in the way of shotguns?

Colt: The pumps and side-by-sides are your two basic types. You're starting to see some lever actions now, but not too many just yet. The Winchester Model 97 clones from China are popular. As for the side-by-sides, the Coach Guns from Stoeger with the 20-inch barrels…and maybe Grandfather's old shotgun, the Stevens that's had the barrels cut down to 20 inches or so.

To customize your shotgun, all you really might need to do is make sure the stock is the right length…

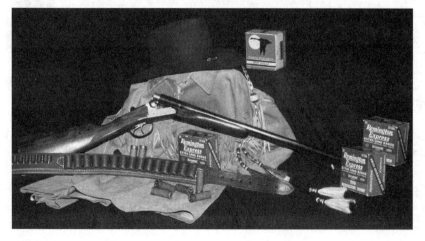

M.D.: And gauge? I'm assuming the 12-gauge rules the roost.

Colt: It does, but the 16-gauge is becoming more popular. The Model 97 was made in 12 and 16-gauge only, and most of the 12s have been bought up as a result of the cowboy action shooting. So there are more 16-gauge guns becoming available, and folks are starting to use them.

It is a smaller diameter shell, and that size difference between the 12 and the 16 can help folks with smaller hands. When you're pulling out and trying to handle two or three or four shells at a time, it can be tough. But with the smaller diameter shotgun shells, it just means the more shells you can hold comfortably.

M.D.: Revolvers and rifles might be easier for some to understand in terms of customizing and modifications, but shotguns?

Colt: I do an action job on the shotguns so they're easier to open and close. I polish the chambers so that the spent shells come out faster, and I can also alter the forcing cones so that the pattern is improved *and* recoil is reduced. I'll install recoil pads (Recoil pads made of natural period materials are permitted) and can shorten stocks, if necessary.

I'll also funnel the opening (chamber throats) of the shotgun so it's faster to load. I'll bevel the top, say, half or two-thirds of the breech, and this just makes the gun faster to load. Rather, you can slip the shells in faster and easier. After I've polished the chambers, all you have to do is shake the gun, and the empty hulls just pop out.

M.D.: Most of the period shotguns came from the manufacturer with a late 1800s version of modified and full chokes built right into the barrels. That is, an integral part of the barrel. Has anything changed today?

Colt: Normally in the type of shooting we do, chokes really aren't necessary; however, some people do put in screw-in chokes. But remember, no external modifications. The screw-in chokes can't be seen. My Model 97 has an internal (screw-in) choke, but you can't see it unless you look right down the barrel.

Usually, I'll take a full, a modified, and an improved cylinder choke with me to the matches. Most of the time, I shoot an improved cylinder. We're shooting close range stationary targets, and if you have an aerial target, it's usually coming up pretty quick. You don't have a lot of distance or time, so that wider pattern is better.

★ ★ ★ ★ ★ ★ ★ ★ ★

The long and short of customized guns in the cowboy action game is that there are limits to what you can do. The real goal is to maintain the spirit of the game, which is to attempt to capture the history and lore of the Old West. In those days, firearms were viewed simply as tools. The gun had a job to do and had to be tough enough to complete the task without fail. Life on the frontier was difficult. There was precious little money left over in a cowboy's budget for things like firearms engraving and modifications. To that end, cowboy action shooters must maintain the outward appearances, even if they spend the money to "slick up" the internal workings.

Simple engraving here and there can add a touch of class, but by and large, a cowboy gun is built for work and the rules of SASS will keep it that way.

... Oh, and chamfer the breech end of the barrels to allow for faster loading. You can also polish the chambers to allow for faster unloading.

Photo courtesy Okeechobee Marshals

Photo courtesy North Alabama Regulators

Chapter 5

The Cutting Edge of Cowboy Shooting

By M.D. Johnson

Honestly, now where would a cowboy be without a knife? I mean, we're talking Annie Oakley without her rifle, or George Patton without his signature ivory-handled Colt Single Action, aren't we?

Since the first Neanderthal hunter-gatherer skinned a wooly mammoth with a stone blade, knives have played an almost indispensable role in the Great Outdoors. Today, many outdoorsmen and women wouldn't think of heading afield without some type of cutting implement, be it a favorite pocketknife, Grandpa's old Buck skinner, or a modern, high-tech collection of strange steels and synthetic handle materials.

Not surprising, given the knife's history and reputation throughout the late 1800s,

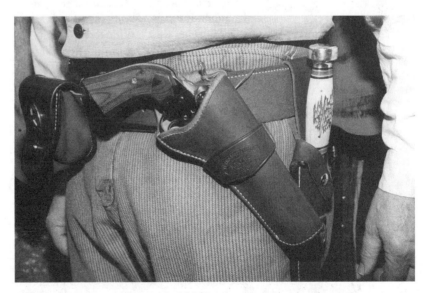

What's a cowboy without a knife? Just a guy with a couple of guns, I guess.

> For knife-makers like Bromley, these projects are not only time-consuming, but each is a labor of love – each one, a little bit better, a little more polished, and a little bit more eye-catching than the one before.

many of the cowboy action shooters of today would feel, well, naked without a blade at their side. Or in their boot. Or in their pocket. Or, perhaps hanging around their neck on a leather tie. Regardless, though, of where it's carried, knives are to many of the SASS shooters as much a part of the image that is the Old West as is their western garb or their Yellow Boy rifles.

"At the shooting events, the knives are part of the ambiance. They're part of the Period," said knife-maker Peter Bromley. Heralding from Spokane, Washington, Bromley, 61, has been making knives now for more than three decades, and has, for the past several years, catered to countless members of SASS looking to round out their portrayal of the rough-and-tumble time that was the Old West.

A carpet and vinyl layer by trade, Bromley's love affair with edged steel began many, many winters ago.

"I've loved knives since I was a little bitty tyke," he said. "And I've always had a project. I've always been fixing something or building something. I was watching a guy at a county fair; he was forging dinner gongs and ornamental stuff. You know, beating hot steel. And I just thought that was neat. So I got a forge and an anvil and I started doing that…but there wasn't any money in that. I was kind of looking for a paying hobby.

"Well, I had this old file that I was going to throw away," he continued, "and I thought I'd make a knife out of it. When I was finished with it, I looked at it and thought – "Peter, you can do better than that." It was pretty rough. Well, that was the beginning. I just kept on going. There really wasn't anyone around that I could ask questions. There weren't that many knife-makers, and very few books on the subject. So there for a long time, I was pretty much self-taught. Now, there's an abundance of books."

Building a Knife

Look at any custom-made knife and it doesn't take long before you realize that each piece is a work of art in and of itself. For knife-makers like Bromley, these projects are not only time-consuming, but each is a labor of love – each one, a little bit better, a little more polished, and a little bit more eye-catching than the one before. Hours, even days, are spent shaping and grinding, forming and polishing, until all of the pieces form a single masterpiece.

That said, where do these artisans begin? For Bromley, it all starts with the steel.

"I buy my steel here at the local spring shop," he said. "They build springs and so forth. It's primarily 5160 in terms of alloy, but it's a spring steel. I use 1084, also. The properties in those steels make them very tough. Those numbers – 5160, 1084, 1095 – are a type of steel. All steels have a designator. They use numbers instead of a name. It's the composition of the steel."

He continued. "I work strictly with hard carbon steel. I don't work with stainless steel. I don't have anything bad to say about it, but, first, it wouldn't be from the period. (*Period* meaning that the object, knife or otherwise, could have been found during the late 1800s, the historical timeframe of the cowboy action shooters.)

"High carbon steels, you can heat treat them yourself. The recipe for heat treating them is pretty simple. When you get into stainless steels, it gets very involved. Most knife-makers who build stainless knives send them off to a heat treater to have them properly heat treated. The recipe for heat treating stainless is kind of exotic."

For many, to view a knife is to view a blade; however, knife-makers will tell you in no uncertain terms that there's a hell of a lot more to a knife than just a sharpened piece of high-carbon steel. In fact, one of the most decorative elements of any knife is that part easiest to get a grip on – the handle.

"I enjoy working with any of the natural materials," said Bromley. "Any of the hardwoods, like ebony or rosewood. Both are very period. Ivory and bone, too. We use a lot of ivory and bone, as well as antler or stag. I've found that when you're making period knives, if you're using plastic or some other phony stuff on the handles, they don't sell. Guys want it to look authentic."

All of this work – blade, handle, engraving, ornamentation, accessorizing – understandably takes time. Anything, as any knifemaker worth his or her salt will tell you, worth doing is worth doing right. And doing it right, they'll continue, doesn't necessarily mean doing it quickly.

"For a fancy bowie, I can do one in about three days," said Bromley. "I've spent as much as 40 hours on a knife, but a simple hunting knife – a 3-1/2 inch drop point or something like that – I can make in one day. Start to finish, one day. But something you want to consider is the fact that I've been doing this a long time. There aren't a lot of wasted moves. And over the years, I've built up my machine shop to where I can go from machine to machine and do the different steps. I don't have to break a machine down in order to switch it over."

As is the case with many, perhaps the majority, of the gear-related items that a cowboy action shooter may take or wear to a match, knives can run the gamut, price-wise, from reasonably inexpensive to Catch-Your-Breath spendy. The sticker, says Bromley, depends on what you want to spend and if you want to have a fancy knife to hang on your belt or stick in your boot.

"I have some simple hunting knives for around $135, but then when you get up into the Damascus bowie knives – the real fancy knives – you're looking at $900," he said. "I do a lot of custom work, but a lot of the knives that I make, well, they just make me happy. I do a lot of replicas. I do combinations, too. Take this theme from this knife and that theme from that knife, and kind of marry them and put them together.

"If the handles on one knife are mammoth ivory, that's going to be spendy, of course," Bromley explained. "If there's fancy file work on the back of the blade and around the handle, that adds labor. If the guard isn't just an oval guard, but is a fancy shape with some file work. Well, it basically gets down to labor – and how long it takes to build the knife. Some Bowies, they're involved."

Knives come in all shapes, sizes and price ranges. Pick the one that best suits your character.

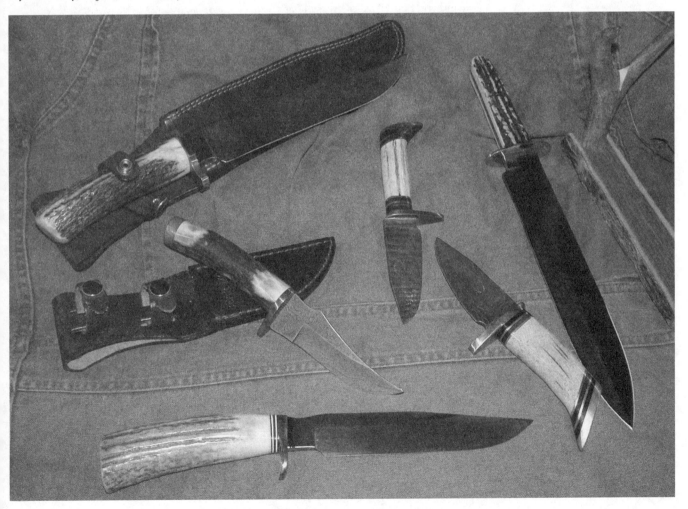

Just like these Old West gunfighters have their Single Action Shooting Society, so, too, do the knife-makers have their organizations. And again, like SASS, these knife-making groups provide their members an opportunity to put their talents and their love of the hobby on display. One such organization is the American Bladesmithing Society, or ABS. A vested member of the ABS, Bromley explains that the society's final exam, for lack of a better phrase, is nothing short of impressive. And difficult, too.

"The first thing you have to do is cut a 1-inch diameter, free-hanging hemp rope. Just swing the rope over a tree, and then cut it in half with one cut," said Bromley. "Then, you chop two 2x4s in half. Then, you have to be able to shave the hair on your arm with it. And you're not allowed to sharpen the blade during the test."

"After you've chopped the 2x4s and shaved your arm, then you lock the blade in a vise and you bend it 90 degrees. That's the performance part. You send five knives, including that bent knife, to the judges. There's seven judges. They look at the work, and either say 'yes' or 'no.' I did this two or three years ago."

Impressive? Yes, but not surprisingly qualifications for a tool that for many a cowpoke meant the difference between life and death.

The Cadillac of Knives – The Bowie

Some might ask – Why knives for an organization that focuses on shooting and the shooting skills applicable to the Old West? And why, particularly, this famous – and infamous – Bowie knife? According to Bromley, there's a ton of history behind the legendary Bowie, and it's in large part this history that makes the Bowie so appealing to the cowboy action shooters of today.

"In 1827," relates Bromley, "Bowie was involved in a duel on a sandbar outside of Naches, Mississippi. And he killed a guy with a big knife. So the American press picked up on this and it made a big splash in all the Eastern newspapers. This duel, and how Mister Jim Bowie had killed this guy with this big knife. After that, everyone referred to the big knives, then, as Bowie knives."

But there's a reason, says Bromley, that Jim Bowie might have had this knife on his belt on the fateful day in 1827.

"When Jim Bowie was in this duel, this was at a period in time when guns were one-shot pistols, and you prayed to God the sumbitch went off," Bromley says with a laugh. "But once you fired your bullet, what were you gonna do? So the fighters might have several pistols, but your back-up, of course, was a knife. Everyone carried a knife. Not just out in the rural areas, but everyone. As guns got better, though, knives got smaller and scarcer."

Other than the fact that this particular large, edged weapon was owned and wielded by a fellow of the name Bowie, what then makes a Bowie knife a Bowie knife? Often, and in some cases incorrectly, folks have taken to calling any large knife a Bowie; however, says Bromley, there's surprisingly more than meets the eye when searching for such a definition. Or rather, less.

"Bowie knives are fighting knives," he said. "The guard on a Bowie knife is not just below the handle; it's above AND below the handle. That classifies it as a fighting knife. The guard helps protect

Every knife needs a sheath. Why should it not match your gunbelt?

your hand. Hunting knives, on the other hand, will have just a tang that comes down below to protect your finger."

He continued. "Generally, I would say that the blade length is going to be 6- to 6-1/2 inches. And that's another misconception. Everyone thinks that a Bowie knife is a big, huge, beastie thing, and that's just not true. They really weren't. If you go back and look at all the pictures, the majority of the Bowie knives had a 7- to 8-inch blade. You get a 10-inch blade, and you're talking about a lot of weight to be carrying around…and those guys carried them on a daily basis."

But, as you might suspect, all Bowie knives aren't created equal. There are large Bowies and small Bowies, the smaller models often seen carried, handle outward and on display, in an action shooter's boot. "All part of the costume," said Bromley. Too, identically-sized Bowies can, as Bromley explained, be of different styles. There are Bowies whose blades have *clips*, or somewhat dropped points. There are spear point Bowies – sans clip – which are often referred to as California Bowies. These, said Bromley, were very distinctive in appearance, and were made beginning back in the Gold Rush days of the late 1840s until the turn of the century. Perhaps uncharacteristically when one thinks of the huge hunk of steel carried by Sylvester Stallone in the *Rambo* series, these California Bowies sported blades of about 6 inches.

"These knives were extremely high quality," said Bromley. "And if you can get a hold of one of these knives today, you're talking several thousand dollars."

Looking Good

It's raining at the End of Trail, a half-day steady fall that drives the dust into the ground and turns Main Street into an ankle-deep quagmire. Still, the matches go on. As the sun drops into the Pacific, the streets return to normal. The skies brighten, and quiet reigns. And the shooters? They've retired to a lamp-lit canvas hootch to clean six-guns and hang clothing to dry. Still encased in their damp cowhide scabbards, their Bowies are laid in the corner to be retrieved and worn in the morning.

Sound right? Wrong! It makes no sense, pardner, to spend $500 on a work-of-art blade, only to mistreat the piece by opening the door to, among other nasties, old Mister Rust. As with any tool or piece of equipment, knives too need care and attention, regardless of whether they've been put through a thunderstorm or simply have seen a lot of miles.

"Being that it's high carbon steel, you don't want to put it away wet. You want to dry it off. A little bit of oil every now and then. But the main thing is to keep it dry 'cause it will rust," said Bromley.

And what about that shave-with-it razor edge? Sooner or later, your knife is going to dull, and then what?

"I'd suggest using a sharpening stone," said Bromley. "Or what's popular with a lot of folks are the Lansky Sharpeners, where you can lock in the sharpening angle."

But knife care doesn't end with a drying towel and the programmed stones of a Lansky Sharpening System.

"Maintenance on the handle depends on the material," said Bromley. "With ivory, you want to maintain about an 8 percent moisture content. So with ivories, you need to put a little oil on 'em and rub it in real well about three times a year. By oil, don't use a petroleum-based oil. Olive oil works well. But ivories, if they get dry, can crack. Sudden temperature changes, too. You can't take an ivory-handled knife, throw it up on the dashboard of your truck, and then take it into a cool room. That's really hard on ivory. With the exotic woods – ebony and rosewood – you want to use the oils, too. There's that moisture content you want to maintain."

Storage, said Bromley, depends largely on who you listen to.

"A lot of knife makers recommend not storing the blade in the scabbard," he warns. "They claim that the acids used in tanning the leather (scabbard) are detrimental to the metal; however, I'm not saying that's wrong, but I've had knives in scabbards for a long time, and I don't see any pitting or anything like that. Still, that's what is recommended."

It makes no sense, pardner, to spend $500 on a work-of-art blade, only to mistreat the piece by opening the door to, among other nasties, old Mister Rust.

Photo courtesy Dry Gulch Desperados

Photo courtesy Boneyard Creek Regulators

Photo courtesy Homesteaders Shooting Club

Photo courtesy Gold Coast Gunslingers

Photo courtesy Gila Rangers

What'll it be, Pilgrim? Black Powder or Smokeless?

Chapter 6

What'll it be, Pilgrim? Black Powder or Smokeless?

By John Taffin

All of the sixguns, leverguns, and shotguns used for cowboy action shooting under SASS (Single Action Shooting Society) rules must be authentic 19th-century firearms or replicas thereof. Most of us grew up watching our heroes handle these firearms with unbelievable and impossible skill in the movies and on television. We cannot duplicate their exploits, however, we can thoroughly enjoy the greatest firearms ever to come from the mind of man. These firearms were built originally for black powder use in the latter third of the 1800s, but many of them saw more black powder blanks than real cartridges as dozens of our B western heroes fired thousands of non-recoiling, smoke-producing rounds as they cleaned up the mythical Old West.

One of the great attributes of CAS is the encouragement of our imaginations as we become the heroes we came close

Treat and respect every firearm at all times as if it was loaded.

– SASS Shooters Handbook, April 2004

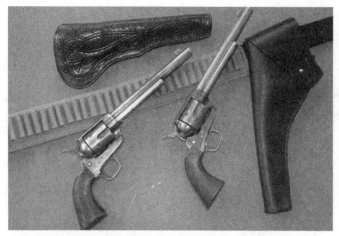

(top, left) These two old Colts from 1879 and 1881 are for black powder only. (top, right) Of these four original 1st Generation Colts, two were originally designed for black powder use, while two arrived after the advent of smokeless powder.

(bottom, left) Black powder only for this pair of 1st Generation Colt Single Action Armies. Leather by Will Ghormley. (bottom, right) Whether the choice is black powder or smokeless, custom leather such as these rigs from El Paso Saddlery, is part of the great attraction of cowboy action shooting.

to worshiping when we were kids. Imagination is, in fact, a great part of CAS when it comes to choosing aliases, firearms, leather, and costuming. There are many decisions to be made and most of us make several choices as to which firearms to use before we comfortably settle in to cowboy action shooting. Not only do we have all of these choices, we also have several shooting categories to choose from and also to decide just how authentic we wish to be. That authenticity extends to our choice of firearms as well as to whether we will shoot black powder, including black powder substitutes, or smokeless powder cartridges. Even this choice can become complicated as we can choose to shoot black powder cartridges in replicas of black powder firearms, smokeless powder cartridges in modern firearms, or any combination thereof. It is certainly not unusual to see competitors using black powder cartridges in thoroughly modern Ruger Vaqueros, which are not a replica of any 19th century sixgun. Under SASS rules, Rugers, complete with transfer bar safety and often constructed of stainless steel, both of which are 100 years removed from the second half of the 19th-century, are wisely allowed in cowboy action shooting.

As this is written, SASS has established seven categories for shooters to choose from most of which are based upon the sixguns being used and/or how they are being shot. Modern was set up to allow the use of adjustable-sighted sixguns, such as the immensely popular Ruger Blackhawk, while Traditional is for fixed-sighted sixguns such as the Colt Single Action and the Ruger Vaquero. Both of these categories may be shot one-handed or using two hands. Frontier Cartridge may be shot only with traditional firearms and only with black powder or black powder substitute loads. Both Duelist and Gunfighter are strictly one-handed propositions with the former being shot using one sixgun at a time while the latter requires both sixguns to be drawn and shot alternately. Frontiersman allows only the use of percussion revolvers, which must be shot duelist style.

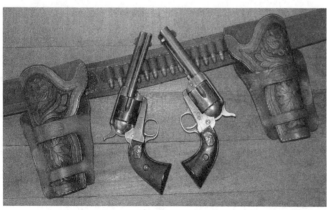
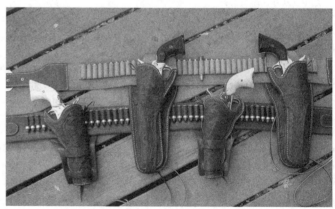

What'll it be, Pilgrim? Black Powder or Smokeless?

Finally we come to the newest category, Classic, or as it is usually referred to, Classic Cowboy, which requires Traditional sixguns shot duelist style, double barrel shotguns with external hammers, and leverguns, whether real or replicas, dating no later than 1873. Normally this would require using replicas of the 1860 Henry, 1866 Yellow Boy, and the 1873 Winchester. Only two categories, Frontier Cartridge and Frontiersman require black powder loads. However there are no rules to prevent the use of black powder in all other categories. Many Traditionalists, Duelists, Gunfighters, and Classic Cowboys use black powder loads, but it is rare to find anyone using black powder in the Modern category. So what'll it be Pilgrim? Black powder or smokeless? Or both? We will look at several things to consider.

Choosing Firearms: Fortunately, in my vocation as a gun writer, I am able to test just about every conceivable firearm in general and especially those applicable to cowboy action shooting. I've been able to shoot all replicas currently available both as to sixguns and leverguns, and most shotguns. I have not found any problems using smokeless powder loads. Earlier Colt-style replicas often had front sights that were too low, causing the sixguns to often shoot very high. This has all been taken care of and now most replicas, as well as the Ruger Vaquero, provide enough front sight height to allow filing in to hit point of aim.

Any of the Colt, Remington, and Smith & Wesson replicas work well with smokeless powder loads. However, when we switch to black powder, we find a vast difference in how they operate. One only has to look at the military tests of the 1870s to see this. The Colt Single Action Army was fired for 200 rounds without cleaning, the barrel was swabbed out, and the tests continued. Both the original Remington and Smith & Wesson revolvers were obviously smokeless powder sixguns built in a black powder age, as their tolerances were tight enough they were quickly affected by black powder fouling, especially the rotation of the cylinder. The same is true today of current replicas; Colt replicas will continue to operate, while the Remington and Smith & Wesson sixguns will often bind before a cylinder full has been fired. Whether one is going to use black powder or smokeless powder should be considered when choosing the sixguns for cowboy action shooting. The Remingtons and Smith & Wessons can be used successfully, however they require some special treatment which will be covered shortly. I have not run into any

This pre-1898 Colt Frontier Six-Shooter should only be used with black powder.

(bottom, left) Whether used with black powder, or smokeless powder the Remington 1875 and Colt 1873, when combined with our imagination can take us back to the Frontier Period. (bottom, right) For use with black powder loads the Remington replicas require special attention during a match. Grips are by Buffalo Brothers.

The Gun Digest® Book of Cowboy Action Shooting

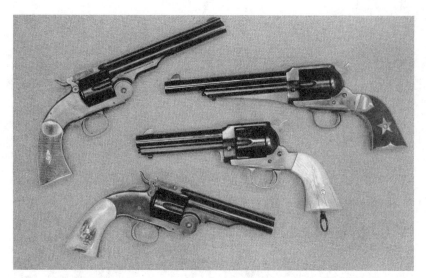

Although originally chambered for black powder cartridges, replica Smith & Wessons and Remingtons can be used with black powder or smokeless powder. Grips by Buffalo Brothers.

(bottom, left) Black Hills offers a full line of CAS loads for shooters. (bottom, right) For those cowboy action shooters who want to experience black powder but do not reload, Ten-X and Cor-Bon offer black powder substitute loads, while Black Dawge and Wind River can provide authentic black powder loads.

operational problems using black powder with any leverguns or shotguns.

Factory Loaded Cartridges: In the early days of CAS, one had to be a reloader in order to provide the cartridges needed for competition under SASS rules, which state loads must use lead alloy bullets with a muzzle velocity under 1,000 fps in a sixgun with 1,400 fps being the upper boundary for leverguns. Even into the 1990s about the only choice available was a few loads for the .38 Special, .44 Special, and .45 Colt. Black powder loads were virtually non-existent.

All of this has changed considerably. Today's CAS shooter can choose from a myriad of properly loaded rounds using lead alloy bullets with flat noses for safe use in leverguns and also meeting the requirements as to muzzle velocity. Many cartridges, which disappeared long before World War II, have also been resurrected and chambered in single-action sixguns and leverguns or both. Black Hills Ammunition,

Ten-X, Ultramax, PMC, MagTech, Winchester, CCI-Speer, and Hornady all offer cowboy action shooting loads, with the first two companies offering virtually every possible cartridge. Loads are available for .45 Colt, .45 Schofield, .44-40, .44 Colt, .44 Russian, .44 Special, .38-40, .38 Long Colt, .38 Special, and even .357 Magnum and .44 Magnum.

In addition to all of these above-mentioned smokeless powder loads, both black powder and black powder substitute loads are also available. Black Dawge and Wind River Trading Co. offer authentic black powder loads in .45 Colt, .45 Schofield, .44-40, .38-40, .44 Russian, and .38 Special, while Ten-X and Cor-Bon offer black powder substitute loads. So even if one does not reload, there should be no problem when it comes to choosing whether to use smokeless or black powder loads.

Reloading For Cowboy Action Shooting: Whether one chooses black powder or smokeless powder loads has a great bearing on the equipment, technique, and bullets to be used. This is covered in greater detail in the article reloading for cowboy action shooting, however herein a few things are highlighted. Smokeless powder loads can be easily assembled with RNFP (round-nosed flat-point) bullets such as those offered by Oregon Trail Bullet Co. Cartridges may be loaded on a single-stage press with powder dispensed by a regular powder measure or on a progressive press the same as cartridges designed for any other purposes.

All this changes, however when we switch to black powder. The dispensing of black powder requires a special powder

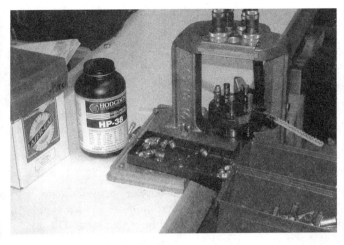
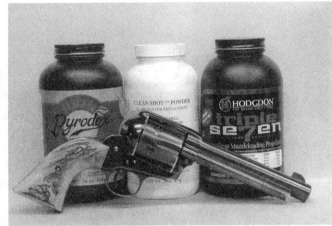

measure, an anti-static measure to prevent a spark that could ignite the black powder.

Powder, Primer, And Bullet Selection: CAS rules require loads that are normally assembled with the faster-burning smokeless powders. These include Alliant's Bullseye, Red Dot, and Unique; Accurate Arms Nitro 100, #2, and #5; Hodgdon's Clays, TiteGroup, HP38, and Universal; and Winchester's 231. Most of these will be relatively clean-burning and require relatively small amounts of powder in large-capacity cases. Black Powder choices include FFg and FFFg grade granulations (the more "F's", the faster-burning) from Goex, Elephant Brand, Kik, Swiss, and Wano. The choice may be limited to what is locally available for each shooter. Add to this the black powder substitutes such as Clean Shot, which is used in most factory-loaded black powder cartridges; and Goex's Clear Shot and Hodgdon's Pyrodex, Select, and Triple 7. Most of these are also offered in either FFg or FFFg. Looking at these powders alone reveals smokeless powder shooters have 11 choices, while the black powder shooter has at least a dozen and a half offerings to pick from. Any of these smokeless powders will work well with any firearm chosen, however it will require some experimenting to find the best black powder or black powder substitute, especially if one chooses to shoot Remington or Smith & Wesson sixguns.

Primers are also a factor, with standard primers being normally used with smokeless powder loads, however magnum primers will be the best choice for reliable ignition with black powder loads. Any of the RNFP bullets from such suppliers as Oregon Trail Bullet Co., AA Ltd., or Meister work well with smokeless powder loads, however, the picture changes with the use of black powder or black powder substitutes. Most machine-cast bullets are harder than necessary or desired for black powder loads and they also use a lubricant that is too hard. One can make it through a match with black powder loads using these bullets, but some extra care is needed, which will be discussed shortly. Meister

(top, left) RCBS's Pro 2000 can be used for quickly reloading smokeless powder loads or for resizing, de-capping, priming, and belling cases for black powder. (top, right) Black Powder substitutes include Pyrodex, Clean Shot, and Triple Seven.

(bottom, left) Original 19th-century loads can be duplicated with Goex black powder, Pyrodex, or Unique. (bottom, right) For use with black powder loads the Remington replicas require special attention during a match. Grips are by Buffalo Brothers.

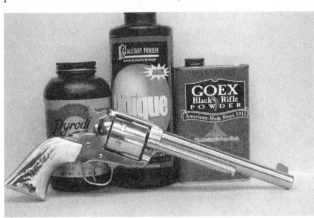
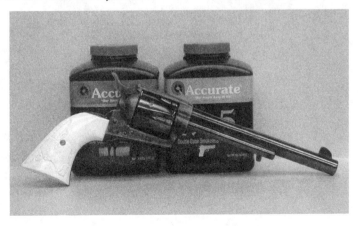

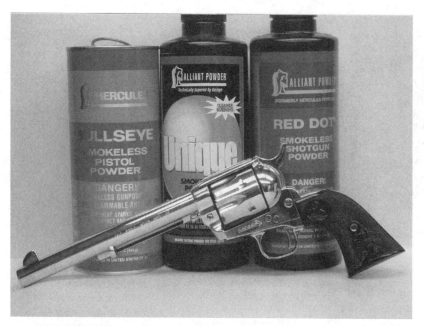

Two of the oldest powders in existence Alliant's Bullseye and Unique are joined by Red Dot as excellent choices for CAS loads.

Hodgdon's lineup of quality CAS powders includes Universal, HP38, and TiteGroup.

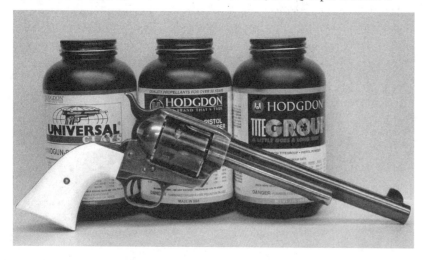

offers their bullets lubed with SPG, a softer lube to help prevent black powder fouling, while Black Dawge offers the best way to go as far as bullets for black powder loads by providing both a softer alloy as well as a soft lube to help prevent fouling.

Shooting A Match: Shooting smokeless powder loads in a cowboy action shooting match requires quality firearms and quality loads. The same is true for black powder shooting however more equipment is needed. When shooting black powder loads, my shooting cart and vehicle contain several more items including patches, solvent, cleaning rods, a Lyman #310 tool, a gallon jug of soapy water, and three everyday items found in the grocery store, a roll of paper towels, Windex, and Q-Tips. Windex is indispensable when it comes to keeping black powder firearms operating.

Most Colt-style replicas and leverguns using black powder loads will keep operating and shooting through an entire five- or six-stage match. However, even they will benefit with some special care between stages. Remingtons and Smith & Wessons, at least in my experience, will not continue operating through an entire match without special care. That special care is Windex. Between stages I soak patches in Windex and then swab out the bores of both sixguns and leverguns. This may not be necessary when using soft alloy bullets with soft lube in Colt sixguns and leverguns; however, it certainly does not hurt.

With Remingtons and Smith & Wessons, even when using the best possible bullet and the cleanest-burning black powder or black powder substitute, I have found no way to avoid special attention in between stages. It is not only necessary to swab out the bores, it is also required that the cylinders be attended to. That large spray bottle of Windex is used to apply liberal amounts of the magic elixir to both the front and back of the cylinder to remove the black powder fouling that restricts smooth rotation. Windex is cheap and may be used liberally. Several squirts are applied all over and a paper towel used to wipe off the excess, and the sixguns are then, hopefully, ready to operate through the next stage.

After The Match: After shooting smokeless powder loads, my firearms can be wiped down with Hoppe's #9 and placed back in the safe to be cleaned sometime in the future whenever I wish to do so. Life is not so simple with firearms used with black powder. When the match is over, I remove the cylinder from any sixguns, spray the chambers with Windex, run another patch down the barrel, spray the entire sixgun as well and then wipe down with a paper towel. Barrels of both levergun and shotgun are soaked liberally with Windex. Leaving a fired case in the chamber will prevent the Windex/black powder fouling liquid from flowing back into the action. When I arrive home all the firearms used for black powder shooting are then thoroughly cleaned with special black powder cleaners such as Black Dawge's Dawge Whizz. A Q-Tip soaked in solvent is used in the hard-to-reach places in the cylinder window, the cylinder ratchet, the bolt notches, around firing pins, the hammer recess, in fact anyplace I can reach with a Q-Tip. After every third match, firearms are completely dismantled and all parts thoroughly cleaned. We can be lazy when it comes to cleaning smokeless powder firearms. However black powder guns allow us no such latitude and MUST be cleaned after every use. Generally speaking, black powder substitutes will produce less fouling and less corrosive action on barrels and cylinders, however it is still required that all firearms, whether loaded with black powder or black powder substitutes, be cleaned after a match.

We are not finished yet! Fired cartridge cases, whether used with black powder or black powder substitutes, also require special attention. Before leaving the range I use a Lyman #310 nutcracker-style hand tool for de-priming black powder cartridges and then place the fired cartridges in the gallon jug of soapy water. The ride home sloshes the empty cases around, beginning the cleaning process. At home, the dirty water and cartridge cases are dumped in the kitchen sink, sprayed with the hose attachment on the sink, and allowed to drain. The cases are then removed from the sink and placed on newsprint to dry, and a Q-Tip is used to remove the black crud from the primer pockets. Cases are then placed in a large Dillon Vibratory Case Cleaner along with any cases used with smokeless powder that may also need to be cleaned. When the cleaning is accomplished, I know which are black powder cases by the fact they have already had the primer removed.

Whether to use smokeless powder or black powder loads is a difficult decision. The smokeless powder loads are certainly more convenient; however, black powder loads are more authentic. An extra-added bonus with the use of black powder is the spiritual connection to the past every time the hammer falls, the primer ignites the powder, and I feel and experience the resulting Boom! and cloud of smoke. Because the choice is so difficult, it is one I choose not to make. I have found the simple solution. In our local club we can shoot through twice. Sometimes I shoot smokeless in both categories; other times I go with black. However, I have found that by shooting black powder loads first in Duelist category followed by smokeless powder loads in Classic Cowboy category in the same stage, I do not have to make the decision, I reap the benefits of both, and following the black powder loads with smokeless powder loads helps to reduce fouling.

The question may arise as to whether black powder and smokeless powder loads will shoot to the same point of aim? I have not found this to be a problem. In fact my most-used loads with smokeless and black powder both are in the same muzzle velocity range. For example, by using 8.0 grains of Unique with 180-, 200-, or 250-grain bullets in the .38-40, .44-40, and .45 Colt respectively for my smokeless powder loads and 33.0-35.0 grains of black powder or a black powder substitute with the same bullets and calibers, my point of impact remains the same or nearly so it makes no difference in a cowboy action shooting match.

> Throughout this manual, blackpowder means blackpowder, Pyrodex, Black Mag, or comparable propellants intended for muzzle loading firearms.
> – SASS Shooters Handbook, April 2004

Whether using black powder or black powder substitute loads, Windex is indispensable.

Photo courtesy Rockford Regulators

Photo courtesy Rockford Regulators

Photo courtesy Rockford Regulators

Photo courtesy Rockford Regulators

Photo courtesy Illinois River City Regulators and Chillicothe Sportsmen's Club

Photo courtesy Rockford Regulators

Photo courtesy Rockford Regulators

Chapter 7

Reloading for Cowboy Action Shooting

By John Taffin

The firearms typically used in cowboy action shooting must have been in existence prior to 1899. SASS (Single Action Shooting Society), the largest and oldest cowboy action shooting organization, allows for the use of original single-action sixguns, leverguns, and shotguns or replicas thereof.

Cartridges, on the other hand are a different story. The pre-1899 cartridges available today include .45 Colt, .45 Schofield, .44-40, .44 Russian, .44 Colt, .38-40, .38 Long Colt, and .32-20. The .41 Long Colt also belongs in this group, however new brass is just now becoming available and we have yet to see any replicas chambered in .41LC. This situation should

Properly tailored reloads usually spell success in cowboy action shooting matches.

Taffin's most-used loads for both cowboy action shooting and everyday use are assembled with Unique and Oregon Trail RNFP bullets in .45 Colt, .44-40, and .38-40.

(bottom, left) Thanks to Black Hills and Starline, cowboy action shooters now have brass for reloading the .38 Long Colt, .44 Colt, .44 Russian, and the .45 Schofield. (bottom, right) Winchester's 231 and Alliant's Red Dot and Bullseye are excellent choices for CAS loads.

have changed by the time you read this. Other cartridges are allowed if they are loaded to SASS specifications even though they did not arrive on the scene until after 1898. These include the .38 Special (1899), .44 Special (1907), .357 Magnum (1935), .44 Magnum (1955), .41 Magnum (1964), and the .32 Magnum (1984). All cartridges used in CAS under SASS rules, whether they were developed before or after, must adhere to certain specifications. Those specifications state bullets must be of a lead alloy. They may have no jackets, half jackets, plating, or gas checks; and whatever the cartridge chosen, muzzle velocities must be under 1,000 fps when fired from a revolver and less than 1,400 fps when used in a levergun.

Original cartridge-firing firearms now available in replica form include the Colt Single Action Army, Bisley Model, Cartridge Conversion, Colt 1871-72 Open-Top; Remington Models 1875 and 1890; and Smith & Wesson's Schofield Model and Model #3 Russian. Replica leverguns offered today are the early Winchesters, Models 1860 Henry, 1866 Yellow Boy, 1873, and 1892. Originally the 1894 Winchester was not chambered in the sixgun cartridges required under SASS rules, however today it can be found chambered in .45 Colt, .44-40, .44 Magnum, and .357 Magnum.

Other firearms are given special dispensation even though they are not replicas. These include the currently manufactured Marlin 1894s which has been produced in .45 Colt, .44-40, .44 Magnum, .357 Magnum, .38 Special, .32-20, .25-20, and just introduced as this is written, the .32 Magnum. On the sixgun side relatively "modern" single actions with transfer bar safeties, such as the Ruger Vaquero, EAA Bounty Hunter, Colt Cowboy, and the Freedom Arms Model 97 are also allowed. A special Modern competition category allows the use of sixguns with adjustable sights. This mainly accommodates those shooters with Ruger Blackhawks, however it also covers the Colt New Frontier, the Freedom Arms Model 97, the Uberti Buckhorn, and replicas of the Colt and Bisley Flat-Top Target revolvers.

Black powder was the propellant used in all of the mentioned cartridges introduced prior to 1899, however both the .38 Special and the .44 Special were also originally loaded with black powder even though they were developed after 1898. The original 19th century cartridge cases did not have the solid bases found on today's cartridges but were of the balloon-head style with an unsupported primer pocket extending above the rather thin interior base. Today's cartridge cases are definitely stronger, however the original cases had more capacity. I have been able to locate a sufficient number of old-style balloon-head brass cases for several of the original cartridges in order to duplicate the original loads using today's components.

With FFg Goex black powder the .45 Colt, .44-40, and .38-40 were all loaded with the original 40-grain load and bullets

of 255, 200, and 180 grains respectively. The results were quite surprising. Using Magnum Pistol Primers, and 7-1/2-inch barreled sixguns, all three loads were over 1,000 fps muzzle velocities. Even with the components used in the 1870s these must have indeed been serious loads. In fact so much so, the Army dropped the .45 Colt load back to 30 grains of powder for military use, while the civilian load was leveled off at 35 grains. This tells me for those who are truly concerned about shooting authentic loads in these three calibers, the muzzle velocities should be at least 800 fps. Duplicating the original loads in the .45 Schofield (880 fps), and the .44 Russian (800) fps, also tells us today's loads should at least be in the 700-750 fps range.

For those who do not reload, Black Hills Ammunition has led the way in offering cowboy action shooting loads using Starline Brass. Reloaders have also reaped the benefits as we now have exceptional quality brass in virtually every caliber/cartridge originally offered in the pre-1899 time period covered by cowboy action shooting. This includes .45 Colt, .45 S&W, .44-40, .44 Russian, .44 Colt, .38-40, .38 Long Colt, .32-20, and just now, the .41 Long Colt.

Most of my loads for cowboy action shooting are assembled with RCBS's Pro 2000 Progressive Press. I have been using it for several years and for several reasons. I especially like the primer feeding system, as instead of a vertical tube holding 100 primers stacked on top of each other, the Pro 2000 utilizes plastic strips holding 25 primers that are fed horizontally. The strips can be purchased already loaded with CCI primers and can then be reloaded with any manufacturer's primers using the special

(top, left) Even such modern cartridges as the .38 Special, .44 Special, .357 Magnum, and the .44 Magnum can be loaded for cowboy action shooting. (top, right) Oregon Trail offers a full line of RNFP bullets such as these .45 Colt, .44-40, .38-40, and .38 Special examples.

(bottom, left) Whether using black powder or a black powder substitute for reloading for CAS, safety demands a specially designed black powder measure such as this one by Lyman. (bottom, right) Properly alloyed bullets, complete with two grooves packed with SPG Lube for best results in black powder loads, are available from Black Dawge Cartridge Co.

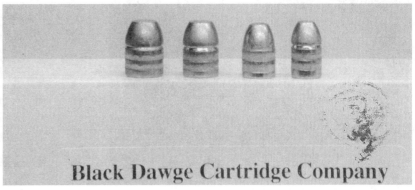

The Gun Digest® Book of Cowboy Action Shooting

tool provided by RCBS. It took awhile to become accustomed to using this tool, however I have now become proficient enough at this task so that after spending several hours reloading the plastic strips I can then spend days loading ammunition without ever having to stop and fill primer tubes.

My three primary cartridges for cowboy action shooting are the .45 Colt, .44-40, and .38-40, all of which can be loaded with the same powder charge. This is especially convenient using the RCBS Pro 2000 because the powder measure is not part of the die plate, but rather stays with the press as dies are changed. The die plate takes about 10 seconds to change, so I keep separate die plates handy already set up for all cartridges I load on the Pro 2000. Most of my loading on the Pro 2000 is for cartridges using large primers. However, if I wish to switch to such small primer cases as the .38 Special, .38 Long Colt, or .32-20, the primer seating punch is easily changed by loosening and tightening one nut. The Pro 2000 is also quite versatile in the fact that the same shell plate handles the .45 Colt, .44-40, .38-40, and .45 Schofield, while a second shell plate can be used for the .44 Russian, .44 Colt, .44 Special, and even the .44 Magnum.

Even the .44-40, .38-40, and .32-20, all being tapered or bottlenecked cartridges, can be loaded on the Pro 2000 even though they are not sized with carbide dies reserved for straight-walled cartridges. It is only necessary to add a preliminary step to properly lube the cartridge cases before sizing. I simply place about 100 cleaned cases in a shallow cardboard tray, lightly apply a spray-on lube, shake and spray again, and they are ready for loading on the progressive. Most of these lubes dry very well enough on their own that with the pressures involved in CAS loads, I do not find it necessary to wipe the cases down before shooting.

I mentioned the use of the same powder charge with the .45 Colt, .44-40, and .38-40. An example of this is 8.0 grains of Unique using bullet weights of 250 grains, 200 or 225 grains, and 180 grains respectively. I have found all of these to be loads that are very close in muzzle velocity to the original black powder loads of these three cartridges. All three provide enough recoil to let the shooter know the sixgun in hand is a big-bore revolver while at the same time not producing punishing recoil. Even someone as hard of hearing as I am (comes from too many early years of shooting without ear protection), can hear the "Clang" when the bullets from these loads hit steel.

Excellent powders for cowboy action shooting loads include, but are not limited to, Alliant's Unique, Bullseye, and Red Dot; Accurate Arms Nitro 100; Hodgdon's, Universal, TiteGroup, and HP-38; and Winchester's WW231.

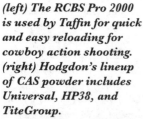

(left) The RCBS Pro 2000 is used by Taffin for quick and easy reloading for cowboy action shooting. (right) Hodgdon's lineup of CAS powder includes Universal, HP38, and TiteGroup.

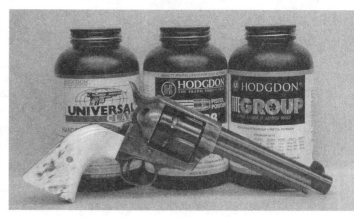

Reloading for Cowboy Action Shooting

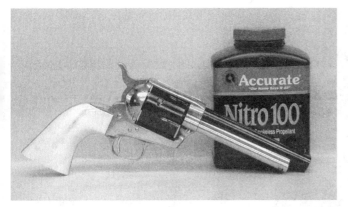

Not only do we have access to excellent brass and a great selection of powder for assembling CAS loads, thanks to such companies as Oregon Trail Bullet Co., we also have a large selection of RNFP bullets to choose from. RNFP stands for round-nosed flat-point, which is the style of bullet used in most CAS loads for one important reason. Safety. The same loads used in sixguns are normally also used in the magazine tubes of leverguns. As the levergun loads are stacked one on top of the other, the nose of each bullet contacts the primer of the cartridge ahead of it. If the nose shape were to be round or pointed, there is a distinct possibility of a cartridge being fired in the magazine tube, which could be disastrous. Safety requires loading only flat-nosed bullets if the cartridge is to be used in a levergun.

Oregon Trail Bullet Co. produces RNFP bullets in .38, .38-40 (which is actually .40 caliber), .44, and .45. Since there is quite a bit of variation in the chamber mouths of .44 and .45 caliber sixguns, Oregon Trail offers both .452" and .454" diameter .45 bullets as well as .427", .429", and .430" diameters in their .44 caliber selection. Normally the largest diameter that will easily chamber will produce the best accuracy. Most recent Colts and Colt replicas chambered in .45 Colt seem to prefer .454" bullets while .452" is usually the best choice for Rugers.

There is so much variation in .44 caliber sixgun chambers that those seeking maximum accuracy will need to experiment. I have found examples from the same manufacturer that would accept nothing larger than .427" bullets while others easily chambered loads assembled with .430" diameter bullets. Whatever works in the sixgun normally also works well enough in the levergun at the distances shot in cowboy action shooting. I have yet to encounter a levergun that would not chamber .45 Colt loads using .454" bullets nor a .44 levergun that would not handle .430" bullets. Although, loads tailor-made for a particular sixgun with RNFP bullets usually pick up 200-300 fps muzzle velocity when used in a longer barreled levergun, some of the milder loads may only gain around 100 fps. Any loads assembled for sixguns under 1,000 fps muzzle velocity can be expected to stay well under 1,400 fps in a levergun.

There are six cartridge-shooting categories currently in existence in cowboy action shooting under SASS rules. Shooters may use smokeless powder or black powder cartridges in any of the following categories: Modern, Traditional, Duelist, Gunfighter, or Classic Cowboy. Black powder is required to shoot in Frontier Cartridge. Black powder not only includes

(top, left) Accurate Arms #1 powder for CAS reloading is Nitro 100 (top, right) 19th century sixguns should only be used with reloads assembled with black powder or a black powder substitute.

With a little experimentation, loads can be tailored to hit the same point of impact using smokeless powder, black powder, or a black powder substitute.

The Gun Digest® Book of Cowboy Action Shooting

The 1860 Army top left was used as the basic platform for the Colt Cartridge Conversion and the 1871-72 Open-Top which then evolved into the Model 1873 Peacemaker. The 1860 is for black powder only however the other three replicas may be used with black powder or smokeless powder.

(bottom, left) The Remington replicas need special attention between stages to keep functioning when used with black powder or a black powder substitute. (bottom, right) These Ruger Blackhawks, all custom built for hunting, also perform well with CAS reloads.

traditional back powder but black powder substitutes as well.

I first started loading smokeless powder cartridges in 1957. It was not long after that I began loading black powder cartridges thinking it was simpler. It wasn't and isn't. Yes it is possible to pack in all the black powder a case will hold, squeeze a bullet on top, and the result will probably be a cartridge that will fire, however the accuracy may be a lot less than desired or expected. For many years my black powder cartridges were re-sized, de-capped, belled, and re-primed, using a single stage press, the cartridges were then placed in a loading block and charged using an adjustable hand measure or flask, and then it was back to the single-stage press for bullet seating and crimping. Reloading black powder cartridges is much simpler today.

The same Pro 2000 and dies are used for black powder as for smokeless powder, however in a much different way. Just as with smokeless powder loads, the Pro 2000 is used for re-sizing, de-capping, priming, and expanding the case mouth. The bullet seating die and RCBS powder measure are backed out as these two steps are bypassed. I normally run several hundred cases at a time, and after the four mentioned operations are accomplished, I move to another part of my loading room where Lyman's Black Powder Measure is mounted. This powder dispenser is designed to prevent the possibility of a spark igniting the black powder in the hopper. Powder measures designed for smokeless MUST NEVER be used with black powder, or black powder substitutes, because of the danger of electric sparking.

Once my cases, which are placed in a loading block, are charged using the Lyman Black Powder Measure, I then place a wad over the powder charge in each cartridge and then move to the single-stage press for bullet seating and crimping. Lately I have been using Walter's Wads, which are cut from a vegetable fiber sheet, between powder and bullet, as it provides two functions: it helps protect the base of the bullet and it also helps to minimize barrel fouling.

Smokeless powder loads are assembled with relatively fast-burning powders, powders that do not even come close to filling up the space below the bullet. These powders are designed to give desired results with small amounts of powder and without using all the case capacity. This is not true of black powder or black powder substitutes. Enough black powder must be used so it is slightly compressed by the wad and the bullet. At no time should there be any air space left in black powder cartridges.

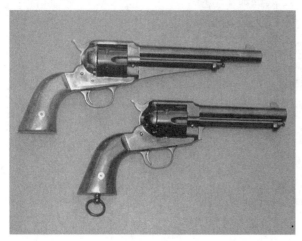

Light Loads For Cowboy Action Shooting?

I've basically been shooting "Cowboy" most of my life. As a teenager, in 1957, I purchased a 1st Generation 4 3/4-inch Colt Single Action Army in .38-40 and it was soon followed by a brand-new 2nd Generation 7 1/2-inch Colt Single Action Army chambered in .45 Colt. The first loads through these guns were standard factory loads whose price tag soon made me realize I needed to reload. I have been reloading the .45 Colt ever since, always using loads that were to the original black powder levels in several Colt Single Actions. I never dreamed of loading the .45 Colt to anything below standard levels.

When I first started participating in organized cowboy action shooting, the .45 Colt using standard level loads was king. To my mind these loads were an important part of our connection to the historical past, as well as being in what SASS has long labeled "The Spirit Of The Game." Then things started to change. A small group of shooters forgot the fun and enjoyment aspect of cowboy action shooting and instead concentrated on what they had to do to win. Everyone knows all things being equal, most of us can shoot much better with loads with little recoil than we can with full-house .45s.

Shooters began looking for lighter recoiling loads in the .45 Colt. To my mind this was a mistake and remains a mistake for two reasons. First, we lose all thought of authenticity when we shoot light loads. I want to hear that sixgun Boom! I want to feel the gentle but authoritative recoil in my hand, and I want to hear a resounding Clang! when the bullet hits the metal target. This, of course, is strictly feeling on my part. There is, however a second and more important reason. I know of three .45 Colt sixguns that have blown apart and the common element in all three was a lighter than standard bullet coupled with a lighter than standard powder charge. Most of us know to never go above maximum listed loads in reloading manuals. At the other end of the spectrum, the recommended starting charge should also be adhered to. There are experts who will tell us it is impossible to blow a sixgun such as the .45 Colt by using a lightweight bullet and a lighter than normal powder charge. That would be the end of the argument except for the fact that just as many experts will tell us it is definitely possible. Personally, I won't take the chance. My sixguns, my hands, and my eyes are too valuable.

A growing number of cowboy action shooters have now taken it to the second level and are shooting .38 Specials. Not just standard .38 Specials using 158-grain bullets at 850 fps, as my wife, even after double carpal tunnel surgery and double thumb surgery does in her Rugers, but .38s loaded with 90- to 125-grain bullets traveling at 400 fps or less. The result is loads that allow one to shoot very quickly with little or no recoil. Very effective, but in no way authentic, and in my mind way off the mark determined by "The Spirit Of The Game."

Some shooters are also using a veritable pinch of powder with added fillers in the loads, which to me is an accident waiting to happen. At no time will I use or ever recommend any type of filler to be used with smokeless powder loads. I'll carry it even further. The only filler that should be used with black powder or black powder substitute loads is a wad or grease cookie between powder and bullet. I've even encountered "black powder" shooters who are using just enough powder with added filler to get the bullet out of the barrel and to the target. What chance does a black powder shooter using authentic 1870s style loads in a .45 Colt have competing against someone using such .38 Special loads that not only do not recoil they barely produce any smoke?

One match found me chuckling to myself as I watched a lovely cowgirl in her 70s shoot black powder, real black powder, loads in a pair of 7 1/2-inch .45 Colt sixguns, while what appeared to be a perfectly healthy fellow in his 40s was shooting .32-caliber sixguns. She appeared to be having a great deal of fun; he was so serious about winning he was absolutely not pleasant to be around. Somehow I felt he was missing something really important about cowboy action shooting and I also wondered what it was he expected to win since no prizes are awarded. CAS should be fun as we let our imagination transport us back in time.

At one time SASS considered placing a minimum muzzle velocity of 650 fps on all loads. Unfortunately, they backed off which gives us the current situation. If recoil is a problem, the answer is not trying to load down a big-bore cartridge. If the standard loads in the .45 Colt are too much, the next step down is the .45 Schofield or .44-40 or .38-40 or .44 Colt or .44 Russian. The .38 Long Colt, .32-20, and the currently popular .38 Special and .32 Magnum should be reserved for younger kids and anyone who truthfully finds it physically difficult to handle larger chamberings. Cowboy action shooting should adhere as much as possible to three basic ideas, authenticity, honesty, and safety. My mom and dad never had to lay down many rules; I knew what they expected from me. The same should be true of cowboy action shooters. The Spirit of the Game should cover just about everything.

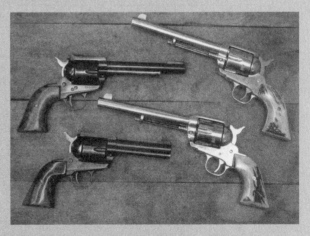

Ruger Blackhawks are the #1 choice for shooting in the Modern category while the Vaqueros take a big share of the Traditional category.

Selected Smokeless Loads for Cowboy Action Shooting

Cartridge/Bullet Weight	Charge/Powder	Barrel Length	Muzzle Velocity
.45 Colt 250-gr.	8.0 gr. Unique	7 1/2"	895 fps
	6.0 gr. Red Dot	7 1/2"	835 fps
	6.0 gr. TiteGroup	7 1/2"	810 fps
	6.0 gr. Nitro 100	7 1/2"	870 fps
	7.0 gr. WW231	7 1/2"	800 fps
.44-40 200-gr.	8.0 gr. Unique	7 1/2"	915 fps
	6.0 gr. Red Dot	7 1/2"	855 fps
	6.0 gr. TiteGroup	7 1/2"	865 fps
	6.0 gr. Nitro 100	7 1/2"	890 fps
	7.0 gr. WW231	7 1/2"	910 fps
.38-40 180-gr.	8.0 gr. Unique	7 1/2"	995 fps
	6.0 gr. Red Dot	7 1/2"	900 fps
	6.0 gr. TiteGroup	7 1/2"	925 fps
	6.0 gr. Nitro 100	7 1/2"	930 fps
	7.0 gr. WW231	7 1/2"	910 fps

Selected Black Powder Loads for Cowboy Action Shooting

Cartridge/Bullet Weight	Charge/Powder	Barrel Length	Muzzle Velocity
.45 Colt 250-gr.	35.0 gr. FFg	7 1/2"	870 fps
	35.0 gr. FFFg	7 1/2"	920 fps
	35.0 gr. Pyrodex P	7 1/2"	930 fps
	35.0 gr. Pyrodex Select	7 1/2"	905 fps
.44-40 200-gr.	35.0 gr. FFg	7 1/2"	860 fps
	35.0 gr. FFFg	7 1/2"	895 fps
	35.0 gr. Pyrodex P	7 1/2"	995 fps
	35.0 gr. Pyrodex Select	7 1/2"	935 fps
.38-40 180-gr.	30.0 gr. FFg	7 1/2"	950 fps
	30.0 gr. FFFg	7 1/2"	975 fps
	30.0 gr. Pyrodex P	7 1/2"	910 fps
	30.0 gr. Pyrodex Select	7 1/2"	985 fps

All black powder loads are by volume not by actual weight.

For an in-depth look at reloading smokeless and black powder cartridges, the reader is referred to my book *Action Shooting Cowboy Style* published by Krause Publications. This book contains a large amount of both smokeless and black powder loads for all cartridges applicable for shooting both sixguns and leverguns.

(top, left) Two replica .45s: The Colt Single Action Army will function much longer with black powder loads than the 1875 Remington. (top, right) Colt Single Actions, whether the standard Model P or the Bisley Model work well with both smokeless and black powder reloads.

The same bullets used for loading smokeless powder cartridges will also work for black powder cartridges loaded for cowboy action shooting. They will not necessarily give the best accuracy, and it will probably be necessary to swab out the barrel in between stages to keep the firearm on target. Fouling around the front of the cylinder will also probably be a factor to be reckoned with. The reason for this is that the machine-cast RNFP bullets normally used with smokeless powder are too hard, have too little lube, and a lube that is also too hard for the best results with black powder. When shooting black powder loads assembled with commercial RNFP bullets, I keep a spray bottle of Windex, cleaning rods, and patches handy. In between stages Windex-soaked patches are run down the barrel and Windex is also sprayed liberally around the front and back to the cylinder. It's cheap, it works, and it keeps sixguns and leverguns operating through an entire match.

Black powder works best with a relatively soft bullet, and lots of soft lube. This has normally meant bullets had to be cast, sized, and lubricated personally rather than purchased. This has all now changed thanks to Stewart Dawge & Associates. This relatively new company, under the Black Dawge label, offers a complete line of black powder cartridges, black powder bullets, and an excellent black powder cleaner known as Dawge Whizz. Their bullets, properly alloyed and lubed with SPG black powder lube, are currently available in a 145-grain .38, 180-grain .38-40, 205-grain .44-40, and a 235-grain .45 Colt. All bullets are of the flat-nosed style for safe use in leverguns.

Reloading black powder cartridges requires extra steps in the loading process, often requires special attention to keep our firearms functioning during a match, and definitely requires we pay strict attention to cleaning all firearms and fired brass after every session. Is it worth it? Cowboy action shooting takes us back to a better time, at least our imagination tells us so. Using frontier-style clothing, leather, and firearms transports us back more than 100 years. Using smokeless powder loads does not detract from this time travel, however black powder loads seem to not only fuel our imagination, but also to spiritually connect us with the past. With smokeless powder or black powder, whatever the choice may be, the reloader gains special satisfaction knowing the match was shot with personally assembled ammunition.

One of the most popular sixguns for CAS is the Ruger Vaquero.

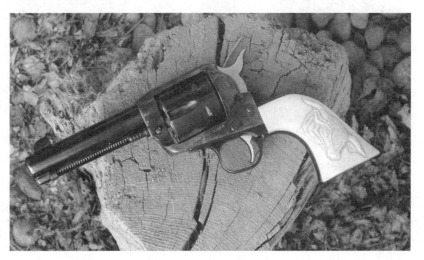

The Gun Digest® Book of Cowboy Action Shooting

Photos courtesy Liberty Prairie Regulators

62   The First Shoot: A New Club Takes Shape

Chapter 8

The First Shoot: A New Club Takes Shape

By Doc Bonecutter

It was in June 1999 that One Shot and I decided we should hold cowboy action shooting matches at our local gun club. Having shot at several other clubs, we figured that hosting matches was a possibility. The Liberty Prairie Regulators finished their inaugural shooting season in September 2000. This article will tell you how we did that and may give you a few ideas if you are of the same mind.

First off, you are going to need a core group of enthusiastic supporters. It takes a lot of work to set up and run a match and the more volunteers you have, the better. When we started shooting CAS we came back to our local gun club

Git yer guns, we're havin' a shootin' contest!

The Gun Digest® Book of Cowboy Action Shooting   **63**

and told everybody about it. We shot our cowboy pistols at the indoor range and people took notice and soon were interested in finding out more. Luckily, two of our most interested converts were the president and secretary of the gun club and they helped to form our core group of Cowboy boosters.

You will also need time and money. It takes a while to build up the supplies and publicity for a local cowboy action shoot.

After we decided to look into hosting our own matches, we began with the facility. Our local gun club has been in existence since 1924 and has active sporting clays and trap leagues. There is a rifle range but other than the shotgun sports, there has been no regular organized shooting events. The far end of the range has an "L"-shaped hill (courtesy of the last glacier) that is perfect as a backdrop for shooting. One arm of the hill is 100 yards long and the other is 75 yards. Since we have no side berms, our major concern was (and still is) safety and splatter. After due consideration and comparison to other clubs, we felt we could safely do up to five stages if we angled the end stages away from the others and limited downrange movement to the first stage only. However, since we are in the middle of the rifle range, we cannot leave any props, targets or stages up between matches so everything has to be portable.

After we had decided that the facility was appropriate, we began selling our idea to the club. We brought in pictures from other clubs and hung them up in the clubhouse. We brought up the idea at a club meeting and the club officers and members were supportive and we got the go ahead to start. I sent away for the SASS Club handbook and we began working with the help of the suggestions and tips contained in it. Other clubs were consulted and Prowler and Sierra Jack Cassidy, as well as others, were very supportive and helpful. We were also fortunate that SASS was at nearby Oshkosh, WI for the DU Great Outdoors Festival in August of 1999 and Hipshot and a great group from Memphis were there not only to give advice

This sport is limited only by your imagination. If you want to build a wagon, build a wagon.

but to serve as wonderful advertisers for cowboy action shooting.

The next step was getting the "stuff." Again, the key is to get as many people involved as possible. One of the gun club members is an excellent welder so we convinced him to spend much of the Wisconsin winter building stands for us. Several members went on scrap hunts for steel plate and another member had a friend with a flame cutter who would work for little more than cost. We ended up with 30 regular targets, as well as a number of shotgun swingers and 4 tombstones with clay bird flippers. Our welder made 22 individual stands and two five-target trees. We made sure to design the stands so that the targets were tilted forward as SASS recommends to minimize splatter and we used rolled steel instead of rebar so there were fewer surfaces for lead to splatter from. The targets and stands were our biggest expense as good, thick steel plate and bars are hard to come by for free. Our other big expense over the winter was buying five timers.

Next we needed to build props and loading/unloading tables. We decided that we would put up three stages for our first shoot and have two scenarios at each stage. That meant we needed six tables. Our original tables were made out of sawhorses and plywood but as the summer progressed we replaced them with custom tables, antique card tables, and plastic round tables from the local builder's supply. The largest prop we made was a jail front using three 4-foot by 10-foot take-down sections and assembling them with clamps and screws each time. Other props such as an outhouse, table, fences and fort pieces (made from prefab 4- by 6-foot stockade fence sections) soon followed.

As spring neared and things began to come together, we began to advertise. After consultation with the other state clubs, we set every third Saturday of the month as our match date and decided to run from April through September. Flyers were made and sent to area sporting good stores. We also took flyers to other state CAS matches as well as gun shows and Primitive swap meets (a fair number of our cowboys came over from the muzzleloading re-enactors).

Our secretary, Chicken Wing, took over the modern telegraph part and affiliated the Regulators with SASS. That got us listed in the *Chronicle* and on the Web site. There are also other links on the Web where clubs and contacts can be listed.

As the third Saturday in April neared, things stepped into high gear. The SASS computer scoring program was tested and we set up the range and did a practice shoot. We printed release forms and scoring sheets and made a full-size John Wayne cut-out into a roadside sign. I wrote stages as I continued to do all summer. Some I made up, others were given to me (Thanks, Piney Woods!), and our members shared some of their favorite scenarios from other places. Things went well and we set up the course on Friday night in 70-degree, sunny conditions. The next morning 22 brave souls showed up in 40-degree, windy, and cloudy conditions. (Gotta love that Wisconsin weather!) Sign-up was at 8:30 and a fairly prolonged shooter's meeting followed at 9:00. The key to the first shoot going smoothly (aside from the preparation) was the experienced shooters who showed up from other clubs. As is the norm in SASS, they took the rookie cowfolk under their wings and helped keep the posses moving along in a safe and smooth manner. Although none of us had had a chance to take the Range Officer

What would the Wild West be without a horse or two. I say put this thing on springs to make the shooting even tougher.

course, we had downloaded the course and followed it and the SASS rules closely. The experienced shooters helped with suggestions and directions (and lent guns and equipment!) whenever they felt they were needed.

As spring turned into summer and more shooters came, we decided to expand to 5 stages to keep the posse size manageable. We had to be a little more creative in using targets since we didn't have enough to put a whole bunch at each station. More tables and props were also necessary and we added those as we could (you do not necessarily need a lot of fancy props–a bottle, plate, rope, apron, etc. can go a long way with a little imagination). We also had to be careful in protecting the 180-degree shooting line in set-up, and splatter is always a problem without individual shooting bays. Proper stand placement and target angles can minimize it, but you can't eliminate it. A bucket of eye and ear protection was available for visitors and cowboys and cowgirls were quick to make sure spectators were protected.

By the end of the season, we had 40 to 45 shooters at each match. We were usually done by 12:30 or 1 p.m. and we retired to the clubhouse to await the computer results. We also set up a long-range target for those who wanted to shoot. We did not offer any formal side matches but gave everybody who so desired a chance to shoot at 250 yards.

The total out-of-pocket cost for our first year was a little over $2500. The club paid for almost half of the cost and a couple of our members bought the rest of the necessary supplies and were paid back over the summer as money from the match fees came in. We charged $12 per shooter and sold hot dogs, beans, and beverages after the match. By the end of the year we had pretty well broke even.

A lot remains to be done for next year and there is a lot of room for improvement. More publicity should be done – there are lots of small local newspapers as well as TV stations that should be contacted. There are lots of gun shows and local events (our float with Saloon gals in the local parade was a big hit!) that we should attend in full cowboy outfits. Our members would like to see a newsletter with match results each month. There has GOT to be a way to get more people to help set-up and take down the stages. The club has ordered 200 railroad ties to build individual shooting bays that will give us a little more flexibility and safety in stage design. (I'm still not sure just WHO is gonna lift the ties to the top of the wall…)

All in all, we had a lot of fun and I would encourage you to do the same.

With a little effort, every shooting range can be made to look like an Old West town.

SUTLER'S ROW

Doug Turnbull Restoration
Big Bore Classics

Turnbull Restoration Big Bore Classics Rifles are constructed using original and new manufactured Model 1886 Winchester & Browning Rifles. Available in calibers: 45-70, 45-90 & 50-110 (50 Express). For more information contact us at:
6680 Route 5 & 20, P.O. Box 471 Bloomfield, NY 14469
Phone: 585-657-6338 Email: turnbullrest@mindspring.com Website: www.turnbullrestoration.com

---

Triple K Manufacturing
IS
Cowboy Action Shooting Leather
Call for your 48-page catalog today! (only $5)

Refundable with Purchase

619-232-2066

Black Hills Gold Ammunition

If you were able to step back in time to the 1800's in Tombstone, Arizona you would want to be prepared. It was a rough time with rough men. You would need the best gear you could find, including ammunition; the type that would never let you down. You would want Black Hills Ammunition in your guns, in your loops and extra in your saddlebags. We won't let you down.

BLACK HILLS AMMUNITION
P.O. Box 3090, Rapid City, SD 57709
Phone: 1-605-348-5150 • Fax: 1-605-348-9827
Web: www.black-hills.com

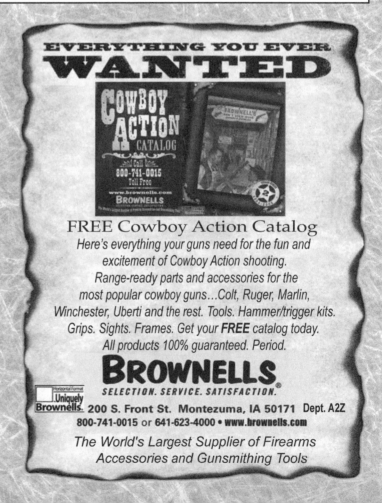

EVERYTHING YOU EVER WANTED

FREE Cowboy Action Catalog
Here's everything your guns need for the fun and excitement of Cowboy Action shooting.
Range-ready parts and accessories for the most popular cowboy guns...Colt, Ruger, Marlin, Winchester, Uberti and the rest. Tools. Hammer/trigger kits. Grips. Sights. Frames. Get your **FREE** catalog today.
All products 100% guaranteed. Period.

BROWNELLS
SELECTION. SERVICE. SATISFACTION.
200 S. Front St. Montezuma, IA 50171 Dept. A2Z
800-741-0015 or 641-623-4000 • www.brownells.com

The World's Largest Supplier of Firearms Accessories and Gunsmithing Tools

SUTLER'S ROW

Bear Track Cases

Designed by an Alaskan bush pilot! Polyurethane coated, zinc plated corners and feet, zinc plated—spring loaded steel handles, stainless steel hinges, high density urethane foam inside with a neoprene seal. Aluminum walls are standard at .070 with riveted ends. Committed to quality that will protect your valuables regardless of the transportation method you use. Exterior coating also protects other items from acquiring "aluminum black." Many styles, colors and sizes available. Wheels come on large cases and special orders can be accommodated. Call for a brochure or visit online.

Bear Track Cases when top quality protection is a must.

BEAR TRACK CASES
314 Highway 239, Freedom, WY 83120
Phone: 307-883-2468 • Fax: 307-883-2005
Web: www.beartrackcases.com

The SIDEWINDER

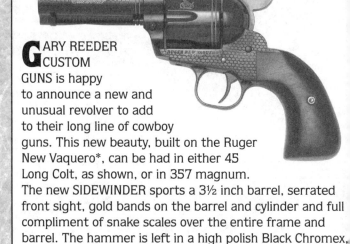

GARY REEDER CUSTOM GUNS is happy to announce a new and unusual revolver to add to their long line of cowboy guns. This new beauty, built on the Ruger New Vaquero*, can be had in either 45 Long Colt, as shown, or in 357 magnum. The new SIDEWINDER sports a 3½ inch barrel, serrated front sight, gold bands on the barrel and cylinder and full compliment of snake scales over the entire frame and barrel. The hammer is left in a high polish Black Chromex, along with the trigger. They finish it off with their Gunfighter Grip and pitch black micarta grips.

$1,195 or $950 on your new Vaquero*

4-6 month deliver in most cases.

GARY REEDER CUSTOM GUNS
2601 E. 7th Avenue, Flagstaff, AZ 86004
Phone: 928-527-4100 or 928-526-3313
Web: www.reedercustomguns.com

* The names Ruger and Vaquero are trademarks of the Sturm, Ruger Firearms Co. Inc.

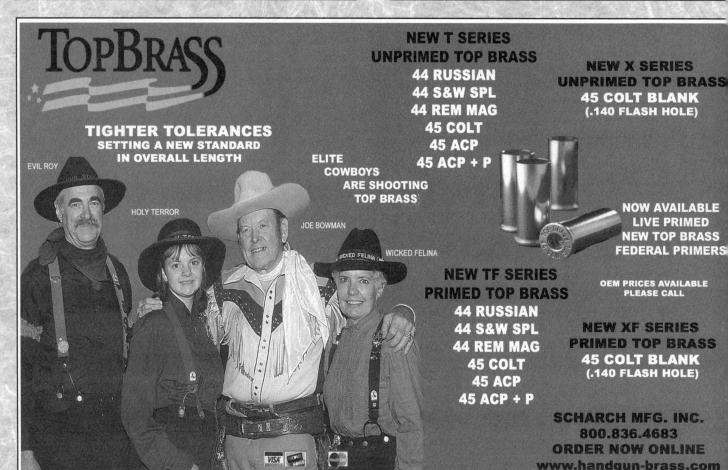

Cowboy-style Firearms & Values

The following catalog information was obtained from
The Standard Catalog of® Firearms, 15th Edition.
Used with permission.

PHOTO CREDITS

Thanks to the Milwaukee Public Museum, 800 W. Wells St., Milwaukee, WI 53233; and the Buffalo Bill Historical Center, Cody Firearms Museum, P.O. Box 1000, Cody, WY 82414, for supplying us with photographs. We also wish to thank the Remington Arms Company for its kind assistance in providing us with photos of out-of-production Remington firearms.

Many thanks to the following who loaned us their firearms to photograph for this book:

Walter C. Snyder	John J. Stimson, Jr.	Jim Supica
Paul Goodwin Creative Services	Nick Niles	William Hammond
Lt. Col. William S. Brophy	Richard M. Kumor, Sr.	Jim Cate
Mike Stuckslager	William F. Krause	John C. Dougan

AUCTION HOUSE CREDITS

The following auction houses were kind enough to allow the catalog to report unusual firearms from their sales. The directors of these auction concerns are acknowledged for their assistance and support.

Amoskeag Auction Company, Inc.
250 Commercial Street, Unit #3011
Manchester, NH 03101
Attention: Jason or Melissa Devine
603-627-7383
603-627-7384 FAX

Old Town Station Ltd.
P.O. Box 15351
Lenexa, KS 66285
Attention: Jim Supica
913-492-3000
913-492-3022 FAX

Little John's Auction Service, Inc.
1740 W. La Veta
Orange, CA 92868
Attention: Carol Watson
714-939-1170
714-939-7955 FAX

Wallis & Wallis
West Street Auction Galleries
Lewes, Sussex, England BN7 2NJ

Bonhams & Butterfields
220 San Bruno Avenue
San Francisco, CA 94103
415-861-7500
415-861-8951 FAX

Rock Island Auction Company
1050 36th Avenue
Moline, IL 61265
Attention: Patrick Hogan
800-238-8022
309-797-1655 FAX

Greg Martin Auctions
660 Third Street, Suit 100
San Francisco, CA 94107
800-509-1988
415-522-5706 FAX

GRADING SYSTEM

In the opinion of the editor, all grading systems are subjective. It is our task to offer the collector and dealer a measurement that most closely reflects a general consensus on condition. The system we present seems to come closest to describing a firearm in universal terms. We strongly recommend that the reader acquaint himself with this grading system before attempting to determine the correct price for a particular firearm's condition. Remember, in most cases condition determines price.

NIB—NEW IN BOX

This category can sometimes be misleading. It means that the firearm is in its original factory carton with all of the appropriate papers. It also means the firearm is new; that it has not been fired and has no wear. This classification brings a substantial premium for both the collector and shooter.

EXCELLENT

Collector quality firearms in this condition are highly desirable. The firearm must be in at least 98 percent condition with respect to blue wear, stock or grip finish, and bore. The firearm must also be in 100 percent original factory condition without refinishing, repair, alterations or additions of any kind. Sights must be factory original as well. This grading classification includes both modern and antique (manufactured prior to 1898) firearms.

VERY GOOD

Firearms in this category are also sought after both by the collector and shooter. Modern firearms must be in working order and retain approximately 92 percent original metal and wood finish. It must be 100 percent factory original, but may have some small repairs, alterations, or non-factory additions. No refinishing is permitted in this category. Antique firearms must have 80 percent original finish with no repairs.

GOOD

Modern firearms in this category may not be considered to be as collectable as the previous grades, but antique firearms are considered desirable. Modern firearms must retain at least 80 percent metal and wood finish, but may display evidence of old refinishing. Small repairs, alterations, or non-factory additions are sometimes encountered in this class. Factory replacement parts are permitted. The overall working condition of the firearm must be good as well as safe. The bore may exhibit wear or some corrosion, especially in antique arms. Antique firearms may be included in this category if their metal and wood finish is at least 50 percent original factory finish.

FAIR

Firearms in this category should be in satisfactory working order and safe to shoot. The overall metal and wood finish on the modern firearm must be at least 30 percent and antique firearms must have at least some original finish or old re-finish remaining. Repairs, alterations, nonfactory additions, and recent refinishing would all place a firearm in this classification. However, the modern firearm must be in working condition, while the antique firearm may not function. In either case the firearm must be considered safe to fire if in a working state.

POOR

Neither collectors nor shooters are likely to exhibit much interest in firearms in this condition. Modern firearms are likely to retain little metal or wood finish. Pitting and rust will be seen in firearms in this category. Modern firearms may not be in working order and may not be safe to shoot. Repairs and refinishing would be necessary to restore the firearm to safe working order. Antique firearms will have no finish and will not function. In the case of modern firearms their principal value lies in spare parts. On the other hand, antique firearms in this condition may be used as "wall hangers" or as an example of an extremely rare variation or have some kind of historical significance.

PRICING SAMPLE FORMAT

NIB	Exc.	V.G.	Good	Fair	Poor
550	450	400	350	300	200

PRICING

The prices given in this book are RETAIL prices

Unfortunately for shooters and collectors, there is no central clearinghouse for firearms prices. The prices given in this book are designed as a guide, not as a quote. This is an important distinction because prices for firearms vary with the time of the year and geographical location. For example, interest in firearms is at its lowest point in the summer. People are not as interested in shooting and collecting at this time of the year as they are in playing golf or taking a vacation. Therefore, prices are depressed slightly and guns that may sell quickly during the hunting season or the winter months may not sell well at all during this time of year. Geographical location also plays an important part in pricing. Political pundits are often heard to say that all politics is local. Well, the same can be said, in many ways, for the price of firearms. For instance, a Winchester Model 70 in a .264 caliber will bring a higher price in the Western states than along the Eastern seaboard. Smaller gauges and calibers seem to be more popular along both coasts and mid-sections of the United States than in the more open western sections of the country.

It is not practical to list prices in this book with regard to time of year or location. What is given is a reasonable price based on sales at gun shows, auction houses, Gun List prices, and information obtained from knowledgeable collectors and dealers. The firearms prices listed in this book are RETAIL PRICES and may bring more or less depending on the variables discussed previously. If you choose to sell your gun to a dealer you will not receive the retail price but a wholesale price based on the markup that particular dealer needs to operate. Also, in certain cases there will be no price indicated under a particular condition but rather the notation "N/A" or the symbol "—." This indicates that there is no known price available for that gun in that condition or the sales for that particular model are so few that a reliable price cannot be given. This will usually be encountered only with very rare guns, with newly introduced firearms, or more likely with antique firearms in those conditions most likely to be encountered. Most antique firearms will be seen in the good, fair and poor categories.

One final note. The prices listed here come from a variety of sources: retail stores, gun shows, individual collectors, and auction houses. Due to the nature of business, one will usually pay higher prices at a retail store than at a gun show. In some cases, auctions will produce excellent buys or extravagant prices, depending on any given situation. Collectors will sometimes pay higher prices for a firearm that they need to fill out their collection while in other circumstances they will not be willing to pay market price if they don't have to have the gun. The point here is that prices paid for firearms is an ever-changing affair based on a large number of variables. The prices in this book are a GENERAL GUIDE as to what a willing buyer and willing seller might agree on. You may find the item for less, and then you may have to pay more depending on the variables of your particular situation.

Sometimes we lose sight of our collecting or shooting goals and focus only on price. Two thoughts come to mind. First, one long time collector told me once that, "you can never pay too much for a good gun." Second, Benjamin Franklin once said, "the bitterness of poor quality lingers long after the sweetness of a low price."

In the final analysis, the prices listed here are given to assist the shooter and collector in pursuing their hobby with a better understanding of what is going on in the marketplace. If this book can expand one's knowledge, then it will have fulfilled its purpose.

A

AGUIRREY ARANZABAL (AYA)
Eibar, Spain
Side-by-Side Shotguns
Current Importers—Armes de Chasse, John Rowe, Fieldsport, New England Custom Gun Service, Ltd., British Game Gun

SIDE-BY-SIDE

Matador Side-by-Side

A 12, 16, 20, 28 or .410 bore boxlock double-barrel shotgun with 26", 28" or 30" barrels, single-selective trigger and automatic ejectors. Blued with a walnut stock. Manufactured from 1955 to 1963.

Exc.	V.G.	Good	Fair	Poor
500	400	350	300	200

NOTE: 28 gauge and .410 add 20 percent.

Matador II Side-by-Side

As above, in 12 or 20 gauge with a ventilated rib.

Exc.	V.G.	Good	Fair	Poor
600	425	375	300	200

Matador III Side-by-Side

As above, with 3" chambers.

NIB	Exc.	V.G.	Good	Fair	Poor
950	750	600	450	350	250

Bolero Side-by-Side

As above, with a non-selective single trigger and extractors. Manufactured until 1984.

Exc.	V.G.	Good	Fair	Poor
500	400	300	250	200

Iberia Side-by-Side

A 12 or 20 gauge Magnum boxlock double-barrel shotgun with 26", 28" or 30" barrels, double triggers and extractors. Blued with a walnut stock.

NIB	Exc.	V.G.	Good	Fair	Poor
600	500	425	325	250	200

Iberia II Side-by-Side

Similar to the above, in 12 or 16 gauge with 28" barrels and 2 3/4" chambers. Still in production.

NIB	Exc.	V.G.	Good	Fair	Poor
600	500	425	325	250	200

Model 106 Side-by-Side

A 12, 16, or 20 gauge boxlock double-barrel shotgun with 28" barrels, double triggers and extractors. Blued with a walnut stock. Manufactured until 1985.

NIB	Exc.	V.G.	Good	Fair	Poor
600	500	400	300	250	200

Model 107-LI Side-by-Side

As above, with the receiver lightly engraved and an English-style stock. In 12 or 16 gauge only.

NIB	Exc.	V.G.	Good	Fair	Poor
700	600	525	450	300	250

Model 116 Side-by-Side
A 12, 16 or 20 gauge sidelock double-barrel shotgun with 27" to 30" barrels, double triggers and ejectors. Engraved, blued with a walnut stock. Manufactured until 1985.

NIB	Exc.	V.G.	Good	Fair	Poor
950	800	600	475	350	275

Model 117 Side-by-Side
As above, with 3" chambers.

NIB	Exc.	V.G.	Good	Fair	Poor
850	700	500	425	300	250

Model 117 "Quail Unlimited" Side-by-Side
As above in 12 gauge only with 26" barrels and the receiver engraved "Quail Unlimited of North America." Forty-two were manufactured.

NIB	Exc.	V.G.	Good	Fair	Poor
1500	1200	875	650	425	300

Model 210 Side-by-Side
An exposed hammer, 12 or 16 gauge, boxlock shotgun with 26" to 28" barrels and double triggers. Blued with a walnut stock. Manufactured until 1985.

NIB	Exc.	V.G.	Good	Fair	Poor
800	675	550	400	325	225

Model 711 Boxlock Side-by-Side
A 12 gauge boxlock double-barrel shotgun with 28" or 30" barrels having ventilated ribs, single-selective trigger and automatic ejectors. Manufactured until 1984.

NIB	Exc.	V.G.	Good	Fair	Poor
900	800	700	500	350	250

Model 711 Sidelock Side-by-Side
As above, with sidelocks. Manufactured in 1985 only.

NIB	Exc.	V.G.	Good	Fair	Poor
1000	900	750	500	400	300

Senior Side-by-Side
A custom order 12 gauge double-barrel sidelock shotgun, gold inlaid and engraved. Made strictly to individual customer's specifications.

NIB	Exc.	V.G.	Good	Fair	Poor
15000	12500	9000	7000	4500	2250

ALLEN, ETHAN
Grafton, Massachusetts

The company was founded by Ethan Allen in the early 1800s. It became a prolific gun-making firm that evolved from Ethan Allen to Allen & Thurber, as well as the Allen & Wheelock Company. It was located in Norwich, Connecticut, and Worcester, Massachusetts, as well as Grafton. It eventually became the Forehand & Wadsworth Company in 1871 after the death of Ethan Allen. There were many and varied firearms produced under all of the headings described above. If one desires to collect Ethan Allen firearms, it would be advisable to educate oneself, as there are a number of fine publications available on the subject.

Side Hammer Navy Revolver
This was a large-frame, military-type revolver that was similar to the Side Hammer Belt Model, chambered for .36 caliber percussion. It features an octagon, 5.5" to 8" barrel with a 6-shot, engraved cylinder. There was an early-production type with a friction catch on the trigger guard. There were approximately 100 manufactured between 1858 and 1861.

Exc.	V.G.	Good	Fair	Poor
—	—	3750	1500	500

Standard Model
1,000 manufactured.

Exc.	V.G.	Good	Fair	Poor
—	—	3250	1250	500

Center Hammer Army Revolver
A large, military-type, single-action revolver that was chambered for .44 caliber percussion. It had a 7.5", half-octagon barrel and a 6-shot, unfluted cylinder. The hammer was mounted in the center of the frame. The finish was blued with a case-colored hammer and trigger guard and walnut grips. The barrel was marked, "Allen & Wheelock. Worchester, Mass. U.S./Allen's Pt's. Jan. 13, 1857. Dec. 15, 1857, Sept. 7, 1858." There were approximately 700 manufactured between 1861 and 1862.

Exc.	V.G.	Good	Fair	Poor
—	—	3750	1500	500

Center Hammer Navy Revolver
Similar to the Army Revolver except chambered for .36 caliber percussion with a 7.5", full-octagon barrel. Examples have been noted with 5", 6", or 8" barrels. Otherwise, it was similar to the Army model.

Exc.	V.G.	Good	Fair	Poor
—	—	3000	1250	500

Center Hammer Percussion Revolver
A single-action revolver chambered for .36 caliber percussion. It had an octagonal, 3" or 4" barrel with a 6-shot, unfluted cylinder. The finish was blued with walnut grips. This model supposedly was made for the Providence, Rhode Island, Police Department and has become commonly referred to as the "Providence Police Model." There were approximately 700 manufactured between 1858 and 1862.

Exc.	V.G.	Good	Fair	Poor
—	—	1250	500	200

.32 Side Hammer Rimfire Revolver
A single-action, spur-trigger, pocket revolver chambered for the .32 caliber rimfire cartridge. It had octagonal barrels from 3" to 5" in length. The finish was blued with flared-butt, walnut grips. It was marked "Allen & Wheelock Worcester, Mass." There were three variations with a total of approximately 1,000 manufactured between 1859 and 1862.

First Model
Rounded top strap.

Exc.	V.G.	Good	Fair	Poor
—	—	800	350	150

Second Model
July 3, 1860 marked on frame.

Exc.	V.G.	Good	Fair	Poor
—	—	700	300	100

Third Model
1858 and 1861 patent dates.

Exc.	V.G.	Good	Fair	Poor
—	—	600	200	100

Vest Pocket Derringer
A small pocket pistol chambered for the .22 rimfire cartridge. It had a 2", part-octagon barrel that swung to the right-hand side for loading. The cartridges were manually extracted. It featured a brass frame with a blued or plated barrel and walnut, bird's-head grips. The barrel was marked "Allen & Co. Makers." This was an extremely small firearm, and there were approximately 200 manufactured between 1869 and 1871.

Exc.	V.G.	Good	Fair	Poor
—	—	700	300	100

.32 Derringer
Similar to the Vest Pocket version, larger in size, and chambered for the .32 rimfire cartridge. It had a part-octagon barrel from 2" to 4" in length that swung to the right for loading. This version featured an automatic extractor. The barrel was marked "E. Allen & Co. Worchester, Mass." This was a very rare firearm, made between 1865 and 1871.

Exc.	V.G.	Good	Fair	Poor
—	—	600	250	100

.41 Derringer
The same size and configuration as the .32 caliber model except it was chambered for the .41 rimfire cartridge with barrel lengths of 2.5" to 2.75" in length. The markings were the same. There were approximately 100 manufactured between 1865 and 1871.

Exc.	V.G.	Good	Fair	Poor
—	—	2000	800	350

Side Hammer Breech-loading Rifle
A unique rifle chambered for .36 to .50 caliber percussion. It was offered with various-length, part-octagon barrels. It had an unusual breech mechanism that was activated by a rotating lever which resembled a water faucet. The barrel was browned with a case-colored lock and a walnut stock. It was marked "Allen & Wheelock/ Allen's Patent July 3, 1855." There were approximately 500 manufactured between 1855 and 1860.

Exc.	V.G.	Good	Fair	Poor
—	—	3250	1500	500

Drop Breech Rifle
This single-shot rifle was chambered for the .22 through the .44 rimfire cartridges. It had a part-octagon barrel from 23" to 28" in length. The breech was activated by the combination trigger guard action lever. Opening the breech automatically ejected the empty cartridge. The external hammer was manually cocked, and it featured an adjustable sight. The barrel was blued with a case-colored frame and a walnut stock. It was marked "Allen & Wheelock/ Allen's Pat. Sept. 18, 1860." There were approximately 2,000 manufactured between 1860 and 1871.

Exc.	V.G.	Good	Fair	Poor
—	—	1250	500	200

Double-Barrel Shotgun
A side-by-side gun chambered for 10 or 12 gauge. The barrel length was 28". It was loaded by means of a trapdoor-type breech that had a lever handle. The finish was blued with checkered walnut stock. There were a few hundred manufactured between 1865 and 1871.

Exc.	V.G.	Good	Fair	Poor
—	—	1650	700	250

ALSOP, C.R.
Middletown, Connecticut
This firearms manufacturer made revolvers during 1862 and 1863. They made two basic models, the Navy and the Pocket model. Some collectors consider the Alsop to be a secondary U.S. martial handgun, but no verifying government contracts are known to exist.

First Model Navy Revolver
A .36 cal. revolver with a 3.5", 4.5", 5.5", or 6.5" barrel length and a 5-shot cylinder. It has a blued finish, wood grips, and a peculiar hump in its backstrap. The first model has a safety device which blocks the spur trigger. This device is found on serial numbers 1-100. Markings are as follows: "C.R. Alsop Middletown, Conn. 1860 & 1861" on the barrel. The cylinder is marked "C.R. Alsop" & "Nov. 26th, 1861"; the side plate, "Patented Jan. 21st, 1862."

Exc.	V.G.	Good	Fair	Poor
—	—	3750	1250	500

Standard Model Navy Revolver
Exactly the same as the First Model without the safety device. They are serial numbered 101 to 300.

Exc.	V.G.	Good	Fair	Poor
—	—	3250	850	300

Pocket Model Revolver
A .31 cal. 5-shot revolver with spur trigger, 4" round barrel, blued finish, and wood grips. It is very similar in appearance to the Navy model but smaller in size. It is marked "C.R. Alsop Middletown, Conn. 1860 & 1861" on the barrel. The cylinder is marked "C.R. Alsop Nov. 26th, 1861." They are serial numbered 1-300.

Exc.	V.G.	Good	Fair	Poor
—	—	1500	600	200

AMERICAN ARMS CO.
Boston, Massachusetts
The history of American Arms is rather sketchy, but it appears the company was formed in 1853 as the G. H. Fox Co. and then became the American Tool & Machine Co. in 1865. In 1870 they formed a new corporation called American Arms Company with George Fox as the principle stockholder. This corporation was dissolved in 1873; a second American Arms Co. was incorporated in 1877 and a third in 1890. It is unclear if these corporations had essentially the same owners, but George H. Fox appears as a principal owner in two of the three. One could assume that financial problems forced them to bankrupt one corporation and reorganize under another. American Arms manufactured firearms in Boston, Massachusetts, from 1866 until 1893. In 1893 they moved to Bluffton, Alabama and manufactured guns until 1901.

Whitmore Model Hammerless Double
Manufactured from 1890 to 1901. It comes in 10, 12, and 16 gauge with 28", 30" or 32" twist, laminated or Damascus barrels. It is marked Whitmore's patent.

Courtesy Nick Niles, Paul Goodwin photo

Exc.	V.G.	Good	Fair	Poor
—	1000	500	250	150

TOP BREAK REVOLVERS
Spur Trigger—Single-Action Five-Shot Revolver
These revolvers were made between 1883 and 1887 in .38 S&W only. They feature an unusual manual ring extractor and double-fluted cylinder. They are nickel plated with hard rubber grips and are marked "American Arms Company Boston Mass."

Exc.	V.G.	Good	Fair	Poor
—	400	250	100	75

Standard Trigger Double-Action Model 1886 Revolver
This model has a standard trigger and trigger guard, comes in .32 short and .38 S&W with a 3.5-inch barrel, in blue or nickel finish. The early models are equipped with the ring extractor and double fluted cylinder. Later variations have a standard star extractor and single fluted cylinder.

Exc.	V.G.	Good	Fair	Poor
—	600	250	100	75

Hammerless Model 1890 Double-Action
These guns were manufactured from 1890 to 1901. It has an adjustable single- or double-stage trigger pull and several unusual safety devices. It comes in .32 and .38 S&W with a 3.25" ribbed barrel, fluted cylinder, nickel finish, hard rubber grips with logo and ivory or mother of pearl grips. It is marked "American Arms Co. Boston/Pat. May 25, 1886." The top strap is marked "Pat. Pending" on early models and "Pat's May 25'86/Mar 11'89/June 17'90" on later models.

Exc.	V.G.	Good	Fair	Poor
—	600	250	100	75

Double-Barrel Derringers
American Arms Co. manufactured a two-barrel derringer-style pocket pistol. The barrels were manually rotated to load and fire the weapon. The pistol had a nickel-plated brass frame, blued barrels, and walnut grips. The markings were as follows: "American Arms Co. Boston, Mass." on one barrel and "Pat. Oct. 31, 1865" on the other barrel. There were approximately 2,000-3,000 produced between 1866 and 1878.

Combination .22 caliber R.F. and .32 caliber R.F.
A two-caliber combination with 3" barrel, square butt only. The most common variation.

Exc.	V.G.	Good	Fair	Poor
—	—	700	300	100

.32 cal. R.F., Both Barrels
3" barrel with square butt.

Exc.	V.G.	Good	Fair	Poor
—	—	900	400	100

.32 caliber R.F., Both Barrels
2-5/8" barrel with bird's-head grips.

Exc.	V.G.	Good	Fair	Poor
—	—	950	450	150

.38 caliber R.F., Both Barrels
2-5/8" barrel with bird's-head grips. A rare variation.

Exc.	V.G.	Good	Fair	Poor
—	—	2250	950	350

.41 caliber R.F., Both Barrels
2-5/8" barrel with square butt only.

Exc.	V.G.	Good	Fair	Poor
—	—	1750	750	200

AMERICAN DERRINGER CORP.
Waco, Texas

Model 1 Derringer
Fashioned after the Remington O/U derringer this is a high quality, rugged pistol. It is built from high tensile strength stainless steel. There are over 60 different rifle and pistol calibers to choose from on special order. The upper barrel can be chambered different from the lower barrel on request. Available in a high polish finish or a satin finish. Offered with rosewood, bacote, walnut, or blackwood grips. Ivory, bonded ivory, stag, or pearl are available at extra cost. Overall length is 4.8", barrel length is 3", width across the frame is .9", width across the grip is 1.2". Typical weight is 15 oz. in .45 caliber. All guns are furnished with French fitted leatherette case. Prices are determined by caliber.

Caliber: .22 Long Rifle through .357 Mag. and .45 ACP

NIB	Exc.	V.G.	Good	Fair	Poor
300	225	150	125	100	75

Calibers: .41 Mag., .44-40, .44 Special, .44 Mag., .45 Long Colt, .410 Bore, .22 Hornet, .223 Rem., 30-30, and .47-70 Gov't.

NIB	Exc.	V.G.	Good	Fair	Poor
375	300	250	200	150	100

NOTE: Add $25 for optional extra high polish finish.

Model 1 Lady Derringer
Similar to the Model 1 but chambered for the .38 Special, .32 Magnum, .45 Colt, or .357 Magnum. Offered in two grades.

Deluxe Grade
High polished stainless steel with scrimshawed ivory grips with cameo or rose design.

NIB	Exc.	V.G.	Good	Fair	Poor
325	250	200	150	100	75

Deluxe Engraved Grade
Same as above but hand engraved in 1880s style.

NIB	Exc.	V.G.	Good	Fair	Poor
650	550	500	450	250	150

NOTE: For .45 Colt and .45/.410 add $75. For .357 magnum add $50.

Model 1 Texas Commemorative
Built with a solid brass frame and stainless steel barrel. Dimensions are same as Model 1. Grips are stag or rosewood and offered in .45 Colt, .44-40, or .38 Special. Barrels marked "Made in the 150th Year of Texas Freedom." Limited to 500 pistols in each caliber.

Caliber: .38 Special

NIB	Exc.	V.G.	Good	Fair	Poor
325	250	200	150	100	75

Calibers: .45 Colt and .44-40

NIB	Exc.	V.G.	Good	Fair	Poor
400	325	250	200	125	100

Deluxe Engraved
Special serial number engraved on backstrap.

NIB	Exc.	V.G.	Good	Fair	Poor
900	750	550	350	250	150

Model 1 NRA 500 Series
Limited edition of 500. Also available in gold and blue finishes over stainless steel.

NIB	Exc.	V.G.	Good	Fair	Poor
350	300	250	200	150	100

Model 1 125th Anniversary Commemorative
Built to commemorate the 125th anniversary of the derringer, 1866 to 1991. Similar to the Model 1 but marked with the patent date December 12, 1865. Brass frame and stainless steel barrel. Chambered for .440-40, .45 Colt, or .38 Special.

NIB	Exc.	V.G.	Good	Fair	Poor
300	250	225	175	125	100

Deluxe Engraved

NIB	Exc.	V.G.	Good	Fair	Poor
650	550	500	450	250	150

Model 4
Similar in appearance to the Model 3 but fitted with a 4.1" barrel. Overall length is 6" and weight is about 16.5 oz. Chambered for 3" .410 bore, .45 Long Colt, .44 Magnum, or .357 Magnum.

NIB	Exc.	V.G.	Good	Fair	Poor
375	300	275	250	200	125

NOTE: For .45-70 add $150. For .44 magnum add $100.

Model 4—Engraved

NIB	Exc.	V.G.	Good	Fair	Poor
1500	1200	—	—	—	—

AMERICAN FRONTIER FIREARMS
Aguanga, California

This firm began importing Italian-made parts for its single-action revolver line in 1996. These parts are then fitted and finished in its California facility. The first of these metallic cartridge revolvers was ready for delivery in late 1996. In addition to its standard guns the company also offers special finishes and is ready to fill special orders. For this reason, only standard prices are given.

1871-72 Open Top Standard Model
Offered in .38 or .44 caliber with non-rebated cylinder. Barrel lengths are 7.5" or 8" in round. Blued finish except silver backstrap and trigger guard. Walnut grips.

NIB	Exc.	V.G.	Good	Fair	Poor
795	625	500	400	—	—

Richards & Mason Conversion 1851 Navy Standard Model
Offered in .38 and .44 calibers with Mason ejector assembly and non-rebated cylinder with a choice of octagon barrels in 4.75", 5.5", or 7.5". Blued finish with blued backstrap and trigger guard. Walnut grips.

NIB	Exc.	V.G.	Good	Fair	Poor
795	325	500	400	—	—

1860 Richards Army Model
Chambered for .44 Colt and .38 caliber. Rebated cylinder with or without ejector assembly. Barrel length is 7.5". High polish blue finish with silver trigger guard and case hardened frame.

NIB	Exc.	V.G.	Good	Fair	Poor
795	325	500	400	—	—

NOTE: Guns shipped without ejector assembly will be supplied with a ramrod and plunger typical of the period.

AMERICAN GUN CO., NEW YORK
Norwich, Connecticut
Maker—Crescent Firearms Co.
Distributor—H. & D. Folsom Co.

NOTE: For a full listing of most of the variations of the Crescent Arms Co., and shotguns marked with American Gun Co. see "Crescent F.A. Co."

Side-by-Side Shotgun
A typical trade gun made around the turn of the century by the Crescent Firearms Co. to be distributed by H. & D. Folsom. These are sometimes known as "Hardware Store Guns," as that is where many were sold. This particular gun was chambered for 12, 16, and 20 gauges and was produced with or without external hammers. The length of the barrels varied, as did the chokes. Some were produced with Damascus barrels; some, with fluid steel. The latter are worth approximately 25 percent more.

Knickerbocker Pistol
(See Knickerbocker)

ARMSCO FIREARMS CORP.
Ankara, Turkey
USA—Des Plaines, Illinois

Built by Huglu Hunting Firearms Corporation in Turkey, which was established in 1927. Armsco is the U.S. representative. First year of business in the U.S. was 2002.

SIDE-BY-SIDE

Model 202B
Boxlock gun offered in 12, 16, 20, and 28 gauge as well as .410 bore with barrel lengths from 22" to 32" depending on gauge. Double triggers. Hand engraved about 50 percent coverage. Fixed chokes or choke tubes. Checkered walnut stock with cheekpiece. Weight is about 6.4 lbs. to 7.3 lbs. depending on gauge.

NIB	Exc.	V.G.	Good	Fair	Poor
520	400	—	—	—	—

Model 202A
Same as above but offered with standard buttstock.

NIB	Exc.	V.G.	Good	Fair	Poor
697	525	—	—	—	—

Model 201A
Offered in gauges from 12 to .410 with sideplates with 50 percent hand engraving. Choice of single or double triggers.

NIB	Exc.	V.G.	Good	Fair	Poor
695	525	—	—	—	—

Model 200A
Boxlock in gauges 12 to .410 with single trigger. Hand engraved 50 percent coverage.

NIB	Exc.	V.G.	Good	Fair	Poor
750	575	—	—	—	—

Model 205A
Offered in gauges 12 to .410 with barrel lengths 22" to 32" depending on gauge. Boxlock frame with 60 percent hand engraving coverage. Single trigger. Checkered walnut stock. Weights are 6.1 lbs. to 6.8 lbs. depending on gauge.

NIB	Exc.	V.G.	Good	Fair	Poor
990	750	—	—	—	—

Model 210AE
Offered in 12, 16, and 20 gauge with single trigger and automatic ejectors. Boxlock frame is 60 percent hand engraved. Optional fixed or choke tubes.

NIB	Exc.	V.G.	Good	Fair	Poor
1250	950	—	—	—	—

Model 210BE
Same as above but with double triggers.

NIB	Exc.	V.G.	Good	Fair	Poor
1150	850	—	—	—	—

ARRIETA S.L. ELQOLBAR
Spain
Importers—Jack J. Jansma, Orvis,
New England Arms, Quality Arms

This company produces a wide variety of double-barrel shotguns in a price range from $450 to above $14,000. It is recommended that highly engraved examples, as well as small bore arms, be individually appraised.

490 Eder
A double-barrel boxlock shotgun with double triggers and extractors. Discontinued in 1986.

Exc.	V.G.	Good	Fair	Poor
475	425	325	250	100

500 Titan
A Holland & Holland-style sidelock double-barrel shotgun with French case hardened and engraved locks. Double triggers on extractors. No longer imported after 1986.

Exc.	V.G.	Good	Fair	Poor
575	500	400	300	150

501 Palomara
As above, but more finely finished. Discontinued in 1986.

Exc.	V.G.	Good	Fair	Poor
700	600	500	400	200

505 Alaska
As above, but more intricately engraved. Discontinued in 1986.

Exc.	V.G.	Good	Fair	Poor
800	700	600	500	250

510 Montana
A Holland & Holland-style sidelock double-barrel shotgun with the internal parts gold-plated.

NIB	Exc.	V.G.	Good	Fair	Poor
2200	1750	1250	850	500	250

550 Field

As above, without the internal parts gold-plated.

NIB	Exc.	V.G.	Good	Fair	Poor
2200	1750	1250	850	500	250

557 Standard

As above, but more finely finished.

NIB	Exc.	V.G.	Good	Fair	Poor
2750	2000	1750	1250	800	400

558 Patria

As above, but more finely finished.

NIB	Exc.	V.G.	Good	Fair	Poor
2650	2150	1750	1250	800	400

560 Cumbre

As above, but featuring intricate engraving.

NIB	Exc.	V.G.	Good	Fair	Poor
2800	2200	1800	1200	800	400

570 Lieja

NIB	Exc.	V.G.	Good	Fair	Poor
3400	2500	2000	1500	750	500

575 Sport

NIB	Exc.	V.G.	Good	Fair	Poor
3750	2750	2250	1700	1200	750

578 Victoria

This model is engraved in the English manner with floral bouquets.

NIB	Exc.	V.G.	Good	Fair	Poor
3500	2750	2000	1250	750	350

585 Liria

As above, but more finely finished.

NIB	Exc.	V.G.	Good	Fair	Poor
3800	3000	2250	1500	900	400

588 Cima

NIB	Exc.	V.G.	Good	Fair	Poor
3800	3000	2250	1500	900	400

590 Regina

NIB	Exc.	V.G.	Good	Fair	Poor
4250	3500	2700	1750	1000	500

595 Principe

As above, but engraved with relief-cut hunting scenes.

NIB	Exc.	V.G.	Good	Fair	Poor
6500	5000	4000	3000	2000	1000

600 Imperial

This double-barrel shotgun has a self-opening action.

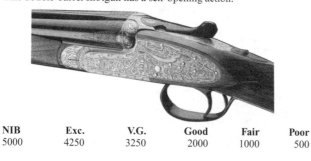

NIB	Exc.	V.G.	Good	Fair	Poor
5000	4250	3250	2000	1000	500

601 Imperial Tiro

As above, but nickel-plated. Fitted with a self-opening action.

NIB	Exc.	V.G.	Good	Fair	Poor
5750	5000	4000	3000	2000	1000

801

A detachable sidelock, self-opening action, double-barrel shotgun engraved in the manner of Churchill.

NIB	Exc.	V.G.	Good	Fair	Poor
7950	7000	6500	4000	3000	1500

802

As above, with Holland & Holland-style engraving.

NIB	Exc.	V.G.	Good	Fair	Poor
7950	7000	6500	4000	3000	1500

803

As above, with Purdey-style engraving.

NIB	Exc.	V.G.	Good	Fair	Poor
5850	5000	4000	3000	2000	1000

871

This model features hand detachable sidelocks with Holland ejectors. Scroll engraving.

NIB	Exc.	V.G.	Good	Fair	Poor
4300	3600	2500	1500	1000	750

872

This model has same features as the Model 871 with the addition of more engraving coverage using a tighter scroll.

NIB	Exc.	V.G.	Good	Fair	Poor
9800	8250	7000	4000	3000	1000

873

This model features hand detachable sidelocks and game scene engraving.

NIB	Exc.	V.G.	Good	Fair	Poor
6850	5800	4500	3000	1500	750

874

Same features as above model but with the addition of a blued frame with gold line outlines.

NIB	Exc.	V.G.	Good	Fair	Poor
8000	6750	5500	4500	3000	1000

875

A custom manufactured sidelock, double-barrel shotgun built solely to the customer's specifications.

NIB	Exc.	V.G.	Good	Fair	Poor
13000	10500	8500	6000	3000	1000

B

BAIKAL
Russia

Baikal TOZ - 34

A 12 or 28 gauge double-barrel shotgun with 26" or 28" barrels, double triggers, cocking indicators and extractors. Blued with a checkered walnut stock. This model was also available with a silver-plated receiver. Mfg. List Price: $465.95

NIB	Exc.	V.G.	Good	Fair	Poor
375	300	250	200	100	75

CURRENTLY IMPORTED BAIKAL SHOTGUNS
Importer—European American Armory

IZH18

This is a single-barrel shotgun chambered for 12, 20, or .410 bore. Choice of 26.5" or 29.5" barrels. Hardwood stock. Ejectors. Introduced in 1999.

NIB	Exc.	V.G.	Good	Fair	Poor
95	75	50	—	—	—

IZK18MAX

Similar to the above model but with polished nickel receiver, vent rib, walnut stock, screw-in chokes, and ejectors. Offered in 12 and 20 gauge as well as .410 bore.

NIB	Exc.	V.G.	Good	Fair	Poor
170	125	100	—	—	—

IZH43

This side-by-side gun is available in 12, 16, 20, 28, and .410 bore. In barrel lengths for 20" to 28" depending on gauge. Internal hammers. Single-selective trigger, ejectors. Walnut stock.

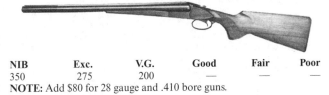

NIB	Exc.	V.G.	Good	Fair	Poor
350	275	200	—	—	—

NOTE: Add $80 for 28 gauge and .410 bore guns.

IZH43K

Introduced in 1999 this is a 12 gauge 3" side-by-side hammer gun with choice of barrel lengths of 18.5", 20", 24", 26", and 28". Single-selective trigger or double trigger. Engraved side plates. Walnut stock with pistol grip. Weight is about 7.3 lbs.

NIB	Exc.	V.G.	Good	Fair	Poor
375	300	250	—	—	—

NOTE: Deduct $40 for double triggers.

MP213 Coach Gun

Similar to the above model but with internal hammers. Single or double triggers. Weight is about 7 lbs.

NIB	Exc.	V.G.	Good	Fair	Poor
275	255	175	—	—	—

NOTE: Deduct $40 for double triggers. Add $80 for 20 gauge.

BAKER GUN & FORGING CO.
Batavia, New York

The Baker Gun & Forging Company was founded in early 1890, by Elias Baker, brother of William Baker. Made from drop forged parts, Baker single and double barrel shotguns quickly gained a reputation for strength and reliability among shooters of the period. Offered in a wide variety of grades, from plain utilitarian to heavily embellished models, Baker shotguns have in recent years become highly collectable. The company was sold on December 24, 1919, to H. & D. Folsom Arms Company of Norwich, Connecticut. The Folsom Company had for almost 20 years been the Baker Company's sole New York City agent and had marketed at least one Baker model that was only made for them. From 1919 to approximately 1923, Folsom continued to assemble and make Baker shotguns. Late model Bakers were made by the Crescent Firearms Company and have serial numbers with an "F" suffix.

The Baker Gun & Forging Company was the first American arms manufacturer to:
1. Make a single barrel trap shotgun.
2. Make a single barrel trap shotgun with a ventilated rib.
3. Make arms with an intercepting firing pin block safety.
4. Make a double barrel shotgun with hammers directly behind the firing pins.
5. Use a long swinging sear that once adjusted gave consistent trigger pull throughout the working life of an arm.

Those Baker shotguns manufactured between 1913 and 1923 that were engraved by Rudolph J. Kornbrath command substantial price premiums over the values listed. Prospective purchasers of Kornbrath decorated Bakers are advised to secure a qualified appraisal prior to acquisition.

Baker Trap Gun

A 12 gauge single barrel boxlock shotgun with either a 30" or 32" barrel. Blued, case hardened with a walnut stock.

Exc.	V.G.	Good	Fair	Poor
1500	1250	900	500	250

Elite Grade

Standard scrollwork and simple game scenes engraved on receiver.

Exc.	V.G.	Good	Fair	Poor
2000	1500	1000	500	250

Superba

Heavily engraved on receiver and sides of barrel breech.

Exc.	V.G.	Good	Fair	Poor
4000	3000	1500	750	500

Expert Grade Double Shotgun

The highest grade shotgun manufactured by the Baker Gun & Forging Company. General specifications as above. The stock of imported English or French walnut. The engraving of full coverage type and partially chiselled. Automatic ejectors and single trigger if requested. Built on special order only.

Exc.	V.G.	Good	Fair	Poor
5000	4000	2000	1500	750

Deluxe Grade Double Shotgun

The designation given those Expert Grade shotguns produced by H. & D. Folsom from 1919 to 1923. Characteristics and values identical to those listed for the Baker Expert Grade Double Shotgun.

Black Beauty Double Shotgun

Made solely for H. & D. Folsom Arms Company. A 12 or 16 gauge double barrel shotgun with sidelocks and 26", 28", 30", or 32" barrels in 12 gauge and 26", 28", or 30" barrels in 16 gauge. The barrels are blued, the receiver is case hardened, the sideplates are finished with black oxide and the stock is walnut. Automatic ejectors and single trigger are extra cost options.

Exc.	V.G.	Good	Fair	Poor
850	750	650	500	250

Grade S Double Shotgun

As above, with simple engraving.

Exc.	V.G.	Good	Fair	Poor
1200	1000	750	400	250

Grade R Double Shotgun

As above, with case hardened sideplates and engraved with simple scrollwork and game scenes.

Exc.	V.G.	Good	Fair	Poor
1500	1250	900	500	300

Paragon Grade Shotgun
As above, with finely cut scrollwork and detailed game scenes engraved on the sideplates. The stock of finely figured walnut.

Exc.	V.G.	Good	Fair	Poor
2000	1750	1200	900	500

Paragon Grade—Model NN
As above, but more finely engraved. Built on special order only. Automatic ejectors.

Exc.	V.G.	Good	Fair	Poor
3000	2250	1400	900	500

Batavia Special
A 12 or 16 gauge double barrel shotgun with sidelocks and 28", 30", or 32" barrels in 12 gauge and 28" or 30" barrels in 16 gauge. Blued, case hardened with a walnut stock and double triggers.

Exc.	V.G.	Good	Fair	Poor
500	325	275	225	175

Batavia Brush Gun
A 12 or 16 gauge double barrel shotgun with sidelocks and 26" barrels. Blued, case hardened with walnut stock. Sling rings and swivels optional.

Exc.	V.G.	Good	Fair	Poor
400	325	275	225	175

Batavia Leader
A 12 or 16 gauge double barrel shotgun with sidelocks and 26", 28", 30", or 32" barrels in 12 gauge and 26", 28", or 30" barrels in 16 gauge. Blued, case hardened with a walnut stock and double triggers.

Exc.	V.G.	Good	Fair	Poor
500	425	375	325	275

Batavia Damascus
As above with Damascus barrels.

Exc.	V.G.	Good	Fair	Poor
400	325	275	225	175

Baker Hammer Gun
A 10, 12, or 16 gauge double barrel shotgun with sidehammers and 30" and 32" barrels in 10 gauge, 26" to 32" barrels in 12 gauge and 26" to 30" barrels in 16 gauge. Browned, case hardened with walnut stock and double triggers.

Exc.	V.G.	Good	Fair	Poor
300	250	175	125	100

Batavia Automatic Rifle
A .22 caliber semi-automatic rifle with a 24" round barrel and a detachable 7-shot magazine. Blued with a walnut stock.

Exc.	V.G.	Good	Fair	Poor
400	300	200	100	50

BAKER, WILLIAM
Marathon, Syracuse and Ithaca, New York
William Baker designed and built double barrel shotguns from approximately 1869 until his death in 1889. His hammerless designs were used by the Baker Gun & Forging Company of Batavia, New York, which was established by his brother Elias in early 1890.

BAKER, M.A.
Fayetteville, North Carolina
In business from 1857 through 1862, Baker produced sporting arms prior to the Civil War. During the Civil War Baker altered muskets and "common rifles." In addition, it is thought that Baker made rifles for the State of North Carolina with lockplates stamped M.A. BAKER/FAYETTEVILLE/N.C. These rifles resembled the U.S. Model 1841 Rifle and had the following characteristics: Overall length 51-1/2"; Barrel length 35-1/8"; Caliber .50. Number made in excess of 65. Prospective purchasers are strongly advised to secure a qualified appraisal prior to acquisition.

Exc.	V.G.	Good	Fair	Poor
—	—	25000	12500	2500

BAKER, THOMAS
Baker shotguns and rifles were extensively imported into the United States during the nineteenth and early twentieth centuries. As these arms are often marked with his address, the following list of the London premises he occupied should prove useful.

1 Stonecutter Street	1838-1844
Bury Street, St. James	1844-1850
34 St. James Street	1850
88 Fleet Street	1851-1881
88 Fleet Street & 21 Cockspur Street	1882-1898
88 Fleet Street & 29 Glasshouse Street	1899-1905
29 Glasshouse Street	1905-1915
64 Haymarket	1915

BALL REPEATING CARBINE
Lamson & Co.
Windsor, Vermont

Ball Repeating Carbine

A .50 caliber lever action repeating carbine with a 20.5" round barrel and 7-shot magazine. The receiver is marked "E.G. Lamson & Co./Windsor, Vt./U.S./Ball's Patent/June 23, 1863/Mar. 15, 1864." Blued, case hardened with a walnut stock. Late production examples of this carbine have been noted with browned or bright barrels. In excess of 1,500 were made between 1864 and 1867.

Exc.	V.G.	Good	Fair	Poor
—	5000	2500	900	400

BALLARD PATENT ARMS
(until 1873; after 1875, see MARLIN)

On Nov. 5, 1861, C.H. Ballard of Worcester, Massachusetts, received a patent for a breechloading mechanism that would remain in production for nearly thirty years. Ballard patented a breechblock that tilted down at its front to expose the breech by activating the lever/triggerguard. During the twelve years that followed, Ballard rifles, carbines, and shotguns were produced by five interrelated companies. Four of these were successive: Ball & Williams, R. Ball & Co. (both of Worcester, Massachusetts), Merrimack Arms & Manufacturing Co. and Brown Manufacturing Company (both of Newburyport, Massachusetts). These four companies produced Ballard arms in a successive serial range (1 through approximately 22,000), all marked upon the top of the frame and the top of the barrel where it joins the frame. In 1863, another company, Dwight, Chapin & Company of Bridgeport, Connecticut, also produced Ballard rifles and carbines in a larger frame size, but in a different serial range (1 through about 1,900), usually marked on the left side of the frame below the agents' mark. The large frame carbines and rifles were produced to fulfill a U.S. War Department contract initially for 10,000 of each, subsequently reduced to 1,000 of each, issued to Merwin & Bray, the sole agents for the Ballard patent arms between 1862 and 1866. Most of the production during this period concentrated on military contracts, either for the U.S. War Department or the state of Kentucky, although the state of New York also purchased 500 for its state militia.

Ballard (Ball & Williams) sporting rifles, second type (Serial numbers 200-1600, and 1600-14,000, interspersed with martial production)

Barrel length 24", 28", or 30", usually octagonal, but part round/part octagonal as well; calibers .32, .38, and .44 rimfire. Markings: BALL & WILLIAMS/Worcester, Mass., BALLARD'S PATENT/Nov. 5, 1861, and MERWIN & BRAY, AGT'S/ NEW YORK, on facets of barrel until about serial no. 9000, thereafter the patent name and date on the right side of the frame and the manufacturer and agents on the left side of the frame. On early production (200 to 1500), the extractor knob is smaller and crescent shaped. Early production (prior to about serial no. 10,000) have solid breechblocks; after that number breechblocks are made in two halves. A few of these arms were made with bronze frames to facilitate engraving and plating. These should command a higher premium.

Exc.	V.G.	Good	Fair	Poor
—	—	1500	650	250

Ballard (Ball & Williams) sporting rifles, third type (Serial numbers 14,000-15,000)

These arms are essentially the same as the second type in characteristics but have Merwin & Bray's alternate percussion mechanism built into the breechblock. The hammer is accordingly marked on the left side "PATENTED JAN. 5, 1864."

Exc.	V.G.	Good	Fair	Poor
—	—	1000	500	200

Ballard (Ball & Williams) military carbines
(Serial numbers 1500-7500, and 8500-10,500)

Overall length 37-1/4"; barrel (bore) length 22"; caliber .44 rimfire. Markings: same as Ballard/Ball & Williams sporting rifles, second type. Additional marks on U.S. War Department purchases include inspector's initials "MM" or "GH" on left side of frame, and "MM" on barrel, breechblock, buttplate, and on left side of buttstock in script within an oval cartouche. Three thousand of the earlier production (serial numbers 1700 through about 5000) of these carbines were sold to the state of Kentucky under an August 1862 contract, extended in April 1863. In November 1863, Kentucky contracted for an additional 1,000 carbines. In the interim, the state of New York purchased 500 for distribution to its militia. The U.S. War Department ordered 5,000 under a contract signed in January of 1864, but Ball & Williams delivered only 1,500 (serial numbers noted in range of 9800 through 10,600) while concentrating production on their more lucrative Kentucky contract. Another 600 of the federal contract were partially inspected (serial numbers about 6500 to 7100-MM in cartouche stock only) but were rejected because the barrels had been rifled prior to proofing; these were sold to Kentucky in September 1864 on an open market purchase. The carbines marked with federal inspection marks usually bring a premium.

Exc.	V.G.	Good	Fair	Poor
—	—	3750	1500	600

Ballard (Ball & Williams) "Kentucky" half-stock rifles

Overall length 45-3/8"; barrel (bore) length 30"; caliber .44 rimfire. These half-stock rifles bear the standard Ball & Williams markings upon their barrels and in addition have the state ownership mark ("KENTUCKY") on the barrel forward of the rear sights. A total of 1,000 (serial numbers about 7100 through 8550) were contracted for by Kentucky in November 1863 and delivered between January and April 1864.

Exc.	V.G.	Good	Fair	Poor
—	—	1750	700	300

Ballard (Dwight, Chapin & Co.) carbines

Overall length 37-3/4"; barrel (bore) length 22"; caliber .56 rimfire. Markings: On left side of round-topped frame "BALLARD'S PATENT/NOV. 5 1861"; on right side of frame "DWIGHT, CHAPIN & CO./BRIDGEPORT CONN." (through serial number about 125, deleted after that number) over "MERWIN & BRAY/AGT'S N.Y." over serial no. Inspection letters "D" frequently appear on carbines with the Dwight, Chapin, & Co. markings, indicative of preliminary inspection by E. M. Dustin, of the U.S. Ordnance Department.

Often mistaken as early Ballard production from a fictitious Fall River, Massachusetts factory, these carbines and their complementing rifles were in fact not placed into production until 1863, as evident by the split, two-piece breechblocks. Both carbines and rifles originated from a contract entered into between the U.S. War Department and Merwin & Bray in October 1862 for 10,000 of each arm, subsequently reduced to 1,000 of each by the Commission on Ordnance and Ordnance Stores. Because Ball & Williams facilities were tied up with Kentucky contracts, Merwin & Bray turned to the small parts maker of Dwight, Chapin & Co. in Bridgeport, Connecticut. Although they tooled for production, they fell short of scheduled delivery dates, and although about 100 carbines had been inspected, no deliveries were accepted (due to caliber problems) by the U.S. government, effectively bankrupting Dwight, Chapin & Co. The completed carbines and unfinished parts were sent to Worcester and assembled by Ball & Williams, and Merwin & Bray sold all 1,000 carbines in Kentucky in April 1864 on an open market purchase.

Exc.	V.G.	Good	Fair	Poor
—	—	1800	750	300

Ballard (Dwight, Chapin & Co.) full-stock rifles

Overall length 53"; barrel (bore) length 30"; caliber .56 rimfire. Markings: same as Dwight, Chapin & Co. carbines, but none found with "DWIGHT, CHAPIN & CO./BRIDGEPORT, CONN." stamping above agents marks. The history of these rifles is the same as the .56 caliber carbines, with serial numbers interspersed in the production of the carbines (1 through 1850). Evidently only about 650 of the rifles were completed of the 1,000 set up. Of these, 35 were sold to a U.S. agent in Florida in February 1864 and 600 to Kentucky in April 1864 with the 1,000 carbines.

Exc.	V.G.	Good	Fair	Poor
—	—	1800	750	300

Ballard (R. Ball) & Co. sporting rifles

Overall length varies according to barrel length; barrel (bore) length usually 24", 28", and 30"; calibers .32, .38, .44, and .46 rimfire. Markings: The frame markings of R. Ball & Co. rifles are similar to Ball & Williams production, only eliminating the Ball & Williams marking on the left side. Cartridge size, e.g. "No. 44", usually also stamped upon the top of the barrel or frame. Merwin & Bray's patented alternate ignition device usually present with left side of hammer usually marked "PATENTED JAN. 5, 1864." Serial numbers (which follow in sequence with Ball & Williams production. i.e. after no. about 15,800) appear on top of barrel and top of frame. After William Williams withdrew from the Ball & Williams partnership in mid-1865, the business continued under the name of R. Ball & Co., with Richard Ball's son-in-law, E.J. Halstead, in charge after the former's paralytic stroke in the fall of 1865.

Courtesy Rock Island Auction Company

Exc.	V.G.	Good	Fair	Poor
—	—	2000	850	300

Ballard (R. Ball) & Co. carbines

Overall length 37-1/4"; barrel (bore) length 22" caliber .44 rimfire. Markings: same as R. Ball & Co. sporting rifles; "No. 44" on top of frame near breech. Although firm evidence is elusive, approximately 1,000 of these carbines were manufactured in anticipation of a Canadian contract, which never came to fruition. Serial numbers are interspersed with sporting rifles, in the 16,400 through 17,700 range. All are equipped with the Merwin & Bray dual ignition block.

Exc.	V.G.	Good	Fair	Poor
—	—	1350	500	200

Ballard (Merrimack Arms & Manufacturing Co.) sporting rifles

Overall length varies with barrel length; usual barrel lengths 24", 28", 30"; calibers .22, .32, .44, .46, .50 rimfire. Markings: Left side of frame marked with both manufacturing and patent marks, "MERRIMACK ARMS & MFG. CO./NEWBURYPORT, MASS." over "BALLARD'S PATENT/ NOV. 5, 1861." Caliber usually marked on top of barrel or frame, e.g. "No. 38" together with serial no. Left side of hammer marked "PATENTED JAN. 5, 1864" if breech fitted with Merwin & Bray's alternate ignition device. In the spring of 1866, Edward Bray of Brooklyn, New York, and former partner of Joseph Merwin purchased the Ballard machinery from R. Ball & Co. and set up a new plant in Newburyport, Massachusetts primarily for the production of sporting rifles. The glut of surplus arms on the market following the American Civil War, however, forced him into bankruptcy in early 1869, after producing only about 2,000 Ballard rifles, carbines and a limited number of 20 gauge shotguns. Serial numbers continue in the sequence of the Ball & Williams/R. Ball & Co. production (serial numbers about 18,000 through 20,300). Prices of these rifles will vary considerably depending on the degree of finish or engraving.

Exc.	V.G.	Good	Fair	Poor
—	—	1750	700	300

Ballard (Merrimack Arms & Manufacturing Co.) carbines

Overall length 37-1/4"; barrel (bore) length 22"; caliber .44 rimfire. Markings: same as Merrimack Arms & Mfg. Co. sporting rifles. In March 1866, the state of New York purchased 100 Ballard carbines (serial numbers about 18,500 to 18,600) for use by its prison guards. In January 1870, an additional 70 (serial numbers 19,400 to 19,500) were purchased from New York City arms merchants Merwin, Hulbert & Co. to arm guards at Sing Sing Prison. Between these two purchases Merrimack Arms & Mfg. Co. had shortened its new "tangless" frames by 1/8", the prime distinction between the two purchases. Despite the rarity of both types of carbines, they do not command high prices.

Exc.	V.G.	Good	Fair	Poor
—	—	1250	500	275

Ballard (Brown Manufacturing Co.) sporting rifles
Dimensions: same as Merrimack Arms & Mfg. Co. sporting rifles. Markings: left side of frame marked with manufacturer, "BROWN MFG. CO. NEWBURYPORT, MASS." over patent, "BALLARD'S PATENT/ NOV. 5, 1861." Serial no. on top of barrel and frame. Upon the failure of Merrimack Arms & Manufacturing Company in early 1869, the plant was purchased by John Hamilton Brown, who continued producing Ballard patent rifles until 1873 in a serial range consecutive with that of its three predecessors (Ball & Williams, R. Ball & Co., and Merrimack Arms & Mfg. Co.). Approximately 2,000 Ballard arms were produced during the period of Brown's manufacture of the Ballard (serial numbers about 20,325 through 22,100). Brown made Ballards tend to exhibit finer finishing than earlier produced rifles, accounting for their average higher value. Special features, such as breakdown facility and side extractors (on .22 cal. rifles) will also positively affect the prices.

Exc.	V.G.	Good	Fair	Poor
—	—	1750	600	300

Ballard (Brown Mfg. Co.) full-stock military rifles
Overall length 52-1/2" barrel (bore) length 30"; caliber .46 rimfire. Markings: The same as Brown Mfg. Co. sporting rifles, with the addition of the caliber marking, "No. 46", on the top of the barrel forward of the rear sight. The cause for the production of the Ballard/Brown military rifle has yet to be determined, but it has been speculated that they were possibly manufactured in anticipation of a sale to France during the Franco-Prussian War. In any event, the sale was not culminated, and many, if not most, of the estimated 1,000 produced were "sporterized" by shortening the forestock and sold by commercial dealers in the United States. Serial numbers concentrate in the 20,500 through 21,600 range, with sporting rifles interspersed in the sequence. Rifles that have not been sporterized command a premium.

Exc.	V.G.	Good	Fair	Poor
—	—	1750	700	300

BALLARD RIFLE AND CARTRIDGE CO.
Cody, Wyoming

All models feature American black walnut stocks, case hardening, and rust blued barrels. There are a number of special order features that are available with these rifles. These extra-cost items should be appraised prior to a sale.

No. 1-3/4 Far West Rifle
Offered with 30" round barrel in standard or heavy weight. Single or double-set triggers, S lever, ring-style lever, blade front sight, and Rocky Mountain rear sight. Offered in calibers from .32-40 to .50-90. Weight with standard 30" barrel is approximately 10.5 lbs., with heavyweight barrel 11.75 lbs.

NIB	Exc.	V.G.	Good	Fair	Poor
1850	1500	—	—	—	—

No. 4-1/2 Mid Range Model
This model features checkered fancy walnut stock, standard or heavy weight half octagon barrel 30" or 32" with single or double-set triggers, pistol grip, hard rubber or steel shotgun butt, horn forend cap, full-loop lever, and globe front sight. Offered in calibers from .32-40 to .40-70. Weight with standard barrel 10.75 lbs. and with heavy barrel 11.5 lbs.

NIB	Exc.	V.G.	Good	Fair	Poor
2650	2000	—	—	—	—

No. 5 Pacific Model
This model features a 30" or 32" octagon barrel in either standard or heavy weight, stocks in rifle or shotgun configuration, double-set triggers, ring lever, blade front sight, and Rocky Mountain rear sight. Calibers from .38-55 to .50-90. Weight with standard 30" barrel is 10.75 lbs., with heavyweight barrel 12 lbs.

NIB	Exc.	V.G.	Good	Fair	Poor
2375	1850	—	—	—	—

No. 7 Long Range Model
This model features a fancy walnut checkered stock with 32" or 34" standard or heavy weight half octagon barrel. Pistol-grip stock with rubber or steel shotgun butt, single or double-set triggers, full-loop lever, horn forend cap, and globe front sight. Calibers from .32-40 to .45-110. Weight with standard 32" barrel 11.75 lbs., with heavyweight barrel 12.25 lbs.

NIB	Exc.	V.G.	Good	Fair	Poor
2650	2000	—	—	—	—

No. 1-1/2 Hunter's Rifle
This model features a 30" round barrel, single trigger, S lever, plain forend, and rifle buttstock. Blade front sight and Rocky Mountain rear sight are standard. Calibers from .32-40 to .50-70. Weight is about 10.5 lbs.

NIB	Exc.	V.G.	Good	Fair	Poor
1650	1250	—	—	—	—

No. 2 Sporting Model
Stocked in plain walnut with crescent butt and offered in 24", 26", 28", or 30" octagon barrel with blade front and Rocky Mountain rear sights. A straight-grip action with S lever, in calibers .38-40, .44-40, and .45 Colt.

NIB	Exc.	V.G.	Good	Fair	Poor
1650	1250	—	—	—	—

No. 3 Gallery Rifle
Chambered for the .22 caliber rimfire cartridge this model features a choice of 24", 26", or 30" lightweight octagon barrel with rifle-style buttstock with steel crescent buttplate, S lever, blade and Rocky Mountain sights. Weight with standard 26" barrel is about 7.5 lbs.

NIB	Exc.	V.G.	Good	Fair	Poor
1650	1250	—	—	—	—

No. 3F Fine Gallery Rifle
Same as above model but with fancy checkered walnut stock, pistol grip, single or double-set triggers, full-loop lever, light Schuetzen buttstock, Globe front sight and gallery tang sight. Weight with standard 26" barrel is approximately 7.75 lbs.

NIB	Exc.	V.G.	Good	Fair	Poor
2650	2000	—	—	—	—

No. 4 Perfection Model
This model features a plain walnut stock with rifle or shotgun butt. Offered in 30" or 32" octagon barrel with blade front sight and Rocky Mountain rear sight. Straight-grip action with single or double-set triggers with S lever or ring lever in calibers from .32-40 to .50-90.

NIB	Exc.	V.G.	Good	Fair	Poor
1850	1500	—	—	—	—

No. 5-1/2 Montana Model
This model has a fancy walnut stock, double-set triggers, and ring lever. Shotgun steel butt. Barrels are either 30" or 32", extra heavy octagon, in calibers .45-70, .45-110, and .50-90. Under barrel wiping rod. Weight is approximately 14.5 lbs.

NIB	Exc.	V.G.	Good	Fair	Poor
2525	2000	—	—	—	—

No. 6 Off-Hand Rifle Model
This rifle features a fancy walnut checkered stock with hand rubbed finish, heavy Schuetzen buttplate, and horn insert on forend. Choice of 30", 32", or 34" half-octagon barrel with Globe front sight. Straight-grip action with double-set triggers, Schuetzen ball, spur lever and deluxe rust blueing. Offered in .22 LR, .32-40, .38-55, .40-65, and .40-70 calibers.

NIB	Exc.	V.G.	Good	Fair	Poor
2950	2350	—	—	—	—

No. 8 Union Hill Model

This model features a 30" or 32" half-octagon standard or heavy barrel, single or double-set triggers, pistol-grip stock with cheekpiece, full-loop lever, hook Schuetzen buttplate and fancy walnut checkered stock. Offered in calibers from .22 LR to .40-70. Weight with standard barrel in .32 caliber 10.5 lbs, with heavyweight barrel in .40 caliber 11.5 lbs. This model is not furnished with sights.

NIB	Exc.	V.G.	Good	Fair	Poor
2650	2000	—	—	—	—

Model 1885 High Wall

This single-shot rifle is chambered for a wide variety of calibers from .18 Bee to .577 Express. Barrel lengths to 34". American walnut stock. Many options to choose from that will affect price. Introduced in 2000.

NIB	Exc.	V.G.	Good	Fair	Poor
1850	1500	—	—	—	—

BERETTA, PIETRO
Brescia, Italy
Importer—Beretta U.S.A. Corp.
Accokeek, Maryland

Fabbrica d'Armi Pierto Beretta, of Gardone Val Trompia, near Milan, Italy is one of the world's oldest industrial concerns. A leading maker of sporting, military, and civilian firearms, this firm has been in existence for almost 500 years. Founded by Bartolomeo Beretta, a master gunbarrel maker, in 1526. His son Giovannino followed his father's footsteps and subsequent generations have developed this firm into a worldwide success. Beretta manufactured its first pistol, the Model 1915, in 1915 as a wartime project.

Spread over 500,000 square feet and employing 2,200 employees this old world firm captured the United States military contract in 1985 for its standard issue sidearm, the Model 92F. These pistols are currently manufactured at Beretta U.S.A.'s plant in Maryland. Besides the affiliate in the United States, Beretta has three others located in France, Greece, and Rome.

The American affiliate was formed in 1977 to handle U.S. demand. A year later it began to manufacture some firearms, namely the Model 92F. At the present time Beretta has delivered more than 250,000 Model 92F pistols to the U.S. military. Beretta continues to produce sidearms for the U.S. military and law enforcement agencies throughout the U.S.

NOTE: In 1994 Beretta changed its model designations with a new nomenclature system that brings back some of the old product names and the addition of new names instead of numbered models. Beretta will continue to use the numbered model designation along with the new product names so that both will complement the other.

Stampede Blue

Introduced in 2003, this single-action revolver is chambered for the choice of .45 Colt, .44-40, or .357 Magnum cartridge. Choice of 4.75", 5.5", or 7.5" barrel. Blued with Beretta case color and black polymer grips. Weight is about 2.3 lbs. depending on barrel length.

NIB	Exc.	V.G.	Good	Fair	Poor
465	365	—	—	—	—

Stampede Nickel

As above but with brushed nickel finish and walnut grips.

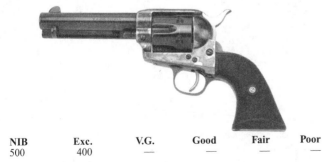

NIB	Exc.	V.G.	Good	Fair	Poor
500	400	—	—	—	—

Stampede Deluxe

As above but with charcoal blue finish and Beretta case color with select walnut grips.

NIB	Exc.	V.G.	Good	Fair	Poor
620	500	—	—	—	—

Model 409 PB

A 12, 16, 20, and 28 gauge boxlock, double-barrel shotgun with 27", 28", or 30" barrels with double triggers and extractors and various choke combinations. Blued with a checkered walnut stock. Manufactured between 1934 and 1964.

Exc.	V.G.	Good	Fair	Poor
775	700	625	500	250

Model 410 E

As above, but more finely finished.

Exc.	V.G.	Good	Fair	Poor
900	825	650	500	275

Model 410

As above, with a 32" Full-choke barrel. Blued with a checkered walnut stock. Introduced in 1934.

Exc.	V.G.	Good	Fair	Poor
1000	925	750	600	300

Model 411 E

The Model 410 with false sideplates and more heavily engraved. Manufactured between 1934 and 1964.

Exc.	V.G.	Good	Fair	Poor
1200	1125	950	800	425

Model 424

A 12 and 20 gauge boxlock shotgun with 26" or 28" barrels, double triggers, various choke combinations, and extractors. Blued with a checkered walnut stock. In 20 gauge it is designated the Model 426 and would be worth an additional $100.

Exc.	V.G.	Good	Fair	Poor
950	875	675	500	225

Model 426 E

As above, with silver inlays and heavier engraving, single-selective trigger and automatic ejectors. Not imported after 1983.

Exc.	V.G.	Good	Fair	Poor
1150	1075	875	700	350

Model 625

A 12 or 20 gauge boxlock, double-barrel shotgun with 26", 28", or 30" barrels, various choke combinations, double triggers and extractors. Moderately engraved and blued with a checkered walnut grip. Imported between 1984 and 1986.

Exc.	V.G.	Good	Fair	Poor
800	750	600	500	250

Silver Hawk

A 10 or 12 gauge boxlock, double-barrel shotgun with 30" barrels, double triggers and extractors. Blued with a silver-finished receiver and a checkered walnut stock. The 10 gauge version would be worth an additional 20 percent. Discontinued in 1967.

Exc.	V.G.	Good	Fair	Poor
500	450	375	250	150

Model 470 Silver Hawk

Introduced in 1997 to commemorate Beretta's 470 years in the gun-making business, this shotgun is offered in either 12 or 20 gauge configurations. The receiver is silver chrome with engraving. The top lever is checkered with a gold inlaid hawk's head. The gun is fitted with a straight grip stock with splinter forearm of select walnut with oil finish. Choice of 26" or 28" barrels with auto ejection or manual extraction. Weight of 12 gauge about 6.5 lbs. The 20 gauge weighs approximately 6 lbs.

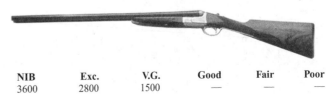

NIB	Exc.	V.G.	Good	Fair	Poor
3600	2800	1500	—	—	—

Model 470 Silver Hawk EL
Introduced in 2002 this model features color case hardened frame with side plates with gold filled game scene engraving. Offered in 12 or 20 gauge with choice of 26" or 28" barrels. Weight is 5.9 lbs. for 20 gauge and 6.5 lbs. for 12 gauge.

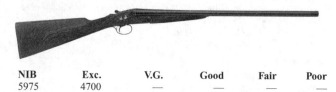

NIB	Exc.	V.G.	Good	Fair	Poor
5975	4700	—	—	—	—

471 Silver Hawk
Introduced in 2003, this side-by-side shotgun has a boxlock receiver and is offered in 12 and 20 gauge with a choice of 26" or 28" barrels. This model is also offered with a choice of pistol grip with beavertail forend or straight grip stock with splinter forend. A straight grip stock with case color receiver is also available at a premium. Select walnut stock with oil finish. Single-selective trigger. Weight is about 6.5 lbs. in 12 gauge and 5.9 lbs. in 20 gauge.

NIB	Exc.	V.G.	Good	Fair	Poor
2875	2250	—	—	—	—

NOTE: Add $350 for straight grip stock with case color receiver.

Model 626 Field Grade
A 12 or 20 gauge boxlock double barrel shotgun with a 26" or 28" barrel, various choke combinations, single trigger and automatic ejectors. Engraved, blued with a checkered walnut stock. Imported between 1984 and 1988.

Exc.	V.G.	Good	Fair	Poor
900	825	700	575	475

626 Onyx
This model is a boxlock side-by-side shotgun offered in 12 gauge and 20 gauge. With choice of 26" or 28" solid rib barrels with screw-in chokes. Double triggers are standard but single trigger is available on request. Receiver is anti-glare black matte finish. Stock is walnut with hand checkering and pistol grip. The 12 gauge weighs 6 lbs. 13 oz. and the 20 gauge weighs 6 lbs. 13 oz.

NIB	Exc.	V.G.	Good	Fair	Poor
1250	950	850	750	500	400

627 EL
This model is offered in 12 gauge only with choice of 26" or 28" solid rib barrels. The walnut is highly figured and fine cut checkered. The receiver is silver with side plates engraved with scroll. Comes with hard case.

NIB	Exc.	V.G.	Good	Fair	Poor
2500	2000	1750	1500	1250	650

627 EELL
Same as above but fitted with scroll engraved side plates with game scenes. Walnut is highly figured with fine line checkering. A straight-grip stock is also offered in this model. Comes with hard case.

NIB	Exc.	V.G.	Good	Fair	Poor
3750	3500	3000	2500	1500	1000

Model FS-1
A single-barrel boxlock shotgun in all gauges and a 26" or 28", full choke barrel. Blued with a checkered walnut stock. This model was also known as the "Companion."

Exc.	V.G.	Good	Fair	Poor
250	225	175	125	90

BERNARDELLI, VINCENZO
Brescia, Italy
Importer—Armsport
Miami, Florida

Established in the 1721, this company originally manufactured military arms and only entered the commercial sporting arms market in 1928.

S. Uberto I Gamecock
A 12, 16, 20, or 28 gauge boxlock side-by-side shotgun with either 25.75" or 27.5" barrels, various chokes, double triggers and extractors. Automatic ejectors were available and would be worth a 20 percent premium. Blued with a checkered stock.

Exc.	V.G.	Good	Fair	Poor
950	700	500	350	250

Brescia
A 12, 16, or 20 gauge sidelock double-barrel shotgun with exposed hammers, various barrel lengths, choke combinations, a sidelock action, double triggers, and manual extractors. Blued with an English-style, checkered walnut stock.

NIB	Exc.	V.G.	Good	Fair	Poor
1850	900	700	450	350	225

Italia
This is a higher grade version of the Brescia.

NIB	Exc.	V.G.	Good	Fair	Poor
2250	1250	750	600	400	250

Italia Extra
This is the highest grade hammer gun that Bernardelli produces.

NIB	Exc.	V.G.	Good	Fair	Poor
5900	2750	1500	1000	750	300

BILLINGS
Location Unknown

Billings Pocket Pistol
A .32 rimfire caliber single-shot spur trigger pistol with a 2.5" round barrel and an unusually large grip. The barrel is stamped "Billings Vest Pocket Pistol Pat. April 24, 1866." Blued with walnut grips. Manufactured between 1865 and 1868.

Exc.	V.G.	Good	Fair	Poor
—	—	3500	1500	550

BISMARCK
Location Unknown

Bismarck Pocket Revolver
A .22 caliber spur trigger revolver with a 3" round ribbed barrel and a 7-shot, unfluted cylinder. Brass frame and the remainder was plated with rosewood grips. The barrel is marked "Bismarck." Manufactured in the 1870s.

Exc.	V.G.	Good	Fair	Poor
—	—	500	200	90

BLAKE, J. H.
New York, New York

Blake Bolt-Action Rifle
A .30-40 Krag caliber bolt-action rifle with a 30" barrel, and a 7-shot magazine. The stock is secured by three barrel bands. Blued with a walnut stock. Manufactured between 1892 and 1910.

Exc.	V.G.	Good	Fair	Poor
—	2750	950	400	200

BLAND, THOMAS & SONS
London, England

Established in 1840, this firm has produced or marketed a wide variety of percussion and cartridge arms. Over the years, the firm has occupied a variety of premises in London, some of them concurrently.

41 Whittall Street	1840-1867
41, 42, 43 Whittall Street	1867-1886
106 Strand	1872-1900
430 Strand	1886-1900
2 William IV Street	1900-1919
4-5 William IV Street	1919-1973
New Row, St. Martin's Lane	1973-

T. Bland & Sons is perhaps best known for their double-barrel rifles and shotguns, which were made in a variety of grades.

BLISS, F. D.
New Haven, Connecticut

Bliss Pocket Revolver

A .25 caliber spur trigger revolver with a 3.25" octagon barrel, 6-shot magazine, and a square butt. Blued with either hard rubber or walnut grips. The barrel is stamped "F.D. Bliss New Haven, Ct." There was an all-brass framed version made early in the production, and this model would be worth approximately 50 percent more than the values listed here for the standard model. Approximately 3,000 manufactured circa 1860 to 1863.

Exc.	V.G.	Good	Fair	Poor
—	—	700	300	100

BLISS & GOODYEAR
New Haven, Connecticut

Pocket Model Revolver

A .28 caliber percussion revolver with a 3" octagonal barrel, 6-shot magazine, unfluted cylinder and a solid frame with a removable side plate. Blued with a brass frame and walnut grips. Approximately 3,000 manufactured in 1860.

Exc.	V.G.	Good	Fair	Poor
—	—	950	450	200

BLUNT & SYMS
New York, New York

Under Hammer Pepperbox

Pepperboxes produced by Blunt & Syms are noteworthy for the fact that they incorporate a ring trigger cocking/revolving mechanism and a concealed under hammer. They were produced in a variety of calibers and the standard finish was blued. Normally these pistols are found marked simply "A-C" on the face of the barrel group. Some examples though are marked "Blunt & Syms New York."

This firm was in business from approximately 1837 to 1855.

Small Frame Round Handle .25-.28 Caliber

Exc.	V.G.	Good	Fair	Poor
—	—	1250	600	200

Medium Frame Round Handle .31 Caliber

Exc.	V.G.	Good	Fair	Poor
—	—	1000	400	150

Round Handle Dragoon .36 Caliber

Exc.	V.G.	Good	Fair	Poor
—	—	2250	850	350

Medium Frame Saw Handle .31 Caliber

Exc.	V.G.	Good	Fair	Poor
—	—	1250	500	250

Saw Handle Dragoon .36 Caliber

Exc.	V.G.	Good	Fair	Poor
—	—	2250	950	400

Dueling Pistol

A .52 caliber percussion single-shot pistol with an octagonal barrel normally of 9" length. Steel furniture with a walnut stock. Barrel marked "B&S New York/Cast Steel."

Exc.	V.G.	Good	Fair	Poor
—	—	1500	650	300

Single-Shot Bar Hammer

A .36 caliber single-shot percussion pistol with a 6" half-octagonal barrel and a bar hammer. Blued or browned with walnut grips. Marked as above.

Exc.	V.G.	Good	Fair	Poor
—	—	900	400	200

Side Hammer Pocket Pistol

A .31 or .35 caliber single-shot percussion pistol with a 2.5" to 6" octagonal barrel. Blued with walnut grips.

Exc.	V.G.	Good	Fair	Poor
—	—	900	400	175

Side Hammer Belt Pistol

As above, in calibers ranging from .36 to .44 with barrel lengths of 4" or 6".

Exc.	V.G.	Good	Fair	Poor
—	—	1000	400	250

Ring Trigger Pistol

A .36 caliber percussion single-shot pistol with a 3" to 5" half-octagonal barrel and a ring trigger. Blued with walnut grips.

Exc.	V.G.	Good	Fair	Poor
—	—	750	350	150

Double Barrel Pistol

A .36 to .44 caliber percussion double barrel pistol with 7.5" barrels and walnut grips. A ring trigger variation of this model is known.

Exc.	V.G.	Good	Fair	Poor
—	—	950	400	150

Double Barrel Under Hammer Pistol

As above, with two under hammers and in .34 caliber with 4" barrels.

Exc.	V.G.	Good	Fair	Poor
—	—	1250	550	200

Derringer Style Pistol

A .50 caliber single-shot percussion pistol with a 3" barrel, German silver mounts and a walnut stock. The lock is marked "Blunt & Syms/New York."

Exc.	V.G.	Good	Fair	Poor
—	—	1250	500	250

BOND ARMS INC.
Grandbury, Texas

Texas Defender

This is a stainless steel over-and-under derringer chambered for a variety of calibers such as .45 Colt/.410, .357 Magnum, 9mm, .45 ACP, and .44 Magnum. Barrels are interchangeable. Grips are laminated black ash or rosewood. Barrel length is 3" with blade front sight and fixed rear sight. Weight is approximately 21 oz. Introduced in 1997.

Exc.	V.G.	Good	Fair	Poor
320	275	—	—	—

BOSS & CO.
London, England
SEE—British Double Guns

BOSWELL, CHARLES
London, England

One of England's more established makers of best-quality rifles and shotguns. In 1988 the company was purchased by an American consortium and the Cape Horn Outfitters of Charlotte, North Carolina, was appointed their sole agent.

Double Rifle, Boxlock

A .300 Holland & Holland, .375 Holland & Holland or .458 Winchester Magnum double-barrel boxlock rifle with double triggers and a walnut stock. Other features were made to the customer's specifications. A .600 Nitro Express version was also available.

Exc.	V.G.	Good	Fair	Poor
40000	32500	25000	17500	—

NOTE: .600 Nitro Express add 25 percent.

Double Rifle, Sidelock

As above, with Holland & Holland-style sidelocks.

Exc.	V.G.	Good	Fair	Poor
55000	40000	30000	20000	—

NOTE: .600 Nitro Express add 25 percent.

Double Barrel Shotguns
SEE—British Double Guns

BOSWORTH, B. M.
Warren, Pennsylvania

Bosworth Under Hammer Pistol

A .38 caliber single-shot percussion pistol with an under hammer and a 6" half-octagonal barrel. The frame is marked "BM Bosworth." Browned with brass grips forming part of the frame. Made circa 1850 to 1860.

Exc.	V.G.	Good	Fair	Poor
—	—	1500	550	200

BRAND
E. Robinson, Maker
New York

Brand Breech Loading Carbine

A .50 rimfire caliber carbine with a 22" barrel secured by one barrel band. The frame is marked "Brand's Patent July 29,1862/E. Robinson Manfr/New York." This carbine was produced in limited numbers, primarily for trial purposes.

Exc.	V.G.	Good	Fair	Poor
—	—	5500	2500	900

BREDA, ERNESTO
Milan, Italy

Andromeda Special

A 12 gauge boxlock shotgun with various barrel lengths and chokes, single-selective triggers and automatic ejectors. Engraved, satin-finished with checkered walnut stock.

Exc.	V.G.	Good	Fair	Poor
950	650	550	425	300

BRITISH DOUBLES
By Douglas Tate

British double barrel shotguns have never been more popular. Tougher laws in Britain have encouraged gun owners there to sell at just the same time as shotgunners here have attained enough sophistication to recognize that even a mid-grade gun such as a Webley is a better weapon than a machine-made American classic.

The result has been unprecedented opportunities for shooters/collectors but also a bit of confusion. Several lessons have emerged but the most important is that traditional methods of evaluating American shotguns will not work for British guns and that each one must be individually evaluated on its own merits.

For instance "Exc., V.G., Good, Fair, & Poor" are almost meaningless with English shotguns because you will frequently find guns which are cosmetically in the first category but which paper thin barrels and out of proof bores have consigned to the last category.

In just the same way that there are only three important elements to game management; habitat, habitat, habitat, there are only three significant elements to appraising British guns; barrels, barrels and barrels. This is because most problems with second-hand British guns when fixed will add value to the gun but replacement barrels are prohibitively expensive. A $4000 gun with sound barrels is a bargain but an identical gun bought for $400 with duff barrels is a dud because it will cost $10,000 for new ones. Barrel condition is then the essential component of value.

If a 12 bore gun was originally proofed at .729 and still measures .729, (this figure represents the interior bore diameter 9 inches from the breech) and if the wall thicknesses—9 inches from the muzzle—are well above the gun trade recommended minimum of 20 thou, then the gun is excellent regardless of its appearance, because cosmetic problems are easily rectified.

If, on the other hand, it was proofed at .729 and now measures .750 and has wall thicknesses in the low teens, it is virtually worthless regardless of how lovely it may look. If you have neither the gauges nor the skills to check these measurements out yourself, send the gun to one of the English gun makers working in North America listed at the end of this essay.

This type of thing is more common than one might think. I learned about such a gun recently which was externally new in the box condition but must have been put away dirty because the barrels were pitted beyond redemption. An unscrupulous seller could easily have the pits lapped out and offered it as a new gun with mirror bores. Only careful gauging would reveal that the gun was out of proof and potentially dangerous.

Also, it is a mistake to think that original condition has the same significance for British as it does for American guns. The most desirable 23,000 / 24,000 serial number Purdeys were built with hard use in mind and consequently left the factory with the wood slightly proud. The idea was that at the end of every season the gun would be returned to the maker for routine maintenance, and also to have the barrels and furniture reblacked, the color case revarnished and the wood refinished as need be.

A philistine seeing two guns, one with proud wood and one with the wood refinished to the metal, might assume the former was a restock and the latter an original gun. Such are the pitfalls for the uninitiated. But the point is that broadly speaking, a properly maintained gun will command a high resale value and completely unfired guns from the golden era are so rare as to be virtual non-existent. The exception: a pair of Boss's from the 1930's sold at Sotheby's in London on Tuesday, May 17th, 1994 for £58,700, over $90,000.

The major distinction between a reconditioned and re-case colored Parker and a sympathetically restored Purdey is that the latter is perfectly acceptable while the former is a corporal offense.

Another significant difference is that model designations mean very little in the U.K. Although most makers offered a variety of models in their catalogues, the actual guns rarely resemble the catalogue pictures and model names almost never appear on the guns themselves. The exception here is W. W. Greener, who offered an unbelievable one hundred and fifty one (151) grades of guns many of which seem to have the model name or number on the gun. Moreover certain models such as the Churchill "Hercules" were of quite different qualities before and after WWII while the model known as the "Utility" in the thirties became the "Regal" in the fifties with out any noticeable change of quality.

To avoid confusion the British—to all intents and purposes—ignore model designation. Instead they have adopted a system which divides any given makers output into boxlock nonejector, boxlock ejector, sidelock nonejector, sidelock ejector, over unders and hammer guns. It's a system that works well for the Brits and one that worked well for Don Gustine in his essay in Birmingham Gunmakers (see pages 162-164.) I hope it is one which will work well here but ultimately, of course, because of their bespoke nature, the only way to evaluate British guns is one at a time.

ENGLISH GUNMAKERS IN NORTH AMERICA

Dale Tate
P.O. Box 3016
Gonzales, CA 93926
(408) 675-2473

David Trevallion
9 Old Mountain Road
Cape Neddick, ME 03902
(207) 361-1130

John F. Rowe
P.O. Box 86
2501 Rockwood Road
Enid, OK 73702
(405) 233-5942

Kirk Merrington
207 Sierra Road
Kerrville, TX 78028
(830) 367-2937

Les Paul
R.R. 1, Roseneath, Ontario
CANADA K0K 2X0
(905) 721-1876

Paul Hodgins
P.O. Box 3546
Logan, UT 84323
(435) 753-2796

Alfred W. Gallifent
P.O. Box 34
Warrington, PA 18976
(215) 343-3974

Following is an alphabetic listing of British makers whose guns are most frequently encountered with dealers and at auctions.

Army & Navy Co-operative Society Limited, London
Started in 1871 as an organization by which military men could buy wine wholesale, the membership soon increased to include diplomats and foreign service bureaucrats, while the catalogue expanded to include every manner of household and sporting goods. Most guns were acquired in the Birmingham trade and many were Webley & Scott products.
   Estimates listed range from guns barely in proof with marginal wall thicknesses to those with barrel specifications as proofed.
Boxlock non-ejectors $1,000 to $3,000
Boxlock ejectors $1,500 to $5,000
Sidelock non-ejectors $2,000 to $7,000
Sidelock ejectors $3,000 to $15,000
Hammer Guns $1,000 to $3,000

Atkin, Henry
The first Henry Atkin was one of James Purdey's original workman, his son started the family business in 1878. J. P. Morgan and Gough Thomas were both Atkin customers because they felt the Atkin's offered the same quality as Purdey's without as high a cost.
   Estimates listed range from guns barely in proof with marginal wall thicknesses to those with barrel specifications as proofed.
Boxlock non-ejectors $1,500 to $4,000
Boxlock ejectors $2,000 to $8,500
Sidelock non-ejectors $2,000 to $10,000
Sidelock ejectors $4,000 to $30,000
Hammer Guns $2,000 to $10,000

Beesley, Frederick
Frederick Beesley served his apprenticeship with Moore and Grey and worked for several London gun makers including James Purdey and Son before establishing his own business in 1879. His claim to fame is the self opening system he patented (No. 31 of 1880) and licensed to James Purdey for "five shillings for every gun made." To this day every side-by-side gun by Purdey is built on this system.
   Estimates listed range from guns barely in proof with marginal wall thicknesses to those with barrel specifications as proofed.
Boxlock non-ejectors $1,500 to $4,000
Boxlock ejectors $2,000 to $8,500
Sidelock non-ejectors $2,000 to $10,000
Sidelock ejectors $4,000 to $30,000
Hammer Guns $2,000 to $10,000
Over & Unders $5,000 to $30,000

Blanch, John
John Blanch apprenticed with Jackson Mortimer and married his master's daughter. Later he working with John Manton. Today the Blanch name is perhaps best remembered for "A Century of Guns" first published in 1909 and written by H. J. Blanch grandson of the founder.
   Estimates listed range from guns barely in proof with marginal wall thicknesses to those with barrel specifications as proofed.
Boxlock non-ejectors $1,500 to $4,000
Boxlock ejectors $2,000 to $8,500
Sidelock non-ejectors $2,000 to $10,000
Sidelock ejectors $4,000 to $30,000
Hammer Guns $2,000 to $10,000

Bland, Thomas
Thomas Bland started in business in 1840 in Birmingham. Bland moved to London in 1875 and occupied a variety of premises close to Charing Cross Station until at least the 1960s. They well known for their wildfowling guns, particularly the "Brent" model which enjoyed a wide following. The Bland firm is still in business in Benton, Pennsylvania.
   Estimates listed range from guns barely in proof with marginal wall thicknesses to those with barrel specifications as proofed.
Boxlock non-ejectors $1,000 to $3,000
Boxlock ejectors $1,500 to $5,000
Sidelock non-ejectors $2,000 to $7,000
Sidelock ejectors $3,000 to $15,000
Hammer Guns $1,000 to $3,000

Boss & Co.
Thomas Boss worked for the great Joseph Manton before becoming an outworker to the London trade. In 1891 John Robertson, a Scotsman, was taken in as a partner. Under Robertson's control the firm established itself as London's best gun maker rivaled only by Purdey's. Beyond intrinsic quality Boss is famous for their single trigger and over-and-under designs which are both widely copied. A scarce 20 bore assisted opening over-and-under by Boss sold as Sotheby's, Glen-eagles sale in August 1998 for $76,500.
   Estimates listed range from guns barely in proof with marginal wall thicknesses to those with barrel specifications as proofed.

Courtesy Bonhams & Butterfields

Boxlock non-ejectors $1,500 to $4,000
Boxlock ejectors $2,000 to $8,500
Sidelock non-ejectors $2,000 to $10,000
Sidelock ejectors $4,000 to $30,000
Hammer Guns $2,000 to $10,000
Over & Unders $20,000 to $100,000

Boswell, Charles
Charles Boswell worked for Thomas Gooch and the Enfield factory before establishing himself in 1872. He was a skillful pigeon shot and the firm's reputation rested for many years on their ability to build live bird guns. The records are currently in the hands of G. R. Beckstead in Florida.
   Estimates listed range from guns barely in proof with marginal wall thicknesses to those with barrel specifications as proofed.
Boxlock non-ejectors $1,000 to $3,000
Boxlock ejectors $1,500 to $5,000
Sidelock non-ejectors $2,000 to $7,000
Sidelock ejectors $3,000 to $15,000
Hammer Guns $1,000 to $3,000

Brazier, Joseph
Current Importer/Distributor FNGB, Colorado Springs, CO
Founded in 1831 and best known for high quality locks, receivers, and components supplied to the English gun trade. The majority of Best Guns have used Brazier components. Today, this firm makes close tolerance CNC parts, Best Guns of its own design. Made to order Best sidelock with interchangeable parts begin at $20,000.

Estimates listed range from guns barely in proof with marginal wall thicknesses to those with barrel specifications as proofed.
Boxlock non-ejectors $2,000 to $3,000
Boxlock ejectors $2,000 to $4,500
Sidelock non-ejectors $20,000 to $25,000
Sidelock ejectors $20,000 to $250,000
Hammer Guns $4,000 to $15,000

Brown, A.A.
Albert Arthur Brown established his business in Whittal St., Birmingham in 1930. The firm has maintained a reputation as one of the finest makers to the trade having built guns for Churchill, H & H and Westley Richards. They still make guns today in Alverchurch, not far from Birmingham.
Estimates listed range from guns barely in proof with marginal wall thicknesses to those with barrel specifications as proofed.
Boxlock non-ejectors $1,000 to $3,000
Boxlock ejectors $1,500 to $5,000
Sidelock non-ejectors $2,000 to $7,000
Sidelock ejectors $3,000 to $15,000

Brown, David McKay
David McKay Brown started his apprenticeship with Alex Martin in Glasgow and completed it with John Dickson in Edinburgh. His renown rest on his ability with traditional Scottish round action guns and his own patent over/under based on a trigger plate action. He works in Bothwell just outside Glasgow. A fine pair of 20 bore assisted opening round action guns by David McKay Brown sold at Sotheby's, Gleneagles sale in August 1998 for $52,200.
Estimates listed range from guns barely in proof with marginal wall thicknesses to those with barrel specifications as proofed.
Round Action & O/U Guns $20,000 to $100,000

Churchill, E.J.
Edwin John Churchill served his time with William Jeffery & Son and was famous as a pigeon shot. Today the firm is best remembered for its 25" barreled guns introduced by Robert Churchill in the 1920s. The firm is still in business in West Wycombe, England.
Estimates listed range from guns barely in proof with marginal wall thicknesses to those with barrel specifications as proofed.
Boxlock non-ejectors $1,500 to $4,000
Boxlock ejectors $2,000 to $8,500
Sidelock non-ejectors $2,000 to $10,000
Sidelock ejectors $4,000 to $30,000
Hammer Guns $2,000 to $10,000
Over & Unders $10,000 to $50,000

Cogswell & Harrison
Benjamin Cogswell claimed to be in business from 1770. The firm's reputation rests on its self-opening game guns. Today this tradition continues with ex-Purdey craftsman Allen Crewe. building fine Beesley action self-openers and Woodward-style O/U's. They are in Royal Berkshire just west of London.
Estimates listed range from guns barely in proof with marginal wall thicknesses to those with barrel specifications as proofed.
Boxlock non-ejectors $1,000 to $3,000
Boxlock ejectors $1,500 to $5,000
Sidelock non-ejectors $2,000 to $7,000
Sidelock ejectors $3,000 to $30,000
Hammer Guns $1,000 to $3,000
Over & Unders $10,000 to $50,000

Dickson, John
John Dickson served his time with J. Wallace in Edinburgh. In 1882 he registered the first of a series of patents which would culminate in the famous Scottish round action gun. Dickson's continue to build these guns to this day at their Frederick Street premises.
Estimates listed range from guns barely in proof with marginal wall thicknesses to those with barrel specifications as proofed.
Boxlock non-ejectors $1,000 to $3,000
Boxlock ejectors $1,500 to $5,000
Sidelock non-ejectors $2,000 to $7,000
Sidelock ejectors $3,000 to $15,000
Hammer Guns $2,000 to $10,000
Round Action Guns $5,000 to $50,000

Evans, William
William Evans worked for both Purdey and H & H before setting up on his own in 1883. Many of the Evans guns appear to have been made by Webley & Scott and other Birmingham gun makers. Today the firm builds its own guns and is located in St. James, central London.
Estimates listed range from guns barely in proof with marginal wall thicknesses to those with barrel specifications as proofed.
Boxlock non-ejectors $1,000 to $3,000
Boxlock ejectors $1,500 to $5,000
Sidelock non-ejectors $2,000 to $7,000
Sidelock ejectors $3,000 to $50,000
Hammer Guns $1,000 to $3,000

Fraser, Daniel
Daniel Fraser apprenticed with Alexander Henry in Edinburgh before opening his own business on Leith St. He is perhaps best remembered for his rifles and distinctive, fancy back boxlocks. The firm he founded is once again in business in Scotland.
Estimates listed range from guns barely in proof with marginal wall thicknesses to those with barrel specifications as proofed.
Boxlock non-ejectors $1,000 to $3,000
Boxlock ejectors $1,500 to $5,000
Sidelock non-ejectors $2,000 to $7,000
Sidelock ejectors $3,000 to $50,000
Hammer Guns $1,000 to $3,000

Grant, Stephen
Stephen Grant was apprenticed to Kavanagh of Dublin before working with Charles Lancaster and Thomas Boss in London. The firm is perhaps best remembered for its distinctive sidelever guns with fluted fences. The guns are made today in Essendon, Herts, England.
Estimates listed range from guns barely in proof with marginal wall thicknesses to those with barrel specifications as proofed.
Boxlock non-ejectors $1,500 to $4,000
Boxlock ejectors $2,000 to $8,500
Sidelock non-ejectors $2,000 to $10,000
Sidelock ejectors $4,000 to $50,000
Hammer Guns $2,000 to $10,000

Gibbs, George
The Gibbs Company has been in Bristol, England since the 1830s. Though they have built many fine shotguns the name is also strongly associated with rifles. The firm is now owned by Ian Crudgington famous for his book *"The British Shotgun, Vol. I & II."*
Estimates listed range from guns barely in proof with marginal wall thicknesses to those with barrel specifications as proofed.
Boxlock non-ejectors $1,000 to $3,000
Boxlock ejectors $1,500 to $5,000
Sidelock non-ejectors $2,000 to $7,000
Sidelock ejectors $3,000 to $15,000
Hammer Guns $1,000 to $3,000

Greener, W.W.
William Greener apprenticed with Burnand of Newcastle before working with John Manton in London. His son, W.W. Greener, took over in 1869 and built his reputation with "a medium-priced weapon of sound workmanship. The name will forever be associated with the "Greener crossbolt." In recent years the company, still based in Birmingham, has built a small quantity of high grade guns.
Estimates listed range from guns barely in proof with marginal wall thicknesses to those with barrel specifications as proofed.
Boxlock non-ejectors $1,000 to $3,000
Boxlock ejectors $1,500 to $50,000
Sidelock non-ejectors $2,000 to $7,000
Sidelock ejectors $3,000 to $100,000
Hammer Guns $1,000 to $3,000

Hellis, Charles
Charles Hellis was established in 1884 in Westbourne Park, London. The most frequently encountered Hellis guns here in the U.S. are probably the 2" 12 bore and "featherweight" models. Charles Hellis is once again doing business from the west end of London.
Estimates listed range from guns barely in proof with marginal wall thicknesses to those with barrel specifications as proofed.

Boxlock non-ejectors $1,000 to $3,000
Boxlock ejectors $1,500 to $5,000
Sidelock non-ejectors $2,000 to $7,000
Sidelock ejectors $3,000 to $15,000

Henry, Alexander

Alexander Henry has been Edinburg's rifle maker since 1853. Between 1860 and 1882 Henry registered over a dozen patents, mostly for falling black and double rifles. Henry built rifles for Queen Victoria, her husband Prince Albert and their son The Duke of Edinburg. The name and records were eventually acquired by Alex Martin of Glasgow and now reside with Dickson's in Edinburg.

Estimates listed range from guns barely in proof with marginal wall thicknesses to those with barrel specifications as proofed.
Boxlock non-ejectors $1,500 to $3,000
Boxlock ejectors $2,000 to $6,000
Sidelock non-ejectors $2,000 to $9,000
Sidelock ejectors $4,000 to $15,000

Holland & Holland

Harris Holland started as a tobacconist but moved into guns around 1848. Famous for presentation quality guns built for figures as diverse as President Theodore Roosevelt and The Nizam of Hydrabad, they continue to trade under the auspices of Channel, the well-known French luxury goods company.

Estimates listed range from guns barely in proof with marginal wall thicknesses to those with barrel specifications as proofed.

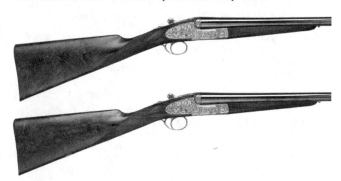

Boxlock non-ejectors $1,5000 to $4,000
Boxlock ejectors $2,000 to $9,000
Sidelock non-ejectors $2,000 to $10,000
Sidelock ejectors $4,000 to $100,000
Hammer Guns $2,000 to $10,000
Over & Unders $8,000 to $100,000

Horsley, Thomas

The firm was founded by Thomas Horsley in about 1832 in York, Yorkshire. Famous for their sliding thumb piece toplever hammer guns they are considered by many to be the best of the provincial gun makers. No longer in business.

Estimates listed range from guns barely in proof with marginal wall thicknesses to those with barrel specifications as proofed.
Boxlock non-ejectors $1,000 to $3,000
Boxlock ejectors $1,500 to $5,000
Sidelock non-ejectors $2,000 to $7,000
Sidelock ejectors $3,000 to $15,000
Hammer Guns $1,000 to $3,000

Horton, William

William Horton was a Burmingham gunmaker who moved to Whitehaven in north-west England before settling in Glasgow in 1863. He died in 1896 but his son Oliver continued registering a series of patents that culminated in the firm's distinctive boxlock gun. Horton was acquired by another Glasgow gunmaker, Arthur Allen, in 1924.

Estimates listed range from guns barely in proof with marginal wall thicknesses to those with barrel specifications as proofed.
Boxlock non-ejectors $1,500 to $3,000
Boxlock ejectors $2,000 to $6,000
Sidelock non-ejectors $2,000 to $9,000
Sidelock ejectors $4,000 to $15,000

Jeffrey, W.J.

William Jackman Jeffery managed Philip Webley's London showroom from 1887 to 1894. The business he established retailed more of the massive .600 double rifles than any other London maker. but these were likely made by Leonard of Birmingham. John Saunders, also of Birmingham, made many of his sidelock ejectors. The company records are with Holland & Holland in London.

Estimates listed range from guns barely in proof with marginal wall thicknesses to those with barrel specifications as proofed.

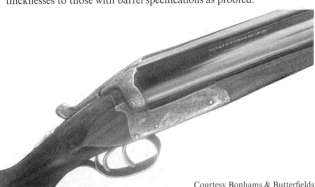

Courtesy Bonhams & Butterfields

Boxlock non-ejectors $1,000 to $3,000
Boxlock ejectors $1,500 to $5,000
Sidelock non-ejectors $2,000 to $7,000
Sidelock ejectors $3,000 to $15,000
Hammer Guns $1,000 to $3,000

Lancaster, Charles

The original Charles Lancaster was a barrel maker for both Joseph Manton and the first James Purdey. In 1878 the business was acquired by A.A. Thorn who established the firm's name with "The Art of Shooting," which ran to at least 14 editions and which he wrote under the pseudonym of "Charles Lancaster." The firm was famous for its four barrel pistols/rifles/shotguns and continues today from Bishopswood, Somerset.

Estimates listed range from guns barely in proof with marginal wall thicknesses to those with barrel specifications as proofed.
Boxlock non-ejectors $1,000 to $3,000
Boxlock ejectors $1,500 to $5,000
Sidelock non-ejectors $2,000 to $7,000
Sidelock ejectors $3,000 to $15,000
Hammer Guns $1,000 to $3,000
Over & Unders $5,000 to $20,000

Lang, Joseph

Joseph Lang worked for Alexander Wilson before starting out on his own in 1821. The firm is best remembered for its "Vena Contracta" gun which had a 12 bore breech that tapered to 16 bore at the muzzle. The company was until recently owned by a Texan but has since returned to England.

Estimates listed range from guns barely in proof with marginal wall thicknesses to those with barrel specifications as proofed.
Boxlock non-ejectors $1,000 to $3,000
Boxlock ejectors $1,500 to $5,000
Sidelock non-ejectors $2,000 to $7,000
Sidelock ejectors $3,000 to $35,000
Hammer Guns $1,000 to $3,000

Lewis, G.E.

George Edward Lewis was born in 1829 and apprenticed in "all branches" of the Birmingham gun trade. His fame rests on his magnum "gun of the period" which was popular with generations of wildfowlers. The firm continues today from Halesowen, West Midlands.

Estimates listed range from guns barely in proof with marginal wall thicknesses to those with barrel specifications as proofed.
Boxlock non-ejectors $1,500 to $4,000
Boxlock ejectors $2,000 to $8,500
Sidelock non-ejectors $2,000 to $10,000
Sidelock ejectors $4,000 to $30,000
Hammer Guns $2,000 to $10,000

MacNaughton & Son

James MacNaughton started in business in 1864 in Edinburgh. His fame rests on his patent Edinburgh round action gun of 1879. The firm is back in business in Edinburgh.

Estimates listed range from guns barely in proof with marginal wall thicknesses to those with barrel specifications as proofed.
Boxlock non-ejectors $1,000 to $3,000
Boxlock ejectors $1,500 to $5,000
Sidelock non-ejectors $2,000 to $7,000
Sidelock ejectors $3,000 to $15,000
Hammer Guns $2,000 to $10,000
Round Action Guns $3,000 to $20,000

Pape, W.R.

William Rochester Pape started his business in 1858 enlarging a game dealership owned by his family. He is credited with the earliest patent for choke boring (1866) and rivals Horsley as the best of the provincial gun makers. A 16 bore Pape, once owned by the Grandson of the firm's founder, sold at Sotheby's, London for $14,904 in March 1999.

Estimates listed range from guns barely in proof with marginal wall thicknesses to those with barrel specifications as proofed.

Courtesy Bonhams & Butterfields

Boxlock non-ejectors $1,000 to $3,000
Boxlock ejectors $1,500 to $15,000
Sidelock non-ejectors $2,000 to $7,000
Sidelock ejectors $3,000 to $15,000
Hammer Guns $1,000 to $3,000

Powell, William

William Powell started out in Birmingham in 1802. Their top "lift up-lever" are considered highly desirable. They continue in Birmingham today.

Estimates listed range from guns barely in proof with marginal wall thicknesses to those with barrel specifications as proofed.
Boxlock non-ejectors $1,000 to $3,000
Boxlock ejectors $1,500 to $5,000
Sidelock non-ejectors $2,000 to $7,000
Sidelock ejectors $3,000 to $35,000
Hammer Guns $1,000 to $3,000

Purdey & Son, James

James Purdey, one of Joseph Manton's earliest gun makers, starting in about 1803. The famous Purdey underbolt, developed in 1863 is perhaps the most widely disseminated of all shotgun patents. Today the company is still considered the world's greatest gun makers. A pair of Purdey 16 bore guns, once were owned by Edward VIII when he was Prince of Wales, sold at Sotheby's, Geneva, in 1991 for $196,428.

Estimates listed range from guns barely in proof with marginal wall thicknesses to those with barrel specifications as proofed.
Boxlock non-ejectors $1,5000 to $4,000
Boxlock ejectors $2,000 to $9,000
Sidelock non-ejectors $2,000 to $10,000
Sidelock ejectors $4,000 to $100,000
Hammer Guns $2,000 to $10,000
Over & Unders $8,000 to $100,000

Richards, William Westley

William Westley Richards founded his own company in 1812 at 82 High St., Birmingham. In 1975 two of the firms workforce developed the famous Anson & Deeley boxlock action which was made hand detachable in 1897. The firm continues in Bournebrook to this day.

Estimates listed range from guns barely in proof with marginal wall thicknesses to those with barrel specifications as proofed.
Boxlock non-ejectors $1,500 to $4,000
Boxlock ejectors $2,000 to $8,500
Sidelock non-ejectors $2,000 to $10,000
Sidelock ejectors $4,000 to $30,000
Hammer Guns $2,000 to $10,000
Over & Unders $10,000 to $100,000

Rigby, John

John Rigby started for himself in Dublin in 1775. The company enjoys a 200-year reputation as fine rifle makers and are famous for their .416 propriety cartridge. They were recently sold and moved to California.

Estimates listed range from guns barely in proof with marginal wall thicknesses to those with barrel specifications as proofed.
Boxlock non-ejectors $1,500 to $4,000
Boxlock ejectors $2,000 to $8,500
Sidelock non-ejectors $2,000 to $10,000
Sidelock ejectors $4,000 to $35,000
Hammer Guns $2,000 to $10,000

Rosson & Co., C. S.

C. S. Rosson was a provincial maker active from the turn of the century in Norwich. They produced a slide opener, self openers built on the Edwin V. Smith patent and a 2" chambered gun they called the "Twentieth Century." They failed in 1957.

Estimates listed range from guns barely in proof with marginal wall thicknesses to those with barrel specifications as proofed.
Boxlock non-ejectors $1,000 to $3,000
Boxlock ejectors $1,500 to $5,000
Sidelock non-ejectors $2,000 to $7,000
Sidelock ejectors $3,000 to $15,000
Hammer Guns $1,000 to $3,000

Scott, W & C

William Scott served an apprenticeship with a Bury St. Edmund's gun maker, possibly Ben or Charles Parker. In 1865 the firm contributed to the perfection of the English gun by developing the standard spindle, which connects the Purdey bolt to the top lever. They no longer trade.

Estimates listed range from guns barely in proof with marginal wall thicknesses to those with barrels specifications as proofed.
Boxlock non-ejectors $1,000 to $3,000
Boxlock ejectors $1,500 to $5,000
Sidelock non-ejectors $2,000 to $7,000
Sidelock ejectors $3,000 to $15,000
Hammer Guns $1,000 to $3,000

Watson Brothers

Watson Brothers date from 1875 and are famous for their small bore guns. In recent years the company has been resuscitated by Mike Louca, who is establishing himself as a builder of round bodied over-and-unders.

Estimates listed range from guns barely in proof with marginal wall thicknesses to those with barrel specifications as proofed.
Boxlock non-ejectors $1,000 to $3,000
Boxlock ejectors $1,500 to $5,000
Sidelock non-ejectors $2,000 to $7,000
Sidelock ejectors $3,000 to $15,000
Hammer Guns $1,000 to $3,000
Over & Unders $30,000 to $100,000

Webley & Scott

Philip Webley began his apprenticeship as a lockmaker in 1827, probably with Ryan & Watson. In 1897 he merged with W. & C. Scott and built semi machine-made shotguns using techniques previously employed on revolvers. The firm ceased operations in 1991.

Estimates listed range from guns barely in proof with marginal wall thicknesses to those with barrel specifications as proofed.
Boxlock non-ejectors $1,000 to $3,000
Boxlock ejectors $1,500 to $5,000
Sidelock non-ejectors $2,000 to $7,000
Sidelock ejectors $3,000 to $15,000
Hammer Guns $1,000 to $3,000

Wilkes, John
Current Importer/Distributor FNGB, Colorado Springs, CO
The first John Wilkes was established in Birmingham in 1830. The firm's reputation rests on the intrinsic high quality of their work. They continue on 79 Beak St., London.

New guns built today have interchangeable parts and locks. Special Series over-and-under sidelock guns in 20 gauge only with custom features retail for $28500. Only 25 are to be built.

Estimates listed range from guns barely in proof with marginal wall thicknesses to those with barrel specifications as proofed.
Boxlock non-ejectors $2,000 to $3,000
Boxlock ejectors $2,000 to $4,500
Sidelock non-ejectors $20,000 to $25,000
Sidelock ejectors $20,000 to $250,000
Hammer Guns $4,000 to $15,000

Woodward, James
James Woodward worked for Charles Moore, becoming a partner before establishing his own company. The firm's reputation rests in large part on its "Automatic" double rifles and to an even greater extent on its over-and-under shotguns, which are the only ones that have ever rivaled Boss's.

Estimates listed range from guns barely in proof with marginal wall thicknesses to those with barrel specifications as proofed.
Boxlock non-ejectors $1,500 to $4,000
Boxlock ejectors $2,000 to $8,500
Sidelock non-ejectors $2,000 to $10,000
Sidelock ejectors $4,000 to $30,000
Hammer Guns $2,000 to $10,000
Over & Unders $20,000 to $200,000

BRNO ARMS
Uhersky Brod, Czech Republic
Importer—Euro Imports

ZP-49
A 12 gauge sidelock double-barrel shotgun with double triggers and automatic ejectors. Blued with a walnut stock. Imported in 1986 only.

Exc.	V.G.	Good	Fair	Poor
950	800	650	450	325

ZP-149
As above, without engraving.

NIB	Exc.	V.G.	Good	Fair	Poor
700	600	500	400	300	200

ZP-349
As above, with the buttstock having a cheekpiece and a beavertail forearm.

Exc.	V.G.	Good	Fair	Poor
700	600	500	350	250

ZBK-100
A single barrel shotgun in 12 or 20 gauge with 27" barrel and walnut stock. Weight is approximately 5.5 lbs.

NIB	Exc.	V.G.	Good	Fair	Poor
250	200	150	—	—	—

BROLIN ARMS
Le Verne, California

This California company began business in 1995 manufacturing 1911-type pistols. These pistols are manufactured and assembled in the U.S. Very little price history has been established. Starting in 1997 the company expanded its product line to include shotguns, single-action revolvers, Mauser rifles, semi-automatic .22 caliber pistols, and a custom shop.
NOTE: This company ceased operations in 1999.

MITCHELL SINGLE-ACTION REVOLVERS
Single-Action Army Model
Offered in 4.75", 5.5", or 7.5" barrel lengths and chambered for the .45 Long Colt, .357 Magnum, or .44-40 calibers. Offered in blue finish with case hardened frame or nickel finish. Also available with dual cylinders, i.e. .45 LC/.45 ACP. Add $50 for nickel finish, and $150 for dual cylinder models.

NIB	Exc.	V.G.	Good	Fair	Poor
450	350	—	—	—	—

BROOKLYN F. A. CO.
Brooklyn, New York

Slocum Pocket Revolver
A .32 caliber spur-trigger revolver with a 3" round barrel. The frame is silver-plated brass and scroll engraved; the remainder is either blued or plated with walnut grips. The barrel is marked "B.A. Co. Patented April 14, 1863." Approximately 10,000 were manufactured in 1863 and 1864. The cylinder has five individual tubes that slide forward to open for loading and then for ejecting the spent cartridges.

Exc.	V.G.	Good	Fair	Poor
—	—	800	300	100

Slocum Unfluted Cylinder Pocket Revolver
As above, but in .22 or .32 caliber with 5- or 7-shot cylinder. Approximately 250 were manufactured in .32 rimfire and 100 in .22 rimfire.

Exc.	V.G.	Good	Fair	Poor
—	—	1000	400	200

NOTE: .22 caliber add 25 percent.

BROWN, A.A.
Birmingham, England
SEE—British Double Guns

BROWN, DAVID MCKAY
Glasgow, Scotland
SEE—British Double Guns

BROWN MANUFACTURING CO.
Newburyport, Massachusetts
Also SEE—Ballard Patent Arms

Southerner Derringer
A .41 caliber spur-trigger single-shot pocket pistol with a pivoted 2.5" or 4" octagonal barrel marked "Southerner." Silver-plated or blued with walnut grips. This pistol was manufactured by the Merrimack Arms Co. from 1867 to 1869 and by the Brown Manufacturing Co. from 1869 to 1873.

Brass Framed 2.5" Barrel

Exc.	V.G.	Good	Fair	Poor
—	—	800	300	125

Iron Frame 2.5" Barrel (Brown Mfg. Only)

Exc.	V.G.	Good	Fair	Poor
—	—	950	400	200

Brass Frame 4" Barrel

Exc.	V.G.	Good	Fair	Poor
—	—	3250	1250	500

Brown Mfg. Co./Merrill Patent Breechloading Rifles
Overall length 54-3/4"; barrel (bore) length 35"; caliber .577. Markings: On breechblock-bolt mechanism, "BROWN MFG. CO. NEWBURYPORT, MASS./PATANTED OCT. 17, 1871." The patent issued to George Merrill in 1871, permitted the Brown Manufacturing Co. to alter probably up to 1,000 English P1853 rifle-muskets to a single-shot breechloading system. The large bolt handle projecting upward at the end of the breech readily distinguishes these arms.

Exc.	V.G.	Good	Fair	Poor
—	—	2000	800	300

BROWNING ARMS CO.
Morgan, Utah

Contrary to popular belief, the firm of Browning Arms has really manufactured only one gun in its long and colorful history. This was the Model 1878 single-shot rifle, which was actually the first gun that the prolific inventor John M. Browning patented. This firm was founded in 1880 as J. M. Browning & Bro. in Ogden, Utah. John Browning is considered by many to be the greatest firearms genius of all time. He created 80 firearms designs and held 128 individual patents. He sold designs to Winchester, Stevens, Remington, and Colt, as well as to the Belgian firm of Fabrique Nationale (FN). He was directly responsible for designing many of the firearms with which we have come to be familiar, including the 1911 Colt Government Model, the 1885 Winchester Single-Shot (evolved from the Model 1878 that was actually Browning-manufactured), the Models 1886, 1892, 1894, and 1895 Lever Action Rifles, as well as the Model 1897 Shotgun. He was also directly responsible for producing the Model 1935 Hi-Power that achieved worldwide service pistol acceptance. In the 1890s Browning had difficulty dealing with the American arms corporations, so he went to Europe and established a lasting relationship with the firm of Fabrique Nationale in Herstal, Belgium. This agreement lasted until 1977 when FN purchased the Browning Company. In the early 1970s, the Browning corporation contracted with the firm of B. C. Miroku in Japan and has since marketed guns produced by them. In 1991 GIAT, a French state-owned firm, purchased FN and Browning. One should be cognizant of the fact that in the opinion of many experts Miroku-produced Browning firearms are as high in quality as any others produced; collector interest dictates greater values on the Belgian-manufactured versions.

Custom Shop BSL
This is a side-by-side shotgun is equiped with Browning sidelock barrel, Holland & Holland-type locks with double trigger and auto ejectors. The gun is assembled and finished by Labeau-Courally. It is offered in both 12 and 20 gauge. Engraved grayed receiver or case colored receiver. Introduced into the Browning product line in 2001.

Case Colored Receiver (BSL Grade LC1)
NIB	Exc.	V.G.	Good	Fair	Poor
10200	—	—	—	—	—

Engraved Gray Receiver (BSL Grade LC2)

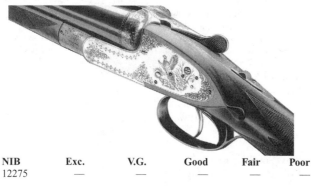

NIB	Exc.	V.G.	Good	Fair	Poor
12275	—	—	—	—	—

BSS
This is a side-by-side, double-barrel shotgun chambered for 12 or 20 gauge. It was offered with a 26", 28", or 30" barrel with various choke combinations. It features a boxlock action and automatic ejectors. Early guns had a nonselective single trigger; late production, a selective trigger. The finish is blued with a checkered walnut stock and beavertail forearm. It was manufactured between 1978 and 1987 by B.C. Miroku.

Exc.	V.G.	Good	Fair	Poor
1200	950	775	650	400

NOTE: Single-selective trigger add 20 percent. 20 gauge add 20 percent.

BSS Sporter
This version features an English-style, straight-grip stock and a splinter forearm. The stock was oil-finished. It was offered with a 26" or 28" barrel.

Exc.	V.G.	Good	Fair	Poor
1200	950	775	650	400

NOTE: For 20 gauge add 20 percent.

BSS Grade II
This version features game scene engraving and a satin, coin finished receiver. It was discontinued in 1984.

Exc.	V.G.	Good	Fair	Poor
1750	1350	1100	850	500

BSS Sidelock
This version features an engraved sidelock action and was offered in 12 or 20 gauge. It was offered with a 26" or 28" barrel and has a straight-grip stock and splintered forearm. It was manufactured in Korea between 1983 and 1987.

NIB	Exc.	V.G.	Good	Fair	Poor
2400	2100	1600	1250	800	500

NOTE: Add 10 percent to above prices for 20 gauge guns.

Model 53
Offered in 1990 this model is a reproduction of the Winchester Model 53 and like the original is chambered for the .32-20 cartridge. This is a limited edition offering confined to 5,000 rifles. It features hand-cut checkering, high-grade walnut stock with full pistol grip and semi-beavertail forend. Pistol grip is fitted with a metal grip cap. Barrel length is 22" and the finish is blue.

NIB	Exc.	V.G.	Good	Fair	Poor
725	625	550	450	325	200

Model 1878
Based on John M. Browning's first patent this single-shot rifle was the only firearm manufactured by the Browning brothers. Offered in several calibers only a few hundred probably exist with the Ogden, Utah, barrel address. This design was later sold to Winchester and sold under that company's name as the Model 1885 High Wall.

Exc.	V.G.	Good	Fair	Poor
4500	3500	2500	1500	500

Model 1885 High Wall
This is a single-shot rifle with falling block action and octagonal free-floating barrel similar to the Model 78. Introduced in 1985. The stock is a high grade walnut with straight grip and recoil pad. Furnished with 28" barrel it is offered in the following calibers: .223, .22-250, .270, .30-06, 7mm Rem. Mag., .45-70 Gov't. Weighs about 8 lbs. 12 oz.

NIB	Exc.	V.G.	Good	Fair	Poor
800	650	550	300	200	100

Model 1885 Low Wall
Introduced in 1995 this rifle is similar to the above but in a more accurate version of the original Low Wall. The thin octagon barrel is 24" in length. Trigger pull is adjustable. The walnut stock is fitted with a pistol grip and schnabel forearm. Offered in .22 Hornet, .223 Rem. and the .243 Win. calibers. Weight is about 6.4 lbs.

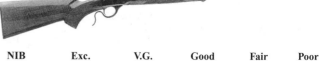

NIB	Exc.	V.G.	Good	Fair	Poor
750	600	500	400	300	150

Model 1885 Low Wall Traditional Hunter
Introduced in 1998 this model is similar to the Low Wall but with a half-octagon half-round 24" barrel chambered for the .357 Magnum, .44 Magnum, and .45 Colt cartridges. Case colored receiver and crescent butt with tang sight are also features. Weight is approximately 6.5 lbs.

NIB	Exc.	V.G.	Good	Fair	Poor
900	750	—	—	—	—

Model 1885 BPCR (Black Powder Cartridge Rifle)
This model was introduced in 1996 for BPCR metallic silhouette shoots. Chambered for the .45-70 or .40-60 caliber the receiver is case colored and the 28" round barrel is fitted with vernier sight with level. The walnut stock has a checkered pistol grip and is fitted with a tang sight. Weight is approximately 11 lbs.

NIB	Exc.	V.G.	Good	Fair	Poor
1500	1300	800	400	300	150

Model 1885 BPCR Creedmore Type
Introduced in 1998 this model is chambered for the 45/90 cartridge and features a 34" heavy half-round barrel with long range tang sight and wind gauge front sight. Weight is approximately 11 lbs. 13 oz.

NIB	Exc.	V.G.	Good	Fair	Poor
1250	1000	—	—	—	—

Model 1885 High Wall Traditional Hunter
This variation of the Model 1885 series was introduced in 1997. It is fitted with an oil finish walnut stock with crescent buttplate. The barrel is octagonal and 28" in length. The rear sight is buckhorn and the rifle is fitted with a tang-mounted peep sight. The front sight is gold bead classic style. The rifle is chambered for the .30-30, .38-55, and .45-70 cartridges. Weight is approximately 9 lbs. In 1998 the .454 Casull caliber was added to this rifle.

NIB	Exc.	V.G.	Good	Fair	Poor
1100	900	700	—	—	—

Model 1886 Grade I
This was a lever action sporting rifle patterned after the Model 1886 Winchester rifle. It was chambered for the .45-70 cartridge and has a 26", octagonal barrel with a full-length, tubular magazine. The finish is blued with a walnut stock and crescent buttplate. There were 7,000 manufactured in 1986.

NIB	Exc.	V.G.	Good	Fair	Poor
1350	950	725	600	450	300

Model 1886 Grade I Carbine

NIB	Exc.	V.G.	Good	Fair	Poor
850	650	550	400	325	250

Model 1886 High Grade
This deluxe version of the Model 1886 features game scene engraving with gold accents and a checkered, select walnut stock. "1 of 3,000" is engraved on the top of the barrel. There were 3,000 manufactured in 1986.

NIB	Exc.	V.G.	Good	Fair	Poor
1600	1150	900	700	550	425

Model 1886 High Grade Carbine

NIB	Exc.	V.G.	Good	Fair	Poor
1200	950	750	600	450	300

Model 1886 Montana Centennial
This version is similar to the High Grade with a different engraving pattern designed to commemorate the centennial of the State of Montana. There were 2,000 manufactured in 1986. As with all commemoratives, it must be NIB with all supplied materials to command collector interest.

NIB	Exc.	V.G.	Good	Fair	Poor
1300	950	750	600	450	375

B-92 Carbine
This is a lever action sporting rifle patterned after the Winchester Model 92. It was chambered for the .357 Mag. and the .44 Mag. cartridges. It has a 20" barrel with an 11-round, tubular magazine. The finish is blued with a walnut stock. It was discontinued in 1986.

Exc.	V.G.	Good	Fair	Poor
400	325	195	150	120

NOTE: Add 10 percent for Centennial Model. For .357 Magnum add 30 percent.

Model 1895 Grade I
This is a lever action sporting rifle chambered in .30-40 Krag and the .30-06 cartridge. It was patterned after the Model 1895 Winchester rifle. It has a 24" barrel and a 4-round, integral box magazine. It has a buckhorn rear sight and a blade front. The finish is blued with a walnut stock. There were 6,000 manufactured in .30-06 and 2,000 chambered for the .30-40 Krag. It was manufactured in 1984.

Exc.	V.G.	Good	Fair	Poor
600	525	450	375	275

NOTE: For .30-06 caliber add 15 percent.

Model 1895 High Grade
This is the deluxe engraved version of the Model 1895. It has gold-inlaid game scenes and a gold-plated trigger and features a checkered select walnut stock. There were 2,000 produced in 1984—1,000 in each caliber.

Exc.	V.G.	Good	Fair	Poor
1000	900	700	575	400

NOTE: For .30-40 caliber deduct 20 percent.

BRUCE & DAVIS
Webster, Massachusetts

Double-Barreled Pistol
A .36 caliber double-barrel percussion pistol with 3" to 6" round barrels. The barrel rib marked "Bruce & Davis." Blued with walnut grips. Manufactured during the 1840s.

Exc.	V.G.	Good	Fair	Poor
—	—	800	350	150

BRUCHET
Ste. Etienne, France

Model A Shotgun
A 12 or .410 bore side-by-side shotgun with double triggers, and automatic ejectors. The barrel lengths and chokes are to customer specifications. Produced on a limited basis (50 per year) since 1982.

NIB	Exc.	V.G.	Good	Fair	Poor
2500	1750	1500	1250	1000	500

Model B
As above, with a finer finish and a spring-assisted action opener. Imported since 1982.

NIB	Exc.	V.G.	Good	Fair	Poor
6750	5250	4000	3000	2250	1250

BRUFF, R.P.
New York, New York

Bruff Pocket Pistol
A .41 caliber single-shot percussion pistol with 2.5" to 3" barrels The pistol is marked "R.P. Bruff NY" in an arch and "Cast Steel." German silver with a checkered walnut stock. Manufactured between 1861 and 1870.

Exc.	V.G.	Good	Fair	Poor
—	—	1500	600	200

BULLARD REPEATING ARMS CO.
Springfield, Massachusetts

Designed by James H. Bullard, the following rifles were manufactured in competition with those produced by the Whitney Arms Company and the Winchester Repeating Arms Company. Approximately 12,000 were made between 1886 and 1890.

Small Frame
A .32-40 and .38-45 caliber lever action rifle with a 26" octagonal barrel and either a half or full length magazine tube. Blued or case hardened with a walnut stock. The receiver is stamped "Bullard Repeating Arms Company/Springfield, Mass., U.S.A. Pat. Aug. 16, 1881." The caliber is marked on top of the frame.

Exc.	V.G.	Good	Fair	Poor
—	3250	1250	600	300

Large Frame

A .40-75 through .45-85 caliber lever action rifle with 28" octagonal barrel. Other features and markings as above. Can be custom ordered in .50-95 and .50-115.

Exc.	V.G.	Good	Fair	Poor
—	4000	1750	800	400

Carbine

A .45-70 caliber lever action rifle with a 22" round barrel and a sliding dust cover on the receiver. Marking and finish as above.

Exc.	V.G.	Good	Fair	Poor
—	6500	3000	1250	500

Musket

A .45-70 caliber lever action rifle with a 30" round barrel with a full-length stock secured by two barrel bands. There is a rod under the barrel, military sights, and the same sliding cover on the receiver as found on the Carbine. There have been examples noted without the manufacturer's markings.

Exc.	V.G.	Good	Fair	Poor
—	5750	2750	1250	500

BULLDOG SINGLE-SHOT PISTOL
Connecticut Arms & Manufacturing Co.
Naubuc, Connecticut

Bulldog

A .44 or .50 caliber single-shot spur trigger pistol with 4" or 6" barrels, and a pivoting breechblock that moves to the left for loading. Blued, case hardened and stamped "Connecticut Arms & Manf. Co. Naubuc Conn. Patented Oct. 25, 1864." There were only a few hundred manufactured, and the .50 caliber, 6" barreled versions would be worth an additional 40 percent. Produced between 1866 and 1868.

Exc.	V.G.	Good	Fair	Poor
—	1500	600	250	150

BURGESS GUN CO.
Buffalo, New York
Also SEE—Colt and Whitney

One of the most prolific 19th century designers was Andrew Burgess who established his own company in 1892. The Burgess Gun Company manufactured slide action shotguns and rifles operated by a unique pistol grip prior to their being purchased by the Winchester Repeating Arms Company in 1899. Arms based on Burgess' patents were manufactured by a variety of American gun makers. Serial numbers for all Burgess shotguns begin at 1000.

12 Gauge Slide Action Shotgun

A 12 gauge slide-action shotgun with a 28" or 30" barrel. Blued with a walnut stock. This model was available with 6 grades of engraving. The values listed are for the standard, plain model.

Burgess engraving grades (1-4)

Exc.	V.G.	Good	Fair	Poor
—	1500	600	250	125

Folding Shotgun

As above, with a 19.5" barrel that is hinged so that it may be folded back against the buttstock.

Exc.	V.G.	Good	Fair	Poor
—	4250	1750	650	300

BUTLER, WM. S.
Rocky Hill, Connecticut

Butler Single-Shot Pistol

A .36 caliber single-shot percussion pocket pistol with a 2.5" barrel and the frame and grip made in one piece. The frame marked "Wm. S. Butler's Patent/Patented Feb.3, 1857."

Exc.	V.G.	Good	Fair	Poor
—	—	900	350	150

C

CASARTELLI, CARLO
Brescia, Italy
Importer—New England Arms Co.
Kittery Point, Maine

Sidelock Shotgun

Custom order sidelock shotgun that is available in any gauge, barrel length, choke, automatic ejectors and single-selective trigger and choice of engraving style.

NIB	Exc.	V.G.	Good	Fair	Poor
15000	13500	10000	8250	6000	4000

CHAPMAN, G. & J.
Philadelphia, Pennsylvania

Chapman Pocket Revolver

A .32 caliber revolver with a 4" round barrel and 7-shot cylinder. The frame is made of brass while the barrel and cylinder are of steel. The barrel is marked "G.& J. Chapman/Philada/Patent Applied For/1861." Manufactured during the 1860s.

Exc.	V.G.	Good	Fair	Poor
—	—	2250	950	250

CHAPIUS
France

RG Progress

A 12, 16, or 20 gauge boxlock shotgun. Most options are available on order.

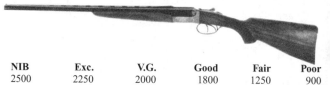

NIB	Exc.	V.G.	Good	Fair	Poor
2500	2250	2000	1800	1250	900

CHICAGO F. A. CO.
Chicago, Illinois

Protector Palm Pistol

A .32 caliber radial cylinder revolver designed to fit in the palm of the hand and to be operated by a hinged lever mounted to the rear of the circular frame. The sideplates are marked "Chicago Firearms Co., Chicago, Ill." and "The Protector." Blued with hard rubber grip panels or nickel-plated with pearl grip panels. Manufactured by the Ames Manufacturing Company.

Courtesy Rock Island Auction Company

Standard Model Nickel-Plated/Black Grips

Exc.	V.G.	Good	Fair	Poor
—	2500	1000	500	250

NOTE: Blued finish add 50 percent. Pearl grips add 20 percent.

CHURCHILL, E. J. LTD.
London, England

Premier Side-by-Side
Similar to the over-and-under gun but with side-by-side barrels. Also offered in 16 gauge as well as 12, 20, and 28 gauge. Weights are about 6.5 lbs. for 12 gauge; 6 lbs. for 16 gauge; and 5.8 lbs. for 20 gauge. Many extra options are available. Seek expert advice prior to a sale.

NIB	Exc.	V.G.	Good	Fair	Poor
36500	—	—	—	—	—

NOTE: Add $3,000 for 28 gauge guns.

CIMARRON F. A. MFG. CO.
Fredericksburg, Texas

In business since 1984 this company imports quality single-action revolvers and rifles from Uberti, Armi San Marco, and Pedersoli.
NOTE: Cimarron also sells Uberti-manufactured blackpowder Colt reproductions, from the Patterson to the Model 1862 Pocket. For prices and specifications on these models see the Uberti section.

Model No. 3 Schofield
This version of the Schofield is manufactured for Cimarron by Armi San Marco in Italy. Its parts are interchangeable with the original. It is offered in several variations and calibers.

Schofield Civilian Model
Fitted with 7" barrel and offered in .44 Russian & .44 Special, .44 WCF, .45 Schofield, .45 Long Colt.

NIB	Exc.	V.G.	Good	Fair	Poor
849	650	—	—	—	—

Schofield Military Model
Essentially the same as the Civilian Model except for its markings.

NIB	Exc.	V.G.	Good	Fair	Poor
849	650	—	—	—	—

Schofield Wells Fargo
Similar to the Military and Civilian Model but fitted with a 5" barrel. Calibers are the same.

NIB	Exc.	V.G.	Good	Fair	Poor
849	650	—	—	—	—

NOTE: For standard nickel finish add $100 and for custom nickel finish add $150.

COLT SINGLE-ACTION ARMY CONFIGURATIONS

Cimarron Arms reproduction of the 1873 Colt Single-Action Army revolver comes in two basic configurations. First is the "Old Model" with the black powder frame screw-in cylinder pin retainer and circular bull's eye ejector head. Second is the "prewar Model" style frame with spring loaded cross-pin cylinder retainer and half moon ejector head. Old Model revolvers are available in authentic old style charcoal blue finish at an extra charge. Unless otherwise stated all of these Colt reproductions are produced by Uberti of Italy. Plain walnut grips are standard unless noted.

Model 1872 Open Top
Offered with 5.5" barrel or 7.5" barrel and chambered for the .38 Colt & S&W Special, .44 Colt & Russian, .45 S&W Schofield. Walnut grips. Choice of early Navy-style brass or later Army steel style grip frame. Finish is blue, charcoal blue, nickel, or original finish.

NIB	Exc.	V.G.	Good	Fair	Poor
469	350	—	—	—	—

General Custer 7th Cavalry Model
Has US military markings and is fitted with 7-1/2" barrel on an Old Model frame. Offered in .45 Long Colt only.

NIB	Exc.	V.G.	Good	Fair	Poor
550	450	350	—	—	—

Rough Rider U.S. Artillery Model
This version of the Old Model is fitted with a 5-1/2" barrel and chambered for .45 Long Colt.

NIB	Exc.	V.G.	Good	Fair	Poor
550	450	350	—	—	—

Frontier Six Shooter
This revolver is offered with a choice of 4-3/4", 5-1/2", or 7-1/2" barrel. It is chambered for .38 WCF, .357 Magnum, .44 WCF, .45 Long Colt, or .45 LC with extra .45 ACP cylinder.

NIB	Exc.	V.G.	Good	Fair	Poor
475	350	—	—	—	—

NOTE: For charcoal blue finish add $40 to NIB price. For extra .45 ACP cylinder add $30. For stainless steel add $50.

Sheriff's Model w/no ejector
Fitted with a 3" barrel and chambered in .44 WCF or .45 Long Colt. Built on an Old Model frame.

NIB	Exc.	V.G.	Good	Fair	Poor
469	350	—	—	—	—

New Sheriff's Model w/ejector
This variation is fitted with a 3-1/2" barrel with ejector and is available in .357 Magnum, .44 WCF, .44 Special, and .45 Long Colt.

NIB	Exc.	V.G.	Good	Fair	Poor
500	400	325	—	—	—

NOTE: For checkered walnut grips add $35.

Wyatt Earp Buntline
This is a limited edition model fitted with a 10" barrel chambered for the .45 Long Colt cartridge. Model P frame. Silver shield inlaid in grip.

NIB	Exc.	V.G.	Good	Fair	Poor
760	600	—	—	—	—

New Thunderer
The frame is based on the Old Model fitted with a bird's-head grip with a choice of plain or checkered walnut grips. Originally offered in 3-1/2" or 4-3/4" barrel lengths; in 1997 5-1/2" barrels were offered. Chambered for .357 Magnum, .44 WCF, .44 Special, or .45 Long Colt/.45 ACP.

NIB	Exc.	V.G.	Good	Fair	Poor
500	400	325	—	—	—

NOTE: For checkered walnut grips add $35.

Thunderer Long Tom
Same as the New Thunderer except for a barrel length of 7.5".

NIB	Exc.	V.G.	Good	Fair	Poor
520	425	350	—	—	—

Lightning
Similar to the Thunderer but with a smaller grip frame. Chambered for the .38 Special cartridge and fitted with 3.5", 4.75", or 5.5" barrel. Finish is blue with case hardened frame.

NIB	Exc.	V.G.	Good	Fair	Poor
389	300	—	—	—	—

Lightning .32s
This model features two cylinders chambered for the .32-20 and the .32 H&R cartridges. Choice of 3.5", 4.75", or 5.5" barrel. Introduced in 2004.

NIB	Exc.	V.G.	Good	Fair	Poor
560	400	—	—	—	—

New Model P
Offered in either Old Model or prewar styles in a choice of 43/4", 5-1/2", or 7-1/2" barrel. Chambered for .32 WCF, .38 WCF, .44 WCF, .44 Special, or .45 Long Colt.

NIB	Exc.	V.G.	Good	Fair	Poor
500	400	325	—	—	—

Stainless Frontier Model P
This model is a Model P in stainless steel. Chambered for the .357 Mag or .45 Colt cartridge. Barrels are 4.75", 5.5", or 7.5". Introduced in 2004.

NIB	Exc.	V.G.	Good	Fair	Poor
600	450	—	—	—	—

A.P. Casey Model P U.S. Cavalry
Fitted with a 7-1/2" barrel and chambered for .45 Long Colt this revolver has US markings (APC) on an Old Model frame.

NIB	Exc.	V.G.	Good	Fair	Poor
499	375	—	—	—	—

Rinaldo A. Carr Model P U.S. Artillery
This is a Model P built on an Old Model frame and chambered for .45 Long Colt and fitted with a 5-1/2" barrel. US markings (RAC).

NIB	Exc.	V.G.	Good	Fair	Poor
499	375	—	—	—	—

Evil Roy Model
This model features a Model P frame with wide square-notch rear sight and wide-width front sight. Slim grips checkered or smooth. Tuned action with lightened trigger. Chambered for the .357 Mag, .45 Colt, or .44-40 cartridge. Barrel lengths are 4.75" or 5.5". Introduced in 2004.

NIB	Exc.	V.G.	Good	Fair	Poor
675	500	—	—	—	—

Model P Jr.
Similar to the Model P but sized 20 percent smaller. Chambered for the .38 Special cartridge and fitted with 3.5" or 4.75" barrels. Blue with case hardened frame.

NIB	Exc.	V.G.	Good	Fair	Poor
490	400	325	—	—	—

Model P Jr. .32s
This model, introduced in 2004, features two cylinders chambered for the .32-20 and the .32 H&R cartridges. Choice of 3.5", 4.75", or 5.5" barrel.

NIB	Exc.	V.G.	Good	Fair	Poor
550	400	—	—	—	—

Cimarron 1880 Frontier Flat Top
Introduced in 1998 this model is a target version of the Colt single-action army. Rear sight is adjustable for windage and front adjustable for elevation. Offered with choice of 4.75", 5.5", or 7.5" barrels and chambered for .45 Colt, .45 Schofield, .44 WCF, and .357 Magnum. Choice of model P frame or pre-war frame.

NIB	Exc.	V.G.	Good	Fair	Poor
480	350	—	—	—	—

Cimarron Bisley
Exact copy of the Colt Bisley with case hardened frame. Choice of 4.75", 5.5", or 7.5" barrels and calibers from .45 Colt, .45 Schofield, .44 WCF, to .357 Magnum. Introduced in 1998.

NIB	Exc.	V.G.	Good	Fair	Poor
525	400	325	—	—	—

Cimarron Bisley Flat Top
Offered in the same barrel lengths and caliber as the standard Bisley with the addition of a windage adjustable rear sight and elevation adjustable front sight. Introduced in 1998.

NIB	Exc.	V.G.	Good	Fair	Poor
525	400	325	—	—	—

El Pistolero
This budget-priced revolver was introduced in 1997 and features a brass backstrap and trigger guard with plain walnut grips. Offered in 4-3/4", 5-1/2", and 7-1/2" barrel lengths. Chambered for .45 Long Colt or .357 Magnum.

NIB	Exc.	V.G.	Good	Fair	Poor
340	250	—	—	—	—

Model 1872 Open Top
This revolver is offered in a number of different calibers and configurations. It is chambered for the .44 SP, .44 Colt, .44 Russian, .45 Schofield, .38 Colt, .38 Special. It can be fitted with Army or Navy grips. Barrel lengths are 4.75", 5.5", or 7.5". Offered in regular blued finish, charcoal blue finish, or original finish.

NIB	Exc.	V.G.	Good	Fair	Poor
530	425	350	—	—	—

NOTE: Add $40 for charcoal finish and $50 for original finish. Add $25 for silver-plated back strap and trigger guard.

RICHARDS CONVERSIONS

Model 1851
Chambered for .38 Special, .38 Colt, and .44 Colt. Fitted with 5" or 7" barrels.

NIB	Exc.	V.G.	Good	Fair	Poor
550	450	—	—	—	—

Model 1861

Chambered for .38 Special, .38 Colt, and .44 Colt. Fitted with 5" or 7" barrels.

NIB	Exc.	V.G.	Good	Fair	Poor
550	450	—	—	—	—

Model 1860

Chambered for .38 Special, .38 Colt, and .44 Colt. Fitted with 5" or 7.5" barrels.

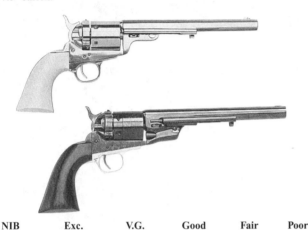

NIB	Exc.	V.G.	Good	Fair	Poor
550	450	—	—	—	—

Relic Finish

Offered by Cimarron as an extra cost item on its revolvers. This finish duplicates the old worn antique finish seen on many used historical Colts.
NOTE: Add $40 to the NIB price for any Cimarron revolver with this finish.

RIFLES

Henry Civil War Model

Offered in .44 WCF or .45 Long Colt with 24-1/4" barrel.

NIB	Exc.	V.G.	Good	Fair	Poor
1150	925	750	—	—	—

NOTE: For charcoal blue or white finish add $80.

Henry Civilian Model

Same as above but without military markings.

NIB	Exc.	V.G.	Good	Fair	Poor
1150	925	750	—	—	—

Model 1866 Yellowboy Carbine

Reproduction of the Winchester model 1866. Fitted with a 19" barrel and chambered for .38 Special, .44 WCF, or .45 Long Colt.

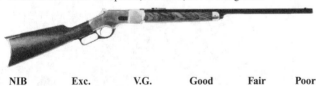

NIB	Exc.	V.G.	Good	Fair	Poor
950	750	600	—	—	—

NOTE: For charcoal blue add $40.

Model 1866 Yellowboy Rifle

Same as above but fitted with a 24-1/4" barrel.

NIB	Exc.	V.G.	Good	Fair	Poor
950	750	600	—	—	—

NOTE: For charcoal blue add $40.

Model 1866 Yellowboy Trapper

As above but with a 16" barrel.

NIB	Exc.	V.G.	Good	Fair	Poor
900	725	600	—	—	—

Winchester Rifle

This lever-action rifle is offered in .357 Magnum, .44 WCF, or .45 Long Colt. Fitted with a 24-1/4" barrel.

NIB	Exc.	V.G.	Good	Fair	Poor
1150	925	750	—	—	—

NOTE: For charcoal blue add $40. For pistol grip option add $140.

Model 1873 Long Range Rifle

Similar to the Model 1873 but fitted with a 30" barrel.

NIB	Exc.	V.G.	Good	Fair	Poor
1075	850	—	—	—	—

NOTE: For pistol grip option add $140. For 1 of 1000 engraving option add $1,250.

Model 1873 Carbine

Same as the standard Model 1873 but fitted with a 19" barrel.

NIB	Exc.	V.G.	Good	Fair	Poor
1025	825	—	—	—	—

NOTE: Add $40 for charcoal blue.

Model 1873 Short Rifle

This model is fitted with a 20" barrel. Production ceased in 1998.

NIB	Exc.	V.G.	Good	Fair	Poor
1150	925	750	—	—	—

NOTE: Add $40 for charcoal blue.

Model 1873 Trapper

As above but with 16" barrel.

NIB	Exc.	V.G.	Good	Fair	Poor
1025	825	—	—	—	—

Billy Dixon Model 1874 Sharps

A reproduction of the Model 1874 Sharps rifle chambered for the .45-70 cartridge. Fitted with a 32" tapered octagon barrel. Stock is hand checkered with oil finish walnut. Double set triggers standard. First introduced to the Cimarron product line in 1997.

NIB	Exc.	V.G.	Good	Fair	Poor
1500	1200	—	—	—	—

Remington Rolling Block

This Remington reproduction was introduced to Cimarron in 1997 and represents the Rolling Block Sporting rifle with 30" tapered octagon barrel and chambered for .45-70 cartridge. Hand-checkered, satin-finished walnut stock.

NIB	Exc.	V.G.	Good	Fair	Poor
1300	1000	—	—	—	—

Adobe Walls Rolling Block

This model is chambered for the .45-70 cartridge and is fitted with a 30" octagon barrel. Hand-checkered walnut stock with hand finishing. Case colored receiver and German silver nose cap. Weight is about 10.13 lbs. Introduced in 2004.

NIB	Exc.	V.G.	Good	Fair	Poor
1415	1050	—	—	—	—

Model 1885 High Wall

Reproduction of the Winchester Model 1885 chambered for .45-70, .45-90, .45-120, .40-65, .348 Win., .30-40 Krag, or .38-55 cartridges. Fitted with a 30" barrel. Walnut stock and case colored receiver.

NIB	Exc.	V.G.	Good	Fair	Poor
995	800	650	—	—	—

Model 1885 Low Wall

Introduced in 2004 this model is chambered for the .22 Long Rifle, .22 Hornet, .30-30, .32-20, .38-40, .357 Mag, .44-40, and .44 Mag cartridges. Hand checkered walnut stock with pistol grip. Octagon barrel is 30" long. Single or double-set trigger.

NIB	Exc.	V.G.	Good	Fair	Poor
1175	850	—	—	—	—

Sharps Silhoutte

Offered in .45-70 or .40-65 calibers with 32" octagon barrel. Introduced in 1998.

NIB	Exc.	V.G.	Good	Fair	Poor
1095	850	700	—	—	—

Quigley Sharps Sporting Rifle

This rifle is chambered for the .45-70 or .45-120 caliber and fitted with a heavy 34" octagon barrel. Introduced in 1998.

NIB	Exc.	V.G.	Good	Fair	Poor
1725	1350	—	—	—	—

Billy Dixon 1874 Sharps

Fitted with a 32" barrel and chambered for the .45-70, .45-90, or the .50-70. Introduced in 1995.

NIB	Exc.	V.G.	Good	Fair	Poor
1620	1250	—	—	—	—

Sharp's No. 1 Sporting Rifle

Plain walnut stock with pistol grip. Fitted with a 32" barrel. Chambered for the .45-70 cartridge.

NIB	Exc.	V.G.	Good	Fair	Poor
1350	1050	—	—	—	—

Springfield Trapdoor Carbine

Based on the famous Springfield design. Chambered for the .45-70.

NIB	Exc.	V.G.	Good	Fair	Poor
995	800	—	—	—	—

Springfield Trapdoor Officer's Model

This is the Officer's version of the Springfield Trapdoor model. Chambered for .45-70.

NIB	Exc.	V.G.	Good	Fair	Poor
1150	900	—	—	—	—

Texas Ranger Carbine

This model is a copy of the Sharps Model 1859 Military Carbine. Round barrel is 22" long. Receiver is case colored. Stock is American black walnut. Chambered for the .45-70 cartridge. Marked "T*S" on the barrel. Introduced in 2004.

NIB	Exc.	V.G.	Good	Fair	Poor
1200	900	—	—	—	—

Pride of the Plains Model

Based on the Sharps Model 1874 Sporting Rifle, this model, chambered for the .45-70 cartridge, features a 32" octagon barrel, hand-checkered walnut stock with pistol grip, coin nickel receiver, Creedmore tang sight, and target front sight with inserts. Introduced in 2004.

NIB	Exc.	V.G.	Good	Fair	Poor
1620	1200	—	—	—	—

Professional Hunter Model

This model is the basic Sharps Model 1874 chambered for the .45-70 cartridge. Fitted with a 32" barrel, case colored receiver, walnut stock with shotgun butt and double-set triggers. Introduced in 2004.

NIB	Exc.	V.G.	Good	Fair	Poor
1160	850	—	—	—	—

Big Fifty Model

Chambered for the .50-90 cartridge and fitted with a 34" half-octagon barrel. Fancy walnut stock with hand checkering and pistol grip. Case colored receiver, German silver nose cap, and Hartford-style Soule Creedmore sights with spirit level and globe front sight. Weight is about 11 lbs. Introduced in 2004.

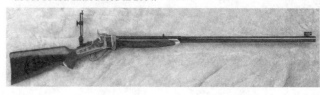

NIB	Exc.	V.G.	Good	Fair	Poor
1890	1400	—	—	—	—

CLARK, F. H.
Memphis, Tennessee

Pocket Pistol

A .41 caliber single-shot percussion pistol with a 3.5" to 5" barrel, German silver mounts and end cap, and the barrel is stamped "F.H. Clark & Co./Memphis." Manufactured in the 1850s and 1860s.

Exc.	V.G.	Good	Fair	Poor
—	—	4250	1750	500

CLASSIC DOUBLES
Tochigi City, Japan
Importer—Classic Doubles International
St. Louis, Missouri

Importer of the Japanese shotgun formerly imported by Winchester as the Model 101 and Model 23. These models were discontinued by Winchester in 1987.

Model 201 Classic

A 12 or 20 gauge boxlock double-barrel shotgun with 26" ventilated-rib barrels, screw-in choke tubes single-selective trigger and automatic ejectors. Blued with checkered walnut stock and beavertail forearm.

NIB	Exc.	V.G.	Good	Fair	Poor
2400	1950	1700	1500	1250	900

COBRA ENTERPRISES, INC.
Salt Lake City, Utah

DERRINGERS

Standard Series

Offered chambered in .22 LR, .22 WMR, .25 ACP, and .32 ACP. Over-and-under barrels are 2.4". Pearl or laminate wood grips. Weight is about 9.5 oz. grips. Introduced in 2002.

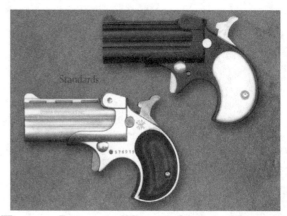

NIB	Exc.	V.G.	Good	Fair	Poor
90	70	—	—	—	—

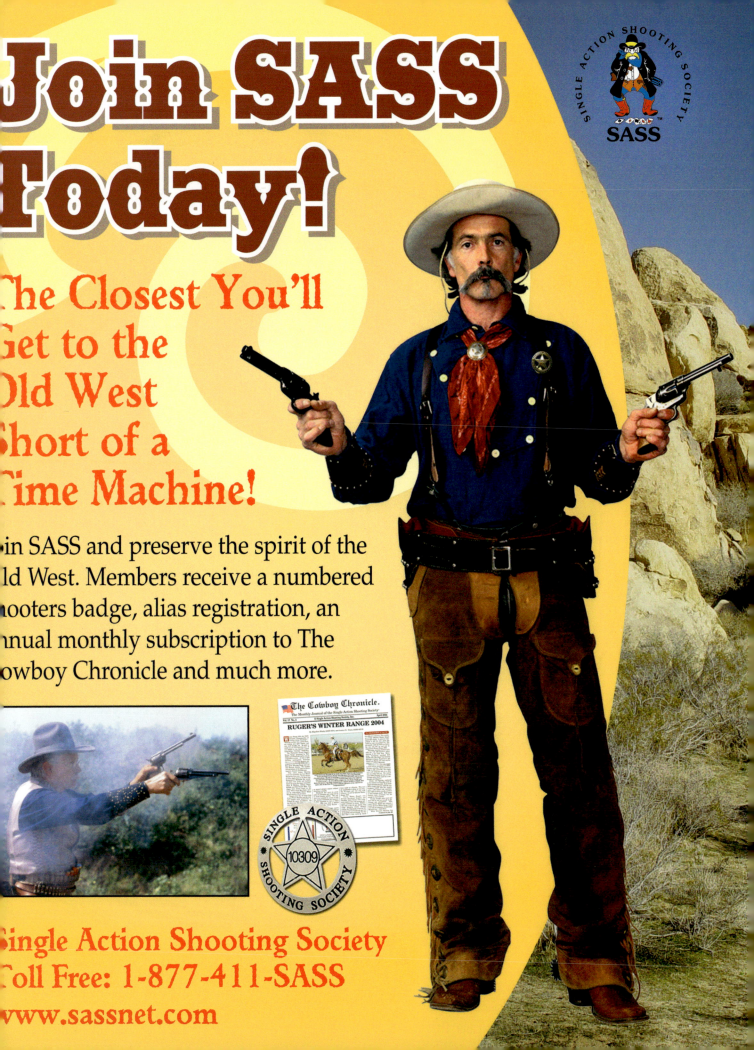

SHOOT! MAGAZINE
Guns and Gear of the Cowboy Era

THE BEST OF WESTERN-ACTION SHOOTING AND THE OLD WEST

VISIT OUR OLD WEST MERCANTILE AT
WWW.SHOOTMAGAZINE.COM

7154 W. State St. 384 Boise, ID 83714 ✶ 1-800-342-0904 or 208 368-9920

THE RUGER NEW VAQUERO
NEW SIZE
NEW FEATURES

RUGER NEW VAQUERO

Original-size, pre-1962 "XR-3" style steel grip frame with checkered "hard rubber" grips, for authentic "Old West" feel and handling.

Traditional beveled cylinder for ease in holstering.

New Ruger reverse indexing pawl (patent pending), enables positive indexing of each chamber with loading gate cutout for easier loading and unloading.

Mid-size steel frame and cylinder scaled down to the same size as the original 1955 Ruger Blackhawk.

New crescent-shaped ejector rod head.

Ruger New Vaquero
NV44 • .45 Colt
Suggested retail price of $583.00

Ruger Stainless New Vaquero
KNV35 • .357 Mag.
Suggested retail price of $583.00

For more than a decade, the Ruger Vaquero has dominated the Cowboy Action Shooting world. These demanding shooters recognize the strength and modern mechanical superiority of Sturm, Ruger's legendary single actions, combined with traditional American styling.

New for 2005, Sturm, Ruger proudly introduces the New Vaquero, which has been redesigned to offer the original "Old West" single action look and feel with new features demanded by competitive shooters. From the past, we've brought back the mid-size cylinder frame and slimmer "XR-3" style grip frame, plus a beveled cylinder and a contoured crescent-shaped ejector rod head. We've engineered a recontoured hammer and new hammer spring for the smoothest, easiest cocking ever. Our new reverse indexing pawl makes loading and unloading faster and easier. Of course, the Ruger New Vaquero still features our patented transfer bar and loading gate interlock for an unprecedented level of security.*

A variety of New Vaquero models are available in .357 Magnum and .45 Colt and barrel lengths of 4 5/8" and 5 1/2". We also offer .45 Colt models with 7 1/2" barrels. Try one today and feel the difference.

*Owners of "old model" (three screw) Ruger single action revolvers manufactured from 1953-1972, and Bearcats with serial numbers below 93-00000 should contact us for details about FREE safety conversions.

STURM, RUGER & CO., INC.
Southport, CT 06890, U.S.A. • www.ruger.com

All Ruger firearms are designed and built with pride by American workers at Ruger factories in the United States of America.
FREE Instruction Manuals are available online at www.ruger.com

RUGER
ARMS MAKERS FOR RESPONSIBLE CITIZENS

Big Bore Series

Chambered for the .22 WMR, .32 H&R Mag., and the .38 Special. Barrel length is 2.75". Choice of black synthetic, laminate oak, or laminate rosewood grips. Chrome or black finish. Weight is about 14 oz.

NIB	Exc.	V.G.	Good	Fair	Poor
110	80	—	—	—	—

Long Bore Series

This series is chambered for the .22 WMR, .38 Special, or the 9mm cartridge. Fitted with a 3.5" barrel. Black synthetic, laminate oak, or laminate rosewood grips. Chrome or black finish. Weight is about 16 oz.

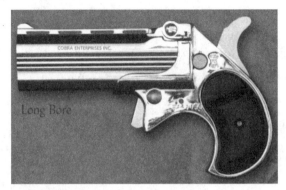

NIB	Exc.	V.G.	Good	Fair	Poor
110	80	—	—	—	—

SEMI-AUTO PISTOLS

C-32/C-380

Chambered for the .32 ACP or .380 cartridges. Fitted with a 2.8" barrel. Chrome or black finish. Magazine capacity is 5 rounds for the .380 and 6 rounds for the .32 ACP. Weight is about 22 oz.

NIB	Exc.	V.G.	Good	Fair	Poor
100	80	—	—	—	—

C-9mm

This is a double-action-only pistol chambered for the 9mm cartridge. Fitted with a 3.3" barrel. Magazine capacity is 10 rounds. Load indicator. Polymer grips. Weight is about 21 oz.

NIB	Exc.	V.G.	Good	Fair	Poor
130	100	—	—	—	—

Patriot .45

This is double-action-only pistol chambered for the .45 ACP cartridge. Barrel length is 3". Frame is black polymer. Slide is stainless steel. Magazine capacity is 6 rounds. Weight is about 20 oz.

NIB	Exc.	V.G.	Good	Fair	Poor
250	200	—	—	—	—

CODY, MICHAEL & SONS
Nashville, Tennessee

Received a contract with the State of Tennessee for "Mississippi" rifles with brass patchboxes in late 1861. Barrel length 36"; caliber .54. Cody often used reworked Model 1817 Rifle barrels and sporting pattern single screw lockplates. Rifles are unmarked except for large engraved serial number on top of breech plug tang.

Prospective purchasers are strongly advised to secure a qualified appraisal prior to acquisition.

Exc.	V.G.	Good	Fair	Poor
—	—	25000	10000	1500

COFER, T. W.
Portsmouth, Virginia

Cofer Navy Revolver

A .36 caliber spur trigger percussion revolver with a 7.5" octagonal barrel and 6-shot cylinder. The top strap is marked "T.W. Cofer's/Patent." and the barrel "Portsmouth, Va." This revolver was manufactured in limited quantities during the Civil War. Prospective purchasers are advised to secure a qualified appraisal prior to acquisition.

NOTE: This revolver is one of the most sought-after Confederate martial arms.

Courtesy Greg Martin Auctions

Exc.	V.G.	Good	Fair	Poor
—	—	100000	35000	5000

COGSWELL
London, England

Cogswell Pepperbox Pistol

A .47 caliber 6-shot percussion pepperbox with case hardened barrels, German silver frame and walnut grips. Normally marked "B. Cogswell, 224 Strand, London" and "Improved Revolving Pistol."

Exc.	V.G.	Good	Fair	Poor
—	—	3500	1250	750

COGSWELL & HARRISON, LTD.
London, England
SEE—British Double Guns

COLT'S PATENT FIRE ARMS MANUFACTURING COMPANY
Hartford, Connecticut

Of all the American firearms manufacturers, perhaps the best known is the Colt Company. Indeed, this recognition is so widespread that some popular writers have used the name Colt to indicate a revolver or semi-automatic pistol.

Originally founded in 1836 as the Patent Arms Manufacturing Company (Paterson, New Jersey) to produce percussion revolvers designed by Samuel Colt, the concern was initially a failure. However, the company formed in 1847 to manufacture revolvers of an improved form was a success. Even after Samuel Colt's death in 1862, his company thrived. With the introduction of the Model 1873 Single-Action Army Revolver, the myth of the Colt became part of the American legend for that revolver was to be used by adventurers, cowboys, farmers, soldiers and a host of others for better than 70 years.

In 1897 the Colt's Patent Fire Arms Manufacturing Company entered into an agreement with John M. Browning to produce self-loading pistols of his design. One result of this association was to be the

.45 caliber Model 1911 Semi-automatic Pistol, which was the standard issue sidearm of the U.S. Armed Forces from 1911 to the late 1980s.

Because of their romance, form and variation, Colt revolvers, pistols and longarms are most sought after by collectors. Due to this, however, caution should be exercised and the opinion of experts should be sought when the purchase of rare or pristine examples is contemplated.

COLT PATERSON MODELS
Paterson, New Jersey

Pocket or Baby Paterson Model No. 1

The Paterson was the first production revolver manufactured by Colt. It was first made in 1837. The Model 1 or Pocket Model is the most diminutive of the Paterson line. The revolver is serial numbered in its own range, #1 through #500. The numbers are not visible without dismantling the revolver. The barrel lengths run from 1.75" to 4.75". The standard model has no attached loading lever. The chambering is .28 caliber percussion and it holds five shots. The finish is all blued, and the grips are varnished walnut. It has a roll-engraved cylinder scene, and the barrel is stamped "Patent Arms Mfg. Co. Paterson N.J.Colt's Pt."

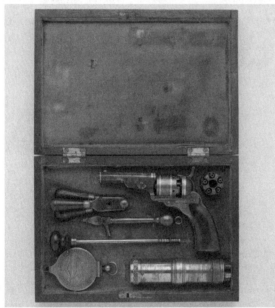

Courtesy Greg Martin Auctions

Exc.	V.G.	Good	Fair	Poor
—	—	30000	12500	—

Belt Model Paterson No. 2

The Belt Model Paterson is a larger revolver with a straight-grip and an octagonal barrel that is 2.5" to 5.5" in length. It is chambered for .31 caliber percussion and holds five shots. The finish is all blued, with varnished walnut grips and no attached loading lever. It has a roll-engraved cylinder scene, and the barrel is stamped "Patent Arms Mfg. Co. Paterson N.J. Colt's Pt." The serial number range is #1-#850 and is shared with the #3 Belt Model. It was made from 1837-1840.

Exc.	V.G.	Good	Fair	Poor
—	—	50000	20000	—

Belt Model Paterson No. 3

This revolver is quite similar to the Model #2 except that the grips are curved outward at the bottom to form a more handfilling configuration. They are serial numbered in the same #1-#850 range. Some attached loading levers have been noted on this model, but they are extremely rare and would add approximately 35 percent to the value.

Exc.	V.G.	Good	Fair	Poor
—	—	75000	30000	—

Ehlers Model Pocket Paterson

John Ehlers was a major stockholder and treasurer of the Patent Arms Mfg. Co. when it went bankrupt. He seized the assets and inventory. These revolvers were Pocket Model Patersons that were not finished at the time. Ehlers had them finished and marketed them. They had an attached loading lever, and the abbreviation "Mfg. Co." was deleted from the barrel stamping. There were 500 revolvers involved in the Ehlers variation totally, and they were produced from 1840-1843.

Exc.	V.G.	Good	Fair	Poor
—	—	50000	20000	—

Ehlers Belt Model Paterson

The same specifications apply to this larger revolver as they do to the Ehlers Pocket Model. It falls within the same 500 revolver involvement and is rare.

Exc.	V.G.	Good	Fair	Poor
—	—	50000	20000	—

Texas Paterson Model No. 5

This is the largest and most sought after of the Paterson models. It is also known as the Holster Model. It has been verified as actually seeing use by both the military and civilians on the American frontier. It is chambered for .36 caliber percussion, holds five shots, and an octagonal barrel that ranges from 4" to 12" in length. It has been observed with and without the attached loading lever, but those with it are rare. The finish is blued, with a case-colored hammer. The grips are varnished walnut. The cylinder is roll-engraved; and the barrel is stamped "Patent Arms Mfg. Co. Paterson, N.J. Colts Pt." Most Texas Patersons are well used and have a worn appearance. One in excellent or V.G. condition would be highly prized. A verified military model would be worth a great deal more than standard, so qualified appraisal would be essential. The serial number range is #1-#1000, and they were manufactured from 1838-1840. The attached loading lever brings approximately a 25 percent premium.

Exc.	V.G.	Good	Fair	Poor
—	—	125000	50000	—

COLT REVOLVING LONG GUNS
1837-1847

First Model Ring Lever Rifle

This was actually the first firearm manufactured by Colt; the first revolver appeared a short time later. There were 200 of the First Models made in 1837 and 1838. The octagonal barrel of the First Model is 32" long and browned, while the rest of the finish is blued. The stock is varnished walnut with a cheekpiece inlaid with Colt's trademark. The ring lever located in front of the frame is pulled to rotate the 8-shot cylinder and cock the hammer. The rifle is chambered for .34, .36, .38, .40, and .44 caliber percussion. The cylinder is roll-engraved, and the barrel is stamped "Colt's Patent/Patent Arms Mfg. Co., Paterson, N. Jersey." This model has a top strap over the cylinder. They were made both with and without an attached loading lever. The latter is worth approximately 10 percent more.

Exc.	V.G.	Good	Fair	Poor
—	—	60000	20000	—

Second Model Ring Lever Rifle

This model is quite similar in appearance to the First Model. Its function is identical. The major difference is the absence of the top strap over the cylinder. It had no trademark stamped on the cheekpiece. The Second Model is offered with a 28" and a 32" octagonal barrel and is chambered for .44 caliber percussion, holding 8 shots. There were approximately 500 produced from 1838-1841. The presence of an attached cheekpiece would add approximately 10 percent to the value.

Exc.	V.G.	Good	Fair	Poor
—	—	40000	12500	—

Model 1839 Shotgun

This model is quite similar in appearance to the 1839 Carbine. It is chambered for 16 gauge and holds six shots. It has a Damascus pattern barrel, and the most notable difference is a 3.5" (instead of a 2.5") long cylinder. There were only 225 of these made from 1839-1841. The markings are the same as on the Carbine.

Exc.	V.G.	Good	Fair	Poor
—	—	25000	10000	—

Model 1839 Carbine

This model has no ring but features an exposed hammer for cocking and rotating the 6-shot cylinder. It is chambered for .525 smoothbore and comes standard with a 24" round barrel. Other barrel lengths have been noted. The finish is blued, with a browned barrel and a varnished walnut stock. The cylinder is roll-engraved, and the barrel is stamped "Patent Arms Mfg. Co. Paterson, N.J.-Colt's Pt." There were 950 manufactured from 1838-1841. Later variations of this model are found with the attached loading lever standard, and earlier models without one would bring approximately 25 percent additional. There were 360 purchased by the military and stamped "WAT" on the stock. These would be worth twice what a standard model would bring. Anyone considering the purchase of one would be well advised to proceed with extreme caution.

Exc.	V.G.	Good	Fair	Poor
—	—	25000	9500	—

Model 1839/1850 Carbine

In 1848 Colt acquired a number of Model 1839 Carbines (approximately 40) from the state of Rhode Island. In an effort to make them marketable they were refinished and the majority fitted with plain cylinders (brightly polished) having integral ratchets around the arbor hole.

Barrel length 24"; caliber .525; barrel browned; cylinder polished; frame blued; furniture case hardened; walnut stock varnished.

Courtesy Little John's Auction Service, Inc.

Exc.	V.G.	Good	Fair	Poor
—	—	35000	12500	—

Model 1854 Russian Contract Musket

In 1854 Colt purchased a large number of U.S. Model 1822 flintlock muskets that the company altered to percussion cap ignition and rifled. The reworked muskets are dated 1854 on the barrel tang and at the rear of the lockplate. In most instances the original manufactory marks, such as Springfield or Harpers Ferry at the rear of the lockplate, have been removed, while the U.S. and eagle between the hammer and bolster remain. The percussion nipple bolster is marked COLT'S PATENT. Some examples have been noted with the date 1858.

Barrel length 42"; caliber .69; lock and furniture burnished bright; walnut stock oil finished.

Exc.	V.G.	Good	Fair	Poor
—	—	4000	1500	750

Breech-loading examples made in two styles are also known. Production of this variation is believed to have only taken place on an experimental basis.

Exc.	V.G.	Good	Fair	Poor
—	—	6500	2500	1000

COLT WALKER-DRAGOON MODELS
Hartford, Connecticut

Walker Model Revolver

The Walker is a massive revolver. It weighs 4 lbs., 9 oz. and has a 9" part-round/part-octagonal barrel. The cylinder holds six shots and is chambered for .44 caliber percussion. There were 1,000 Walker Colts manufactured in 1847, and nearly all of them saw extremely hard use. Originally this model had a roll-engraved cylinder, military inspection marks, and barrel stamping that read "Address Saml. Colt-New York City." Practically all examples noted have had these markings worn or rusted beyond recognition. Because the Walker is perhaps the most desirable and sought-after Colt from a collector's standpoint and because of the extremely high value of a Walker in any condition, qualified appraisal is definitely recommended. These revolvers were serial numbered A, B, C, and D Company 1-220, and E Company 1120.

Exc.	V.G.	Good	Fair	Poor
—	—	300000	150000	50000

Civilian Walker Revolver

This model is identical to the military model but has no martial markings. They are found serial numbered 1001 through 1100.

Exc.	V.G.	Good	Fair	Poor
—	—	300000	150000	50000

Whitneyville Hartford Dragoon

This is a large, 6-shot, .44 caliber percussion revolver. It has a 7.5" part-round/part-octagonal barrel. The frame, hammer, and loading lever are case colored. The remainder is blued, with a brass trigger guard and varnished walnut grips. There were only 240 made in late 1847. The serial numbers run from 1100-1340. This model is often referred to as a Transitional Walker. Some of the parts used in its manufacture were left over from the Walker production run. This model has a roll-engraved cylinder scene, and the barrel is stamped "Address Saml. Colt New York-City." This is an extremely rare model, and much care should be taken to authenticate any contemplated acquisitions.

Exc.	V.G.	Good	Fair	Poor
—	—	60000	35000	18500

Walker Replacement Dragoon

This extremely rare Colt (300 produced) is sometimes referred to as the "Fluck" in memory of the gentleman who first identified it as a distinct and separate model. They were produced by Colt as replacements to the military for Walkers that were no longer fit for service due to mechanical failures. They were large, 6-shot, .44 caliber percussion revolvers with 7.5" part-round/part-octagonal barrels. Serial numbers ran from 2216 to 2515. The frame, hammer, and loading lever are case-colored; the remainder, blued. The grips, which are longer than other Dragoons and similar to the Walkers, are of varnished walnut and bear the inspectors mark "WAT" inside an oval cartouche on one side and the letters "JH" on the other. The frame is stamped "Colt's/Patent/U.S." The letter "P" appears on various parts of the gun. This is another model that should definitely be authenticated before any acquisition is made.

Exc.	V.G.	Good	Fair	Poor
—	—	45000	25000	6000

First Model Dragoon

Another large, 6-shot, .44 caliber percussion revolver. It has a 7.5" part-round/part-octagonal barrel. The frame, hammer, and loading lever are case colored; the remainder, blued with a brass grip frame and square backed trigger guard. The trigger guard is silver-plated on the Civilian Model only. Another distinguishing feature on the First Model is the oval cylinder stop notches. The serial number range is 1341-8000. There were approximately 5,000 made. The cylinder is roll-engraved; and the barrel stampings read "Address Saml. Colt, New York City." "Colt's Patent" appears on the frame. On Military Models the letters "U.S." also appear on the frame.

Military Model

Exc.	V.G.	Good	Fair	Poor
—	—	40000	20000	3500

Civilian Model

Exc.	V.G.	Good	Fair	Poor
—	—	35000	18000	3000

Second Model Dragoon

Most of the improvements that distinguish this model from the First Model are internal and not readily apparent. The most obvious external change is the rectangular cylinder-stop notches. This model is serial numbered from 8000-10700, for a total production of approximately 2,700 revolvers manufactured in 1850 and 1851. There is a Civilian Model, a Military Model, and an extremely rare variation that was issued to the militias of New Hampshire and Massachusetts (marked "MS."). Once again, caution is advised in acquisition.

Civilian Model

Exc.	V.G.	Good	Fair	Poor
—	—	35000	25000	3500

Military Model

Exc.	V.G.	Good	Fair	Poor
—	—	40000	30000	3000

Militia Model

Exc.	V.G.	Good	Fair	Poor
—	—	45000	30000	3000

Third Model Dragoon

This is the most common of all the large Colt percussion revolvers. Approximately 10,500 were manufactured from 1851 through 1861. It is quite similar in appearance to the Second Model, and the most obvious external difference is the round trigger guard. The Third Model Dragoon was the first Colt revolver available with a detachable shoulder stock. There are three basic types of stocks, and all are quite rare as only 1,250 were produced. There are two other major variations we will note—the "C.L." Dragoon, which was a militia-issued model and is rare, and the late-issue model with an 8" barrel. These are found over serial number 18000, and only 50 were produced. Qualified appraisal should be secured before acquisition as many fakes abound.

Civilian Model

Exc.	V.G.	Good	Fair	Poor
—	—	27500	15000	2500

Military Model

Exc.	V.G.	Good	Fair	Poor
—	—	30000	17500	3000

Shoulder Stock Cut Revolvers

Exc.	V.G.	Good	Fair	Poor
—	—	35000	20000	3000

Shoulder Stocks

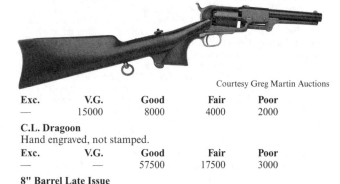

Courtesy Greg Martin Auctions

Exc.	V.G.	Good	Fair	Poor
—	15000	8000	4000	2000

C.L. Dragoon

Hand engraved, not stamped.

Exc.	V.G.	Good	Fair	Poor
—	—	57500	17500	3000

8" Barrel Late Issue

Exc.	V.G.	Good	Fair	Poor
—	—	42500	25000	3000

Hartford English Dragoon

This is a variation of the Third Model Dragoon. The only notable differences are the British proofmarks and the distinct #1-#700 serial number range. Other than these two features, the description given for the Third Model would apply. These revolvers were manufactured in Hartford but were finished at Colt's London factory from 1853-1857. Some bear the hand-engraved barrel marking "Col. Colt London." Many of the English Dragoons were elaborately engraved, and individual appraisal would be a must.

Two hundred revolvers came back to America in 1861 to be used in the Civil War. As with all the early Colts, caution is advised in acquisition.

Exc.	V.G.	Good	Fair	Poor
—	—	25000	12000	3000

Model 1848 Baby Dragoon

This is a small, 5-shot, .31 caliber percussion revolver. It has an octagonal barrel in lengths of 3", 4", 5", and 6". Most were made without an attached loading lever, although some with loading levers have been noted. The frame, hammer, and loading lever (when present) are case colored; the barrel and cylinder, blued. The grip frame and trigger guard are silver-plated brass. There were approximately 15,500 manufactured between 1847 and 1850. The serial range is between 1-5500. The barrels are stamped "Address Saml. Colt/New York City." Some have been noted with the barrel address inside brackets. The frame is marked "Colt's/Patent." The first 10,000 revolvers have the Texas Ranger/Indian roll-engraved cylinder scene; the later guns the stagecoach holdup scene. This is a popular model, and many fakes have been noted.

Stagecoach Holdup Scene

Exc.	V.G.	Good	Fair	Poor
—	—	13000	7000	2000

Texas Ranger/Indian Scene

Exc.	V.G.	Good	Fair	Poor
—	—	12000	6500	2000

NOTE: Attached loading lever add 15 percent.

Model 1849 Pocket Revolver

This is a small, either 5- or 6-shot, .31 caliber percussion revolver. It has an octagonal barrel 3", 4", 5", or 6" in length. Most had loading gates, but some did not. The frame, hammer, and loading lever are case colored; the cylinder and barrel are blued. The grip frame and round trigger guard are made of brass and are silver plated. There are both large and small trigger guard variations noted. This is the most plentiful of all the Colt percussion revolvers, with approximately 325,000 manufactured over a 23-year period, 1850-1873. There are over 200 variations of this model, and one should consult an expert for individual appraisals. There are many fine publications specializing in the field of Colt percussion revolvers that would be helpful in the identification of the variations. The values represented here are for the standard model.

Courtesy Rock Island Auction Company

Exc.	V.G.	Good	Fair	Poor
—	—	1800	1200	300

London Model 1849 Pocket Revolver

Identical in configuration to the standard 1849 Pocket Revolver, the London-made models have a higher quality finish and their own serial number range, 1-11000. They were manufactured from 1853 through 1857. They feature a roll-engraved cylinder scene, and the barrels are stamped "Address Col. Colt/London." The first 265 revolvers, known as early models, have brass grip frames and small round trigger guards. They are quite rare and worth approximately 50 percent more than the standard model that has a steel grip frame and large oval trigger guard.

Exc.	V.G.	Good	Fair	Poor
—	—	1800	1200	300

Model 1851 Navy Revolver

This is undoubtedly the most popular revolver Colt produced in the medium size and power range. It is a 6-shot, .36-caliber percussion revolver with a 7.5" octagonal barrel. It has an attached loading lever. The basic model has a case colored frame hammer, and loading lever, with silver-plated brass grip frame and trigger guard. The grips are varnished walnut. Colt manufactured approximately 215,000 of these fine revolvers between 1850 and 1873. The basic Navy features a roll-engraved cylinder scene of a battle between the navies of Texas and Mexico. There are three distinct barrel stampings—serial number 1-74000, "Address Saml. Colt New York City"; serial number 74001-101000 "Address Saml. Colt. Hartford, Ct."; and serial number 101001-215000 "Address Saml. Colt New York U.S. America." The left side of the frame is stamped "Colt's/Patent" on all variations. This model is also available with a detached shoulder stock, and values for the stocks today are nearly as high as for the revolver itself. Careful appraisal should be secured before purchase. The number of variations within the 1851 Navy model designation makes it necessary to read specialized text available on the subject. We furnish values for the major variations but again caution potential purchasers to acquire appraisals.

Square Back Trigger Guard, 1st Model, Serial #11000

Exc.	V.G.	Good	Fair	Poor
—	—	35000	25000	5500

Square Back Trigger Guard, 2nd Model, Serial #1001-4200

Exc.	V.G.	Good	Fair	Poor
—	—	25000	10000	2500

Small Round Trigger Guard, Serial #420185000

Exc.	V.G.	Good	Fair	Poor
—	—	5000	2500	500

Large Round Trigger Guard, Serial #85001-215000

Exc.	V.G.	Good	Fair	Poor
—	—	4500	2200	500

Martial Model
"U.S." stamped on the left side of frame; inspector's marks and cartouche on the grips.

Exc.	V.G.	Good	Fair	Poor
—	—	12000	4000	1000

Shoulder Stock Variations
1st and 2nd Model Revolver cut for stock only. An expert appraisal is recommended prior to a sale of these very rare variations.

Stock Only

Exc.	V.G.	Good	Fair	Poor
—	—	8000	4000	1250

3rd Model Cut For Stock
Revolver only.

Exc.	V.G.	Good	Fair	Poor
—	—	9500	4000	1250

Stock

Exc.	V.G.	Good	Fair	Poor
—	—	7000	3750	1000

London Model 1851 Navy Revolver
These revolvers are physically similar to the U.S.-made model with the exception of the barrel address, which reads "Address Col. Colt. London." There are also British proofmarks stamped on the barrel and cylinder. There were 42,000 made between 1853 and 1857. They have their own serial-number range, #1-#42,000. There are two major variations of the London Navy, and again a serious purchaser would be well advised to seek qualified appraisal as fakes have been noted.

1st Model
Serial #1-#2,000 with a small round brass trigger guard and grip frame. Squareback guard worth a 40 percent premium.

Exc.	V.G.	Good	Fair	Poor
—	—	4250	1750	700

2nd Model
Serial #2,001-#42,000, steel grip frame, and large round trigger guard.

Exc.	V.G.	Good	Fair	Poor
—	—	4000	1500	600

Hartford Manufactured Variation
Serial numbers in the 42,000 range.

Exc.	V.G.	Good	Fair	Poor
—	—	4500	3000	600

COLT SIDE HAMMER MODELS

Model 1855 Side Hammer "Root" Pocket Revolver
The "Root", as it is popularly known, was the only solid-frame revolver Colt ever made. It has a spur trigger and walnut grips, and the hammer is mounted on the right side of the frame. The standard finish is a case colored frame, hammer, and loading lever, with the barrel and cylinder blued. It is chambered for both .28 caliber and .31 caliber percussion. Each caliber has its own serial number range—1-30000 for the .28 caliber and 1-14000 for the .31 caliber. The model consists of seven basic variations, and the serious student should avail himself of the fine publications dealing with this model in depth. Colt produced the Side Hammer Root from 1855-1870.

Models 1 and 1A Serial #1-384
3.5" octagonal barrel, .28 caliber, roll-engraved cylinder, Hartford barrel address without pointing hand.

Exc.	V.G.	Good	Fair	Poor
—	—	6000	3500	1200

Model 2 Serial #476-25000
Same as Model 1 with pointing hand barrel address.

Exc.	V.G.	Good	Fair	Poor
—	—	1800	1200	500

Courtesy Rock Island Auction Company

Model 3 Serial #25001-30000
Same as the Model 2 with a full fluted cylinder.

Exc.	V.G.	Good	Fair	Poor
—	—	1800	1200	500

Model 3A and 4 Serial #1-2400
.31 caliber, 3.5" barrel, Hartford address, full fluted cylinder.

Exc.	V.G.	Good	Fair	Poor
—	—	2500	1500	600

Model 5 Serial #2401-8000
.31 caliber, 3.5" round barrel, address "Col. Colt New York."

Exc.	V.G.	Good	Fair	Poor
—	—	1800	1200	500

Model 5A Serial #2401-8000
Same as Model 5 with a 4.5" barrel.

Exc.	V.G.	Good	Fair	Poor
—	—	3200	1600	600

Models 6 and 6A Serial #8001-11074
Same as Model 5 and 5A with roll-engraved cylinder scene.

Exc.	V.G.	Good	Fair	Poor
—	—	1800	1200	500

Models 7 and 7A Serial #11075-14000
Same as Models 6 and 6A with a screw holding in the cylinder pin.

Exc.	V.G.	Good	Fair	Poor
—	—	3500	2200	800

COLT SIDE HAMMER LONG GUNS

1855 Sporting Rifle, 1st Model
This is a 6-shot revolving rifle chambered for .36 caliber percussion. It comes with a 21", 24", 27", or 30" round barrel that is part octagonal where it joins the frame. The stock is walnut with either an oil or a varnish finish. The frame, hammer, and loading lever are case colored; the rest of the metal, blued. The hammer is on the right side of the frame. The 1st Model has no forend, and an oiling device is attached to the barrel underlug. The trigger guard has two spur-like projections in front and in back of the bow. The roll-engraved cylinder scene depicts a hunter shooting at five deer and is found only on this model. The standard stampings are " Colt's Pt./1856" and "Address S. Colt Hartford, Ct. U.S.A."

Early Model
Low serial numbers with a hand-engraved barrel marking "Address S. Colt Hartford, U.S.A."

Exc.	V.G.	Good	Fair	Poor
—	—	15000	5500	1500

Production Model

Exc.	V.G.	Good	Fair	Poor
—	—	12000	3000	1000

1855 1st Model Carbine
Identical to the 1st Model Rifle but offered with a 15" and 18" barrel.

Exc.	V.G.	Good	Fair	Poor
—	—	9500	3000	1000

1855 Half Stock Sporting Rifle
Although this rifle is quite similar in appearance and finish to the 1st Model, there are some notable differences. It features a walnut forend that protrudes halfway down the barrel. There are two types of trigger

guards—a short projectionless one or a long model with a graceful scroll. There is a 6-shot model chambered for .36 or .44 caliber or a 5-shot model chambered for .56 caliber. The cylinder is fully fluted. The markings are "Colt's Pt/1856" and "Address Col. Colt/Hartford Ct. U.S.A." There were approximately 1,500 manufactured between 1857 and 1864.

Exc.	V.G.	Good	Fair	Poor
—	—	9500	3500	1000

1855 Full Stock Military Rifle

This model holds 6 shots in its .44 caliber chambering and 5 shots when chambered for .56 caliber. It is another side hammer revolving rifle that resembles the Half Stock model. The barrels are round and part-octagonal where they join the frame. They come in lengths of 21", 24", 27", 31", and 37". The hammer and loading lever are case colored; the rest of the metal parts, blued. The walnut buttstock and full length forend are oil finished, and this model has sling swivels. The cylinder is fully fluted. Military models have provisions for affixing a bayonet and military-style sights and bear the "U.S." martial mark on examples that were actually issued to the military. The standard stampings found on this model are "Colt's Pt/1856" and "Address Col. Colt Hartford, Ct. U.S.A." There were an estimated 9,300 manufactured between 1856 and 1864.

Martially Marked Models

Exc.	V.G.	Good	Fair	Poor
—	—	25000	9500	2000

Without Martial Markings

Exc.	V.G.	Good	Fair	Poor
—	—	8000	3500	1000

1855 Full Stock Sporting Rifle

This model is similar in appearance to the Military model, with these notable exceptions. There is no provision for attaching a bayonet, there are no sling swivels, and it has sporting-style sights. The buttplate is crescent shaped. This model has been noted chambered for .56 caliber in a 5-shot version and chambered for .36, .40, .44, and .50 caliber in the 6-shot variation. They are quite scarce in .40 and .50 caliber and will bring a 10 percent premium. The standard markings are "Colt's Pt/1856" and "Address Col. Colt/Hartford Ct. U.S.A." Production on this model was quite limited (several hundred at most) between the years 1856 and 1864.

Exc.	V.G.	Good	Fair	Poor
—	—	10500	4000	1000

Model 1855 Revolving Carbine

This model is similar in appearance to the 1855 Military Rifle. The barrel lengths of 15", 18", and 21" plus the absence of a forend make the standard Carbine Model readily identifiable. The markings are the same. Approximately 4,400 were manufactured between 1856 and 1864.

Exc.	V.G.	Good	Fair	Poor
—	—	9500	4000	1000

Model 1855 Artillery Carbine

Identical to the standard carbine but chambered for .56 caliber only, it has a 24" barrel, full-length walnut forend, and a bayonet lug.

Exc.	V.G.	Good	Fair	Poor
—	—	17000	5500	1500

Model 1855 British Carbine

This is a British-proofed version with barrel lengths of up to 30". It has a brass trigger guard and buttplate and is chambered for .56 caliber only. This variation is usually found in the 10000-12000 serial number range.

Exc.	V.G.	Good	Fair	Poor
—	—	9000	3750	1000

Model 1855 Revolving Shotgun

This model very much resembles the Half Stock Sporting Rifle but was made with a 27", 30", 33", and 36" smoothbore barrel. It has a 5-shot cylinder chambered for .60 or .75 caliber (20 or 10 gauge). This model has a case-colored hammer and loading lever; the rest of the metal is blued, with an occasional browned barrel noted. The buttstock and forend are of walnut, either oil or varnish-finished. This model has no rear sight and a small trigger guard with the caliber stamped on it. Some have been noted with the large scroll trigger guard; these would add 10 percent to the value. The rarest shotgun variation would be a full stocked version in either gauge, and qualified appraisal would be highly recommended. This model is serial numbered in its own range, #1-#1100. They were manufactured from 1860-1863.

Courtesy Amoskeag Auction Company

.60 Caliber (20 gauge)

Exc.	V.G.	Good	Fair	Poor
—	—	8000	3500	1000

.75 Caliber (10 gauge)

Exc.	V.G.	Good	Fair	Poor
—	—	8000	3500	1000

Model 1861 Single-Shot Rifled Musket

With the advent of the Civil War, the army of the Union seriously needed military arms. Colt was given a contract to supply 112,500 1861-pattern percussion single-shot muskets. Between 1861 and 1865, 75,000 were delivered. They have 40" rifled barrels chambered for .58 caliber. The musket is equipped with military sights, sling swivels, and a bayonet lug. The metal finish is bright steel, and the stock is oil-finished walnut. Military inspector's marks are found on all major parts. "VP" over an eagle is stamped on the breech along with a date. The Colt address and a date are stamped on the lockplate. A large number of these rifles were altered to the Snyder breech loading system for the Bey of Egypt.

Production Model

Exc.	V.G.	Good	Fair	Poor
—	5500	2000	750	450

PERCUSSION REVOLVERS

Model 1860 Army Revolver

This model was the third most produced of the Colt percussion handguns. It was the primary revolver used by the Union Army during the Civil War. Colt delivered 127,156 of these revolvers to be used during those hostilities. This is a 6-shot .44 caliber percussion revolver. It has either a 7.5" or 8" round barrel with an attached loading lever. The frame, hammer, and loading lever are case colored; the barrel and cylinder are blued. The trigger guard and front strap are brass, and the backstrap is blued steel. The grips are one-piece walnut. The early models have the barrels stamped "Address Saml. Colt Hartford Ct." Later models are stamped "Address Col. Saml. Colt New-York U.S. America." "Colt's/Patent" is stamped on the left side of the frame; ".44 Cal.," on the trigger guard. The cylinder is roll engraved with the naval battle scene. There were a total of 200,500 1860 Army Revolvers manufactured between 1860 and 1873.

Courtesy Greg Martin Auctions

Martial Marked Model

Exc.	V.G.	Good	Fair	Poor
—	—	7500	3500	900

Civilian Model

This model is found in either 3- or-4 screw variations and it may or may not be cut for a shoulder stock. Civilian models are usually better finished.

Exc.	V.G.	Good	Fair	Poor
—	—	6000	3000	800

Full Fluted Cylinder Model

Approximately 4,000 Army's were made with full fluted cylinders. They appear in the first 8,000 serial numbers.

Exc.	V.G.	Good	Fair	Poor
—	—	15000	7000	2000

Shoulder Stock 2nd Type (Fluted Cylinder Model)
NOTE: Expert appraisals should be acquired before a sale. These are rare accouterments.

Shoulder Stock 3rd Type (Standard Model)
NOTE: Expert appraisals should be acquired before a sale. These are rare accouterments.

Model 1861 Navy Revolver

This model is a 6-shot, 7.5" round-barreled, .36 caliber percussion revolver. The frame, hammer, and attached loading lever are case colored. The barrel and cylinder are blued. The grip frame and trigger guard are silver-plated brass. The grips are of one-piece walnut. The cylinder has the roll-engraved naval battle scene, and the barrel stamping is "Address Col. Saml. Colt New-York U.S. America." The frame is stamped "Colts/Patent" with "36 Cal." on the trigger guard. There are not many variations within the 1861 Navy model designation, as less than 39,000 were made between 1861 and 1873.

Courtesy Rock Island Auction Company

Civilian Model

Exc.	V.G.	Good	Fair	Poor
—	—	7500	3500	900

Military Model

Marked "U.S." on frame, inspector's cartouche on grip. 650 were marked "U.S.N." on the butt.

Exc.	V.G.	Good	Fair	Poor
—	—	18000	5500	1800

Shoulder Stock Model

Only 100 3rd-type stocks were made. They appear between serial #11000-#14000. These are very rare revolvers. Cautions should be exercised.

Revolver

Exc.	V.G.	Good	Fair	Poor
—	—	17500	5000	1500

NOTE: Expert appraisals should be acquired before a sale.

Stock

Exc.	V.G.	Good	Fair	Poor
—	—	9500	4250	1000

NOTE: Expert appraisals should be acquired before a sale. These are rare accouterments.

Fluted Cylinder Model

Approximately the first 100 were made with full fluted cylinders.

Exc.	V.G.	Good	Fair	Poor
—	—	45000	7500	2000

NOTE: Expert appraisals should be acquired before a sale. These are very rare.

Model 1862 Pocket Navy Revolver

This is a smaller, 5-shot, .36 caliber percussion revolver that resembles the configuration of the 1851 Navy. It has a 4.5", 5.5", or 6.5" octagonal barrel with an attached loading lever. The frame, hammer, and loading lever are case colored; the barrel and cylinder, blued. The grip frame and trigger guard are silver-plated brass; and the one-piece grips, of varnished walnut. The stagecoach holdup scene is roll-engraved on the cylinder. The frame is stamped "Colt's/Patent"; and the barrel, "Address Col. Saml. Colt New-York U.S. America." There were approximately 19,000 manufactured between 1861 and 1873. They are serial numbered in the same range as the Model 1862 Police. Because a great many were used for metallic cartridge conversions, they are quite scarce today.

The London address model with blued steel grip frame would be worth more than the standard model.

Standard Production Model

Exc.	V.G.	Good	Fair	Poor
—	—	3000	1200	500

NOTE: Longer barrels will bring a premium over the 4.5" length.

Model 1862 Police Revolver

This is a slim, attractively designed revolver that some consider to be the most aesthetically pleasing of all the Colt percussion designs. It has a 5-shot, half-fluted cylinder chambered for .36 caliber. It is offered with a 3.5", 4.5", 5.5", or 6.5" round barrel. The frame, hammer, and loading lever are case colored; the barrel and cylinder, blued. The grip frame is silver-plated brass; and the one-piece grips, varnished walnut. The barrel is stamped "Address Col. Saml Colt New-York U.S. America"; the frame has "Colt's/Patent" on the left side. One of the cylinder flutes is marked "Pat Sept. 10th 1850." There were approximately 28,000 of these manufactured between 1861 and 1873. Many were converted to metallic cartridge use, so they are quite scarce on today's market.

The London address model would be worth approximately twice the value of the standard model.

Standard Production Model

Exc.	V.G.	Good	Fair	Poor
—	—	2250	1000	400

NOTE: Longer barrels will bring a premium over the 3.5" or 4.5" length.

METALLIC CARTRIDGE CONVERSIONS

Thuer Conversion Revolver

Although quite simplistic and not commercially successful, the Thuer Conversion was the first attempt by Colt to convert the percussion revolvers to the new metallic cartridge system. This conversion was designed around the tapered Thuer cartridge and consists of a ring that replaced the back part of the cylinder, which had been milled off. This ring is stamped "Pat. Sep. / 15. 1868." The ejection position is marked with the letter "E." These conversions have rebounding firing pins and are milled to allow loading from the front of the revolver. This conversion was undertaken on the six different models listed; and all other specifications, finishes, markings, etc., not directly affected by the conversion would be the same as previously described. From a collectible and investment standpoint, the Thuer Conversion is very desirable. Competent appraisal should be secured if acquisition is contemplated.

Model 1849 Pocket Conversion

Exc.	V.G.	Good	Fair	Poor
—	—	12500	4000	2000

Model 1851 Navy Conversion

Exc.	V.G.	Good	Fair	Poor
—	—	15000	5000	2000

Model 1860 Army Conversion

Exc.	V.G.	Good	Fair	Poor
—	—	17500	6000	2000

Model 1861 Navy Conversion

Exc.	V.G.	Good	Fair	Poor
—	—	17500	6000	2000

Models 1862 Police Conversion

Exc.	V.G.	Good	Fair	Poor
—	—	11500	3500	1500

Model 1862 Pocket Navy Conversion

Exc.	V.G.	Good	Fair	Poor
—	—	11500	3500	1500

NOTE: Blued models will bring higher prices than nickel models in the same condition.

Richards Conversion, 1860 Army Revolver

This was Colt's second attempt at metallic cartridge conversion, and it met with quite a bit more success than the first. The Richards Conversion was designed for the .44 Colt cartridge and has a 6-shot cylinder and an integral ejector rod to replace the loading lever that had been removed. The other specifications pertaining to the 1860 Army Revolver remain as previously described if they are not directly altered by the conversion. The Richards Conversion adds a breechplate with a firing pin and its own rear sight. There were approximately 9,000 of these Conversions manufactured between 1873 and 1878.

Civilian Model

Exc.	V.G.	Good	Fair	Poor
—	—	5250	2000	600

Martially Marked Variation

This variation is found with mixed serial numbers and a second set of conversion serial numbers. The "U.S." is stamped on the left side of the barrel lug, and inspector's cartouche appears on the grip. This is a very rare Colt revolver.

Courtesy Little John's Auction Service, Inc., Paul Goodwin photo

Exc.	V.G.	Good	Fair	Poor
—	—	15000	7000	2000

NOTE: Blued models will bring higher prices than nickel models in the same condition.

Transition Richards Model

This variation is marked by the presence of a firing pin hammer.

Exc.	V.G.	Good	Fair	Poor
—	—	6000	3000	1200

NOTE: Blued models will bring higher prices than nickel models in the same condition.

Richards-Mason Conversion, 1860 Army Revolver

This conversion is different from the Richards Conversion in a number of readily apparent aspects. The barrel was manufactured with a small lug much different in appearance than seen on the standard 1860 Army. The breechplate does not have its own rear sight, and there is a milled area to allow the hammer to contact the base of the cartridge. These Conversions were also chambered for the .44 Colt cartridge, and the cylinder holds 6 shots. There is an integral ejector rod in place of the loading lever. The barrels on some are stamped either "Address Col. Saml. Colt New-York U.S. America" or "Colt's Pt. F.A. Mfg. Co. Hartford, Ct." The patent dates 1871 and 1872 are stamped on the left side of the frame. The finish of these revolvers, as well as the grips, were for the most part the same as on the unconverted Armies; but for the first time, nickel-plated guns are found. There were approximately 2,100 of these Conversions produced in 1877 and 1878.

Exc.	V.G.	Good	Fair	Poor
—	—	6000	2500	800

NOTE: Blued models will bring higher prices than nickel models in the same condition.

Richards-Mason Conversions 1851 Navy Revolver

These revolvers were converted in the same way as the 1860 Army previously described, the major difference being the caliber .38, either rimfire or centerfire. Finishes are mostly the same as on unconverted revolvers, but nickel-plated guns are not rare.

Production Model Serial #1-3800

Exc.	V.G.	Good	Fair	Poor
—	—	4500	2000	800

U.S. Navy Model Serial #41000-91000

"USN" stamped on butt; steel grip frame.

Exc.	V.G.	Good	Fair	Poor
—	—	7000	3000	1000

NOTE: Blued models will bring higher prices than nickel models in the same condition.

Richards-Mason Conversion 1861 Navy Revolver

The specifications for this model are the same as for the 1851 Navy Conversion described above, with the base revolver being different. There were 2,200 manufactured in the 1870s.

Standard Production Model Serial #100-3300

Exc.	V.G.	Good	Fair	Poor
—	—	4250	1500	500

U.S. Navy Model Serial #1000-9999

Exc.	V.G.	Good	Fair	Poor
—	—	6500	3500	1000

NOTE: Blued models will bring higher prices than nickel models in the same condition.

Model 1862 Police and Pocket Navy Conversions

The conversion of these two revolver models is the most difficult to catalogue of all the Colt variations. There were approximately 24,000 of these produced between 1873 and 1880. There are five basic variations with a number of sub-variations. The confusion is usually caused by the different ways in which these were marked. Depending upon what parts were utilized, caliber markings could be particularly confusing. One must also consider the fact that many of these conversion revolvers found their way into secondary markets, such as Mexico and Central and South America, where they were either destroyed or received sufficient abuse to obliterate most identifying markings. The five basic variations are all chambered for either the .38 rimfire or the .38 centerfire cartridge. All held 5 shots, and most were found with the round roll-engraved stagecoach holdup scene. The half-fluted cylinder from the 1862 Police is quite rare on the conversion revolver and not found at all on some of the variations. The finishes on these guns were pretty much the same as they were before conversion, but it is not unusual to find nickel-plated specimens. Blued models will bring a premium over nickel in the same condition. The basic variations are as follows.

Round Barrel Pocket Navy with Ejector

Exc.	V.G.	Good	Fair	Poor
—	—	3500	1600	800

3.5" Round Barrel Without Ejector

Exc.	V.G.	Good	Fair	Poor
—	—	2500	1000	300

4.5" Octagonal Barrel Without Ejector

Exc.	V.G.	Good	Fair	Poor
—	—	3000	1200	400

NOTE: Blued models will bring higher prices than nickel models in the same condition.

Model 1862 Pocket Navy Octagon Barrel with Ejector

Exc.	V.G.	Good	Fair	Poor
—	—	3250	1500	600

NOTE: Half-fluted cylinder add 20 percent.

Model 1862 Police Round Barrel with Ejector

Exc.	V.G.	Good	Fair	Poor
—	—	3250	1500	600

NOTE: Blued models will bring higher prices than nickel models in the same condition.

Model 1871-1872 Open Top Revolver

This model was the first revolver Colt manufactured especially for a metallic cartridge. It was not a conversion. The frame, 7.5" or 8" round barrel, and the 6-shot cylinder were produced for the .44 rimfire metallic cartridge. The grip frame and some internal parts were taken from the 1860 Army and the 1851 Navy. Although this model was not commercially successful and was not accepted by the U.S. Ordnance Department, it did pave the way for the Single-Action Army that came out shortly thereafter and was an immediate success. This model is all blued, with a case colored hammer. There are some with silver-plated brass grip frames, but most are blued steel. The one-piece grips are of varnished walnut. The cylinder is roll-engraved with the naval battle scene. The barrel is stamped "Address Col. Saml. Colt New-York U.S. America." The later production revolvers are barrel stamped "Colt's Pt. F.A. Mfg. Co. Hartford, Ct. U.S.A." The first 1,000 revolvers were stamped "Colt's/Patent." After that, 1871 and 1872 patent dates appeared on the frame. There were 7,000 of these revolvers manufactured in 1872 and 1873.

Courtesy Rock Island Auction Company

1860 Army Grip Frame

Exc.	V.G.	Good	Fair	Poor
—	—	10000	3000	800

1851 Navy Grip Frame

Exc.	V.G.	Good	Fair	Poor
—	—	11500	4000	1200

NOTE: Blued models will bring higher prices than nickel models in the same condition.

COLT DERRINGERS AND POCKET REVOLVERS

NOTE: A surprising number of Colt pistols are still found in their original boxes, even older models. This can add 100 percent to the value of the pistol.

First Model Derringer

This is a small all-metal single-shot. It is chambered for the .44 rimfire cartridge. The 2.5" barrel pivots to the left and downward for loading. This model is engraved with a scroll pattern and has been noted blued, silver, or nickel-plated. The barrel is stamped "Colt's Pt. F.A. Mfg. Co./Hartford Ct. U.S.A/ No.1." ".41 Cal." is stamped on the frame under the release catch. There were approximately 6,500 of this model manufactured from 1870-1890. It was the first single-shot pistol Colt produced.

Courtesy Rock Island Auction Company

Exc.	V.G.	Good	Fair	Poor
—	—	2500	1200	400

Second Model Derringer

Although this model has the same odd shape as the First Model, it is readily identifiable by the checkered varnished walnut grips and the "No 2" on the barrel after the address. It is also .41 rimfire and has a 2.5" barrel that pivots in the same manner as the First Model. There were approximately 9,000 of these manufactured between 1870 and 1890.

Exc.	V.G.	Good	Fair	Poor
—	—	2000	900	400

Third Model Derringer

This model was designed by Alexander Thuer who was also responsible for Colt's first metallic cartridge conversion. It is often referred to as the "Thuer Model" for this reason. It is also chambered for the .41 rimfire cartridge and has a 2.5" barrel that pivots to the right (but not down) for loading. The Third Model has a more balanced appearance than its predecessors, and its commercial success (45,000 produced between 1875 and 1910) reflects this. The barrel on this model is stamped "Colt" in small block letters on the first 2,000 guns. The remainder of the production features the "COLT" in large italicized print. The ".41 Cal." is stamped on the left side of the frame. This model will be found with the barrel blued or plated in either silver or nickel and the bronze frame plated. The grips are varnished walnut.

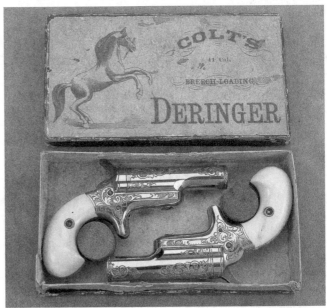

Courtesy Little John's Auction Service, Inc.

First Variation, Early Production

This has a raised area on the underside of the frame through which the barrel screw passes, and the spur is not angled. Small block "Colt" lettering on barrel.

Exc.	V.G.	Good	Fair	Poor
—	—	6500	2200	1000

First Variation, Late Production

This is similar to early production but has large italicized "COLT" on barrel.

Exc.	V.G.	Good	Fair	Poor
—	—	3250	1500	600

Production Model

Exc.	V.G.	Good	Fair	Poor
—	—	800	400	200

NOTE: Blued models will bring a premium over nickel in the same condition.

House Model Revolver

There are two basic versions of this model. They are both chambered for the .41 rimfire cartridge. The 4-shot version is known as the "Cloverleaf" due to the shape of the cylinder when viewed from the front. Approximately 7,500 of the nearly 10,000 House revolvers were of this 4-shot configuration. They are offered with a 1.5" or 3" barrel. The 1.5" length is quite rare, and some octagonal barrels in this length have been noted. The 5-shot round-cylinder version accounts for the rest of the production. It is found with serial numbers over 6100 and is offered with a 2-7/8" length barrel only. This model is stamped on the top strap "Pat. Sept. 19, 1871." This model has brass frames that were sometimes nickel-plated. The barrels are found either blued or plated. The grips are varnished walnut or rosewood. There were slightly fewer than 10,000 of both variations manufactured from 1871-1876.

Cloverleaf with 1.5" Round Barrel

Exc.	V.G.	Good	Fair	Poor
—	—	3000	1250	400

NOTE: Blued models will bring a premium over nickel in the same condition.

Cloverleaf with 3" Barrel

Exc.	V.G.	Good	Fair	Poor
—	—	1500	500	200

House Pistol with 5-Shot Round Cylinder

Exc.	V.G.	Good	Fair	Poor
—	—	1300	500	200

Open Top Pocket Revolver

This is a .22-caliber rimfire, 7-shot revolver that was offered with either a 2-3/8" or a 2-7/8" barrel. The model was a commercial success, with over 114,000 manufactured between 1871 and 1877. There would undoubtedly have been a great deal more sold had not the cheap copies begun to flood the market at that time, forcing Colt to drop this model from the line. This revolver has a silver or nickel-plated brass frame and a nickel-plated or blued barrel and cylinder. The grips are varnished walnut. The cylinder bolt slots are found toward the front on this model. "Colt's Pt. F.A. Mfg. Co./Hartford, Ct. U.S.A." is stamped on the barrel and ".22 Cal." on the left side of the frame.

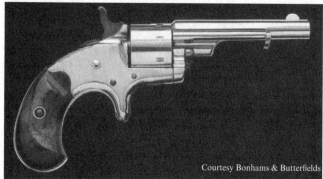

Courtesy Bonhams & Butterfields

Early Model with Ejector Rod

Exc.	V.G.	Good	Fair	Poor
—	—	1750	800	400

Production Model without Ejector Rod

Exc.	V.G.	Good	Fair	Poor
—	—	600	300	150

NOTE: Blued models will bring a premium over nickel in the same condition.

New Line Revolver .22

This was the smallest framed version of the five distinct New Line Revolvers. It has a 7-shot cylinder and a 2.25" octagonal barrel. The frame is nickel-plated, and the balance of the revolver is either nickel-plated or blued. The grips are of rosewood. There were approximately 55,000 of these made from 1873-1877. Colt also stopped production of the New Lines rather than try to compete with the "Suicide Specials." "Colt New .22" is found on the barrel; and ".22 Cal.," on the frame. The barrel is also stamped "Colt's Pt. F.A. Mfg.Co./Hartford, Ct. U.S.A."

1st Model
Short cylinder flutes.

Exc.	V.G.	Good	Fair	Poor
—	—	600	300	150

2nd Model
Long cylinder flutes.

Exc.	V.G.	Good	Fair	Poor
—	—	500	250	125

NOTE: Blued models will bring higher prices than nickel models in the same condition.

New Line Revolver .30

This is a larger version of the .22 New Line. The basic difference is the size, caliber, caliber markings, and the offering of a blued version with case colored frame. There were approximately 11,000 manufactured from 1874-1876.

Exc.	V.G.	Good	Fair	Poor
—	—	600	300	150

NOTE: Prices above are for nickel finish. Blued models will bring a premium of 100 percent.

New Line Revolver .32

This is the same basic revolver as the .30 caliber except that it is chambered for the .32-caliber rimfire and .32-caliber centerfire and is so marked. There were 22,000 of this model manufactured from 1873-1884. This model was offered with the rare 4" barrel, and this variation would be worth nearly twice the value of a standard model.

Exc.	V.G.	Good	Fair	Poor
—	—	600	300	150

NOTE: Prices above are for nickel finish. Blued models will bring a premium of 100 percent.

New Line Revolver .38

There were approximately 5,500 of this model manufactured between 1874 and 1880. It is chambered for either the .38 rimfire or .38 centerfire caliber and is so marked. This model in a 4" barrel would also bring twice the value.

Courtesy Rock Island Auction Company

Exc.	V.G.	Good	Fair	Poor
—	—	800	400	200

NOTE: Blued models will bring a premium over nickel in the same condition.

New Line Revolver .41

This is the "Big Colt," as it was sometimes known in advertising of its era. It is chambered for the .41 rimfire and the .41 centerfire and is so marked. The large caliber of this variation makes this the most desirable of the New Lines to collectors. There were approximately 7,000 of this model manufactured from 1874-1879. A 4"-barreled version would again be worth a 100 percent premium.

Exc.	V.G.	Good	Fair	Poor
—	—	900	400	200

NOTE: Prices above are for nickel finish. Blued models will bring a premium of 100 percent.

New House Model Revolver

This revolver is similar to the other New Lines except that it features a square-butt instead of the bird's-head configuration, a 2.25" round barrel without ejector rod, and a thin loading gate. It is chambered for the .32 (rare), .38, and the .41 centerfire cartridges. The finish was either full nickel-plated or blued, with a case colored frame. The grips are walnut, rosewood or (for the first time on a Colt revolver) checkered hard rubber, with an oval around the word "Colt." The barrel address is the same as on the other New Lines. The frame is marked "New House," with the caliber. There were approximately 4,000 manufactured between 1880-1886. .32 caliber model would bring a 10 percent premium.

Exc.	V.G.	Good	Fair	Poor
—	—	1000	450	250

NOTE: Prices above are for nickel finish. Blued models will bring a premium of 100 percent.

New Police Revolver

This was the final revolver in the New Line series. It is chambered for .32, .38, and .41 centerfire caliber. The .32 and .41 are quite rare. It is offered in barrel lengths of 2.25", 4.5", 5.5", and 6.5". An ejector rod is found on all but the 2.5" barrel. The finish is either nickel or blued and case colored. The grips are hard rubber with a scene of a policeman arresting a criminal embossed on them; thusly the model became known to collectors as the "Cop and Thug" model. The barrel stamping is as the other New Lines, and the frame is stamped "New Police .38." There were approximately 4,000 of these manufactured between 1882-1886.

Long Barrel Model with Ejector

Exc.	V.G.	Good	Fair	Poor
—	—	3250	1400	700

NOTE: The .32 and .41 caliber versions of this model will bring a 40-50 percent premium. Blued models and models with 5.5" or 6.5" barrels will bring a premium. Short barrel model will bring about 50 percent of the listed prices.

COLT'S SINGLE-ACTION ARMY REVOLVER

The Colt Single-Action Army, or Peacemaker as it is sometimes referred to, is one of the most widely collected and recognized firearms in the world. With few interruptions or changes in design, it has been manufactured from 1873 until the present. It is still available on a limited production basis from the Colt Custom Shop. The variations in this model are myriad. It has been produced in 30 different calibers and barrel lengths from 2.5" to 16", with 4.75", 5.5", and 7.5" standard. The standard finish is blued, with a case colored frame. Many are nickel-plated. Examples have been found silver- and gold-plated, with combinations thereof. The finest engravers in the world have used the SAA as a canvas to display their artistry. The standard grips from 1873-1883 were walnut, either oil-stained or varnished. From 1883 to approximately 1897, the standard grips were hard rubber with eagle and shield. After this date, at serial number 165000, the hard rubber grips featured the Rampant Colt. Many special-order grips were available, notably pearl and ivory, which were often checkered or carved in ornate fashion. The variables involved in establishing values on this model are extreme. Added to this, one must also consider historical significance, since the SAA played a big part in the formative years of the American West. Fortunately for those among us interested in the SAA, there are a number of fine publications available dealing exclusively with this model. It is my strongest recommendation that they be acquired and studied thoroughly to prevent extremely expensive mistakes. The Colt factory records are nearly complete for this model, and research should be done before acquisition of rare or valuable specimens.

For our purposes we will break down the Single-Action Army production as follows:
Antique or Black Powder, 1873-1898, serial number 1175000
  The cylinder axis pin is retained by a screw in the front of the frame.
Prewar, 1899-1940, serial number 175001-357859
  The cylinder axis pin is retained by a spring-loaded button through the side of the frame. This method is utilized on the following models, as well.
Postwar 2nd Generation, 1956-1978, serial number 0001SA-99999SA
3rd Generation, 1978-Present, serial #SA1001.

A breakdown of production by caliber will follow the chapter. It is important to note that the rarer calibers and the larger calibers bring higher values in this variation.

Anyone wishing to procure a factory letter authenticating a Single-Action Army should do so by writing to: COLT HISTORIAN, P.O. BOX 1868, HARTFORD, CT 06101. There is a charge of $50 per serial number for this service. If Colt cannot provide the desired information, $10 will be refunded. Enclose the Colt model name, serial number, and your name and address, along with the check.

NOTE: A surprising number of Colt pistols are still found in their original boxes, even older models. This can add 100 percent to the value of the pistol. As a rule of thumb nickel guns will bring a deduction of 20 percent to 30 percent. For revolvers with 4.75" barrels add 10 percent to 15 percent. For checkered grips add 20 percent.

COLT ANTIQUE SINGLE-ACTION ARMY REVOLVER

1st Year Production "Pinched Frame" 1873 Only

It is necessary to categorize this variation on its own. This is one of the rarest and most interesting of all the SAAs—not to mention that it is the first. On this model the top strap is pinched or constricted approximately one-half inch up from the hammer to form the rear sight. The highest surviving serial number having this feature is #156, the lowest #1. From these numbers, it is safe to assume that the first run of SAAs were all pinched-frame models; but there is no way to tell how many there were, since Colt did not serial number the frames in the order that they were manufactured. An educated guess would be that there were between 50 and 150 pinched frame guns in all and that they were all made before mid-July 1873. The reason for the change came about on the recommendation of Capt. J.R. Edie, a government inspector who thought that the full fluted top strap would be a big improvement in the sighting capabilities of the weapon. The barrel length of the first model is 7.5"; the standard caliber, .45 Colt; and the proper grips were of walnut. The front sight blade is German silver. Needless to say, this model will rarely be encountered; and if it is, it should never be purchased without competent appraisal.

Exc.	V.G.	Good	Fair	Poor
—	85000	55000	32000	10000

Early Military Model 1873-1877

The serial number range on this first run of military contract revolvers extends to #24000. The barrel address is in the early script style with the # symbol preceding and following. The frame bears the martial marking "US," and the walnut grips have the inspector's cartouche stamped on them. The front sight is steel as on all military models; the barrel length, 7.5". The caliber is .45 Colt, and the ejector rod head is the bull's-eye or donut style with a hole in the center of it. The finish features the military polish and case colored frame, with the remainder blued. Authenticate any potential purchase; many spurious examples have been noted.

Exc.	V.G.	Good	Fair	Poor
55000	45000	35000	17000	6000

NOTE: Certain 3-digit and 4-digit serial numbers will command a substantial premium. Seek an expert appraisal prior to sale.

Early Civilian Model 1873-1877

This model is identical to the Early Military Model but has no military acceptance markings or cartouches. Some could have the German silver front sight blade. The early bull's-eye ejector rod head is used on this model. The Civilian Model has a higher degree of polish than is found on the military models, and the finish on these early models could be plated or blued with a case colored frame. This model also has a script barrel address. The grips are standard one-piece walnut. Ivory-grip models are worth a premium.

Exc.	V.G.	Good	Fair	Poor
35000	28000	16000	12000	6000

NOTE: Certain 3-digit and 4-digit serial numbers will command a substantial premium. Seek an expert appraisal prior to sale.

.44 Rimfire Model 1875-1880

This model was made to fire the .44 Henry Rimfire cartridge. It was to be used as a compatible companion sidearm to the Henry and Winchester 1866 rifles that were used extensively during this era. However, this was not the case; and the .44 Rimfire was doomed to economic failure as soon as it appeared on the market. By that time, it had already been established that large-caliber centerfire cartridges were a good deal more efficient than their rimfire counterparts. The large-caliber rimfires were deemed obsolete before this Colt ever hit the market. The result of this was that Colt's sales representatives sold most of the production to obscure banana republics in South and Central America, where this model received much abuse. Most had the original 7.5" barrels cut down; and nearly all were denied even the most basic maintenance, making the survival rate of this model quite low. All this adds to its desirability as a collector's item and makes the risk of acquiring a fake that much greater. This model is unique in that it was the only SAA variation to have its own serial number range, starting with #1 and continuing to #1892, the latest known surviving specimen.

The block style barrel markings were introduced during this production run. At least 90 of these revolvers were converted by the factory to .22 rimfire, and one was shipped chambered for .32 rimfire.

Exc.	V.G.	Good	Fair	Poor
45000	37000	20000	8000	3500

Late Military Model 1878-1891

The later Military Models are serial numbered to approximately #136000. They bear the block-style barrel address without the # prefix and suffix. The frames are marked "US," and the grips have the inspector's cartouche. The finish is the military-style polish, case colored frame; and the remainder, blued. Grips are oil-stained walnut. On the military marked Colts, it is imperative that potential purchases be authenticated as many fakes have been noted.

Exc.	V.G.	Good	Fair	Poor
30000	22000	12000	8000	5000

NOTE: Revolvers produced from 1878 to 1885 will command a premium. Seek an expert appraisal prior to sale.

Artillery Model 1895-1903

A number of "US" marked SAAs were returned either to the Colt factory or to the Springfield Armory, where they were altered and refinished. These revolvers have 5.5" barrels and any combination of mixed serial numbers. They were remarked by the inspectors of the era and have a case colored frame and a blued cylinder and barrel. Some have been noted all blued within this variation. This model, as with the other military marked Colts, should definitely be authenticated before purchase. Some of these revolvers fall outside the 1898 antique cutoff date that has been established by the government and, in our experience, are not quite as desirable to investors. They are generally worth approximately 20 percent less.

Exc.	V.G.	Good	Fair	Poor
18000	12500	8000	4000	3000

London Model

These SAAs were manufactured to be sold through Colt's London Agency. The barrel is stamped "Colt's Pt. F.A. Mfg. Co. Hartford, Ct. U.S.A. Depot 14 Pall Mall London." This model is available in various barrel lengths. They are generally chambered for .45 Colt, .450 Boxer, .450 Eley, .455 Eley, and rarely .476 Eley, the largest of the SAA chamberings. A good many of these London Models were cased and embellished, and they should be individually appraised. This model should be authenticated as many spurious examples have been noted.

Exc.	V.G.	Good	Fair	Poor
22000	15000	10000	4500	2000

NOTE: Revolvers chambered for .476 Eley will command a 100 percent premium.

Frontier Six-Shooter 1878-1882

Several thousand SAAs were made with the legend "Colt's Frontier Six Shooter" acid-etched into the left side of the barrel instead of being stamped. This etching is not deep, and today collectors will become ecstatic if they discover a specimen with mere vestiges of the etched panel remaining. These acid-etched SAAs are serial numbered #45000-#65000. They have various barrel lengths and finishes, but all are chambered for the .44-40 caliber.

Courtesy Little John's Auction Service, Inc., Paul Goodwin photo

Exc.	V.G.	Good	Fair	Poor
42500	22000	14000	8000	6000

Sheriff's or Storekeeper's Model 1882-1898

This model was manufactured with a short barrel (2.5"-4.75"). Most have 4" barrels. It features no ejector rod or housing, and the frame is made without the hole in the right forward section to accommodate the ejector assembly. The Sheriff's or Storekeeper's Model is numbered above serial #73000. It was manufactured with various finishes and chambered for numerous calibers. This model continued after 1898 into the smokeless or modern era. Examples manufactured in the prewar years are worth approximately 20 percent less. Although faking this model is quite difficult, it has been successfully attempted.

Exc.	V.G.	Good	Fair	Poor
37000	24000	12000	7000	3000

Flattop Target Model 1888-1896

This model is highly regarded and sought after by collectors. It is not only rare (only 925 manufactured) but is an extremely attractive and well-finished variation. It is chambered for 22 different calibers from .22 rimfire to .476 Eley. The .22 rimfire, .38 Colt, .41, and .45 Colt are the most predominant chamberings. The 7.5" barrel length is the most commonly encountered.

The serial number range is between #127000-#162000. Some have been noted in higher ranges. The finish is all blued, with a case colored hammer. The checkered grips are either hard rubber or walnut. The most readily identifying feature of the flattop is the lack of a groove in the top strap and the sight blade dovetailed into the flattop. The front sight has a removable blade insert. The values given are for a standard production model chambered for the calibers previously mentioned as being the most common. It is important to have other calibers individually appraised as variance in values can be quite extreme.

Courtesy Little John's Auction Service, Inc.

Exc.	V.G.	Good	Fair	Poor
35000	25000	15000	8000	4000

NOTE: Nickel models will command a premium.

Bisley Model 1894-1915

This model was named for the target range in Great Britain, where their National Target Matches were held since the nineteenth century. The model was designed as a target revolver with an odd humped-back grip that was supposed to better fill the hand while target shooting. It is also easily identified by the wide low profile hammer spur, wide trigger, and the name "Bisley" stamped on the barrel. The Bisley production fell within the serial number range #165000-#331916. There were 44,350 made.

It was offered in 16 different chamberings from .32 Colt to .455 Eley. The most common calibers were .32-20, .38-40, .41, .44-40, and .45 Colt. The barrel lengths are 4.75", 5.5", and 7.5". The frame and hammer are case-colored; the remainder, blued. Smokeless powder models produced after 1899 utilized the push-button cylinder pin retainer. The grips are checkered hard rubber. This model was actually designed with English sales in mind; and though it did sell well over there, American sales accounted for most of the Bisley production. The values we provide here cover the standard calibers and barrel lengths. Rare calibers and/or other notable variations can bring greatly fluctuating values, and qualified appraisals should be secured in such cases.

Exc.	V.G.	Good	Fair	Poor
10000	7000	4000	2500	1200

NOTE: Bisleys manufactured before 1898 are worth approximately 50 percent more.

Bisley Model Flattop Target 1894-1913

This model is quite similar to the Standard Bisley Model, with the flattop frame and dovetailed rear sight feature. It also has the removable front sight insert. It has an all-blued finish with case-colored hammer only and is available with a 7.5" barrel. Smokeless powder models produced after 1899 utilized the push-button cylinder pin retainer. The calibers are the same as the standard Bisley. Colt manufactured 976 of these revolvers. The advice regarding appraisal would also apply.

Exc.	V.G.	Good	Fair	Poor
25000	16000	9500	3500	1800

NOTE: Nickel models will command a premium.

Standard Civilian Production Models 1876-1898

This final designated category for the black powder or antique SAAs includes all the revolvers not previously categorized. They have barrel lengths from 4.75", 5.5", and 7.5" and are chambered for any one of 30 different calibers. The finishes could be blued, blued and case colored, or plated in nickel, silver, gold, or combinations thereof. Grips could be walnut, hard rubber, ivory, pearl, stag, or bone. The possibilities are endless. The values given here are for the basic model, and we again strongly advise securing qualified appraisal when not completely sure of any model variation.

Exc.	V.G.	Good	Fair	Poor
27000	18000	12000	8000	3000

NOTE: For Standard Civilian Production Models with screw-in frame, serial number to 163,000 add a 25 percent to 100 percent premium depending on year built. Seek an expert appraisal prior to sale.

NOTE: At this time it is important to note that the Colt's Single-Action Army Revolvers we have discussed to this point are in the antique category as established by our federal government. The arbitrary cutoff date of 1898 has been established, and any weapon made prior to this date is considered an antique and, as such, not subject to the restraints placed on collectors and dealers by the Gun Control Act of 1968. This is important because firearms falling into this category will usually bring higher values due to the demand by pure investors who do not relish paperwork on collectible investments. There will be those who disagree with me on this line of reasoning, but my experience tells me that it is correct.

COLT PREWAR SINGLE-ACTION ARMY REVOLVER 1899-1940

NOTE: A surprising number of Colt pistols are still found in their original boxes, even older models. This can add 100 percent to the value of the pistol.

Standard Production Prewar Models

The 1899 cutoff has been thoroughly discussed, but it is interesting to note that the actual beginning production date for smokeless models was 1900. The Prewar Colts are, all in all, quite similar to the antiques—the finishes, barrel lengths, grips, etc. Calibers are also similar, with the exception of the obsolete ones being dropped and new discoveries added. The most apparent physical difference between the smokeless powder and black powder models is the previously discussed method of retaining the cylinder axis pin. The prewar Colts utilized the spring-loaded button through the side of the frame. The black powder models utilized a screw in the front of the frame. The values we furnish for this model designation are for these standard models only. The serial number range on the prewar SAAs is 175001-357859. Note that any variation can have marked effects on value fluctuations, and qualified appraisal should be secured.

Exc.	V.G.	Good	Fair	Poor
11500	6750	4000	2500	1500

Long Fluted Cylinder Model 1913-1915

Strange as it may seem, the Colt Company has an apparent credo they followed to never throw anything away. That credo was never more evident than with this model. These Long Flute Cylinders were actually left over from the model 1878 Double-Action Army Revolvers. Someone in the hierarchy at Colt had an inspiration that drove the gunsmiths on the payroll slightly mad: to make these cylinders fit the SAA frames. There were 1,478 of these Long Flutes manufactured. They are chambered for the .45 Colt, .38-40, .32-20, .41 Colt, and the .44 Smith & Wesson Special. They were offered in the three standard barrel lengths and were especially well-polished, having what has been described as Colt's "Fire Blue" on the barrel and cylinder. The frame and hammer are case colored. They are fitted with checkered hard rubber grips and are particularly fine examples of Colt's craft.

Exc.	V.G.	Good	Fair	Poor
15000	8500	6000	3250	2000

COLT POSTWAR SINGLE-ACTION ARMY REVOLVER

Standard Postwar Model 1956-1975

In 1956 the shooting and gun-collecting fraternity succeeded in convincing Colt that there was a market for a re-introduced SAA. The revolver was brought back in the same external configuration. The only changes were internal. The basic specifications as to barrel length and finish availability were the same. The calibers available were .38 Special, .357 Magnum, .44 Special, and .45 Colt. The serial number range of the re-introduced 2nd Generation, as it is sometimes known, Colt is #000ISA-73000SA. Values for the standard postwar Colts are established by four basic factors: caliber (popularity and scarcity), barrel length, finish, and condition. Shorter barrel lengths are generally more desirable than the 7.5". The .38 Special is the rarest caliber, but the .45 Colt and .44 Special are more sought after than the .357 Magnum. Special feature revolvers, such as the 350 factory-engraved guns produced during this period, must be individually appraised. The ivory situation in the world today has become quite a factor, as ivory grips are found on many SAAs. We will attempt to take these factors into consideration and evaluate this variation as accurately and clearly as possible. Remember as always, when in doubt secure a qualified appraisal.

NOTE: 4.75" barrel add 25 percent. 5.5" barrel add 15 percent. Nickel finish add 20 percent. Ivory grips add $250.

7.5" Barrel Model

.38 Special

NIB	Exc.	V.G.	Good	Fair	Poor
2450	1850	1200	900	700	600

.357 Magnum

NIB	Exc.	V.G.	Good	Fair	Poor
1850	1350	900	750	700	650

.44 Special

NIB	Exc.	V.G.	Good	Fair	Poor
2950	2250	1750	1100	1000	750

.45 Colt

NIB	Exc.	V.G.	Good	Fair	Poor
2000	1650	1400	1000	900	750

Sheriff's Model 1960-1975

Between 1960 and 1975, there were approximately 500 Sheriff's Models manufactured. They have 3" barrels and no ejector rod assemblies. The frames were made without the hole for the ejector rod to pass through. They were blued, with case colored frames; 25 revolvers were nickel-plated and would bring a sizable premium if authenticated. The barrels are marked "Colt Sheriff's Model." The serial number has an "SM" suffix. They are chambered for the .45 Colt cartridge.

NIB	Exc.	V.G.	Good	Fair	Poor
3000	2200	1800	1200	850	600

NOTE: Nickel finish add 20 percent.

Buntline Special 1957-1975

The "Buntline Special" was named after a dime novelist named Ned Buntline, who supposedly gave this special long barrel revolver to Wyatt Earp. The story is suspected to be purely legend as no Colt records exist to lend it credence. Be that as it may, the Colt factory decided to take advantage of the market and produced the 12" barreled SAA from 1957-1974. There were approximately 3,900 manufactured. They are chambered for the .45 Colt cartridge and are offered in the blued and case colored finish. Only 65 Buntlines are nickel-plated, making this an extremely rare variation that definitely should be authenticated before purchase. Walnut grips are the most commonly noted, but they are also offered with the checkered hard rubber grips. The barrels are marked on the left side "Colt Buntline Special .45."

NIB	Exc.	V.G.	Good	Fair	Poor
1950	1400	1100	750	600	500

NOTE: Nickel finish add 60 percent.

New Frontier 1961-1975

The New Frontier is readily identified by its flattop frame and adjustable sight. It also has a high front sight. Colt manufactured approximately 4,200 of them. They are chambered for the .357 Magnum, .45

Colt, .44 Special (255 produced), and rarely (only 49 produced) in .38 Special. A few were chambered for the .44-40 cartridge. The 7.5" barrel length is by far the most common, but the 4.75" and 5.5" barrels are also offered. The standard finish is case colored and blued. Nickel-plating and full blue are offered but are rarely encountered. Standard grips are walnut. The barrel is stamped on the left side "Colt New Frontier S.A.A." The serial has the "NF" suffix.

NIB	Exc.	V.G.	Good	Fair	Poor
1850	1400	1000	800	600	500

NOTE: 4.75" barrel add 25 percent. 5.5" barrel add 20 percent. Full Blue add 50 percent. .38 Special add 50 percent. .44 Special add 30 percent. 44-40 add 30 percent.

New Frontier Buntline Special 1962-1967

This model is rare, as Colt only manufactured 70 during this five-year period. They are similar to the standard Buntline, with a 12" barrel. They are chambered for .45 Colt only.

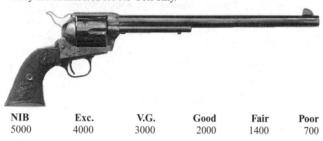

NIB	Exc.	V.G.	Good	Fair	Poor
5000	4000	3000	2000	1400	700

COLT THIRD GENERATION SINGLE-ACTION ARMY 1976-1981

In 1976 Colt made some internal changes in the SAA. The external configuration was not altered. The serial number range began in 1976 with #80000SA, and in 1978 #99999SA was reached. At this time the suffix became a prefix, and the new serial range began with #SA01001. This model's value is determined in much the same manner as was described in the section on the 2nd Generation SAAs. Caliber, barrel length, finish, and condition are once again the four main determining factors. The prevalence of special-order guns was greater during this period, and many more factory-engraved SAAs were produced. Colt's Custom Shop was quite active during this period. We feel that it is not advisable to undertake evaluation of specially embellished guns and strongly advise that competent appraisal be secured on any firearms that deviate from the standard. There are, quite frankly, too many fraudulent Colt SAAs out there; and the financial risks are great.

NOTE: 4.75" barrel add 25 percent. 5.5" barrel add 10 percent. Nickel plated add 10 percent. Ivory grips add $250.

7.5" Barrel

.357 Magnum

NIB	Exc.	V.G.	Good	Fair	Poor
1400	1150	895	750	600	500

.44-40

NIB	Exc.	V.G.	Good	Fair	Poor
1500	1250	900	750	600	500

.44-40 Black Powder Frame (Screw Retaining Cylinder Pin)

NIB	Exc.	V.G.	Good	Fair	Poor
1700	1400	1150	1000	800	600

.44 Special

NIB	Exc.	V.G.	Good	Fair	Poor
1400	1200	900	700	550	500

.45 Colt

NIB	Exc.	V.G.	Good	Fair	Poor
1500	1300	900	750	600	500

Sheriff's Model 3rd Generation

This model is similar to the 2nd Generation Sheriff's Model. The serial number and the fact that this model is also chambered for the .44-40 are the only external differences. Colt offered this model with interchangeable cylinders—.45 Colt/.45 ACP or .44-40/.44 Special—available in 3" barrel, blued and case colored finish standard.

NIB	Exc.	V.G.	Good	Fair	Poor
1050	875	750	600	450	400

NOTE: Interchangeable cylinders add 30 percent. Nickel finish add 10 percent. Ivory grips add $250.

Buntline Special 3rd Generation

This is the same basic configuration as the 2nd Generation with the 12" barrel. Standard finish blued and case-colored, it is chambered for .45 Colt and has checkered hard rubber grips.

NIB	Exc.	V.G.	Good	Fair	Poor
1050	875	750	600	450	400

NOTE: Nickel finish add 10 percent.

New Frontier 3rd Generation

This model is similar in appearance to the 2nd Generation guns. The 3rd Generation New Frontiers have five-digit serial numbers; the 2nd Generation guns, four-digit numbers. That and the calibers offered are basically the only differences. The 3rd Generations are chambered for the .44 Special and .45 Colt and are rarely found in .44-40. Barrel lengths are 7.5" standard, with the 4.75" and 5.5" rarely encountered.

NIB	Exc.	V.G.	Good	Fair	Poor
950	725	650	550	500	400

NOTE: .44-40 add 20 percent. 4.75" barrel add 35 percent. 5.5" barrel add 25 percent.

COLT CURRENT PRODUCTION SINGLE-ACTION ARMY 1982-PRESENT

Standard Single-Action Army

The SAA, it is sad to note, has all but faded from the firearms picture. They are currently available as a special-order custom shop proposition. The cost is great; and the availability, low. The heyday of one of the most venerable firearms of them all is pretty much at an end. The SAAs have been available in .357 Magnum, .38-40, .44-40, .44 Special, and .45 Colt. Barrels were available in 3" through 10" lengths. The finishes are nickel-plated and blued, with case-colored frames. A number of optional finishes are available on request. Grips are available on a custom order basis. This model is available on special-order only.

NOTE: As of 2000 the Custom Shop is offering this revolver in the following configurations:

P1840—Blued .45 Colt with 4.75" barrel
P1841—Nickel .45 Colt with 4.75" barrel
P1850—Blued .45 Colt with 5.5" barrel
P1856—Nickel .45 Colt with 5.5" barrel
P1940—Blued .44-40 with 4.75" barrel
P1941—Nickel .44-40 with 4.75" barrel
P1950—Blued .44-40 with 5.5" barrel
P1956—Nickel .44-40 with 5.5" barrel
P1640—Blued .357 Magnum with 4.75" barrel
P1650—Blued .357 Magnum with 5.5" barrel

Optional Features:

Nickel finish add $125. Royal blue finish add $200. Mirror brite finish add $225. Gold plate add $365. Silver plate add $365. Class A engraving add $875. Class B engraving add $1,200. Class C engraving add $1,500. Class D engraving add $1,750. Buntline engraving add 15 percent.

NIB	Exc.	V.G.	Good	Fair	Poor
1375	1100	850	—	—	—

Colt Cowboy (CB1850)

Introduced in 1998 this model is a replica of the Single-Action Army that features a modern transfer bar safety system. Offered with 5.5" barrel and chambered for .45 Colt. Sights are fixed with walnut grips. Blued barrel with case colored frame. Weight is about 42 oz.

NIB	Exc.	V.G.	Good	Fair	Poor
650	500	—	—	—	—

Colt Single-Action Army "The Legend"
A limited-edition revolver built to commemorate Colt's official PRCA sponsorship. Limited to 1,000. Chambered for .45 Long Colt fitted with a 5-1/2" barrel. Nickel finish Buffalo horn grips with gold medallions. Machine engraved and washed in gold.

NIB	Exc.	V.G.	Good	Fair	Poor
2750	2250	—	—	—	—

COLT SCOUT MODEL SINGLE-ACTION ARMY

NOTE: A surprising number of Colt pistols are still found in their original boxes, even older models. This can add 100 percent to the value of the pistol.

Frontier Scout 1957-1971
This is a scaled-down version of the SAA that is chambered for the .22 LR with an interchangeable .22 Magnum cylinder. It is offered with a 4.25", 4.75", or a 9.5" barrel. The frame is alloy. First year production frame were duotone with frame left in the white and the balance of the revolver blued. All blue models and wood grips became available in 1958. In 1961 the duotone model was dropped from production. A .22 Magnum model was first offered in 1959. In 1964 dual cylinders were introduced. These revolvers have "Q" or "F" serial number suffixes. In 1960 the "K" series Scout was introduced and featured a heavier frame, nickel plating, and wood grips. The majority of commemorative revolvers are of this type. This series was discontinued in 1970. Prices are about 15 percent higher than for the "Q" and "F" series guns.

NIB	Exc.	V.G.	Good	Fair	Poor
450	325	200	175	125	90

NOTE: 9.5" Buntline add 50 percent. Extra cylinder add 10 percent.

Peacemaker Scout & New Frontier
This model is similar to the Frontier Scout, with a steel case-colored or blued frame. Fitted with old style black plastic eagle grips. The barrel lengths offered are 4.75", 6", or 7.5" (Buntline model). It also has an interchangeable .22 Magnum cylinder. Most of these revolvers had a "G" suffix although some built in 1974 had a "L" suffix. In 1982 through 1986 a New Frontier model with cross-bolt safety was offered. This model is often referred to as the "GS" series. This revolver was offered with adjustable sights only. No Peacemakers were offered in this series.

NIB	Exc.	V.G.	Good	Fair	Poor
550	475	300	200	150	100

Scout Model SAA 1962-1971
This is basically a scaled-down version of the SAA chambered for the .22 LR cartridge. This model is offered with a 4.75", 6", or 7" barrel. The earlier production has case-colored frames with the remainder blued; later production is all blued. Grips are checkered hard rubber. This model was discontinued in 1986.

NIB	Exc.	V.G.	Good	Fair	Poor
400	275	200	150	100	75

COLT ANTIQUE LONG ARMS

Berdan Single-Shot Rifle
This is a scarce rifle on today's market. There were approximately 30,200 manufactured, but nearly 30,000 of them were sent to Russia. This rifle was produced from 1866-1870. It is a trapdoor-type action chambered for .42 centerfire. The standard model has a 32.5" barrel; the carbine, 18.25". The finish is blued, with a walnut stock. This rifle was designed and the patent held by Hiram Berdan, Commander of the Civil War "Sharpshooters" Regiment. This was actually Colt's first cartridge arm. The 30,000 rifles and 25 half-stocked carbines that were sent to Russia were in Russian Cyrillic letters. The few examples made for American sales have Colt's name and Hartford address on the barrel.

Rifle Russian Order
30,000 manufactured.

Exc.	V.G.	Good	Fair	Poor
—	2000	750	450	—

Carbine Russian Order
25 manufactured.

Exc.	V.G.	Good	Fair	Poor
—	5500	3000	1250	—

Rifle U.S. Sales
100 manufactured.

Exc.	V.G.	Good	Fair	Poor
—	5000	2250	1250	—

Carbine U.S. Sales
25 manufactured.

Exc.	V.G.	Good	Fair	Poor
—	9500	4500	2000	—

Colt-Franklin Military Rifle
This is a rifle that was not a successful venture for Colt. The patents were held by William B. Franklin, a vice-president of the company. This was a bolt-action rifle with a primitive, gravity-fed box magazine. It is chambered for the .45-70 government cartridge, has a 32.5" barrel, and is blued, with a walnut stock. The rifle has the Colt Hartford barrel address and is stamped with an eagle's head and U.S. inspectors marks. There were only 50 of these rifles produced, and it is believed that they were prototypes intended for government sales. This was not to be, and production ceased after approximately 50 were manufactured in 1887 and 1888.

Exc.	V.G.	Good	Fair	Poor
—	8000	4500	2000	—

Colt-Burgess Lever-Action Rifle
This represented Colt's only attempt to compete with Winchester for the lever-action rifle market. It is said that when Winchester started to produce revolving handguns for prospective marketing, Colt dropped the Burgess from its line. This rifle is chambered for .44-40. It has a 25.5" barrel and a 15-shot tubular magazine. The Carbine version has a 20.5" barrel and 12-shot magazine. The finish is blued, with a case-colored hammer and lever. The stock is walnut with an oil finish. The Colt Hartford address is on the barrel, and "Burgess Patents" is stamped on the bottom of the lever. There were 3,775 rifles manufactured—1,219 with round barrels and 2,556 with octagonal barrels. There were also 2,593 Carbines. The Burgess was produced from 1883-1885.

Rifle, Octagonal Barrel

Exc.	V.G.	Good	Fair	Poor
—	—	3500	1500	550

Rifle, Round Barrel

Exc.	V.G.	Good	Fair	Poor
—	—	3500	1500	550

Carbine

Exc.	V.G.	Good	Fair	Poor
—	—	5000	2000	950

Baby Carbine, Lighter Frame and Barrel (RARE)

Exc.	V.G.	Good	Fair	Poor
—	—	6000	2500	1150

Lightning Slide-Action, Medium-Frame

This was the first slide-action rifle Colt produced. It is chambered for .32-20, .38-40, and .44-40 and was intended to be a companion piece to the SAAs in the same calibers. The rifle has a 26" barrel with 15-shot tube magazine; the carbine, a 20" barrel with 12-shot magazine. The finish is blued, with case-colored hammer; the walnut stock is oil-finished; and the forend, usually checkered. The Colt name and Hartford address are stamped on the barrel along with the patent dates. There were approximately 89,777 manufactured between 1884 and 1902.

Rifle

Exc.	V.G.	Good	Fair	Poor
—	2500	1250	750	400

Carbine

Exc.	V.G.	Good	Fair	Poor
—	3500	1750	800	500

Military Rifle or Carbine

.44-40 caliber, short magazine tube, bayonet lug, and sling swivels.

Exc.	V.G.	Good	Fair	Poor
—	4250	2000	1000	600

Baby Carbine, 1 lb., Lighter Version of Standard Carbine

Courtesy Richard M. Kumor, Sr.

Exc.	V.G.	Good	Fair	Poor
—	5000	2500	1250	750

San Francisco Police Rifle

.44-40 caliber, #SFP 1-SFP401 on bottom tang.

Exc.	V.G.	Good	Fair	Poor
—	3250	1250	800	500

Lightning Slide-Action Small-Frame

This is a well-made rifle and the first of its type that Colt manufactured. It is chambered for the .22 Short and Long. The standard barrel length is 24"; the finish, blued with a case-colored hammer. The stock is walnut; some were checkered; some, not. The barrel is stamped with the Colt name and Hartford address and the patent dates. There were 89,912 manufactured between 1887 and 1904.

Exc.	V.G.	Good	Fair	Poor
2750	1250	700	500	300

Lightning Slide-Action, Large-Frame

This rifle is similar in appearance to the medium-frame Lightning, though larger in size. It is chambered in larger rifle calibers of the era, from .38-56 up to .50-95 Express. The larger calibers are more desirable from a collector's standpoint. The rifle has a 28" barrel; the carbine, a 22" barrel. The finish is blued, with a case-colored hammer. The stock is oiled walnut; the forend, checkered. The Colt name and Hartford address are stamped on the barrel along with the patent dates. This rifle is quite large and has come to be known as the "Express model." Colt manufactured 6,496 between 1887 and 1894.

Rifle, 28" Octagonal Barrel

Exc.	V.G.	Good	Fair	Poor
—	4500	2000	750	500

Rifle, 28" Round Barrel

Exc.	V.G.	Good	Fair	Poor
—	4000	1750	750	500

Carbine, 22" Barrel

Exc.	V.G.	Good	Fair	Poor
—	7500	3500	1500	750

Baby Carbine, 22" Barrel 1 lb. Lighter

Exc.	V.G.	Good	Fair	Poor
—	10000	5000	2250	950

Model 1878 Double-Barrel Shotgun

This model is chambered in 10 or 12 gauge and has 28", 30", or 32" barrels. It is a sidelock double-trigger hammer gun with case-colored locks and breech. The barrels are browned Damacus-patterned. The checkered walnut stock is varnished or oil-finished. The Colt's Hartford address is stamped on the barrel rib; and Colt's name, on the lock. This has been regarded as one of the finest shotguns made in America, although Colt had difficulty competing with the less expensive European imports of the day. They ceased production after only 22,690 were manufactured between 1878 and 1889.

Exc.	V.G.	Good	Fair	Poor
—	1250	600	400	250

NOTE: Fully engraved model add 300 percent.

Model 1883 Double-Barrel Shotgun

This model is a hammerless boxlock, chambered for 10 or 12 gauge. The barrels are 28", 30", or 32"; and it features double triggers. The frame and furniture are case-colored; the barrels, browned with Damascus pattern. The checkered walnut stock is varnished or oil-finished. Colt's Hartford address is stamped on the barrel rib. "Colt" is stamped on each side of the frame. Again, as in the Model 1878, this is rated as one of the finest of all American-made shotguns. There were many special orders, and they require individual appraisal. Colt manufactured 7,366 of these guns between 1883 and 1895.

Exc.	V.G.	Good	Fair	Poor
—	1750	800	500	250

NOTE: Fully engraved model add 300 percent.

Double-Barrel Rifle

This is one of the rarest of all Colt firearms and is a prize for the Colt collector. There were only 35 of these guns manufactured. They were said to be the special interest of Caldwell Hart Colt, Samuel Colt's son, who was an avid arms collector. It is said that most of the 35 guns produced wound up in his collection or those of his friends. This gun is chambered for .45-70 or one of the larger variations thereof. It is an exposed hammer sidelock with double triggers. The locks, breech, and furniture are case-colored; the barrels, browned or blued. The barrels are 28" in length, and the checkered stock was oil-finished or varnished walnut. The barrel rib is stamped with the Colt name and Hartford address. The locks are also stamped "Colt." One must exercise extreme caution in dealing with this model as there have been model 1878 Shotguns converted into double rifles. Colt manufactured the 35 guns over the period 1879-1885.

Exc.	V.G.	Good	Fair	Poor
—	25000	10000	5000	1500

COLT DOUBLE-ACTION REVOLVERS

Model 1877 "Lightning" and "Thunderer"

The Model 1877 was Colt's first attempt at manufacturing a double-action revolver. It shows a striking resemblance to the Single-Action Army. Sales on this model were brisk, with over 166,000 produced between 1877 and 1909. Chambered for two different cartridges, the .38 Colt, known as the "Lightning", and .41 Colt, as the "Thunderer." The standard finishes are blued, with case-colored frame and nickel plate. The bird's-head grips are of checkered rosewood on the early guns and hard rubber on the majority of the production run. The barrel lengths most often encountered are 2.5" and 3.5" without an ejector rod, and 4.5" and 6" with the rod. Other barrel lengths from 1.5" through 10" were offered. The Model 1877 holds 6 shots in either caliber. There were quite a few different variations found within this model designation. Values furnished are for the standard variations. Antiques made before 1898 would be more desirable from an investment standpoint.

NOTE: .41 Caliber "Thunderer" add 10 percent. Over 6" barrel add 50 percent. London barrel address add 20 percent. .32 caliber add 50 percent. Rosewood grips add 10 percent.

Without Ejector, 2.5" and 3.5" Barrel

Exc.	V.G.	Good	Fair	Poor
3000	2000	1000	500	350

With Ejector, 4.5" and 6" Barrel

Exc.	V.G.	Good	Fair	Poor
3000	1800	1000	750	450

NOTE: Premium for blued guns-25 percent. Premium for shorter than 2-1/2"-50 percent.

Model 1878 "Frontier"
This model is a large and somewhat ungainly looking revolver. It has a solid frame with a removable trigger guard. The cylinder does not swing out, and there is a thin loading gate. It has bird's-head grips made of checkered hard rubber; walnut would be found on the early models. The finish is either blued and case-colored or nickel-plated. The Model 1878 holds 6 shots, and the standard barrel lengths are 4.75", 5.5", and 7.5" with an ejector assembly and 3", 3.5", and 4" without. The standard chamberings for the Model 1878 are .32-20, .38-40, .41 Colt, .44-40, and .45 Colt. This model was fairly well received because it is chambered for the large calibers that were popular in that era. Colt manufactured 51,210 between 1878 and 1905. Antique models made before 1898 would be more desirable from an investment standpoint.

NOTE: Add a 15 percent premium for blued revolvers. Add 10 percent to 50 percent premium for calibers other than .44-40 or .45.

Model 1878 "Frontier" Standard
Exc.	V.G.	Good	Fair	Poor
4200	3000	1200	800	400

Model 1878 "Frontier" Omnipotent
This is a special order version of the model above with the name "Omnipotent" stamped on the barrel.

Exc.	V.G.	Good	Fair	Poor
16000	10000	6000	3000	1000

Sheriff's Model
Chambered for .44-40 or .45 Colt with barrels lengths of 3.5" or 4".

Exc.	V.G.	Good	Fair	Poor
6000	4000	2000	1000	800

Model 1902 (Philippine or Alaskan Model)
This is a U.S. Ordnance contract Model 1878. It has a 6" barrel and is chambered for .45 Colt. The finish is blued, and there is a lanyard swivel on the butt. This model bears the U.S. inspector's marks. It is sometimes referred to as the Philippine or the Alaskan model. The trigger guard is quite a bit larger than standard.

Courtesy Bonhams & Butterfields

Exc.	V.G.	Good	Fair	Poor
5500	3500	1800	1000	600

Model 1889 Navy-Civilian Model
The 1889 Navy is an important model from a historical standpoint as it was the first double-action revolver Colt manufactured with a swing-out cylinder. They produced 31,000 of them between 1889 and 1894. The Model 1889 is chambered for the .38 Colt and the .41 Colt cartridges. The cylinder holds 6 shots. It is offered with a 3", 4.5", or 6" barrel; and the finish was either blued or nickel-plated. The grips are checkered hard rubber with the "Rampant Colt" in an oval molded into them. The patent dates 1884 and 1888 appear in the barrel marking, and the serial numbers are stamped on the butt.

Exc.	V.G.	Good	Fair	Poor
3000	1500	1000	600	300

NOTE: Add premium for blued models. For 3" barrel add 20 percent.

Model 1889 U.S. Navy—Martial Model
This variation has a 6" barrel, is chambered for .38 Colt, and is offered in blued finish only. "U.S.N." is stamped on the butt. Most of the Navy models were altered at the Colt factory to add the Model 1895 improvements. An original unaltered specimen would be worth as much as 50 percent premium over the altered values listed.

Exc.	V.G.	Good	Fair	Poor
9000	5000	2500	1000	500

Model 1892 "New Army and Navy"—Civilian Model
This model is similar in appearance to the 1889 Navy. The main differences are improvements to the lockwork function. It has double bolt stop notches, a double cylinder locking bolt, and shorter flutes on the cylinder. The .38 Smith & Wesson and the .32-20 were added to the .38 Colt and .41 Colt chamberings. The checkered hard rubber grips are standard, with plain walnut grips found on some contract series guns. Barrel lengths and finishes are the same as described for the Model 1889. The patent dates 1895 and 1901 appear stamped on later models. Colt manufactured 291,000 of these revolvers between 1892 and 1907. Antiques before 1898 are more desirable from an investment standpoint.

Exc.	V.G.	Good	Fair	Poor
2000	800	500	200	100

NOTE: For 3" barrel add 20 percent.

Model 1892 U.S. Navy—Martial Model
Exc.	V.G.	Good	Fair	Poor
3500	2000	800	600	400

Model 1892 U.S. Army—Martial Model
Exc.	V.G.	Good	Fair	Poor
3500	2000	800	600	400

Model 1896/1896 Army
Exc.	V.G.	Good	Fair	Poor
3500	2000	800	600	400

Model 1905 Marine Corps
This model is a variation of the New Army and Navy Model. It was derived from the late production with its own serial range #10001-10926. With only 926 produced between 1905 and 1909, it is quite rare on today's market and is eagerly sought after by Colt Double-Action collectors. This model is chambered for the .38 Colt and the .38 Smith & Wesson Special cartridges. It holds 6 shots, has a 6" barrel, and is offered in a blued finish only. The grips are checkered walnut and are quite different than those found on previous models. "U.S.M.C." is stamped on the butt; patent dates of 1884, 1888, and 1895 are stamped on the barrel. One hundred twenty-five of these revolvers were earmarked for civilian sales and do not have the Marine Corps markings; these will generally be found in better condition. Values are similar.

Courtesy Faintich Auction Services, Inc., Paul Goodwin photo

Exc.	V.G.	Good	Fair	Poor
4500	3500	2000	1500	750

REPRODUCTION COLT PERCUSSION REVOLVERS

Walker
Made from 1979 to 1981; serial numbers 1200-4120 and 32256 to 32500.

NIB	Exc.	V.G.
895	750	500

Walker Heritage Model
NIB
950

First Model Dragoon
Made from 1980 to 1982; serial numbers 24100-34500.

NIB	Exc.	V.G.
395	300	100

Second Model Dragoon
Made from 1980 to 1982; serial numbers as above.

NIB	Exc.	V.G.
395	300	100

Third Model Dragoon
Made from 1980 to 1982; serial numbers as above.

NIB	Exc.	V.G.
395	300	100

Model 1848 Pocket Pistol
Made in 1981; serial numbers 16000-17851.

NIB	Exc.	V.G.
425	300	100

Model 1851 Navy Revolver
Made from 1971 to 1978; serial numbers 4201-25100 and 24900-29150.

NIB	Exc.	V.G.
395	400	325

Model 1860 Army Revolver
Made from 1978 to 1982; serial numbers 201000-212835.

NIB	Exc.	V.G.
550	500	475

Model 1861 Navy Revolver
Made during 1980 and 1981; serial numbers 40000-43165.

NIB	Exc.	V.G.
500	450	400

Model 1862 Pocket Pistol
Made from 1979 to 1984; serial numbers 8000-58850.

NIB	Exc.	V.G.
425	350	300

Model 1862 Police Revolver
Made from 1979 to 1984; serial numbers in above range.

NIB	Exc.	V.G.
425	400	300

NOTE: The above revolvers were manufactured in a variety of styles (cylinder form, stainless steel, etc.) that affect prices. Factory engraved examples command a considerable premium over the prices listed above.

COLT BLACKPOWDER ARMS
Brooklyn, New York

These blackpowder revolvers and rifles are made under license from Colt.

1842 Paterson Colt No. 5 Holster Model
This model is a copy of the No. 5 Holster model and is chambered for the .36 caliber ball. Fitted with a 7.5" octagon barrel. Hand engraved. This is a special order revolver.

NIB	Exc.	V.G.	Good	Fair	Poor
3000	—	—	—	—	—

Walker
This .44 caliber large-frame revolver is fitted with a 9" barrel.

NIB	Exc.	V.G.	Good	Fair	Poor
475	400	350	300	200	150

Walker 150th Anniversary Model
Marked "A Company No. 1" in gold. Introduced 1997.

NIB	Exc.	V.G.	Good	Fair	Poor
600	500	—	—	—	—

Whitneyville Hartford Dragoon
Similar in appearance to the Walker colt this revolver is fitted with a 7-1/2" barrel and a silver plated iron backstrap and trigger guard. This is a limited edition with a total of 2,400 guns built with serial numbers between 1100 through 1340.

NIB	Exc.	V.G.	Good	Fair	Poor
475	400	350	300	200	150

Marine Dragoon
Special limited edition presentation grade in honor of U.S. Marine Corps.

NIB	Exc.	V.G.	Good	Fair	Poor
895	—	—	—	—	—

3rd Model Dragoon
Another large-frame revolver with 7-1/2" barrel with a brass backstrap, 3-screw frame, and unfluted cylinder.

NIB	Exc.	V.G.	Good	Fair	Poor
475	400	350	300	200	150

Steel Backstrap

NIB	Exc.	V.G.	Good	Fair	Poor
500	425	375	325	200	150

Fluted Cylinder

NIB	Exc.	V.G.	Good	Fair	Poor
510	435	375	325	200	150

Cochise Dragoon
This is a commemorative issue Third Model with gold inlay frame and barrel with special grips.

NIB	Exc.	V.G.	Good	Fair	Poor
895	—	—	—	—	—

Colt 1849 Model Pocket
A small-frame revolver chambered in .31 caliber with a 4" barrel. Fitted with one-piece walnut grips.

NIB	Exc.	V.G.	Good	Fair	Poor
435	375	325	275	200	150

Colt 1851 Model Navy
This is medium-frame revolver chambered in .36 caliber with 71/2" barrel. Walnut grips and case color frame.

NIB	Exc.	V.G.	Good	Fair	Poor
435	375	325	275	200	150

Colt 1851 Model Navy with Dual Cylinder

NIB	Exc.	V.G.	Good	Fair	Poor
475	400	350	300	200	150

Colt Model 1860 Army
This model is chamber in .44 caliber with roll engraved cylinder and one piece walnut grips. Barrel length is 8".

NIB	Exc.	V.G.	Good	Fair	Poor
435	375	325	275	200	150

Colt Model 1860 Army with Dual Cylinder

NIB	Exc.	V.G.	Good	Fair	Poor
475	400	350	300	200	150

Colt Model 1860 Army—Fluted Cylinder

NIB	Exc.	V.G.	Good	Fair	Poor
450	400	350	300	200	150

Colt 1860 Officer's Model
This is a deluxe version of the standard 1860 with a special blued finish and gold crossed sabres. This is a 4-screw frame with 8" barrel and 6-shot rebated cylinder.

NIB	Exc.	V.G.	Good	Fair	Poor
675	575	450	375	250	150

Colt Model 1860 Army Gold U.S. Cavalry
Features a gold engraved cylinder and gold barrel bands.

NIB	Exc.	V.G.	Good	Fair	Poor
650	575	450	375	250	150

Stainless Steel

NIB	Exc.	V.G.	Good	Fair	Poor
475	400	350	300	200	150

Colt 1860 Heirloom Edition
This is an elaborately engraved revolver done in the Tiffany-style and fitted with Tiffany-style grips.

NIB	Exc.	V.G.	Good	Fair	Poor
5000	—	—	—	—	—

Colt Model 1861 Navy
This .36 caliber revolver features a 7-1/2" barrel with engraved cylinder, case colored frame and one piece walnut grips.

NIB	Exc.	V.G.	Good	Fair	Poor
450	400	350	300	200	150

Colt Model 1861 Navy General Custer
Same as above but with engraved frame and cylinder.

NIB	Exc.	V.G.	Good	Fair	Poor
975	850	700	500	300	200

Colt Model 1862 Pocket Navy
This small-frame revolver is fitted with a round engraved cylinder with a 5" octagon barrel with hinged loading lever. Chambered for .36 caliber.

NIB	Exc.	V.G.	Good	Fair	Poor
435	375	325	275	200	150

Colt Model 1862 Trapper-Pocket Police
This small-frame revolver is fitted with a 3-1/2" barrel, silver backstrap, and trigger guard. The cylinder is semi-fluted and chambered in .36 caliber.

NIB	Exc.	V.G.	Good	Fair	Poor
435	375	325	275	200	150

COLTON MANUFACTURING CO.
Toledo, Ohio

The Colton Manufacturing Co. provided Sears with its first American-made hammerless house brand double. Sears advertised their sidelock hammerless gun as "the equal of any gun made, regardless of price" in their 1900 Fall catalog No. 110. There were four models: three side-plated boxlock-types and a unique unitized coil spring driven striker assembly version. All these, especially the latter, were designed to be mass produced. Many of the distinctive sidelock-within-a-sideplated model were produced but they are seldom seen today either because they were used-up or did not hold up well and were scrapped. Sears replaced Colton with the more traditional design Fryberg gun in 1902. Values depend on grade. There appear to be a least two levels of quality and condition ranging from $300 to $1,500. Colton-marked guns are scarce.

Courtesy Nick Niles, Paul Goodwin photo

COMBLAIN
Belgium and Brazil

Single-Shot Rifle

A 11x53Rmm caliber rifle with a falling block-action. Manufactured both in a hammerless and hammer version. Full stock secured by two barrel bands.

Exc.	V.G.	Good	Fair	Poor
750	650	500	350	250

CONNECTICUT ARMS CO.
Norfolk, Connecticut

Pocket Revolver

A .28 caliber spur trigger revolver with 3" octagonal barrel, 6-shot un-fluted cylinder, using a cup-primed cartridge and loads from the front of the cylinder. There is a hinged hook on the side of the frame under the cylinder that acts as the extractor. Silver-plated brass, blued with walnut grips. The barrel is marked "Conn. Arms Co. Norfolk, Conn." Approximately 2,700 manufactured in the 1860s.

Exc.	V.G.	Good	Fair	Poor
—	—	750	300	100

CONNECTICUT VALLEY ARMS CO.
Norcross, Georgia

SHOTGUNS

Brittany 11 Shotgun

A .410 bore double-barrel percussion shotgun with 24" barrels, double triggers and a walnut stock.

NIB	Exc.	V.G.	Good	Fair	Poor
170	150	125	100	75	50

Trapper Shotgun

This is a single barrel 12 gauge shotgun with a 28" barrel. The stock is a straight grip hardwood with checkering. Supplied with three interchangeable chokes. Weighs about 6 lbs.

NIB	Exc.	V.G.	Good	Fair	Poor
225	200	175	150	100	75

Classic Turkey Double-Barrel Shotgun

This is a 12 gauge percussion breech-loading shotgun with 28" barrel. The checkered stock is European walnut with straight grip. Weighs about 9 lbs.

NIB	Exc.	V.G.	Good	Fair	Poor
325	275	225	150	125	100

PISTOLS

Philadelphia Derringer
A .45 caliber single-shot percussion pistol with a 3.25" barrel and walnut stock.

NIB	Exc.	V.G.	Good	Fair	Poor
75	65	50	40	30	20

Sheriff's Model
A .36 caliber percussion revolver, nickel-plated with walnut grips.

NIB	Exc.	V.G.	Good	Fair	Poor
225	200	175	150	125	100

3rd Model Dragoon

NIB	Exc.	V.G.	Good	Fair	Poor
225	200	175	150	125	100

Colt Walker Replica

NIB	Exc.	V.G.	Good	Fair	Poor
275	250	225	200	175	150

Remington Bison

NIB	Exc.	V.G.	Good	Fair	Poor
250	225	200	175	150	125

Pocket Police

NIB	Exc.	V.G.	Good	Fair	Poor
135	110	100	85	65	45

Pocker Revolver
Chambered for .31 caliber. Fitted with 4" octagon barrel. Cylinder holds five bullets. Solid brass frame. Weighs about 15 oz.

NIB	Exc.	V.G.	Good	Fair	Poor
125	100	85	75	60	50

Wells Fargo

NIB	Exc.	V.G.	Good	Fair	Poor
165	145	125	100	75	50

1851 Navy

NIB	Exc.	V.G.	Good	Fair	Poor
135	110	100	85	65	45

1861 Navy

NIB	Exc.	V.G.	Good	Fair	Poor
150	135	110	90	75	50

1860 Army

NIB	Exc.	V.G.	Good	Fair	Poor
220	200	175	150	125	100

1858 Remington

NIB	Exc.	V.G.	Good	Fair	Poor
175	150	125	100	75	50

1858 Remington Target
As above, but fitted with adjustable sights.

NIB	Exc.	V.G.	Good	Fair	Poor
235	200	175	125	100	75

Bison
A 6-shot .44 caliber revolver with 10-1/4" octagonal barrel. Solid brass frame. Weighs about 48 oz.

NIB	Exc.	V.G.	Good	Fair	Poor
160	130	100	85	75	50

CONTENTO/VENTUR
Importer—Ventura
Seal Beach, California

This high-grade, double-barrel shotgun is no longer imported.

SIDE-BY-SIDE

Model 51
A 12, 16, 20, 28, and .410 bore boxlock double-barrel shotgun with 26", 28", 30", and 32" barrels, various chokes, extractors and double triggers. Checkered walnut stock. Introduced in 1980 and discontinued in 1985.

Exc.	V.G.	Good	Fair	Poor
500	350	300	225	150

Model 52
As above in 10 gauge.

Exc.	V.G.	Good	Fair	Poor
500	350	300	225	150

Model 53
As above, with scalloped receiver, automatic ejectors and available with a single-selective trigger. Discontinued in 1985.

Exc.	V.G.	Good	Fair	Poor
550	400	350	250	200

NOTE: Single-selective trigger add 25 percent.

Model 62
A 12, 20, or 28 gauge Holland & Holland sidelock shotgun with various barrel lengths and chokes, automatic ejectors, cocking indicators, a floral engraved receiver, a checkered, walnut stock. Discontinued in 1982.

Exc.	V.G.	Good	Fair	Poor
950	800	750	600	450

Model 64
As above, but more finely finished. No longer in production.

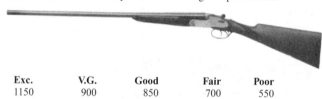

Exc.	V.G.	Good	Fair	Poor
1150	900	850	700	550

CONTINENTAL ARMS CO.
Liege, Belgium

Double Rifle
A .270, .303, .30-40, .30-06, .348, 375 H&H, .400 Jeffreys, .465, .475, .500, and .600 Nitro Express caliber Anson & Deeley boxlock double-barreled rifle with 24" or 26" barrels, and double triggers. Checkered walnut stock.

Exc.	V.G.	Good	Fair	Poor
6500	4500	3750	3000	2250

CONTINENTAL ARMS CO.
Norwich, Connecticut

Pepperbox
A .22 caliber 5-barrel pepperbox with a spur trigger and 2.5" barrels marked "Continental Arms Co. Norwich Ct. Patented Aug. 28, 1866." Some examples of this pistol are to be found marked "Ladies Companion."

Exc.	V.G.	Good	Fair	Poor
—	1850	850	350	250

COOK & BROTHER
RIFLES AND CARBINES
New Orleans

In early 1861, Ferdinand W.C. Cook and his brother, Francis L. Cook, both English emigres, joined to form Cook & Brother in New Orleans to manufacture rifles and carbines following the English P1853 series for the newly seceded state of Louisiana and its neighbors. Between

June 1861 and the federal occupation of New Orleans in April 1862, this firm produced about 200 cavalry and artillery carbines and about 1000 rifles. Having successfully moved the armory's machinery before federal occupation, the firm continued manufacture of rifles in Selma, Alabama, during 1862, probably completing another 1,000 rifles with the New Orleans lock markings from the parts brought with them. Re-established in Athens, Georgia, in early 1863, the firm continued to build both carbines and rifles, manufacturing more than 5,500 above the New Orleans production through 1864. The firm's products were clearly among the best small arms made within the Confederacy.

Cook & Brother Rifles (New Orleans & Selma production)
Overall length 48-3/4"; barrel length 33"; caliber .58. Markings: representation of a Confederate flag ("Stars & Bars") and "COOK & BROTHER/N.O./1861 (or) 1862" on lock; same usually on barrel, together with serial number and "PROVED" near breech. Rifles in the early production have long range rear sights and unusual two piece block and blade front sights as well as an integral bayonet lug with guide on right side of barrel. Later production utilizes a brass clamping ring for the bayonet, a block open rear sight and a simple block and blade front sight. Earlier production will claim a premium if in good condition.

Exc.	V.G.	Good	Fair	Poor
—	—	30000	12500	3000

Cook & Brother Carbines (New Orleans production)
Overall length 40" (artillery), 37" (cavalry); barrel length 24" (artillery), 21" to 21-1/2" (cavalry); caliber .58. Markings: As on Cook & Brother rifles (New Orleans production) artillery and cavalry carbines were produced in New Orleans in a separate serial range from the rifles. Total production is thought not to have exceeded 225, divided evenly between 1861 and 1862 dates. In addition to the overall and barrel lengths, the main difference between the artillery and cavalry carbines is the manner in which they were carried. The former bears standard sling rings on the upper band and the trigger guard strap, the latter has a bar with a ring on the left side of the stock. Both are exceedingly rare.

Exc.	V.G.	Good	Fair	Poor
—	—	17500	6500	5000

Cook & Brother Rifles (Athens production)
Overall length 49"; barrel length 33"; caliber .58. Markings: representation of a Confederate flag ("Stars & Bars") and "COOK & BROTHER/ATHENS GA./date (1863 or 1864), and serial number on lock; "PROVED" and serial number near breech; serial number on various metal parts. After re-establishing their plant at Athens, Georgia, in the spring of 1863, Cook & Brother continued to manufacture rifles in a consecutive serial range after their New Orleans/Selma production (beginning about serial number 2000) and continued to make arms well into 1864 (through at least serial number 7650) until Sherman's army threatened the plant and necessitated the employment of its workforce in a military capacity as the 23rd Battalion Georgia State Guard.

Exc.	V.G.	Good	Fair	Poor
—	—	17500	7500	3000

Cook & Brother Carbines (Athens production)
Overall length 40" (artillery) or 37" (cavalry); barrel lengths 24" (artillery) or 21" to 21-1/2" (cavalry); caliber .58. Markings: same as on Athens production rifles. Artillery and cavalry carbines were manufactured in the same serial range as the Athens production rifles (about 2000 through 7650). As in New Orleans production, the artillery and cavalry carbines are distinguished from one another by their respective lengths. Unlike New Orleans/Selma production, however, some of the cavalry carbines are mounted with sling swivels of the artillery style, while others bear the sling ring on the left side and additionally have a swivel ring to secure the ramrod.

Exc.	V.G.	Good	Fair	Poor
—	—	22500	8000	3500

COOPER, J. M. & CO.
Philadelphia, Pennsylvania

Pocket Revolver
A .31 caliber percussion double-action revolver with 4", 5", or 6" octagonal barrel, and a 6-shot unfluted cylinder. Blued with walnut grips. During the first two years of production they were made in Pittsburgh, Pennsylvania, and were so marked. Approximately 15,000 were manufactured between 1864 and 1869.

Exc.	V.G.	Good	Fair	Poor
—	—	1500	600	150

NOTE: Pittsburgh-marked models add 20 percent.

COPELAND, FRANK
Worcester, Massachusetts

Copeland Pocket Revolver .22
A .22 cartridge spur trigger revolver with a 2.5" barrel, 7-shot magazine, an unfluted cylinder and lock notches on the front. Frame is brass, blued walnut, or rosewood grips. The barrel marked "F. Copeland, Worcester, Mass." Manufactured in the 1860s.

Exc.	V.G.	Good	Fair	Poor
—	650	300	125	100

Copeland .32 Revolver
A .32 caliber spur trigger revolver with a 5-shot fluted cylinder and an iron frame. Nickel-plated. The barrel marked "F. Copeland, Sterling, Mass." Manufactured in the 1860s.

Exc.	V.G.	Good	Fair	Poor
—	650	300	150	75

CRESCENT F. A. CO.
Norwich, Connecticut

Text and prices by Nick Niles

The company made good quality inexpensive single and double-barrel shotguns at its Norwich works, beginning about 1892. It was bought by H&D Folsom of New York City, large importers and distributors of firearms and sporting goods, so they could add an American-made sidelock hammer, side-by-side to their extensive range of imported guns. The Crescent guns were offered in 12, 16, 20, and 28 gauges and later, 44XL shot caliber with Damascus twist laminated or Armory steel barrels depending on the shooter's wants. In 1898 VL&D said these were the best American hammer guns in the market for the money.

Huge quantities of these "Hardware Guns" were produced in a profusion of private brands as well as in Folsom's house brand "American Gun Co. of NY." In 1922 the Crescent brand replaced the "American Gun Co. of NY" and can be found on many thousands of doubles. In 1905 Crescent's first hammerless sidelock was introduced as the American Gun Co. "Knickerbocker" Model No. 6. This very popular model became the Crescent "Peerless" No. 6 in 1922. In 1928 it became the Crescent "Empire" No. 60 and in 1931 the Crescent-Davis "New Empire" No. 88, "New Empire" No. 9, and "Empire" No. 9.

Crescent was bought by J. Stevens Arms Co., Division of Savage Arms Corp. about 1930. It was merged with Davis-Warner Arms Corp. successors to N.R. Davis & Sons Co. and became Crescent-Davis Arms Corp. In 1932 the operation was moved to the Stevens plant at Springfield, Mass. where some sidelock doubles were assembled, Crescent-Davis brand guns remained in Steven's full line catalog until 1941 but from 1937 to 1941 the doubles sold in the C-D brand were on either Stevens or Davis boxlock frames.

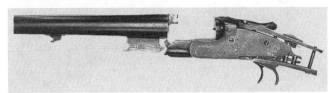

DOUBLES

Triumph—Hammerless Boxlock

Exc.	V.G.	Good	Fair	Poor
700	600	400	300	200

Model 2655—Laminated Barrels Hammer Sidelock

Exc.	V.G.	Good	Fair	Poor
500	400	300	200	150

Model 2665—Damascus Barrels Hammer Sidelock

Exc.	V.G.	Good	Fair	Poor
500	400	300	200	150

Crescent American Hammer Gun No. 0—Hammer Sidelock

Exc.	V.G.	Good	Fair	Poor
350	300	250	200	100

American Machine Made 2641—Hammer Sidelock

Exc.	V.G.	Good	Fair	Poor
400	350	300	250	200

American Machine Made 2650—Hammer Sidelock

Exc.	V.G.	Good	Fair	Poor
500	400	350	300	250

American Machine Made 2660—Damascus Barrels Hammer Sidelock

Exc.	V.G.	Good	Fair	Poor
600	500	450	350	300

American Gun Co. NY No. 1 Armory—Hammerless Sidelock

Exc.	V.G.	Good	Fair	Poor
400	300	250	200	100

American Gun Co. NY No. 2—Hammerless Sidelock

Exc.	V.G.	Good	Fair	Poor
500	400	300	250	200

American Gun Co. No. 3—Damascus Barrels Hammer Sidelock

Exc.	V.G.	Good	Fair	Poor
600	500	400	300	250

American Gun Co. No. 4—Hammer Sidelock

Exc.	V.G.	Good	Fair	Poor
700	600	500	400	300

American Gun Co. No. 5—Damascus Barrels Hammer Sidelock

Exc.	V.G.	Good	Fair	Poor
800	700	600	450	350

Folsom Arms Co. No. 0 Armory—Hammer Sidelock

Exc.	V.G.	Good	Fair	Poor
400	300	250	200	100

Folsom Arms Co. No. 2—Hammer Sidelock

Exc.	V.G.	Good	Fair	Poor
500	400	300	200	150

Folsom Arms Co. No. 3—Damascus Barrel

Exc.	V.G.	Good	Fair	Poor
600	450	350	300	200

Knickerbocker No. 6 Armory—Hammerless Sidelock

Courtesy Nick Niles, Paul Goodwin photo

Exc.	V.G.	Good	Fair	Poor
400	300	250	200	100

Knickerbocker No. 7—Hammerless Sidelock

Exc.	V.G.	Good	Fair	Poor
400	300	250	200	100

Knickerbocker No. 8—Damascus Barrels Hammerless Sidelock

Exc.	V.G.	Good	Fair	Poor
500	400	300	250	200

New Knickerbocker Armory—Hammerless Sidelock

Exc.	V.G.	Good	Fair	Poor
400	300	250	200	100

New Knickerbocker WT—Hammerless Sidelock

Courtesy Nick Niles, Paul Goodwin photo

Exc.	V.G.	Good	Fair	Poor
450	350	250	200	150

New Knickerbocker Damascus Barrels—Hammerless Sidelock

Exc.	V.G.	Good	Fair	Poor
500	400	300	250	200

American Gun Co. Small Bore No. 28—Straight Stock Hammer Sidelock

Exc.	V.G.	Good	Fair	Poor
800	700	600	400	300

American Gun Co. Small Bore No. 44—Straight Stock Hammer Sidelock

Exc.	V.G.	Good	Fair	Poor
900	750	650	450	350

American Gun Co. No. 0—Armory Straight Stock—Hammer Sidelock

Exc.	V.G.	Good	Fair	Poor
350	300	250	200	100

American Gun Co. No. 28—Nitro Straight Stock—Hammer Sidelock

Exc.	V.G.	Good	Fair	Poor
800	650	550	400	300

American Gun Co. No. 44—Nitro Straight Stock—Hammer Sidelock

Exc.	V.G.	Good	Fair	Poor
900	750	600	450	350

American Gun Co. Midget Field No. 28—Hammer Sidelock

Exc.	V.G.	Good	Fair	Poor
800	650	400	400	300

American Gun Co. Midget Field No. 44—Hammer Sidelock

Exc.	V.G.	Good	Fair	Poor
900	750	650	500	350

Crescent 1922 Model No. 66—Quali—Hammerless Sidelock

Exc.	V.G.	Good	Fair	Poor
600	500	450	350	250

Crescent Firearms Co. No. 0—Hammer Sidelock

Exc.	V.G.	Good	Fair	Poor
400	350	250	200	150

Crescent Firearms Co. No. 0—Nickel—Hammer Sidelock

Exc.	V.G.	Good	Fair	Poor
500	400	350	250	200

Crescent Firearms Co. No. 6—Peerless—Hammerless Sidelock

Exc.	V.G.	Good	Fair	Poor
400	350	250	200	150

Crescent Firearms Co. No. 6E—Peerless Engraved—Hammerless Sidelock

Exc.	V.G.	Good	Fair	Poor
600	450	350	250	200

Crescent Firearms Co. No. 66—Quali—Hammerless Sidelock

Exc.	V.G.	Good	Fair	Poor
650	500	400	300	200

Crescent Firearms Co. No. 60—Empire—Hammerless Sidelock

Exc.	V.G.	Good	Fair	Poor
450	400	350	300	200

Crescent Firearms Co. No. 6—Peerless—Hammerless Sidelock

Courtesy Nick Niles, Paul Goodwin photo

Exc.	V.G.	Good	Fair	Poor
400	350	300	200	150

Crescent Firearms Co. No. 44—Improved—Hammer Sidelock

Exc.	V.G.	Good	Fair	Poor
700	600	500	400	300

Crescent Empire No. 60—Hammerless Sidelock

Exc.	V.G.	Good	Fair	Poor
350	300	250	200	100

New Crescent Empire Red Butt—Hammerless Sidelock

Exc.	V.G.	Good	Fair	Poor
400	350	250	200	150

Crescent New Empire No. 88—Hammerless Sidelock

Exc.	V.G.	Good	Fair	Poor
400	350	250	200	150

Crescent New Empire No. 9—Hammerless Sidelock

Exc.	V.G.	Good	Fair	Poor
350	300	250	200	100

Crescent Certified Empire No. 60—Hammerless Sidelock

Exc.	V.G.	Good	Fair	Poor
400	300	250	200	150

Crescent Certified Empire No. 9—Hammerless Sidelock

Exc.	V.G.	Good	Fair	Poor
450	350	300	250	200

Crescent Certified Empire No. 88—Hammerless Sidelock

Exc.	V.G.	Good	Fair	Poor
500	450	400	350	300

Crescent Davis No. 600—Hammerless Boxlock

Courtesy Nick Niles, Paul Goodwin photo

Exc.	V.G.	Good	Fair	Poor
400	350	300	250	200

Crescent Davis No. 900—Hammerless Boxlock

Exc.	V.G.	Good	Fair	Poor
500	450	400	350	300

Revolver

A typical S&W copy made by Crescent in Norwich, Connecticut. It was a top-break, double-action, that was found either blued or nickel-plated with checkered, black hard rubber grips. The cylinder held 5 shots and was chambered for the .32 S&W cartridge.

Exc.	V.G.	Good	Fair	Poor
200	150	125	85	40

BRAND NAMES USED BY CRESCENT ARMS

American Bar Lock Wonder made for Sears, Roebuck & Co.
American Boy made for Townley Metal & Hardware Co.
American Gun Co. (H & D Folsom house brand)
American Gun Company of New York
American Nitro
Armory Gun Co.
Baker Gun Co. (if no foreign proof marks)
T. Barker New York-if a sidelock hammerless double without proofs.
Bellmore Gun Co.
Berkshire No. 3000 made for Shapleigh Hardware Co. of St. Louis, MO
Black Beauty-hammerless doubles
Bluefield Clipper
Bluegrass Arms Co. made for Belknap Hardware Co. of Louisville, KY
Blue Whistler
Bridge Black Prince
Bridge Gun Co.
Bridge Gun Works
Bridgeport Arms Co. (if no foreign proof marks)
Bright Arms Co.
Canadian Belle
Carolina Arms Co. made for Smith Wadsworth Hardware Co. of Charlotte, NC
Caroline Arms
Central Arm Co. made for Shapleigh Hardware Co. of St. Louis, MO
Chatham Arms Co.
Cherokee Arms Co. made for C. M. McClung Co. of Knoxville, TN
Chesapeake Gun Co.
Chicago Long Range Wonder 1908-1918 made for Sears, Roebuck & Co. of Chicago, IL
Colonial
Columbian New York Arms Co.
Compeer made for Van Camp Hardware & Iron Co. of Indianapolis, IN
Connecticut Arms Co.
Cumberland Arms Co.
Crescent Fire Arms Co.
Creve Cour (if no foreign proof marks) made for Isaac Walker Hardware Co. of Peoria, IL
Cruso
Daniel Boone Gun Co. made for Belknap Hardware Co. of Louisville, KY
Delphian Arms Co. (some models without foreign proof marks) made for Supplee-Biddle Hardware Co. of Philadelphia, PA
Delphian Manufacturing Co. (some models)
Diamond Arms Co. (some models) made for Shapleigh Hardware Co. of St. Louis, MO
Dunlap Special made for Dunlap Hardware Co. of Macon, GA
E.C. Mac made for E.C. Meacham Arms Co. of St. Louis, MO
Elgin Arms Co. made for Strauss & Schram and Fred Biffar & Co. both of Chicago, IL
Elmira Arms Co.
Empire Arms Co. made for Sears, Roebuck & Co. of Chicago, IL
Empire State Arms Co.
Enders Oakleaf made for Shapleigh Hardware Co. of St. Louis, MO
Enders Special Service made for Shapleigh Hardware Co.
Enders Royal Service made for Shapleigh Hardware Co.
Essex made for Belknap Hardware Co. of Louisville, KY
Excel made for Montgomery Ward & Co. of Chicago, IL
Farwell Arms Co. made for Farwell, Ozmun & Kirk of St. Paul, MN
Faultless made for John M. Smythe Co. of Chicago, IL
Faultless Goose Gun made for John M. Smyth Co. of Chicago, IL
Field after 1894, The
Folsom Arms Co. (also used by H & D Folsom on Belgian imports)
F.F. Forbes (H & D Folsom house brand)

Fort Pitt Arms Co.
Fremont Arms Co. (also used on Belgian imports)
Gold Medal Wonder
Greenfield (some models) made for Hibbard, Spencer, Bartlett & Co. of Chicago, IL
H.B.C. (some models) made for Hudson's Bay Co. of Canada.
H.S.B. & Co. (some models) made for Hibbard, Spencer, Bartlett & Co. of Chicago, IL
Hanover Arms Co. (if no foreign proof marks)
S.H. Harrington (if no foreign proof marks)
Hartford Arms Co. made for both Simmons Hardware and Shapleigh Hardware Co. of St. Louis, MO
Harvard (H & D Folsom house brand)
Hermitage (some models) made for Grey-Dusley Hardware Co. of Nashville, TN
Hip Spe Bar (some models) made for Hibbard, Spencer, Bartlett & Co. of Chicago, IL
Hibbard (some models) made for Hibbard, Spencer, Bartlett & Co. of Chicago, IL
Howard Arms Co. made for Fred Biffar & Co. of Chicago, IL
Hudson (some models) made for Hibbard, Spencer, Bartlett & Co. of Chicago, IL
Hunter made for Belknap Hardware Co. Louisville, KY
Interstate Arms Co. made for Townley Metal & Hardware Co. of Kansas City, MO
Jackson Arms Co. made for C.M. McClung & Co. of Knoxville, TN
Joseph Arms Co. Norwich, Conn.
K K and Keen Kufter (some models) made for Shapleigh Hardware Co. of St. Louis, MO
Kingsland Special and Kingsland 10 Star made for Geller, Ward & Hasner of St. Louis, MO
Kirk Gun Co. made for Farwell, Ozmun & Kirk of St. Paul, MN
Knickerbocker (up to 1915, H & D Folsom house brand)
Knockabout (before 1925) made for Montgomery Ward & Co. of Chicago, IL
Knoxall (only hammerless doubles)
Laclede Gun Co.
Lakeside made for Montgomery Ward & Co. of Chicago, IL
Leader Gun Co. made for Charles Williams Stores of New York, NY
Lee's Special and Lee's Munner Special made for Lee Hardware Co. of Salina, KS
Long Range Marvel, Long Range Winner, and Long Range Wonder made between 1893 to 1909 for Sears, Roebuck & Co. of Chicago, IL F.A. Loomis
Marshwood
Massachusetts Arms Co. made before 1920 for Blish, Mizet and Silliman Hardware Co. of Atchison, KS
Mears (if no foreign proof marks)
Metropolitan made for Siegal-Cooper Co. of New York, NY
Minnesota Arms Co. made for Farwell, Ozmun, Kirk & Co. of St. Paul, MN
Mississippi Arms Co. St. Louis (some models) made for Shepleigh Hardware Co. of St. Louis, MO
Mississippi Valley Arms Co. (some models) made for Shapleigh Hardware Co. of St. Louis, MO
Mohawk made for Glish, Mizet and Lilliman Hardware Co. of Atchinson, KS
Monitor
Murdock, R. National Firearms Co. (some models)
National Arms Co. hammer doubles (without foreign proof marks) and hammerless doubles made for May Hardware Co. of Washington, D.C. and Moskowitz and Herbach Co. of Philadelphia, PA
New Britain Arms Co.'s Monarch
New Elgin Arms Co.
New Empire
New England (some models after 1914) made for Sears, Roebuck & Co.
New England Arms Co. (some models)
Newport Model CN made for Hibbard, Spencer, Bartlett and Co. of Chicago
Newport Model WN (some models) made for Hibbard, Spencer, Bartlett and Co. of Chicago
New Rival made for Van Camp Hardware and Iron Co. of Indianapolis, IN

New York Arms Co. made for Garnet Carter Co. of Chattanooga, TN
New York Machine Made (some models)
New York Match Gun (some models)
New York Nitro Hammerless
Nitro Bird made for Conover Hardware Co. of Kansas City, MO
Nitro Hunter made for Belknap Hardware Co. of Louisville, KY
Nitro King 1908 to 1917 made for Sears, Roebuck & Co. of Chicago, IL
Norwich Arms Co.
Not-Noc Manufacturing Co. made for Belknap Hardware Co. of Louisville, KY and Canton Hardware Co. of Canton, OH
Osprey made for Lou J. Eppinger, Detroit, MI
Oxford made for Belknap Hardware Co. of Louisville, KY
Peerless (H & D Folsom house brand)
Perfection made for H. G. Lipscomb & Co. of Nashville, TN
Piedmont made for Piedmont Hardware Co. of Danville, PA
Piedmont Arms Co.
Pioneer Arms (if no foreign proof marks) made for Kruse and Baklmann Hardware Co. of Cincinnati, OH
Quail (H & D Folsom house brand)
Queen City made for Elmira Arms Co. of Elmira, NY
Red Chieftan (model 60) made for Supplee Biddle Hardware Co. of Philadelphia, PA
Rev-O-Noc (some models) made for Hibbard, Spencer, Bartlett & Co. of Chicago, IL
Rich-Con made for Richardson & Conover Hardware Co.
Charles Richter (some models) made for New York Sporting Goods Co. of New York, NY
Rickard Arms Co. made for J. A. Rickard Co. of Schenectady, NY
Rival (some models) made for Van Camp Hardware and Iron Co. of Indianapolis, IN
Rocket Special
Royal Service made for Shapleigh Hardware Co. of St. Louis, MO
Rummel Arms Co. made for A. J. Rummel Arms Co. of Toledo, OH
Ruso (if no foreign proof marks)
St. Louis Arms Co. (sidelock hammerless doubles) made for Shapleigh Hardware Co. of St. Louis, MO
Seminole (hammerless) unknown
Shue's Special made for Ira M. Shue of Hanover, PA
Smithsonian (some models)
John M. Smythe & Co. made for John M. Smythe Hardware Co. of Chicago, IL
Southern Arms Co. (some models)
Special Service made for Shapleigh Hardware Co. of St. Louis, MO
Spencer Gun Co. made for Hibbard, Spencer, Bartlett & Co. of Chicago, IL
Sportsman (some models) made for W. Bingham & Co. of Cleveland, OH
Springfield Arms Co. used until 1930. (H & D Folsom house brand). This brand was also used by Stevens and James Warner guns.
Square Deal made for Stratton, Warren Hardware Co. of Memphis, TN
Star Leader (some models)
State Arms Co. made for J.H. Lau & Co. of New York, NY
Sterling Arms Co.
Sullivan Arms Co. made for Sullivan Hardware Co. of Anderson, SC
Superior (some models) made for Paxton & Gallagher Co. of Omaha, NE
Syco (some models) made for Wyeth Hardware Co. of St. Joseph, MO
Ten Star & Ten Star Heavy Duty (if no foreign proof marks) made for Geller, Ward & Hasner Co. of St. Louis, MO
Tiger (if no foreign proof marks) made for J.H. Hall & Co. of Nashville, TN
Townley's Pal and Townley's American Boy made for Townley Metal & Hardware Co. of Kansas City, MO
Trap's Best made for Watkins, Cottrell Co. of Richmond, VA
Triumph (some models) made for Sears, Roebuck & Co. of Chicago, IL
Tryon Special (some models) made for Edward K. Tryon Co. of Philadelphia, PA
U.S. Arms Co. (if no foreign proof marks) made for Supplee-Biddle Hardware Co. of Philadelphia, PA
U.S. Field
Utica Firearms Co. (some models) made for Simmons Hardware Co. of St. Louis, MO

Victor & Victor Special made for Hibbard, Spencer, Bartlett & Co. of Chicago, IL
Virginia Arms Co. made for Virginia-Carolina Co. of Richmond, VA
Volunteer (some models) made for Belknap Hardware Co. of Louisville, KY
Vulcan Arms Co. made for Edward K. Tryon Co. of Philadelphia, PA
Warren Arms Co. (if no foreign proof marks)
Washington Arms Co. (some models)
Wauregan (some models)
Wautauga (some models) made for Wallace Hardware Co. Morristown, TN
Wildwood made for Sears, Roebuck & Co. of Chicago, IL
Wilkinson Arms Co. (if no foreign proof marks) made for Richmond Hardware Co. of Richmond, VA
Wilshire Arms Co. made for Stauffer, Eshleman & Co. of New Orleans, LA
Winfield Arms Co. (H & D Folsom house brand)
Winoca Arms Co. made for Jacobi Hardware Co. of Philadelphia, PA
Witte Hardware Co. (some models) made for Witte Hardware Co. of St. Louis, MO
Wolverine Arms Co. made for Fletcher Hardware Co. of Wilmington, NC
Worthington Arms Co. made for George Worthington Co. of Cleveland, OH

CRISPIN, SILAS
New York, New York

Crispin Revolver

A .32 Crispin caliber 5- or 6-shot revolver produced in limited quantities. Some are marked "Smith Arms Co., New York City. Crispin's Pat. Oct. 3, 1865." The most noteworthy feature of these revolvers is that the cylinder is constructed in two pieces so that the belted Crispin cartridge can be used. It is believed that these revolvers were only made on an experimental basis, between 1865 and 1867.

Exc.	V.G.	Good	Fair	Poor
—	—	18000	7000	2500

CUMMINGS, O. S.
Lowell, Massachusetts

Cummings Pocket Revolver

A .22 caliber spur trigger revolver with a 3.5" ribbed round barrel, and a 7-shot fluted cylinder. Nickel-plated with rosewood grip. The barrel is stamped "O.S. Cummings Lowell, Mass." Approximately 1,000 manufactured in the 1870s.

Exc.	V.G.	Good	Fair	Poor
—	650	300	150	100

CUMMINGS & WHEELER
Lowell, Massachusetts

Pocket Revolver

Similar to the Cummings Pocket Revolver with subtle differences such as the length of the flutes on the cylinder and the size and shape of the grip. The barrel is slightly longer and is marked "Cummings & Wheeler, Lowell, Mass."

Exc.	V.G.	Good	Fair	Poor
—	700	350	150	100

D

DAKIN GUN CO.
San Francisco, California

Model 100

A 12 and 20 gauge boxlock double-barrel shotgun with 26" or 28" barrels, various chokes, extractors and double triggers. Engraved, blued, with a checkered walnut stock. Manufactured in the 1960s.

Exc.	V.G.	Good	Fair	Poor
400	325	275	200	100

Model 147

As above, with ventilated rib barrels.

Exc.	V.G.	Good	Fair	Poor
450	375	250	200	100

Model 160

As above with a single-selective trigger.

Exc.	V.G.	Good	Fair	Poor
475	400	350	250	150

Model 215

As above, but more finely finished.

Exc.	V.G.	Good	Fair	Poor
950	850	700	500	250

Model 170

A 12, 16, and 20 gauge Over/Under shotgun with 26" or 28" ventilated rib barrels, various chokes, and double triggers. Blued and lightly engraved. Discontinued in the 1960s.

Exc.	V.G.	Good	Fair	Poor
500	425	350	275	150

DAKOTA ARMS, INC.
Sturgis, South Dakota

This company was formed by Don Allen. He was a fine craftsmen in the field of custom rifles. The company offers four basic models with a number of options to fit the customers' needs or wants. The workmanship and materials are of the highest quality. They have been in business since 1987.

NOTE: All prices are base prices. Dakota offers a number of extra cost options that can greatly affect the value of its rifles and shotguns.

Model 10 Single-Shot

Built on a single-shot falling action this rifle features a 23" barrel and choice of XX grade wood with oil finish. Fine line checkering, steel gripcap, and 1/2" recoil pad are also standard. Weighs about 5.5 lbs.

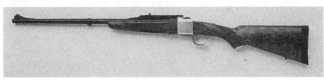

NIB	Exc.	V.G.	Good	Fair	Poor
3495	2500	1750	—	—	—

Little Sharps Rifle

Introduced in 2003 this is a smaller version (20 percent) of the full size Sharps rifle. Standard rifle has a 26" octagon barrel, straight grips stock with XX walnut, steel buttplate and blade front sight. Offered in calibers from .17 HMR to .30-40 Krag. Weight is around 8 lbs.

NIB	Exc.	V.G.	Good	Fair	Poor
3000	—	—	—	—	—

SHOTGUNS

Dakota American Legend

Introduced in 1996, this side-by-side shotgun is offered in 12, 20 and 28 gauge, and .410 bore with 27" barrels, concave rib, splinter forearm, double triggers, straight grips stock, and full scroll engraving on the frame. Many additional extra cost options are offered that can greatly affect the price. The base price is listed.

NIB	Exc.	V.G.	Good	Fair	Poor
18000	14000	—	—	—	—

Dakota Shotgun
Similar to the American Legend but offered in two grades of finish. These new grades were first offered in 1997.

Classic Grade
This grade features a case colored round-action with straight grip and fancy walnut oil finish stock. Forearm is splinter type. Double trigger standard with choice of chokes. This model is no longer in production.

NIB	Exc.	V.G.	Good	Fair	Poor
7950	12500	—	—	—	—

Premier Grade
This grade features a case colored round-action with 50 percent engraving coverage. Exhibition grade English walnut stock with straight grip and splinter forearm. Oil rubbed finish. Double triggers are standard with choice of chokes.

NIB	Exc.	V.G.	Good	Fair	Poor
13950	9500	—	—	—	—

NOTE: Add 10 percent for 28 gauge and .410 bore.

DALY, CHARLES
Importer—KBI, Inc.
Harrisburg, Pennsylvania

An importer of German, Japanese, and Italian shotguns and combination guns.

Superior Side-by-Side
A boxlock over-and-under with an Anson & Deeley boxlock action and double triggers. Blued with a walnut stock. Not manufactured after 1933.

Exc.	V.G.	Good	Fair	Poor
1200	850	650	450	250

Empire Side-by-Side
As above, but engraved with a better grade of walnut.

Exc.	V.G.	Good	Fair	Poor
2500	2000	1750	1250	600

Diamond Grade Side-by-Side
A deluxe version of the above.

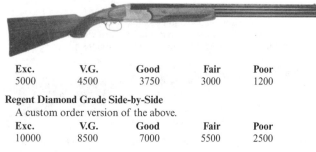

Exc.	V.G.	Good	Fair	Poor
5000	4500	3750	3000	1200

Regent Diamond Grade Side-by-Side
A custom order version of the above.

Exc.	V.G.	Good	Fair	Poor
10000	8500	7000	5500	2500

CHARLES DALY, B.C. MIROKU GUNS

Empire Grade Side-by-Side
A 12, 16, and 20 gauge Anson and Deeley boxlock shotgun with 26", 28", and 30" barrels, various chokes, extractors, and a single trigger. Blued with a checkered walnut stock. Manufactured between 1968 and 1971.

Exc.	V.G.	Good	Fair	Poor
600	450	300	200	100

NOTE: Add 10 percent for ventilated rib barrels and/or 20 gauge.

Superior Grade Single Barrel Trap
A 12 gauge boxlock shotgun with 32" or 34" ventilated rib barrels, Full choke, and automatic ejector. Blued with Monte Carlo walnut stock. Manufactured between 1968 and 1976.

Exc.	V.G.	Good	Fair	Poor
550	500	450	350	200

SIDE-BY-SIDE GUNS

Field Hunter
A side-by-side boxlock gun chambered for 10, 12, 20, 28 and .410. Barrel length from 26" to 32" depending on gauge. Extractors are standard. Add $100 for ejectors. Weight from 8.75 lbs. to 6.75 lbs. depending on gauge. Nickel receiver with game scene engraving.

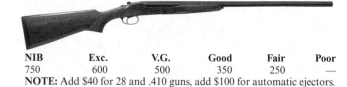

NIB	Exc.	V.G.	Good	Fair	Poor
750	600	500	350	250	—

NOTE: Add $40 for 28 and .410 guns, add $100 for automatic ejectors.

Superior Hunter
A 12, 20, and 28 gauge as well as .410 bore boxlock double-barrel shotgun with 26" or 28" barrels, various chokes, a boxlock action and single trigger. Blued with a walnut stock. In 2002 this model was offered in 10 gauge with 28" barrels.

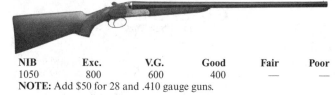

NIB	Exc.	V.G.	Good	Fair	Poor
1050	800	600	400	—	—

NOTE: Add $50 for 28 and .410 gauge guns.

Empire Side-by-Side
Offered in 12 and 20 gauge with 26" or 28" barrels. Chokes are fixed. Weight is about 7 lbs. Silver receiver with game scene engraving, straight stock, splinter forearm, automatic ejectors.

NIB	Exc.	V.G.	Good	Fair	Poor
1350	1000	750	500	—	—

Diamond Side-by-Side
Offered in 12, 20, 28, and .410 with 26" or 28" barrels and fixed chokes. Fancy walnut straight grip stock, hand detachable sidelocks, 100 percent hand engraving coverage. Hand fit and finished. Weight for 12 and 20 gauge guns is about 6.75 lbs., while the 28 and .410 guns weigh about 5.75 lbs. This model is generally made on special order only.

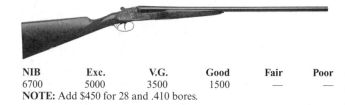

NIB	Exc.	V.G.	Good	Fair	Poor
6700	5000	3500	1500	—	—

NOTE: Add $450 for 28 and .410 bores.

Country Squire Side-by-Side Folding
This model features a folding stock with 25.5" barrels, gold double triggers and walnut stock. Chokes are Full and Full.

NIB	Exc.	V.G.	Good	Fair	Poor
475	375	275	—	—	—

Country Squire Over-and-Under Folding
Same as the model above but with over-and-under vent-rib barrels 25.5" in length.

NIB	Exc.	V.G.	Good	Fair	Poor
550	450	325	—	—	—

DAN ARMS OF AMERICA
Allentown, Pennsylvania

These are Italian-made shotguns manufactured by Silmer and imported by Dan Arms of America. They were no longer produced after 1988.

SIDE-BY-SIDES

Field Grade
A boxlock shotgun chambered for all gauges with 26" or 28" barrels, various choke combinations, double triggers and extractors. Blued with a walnut stock.

Exc.	V.G.	Good	Fair	Poor
300	265	225	150	125

Deluxe Field Grade
As above, with a single trigger and automatic ejectors.

Exc.	V.G.	Good	Fair	Poor
450	400	325	250	200

DANCE & BROTHERS CONFEDERATE REVOLVERS
Columbia, Texas

J.H., G.P., and D.E. Dance began production of percussion revolvers for the Confederate States of America in Columbia, Texas, in mid-1862, moving to Anderson, Texas, in early 1864. Based on surviving serial numbers, the combined output at both places did not exceed 350 pistols. Most of these were in the "Army" (.44 caliber) size but a limited number of "Navy" (.36 caliber) were also manufactured. Nearly all are distinguished by the absence of a "recoil shield" on the frame behind the cylinders. As Colt M1851 "Navy" revolvers closely resemble the Dance Navy revolvers, great care must be exercised in examining revolvers purported to be Dance Navies.

.44 Caliber

Exc.	V.G.	Good	Fair	Poor
—	—	62500	18500	5000

.36 Caliber

Exc.	V.G.	Good	Fair	Poor
—	—	67500	20000	7000

DARNE, S. A.
St. Etienne, France

Darne Side-by-Side Shotguns
A 12, 16, 20, or 28 gauge sliding breech double-barrel shotgun manufactured in a variety of barrel lengths and with numerous optional features. Manufactured from 1881 to 1979.

Model R11

Exc.	V.G.	Good	Fair	Poor
1000	900	750	600	350

Model R15

Exc.	V.G.	Good	Fair	Poor
2500	2000	1750	1500	750

Model V19

Exc.	V.G.	Good	Fair	Poor
3250	3000	2750	2250	1250

Model V22

Exc.	V.G.	Good	Fair	Poor
3750	3500	3000	2500	1200

Model V Hors Series No. I

Exc.	V.G.	Good	Fair	Poor
4500	4000	3750	3250	1500

DAVENPORT FIREARMS CO.
Providence, Rhode Island
Norwich, Connecticut

DOUBLE-BARREL SHOTGUNS
Text and prices by Nick Niles

William Hastings Davenport's company also made and marked double-barrel, visible hammer guns in Providence, R.I. on Orange St., 1880-1882 and in Norwich, Conn. ca. 1890-1909. All are monbloc designs of which there were four models. The 1st model made at Providence, ca. 1881, had hammers rising out of the boxlock frame. The 2nd model, made in Norwich, Conn. about 1898, is a typical boxlock. The 3rd model made in Norwich, Conn., ca. 1909, has small sidelocks set in larger boxlock frames. Its barrels have unnotched extensions and notched underlugs. The 4th model, also from Norwich, possibly made after the 1901 takeover by Hopkins & Allen, also has sidelocks set in boxlock frames but the barrels have half moon lugs and notched barrel extensions. Few Davenport doubles are seen although single barrel guns are often found.

1st Model

Exc.	V.G.	Good	Fair	Poor
1000	800	500	400	300

2nd Model

Exc.	V.G.	Good	Fair	Poor
600	400	300	200	150

3rd Model

Exc.	V.G.	Good	Fair	Poor
1000	800	500	400	300

4th Model

Exc.	V.G.	Good	Fair	Poor
800	400	300	250	200

Single Barrel Shotgun
A 10, 12, 16, or 20 gauge side-hammer single-barrel shotgun with 26" to 36" barrels and extractors. Blued, case hardened with a walnut stock. Manufactured from approximately 1880 to 1915.

Exc.	V.G.	Good	Fair	Poor
—	400	300	150	75

8 Gauge Goose Gun
As above, in 8 gauge.

Exc.	V.G.	Good	Fair	Poor
—	500	250	175	100

DAVIDSON F. A.
Eibar, Spain
Arms bearing this name were manufactured in Spain by Fabrica De Armas.

Model 63B
A 12, 16, 20, 28, or .410 bore double-barrel boxlock shotgun with 25" to 30" barrels. Engraved, nickel-plated with a walnut stock. Made from 1963 to 1976.

Exc.	V.G.	Good	Fair	Poor
325	225	200	150	100

Model 69 SL
A 12 or 20 gauge sidelock double-barrel shotgun with 26" or 28" barrels and finished as above.

Exc.	V.G.	Good	Fair	Poor
400	350	300	225	125

Stagecoach Model 73
A 12 or 20 gauge Magnum sidelock double-barrel shotgun with 20" barrels and exposed hammers.

Exc.	V.G.	Good	Fair	Poor
275	225	175	150	100

DAVIS, N.R. & CO., DAVIS, N.R. & SONS
Manufacturer of percussion, and later, cartridge shotguns from 1853 to 1919. The cartridge shotguns embodied Nathan R. Davis' patented improvements of 1879, 1884, and 1886. Though only made in plain, serviceable grades, Davis shotguns were extremely well made and lived up to the company's motto "As Good as the Best."

Grade A and B Hammerless Shotguns
Made in 12 or 16 gauge with 28", 30", or 32" barrels.

Exc.	V.G.	Good	Fair	Poor
750	600	400	200	100

Grade C Hammerless Shotgun
Made in 10 gauge with 30" or 32" barrels.

Exc.	V.G.	Good	Fair	Poor
750	600	400	200	100

Grade D and DS Hammer Shotguns
Made in 12 or 16 gauge with 28", 30", or 32" barrels.

Exc.	V.G.	Good	Fair	Poor
750	600	400	200	100

Grade E and F Single-Barrel Shotguns
Made in 12 or 16 gauge with 30" or 32" barrels.

Exc.	V.G.	Good	Fair	Poor
250	200	100	75	50

N.R. DAVIS BRANDS

1st Button Opener—Hammer Boxlock

Exc.	V.G.	Good	Fair	Poor
400	300	250	150	100

1st Sidelever—Hammer Boxlock

Exc.	V.G.	Good	Fair	Poor
400	300	250	150	100

2nd Sidelever—Hammer Boxlock

Exc.	V.G.	Good	Fair	Poor
400	300	250	150	100

1st Toplever—Hammer Boxlock

Exc.	V.G.	Good	Fair	Poor
400	300	250	150	100

2nd Toplever—Hammer Boxlock

Exc.	V.G.	Good	Fair	Poor
400	300	250	150	100

3rd Toplever—Hammer Boxlock

Exc.	V.G.	Good	Fair	Poor
400	300	250	150	100

1879 1st Model—Hammer Boxlock

Exc.	V.G.	Good	Fair	Poor
400	300	250	150	100

1879 2nd Model—Damascus Barrels—Hammer Boxlock

Exc.	V.G.	Good	Fair	Poor
400	300	250	150	100

1885 "Hammerless"—Hammerless Boxlock

Exc.	V.G.	Good	Fair	Poor
400	300	250	150	100

1886 Rival—Hammerless Boxlock

Exc.	V.G.	Good	Fair	Poor
300	250	200	150	100

1886 Rival Improved—Hammerless Boxlock

Exc.	V.G.	Good	Fair	Poor
300	250	200	150	100

1897 "G"—Hammer Sidelock

Exc.	V.G.	Good	Fair	Poor
300	250	200	150	100

N.R. DAVIS & SONS BRAND

Hammerless 1900—Hammerless Boxlock

Exc.	V.G.	Good	Fair	Poor
300	250	200	150	100

Hammerless A—Damascus Barrels—Hammerless Boxlock

Exc.	V.G.	Good	Fair	Poor
300	250	200	150	100

Hammerless B—Hammerless Boxlock

Exc.	V.G.	Good	Fair	Poor
300	250	200	150	100

Hammerless C—Engraved Damascus Barrel—Hammerless Boxlock

Exc.	V.G.	Good	Fair	Poor
350	300	250	150	100

Hammerless D—Engraved—Hammerless Boxlock

Exc.	V.G.	Good	Fair	Poor
400	350	300	250	200

New Model—Hammerless Boxlock

Exc.	V.G.	Good	Fair	Poor
300	250	200	150	100

"D.S." Straight Stock—Engraved—Hammerless Boxlock

Exc.	V.G.	Good	Fair	Poor
300	250	200	150	100

Davis Special—Hammerless Boxlock

Exc.	V.G.	Good	Fair	Poor
800	600	500	400	250

Davis "B" Manga Steel—Hammerless Boxlock

Exc.	V.G.	Good	Fair	Poor
800	600	500	400	250

DAVIS-WARNER BRANDS
SEE—Davis-Warner

CRESCENT-DAVIS BRANDS

Model No. 600—Hammerless Boxlock

Exc.	V.G.	Good	Fair	Poor
600	500	300	200	100

Model No. 900—Hammerless Boxlock

Exc.	V.G.	Good	Fair	Poor
600	500	300	200	100

DAVIS & BOZEMAN
Central, Alabama

Pattern 1841 Rifle
A .58 caliber single-shot percussion rifle with a 33" round barrel, full walnut stock, two barrel bands, brass furniture and an iron ramrod.

The lock marked "D. & B. Ala." as well as the serial number and date of manufacture. Prospective purchasers are advised to secure a qualified appraisal prior to acquisition.

Exc.	V.G.	Good	Fair	Poor
—	—	35000	15000	3500

DAVIS INDUSTRIES
Mira Loma, California

This company was founded in 1987 by Jim Davis in Chino, California. The company ceased operations in 2001. Remaining stocks and production machinery purchased by Cobra Enterprises, 1960 S. Milestone Drive, Suite F, Salt Lake City, UT 84104.

D-Series Deringer
A .22 LR, .22 WMR, .25 ACP and .32 ACP caliber double-barrel Over/Under derringer with 2.4" barrels. Black Teflon or chrome-plated finish with laminated wood grips. Weighs approximately 9.5 oz.

NIB	Exc.	V.G.	Good	Fair	Poor
60	50	40	30	25	20

Big Bore D-Series
Similar to the above model but chambered for the .38 Special and .32 H&R Magnum. Barrel length is 2.75". Weighs about 11.5 oz.

NIB	Exc.	V.G.	Good	Fair	Poor
80	60	45	30	25	20

Long Bore D-Series
Introduced in 1994 this two-shot pistol is chambered for the .22 LR, .22 WMR, .32 ACP, .32 H&R Mag., .380 ACP, 9mm, and .38 Special cartridges. Barrel length is 3.75", overall length is 5.65" and weight is approximately 13 oz.

NIB	Exc.	V.G.	Good	Fair	Poor
80	60	45	30	25	20

DAVIS-WARNER ARMS CORPORATION
Norwich, Connecticut

Established in 1917, when N.R. Davis & Sons purchased the Warner Arms Company. Manufactured shotguns, as well as revolvers and semi-automatic pistols. Ceased operations in 1930. The Crescent Arms Company purchased the proprietary rights to the name and briefly assembled shotguns under the name (probably from parts acquired in the purchase) until Crescent was in turn purchased by J.C. Stevens.

Initially, the Davis-Warner shotguns were identical to those made by Davis, (page 360), but they subsequently made a Davis Grade B.S. Hammerless, Davis-Warner Expert and Davis Grade D.S. The pistols made by the company included .32 caliber revolvers and two Browning Patent semi-automatics made in Belgium for the company.

Davis Grade B.S. Hammerless Shotgun
Made in 12, 16, or 20 gauge with 28", 30", or 32" barrels.

Courtesy William Hammond

Exc.	V.G.	Good	Fair	Poor
750	600	400	200	100

Davis-Warner Expert Hammerless
Made in 12, 16, or 20 gauge with 26", 28", 30", or 32" barrels.

Exc.	V.G.	Good	Fair	Poor
750	600	400	200	100

"BS"—Hammerless Boxlock

Exc.	V.G.	Good	Fair	Poor
300	250	200	150	100

"Maximin"—Hammerless Boxlock

Exc.	V.G.	Good	Fair	Poor
400	300	250	200	150

"DS"—Hammerless Boxlock

Exc.	V.G.	Good	Fair	Poor
300	250	200	150	100

Deluxe—Hammerless Boxlock

Exc.	V.G.	Good	Fair	Poor
300	250	200	150	100

Premier—Hammerless Boxlock

Exc.	V.G.	Good	Fair	Poor
300	250	200	150	100

Peerless Ejector—Hammerless Boxlock

Courtesy Nick Niles, Paul Goodwin photo

Exc.	V.G.	Good	Fair	Poor
400	300	250	200	150

Hypower—Hammerless Boxlock

Exc.	V.G.	Good	Fair	Poor
400	300	250	200	150

Ajax—Hammerless Boxlock

Exc.	V.G.	Good	Fair	Poor
300	250	200	150	100

Certified (Savage)

Courtesy Nick Niles, Paul Goodwin photo

Exc.	V.G.	Good	Fair	Poor
400	300	250	150	100

Deluxe Special (Model 805)—Automatic Ejectors

Exc.	V.G.	Good	Fair	Poor
500	400	300	200	150

Premier Special (Model 802)

Exc.	V.G.	Good	Fair	Poor
500	400	300	200	150

Premier (Model 801)

Exc.	V.G.	Good	Fair	Poor
400	300	250	150	100

Ajax (Model 800)

Exc.	V.G.	Good	Fair	Poor
400	300	250	150	100

Davis-Warner Swing Out Revolver
Double-action .32 caliber revolver with a 5" or 6" barrel.

Exc.	V.G.	Good	Fair	Poor
150	125	100	75	50

DAW, G. H.
London, England

Daw Revolver
A .38 caliber double-action percussion revolver with a 5.5" barrel marked "George H. Daw, 57 Threadneedle St. London, Patent No. 112." Blued, with walnut grips. Manufactured in the 1860s.

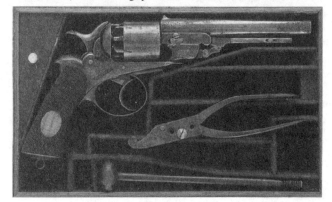

Exc.	V.G.	Good	Fair	Poor
—	5000	3000	1750	1000

DEANE, ADAMS & DEANE
London, England
SEE—Adams

DEANE-HARDING
London, England

Deane-Harding Revolver
A .44 caliber percussion revolver with a 5.25" barrel and 5-shot cylinder. Blued, case hardened with walnut grips. Manufactured during the late 1850s.

Exc.	V.G.	Good	Fair	Poor
—	7500	1750	1250	800

DERINGER REVOLVER AND PISTOL CO.
Philadelphia, Pennsylvania

After Henry Deringer's death, his name was used by I.J. Clark who manufactured rimfire revolvers on Charles Foehl's patents between 1870 and 1879.

Deringer Model I
A .22 caliber spur trigger revolver with a hinged octagonal barrel and 7-shot cylinder. Manufactured circa 1873.

Exc.	V.G.	Good	Fair	Poor
—	—	450	200	150

Deringer Model II
As above, with a round barrel and also available in .32 caliber.

Exc.	V.G.	Good	Fair	Poor
—	—	350	175	100

Centennial 1876
A .22, .32, or .38 caliber solid frame revolver.

Exc.	V.G.	Good	Fair	Poor
—	—	800	450	200

HENRY DERINGER RIFLES AND PISTOLS
Philadelphia, Pennsylvania

Henry Deringer Sr. and his son, Henry Jr., were well established in Philadelphia by the close of the War of 1812, having made both sporting and military rifles at that place since the turn of the century. Henry Jr. continued in the gun trade until the outbreak of the American Civil War, primarily producing flintlock and percussion military rifles, at least 2,500 "Northwest guns" and 1,200 rifles for the Indian trade, a few percussion martial pistols, but most importantly the percussion pocket pistols that became so popular that they took on his misspelled name as a generic term, the "derringers."

Deringer U.S. Navy Contract "Boxlock" Pistols
Overall length 11-5/8"; barrel length 6"; caliber .54. Markings: on lockplate, "US/DERINGER/ PHILADELIA" or merely "DERINGER/PHILADEL'A" in center, the tail either plain or marked "U.S.N./(date)"; barrels sometimes marked with U.S. Navy inspection marks.
Deringer was granted a contract with the U.S. Navy in 1845 for 1,200 of the new "boxlock" percussion pistols also made by Ames. All of these appear to have been delivered. From the extra parts, Deringer is thought to have assembled several hundred extra pistols, some of which he rifled. The latter bring a premium, even though quantities remain enigmatic.

Exc.	V.G.	Good	Fair	Poor
—	3500	1400	1100	750

Deringer Percussion Pocket Pistols
Overall length varies with barrel length; barrel length 1-1/2" to 6" in regular 1/8" gradiants; caliber .41 (usually, other calibers known). Markings: "DERINGER/PHILADELA" on back action lock and rear section of top barrel flat; "P" impressed in circle with serrated edges on left side of breech; agent marks occasionally on top of barrel.
The most famous of Henry Deringer's products, an estimated 15,000 were produced between the Mexican War through the Civil War, usually in pairs. The popularity of the pistol is attested in the large number of imitations and the nickname "Derringer" applied to them, even when clearly not Deringer's products. Prices can fluctuate widely based on agent marks occasionally found on barrel. Care is advised in purchasing purported "true" derringers.

Exc.	V.G.	Good	Fair	Poor
—	4500	1600	1200	800

Principal Makers of Deringer-Style Pocket Pistols
William AFFLERBACH, Philadelphia, PA
Balthaser AUER, Louisville, KY
Frederick BEERSTECHER, Philadelphia and Lewisburg, PA
Franz J. BITTERLICH, Nashville, TN
BLUNT & SYMS, New York, NY
Richard P. BRUFF, New York, NY
Jesse S. BUTTERFIELD, Philadelphia, PA
Daniel CLARK, Philadelphia, PA
Richard CONSTABLE, Philadelphia, PA
DELONG & SON, Chattanooga, TN
MOSES DICKSON, Louisville, KY
Horace E. DIMICK, St. Louis, MO
Gustau ERICHSON, Houston, TX
B.J. EUSTACE & Company, St. Louis, MO
James E. EVANS, Philadelphia, PA
W.S. EVANS, Philadelphia, PA
FIELD, LANGSTROTH & Company, Philadelphia, PA
Daniel FISH, New York, NY
FOLSOM BROTHERS & Company, New Orleans, LA
August G. GENEZ, New York, NY
George D. H. GILLESPIE, New York, NY
Frederick G. GLASSICK, Memphis, TN
James GOLCHER, Philadelphia, PA
Joseph GRUBB & Company, Philadelphia, PA
John H. HAPPOLDT, Charlestown, SC
John M. HAPPOLDT, Columbus, George, and Charlestown, SC
HAWS & WAGGONER, Columbia, SC
HODGKINS & SONS, Macon, GA
Louis HOFFMAN, Vicksburg, MS
HYDE & GOODRICH, New Orleans, LA
Joseph JACOB, Philadelphia, PA

William W. KAYE, Philadelphia, PA
Benjamin KITTERIDGE, Cincinnati, OH
Peter W. KRAFT, Columbia, SC
John KRIDER, Philadelphia, PA
Jacob KUNTZ, Philadelphia, PA
Martille La FITTE, Natchitoches, LA
A. Frederichk LINS, Philadelphia, PA
C. LOHNER, Philadelphia, PA
John P. LOWER, Denver, CO
A.R. MENDENHALL, Des Arc, AK
John MEUNIER, Milwaukee, WI
William D. MILLER, New York, NY
MURPHY & O'CONNELL, New York, NY
—— NEWCOMB, Natchez, MS
Charles A. OBERTEUFFER, Philadelphia, PA
Stephen O'DELL, Natchez, MS
Henry C. PALMER, St. Louis, MO
R. PATRICK, New York, NY
REID & TRACY, New York, NY
William ROBERTSON, Philadelphia, PA
ROBINSON & KRIDER, Philadelphia, PA
Ernst SCHMIDT & Company, Houston, TX
SCHNEIDER & GLASSICK, Memphis, TN
W.A. SEAVER, New York, NY
Paul J. SIMPSON, New York, NY
SLOTTER & Company, Philadelphia, PA
Patrick SMITH, Buffalo, NY
SPRANG & WALLACE, Philadelphia, PA
Adam W. SPIES, New York, NY
Casper SUTER, Selma, AL
Jacob F. TRUMPLER, Little Rock, AK
Edward TRYON, Jr., Philadelphia, PA
George K. TRYON, Philadelphia, PA
TUFTS & COLLEY, New York, NY
WOLF, DASH & FISHER, New York, NY
Alfred WOODHAM, New York, NY
Andrew WURFFLEIN, Philadelphia, PA
John WURFFLEIN, Philadelphia, PA

Agent Names Found On Deringer Pocket Pistols
W.C. ALLEN, San Francisco, CA
W.H. CALHOUN, Nashville, TN
CANFIELD & BROTHERS, Baltimore, MD
F. H. CLARK & CO., Memphis, TN
COLEMAN & DUKE, Cahaba, AL
M.W. GALT & BROTHER, Washington, DC
J.B. GILMORE, Shreveport, LA
A.B. GRISWOLD & CO., New Orleans, LA
HYDE & GOODRICH, New Orleans, LA
LULLMAN & VIENNA, Memphis, TN
A.J. MILLSPAUGH, Shreveport, LA
H.G. NEWCOMB, Natchez, MS
A.J. PLATE, San Francisco, CA
J.A. SCHAFER, Vicksburg, MS
S.L. SWETT, Vicksburg, MS
A.J. TAYLOR, San Francisco, CA
WOLF & DURRINGER, Louisville, KY

DEVISME, F. P.
Paris, France

One of the more popular French gunsmiths of the mid-19th century, F.P. Devisme manufactured a wide variety of firearms including single-shot percussion pistols, double-barrel percussion rifles and shotguns, percussion revolvers and cane guns. After 1858 this maker manufactured cartridge weapons of the same style as his percussion arms. The quality of all of his products is uniformly high and it is impossible to provide generalized price guide. Prospective purchasers are advised to secure a qualified appraisal prior to acquisition.

DICKINSON, E. L. & J.
Springfield, Massachusetts

Ranger
A .32 caliber spur trigger revolver with a 6-shot cylinder.

Exc.	V.G.	Good	Fair	Poor
—	—	450	200	100

Single-Shot
A .32 caliber single-shot pistol with a 3.75" hinged barrel, silver plated brass frame, blued barrel and walnut grips.

Exc.	V.G.	Good	Fair	Poor
—	—	650	250	100

DICKSON, JOHN
Edinburg, Scotland
SEE—British Double Guns

DIMICK, H.E.
St. Louis, Missouri

While this maker is primarily known for half stock Plains Rifles, he also manufactured a limited number of percussion pistols. These vary in length, caliber, stock form and type of furniture. The values listed should only be used as a rough guide. Prospective purchasers should secure a qualified appraisal prior to acquisition. Active 1849 to 1873.

Exc.	V.G.	Good	Fair	Poor
—	—	5000	2000	900

DOUG TURNBULL RESTORATION, INC.
Bloomfield, New York

This company began operation in 1983 as a one-man shop. Today the company numbers 14 people and does finish work for most major firearms manufacturers. The company also installs Miller single triggers. The models listed are a series of special run firearms produced by Turnbull.

DT Colt
This model is a current Colt SAA reworked to look like the pre-1920 SAA. Assigned serisl numbers beginning with 001DT these revolversd are offered in .45 Colt, .44-40, and .38-40 calibers. Barrel lengths are 4.75", 5.5", and 7.5". The standard DT has color case hardened frame and the rest of the gun charcoal blue. Cylinder flutes are enlarged and the fron of the of the cylinder is beveled. Many special optios offered which will affect cost. Prices listed are for standard revolvers.

Year Offered—1998

NIB	Exc.	V.G.	Good	Fair	Poor
1495	—	—	—	—	—

Year Offered—1999

NIB	Exc.	V.G.	Good	Fair	Poor
1995	—	—	—	—	—

Year Offered—2000

NIB	Exc.	V.G.	Good	Fair	Poor
2200	—	—	—	—	—

EHBM Colt
This is a Colt SAA current production revolver limited to 50 guns chambered for the .45 Colt and fitted with a 5.5" barrel. Special features. Serial numbers EHBM01 to EHBM50. First offered in 2000.

NIB	Exc.	V.G.	Good	Fair	Poor
2150	—	—	—	—	—

Smith & Wesson No. 3 Schofield
Introduced in 2002 this is a special new production S&W Schofield with special serial numbers with a "DTR" prefix starting with serial number 0001. The frame, barrel, and cylinder are charcoal blued while the trigger, trigger guard, and barrel latch are bone color case hardened. Factory wood grips are standard. Engraving is optional.

NIB	Exc.	V.G.	Good	Fair	Poor
1995	—	—	—	—	—

Colt/Winchester Cased Set
A cased set with a Colt Model 1873 engraved revolver and a Winchester Model 1894. Colt is chambered for the .45 Colt cartridge and fitted with a 7.5" barrel. Engraving is "B" coverage. Model 1894 is chambered for the .45 Colt cartridge and is in the saddle ring configuration. Engraving pattern is #9 with deer. Checkered walnut stock. Limited to five sets total. Serial numbers 160DT to 164DT.

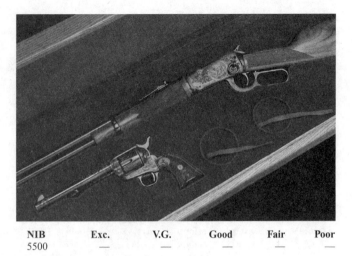

NIB	Exc.	V.G.	Good	Fair	Poor
5500	—	—	—	—	—

General Patton Colt

This limited run of engraved Colt Model 1873 single-action army revolvers is fitted with ivory grips and full-coverage engraving. Chambered for the .45 Colt cartridge and fitted with a 4.75" barrel. Helfricht-style engraving. Silver-plated finish. Limited to 10 revolvers total. Serial numbers GP01 to GP10.

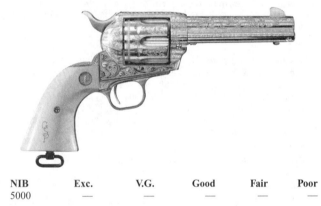

NIB	Exc.	V.G.	Good	Fair	Poor
5000	—	—	—	—	—

Theodore Roosevelt Colt

This Colt single-action army revolver features carved ivory grips, full coverage engraving with gold cylinder, hammer and ejector rod. Chambered for the .44-40 cartridge and fitted with a 7.5" barrel. Nimschke-style engraving. Balance of gun is silver plated. Supplied with fitted case. Limited to 25 revolvers total. Serial numbers TR01 to TR25.

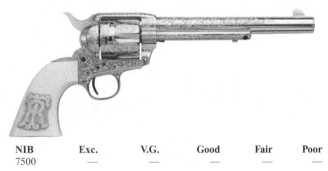

NIB	Exc.	V.G.	Good	Fair	Poor
7500	—	—	—	—	—

DRISCOLL, J.B.
Springfield, Massachusetts

Single-Shot Pocket Pistol

A small pistol chambered for .22 rimfire. It has a 3.5" octagonal barrel that pivots downward for loading after a trigger-like hook under the breech is pulled. It has a spur trigger, silver-plated brass frame, and a blued barrel. The square butt is flared at the bottom, and the grips are walnut. There were approximately 200 manufactured in the late 1860s.

Exc.	V.G.	Good	Fair	Poor
—	—	900	350	100

DUMOULIN
Herstal, Belgium
Importer—Midwest Gunsport
Zebulon, North Carolina

The guns produced by Ernest Dumoulin are essentially handmade to the customer's order. They are of the highest quality, both in materials and workmanship. There are many options available that have a tremendous impact on value fluctuations. The models and values listed here are base prices. If a sale or purchase is contemplated, individual competent appraisal should be secured.

SHOTGUNS

Europa Model

A side-by-side double-barrel chambered for 12, 20, and 28 gauge and .410 bore. It is available in any length barrel and choke combination, with an Anson & Deeley boxlock action and automatic ejectors. One has the option of double or single-selective triggers and a choice of six different moderate engraving patterns. The select walnut stock is oil-finished. This model was introduced in 1989. Basis values are listed.

NIB	Exc.	V.G.	Good	Fair	Poor
3500	2750	1950	1250	800	—

Leige Model

A side-by-side double chambered for 12, 16, 20, and 28 gauge. It is similar to the Europa, with a greater degree of finish and more engraving. The walnut is of a higher grade. This model was introduced in 1986.

NIB	Exc.	V.G.	Good	Fair	Poor
5750	4200	2750	1500	950	—

Continental Model

A side-by-side chambered for 12, 20, and 28 gauge and .410. Barrel lengths and chokes are on a custom-order basis. This is a true sidelock action with automatic ejectors and choice of triggers. There are six different engraving patterns, and the stock is made of high grade, hand-checkered, oil-finished walnut. This model was introduced in 1989.

NIB	Exc.	V.G.	Good	Fair	Poor
7500	6000	4500	3000	1500	—

Etendart Model

A side-by-side chambered for 12, 20, and 28 gauge. This best grade side-by-side is built on a purely made-to-order basis. It is profusely engraved and uses exhibition grade walnut in its stock. There are 12 different engraving patterns from which to choose, and the cost is according to embellishments chosen. Values given here are for the basic model.

NIB	Exc.	V.G.	Good	Fair	Poor
14500	11000	8500	4000	3000	—

E

E.M.F. CO., INC.
Santa Ana, California
SEE—Uberti, Aldo

An importer and a distributor of quality Italian-made reproduction firearms. Its offerings are listed in the section dealing with Aldo Uberti firearms. Included are new products for this company as of 1997.

Hartford Bisley
This single-action revolver is fitted with a Colt Bisley grip. Chambered for .45 Long Colt as well as .32-20, .357 Magnum, .38-40, and .44-40 calibers. Barrel lengths are 4-3/4", 5-1/2", and 7-1/2". Plain walnut grips.

NIB	Exc.	V.G.	Good	Fair	Poor
450	350	—	—	—	—

Hartford Express
A single Colt SAA frame and barrel with a Colt Lightning-style grip. Chambered for .45 Long Colt in 4-3/4", 5-1/2", or 7-1/2" barrel lengths.

NIB	Exc.	V.G.	Good	Fair	Poor
450	350	—	—	—	—

Hartford Pinkerton
This model features a 4" barrel with ejector and a bird's-head grip. Chambered for 45 Long Colt, .32-20, .357 Magnum, .38-40, .44-40, and .44 Special.

NIB	Exc.	V.G.	Good	Fair	Poor
450	350	—	—	—	—

ECLIPSE
Enterprise Gun Works
Pittsburgh, Pennsylvania

Single-Shot Derringer
This pocket pistol was made by the firm of James Bown & Son, doing business as the Enterprise Gun Works. It is chambered for .22 or .32-caliber rimfire cartridges. A few in .25 rimfire have been noted and would add approximately 25 percent to the values listed. The barrel is 2.5" in length and is part-round/part-octagonal. It pivots sideways for loading. It has a spur trigger and a bird's-head grip. The barrel is stamped "Eclipse." It is made of nickel-plated iron, with walnut grips. There were approximately 10,000 manufactured between 1870 and 1890.

Exc.	V.G.	Good	Fair	Poor
—	600	250	100	75

ELLS, JOSIAH
Pittsburgh, Pennsylvania

Pocket Revolver
Three distinct variations of this percussion revolver. They are chambered for .28 and .31 caliber and have 6-shot unfluted cylinders. They have been noted with 2.5", 3", and 3.75" octagonal barrels.

Model 1
The first model has an open-topped frame and is chambered for .28 caliber. The cylinder holds 5 or 6 shots, and the hammer is of the bar type. It was offered with a 2.5" or 3" barrel. The markings are "J. Ells; Patent; 1854." There were approximately 625 manufactured between 1857 and 1859.

Exc.	V.G.	Good	Fair	Poor
—	1500	650	300	200

Model 2
The second model is similar to the first, with a solid-topped frame. They have 5-shot cylinders and 3.75" long barrels. There were approximately 550 manufactured.

Exc.	V.G.	Good	Fair	Poor
—	1500	650	300	200

Model 3
The third model is radically different from its forerunners. It has a closed-top frame and a conventional spur-type hammer that strikes from the right side. It functions either as a double- or single-action. It is chambered for .28 caliber and has a 5-shot cylinder and a 3.75" barrel. There were only about 200 manufactured between 1857 and 1859.

Exc.	V.G.	Good	Fair	Poor
—	1750	950	400	200

ERA
Brazil

Era Double Barrel Shotgun
An inexpensive shotgun chambered for 12 and 20 gauge, as well as .410. It was offered with 26", 28", or 30" barrels with various choke combinations. It has double triggers and extractors, with a checkered hardwood pistol-grip stock. This gun is also available as a Quail model with a 20" barrel and as a Riot model with an 18" barrel. These two models are not offered in .410 bore.

Exc.	V.G.	Good	Fair	Poor
200	150	125	100	75

ERICHSON, G.
Houston, Texas

Erichson Pocket Pistol
A close copy of the Philadelphia-style Henry Deringer. It is chambered for .45-caliber percussion and has a 3.25" barrel. The mountings are German silver and not engraved; the stock is walnut. The hammer is

deeply fluted; and the forend, carved. The barrel is marked "G. Erichson / Houston, Texas." The number produced is unknown, but examples are scarce. They were manufactured in the 1850s and 1860s.

Exc.	V.G.	Good	Fair	Poor
—	—	6000	3000	1000

ESCODIN, M.
Eibar, Spain

This company made a Smith & Wesson revolver copy from 1924 through 1931. It is chambered for the .32 and the .38 Special. The only marking is a coat of arms stamped on the left side of the frame.

Exc.	V.G.	Good	Fair	Poor
175	125	100	75	50

EUROARMS OF AMERICA
Winchester, Virginia

An importer of blackpowder muzzle-loading firearms, primarily replicas of early American weapons.

REVOLVERS

1851 Navy
A replica of the Colt revolver chambered for .36 or .44 caliber percussion. It has a squareback, silver-plated trigger guard and a 7.5" barrel.

NIB	Exc.	V.G.	Good	Fair	Poor
175	125	110	80	65	45

1851 Navy Police Model
Chambered for .36 caliber with a 5-shot, fluted cylinder and a 5.5" barrel.

NIB	Exc.	V.G.	Good	Fair	Poor
175	125	110	80	65	45

1851 Navy Sheriff's Model
A 5" barrelled version of the Navy Model.

NIB	Exc.	V.G.	Good	Fair	Poor
150	100	80	60	50	35

1851 "Schneider & Glassick" Navy
A replica of the Confederate revolver chambered for .36 or .44 caliber percussion.

NIB	Exc.	V.G.	Good	Fair	Poor
150	100	80	60	50	35

1851 "Griswold & Gunnison" Navy
A replica of this Confederate revolver chambered for .36 or .44 caliber percussion.

NIB	Exc.	V.G.	Good	Fair	Poor
150	90	75	60	40	25

1862 Police
A replica of the Colt Model 1862 chambered for .36 caliber percussion, with a 7.5" barrel and a steel frame.

NIB	Exc.	V.G.	Good	Fair	Poor
175	125	110	90	65	45

1860 Army
A replica of the Colt revolver chambered for .44 caliber percussion. It was offered with a 5" or 8" barrel.

NIB	Exc.	V.G.	Good	Fair	Poor
175	125	100	75	50	30

1861 Navy
A replica of the Colt revolver chambered for .36 caliber percussion.

NIB	Exc.	V.G.	Good	Fair	Poor
175	135	110	80	60	40

1858 Remington Army or Navy
Replicas of the Remington percussion revolvers chambered for .26 or .44 caliber.

NIB	Exc.	V.G.	Good	Fair	Poor
200	150	125	100	75	50

RIFLES
The following rifles are modern replicas of early American and British firearms. They are of good quality and are quite serviceable. There is little collector interest, and we list them along with their values.

Buffalo Carbine

NIB	Exc.	V.G.	Good	Fair	Poor
400	350	300	250	175	100

1862 Remington Rifle

NIB	Exc.	V.G.	Good	Fair	Poor
300	250	225	200	125	60

Zouave Rifle

NIB	Exc.	V.G.	Good	Fair	Poor
325	275	225	175	125	90

EUROPEAN AMERICAN ARMORY CORP.
Importers
Sharpes, Florida

EAA Bounty Hunter Shotgun—External Hammers
This is a side-by-side shotgun with external hammers chambered for 10, 12, 16, 20, 28, and .410 bores. It is offered in barrel lengths of 20", 24", and 26".

NIB	Exc.	V.G.	Good	Fair	Poor
375	300	250	—	—	—

EAA Bounty Hunter Shotgun—Traditional
Same as above but with internal hammers. Offered in 12 or 20 gauge.

NIB	Exc.	V.G.	Good	Fair	Poor
300	250	200	—	—	—

EAA Saba
This model is a side-by-side shotgun that features an engraved silver boxlock receiver, double or single triggers, selective ejectors, solid raised matted rib, and select European walnut checkered stock. Offered in 12, 20, and 28 gauge as well as .410 bore. Barrel length are 26" and 28" with fixed chokes.

NIB	Exc.	V.G.	Good	Fair	Poor
775	600	500	400	300	250

EVANS REPEATING RIFLE CO.
Mechanic Falls, Maine

Incorporated in 1873, this firm produced repeating rifles based upon patents issued to Warren R. Evans (1868-1871) and later George F. Evans (1877, 1878 and 1879). The most distinctive feature of these arms is that they used a butt magazine operating on the principle of an Archimedean screw. Distributed by Merwin, Hulbert & Company, as well as Schuyler, Hartley & Graham, Evans rifles met with some success. One of their earliest advocates was William F. Cody (Buffalo Bill). The company ceased operations in 1879, after approximately 15,000 arms had been made.

Lever-Action Rifle
This rifle is totally unique for a number of reasons. It holds the most rounds of any repeating rifle that did not have a detachable magazine, with capacities up to 38 rounds on some models. This rifle was chambered for its own cartridge—the .44 Evans of which there were two versions: a 1" cartridge in the "Old Model" and the "Transition Model" and a 1.5" cartridge in the "New Model." The finish on these rifles is blued, with nickel-plated levers and buttplates noted on some examples. The stocks are walnut. There were approximately 12,250 of all models manufactured between 1873 and 1879.

Old Model
This variation is chambered for the 1" .44 Evans cartridge and has a butt stock that covers only the top half of the revolving 34-shot maga-

zine located in the butt of the rifle. The buttplate appears as if it is reversed, and the markings on the "Old Model" are "Evans Repeating Rifle/Pat. Dec. 8, 1868 & Sept. 16, 1871." There are three versions of the Old Model as follows. They were manufactured between 1874 and 1876 and serial numbered 1-500.

Military Musket
This version has a 30" barrel, with two barrel bands and provisions for a bayonet. There were only 50 estimated manufactured.

Exc.	V.G.	Good	Fair	Poor
—	—	3500	1500	500

Sporting Rifle
Approximately 300 of this model produced with a 26", 28", or 30" octagonal barrel.

Exc.	V.G.	Good	Fair	Poor
—	—	1850	800	400

Carbine
This variation has a 22" barrel, with one barrel band and a sling swivel. There were 150 produced.

Exc.	V.G.	Good	Fair	Poor
—	—	3000	1150	500

Transitional Model
Has a buttstock that covers both the top and bottom of the rotary magazine, with an exposed portion in the middle of the butt. The buttplate does not have the backward appearance, and the barrel is marked "Evans Repeating Rifle Mechanic Falls Me./Pat Dec. 8, 1868 & Sept. 16, 1871." This version was manufactured in 1876 and 1877 and was serial numbered between 500-2185, for a total of approximately 1,650 manufactured.

Military Musket
Has a 30" barrel and two barrel bands. 150 were produced.

Exc.	V.G.	Good	Fair	Poor
—	—	2750	1200	450

Carbine
Four hundred-fifty of these were produced, with a 22" barrel and one barrel band.

Exc.	V.G.	Good	Fair	Poor
—	—	2250	700	375

Sporting Rifle
Has a 26", 28", or 30" barrel. There were 1,050 produced.

Exc.	V.G.	Good	Fair	Poor
—	—	1750	800	300

"Montreal Carbine"
A special issue marked "Montreal," sold by R.H. Kilby, Evans' Canadian sales agent. There were between 50 and 100 produced.

Exc.	V.G.	Good	Fair	Poor
—	—	2750	1150	450

New Model
Approximately 10,000 of the New Model were produced, chambered for the 1.5" .44 Evans cartridge with a magazine capacity reduced to 28. The frame was redesigned and rounded at the top, and the forend fit flush to the receiver. The lever and hammer are streamlined, and there is a dust cover over the loading gate. The markings are the same as on the Transitional Model with "U.S.A." added to the last line. This version was not serial numbered, and any numbers found are assembly numbers only.

Military Musket
3,000 produced, with a 30" barrel and two barrel bands.

Exc.	V.G.	Good	Fair	Poor
—	—	3250	1250	450

Carbine
4,000 produced with a 22" barrel, one barrel band, and a sling swivel.

Exc.	V.G.	Good	Fair	Poor
—	—	1750	750	400

Sporting Rifle
3,000 produced with 26", 28", or 30" octagonal barrels.

Exc.	V.G.	Good	Fair	Poor
—	—	2000	800	400

EVANS, J. E.
Philadelphia, Pennsylvania

Evans Pocket Pistol
A copy of the Philadelphia-made Henry Deringer pistol and is chambered for .41 caliber. It utilizes the percussion ignition system and has barrels from 2.5" to 3" in length. The stock is of walnut with a checkered grip, and the mountings are scroll engraved German silver. The barrel is marked "J.E. Evans Philada." These pistols were manufactured in the 1850s.

Exc.	V.G.	Good	Fair	Poor
—	—	1750	700	350

EVANS, WILLIAM
London, England
SEE—British Double Guns

EXCAM
Hialeah, Florida

An importer of firearms; not a manufacturer. The Erma and Uberti products imported by this company are under their own heading in this book. The other products that they imported are listed here. They are no longer in business.

TA 76
Patterned after the Colt Single Action Army and is chambered for the .22 rimfire cartridge. It has a 4.75", 6", or 9" barrel and blue finish with wood grips. It is offered with brass trigger guard and backstrap and also offered chrome-plated. A combo model with an extra .22 Magnum cylinder is available and would add 10 percent to the listed values.

Exc.	V.G.	Good	Fair	Poor
100	75	65	40	25

TA 38 Over-and-Under Derringer
A two-shot derringer patterned after the Remington derringer. It is chambered for the .38 Special cartridge, has 3" barrels that pivot upward for loading, and is blued with checkered nylon grips. This model was discontinued in 1985.

Exc.	V.G.	Good	Fair	Poor
100	75	65	40	25

EXEL ARMS OF AMERICA
Gardner, Massachusetts
SEE—Lanber
Laurona & Ugartechia

This firm was engaged in the import of Spanish shotguns. They ceased importing them in 1967, and the specific models will be found listed under the manufacturers' names.

Just a Reminder

The prices in this section are designed as a guide, not a quote. This is an important distinction because prices for firearms vary with the time of the year and geographical location.

F

F.I.E.
Hialeah, Florida

Firearms Import and Export was engaged in the business of importing the Franchi shotgun (which is listed under its own heading) and the Arminius revolver (which is made in Germany). They were also distributors for the Titan semi-automatic pistols, which are manufactured in the U.S.A. They were also importing a series of 9mm pistols from Italy that are produced by Tanfoglio and known as the TZ series. F.I.E. was no longer in business as of 1990.

D38 Derringer
A two-shot, Over/Under, Remington-style derringer chambered for the .38 Special cartridge. It is chrome-plated and was dropped from the line in 1985.

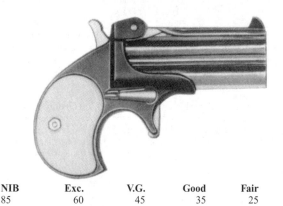

NIB	Exc.	V.G.	Good	Fair	Poor
85	60	45	35	25	20

D86 Derringer
A single-shot derringer with a 3" barrel. It is chambered for the .38 Special cartridge and is chrome-plated. There is an ammnition storage compartment in the butt and a transfer bar safety that makes it safer to carry. This model was introduced in 1986.

NIB	Exc.	V.G.	Good	Fair	Poor
100	80	65	50	35	20

SINGLE-ACTION ARMY REPLICA REVOLVERS

There is a series of single-action, .22 caliber revolvers that were patterned after the Colt Single-Action Army. They were manufactured in the U.S.A. or Brescia, Italy. They are inexpensive and of fair quality. The differences between these models are basically barrel lengths, type of sights, and finish. They all are chambered for the .22 LR and have interchangeable .22 Magnum cylinders. We list them for reference purposes.

Cowboy

NIB	Exc.	V.G.	Good	Fair	Poor
100	75	50	40	35	20

Gold Rush

NIB	Exc.	V.G.	Good	Fair	Poor
150	125	100	80	75	50

Texas Ranger

NIB	Exc.	V.G.	Good	Fair	Poor
100	85	75	50	35	20

Buffalo Scout

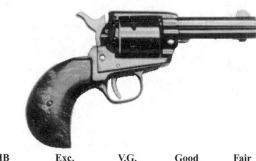

NIB	Exc.	V.G.	Good	Fair	Poor
95	80	70	50	35	20

Legend S.A.A.

NIB	Exc.	V.G.	Good	Fair	Poor
125	110	85	65	50	30

Hombre

A single-action made in Germany by Arminius. It is patterned after the Colt Single-Action Army revolver. The Hombre is chambered for the .357 Magnum, .44 Magnum, and .45 Colt cartridges. It is offered with a 5.5", 6", or 7.5" barrel, case-colored frame, and blued barrel and cylinder, with smooth walnut grips. The backstrap and trigger guard are offered in brass and will bring a 10 percent premium.

NIB	Exc.	V.G.	Good	Fair	Poor
225	200	175	125	100	75

Single-Shot
Brazilian made and chambered for 12 or 20 gauge and .410. It is a single-barreled break open, with 25" through 30" barrel and various chokes. It is blued with a wood stock and was introduced in 1985.

NIB	Exc.	V.G.	Good	Fair	Poor
100	80	60	45	35	25

S.O.B.
Similar to the single-shot, with an 18.5" barrel and a pistol grip instead of a standard stock. This model was discontinued in 1984.

NIB	Exc.	V.G.	Good	Fair	Poor
100	80	60	45	35	25

Brute
A side-by-side chambered for 12 and 20 gauge and .410. It has 19" barrels, double triggers, and extractors. It has a wood stock and was dropped from the line in 1984.

NIB	Exc.	V.G.	Good	Fair	Poor
200	175	125	100	75	50

FABARM
Brescia, Italy
Importer—Heckler & Koch, Inc.
Sterling, Virginia

In 1998 H&K took over the importation of the Fabarm shotgun line in the U.S.

SINGLE-SHOT SHOTGUNS

Omega Standard
Has an alloy receiver and is chambered for 12 and 20 gauge, as well as .410. It has 26" or 28" barrels with various chokes. The finish is black with a beech stock. It was produced in 1989.

NIB	Exc.	V.G.	Good	Fair	Poor
150	125	100	75	50	40

Omega Goose Gun
Chambered for 12 gauge only, with a 35.5" full-choke barrel.

NIB	Exc.	V.G.	Good	Fair	Poor
160	140	125	100	75	50

SIDE-BY-SIDE GUNS

Classic Lion Grade I
Offered in 12 gauge with 3" chambers, single-selective trigger, auto-ejectors, walnut stock, buttplate, and fitted with 26" barrels. Weight is about 7 lbs.

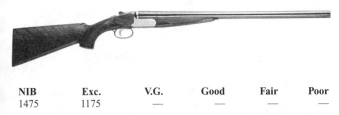

NIB	Exc.	V.G.	Good	Fair	Poor
1475	1175	—	—	—	—

Classic Lion Grade II
Similar to the Grade I but with the addition of oil finished stock and removable sideplates with game scene engraving. Weight is 7.2 lbs.

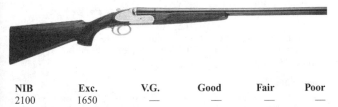

NIB	Exc.	V.G.	Good	Fair	Poor
2100	1650	—	—	—	—

Classic Lion Elite
Introduced in 2002, this 12 gauge model features 26" or 28" barrels with case colored receiver and straight grip stock. Fixed chokes. Weight is about 7 lbs.

NIB	Exc.	V.G.	Good	Fair	Poor
1600	1200	—	—	—	—

FARQUHARSON, JOHN
London, England

Not a gunmaker but the designer of what is perhaps the finest single-shot action ever developed. It was patented on May 25, 1872, and has been used as the basis for some of the world's best single-shot rifles manufactured by top English gunmakers throughout the years. There will be references to this action under sections dealing with these makers.

FARROW ARMS CO.
Holyoke, Massachusetts
Mason, Tennessee

Farrow Falling Block Rifle
Designed by W.M. Farrow, a target shooter who had worked on the Ballard rifles for the Marlin company. The Farrow rifles are chambered for various calibers and have barrel lengths from 28"-36" of octagonal configuration. They feature tang sights and are either all blued or have a nickel-plated receiver. The stocks are walnut. There were two grades offered that varied according to the grade of wood used. These rifles are quite scarce on today's market, and the number manufactured between 1885 and 1900 is unknown.

No. 1 Model
Fancy walnut with checkering and a Schutzen buttplate.

Exc.	V.G.	Good	Fair	Poor
—	—	10000	4000	1750

No. 2 Model
Plainer wood and no checkering.

Exc.	V.G.	Good	Fair	Poor
—	—	9000	3000	1400

FERLACH
Ferlach, Austria

Text by Joseph M. Cornell Ph.D., A.M.A.

The history of gun making in Ferlach began in the early 1500s and continues to the present. Today, there are 13 companies making guns in this beautiful city of about 5,000 inhabitants, which is located in a remote corner of southern Austria. These companies make guns that are among the world's most beautiful and finest. Their price range, at the low end, for a bolt-action rifle is from $5,000 to the high end, for one of their high art guns, at $500,000, or perhaps even more.

These companies are family groupings. Many of these families have been making guns for centuries. For them, gun making is an all-consuming tradition. Some of the best known of these families, and most often encountered in the United States, have names such as Just, Hauptmann, Winkler, Michelitsch, Hambrusch, Scheiring, and Borovnik, etc. Other less well-known makers include Juch, Fanzoj, Glanzig, Koschat, Hofer and Zauner. Some of the companies from the past, such as Franz Sodia are no longer in business and guns from these now extinct companies will be occasionally encountered. But whether or not the families are still in business, Ferlach guns are some of the most beautiful and remarkable examples of the gunmaker's art that are to be found anywhere in the world. A Ferlach gun can be recognized, although not always easily, by the following:
1. Many times the city name "Ferlach" will be found on the gun.
2. Many times a recognizable Ferlach maker's name will be found on the guns, such as ones listed above, but not all Ferlach-made guns will have a maker's name on the gun.
3. Ferlach guns are usually made in the typical "German" style.
4. Ferlach guns usually have a unique type of serial number, which contains a two-digit number followed by a period, ".", e.g. XX.XXX. This serial number can sometimes by used to identify the maker.

Along with the companies in Ferlach, which make guns, there is also a Gunmaker's Consortium, which is owned by 12 of these companies. This Consortium provides a variety of services and products for gun makers both in Ferlach and in other locations as well. The Consortium acts as an engineering and mechanical "Center" that is an essential resource for many of the Ferlach gun makers. The Consortium uses three basic types of the steel to make the barrels: Boehler Antinit, Blitz and Super Blitz. The latter allows the thickness of the barrels to be reduced to a minimum, thus reducing the gun's final weight. Antinit is the most often encountered steel and the least expensive of the steel used in Ferlach guns.

While it is not generally known, many of the makers outside Ferlach, who make some of the world's most expensive guns, do not make their own barreled actions. They buy the actions and put their names on them. This is not true of the Ferlach maker. The actions used in their guns, with the exception of bolt-action rifles, are made right there in Ferlach by the Consortium and then finished by the individual maker. This allows for maximum efficiency and the technical control of the guns being made.

Ferlach gun makers produce almost all types of hunting weapons; these include bolt-action rifles, double rifles, three barreled rifles, drillings, shotguns, guns combining both rifles and shotguns called "combination guns", four barreled guns and even five barreled guns. Ferlach makers are very talented gunsmiths and as a result not only can they make the finest possible guns but they are also able to make guns that would be difficult or impossible for other makers to construct. Furthermore, Ferlach is one of the few centers of gun making in the world where it is still possible to order guns in almost any configuration and in almost any caliber from the small .22 LR to the .600 nitro express or even larger.

In addition to the companies that manufacture guns, Ferlach is the home of many of the world's best engravers. Many of the Ferlach makers have in-house engravers but many do not and almost all the companies send out work for special situations. A list of some of the engravers whose work will be found on Ferlach guns would include names such as Krondofer, Mack, Orou, Schaschl, Singer, Maurer, Widmann, Stogner, de Florian, Plucher and Obiltschnig.

Almost all Ferlach guns are "custom" made guns. This makes each gun somewhat unique, which makes their valuation difficult. There is, however, as with other gunmakers, almost always a relationship between quality, complexity of construction, functionality, beauty, rarity and value/pricing.

It is suggested for proper pricing and evaluation of Ferlach-made guns that an expert be consulted.

FLETCHER BIDWELL, LLC
Viroqua, Wisconsin

Spencer 1860 Military Carbine

Introduced in 2001 this is a faithful reproduction of the original Spencer Carbine. It is chambered for the .56-50 black powder cartridge but in centerfire. Fitted with a blued 22" round barrel. Magazine capacity is 7 rounds in butt tube. Bone charcoal case hardened receiver. Walnut stock. Blade front sight with ladder rear sight adjustable to 800 yards. Weight is about 9 lbs. Built in U.S.

NIB	Exc.	V.G.	Good	Fair	Poor
2395	1850	—	—	—	—

FLORENCE ARMORY
Florence, Guilford Counry, North Carolina

Founded in 1862 as a repair facility to alter sporting arms for military use. Majority of work done by H.C. Lamb & Company. In 1862, Captain Z. Coffin ordered stocks, barrels and locks to assemble newly made rifles. Furniture of these arms varied, either being supplied by Glaze & Company or being the remainders from Searcy & Moore's production. Number made estimated to be in excess of 300 rifles in both .50 and .54 calibers. These arms (particularly the barrels) exhibit characteristics of North Carolina contract pieces.
Prospective purchasers are strongly advised to secure an expert appraisal prior to acquisition.

Exc.	V.G.	Good	Fair	Poor
—	—	25000	10000	4000

FOEHL, C.
Philadelphia, Pennsylvania

Foehl Derringer

A .41 caliber percussion single-shot pistol with a 2" barrel, German silver mounts and a walnut stock. The lock marked "C. Foehl."

Exc.	V.G.	Good	Fair	Poor
—	—	1750	750	300

FOEHL & WEEKS
Philadelphia, Pennsylvania

Columbian

A .32 or .38 caliber revolver marked with the patent date "20 January 1891."

Exc.	V.G.	Good	Fair	Poor
—	350	150	75	50

FOGARTY
American Repeating Rifle Co.
Boston, Massachusetts

Fogarty Repeating Rifle and Carbine

A limited number of repeating rifles and carbines based upon Valentine Fogarty's patents were produced between 1866 and 1867. The calibers of these arms varies and the normal barrel lengths are 20" and 28". Blued, casehardened with walnut stocks. The American Repeating Rifle Company was purchased by the Winchester Repeating Arms Company in 1869. Prospective purchasers are advised to secure a qualified appraisal prior to acquisition.

Rifle

Exc.	V.G.	Good	Fair	Poor
—	—	7500	3750	1250

Carbine

Exc.	V.G.	Good	Fair	Poor
—	—	7500	3750	1250

FOLSOM, H.
St. Louis, Missouri

Derringer

A .41 caliber single-shot percussion pocket pistol with a 2.5" barrel, German silver mounts and a walnut stock. The barrel marked "H. Folsom."

Exc.	V.G.	Good	Fair	Poor
—	—	800	350	275

FOLSOM, H&D ARMS CO.

Double-Barrel Shotguns

Large distributor of double and single barrel shotguns produced by Crescent Firearms Co., Norwich, Connecticut. Folsom owned and later sold to Savage Arms Co. the Crescent Firearms Co., Davis Warner Co., and Baker Gun Co. around 1930. For more information see also Crescent Firearms Co.

FOREHAND & WADSWORTH
Worcester, Massachusetts

Established in 1871 and operated under the above name until 1890 when it became the Forehand Arms Company. Hopkins & Allen purchased the company in 1902.

Single-Shot Derringer

A .22 caliber single-shot pocket pistol with a 2" half-octagonal pivoted barrel, spur trigger and nickel- or silver-plated frame. Walnut grips. The barrel marked "Forehand & Wadsworth Worcester."

Exc.	V.G.	Good	Fair	Poor
—	1250	500	250	100

Single-Shot .41 Derringer

As above in .41 caliber with a 2.5" round barrel.

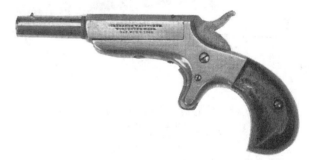

Courtesy Milwaukee Public Museum, Milkwaukee, Wisconsin.

Exc.	V.G.	Good	Fair	Poor
—	—	850	450	200

Side Hammer .22
A .22 caliber spur trigger revolver with a 2.25" to 4" octagonal barrel and 7-shot cylinder. Blued or nickel-plated with walnut grips.

Exc.	V.G.	Good	Fair	Poor
—	600	450	200	100

Center Hammer
A .32 caliber spur trigger revolver with a 3.5" octagonal barrel and 6-shot cylinder. Blued or nickel-plated with rosewood or walnut grips. The top strap commonly found marked "Terror."

Courtesy Milwaukee Public Museum, Milkwaukee, Wisconsin.

Exc.	V.G.	Good	Fair	Poor
—	500	400	200	100

Old Model Army Single-Action Revolver
A .44 Russian caliber revolver with a 7.5" round barrel and 6-shot cylinder. The barrel marked "Forehand & Wadsworth, Worchester, Mass. U.S. Patd. Oct. 22, '61, June 27, '71 Oct. 28, '73." Blued with walnut grips. Approximately 250 were manufactured between 1872 and 1878.

Exc.	V.G.	Good	Fair	Poor
—	—	3250	2000	500

New Model Army Single-Action Revolver
Similar to the above, with a 6.5" barrel and half-cock notch on the hammer. Approximately 250 were made between 1878 and 1882.

Exc.	V.G.	Good	Fair	Poor
—	—	3500	2250	500

Double-Action Revolver
A .32 or .38 caliber double-action revolver with a 3.5" barrel and 6-shot cylinder. The .32 caliber version marked "Forehand & Wadsworth Double-Action", and the .38 caliber "American Bulldog." Manufactured from 1871 to 1890.

Exc.	V.G.	Good	Fair	Poor
—	—	500	200	100

British Bulldog
A solid frame double-action revolver similar to the above.

Exc.	V.G.	Good	Fair	Poor
—	—	200	125	75

British Bulldog .44
As above in .44 S&W caliber with a 5" barrel and 5-shot cylinder.

Exc.	V.G.	Good	Fair	Poor
—	—	200	125	75

Swamp Angel
A .41 caliber single-action revolver with a 3" barrel and 5-shot cylinder. The top strap marked "Swamp Angel."

Exc.	V.G.	Good	Fair	Poor
—	—	200	100	50

Forehand Arms Co. 1898-1902
Perfection Automatic
A .32 or .38 caliber double-action revolver with a hinged barrel and cylinder assembly. Varying barrel lengths. Blued or nickel-plated with hard rubber grips.

Exc.	V.G.	Good	Fair	Poor
—	250	100	75	50

Double-Barrel Shotguns
Good quality hammer and hammerless doubles but few produced until taken over by Hopkins and Allen Firearms Co. Values from $100 to $1,000 depending on grade and condition.

FOWLER, B. JR.
Hartford, Connecticut

Percussion Pistol
A .38 caliber single-shot percussion pistol with a 4" half octagonal barrel, iron frame and maple grips. The barrel marked "B. Fowler, Jr." Manufactured between 1835 and 1838.

Exc.	V.G.	Good	Fair	Poor
—	950	500	300	150

FOX, A. H.
Philadelphia, Pennsylvania

Ansley H. Fox established the Fox Gun Company in Baltimore, Maryland, in 1896. Subsequently, he made arms under the name Philadelphia Gun Company. As of 1905, he operated under the name A.H. Fox. In 1930, this company was purchased by the Savage Arms Company who continued manufacturing all grades of Fox shotguns. As of 1942, the Savage Company only made the plainer grades.
NOTE: Fox Model B double shotguns see Savage Arms Co.

Sterlingworth
A 12, 16, or 20 gauge boxlock double-barrel shotgun with 26", 28", or 30" barrels, double triggers and extractors. Automatic ejectors were also available and would add approximately 30 percent to the values listed. Blued, casehardened with a walnut stock. Manufactured from 1911 to 1946.

Courtesy Nick Niles, Paul Goodwin photo.

Exc.	V.G.	Good	Fair	Poor
1250	1000	800	500	275

NOTE: 20 gauge add 50 percent.

Sterlingworth Deluxe
As above, with an ivory bead, recoil pad and optional 32" barrel.

Exc.	V.G.	Good	Fair	Poor
1450	1250	1000	700	400

NOTE: 20 gauge add 50 percent.

SP Grade
A 12, 16, or 20 gauge boxlock double-barrel shotgun with varying length barrels, double triggers and extractors.

Exc.	V.G.	Good	Fair	Poor
1000	850	750	450	225

NOTE: 20 gauge add 35 percent. Automatic ejectors add 15 percent.

HE Grade
Similar to the early A Grade and offered in 12 and 20 gauge. Chambers were 2-1/4" standard with 3" chambers available on request. This model is marked on the barrel "Not Warranted." This referred to pattern density, not barrel quality. Only sixty 20 gauge HE Grades appear in factory records. Manufactured from 1923 to 1942.

Exc.	V.G.	Good	Fair	Poor
2500	2150	1750	1000	650

NOTE: Single-selective trigger add 20 percent.

High Grade Guns A-FE
The Fox Company as well as the Savage Arms Company produced a variety of shotguns decorated in varying grades. They were available in 12, 16, and 20 gauge. As the value for these arms depends on the particular features of these arms, prospective purchasers are advised to secure a qualified appraisal prior to acquisition.

A Grade
Built from 1905 to 1942

Exc.	V.G.	Good	Fair	Poor
1450	1150	850	600	400

AE Grade (Automatic Ejectors)
Built from 1905 to 1946.

Exc.	V.G.	Good	Fair	Poor
1750	1450	1150	900	700

B Grade
Built from 1905 to 1918.

Exc.	V.G.	Good	Fair	Poor
2400	2100	1600	1100	500

BE Grade
Built from 1905 to 1918.

Exc.	V.G.	Good	Fair	Poor
2800	2500	2000	1500	900

C Grade
Built from 1905 to 1913.

Exc.	V.G.	Good	Fair	Poor
2600	2200	1700	1100	550

CE Grade
Built from 1905 to 1946.

Exc.	V.G.	Good	Fair	Poor
3000	2600	2100	1550	950

XE Grade
Built from 1914 to 1945.

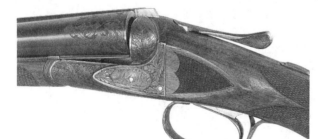

Exc.	V.G.	Good	Fair	Poor
5500	5000	3500	1850	1100

D Grade
Built from 1906 to 1913.

Exc.	V.G.	Good	Fair	Poor
8000	7000	4500	2500	1000

DE Grade
Built from 1906 to 1945.

Exc.	V.G.	Good	Fair	Poor
8500	7500	5000	3000	1500

F Grade
Built from 1906 to 1913.

Exc.	V.G.	Good	Fair	Poor
22500	15000	8000	5000	3000

FE Grade
Built from 1906 to 1940.

Exc.	V.G.	Good	Fair	Poor
25000	18500	10000	7000	5000

Single Barrel Trap Guns
A 12 gauge single barrel boxlock shotgun with 30" or 32" ventilated rib barrels and automatic ejector. There were approximately 571 single-barrel trap guns manufactured. Produced in four grades:

J Grade
Built from 1919 to 1936.

Exc.	V.G.	Good	Fair	Poor
2350	1950	1250	950	600

K Grade
Built from 1919 to 1931. Approximately 75 built.

Exc.	V.G.	Good	Fair	Poor
3500	2750	2000	1500	950

L Grade
Built from 1919 to 1931. Approximately 25 built.

Exc.	V.G.	Good	Fair	Poor
4750	3300	2700	1950	1200

M Grade
Built from 1919 to 1932. A total of 9 guns built.

Exc.	V.G.	Good	Fair	Poor
11500	8750	5500	4000	2500

CURRENTLY MANUFACTURED A.H. FOX SHOTGUNS

In 1993 the Connecticut Manufacturing Company of New Britain, Connecticut, announced the production of the A.H. Fox shotgun in 20 gauge exclusively. The gun is hand-built and constructed to the same dimensions and standards as the original Fox. The gun is offered in five grades with many standard features and several optional ones as well. Each shotgun is built to order. Because these guns are newly built and have no pricing history, only manufacturer's retail price for the base gun will be given. Extra sets of barrels, single triggers, and other extra costs options will greatly affect price.

CE Grade
Receiver engraved with fine scroll and game scene engraving with Turkish Circassian walnut stock, fine line hand checkering. Choice of full, half, or straight grip with splinter forend. Double triggers, automatic ejectors, automatic safety, choice of chokes, and barrel lengths in 26, 28, and 30 inches.

Retail price: $5,650

XE Grade
Same features as above with the addition of chiseled scroll work with engraved game scenes and higher quality Circassian walnut.

Retail price: $8,500

DE Grade
Same features as above with more intricate and extensive engraving. Even higher quality wood with diamond pattern checkering.

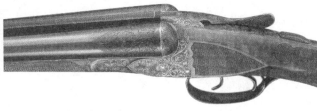

Retail price: $12,500

FE Grade
This grade features gold inlays and distinctive scroll work. Best quality wood with very fine line diamond pattern checkering.

Retail price: $17,500

Exhibition Grade
This is the company's highest grade and features any optional detail the customer desires including custom engraving and exhibition quality wood. Each Exhibition Grade Fox will be unique and should be appraised on an individual basis.
Retail price: $25,000

FRANCHI, L.
Brescia, Italy
Importer—Benelli USA

SIDE-BY-SIDE-SHOTGUNS

Astore
A 12 gauge boxlock shotgun manufactured in a variety of barrel lengths with double triggers and automatic ejectors. Blued with a straight walnut stock. Manufactured from 1937 to 1960.

NIB	Exc.	V.G.	Good	Fair	Poor
1100	900	750	500	350	200

Astore II
As above, but more finely finished.

NIB	Exc.	V.G.	Good	Fair	Poor
1350	1100	900	700	450	250

Astore 5
As above, but more finely finished.

NIB	Exc.	V.G.	Good	Fair	Poor
2250	1750	1250	950	600	300

Airone
Similar to the Astore. Manufactured during the 1940s.

NIB	Exc.	V.G.	Good	Fair	Poor
1300	1050	950	750	500	250

Sidelock Double-Barrel Shotguns
A 12, 16, or 20 gauge sidelock double-barrel shotgun manufactured in a variety of barrel lengths with a single-selective trigger and automatic ejectors. Produced in the following grades they differ as to engraving coverage and quality of wood:

Condor

NIB	Exc.	V.G.	Good	Fair	Poor
7500	6500	4500	3500	2500	1250

Imperial

NIB	Exc.	V.G.	Good	Fair	Poor
10000	8500	6000	4500	3250	1500

Imperiales

NIB	Exc.	V.G.	Good	Fair	Poor
10500	9000	6500	5000	3500	1500

No. 5 Imperial Monte Carlo

NIB	Exc.	V.G.	Good	Fair	Poor
15000	12500	9000	7500	5000	2000

No. 11 Imperial Monte Carlo

NIB	Exc.	V.G.	Good	Fair	Poor
16000	13500	10000	8000	5500	2000

Imperial Monte Carlo Extra

NIB	Exc.	V.G.	Good	Fair	Poor
20000	17500	12500	9500	7500	3500

Highlander
Introduced in 2003 this model features either a 12, 20, or 28 gauge gun fitted with 26" barrels and fixed chokes. Select walnut straight grip stock with splinter forend. Coin finished steel receiver. Single trigger. Weight is 6.4 lbs. for 12 gauge; 5.8 lbs. for 20 gauge, and 5.7 lbs. for 28 gauge.

NIB	Exc.	V.G.	Good	Fair	Poor
1800	1300	—	—	—	—

NOTE: Add $150 for 28 gauge.

FRANCOTTE, A.
Liege, Belgium
For pistols and revolvers SEE—AFC.

Jubilee
A 12, 16, 20, and 28 gauge Anson & Deeley boxlock double-barrel shotgun with various barrel lengths and chokes, automatic ejectors, double triggers and walnut stock.

Exc.	V.G.	Good	Fair	Poor
1650	1350	1100	850	450

No. 14

Courtesy William Hammond

Exc.	V.G.	Good	Fair	Poor
2250	1850	1600	1300	650

No. 18

Exc.	V.G.	Good	Fair	Poor
2750	2250	2000	1500	750

No. 20

Exc.	V.G.	Good	Fair	Poor
3250	2500	2250	1750	900

No. 25

Exc.	V.G.	Good	Fair	Poor
3750	3000	2750	2000	1000

No. 30

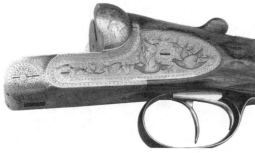

Courtesy William Hammond

Exc.	V.G.	Good	Fair	Poor
4800	4000	3500	3000	1500

Eagle Grade No. 45

Exc.	V.G.	Good	Fair	Poor
3750	3000	2500	2000	1000

Knockabout

A plain version of the Jubilee Model in 12, 16, 20, and 28 gauge and .410 bore.

Exc.	V.G.	Good	Fair	Poor
1250	1100	850	650	500

NOTE: 20 gauge add 20 percent; 28 gauge add 30 percent; .410 add 40 percent.

Sidelock Side-by-Side

A 12, 16, 20, and 28 gauge and .410 bore sidelock shotgun ordered per customer's specifications. Extensive scroll engraving, deluxe walnut stock and finely checkered. The .410 will bring a premium of from $1,200-$1,500.

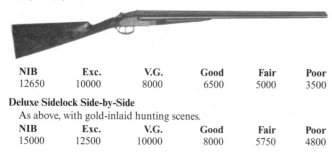

NIB	Exc.	V.G.	Good	Fair	Poor
12650	10000	8000	6500	5000	3500

Deluxe Sidelock Side-by-Side

As above, with gold-inlaid hunting scenes.

NIB	Exc.	V.G.	Good	Fair	Poor
15000	12500	10000	8000	5750	4800

FRANCOTTE, A.
Liege, Belgium
CURRENTLY IMPORTED SHOTGUNS AND RIFLES
Importer—Armes De Chasse
Chadds Ford, Pennsylvania

Francotte currently imports side-by-side boxlock or sidelock shotguns, double rifles, and single-shot rifles as well as bolt-action rifles into the United States through Armes De Chasse. These shotguns and rifles are all custom built to the customer's specifications. Gauge (including 24 and 32 gauge), caliber, barrel length, engraving, wood type and style are all individually produced. No two are alike. These shotguns and rifles should be individually appraised before the sale. Prices listed reflect a range that the original buyer paid and also reflect the value of the changing dollar.

Custom Side-by-Side Shotguns

Available in 12, 16, 20, 28 gauge and .410 bore in either boxlock or sidelock actions. Barrel length, engraving, wood type and style are at the customer's discretion. Retail prices range from:
Basic Boxlock with 27.5" barrels and walnut stock with double triggers in 12, 16, and 20 gauge without engraving—$15,000
Basic Boxlock in 28 gauge or .410 bore without engraving—$11,000
Basic Boxlock with 26.5" or 28" barrels and deluxe walnut stock with scroll engraving, and double triggers in 12, 16, and 20 gauge—$20,000
Basic Boxlock in 28 gauge or .410 bore—$25,000
Prices for 24 and 32 gauge are extra. These prices do not include engraving.

Custom Double Rifles

These custom built double rifles are offered in calibers from 9.3x74R to .470 Nitro Express in boxlock or sidelock actions. Barrel length, engraving, wood type and style are at the customer's discretion. Retail prices range from:
Prices for 24 and 32 gauge are extra. These prices do not include engraving.
Boxlock in 9.3x74R, 8x57JRS and other European calibers-$11,800
Boxlock in .375 H&H and .470 NE—$15,700
Sidelock in 9.3x74R, etc.—$23,700. Sidelock in large calibers—$28,500

Custom Single-Shot Mountain Rifles

These single-shot rifles are offered in rimmed cartridges but rimless cartridge rifles can be built on special request. Barrel length, engraving, wood type and style are at the customer's discretion. Retail prices range from:
Boxlock in rimmed calibers—Prices start at $10,000
Sidelock in 7x65R and 7mm Rem. Mag.—Prices start at $21,000

FRANKLIN, C. W.
Liege, Belgium

Manufacturer of utilitarian shotguns with either exposed or enclosed hammers. Circa 1900.

Single-Barrel

Exc.	V.G.	Good	Fair	Poor
150	75	50	35	20

Damascus Barrel Double

Exc.	V.G.	Good	Fair	Poor
250	150	125	100	65

Steel Barrel Double

Exc.	V.G.	Good	Fair	Poor
300	175	150	125	90

FREEDOM ARMS
Freedom, Wyoming

PREMIER AND FIELD GRADE REVOLVERS

Both grades use the same materials and machining tolerances. The difference is in the finish, standard components, and warranty.
The Premier Grade has a bright brushed finish, screw adjustable rear sight, laminated hardwood grips, and a limited lifetime warranty.
The Field Grade has a matte finish, adjustable rear sight for elevation only, Pachmayr rubber grips, and a one year warranty.

FREEMAN, AUSTIN T.
Hoard's Armory
Watertown, New York

Freeman Army Model Revolver

A .44 caliber percussion revolver with a 7.5" round barrel and a 6-shot unfluted cylinder with recessed nipples. Blued, casehardened rammer and hammer, and walnut grips. The frame is marked "Freeman's Pat. Dec. 9, 1862/Hoard's Armory, Watertown, N.Y." Several thousand were manufactured in 1863 and 1864.

Exc.	V.G.	Good	Fair	Poor
—	—	5000	2000	500

FRIGON
Clay Center, Kansas

An importer of guns manufactured by Marocchi of Italy.

FT I

A 12 gauge boxlock single-barrel shotgun with a 32" or 34" ventilated rib barrel, full choke, automatic ejector and interchanged stock. Blued. Introduced in 1986.

NIB	Exc.	V.G.	Good	Fair	Poor
950	750	650	550	450	300

FUNK, CHRISTOPH
Suhl, Germany

Christoph Funk began his gun business before 1900. The vast majority of long guns were best quality. Some collectors believe that J.P. Sauer built receivers for Funk but this is not known for certain. Funk produced shotguns, shotgun-rifle combinations, and double rifles. Some were exported to England and the U.S. Most of the U.S. imports are in the more common North American calibers such as .300 Savage, 30-30, 32-20 Winchester, and 12 or 16 gauge. Most are found with only a right-hand extension arm which locks into the receiver, but some higher grades have both extension arms. The quality of these guns is extremely high. Guns were probably not made after 1940. Quality of engraving and caliber determines value. American calibers will command a higher price. Prices listed are for American calibers.

Courtesy Jim Cate

Exc.	V.G.	Good	Fair	Poor
2800	2000	1250	600	400

FYRBERG, ANDREW
Worcester and Hopkinton, Massachusetts

Double-Barrel Shotguns

Fyrberg did work for Iver Johnson and C.S. Shattuck Co. of Hatfield, Mass. He began producing a hammerless double about 1902, a well designed boxlock with coil mainsprings. An estimated 2,000 were produced at Hopkinton and Worcester, Mass. Some have been made at Meriden, Conn. Sears cataloged the Fyrberg guns in 1902 to about 1908.

Exc.	V.G.	Good	Fair	Poor
500	400	300	200	150

Revolvers

A 3"-barreled .32 caliber and a 3.5" .38 caliber revolver with round ribbed barrels and round butts. The grips bear the trademark, "AFCo." This model was most likely made by Iver Johnson for Andrew Fyrburg.

Exc.	V.G.	Good	Fair	Poor
200	125	100	75	50

G

GALEF
Zabala Hermanos & Antonio Zoli
Spain

Zabala Double

A 10, 12, 16, and 20 caliber boxlock shotgun with a 22" to 30" barrel and various chokes. Hardwood stock.

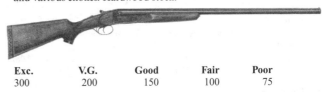

Exc.	V.G.	Good	Fair	Poor
300	200	150	100	75

Companion

A folding 12 to .410 bore single-shot underlever shotgun with a 28" or 30" barrel.

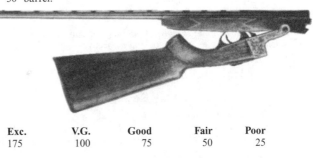

Exc.	V.G.	Good	Fair	Poor
175	100	75	50	25

GALLAGER
Richardson & Overman
Philadelphia, Pennsylvania

Gallager Carbine

A .50 caliber single-shot percussion carbine with a 22.25" barrel, saddle ring and walnut stock. Blued and case hardened. Approximately 23,000 were made during the Civil War.

Percussion Model

As above, in .56-62 rimfire caliber. Approximately 5,000 of this model were made.

Exc.	V.G.	Good	Fair	Poor
—	3250	2000	1250	500

Spencer Cartridge Model

Exc.	V.G.	Good	Fair	Poor
—	2750	1500	950	400

GAMBA, RENATO
Gardone V. T., Italy
Importer—Gamba, USA
New York, New York

SIDE-BY-SIDE SHOTGUNS

Hunter Super

A 12 gauge Anson & Deeley boxlock double-barrel shotgun with a variety of barrel lengths and chokes, double triggers and extractors. Engraved and silver-plated.

NIB	Exc.	V.G.	Good	Fair	Poor
1250	900	700	550	450	250

Principessa

A 12 or 20 gauge boxlock shotgun. Engraved, checkered stock.

NIB	Exc.	V.G.	Good	Fair	Poor
1850	1250	900	700	500	250

Oxford 90
A 12 or 20 gauge sidelock shotgun with various barrel lengths and chokes, the Purdey locking system, double triggers, and automatic ejectors. Walnut stock.

NIB	Exc.	V.G.	Good	Fair	Poor
4250	3250	1700	900	600	300

Oxford Extra
Same as above but with fine engraving.

NIB	Exc.	V.G.	Good	Fair	Poor
5200	4000	2250	1500	900	450

Gamba 624 Prince
Fitted with a Wesley Richards-type frame, select walnut stock, and fine hand engraving. Offered in 12 gauge with 28" barrels.

NIB	Exc.	V.G.	Good	Fair	Poor
4800	3900	2500	1500	850	400

Gamba 624 Extra
Same as above but with deep floral engraving.

NIB	Exc.	V.G.	Good	Fair	Poor
8000	5000	4500	2500	1250	600

London
A 12 or 20 gauge Holland & Holland sidelock shotgun with various barrel lengths and chokes, double or single-selective trigger, automatic ejectors. Walnut stock.

NIB	Exc.	V.G.	Good	Fair	Poor
7000	5500	4500	2500	1250	700

London Royal
As above with engraved hunting scenes.

NIB	Exc.	V.G.	Good	Fair	Poor
8000	6500	5000	3750	2000	950

Ambassador Gold and Black
A 12 and 20 gauge Holland & Holland sidelock shotgun with various barrel lengths and choke combinations, single-selective trigger, automatic ejectors, and a single gold line engraved on the barrels and the frame. Walnut stocks.

NIB	Exc.	V.G.	Good	Fair	Poor
25000	19000	13500	9500	5000	2500

Ambassador Executive
Gamba's best quality shotgun produced in 12 or 20 gauge to the customer's specifications.

NIB	Exc.	V.G.	Good	Fair	Poor
28000	20000	15000	10000	5000	2500

GARBI
Eibar, Spain
Importer—W. L. Moore and Co.
Scottsdale, Arizona

Model 51-B
A 12 gauge boxlock shotgun, also available in 16 and 20 gauge, with double triggers, automatic ejectors, case hardened or coin-finished receiver and walnut stock.

NIB	Exc.	V.G.	Good	Fair	Poor
1750	1200	850	600	—	—

Model 62-B
A 12 gauge sidelock shotgun, also chambered for 16 and 20 gauge with double triggers, extractors and cocking indicators. Engraved, case hardened or coin-finished receiver and walnut stock.

NIB	Exc.	V.G.	Good	Fair	Poor
1500	1050	850	650	—	—

Model 71
A 12, 16, or 20 gauge Holland & Holland sidelock shotgun with various barrel lengths and choke combinations, automatic ejectors and a single-selective trigger. Engraved with fine English-style scrollwork and walnut stock. Discontinued in 1988.

NIB	Exc.	V.G.	Good	Fair	Poor
2500	2000	1800	1500	—	—

Model 100
A 12, 16, or 20 gauge Holland & Holland sidelock shotgun with chopper-lump barrels, automatic ejectors, and a single trigger. Engraved in the Purdey style, with walnut stock.

NIB	Exc.	V.G.	Good	Fair	Poor
3500	3000	2500	2000	—	—

Model 101
As above, with floral engraving. Discontinued in 1988 in this form, then furnished with hand-engraved Continental scroll with round body action.

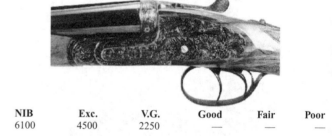

NIB	Exc.	V.G.	Good	Fair	Poor
6100	4500	2250	—	—	—

Model 102
As above, with Holland & Holland style, engraving and also in 28 gauge. Discontinued in 1988.

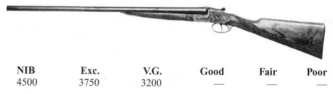

NIB	Exc.	V.G.	Good	Fair	Poor
4500	3750	3200	—	—	—

Model 103A
This model has Purdey-style engraving with high grade wood and checkering.

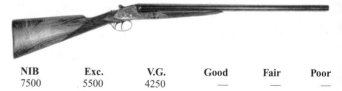

NIB	Exc.	V.G.	Good	Fair	Poor
7500	5500	4250	—	—	—

Model 103A Royal
Same as above but with special high quality engraving, very fancy wood, hand matted rib.

NIB	Exc.	V.G.	Good	Fair	Poor
11000	7750	6000	—	—	—

Model 103B

In 12, 16, 20, or 28 gauge, Holland & Holland sidelock shotgun with various barrel lengths and choke combinations, chopper-lump barrels, Holland & Holland easy-opening mechanism, automatic ejectors, single-selective trigger, and Purdey-type scroll engraving.

NIB	Exc.	V.G.	Good	Fair	Poor
10500	7750	6000	—	—	—

Model 103B Royal

Same as above but with high quality engraving, very fancy wood, hand matted rib.

NIB	Exc.	V.G.	Good	Fair	Poor
14750	11000	8000	—	—	—

Model 120

As above, with engraved hunting scenes. Discontinued in 1988.

NIB	Exc.	V.G.	Good	Fair	Poor
7500	6000	4000	—	—	—

Model 200

As above, Magnum proofed, double locking screws and 100 percent floral scroll engraving.

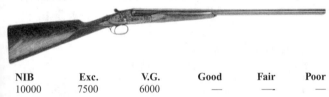

NIB	Exc.	V.G.	Good	Fair	Poor
10000	7500	6000	—	—	—

Model Special

A special order gun. Seek an expert appraisal prior to a sale.

NIB	Exc.	V.G.	Good	Fair	Poor
N/A	—	—	—	—	—

Express Rifle

This is a best-quality sidelock side-by-side double rifle. Stock has pistol grip and cheekpiece. Choice of English scroll or floral engraving. Calibers are 7x65R, 9.3x74R, or .375 H&H.

NIB	Exc.	V.G.	Good	Fair	Poor
21000	15000	12000	—	—	—

GATLING ARMS CO.
Birmingham, England

Established in 1888, this company remained in operation until approximately 1890. Although primarily involved with the marketing of Gatling Guns, it did market the one revolver listed.

Kynoch-Dimancea

A .38 or .45 caliber double-action hammerless revolver with a 6-shot cylinder. The loading system is rather unusual—a spur that resembles a hammer is pulled down, allowing the barrel and cylinder to pivot and to be pulled forward. During this motion the empty cases are ejected and new ones could be inserted. Marked "The Gatling Arms and Ammunition Co. Birmingham"; some are also marked "Dimancea Patent."

Exc.	V.G.	Good	Fair	Poor
—	1750	700	500	325

GEM
Bacon Arms Company
Norwich, Connecticut
SEE—Bacon Arms Company

Gem Pocket Revolver

A .22 caliber spur trigger revolver with a 1.25" octagonal barrel. The frame is iron, engraved, nickel-plated, with walnut or ivory grips. The barrel marked "Gem." Manufactured between 1878 and 1883.

Exc.	V.G.	Good	Fair	Poor
—	—	1750	600	300

GENEZ, A. G.
New York, New York

Located at 9 Chambers Street, Genez made a wide variety of firearms during his working life (ca. 1850 to 1875). The most commonly encountered of his arms today are single-shot percussion pistols and percussion double-barrel shotguns. More rarely seen are single-shot percussion target rifles. A number of the arms he made were decorated by Louis D. Nimschke. Genez products signed by Nimschke command considerable premiums over the values for the standard firearms listed and prospective purchasers of Nimschke engraved pieces are strongly advised to secure a qualified appraisal prior to acquisition.

Double-Barrel Shotgun

Most often encountered in 12 gauge with varying barrel lengths; blued steel furniture, and walnut stock.

Exc.	V.G.	Good	Fair	Poor
—	—	2250	1500	500

Pocket Pistol

A .41 caliber single-shot percussion pistol with a 3" barrel, German silver mountings and a walnut stock. Manufactured in the 1850s and 1860s.

Exc.	V.G.	Good	Fair	Poor
—	—	3500	1250	500

GEORGIA ARMORY
Milledgeville, George

Established in 1862, this concern produced a rifle based upon the U.S. Model 1855 Harper's Ferry Rifle. Nearly identical in all respects to the Harpers Ferry, the Georgia Armory rifle had a lockplate patterned after the U.S. Model 1841 Rifle. Lock marked "G.A. ARMORY" over the date (1862 or 1863). Buttplate tangs marked with serial numbers. The highest known serial number is 309. These rifles were fitted with saber bayonets.

Prospective purchasers are strongly advised to secure an expert appraisal prior to acquisition.

Exc.	V.G.	Good	Fair	Poor
—	—	50000	20000	5000

GIBBS
New York, New York

Gibbs Carbine

A .52 caliber single-shot percussion carbine with a sliding 22" round barrel. Blued, case hardened with a walnut stock. The lock marked with an American eagle and "Wm. F. Brooks/Manf New York/1863." The breech marked "L.H. Gibbs/Patd/Jany 8, 1856." There were only 1,050 produced.

Exc.	V.G.	Good	Fair	Poor
—	—	5000	2000	500

GIBBS RIFLE COMPANY
Martinsburg, West Virginia
SEE ALSO—Parker Hale

This company imports Parker Hale black powder replicas and WW II surplus military firearms such as the Mauser Model 1888, Model 71/84, and the Israeli K98. The company also produced historical remakes and specialty rifles.

GILLESPIE
New York, New York

Derringer Type Pocket Pistol

A .41 caliber single-shot percussion pistol with a 2.5" barrel and a walnut stock. Manufactured from 1848 to 1870.

Exc.	V.G.	Good	Fair	Poor
—	—	2500	1200	500

GOVERNOR
Norwich, Connecticut

Governor Pocket Revolver
A .22 caliber spur trigger revolver with a 3" barrel and 7-shot cylinder. These revolvers were made from modified Bacon pepperboxes. The top strap marked "Governor." Manufactured from approximately 1868 to 1874.

Exc.	V.G.	Good	Fair	Poor
—	—	650	250	100

GRANGER, G.
St. Etienne, France
Importer—Wes Gilpin
Dallas, Texas

Side-by-Side Shotgun
A custom-order 12, 16, and 20 gauge boxlock double-barrel shotgun. Manufactured since 1902. This is a custom order shotgun and an independent appraisal is strongly recommended. Because the gun is imported the value of the dollar frequently determines price movement.

Exc.	V.G	Good	Fair	Poor
15000	12000	8000	4000	1500

GRANT, STEPHEN
London, England
SEE—British Double Guns

GREAT WESTERN ARMS COMPANY

A certain amount of confusion surrounds Great Western Arms Company firearms. Collectors believe that this company's Colt single-action and Remington derringer look-alikes were produced in Italy or Spain and imported into the U.S. under the West Coast distributor H.Y. Hunter. In fact, all major components were built of the finest alloys using investment castings and assembled in Los Angeles, California. Great Western offered an extensive variety of combinations of caliber, finish, and grips. Auxiliary cylinders were offered as well in the following chambers: .44 Special/.44-40/.44 Magnum, .357/.38 Special and .45 ACP/.45 Long Colt. The company made available to its customers several grades and styles of engraving.

During the 10 years that Great Western was in business the quality of its firearms was inconsistent due to uncertain management and finances. This left the company's reputation damaged and allowed Colt and Ruger to dominate the single-action market. By 1961 Great Western Arms Company was no longer able to compete. Despite the company's unstable history there is a small but growing collector interest in these firearms. Approximately 22,000 single-action revolvers were built and less than 3,500 derringers were manufactured from 1953 to 1961.

Standard barrel lengths were: 4-3/4, 5-1/2, and 7-1/2 inches.
Standard calibers were: .38 Special, .357 Magnum, .357 Atomic, .44 Special, .44-40, .44 Magnum, .45 Long Colt, and .22 Long Rifle.
Standard finishes were: Case hardened frame and blued barrel and cylinder, or all blue finish.
NOTE: For guns to be in NIB condition they must have original boxes and paper work. Factory engraved guns must be supported by some type of invoice, letter, or other provenance to realize full value.

Centerfire Single-Action

Courtesy John C. Dougan

Exc.	V.G.	Good	Fair	Poor
500	425	350	250	200

.22 Long Rifle Single-Action

Exc.	V.G.	Good	Fair	Poor
335	295	250	200	150

Target Model
Flattop with micro sights.

Exc.	V.G.	Good	Fair	Poor
550	475	400	300	225

Fast Draw Model
Brass backstrap and trigger guard.

Exc.	V.G.	Good	Fair	Poor
550	475	400	300	225

Deputy Model
4" barrel with full length sight rib.

Exc.	V.G.	Good	Fair	Poor
1000	850	750	650	550

NOTE: For calibers other than standard such as .22 Hornet, .32-20, .45 ACP, .22 Magnum, .30 Carbine add 10 percent premium. For factory plated pistols add 10 percent. For factory cased pistols add 20 percent. For Sheriff's Model or Buntline Special add 15 percent. For factory ivory grips add $175; for stag grips add $95, and for pearl grips add $150. Factory-engraved guns will add $750 to $3,500 to above prices depending on coverage.

Unassembled Kit Gun—In the White

N.I.B.	Exc.	V.G.	Good	Fair
350	300	—	—	—

NOTE: Assembled Kit Gun will bring between $100 and $200 depending on condition.

Derringer Model .38 Special & .38 S&W

Exc.	V.G.	Good	Fair	Poor
300	250	200	150	100

Derringer Model—.22 Magnum RF

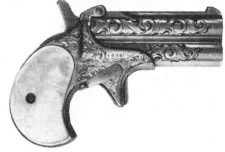

Courtesy John C. Dougan

Exc.	V.G.	Good	Fair	Poor
400	350	250	200	150

NOTE: Factory-engraved Derringers add $350 to $500.

GREIFELT & CO.
Suhl, Germany

SIDE-BY-SIDE SHOTGUNS

Model 22
A 12 or 20 gauge boxlock double-barrel shotgun with 28" or 30" barrels, sideplates, double triggers and extractors. Blued, case hardened with a walnut stock. Manufactured after 1945.

Exc.	V.G.	Good	Fair	Poor
2250	1800	1500	1200	750

Model 22E
As above, with automatic ejectors.

Exc.	V.G.	Good	Fair	Poor
2500	2000	1500	1200	750

Model 103

A 12 and 16 gauge boxlock shotgun with a 28" or a 30" barrel, double triggers and extractors. Walnut stock with a pistol or straight English-style grip. Post-war model.

Exc.	V.G.	Good	Fair	Poor
2250	1800	1500	1200	750

Model 103E

As above, with automatic ejectors.

Exc.	V.G.	Good	Fair	Poor
2500	2000	1500	1200	750

GRISWOLD & GRIER
SEE—Griswold & Gunnison

GRISWOLD & GUNNISON
Griswoldville, Georgia

1851 Navy Type

A .36 caliber percussion revolver with a 7.5" barrel and 6-shot cylinder. The frame and grip straps made of brass and the barrel as well as cylinder made of iron. Approximately 3,700 were made between 1862 and 1864, for the Confederate government.

NOTE: This revolver is sometimes referred to as the Griswold and Grier.

Exc.	V.G.	Good	Fair	Poor
—	—	30000	10000	2500

GROSS ARMS CO.
Tiffin, Ohio

Pocket Revolver

A .25 and .30 caliber spur trigger revolver with a 6" octagonal barrel, a 7-shot cylinder and marked "Gross Arms Co., Tiffin, Ohio." Blued, with walnut grips. Only a few hundred were manufactured between 1864 and 1866.

Exc.	V.G.	Good	Fair	Poor
—	—	1500	550	300

GRUBB, J. C. & CO.
Philadelphia, Pennsylvania

Pocket Pistol

A .41 caliber single-shot percussion pistol with various barrel lengths. German silver, walnut stock and engraved lock and trigger guard. The lock is marked "J.C. Grubb." Several hundred were manufactured between 1860 and 1870.

Exc.	V.G.	Good	Fair	Poor
—	—	1250	650	300

GUEDES-CASTRO
Steyr, Austria

Model 1885

An 8x60mm Guedes single-shot dropping block rifle with a 28" barrel, full-length walnut stock and iron mounts. Made in Austria under contract for the Portuguese army in 1885.

Exc.	V.G.	Good	Fair	Poor
650	400	350	250	125

GUION, T. F.
New Orleans, Louisiana

Pocket Pistol

A .41 caliber single-shot percussion pistol with a 2.5" barrel, German silver mountings, and a walnut stock. Manufactured in the 1850s.

Exc.	V.G.	Good	Fair	Poor
—	—	1750	500	275

H

H.J.S. INDUSTRIES, INC.
Brownsville, Texas

Frontier Four Derringer

A .22 caliber four-barreled pocket pistol with 2.5" sliding barrels, stainless steel frame and barrel grip and walnut grips.

Exc.	V.G.	Good	Fair	Poor
150	100	75	50	25

Lone Star Derringer

A .38 Special caliber single-shot spur trigger pistol with a 2.5" barrel. Stainless steel with wood grips.

Exc.	V.G.	Good	Fair	Poor
175	125	100	75	50

H&R 1871, LLC
Gardner, Massachusetts
SEE—Harrington & Richardson

HALL, ALEXANDER
New York, New York

Revolving Rifle

A .58 caliber percussion revolving rifle with a 15-shot open centered cylinder. The frame was made of brass, the barrel and cylinder of iron and the stock of walnut. Manufactured during the 1850s in limited quantities. Prospective purchasers should secure a qualified appraisal prior to acquisition. This is a very rare firearm.

Exc.	V.G.	Good	Fair	Poor
—	—	22500	9500	3000

HALL-NORTH
Middletown, Connecticut

Model 1840 Carbine

This carbine was manufactured by Simeon North and was chambered for .52 caliber percussion. It is a single-shot, breech-loading, smoothbore with a 21" round barrel. It has a full-length stock held on by two barrel bands. There is a ramrod mounted under the barrel, and the mountings are of iron. The lock is case hardened, and the barrel is brown. The stock is walnut. The markings are "US/S. North/Midltn/Conn." There are two distinct variations, both produced under military contract.

Type 1 Carbine

This model has a squared, right-angled breech lever mounted on the trigger plate. There were 500 of these manufactured in 1840.

Exc.	V.G.	Good	Fair	Poor
—	—	7500	3000	1200

Type 2 Carbine

This variation features a curved, breech-operating lever that is known as a fishtail. There were approximately 6,000 of these manufactured from 1840 to 1843. Some have an 8" bar and ring.

Exc.	V.G.	Good	Fair	Poor
—	—	5000	2000	750

HAMBUSH, JOSEPH
Ferlach, Austria

Boxlock Side-by-Side Shotgun

A custom-order boxlock double-barrel shotgun chambered for all gauges, single-selective or double trigger and automatic ejectors. It features workmanship of a high order, and all specification could vary with the customer's wishes. Engraved with hunting scenes. This is a rare gun and is not often encountered on today's market.

Exc.	V.G.	Good	Fair	Poor
1750	1000	800	550	350

NOTE: Pricing is only estimated as not enough are traded to provide accurate values.

Sidelock Side-by-Side Shotgun
Similar to the above, but features a full sidelock-action.

Exc.	V.G.	Good	Fair	Poor
3500	2000	1800	1500	1250

HAMMERLI, SA
Lenzburg, Switzerland

Dakota
A single-action revolver based on the Colt SAA design. It has a solid frame and is loaded through a gate. It is chambered for .22 LR, .357 Magnum .44-40, and .45 Colt and was offered with barrel lengths of 5", 6", and 7.5". It has a 6-shot cylinder and is blued, with a brass trigger guard and walnut grips.

Exc.	V.G.	Good	Fair	Poor
150	125	100	75	50

Large Calibers

Exc.	V.G.	Good	Fair	Poor
225	175	150	125	100

Super Dakota
Similar to the Dakota but is chambered for .41 and .44 Magnum, with adjustable sights.

Exc.	V.G.	Good	Fair	Poor
275	225	175	150	100

Virginian
Basically a more deluxe version of the Dakota. It is chambered for the .357 and .45 Colt cartridge. The trigger guard and back strap are chrome plated, with the frame case colored and the remainder blued. This model features the "Swissafe" safety system that allows the cylinder axis pin to be locked back to prevent the hammer from falling.

Exc.	V.G.	Good	Fair	Poor
300	250	200	175	125

HAMMOND BULLDOG
Connecticut Arms & Mfg. Co.
Naubuc, Connecticut

Hammond Bulldog
A .44 rimfire single-shot spur trigger pistol with a 4" octagonal barrel that pivots to open. Blued with checkered walnut grips. Manufactured from 1864 to approximately 1867.

Exc.	V.G.	Good	Fair	Poor
—	1250	500	375	250

HANKINS, WILLIAM
Philadelphia, Pennsylvania

Pocket Revolver
A .26 caliber spur trigger percussion revolver with a 3" octagonal barrel, and a 5-shot unfluted cylinder. Blued with walnut grips. Approximately 650 were manufactured in 1860 and 1861.

Exc.	V.G.	Good	Fair	Poor
—	—	2750	1250	500

HANUS, BILL
Newport, Oregon

Bill Hanus Classic
Built in Spain by Ignacio Ugartechea these side-by-side shotguns are offered in 16, 20, 28 gauge, as well as .410 bore. They are fitted with 27" barrel with concave ribs and are choked IC/M. Stock is straight grip with splinter forearm. Double triggers are standard as are automatic ejectors.

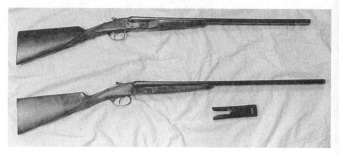

NIB	Exc.	V.G.	Good	Fair	Poor
1600	1250	—	—	—	—

HARRINGTON & RICHARDSON, INC.
Worcester, Massachusetts
Established in 1877 by G.H. Harrington and W.A. Richardson. The arms originally produced by this company were marketed under the trade name Aetna. The firm is now located in Gardner, Massachusetts.
NOTE: In November 2000 the Marlin Firearms Company purchased the assets of Harrington & Richardson. This new company is now known as H&R 1871, LLC.

Model No. 1
A .32 or .38 caliber spur-trigger single-action revolver with a 3" octagonal barrel, solid frame, a 7-shot or a 5-shot cylinder, depending on the caliber. Nickel-plated with checkered rubber bird's-head grips. Barrel marked "Harrington & Richardson Worcester, Mass." Approximately 3,000 were manufactured in 1877 and 1878.

Exc.	V.G.	Good	Fair	Poor
300	250	200	125	75

Model 1-1/2
A .32 caliber spur-trigger, single-action revolver with a 2.5" octagonal barrel and a 5-shot cylinder. Nickel-plated, round-butt rubber grips with an "H&R" emblem molded in. Approximately 10,000 were manufactured between 1878 and 1883.

Exc.	V.G.	Good	Fair	Poor
175	150	125	75	50

Model 2-1/2
As above, with a 3.25" barrel and a 7-shot cylinder. Approximately 5,000 were manufactured between 1878 and 1883.

Exc.	V.G.	Good	Fair	Poor
175	150	125	75	50

Model 3-1/2
Similar to the Model 2-1/2 except in .38 rimfire caliber with a 3.5" barrel and a 5-shot cylinder. Approximately 2,500 were manufactured.

Exc.	V.G.	Good	Fair	Poor
200	175	150	100	75

Model 4-1/2
A .41 rimfire caliber spur trigger revolver with a 2.5" barrel and 5-shot cylinder. Approximately 1,000 were manufactured.

Exc.	V.G.	Good	Fair	Poor
250	200	175	125	90

Model 1880
A .32 or .38 S&W centerfire caliber double-action revolver with a 3" round barrel, a solid frame, and a 5- or 6-shot cylinder, depending on the caliber. Nickel-plated with hard rubber grips. Marked "Harrington & Richardson Worchester, Mass." Approximately 4,000 were manufactured between 1880 and 1883.

Exc.	V.G.	Good	Fair	Poor
250	200	175	125	90

The American Double-Action
A .32, .28, or .44 centerfire caliber double-action revolver with a 2.5", 4.5", or 6" round or octagonal barrel, a 5- or 6-shot fluted cylinder, depending on the caliber, and solid frame, nickel-plated, with some blue models noted. The grips are hard rubber. Marked "The American Double Action." Some noted are marked "H&R Bulldog." Approximately 850,000 were manufactured between 1883 and 1940.

Exc.	V.G.	Good	Fair	Poor
125	100	85	65	40

The Young America Double-Action
A .22 rimfire or .32 S&W centerfire caliber, double-action revolver, with 2", 4.5", or 6" round or octagonal barrels, solid frame, and a 5- or 7-shot cylinder, depending on the caliber. Blued or nickel-plated, with hard rubber grips. Marked "Young America Double Action" or "Young America Bulldog." Approximately 1,500,000 were manufactured between 1884 and 1941.

Exc.	V.G.	Good	Fair	Poor
125	100	85	65	40
Exc.	V.G.	Good	Fair	Poor
300	250	200	150	100

First Model Hand Ejector
A .32 or .38 centerfire caliber double-action revolver with a 3.25" ribbed round barrel. This version does not feature the automatic ejection found on later models. Nickel-plated, with hard rubber grips. The company name is marked on the barrel. Approximately 6,000 were manufactured between 1886 and 1888.

Exc.	V.G.	Good	Fair	Poor
200	150	125	90	65

Model 1 Double-Action Revolver
A .32, .32 Long, and the .38 S&W caliber double-action revolver with a 3.25" ribbed round barrel, and a 5- or 6-shot cylinder, depending on the caliber. Nickel-plated, with hard rubber grips. Approximately 5,000 were manufactured between 1887 and 1889.

Exc.	V.G.	Good	Fair	Poor
175	145	110	80	50

Topper
A single-shot, break-open shotgun chambered for various gauges with various barrel lengths, chokes. Blued, with a hardwood stock. Introduced in 1946.

Exc.	V.G.	Good	Fair	Poor
145	95	75	60	40

Model 088
An external hammer single-shot, break-open shotgun chambered for all gauges with various barrel lengths, chokes and an automatic ejector. Blued, with a case colored frame and hardwood stock.

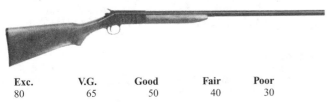

Exc.	V.G.	Good	Fair	Poor
80	65	50	40	30

Model 099
As above, but matte, electroless, nickel-plated.

Exc.	V.G.	Good	Fair	Poor
110	95	75	60	40

Model 162
A 12 or 20 gauge boxlock single-shotgun with a 24" barrel with rifle sights.

Exc.	V.G.	Good	Fair	Poor
125	100	80	65	45

Model 176
A 10-gauge, 3.5" Magnum caliber boxlock single barrel shotgun with a heavyweight 36" barrel and a Full choke. Manufactured between 1977 and 1985.

Exc.	V.G.	Good	Fair	Poor
125	100	80	65	45

Long Tom Classic
Introduced in 1996 this limited edition single-barrel shotgun features a case hardened frame with 32" Full choked barrel. Stock is hand-checkered black walnut with crescent buttplate. Chambered for 12 gauge. Weight is about 7.5 lbs. About 1,000 of these shotguns will be built each year.

NIB	Exc.	V.G.	Good	Fair	Poor
300	250	—	—	—	—

Model 171
A reproduction of the Model 1873 Trapdoor Springfield Carbine with a 22" barrel. Blued, with a case colored receiver and a walnut stock.

Exc.	V.G.	Good	Fair	Poor
300	250	200	150	100

Model 171-DL
As above, but more finely finished.

Exc.	V.G.	Good	Fair	Poor
350	300	250	200	125

100th Anniversary Officer's Model
A commemorative replica of the Officer's Model 1873 Trapdoor Springfield Rifle, with a 26" barrel. Engraved, and an anniversary plaque mounted on the stock. Blued, with a case colored receiver and a pewter forend tip. There were 10,000 manufactured in 1971. As with all commemoratives, this model is desirable only when NIB with all supplied material.

NIB	Exc.	V.G.	Good	Fair	Poor
450	350	300	275	200	125

Custer Memorial Issue
A limited production issue commemorating George Armstrong Custer's Battle of the Little Bighorn. Heavily engraved and gold inlaid with a high-grade checkered walnut stock. Furnished in a mahogany display case that included two books dealing with the subject. There were two versions produced—an Officer's Model, of which 25 were issued commemorating the 25 officers that fell with Custer, and another version commemorating the 243 enlisted men who lost their lives at the Little Bighorn. As with all commemoratives, to be collectible they must be NIB with all furnished material.

Officer's Model
25 manufactured.

NIB	Exc.	V.G.	Good	Fair	Poor
2700	2000	1500	1000	600	400

Enlisted Men's Model
243 manufactured.

NIB	Exc.	V.G.	Good	Fair	Poor
1500	1000	750	500	350	250

Model 174
A plain copy of the Springfield Model 1873 Carbine in .45-70 caliber with a 22" barrel. Manufactured in 1972.

Exc.	V.G.	Good	Fair	Poor
400	350	300	250	175

Model 178
A copy of the Springfield Model 1873 rifle with a 32" barrel. Manufactured from 1973 to 1984.

Exc.	V.G.	Good	Fair	Poor
325	300	250	200	125

HARRIS GUNWORKS
Phoenix, Arizona

Antietam Sharps Rifle
This is a replica of the Sharps Model 1874 sidehammer introduced in 1994. Chambered for the .40-65 or the .45-70. Choice of 30" or 32" octagon or round barrel. Stock is fancy walnut with either straight, pistol grip, or Creedmoor with schnabel forearm. Many optional sights offered. Weight is about 11.25 lbs.

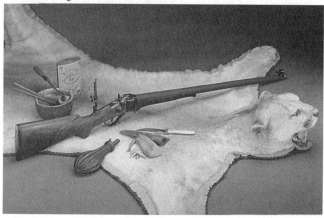

NIB	Exc.	V.G.	Good	Fair	Poor
2400	1850	1200	—	—	—

HAWES
Los Angeles, California

An importer of handguns primarily made in Europe
J. P. Sauer also made a Western-styled series for Hawes based in appearance on the Colt Single-Action Army.

Silver City Marshal
A .22 LR or .22 rimfire Magnum caliber single-action revolver with a 5.5" barrel, 6-shot cylinder, and fixed sights.

Exc.	V.G.	Good	Fair	Poor
125	100	75	50	25

Western Marshal
A .357 Magnum, .44 Magnum, .45 Colt, .45 ACP, .44-40, 9mm, .22 LR, and .22 rimfire Magnum single-action revolver with fixed sights. Blued.

Exc.	V.G.	Good	Fair	Poor
175	150	125	100	75

Texas Marshal
As above, but nickel plated.

Exc.	V.G.	Good	Fair	Poor
185	160	135	100	75

Montana Marshal
The Western Marshal with a brass backstrap and trigger guard.

Exc.	V.G.	Good	Fair	Poor
175	150	125	100	75

Chief Marshal
A .357 Magnum, .44 Magnum, and the .45 Colt caliber revolver with a 6.5" barrel, and 6-shot cylinder and adjustable sights. Blued.

Exc.	V.G.	Good	Fair	Poor
175	150	125	100	75

Federal Marshal
A 6-shot single-action revolver in .357 Magnum, .44 Magnum, and the .45 Colt caliber.

Exc.	V.G.	Good	Fair	Poor
175	150	125	100	75

HENRY REPEATING ARMS COMPANY
Brooklyn, New York

Henry Lever-Action
Chambered for the .22 LR, Long, and Short cartridges It is fitted with a 18.25" barrel and weighs 5.5 lbs. Magazine capacity is 15 for the .22 LR cartridge. Rear sight is adjustable and the front sight is hooded.

NIB	Exc.	V.G.	Good	Fair	Poor
270	175	125	—	—	—

Henry Carbine
Similar to the above model but with an overall length of 34". It features a large loop lever.

NIB	Exc.	V.G.	Good	Fair	Poor
280	175	125	—	—	—

Henry Youth Model
Similar to the carbine model above but with an overall length of 33".

NIB	Exc.	V.G.	Good	Fair	Poor
270	175	125	—	—	—

Henry Golden Boy
This lever-action rifle is chambered for the .22 LR, Short, or Long cartridges as well as the .22 WRM cartridge in a seperate model. Fitted with a brass receiver and 20" octagon barrel. Walnut stock. Weight is about 6.75 lbs.

NIB	Exc.	V.G.	Good	Fair	Poor
400	300	250	—	—	—

NOTE: Add $70 for .22 WRM model or .17 HMR. Add $20 for large loop lever. Add $600 for hand-engraved model.

Henry Pump-Action Rifle
Introduced in 1999 this .22 caliber is fitted with a 18.25" barrel and chambered for the .22 LR cartridge. Walnut stock and adjustable rear sight. Weight is approximately 5.5 lbs.

NIB	Exc.	V.G.	Good	Fair	Poor
250	200	—	—	—	—

HIGH STANDARD MANUFACTURING CORPORATION
New Haven, Hamden, and East Hartford, Connecticut

The High Standard Manufacturing Company was established in 1926, by Carl Swebilius and Gustave Beck to produce drills and machine tools. In 1932, the firm purchased the Hartford Arms & Equipment Company (q.v.) and began the manufacture of the latter's Model 1925 Semi-automatic Pistol as the Hi-Standard Model "B."

Throughout the High Standard Manufacturing Corporation's business life, its products were highly regarded for both their design and quality. While the company was originally located in New Haven, during WWII High Standard operated plants in New Haven and Hamden. After the war the operations were consolidated in Hamden. In 1968 the company was sold to the Leisure Group, Inc. The Leisure Group sold High Standard to High Standard, Inc. in January 1978. A final move was made to East Hartford, Connecticut, in 1977 where it remained until the doors closed in late 1984. In the spring of 1993 the High Standard Manufacturing Co, Inc. of Houston, Texas, acquired the company assets and trademarks as well as the .22 Target Pistols. These original assets were transfered from Connecticut to Houston, Texas, in July 1993. The first shipments of Houston manufactured pistols began in March 1994. Prices listed here are separated for both the Connecticut and Houston models. Collectors will pay a premium for the Connecticut pistols.

Model descriptions, photos, and prices by John J. Stimson, Jr.

BLACKPOWDER REVOLVERS
These guns were a series of .36 caliber cap-and-ball revolvers that began production in 1974 and ran through 1976. These are reproductions of the Confederate copies of the Colt Model 1851 Navy. Note most Confederate copies of the Colt had round barrels, not octagonal as found on Colts. The frames were made by High Standard and the balance of the parts by Uberti. The guns were assembled and finished by High Standard.

Griswold & Gunnison
Blued finish with a brass frame. Six-shot single-action. Commemorative gun came wtih a pine presentation case and a brass belt plate depicting the Georgia state seal.
Catalog number 9331 (Serial numbers 00501 through 02600)
Catalog number 9333 Commemorative (Serial numbers 00001 through 00500)

Exc.	V.G.
330	160

NOTE: Price is for gun in case with accessories. Deduct $100 for gun only in Exc. condition.

HOPKINS & ALLEN
Norwich, Connecticut
ALSO SEE—Bacon Arms Co. & Merwin Hulbert & Co.

Established in 1868, this company produced a variety of spur trigger revolvers in .22, .32, .38, or .41 caliber often marked with trade names such as: Acme, Blue Jacket, Captain Jack, Chichester, Defender, Dictator, Hopkins & Allen, Imperial Arms Co., Monarch, Mountain Eagle, Ranger, Tower's Police Safety, Universal and XL.

Some of these revolvers are hinged-frame, double-action break-opens with round-ribbed barrels of various lengths. Blued or nickel-plated, with checkered plastic grips.

Exc.	V.G.	Good	Fair	Poor
—	—	400	175	75

Derringer
A .22 caliber single-shot pistol with a hinged 1.75" barrel that pivots downwards for loading. Blued or nickel-plated with walnut, ivory, or pearl grips. The frame marked, "Hopkins & Allen Arms Co., Norwich, Conn. U.S.A." Several hundred were manufactured in the 1880s and 1890s.

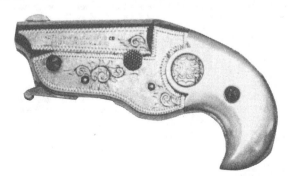

Exc.	V.G.	Good	Fair	Poor
—	—	2250	850	300

I

IGA
Veranopolis, Brazil
Importer—Stoeger Industries
Accokeek, Maryland

Single-Barrel Shotgun

A 12 or 20 gauge or .410 bore single barrel shotgun with an exposed hammer, 28" barrel and hardwood stock.

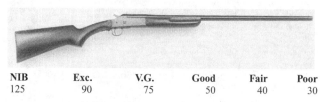

NIB	Exc.	V.G.	Good	Fair	Poor
125	90	75	50	40	30

Single-Barrel Shotgun Youth Model

Offered in 20 gauge and .410 bore this model features a 22" barrel and shorter than standard buttstock. Weighs 5 lbs.

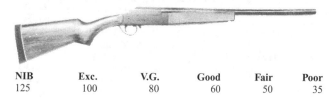

NIB	Exc.	V.G.	Good	Fair	Poor
125	100	80	60	50	35

Coach Gun

A 12 and 20 gauge as well as .410 bore boxlock double-barrel shotgun with 20" barrels, double triggers and extractors. Blued with a hardwood stock.

NIB	Exc.	V.G.	Good	Fair	Poor
400	325	250	150	100	75

NOTE: Add $50 for nickel finish. Add $60 for engraved butt stock.

IRVING, W.
New York, New York

Single-Shot Derringer

A .22 caliber spur trigger single-shot pistol with a 2.75" half octagonal barrel. Silver plated brass frame, blued barrel and rosewood grips. The barrel marked "W. Irving." Manufactured in the 1860s. The .32 caliber variation has a 3" barrel and is worth approximately 40 percent more than the values listed.

Exc.	V.G.	Good	Fair	Poor
—	—	900	300	125

POCKET REVOLVER

1st Model

A .31 caliber spur trigger percussion revolver with a 3" octagonal barrel, 6-shot cylinder and brass frame. The barrel marked "W. Irving." Approximately 50 were made between 1858 and 1862.

Exc.	V.G.	Good	Fair	Poor
—	—	2000	750	250

2nd Model

A .31 caliber percussion revolver with a 4.5" round barrel, loading lever and either brass or iron frame. The barrel marked "Address W. Irving. 20 Cliff St. N.Y." Approximately 600 manufactured with a brass frame and 1,500 with a frame of iron. The brass-frame version will bring a premium of about 35 percent.

Exc.	V.G.	Good	Fair	Poor
—	—	1150	400	200

IRWINDALE ARMS, INC.
Irwindale, California
SEE—AMT

ISRAELI MILITARY INDUSTRIES
Israel

Civilian firearms manufactured by this firm have been and are being retailed by Action Arms Limited, Magnum Research, and Mossberg.

ITHACA GUN CO.
Ithaca, New York

The following material was supplied by Walter C. Snyder and is copyrighted in his name. Used with the author's permission.

The Ithaca Gun Company was founded by William Henry Baker, John VanNatta, and Dwight McIntyre. Gun production started during the latter half of 1883 at an industrial site located on Fall Creek, Ithaca, New York. Leroy Smith joined the company by 1885 and George Livermore joined the firm in 1887. By 1894 the company was under the exclusive control of Leroy Smith and George Livermore. Many of the company's assets were purchased by the Ithaca Acquisition Corporation in 1987 and moved to King Ferry, New York, where it operated until May, 1996. Ithaca Acquisition's assets were purchased in 1996 by the Ithaca Gun Company, LLC and they continue operations to this day at the King Ferry site.

HAMMER MODELS

Ithaca Baker Model

The first model produced by the company was designed by W.H. Baker and was manufactured from 1883 through 1887. It was offered in six grades; Quality A ($35) through Quality F ($200) in either 10 or 12 gauge. All Ithaca-produced Baker models had exposed hammers. Grades above Quality B are seldom encountered and an expert appraisal is recommended.

Quality A

Courtesy Walter C. Snyder

Exc.	V.G.	Good	Fair	Poor
900	500	300	200	100

Quality B

Exc.	V.G.	Good	Fair	Poor
1200	700	350	200	100

New Ithaca Gun

The New Ithaca Gun was introduced in 1888 and discontinued during 1915. Like its predecessor, it was introduced in the same seven grades, Quality A through Quality F. Later, the Quality F was discontinued. By 1900, a "Condensed Steel" barreled model, named Quality X, was introduced. The New Ithaca Gun was produced in gauges 10, 12, and 16, and very rarely, 20. Lower grade models carried the logo, "New Ithaca Gun", usually within a banner, on each side of the frame. Like its predecessor, grades above Quality B are seldom encountered, and an expert appraisal is recommended. Sixteen gauge guns command a 30 percent price premium. The extremely rare 20 gauge model requires an expert appraisal.

Quality A

Courtesy Walter C. Snyder

Exc.	V.G.	Good	Fair	Poor
1000	700	250	150	100

Quality AA

Exc.	V.G.	Good	Fair	Poor
1000	700	300	150	100

Quality B

Exc.	V.G.	Good	Fair	Poor
1200	800	400	200	100

Quality X

Exc.	V.G.	Good	Fair	Poor
1200	800	400	200	100

NOTE: Sixteen gauge guns command a 30 percent premium. The extremely rare 20 gauge model requires an expert appraisal.

The "New Double Bolted Hammer Gun"

During 1915, the Ithaca Gun Company replaced the New Ithaca Gun with a model it referred to as "our new model two bolt hammer gun." The new hammer gun had coil springs powering the external hammers. The "two bolt" lock up was accomplished by a bottom bolt and by the top lever engagement with the rear nub of the rib extension. Lower grade models were marked on both sides of the frame with a setter dog and the logo, "Ithaca Gun Co." The 1915 catalog is the last year hammer guns were advertised but the old records indicate a few were sold as late as 1919.

Grades offered were X, A, AA, B, C, D, and E. The 1915 catalogue advertised a price of $29 for an A Quality model and $150 for the elaborately engraved Quality E. All grades were available in 10, 12, and 16 gauges. Like the New Ithaca Gun, grades above Quality B are seldom encountered, and an expert appraisal is recommended. Sixteen gauge guns command a 30 percent price premium. The extremely rare 20 gauge model requires an expert appraisal.

Quality A

Exc.	V.G.	Good	Fair	Poor
1200	800	300	200	100

Quality AA

Exc.	V.G.	Good	Fair	Poor
1500	1000	400	200	100

Quality B

Exc.	V.G.	Good	Fair	Poor
1500	1000	400	200	100

Quality X

Exc.	V.G.	Good	Fair	Poor
1500	1000	450	200	100

HAMMERLESS MODELS

The first hammerless Ithaca gun was introduced in 1888. All Ithaca double guns were discontinued in 1948.

The gauge and grade can usually be found on the left front corner of the water table of the frame, the serial number is usually found on the right side of the same water table, on the barrel flats, and on the forend iron.

Crass Model

The Crass Model, named after Ithaca's Frederick Crass who designed it, was introduced in 1888. It was offered in Quality 1 through Quality 7. The Quality 1P, a model with no engraving, was introduced in 1898. The Crass Model underwent three major frame redesigns before it was discontinued during 1901. The gun was available in 10, 12, and 16 gauge. Automatic ejectors were introduced in 1893 and were available in any quality gun at extra cost.

NOTE: Sixteen gauge guns will command a 20 percent price premium. Guns above Quality 4 are seldom encountered, and an expert appraisal is necessary. For automatic ejectors add $250. The serial number range for the Crass Model is approximately 7000 to 50000.

Quality 1

Exc.	V.G.	Good	Fair	Poor
800	500	350	200	100

Quality 1-1/2

Exc.	V.G.	Good	Fair	Poor
800	500	350	200	100

Quality 1P

Exc.	V.G.	Good	Fair	Poor
800	500	350	200	100

Quality 2

Courtesy Walter C. Snyder

Exc.	V.G.	Good	Fair	Poor
1200	800	550	200	100

Quality 3

Exc.	V.G.	Good	Fair	Poor
1700	1200	700	300	100

Quality 4

Exc.	V.G.	Good	Fair	Poor
2000	1750	1000	300	100

Lewis Model

Chester Lewis, an Ithaca Gun employee, was credited with the design of the gun that now bears his name. The gun was bolted through the rib extension in addition to the traditional under bolt. The model was available from 1901 through 1906, and was offered in Qualities 1 through 7. It was made in 10, 12, and 16 gauge, and after 1906, 20 gauge. Automatic ejectors were offered at added cost.

Qualities offered: 1, 1 Special, 1-1/2, 2, 3, 4, 5, 6, 7. The 1 Special had Nitro Steel barrels.

NOTE: Automatic ejectors add about $250 to grades below Quality 4. The serial number range for the Lewis Model is approximately 55000 to 123600.

Quality 1

Exc.	V.G.	Good	Fair	Poor
800	500	300	150	100

Quality 1 Special

Courtesy Walter C. Snyder

Exc.	V.G.	Good	Fair	Poor
800	500	300	150	100

Quality 1-1/2

Exc.	V.G.	Good	Fair	Poor
850	550	300	150	100

Quality 2

Exc.	V.G.	Good	Fair	Poor
1000	600	400	200	100

Quality 3

Exc.	V.G.	Good	Fair	Poor
1700	1400	800	400	100

Quality 4

Exc.	V.G.	Good	Fair	Poor
2500	2200	1800	400	100

Quality 5

Exc.	V.G.	Good	Fair	Poor
3500	3000	2000	700	300

Quality 6

Exc.	V.G.	Good	Fair	Poor
6000	4500	3000	700	300

Quality 7

Exc.	V.G.	Good	Fair	Poor
6000	4500	3000	700	300

Minier Model

The Minier Model, named after Ithaca's David Minier, was introduced in 1906 and was available through 1908. It was offered in Qualities Field through 7 and any grade could be ordered with ejectors. The Minier Model was the first Ithaca gun to use coil springs to power the internal hammers. This model was triple bolted, e.g., two fastenings at the rib extension and the under bolt. Gauges 10, 12, 16, and 20 were offered.

Grades offered: Field, 1, 1 Special, 1-1/2, 2, 3, 4, 5, 6, 7.

NOTE: Automatic ejectors add $250 to guns below Quality 4. The serial number range for the Minier Model is approximately 130000 to 151000.

Field Grade

Exc.	V.G.	Good	Fair	Poor
1000	500	300	150	100

Quality 1

Exc.	V.G.	Good	Fair	Poor
1000	500	300	150	100

Quality 1 Special

Exc.	V.G.	Good	Fair	Poor
1000	500	300	150	100

Quality 1-1/2

Exc.	V.G.	Good	Fair	Poor
1000	550	300	150	100

Quality 2

Exc.	V.G.	Good	Fair	Poor
1200	600	400	200	100

Quality 3

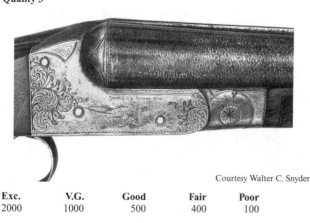

Courtesy Walter C. Snyder

Exc.	V.G.	Good	Fair	Poor
2000	1000	500	400	100

Quality 4

Exc.	V.G.	Good	Fair	Poor
2500	1200	800	400	100

Quality 5

Exc.	V.G.	Good	Fair	Poor
3500	2500	1500	700	300

Quality 6

Exc.	V.G.	Good	Fair	Poor
5000	4000	1500	700	300

Quality 7

Exc.	V.G.	Good	Fair	Poor
6500	4000	1500	700	300

Flues Model

The Flues Model Ithaca gun was built on a three-piece lock mechanism invented and patented by Emil Flues. Introduced in 1908, it remained in production through 1926 when it was replaced by the Ithaca New Double. It was offered in gauges 10, 12, 16, 20, and 28, and enjoyed the longest production life of any Ithaca double gun. Several grades were offered beginning with the Field grade and ending with the Sousa Special. The Flues Model had the same bolting system as used on the Minier Model. Any grade could have been ordered with automatic ejectors at extra cost. A single-selective trigger made by the Infallible Trigger company was offered after 1914 and was the first single trigger offered from the company.

Qualities offered were: Field, 1, 1 Special, 1-1/2, 2, 3, 4, 5, 6, 7, and Sousa.

NOTE: Add $200 for factory-ordered single trigger, add $200 for automatic ejectors on grades lower than Grade 4. Small gauges command a price premium. A 20 gauge gun may command up to a 50 percent price premium; a 28 gauge field grade perhaps as much as 200 percent. The serial number range for the Flues is approximately 175000 to 399000. Expert appraisals are recommended on higher-grade, small-gauge models as they are seldom encountered.

Field Grade

Courtesy Walter C. Snyder

Exc.	V.G.	Good	Fair	Poor
1000	600	300	150	100

Grade 1

Exc.	V.G.	Good	Fair	Poor
1000	750	400	150	100

Grade 1 Special

Exc.	V.G.	Good	Fair	Poor
1000	750	400	150	100

Grade 1-1/2

Exc.	V.G.	Good	Fair	Poor
1100	750	400	150	100

Grade 2

Exc.	V.G.	Good	Fair	Poor
1200	800	400	200	100

Grade 3

Exc.	V.G.	Good	Fair	Poor
2000	1500	800	300	100

Grade 4

Exc.	V.G.	Good	Fair	Poor
2000	1600	1200	300	100

Grade 5

Exc.	V.G.	Good	Fair	Poor
2500	2000	1500	500	200

Grade 6

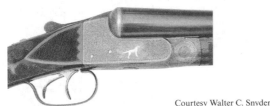
Courtesy Walter C. Snyder

Exc.	V.G.	Good	Fair	Poor
10000	5000	2500	1000	300

Grade 7

Exc.	V.G.	Good	Fair	Poor
9000	4500	2000	1000	300

Sousa

Exc.	V.G.	Good	Fair	Poor
15000	10000	6000	3000	N/A

The New Ithaca Double

The New Ithaca Double, commonly referred to as the NID, was manufactured from 1926 to 1948. It has the distinction of being the last double gun manufactured by the factory. The NID was bolted by a single rotary top bolt and was considered of all Ithaca double guns manufactured up to that time. External cocking indicators were standard on all NID models until about 1934, when they were eliminated from the design. Selective and non-selective single triggers and automatic ejectors were optional at additional costs. A special variation of the NID was introduced in 1932 to accommodate 10 gauge 3-1/2" magnum ammunition and was named, appropriately, the Magnum 10. All NID were available in grades Field, 1, 2, 3, 4, 5, 7, and Sousa (renamed the $1,000 grade after 1936). Gauges Magnum 10, standard 10, 12, 16, 20, 28, and .410 bore were offered.

NOTE: Like most collectible double guns, the smaller gauges command a price premium over the 12 gauge model. A 16 gauge field grade may command a 25 percent price premium, a 20 gauge field grade may command up to a 50 percent price premium, and the 28 gauge, and .410 caliber field-grade models perhaps as much as 250-300 percent. It is recommended that an expert opinion be sought for the valuation of high-grade, small-gauge models. Of late, the Magnum 10 gauge model also commands a price premium. Few of these guns trade, and the advice of an expert appraiser is suggested. Non-selective single trigger add $150. Single-selective trigger add $250. Ventilated-rib add $300. Automatic ejectors for grade below Grade 4 add $300. Beavertail forearm add $200. Monte Carlo buttstock add $300.

Field Grade

Exc.	V.G.	Good	Fair	Poor
1000	700	350	150	100

Grade 1

Exc.	V.G.	Good	Fair	Poor
1250	750	400	200	100

Grade 2

Exc.	V.G.	Good	Fair	Poor
1500	800	650	300	100

Courtesy Walter C. Snyder

Grade 3

Exc.	V.G.	Good	Fair	Poor
2500	1500	1000	400	100

Grade 4

Exc.	V.G.	Good	Fair	Poor
3000	2500	1500	400	100

Grade 5

Courtesy Walter C. Snyder

Exc.	V.G.	Good	Fair	Poor
4000	3200	2000	700	200

Grade 7

Exc.	V.G.	Good	Fair	Poor
10000	7000	4000	1000	300

Sousa Grade

Exc.	V.G.	Good	Fair	Poor
20000	10000	6000	3000	500

THE NEW ITHACA DOUBLE (MODERN-1999)

Reborn in 1999 under the company name Ithaca Classic Doubles of Victor, New York, the reintroduction of the NID will begin with serial number 470000. The last recorded production number from the Ithaca factory for NID was 469999. Only about 50 guns will be produced per year.

Special Field Grade

This side-by-side double is offered in 16, 20, 28, and .410 bore with a choice of matted rib barrel lengths of 26", 28", or 30". Ivory bead front sight. The action is case colored with light line border engraving. The stock is feather crotch black walnut with 22 lpi checkering. Choice of pistol or straight grip. Double trigger is standard. Weight in 20 gauge is about 5 lbs. 14 oz. 28 gauge is about 5 lbs. 8 oz., and .410 bore weighs about 5 lbs. 5 oz.

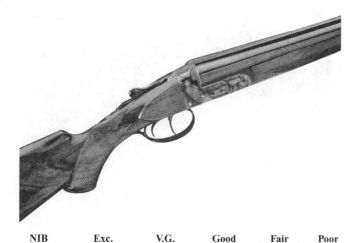

NIB	Exc.	V.G.	Good	Fair	Poor
6000	4750	—	—	—	—

Grade 4E
This model is also available in 16, 20, 28, and .410 with 26", 28", and 30" barrels. This model has gold plated triggers jeweled barrel flats and hand tuned locks. Black walnut stock has 28 lpi checkering with a fleur-de-lis pattern. Pistol or straight grip stock. Action is hand engraved with three game scenes and bank note scroll. Case colored frame.

NIB	Exc.	V.G.	Good	Fair	Poor
8000	6000	—	—	—	—

Grade 7E
This model has all of the gauges and barrel lengths of the above guns. Action is hand engraved with gold two tone inlays. Exhibition grade black walnut stock with elaborate patterns. Custom built dimensions.

NIB	Exc.	V.G.	Good	Fair	Poor
11000	8750	—	—	—	—

Sousa Grade
This model, available in the same gauges and barrel lengths as the above guns is stocked with presentation grade black walnut, hand carved with 32 lpi checkering. The action is hand engraved with bank note scroll and gold inlays. The entire gun is hand fitted and polished. Extremely limited availability. Special order only.

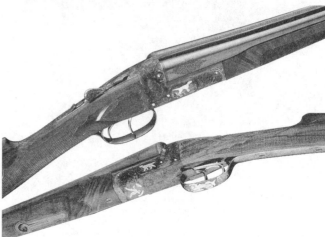

The famous Sousa mermaid in raised gold inlay

NIB	Exc.	V.G.	Good	Fair	Poor
18000	—	—	—	—	—

LEFEVER ARMS COMPANY, INC.
During 1921, Ithaca Gun, under the name "The Lefever Arms Company, Inc." introduced a line of lower-cost, boxlock guns. See the Lefever Arms Company section of this book for prices concerning those guns.

WESTERN ARMS CORPORATION
During 1929 the Ithaca Gun Company created the Western Arms Corporation, which introduced a new, low-cost double gun. That new double gun was named The Long Range Double and it was produced in 12, 16, and 20 gauges, and .410 caliber. Twenty gauge guns often command a 20 percent premium, a .410 caliber can command up to a 250 percent premium. This model was last made at the start of World War II.

The Long Range Double
The Long Range Double had walnut stocks that were not checkered.

Exc.	V.G.	Good	Fair	Poor
450	350	200	150	N/A

NOTE: Single trigger guns will add $100 and automatic ejectors will add $200.

The Long Range Double Deluxe
Usually made exclusively for the Montgomery Ward Company and sold by them under the name, Western Field Deluxe. This model had a line checkering pattern at the grip and on the splinter forend. Many of the Ithaca produced Western Field Deluxe guns had automatic ejectors and that fact was stamped into the right barrel.

Exc.	V.G.	Good	Fair	Poor
450	350	300	150	N/A

NOTE: Single triggers add $100. Automatic ejectors add $200.

IVER JOHNSON ARMS, INC.
Middlesex, New Jersey
SEE—AMAC

Established in 1883 in Fitchburg, Massachusetts, this company has produced a wide variety of firearms during its existence.

Trade Name Revolvers

A series of spur trigger revolvers were made by Iver Johnson bearing only the trade names such as those that follow: Encore, Eclipse, Favorite, Tycoon, and Eagle. In general, the value for these revolvers is as follows:

Exc.	V.G.	Good	Fair	Poor
200	170	120	95	65

SHOTGUNS

Hercules Grade

A boxlock double-barrel shotgun manufactured in a variety of gauges with 26" to 32" barrels, double triggers and extractors. Blued with a walnut stock.

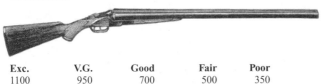

Exc.	V.G.	Good	Fair	Poor
1100	950	700	500	350

NOTE: Add premium for following features:
- Single trigger—200 percent
- Ejectors—200 percent
- 28 gauge—200 percent
- .410 bore—150 percent
- 20 gauge—75 percent
- 16 gauge—10 percent
- Engraving—200 percent
- Vent-rib—25 percent

Skeeter Model

As above, but more finely finished. Discontinued in 1946.

Exc.	V.G.	Good	Fair	Poor
2000	1500	1000	750	500

NOTE: Add premium for following features:
- Single trigger—200 percent
- Ejectors—200 percent
- 28 gauge—200 percent
- .410 bore—150 percent
- 20 gauge—75 percent
- 16 gauge—10 percent
- Engraving—200 percent
- Vent-rib—25 percent

Just a Reminder

An "N/A" or "—" instead of a price indicates that there is no known price avialable for that gun in that condition, or the sales for that particular model are so few that a reliable price cannot be given.

L

LEFEVER ARMS CO.
Syracuse, New York

Founded by Dan Lefever, who was a pioneer in the field of breech-loading firearms. This company was founded in 1884, with Lefever as the president. He was referred to as "Uncle Dan" within the firearms industry. He was responsible for many improvements in the double-barrel shotgun design. He developed the automatic hammerless system in the late 1880s. He also developed a compensating action that allowed simple adjustments to compensate for action wear. In 1901 he was forced out of the company and organized another company—the D.M. Lefever, Sons & Company—also in Syracuse. Dan Lefever died in 1906, and his new company went out of business. The original company was acquired by Ithaca in 1916. They continued to produce Lefever guns until 1948.

Sideplated Shotgun

A double-barrel, side-by-side shotgun chambered for 10, 12, 16, or 20 gauge. It was offered with 26", 28", 30", or 32" barrels with various choke combinations. The barrels are either Damascus or fluid steel. Damascus guns have become collectible and in better condition—very good to excellent—can bring nearly the same price as the fluid-steel guns. It features a fractional sidelock because the hammers were mounted in the frame and the sears and cocking indicators were mounted on the sideplates. After serial number 25,000, the entire locking mechanism was frame mounted and only the cocking indicators remained on the side plates. Double triggers are standard. The finish is blued, with a checkered walnut stock. There are a number of variations that differ in the amount of ornamentation and the quality of materials and workmanship utilized in their construction. Automatic ejectors are represented by the letter "E" after the respective grade designation. This shotgun was manufactured between 1885 and 1919. We strongly recommend that a qualified appraisal be secured if a transaction is contemplated.

NOTE: 20 gauge add 25 percent. Single-selective trigger add 10 percent.

DS Grade

Exc.	V.G.	Good	Fair	Poor
1250	1000	800	500	300

DSE Grade

Exc.	V.G.	Good	Fair	Poor
1750	1400	1150	700	500

H Grade

Exc.	V.G.	Good	Fair	Poor
1400	1100	850	550	350

HE Grade

Exc.	V.G.	Good	Fair	Poor
2200	1750	1450	900	650

G Grade

Exc.	V.G.	Good	Fair	Poor
1700	1350	1100	700	425

GE Grade

Exc.	V.G.	Good	Fair	Poor
2600	2000	1700	1000	650

F Grade
Exc.	V.G.	Good	Fair	Poor
2200	1750	1450	900	650

FE Grade
Exc.	V.G.	Good	Fair	Poor
3200	2500	2100	1300	800

E Grade
Exc.	V.G.	Good	Fair	Poor
3500	2800	2300	1400	900

EE Grade
Exc.	V.G.	Good	Fair	Poor
4600	3700	3000	1850	1150

D Grade
Exc.	V.G.	Good	Fair	Poor
4500	3500	2900	1800	1100

DE Grade
Exc.	V.G.	Good	Fair	Poor
7000	5600	4500	2800	1750

C Grade
Exc.	V.G.	Good	Fair	Poor
6000	4800	4000	2400	1500

CE Grade
Exc.	V.G.	Good	Fair	Poor
8500	6800	5500	3400	2100

B Grade
Exc.	V.G.	Good	Fair	Poor
8000	6400	5200	3200	2000

BE Grade
Exc.	V.G.	Good	Fair	Poor
10000	8000	6500	4000	2500

A Grade
Exc.	V.G.	Good	Fair	Poor
15000	12000	10000	6000	3700

AA Grade
Exc.	V.G.	Good	Fair	Poor
20000	16000	13000	8000	5000

There was also an Optimus Grade and a Thousand Dollar Grade offered. These are extremely high-grade, heavily ornamented firearms inlaid with precious metals. They are extremely rare, and evaluating them on a general basis is impossible.

LEFEVER ARMS COMPANY, INC. (ITHACA)

During 1916, the Ithaca Gun company purchased the gunmaking assets of the Syracuse, New York based, Lefever Arms Company. Between then and World War I, they continued to manufacture the same sideplate gun that had been made in Syracuse until about 1919 when they were discontinued. Prices for those guns are listed above. During 1921, Ithaca Gun Company, under the name the Lefever Arms Company, Inc., introduced a line of lower costs, boxlock guns. Eventually, six different models were produced. Ithaca's Lefever guns were produced in 12, 16, and 20 gauges, and in .410 bore. Twenty gauge guns often command a price premium of 50 percent; a .410 bore gun may command up to a 200 percent premium.

Nitro Special
A side-by-side, double-barrel shotgun chambered for 12, 16, or 20 gauge, as well as .410. The barrels were offered in lengths of 26" to 32" with various choke combinations. It features a boxlock action with double triggers and extractors standard. The finish is blued, with a case-colored receiver and a checkered walnut stock. This model was manufactured between 1921 and 1948 and, incredible as it may seem, its price at introduction was $29.

Exc.	V.G.	Good	Fair	Poor
600	400	250	200	—

NOTE: Single-selective trigger add $100 Automatic ejectors add $200

Long Range Single-Barrel Trap and Field (Model 2)
Manufactured from 1927 to 1947, the Model 2 was a single-barrel gun with no rib. Like the Nitro Special, it had walnut stocks that were line cut checkered at the grip area of the buttstock and on the forend.

Exc.	V.G.	Good	Fair	Poor
500	300	200	100	—

Single-Barrel Trap Ventilated Rib (Model 3)
Manufactured from 1927 to 1942, the Model 3 was a single-barrel gun with the same ventilated rib that was used on the "Knick" trap gun. The walnut stocks had line cut checkering at the grip area of the buttstock and on the forend.

Exc.	V.G.	Good	Fair	Poor
1200	500	250	100	—

Double-Barrel Ventilated Rib Trap (Model 4)
Manufactured during 1929 but catalogued until 1939, the Model 4 was a double-barrel gun with a ventilated rib barrel. The walnut stocks had line cut checkering at the grip area of the buttstock and on the beavertail forend. Only about 200 units were produced.

Exc.	V.G.	Good	Fair	Poor
2000	1200	1000	700	—

A Grade (Model 5)
Manufactured from 1936 to 1939, the A Grade was a double-barreled gun. The walnut stocks had pointed checkering cut at the grip area of the buttstock and on the splinter forend. A line engraving outlined its nicely sculptured frame.

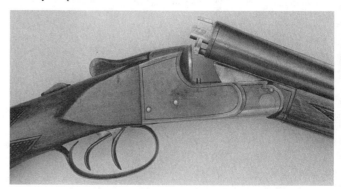

Courtesy Walter C. Snyder

Exc.	V.G.	Good	Fair	Poor
900	600	400	300	—

NOTE: Single trigger add $200, automatic ejectors add $200, beavertail forend add $300.

LEFEVER, D. M., SONS & COMPANY
Syracuse, New York

"Uncle Dan" Lefever founded the Lefever Arms Company in 1884. In 1901 he was forced out of his company and founded the D.M. Lefever, Sons & Company. He continued to produce high-grade, side-by-side shotguns, but of a totally new boxlock design. There were approximately 1,200 shotguns of all variations produced during this period, making them extremely rare and difficult to evaluate on a general basis. We list the models and average values but strongly suggest securing qualified appraisal if a transaction is contemplated.

Lefever Double-Barrel Shotgun
A side-by-side, double-barrel shotgun chambered for 12, 16, or 20 gauge. It was offered with various-length barrels and choke combinations that were made to order. It features double triggers and automatic ejectors. A single-selective trigger was available as an option. The finish is blued, with a checkered walnut stock. The individual grades differ in the amount of ornamentation and the general quality of the materials and workmanship utilized in their construction. This model was discontinued in 1906.

NOTE: Single-selective trigger add 25 percent. 20 gauge add 50 percent.

O Excelsior Grade—Extractors

Exc.	V.G.	Good	Fair	Poor
2500	2000	1650	950	700

Excelsior Grade—Auto Ejectors

Exc.	V.G.	Good	Fair	Poor
3000	2500	2000	1250	900

F Grade, No. 9

Exc.	V.G.	Good	Fair	Poor
3000	2750	2250	1500	1100

E Grade, No. 8

Exc.	V.G.	Good	Fair	Poor
4000	3500	3000	2400	1700

D Grade, No. 7

Exc.	V.G.	Good	Fair	Poor
4500	3900	3400	2750	2000

C Grade, No. 6

Exc.	V.G.	Good	Fair	Poor
5000	4500	3750	3000	2500

B Grade, No. 5

Exc.	V.G.	Good	Fair	Poor
6500	5750	4800	3500	3000

AA Grade, No. 4

Exc.	V.G.	Good	Fair	Poor
9000	7800	6500	4200	2750

There are an "optimus" and an "Uncle Dan" grade, which are top-of-the-line models, that features extremely high quality in materials and workmanship and a great deal of ornamentation. This firearm is extremely rare and seldom found in today's market. It is impossible to evaluate it on a general basis.

SHOTGUNS

Any side-by-side or single-shot shotgun typical of the period from approximately 1860 until 1899 without automatic ejectors, is allowed. Lever or slide-action single barrel, tubular feed, exposed hammer shotguns of the period are allowed, whether original or replicas. Military configurations are not allowed. Certain shooting categories require a specific type of shotgun and ammunition to be used.

– SASS Shooters Handbook, February 2005

M

MARLIN FIREARMS CO.
New Haven, Connecticut

Ballard Rifles

Established by John Mahlon Marlin in 1863. Marlin manufactured pistols until 1875 when he began production of Ballard rifles. In 1881 he made his first lever-action repeating rifle for which his company became famous.

The Marlin Firearms Company has the distinction of being the oldest family owned firearms company in the United States.

The Ballard single-shot rifle was invented by C.H. Ballard of Worcester, Massachusetts. It was patented in 1861. The first of the Ballard rifles was manufactured by the Ball and Williams Co. of Worchester, Massachusetts. In 1866 Merwin and Bray purchased the firm, calling it Merrimack Arms Company, and operated until 1869, when they sold it to the Brown Manufacturing Company of New York City. This venture took a decidedly negative turn, and in 1873 mortgage foreclosure forced the sale to Schoverling and Daly of New York City. These gentlemen were arms dealers, not manufacturers, so they entered into an agreement with John M. Marlin to produce the Ballard rifle. The rifles produced during this period are regarded as some of the finest single-shots ever made, and the venture finally became successful. In 1881 the business became incorporated as the Marlin Firearms Company, and the Ballard was produced under this banner until it was discontinued around the year 1891. The popularity of the repeating rifle simply eroded the demand for the fine single-shot until it was no longer a profitable venture.

BALL & WILLIAMS BALLARDS

First Model

This model was the first Ballard produced. It was introduced in 1861 and was offered with a 24" or 28" octagonal barrel. The frame is case colored, and the barrel is blued. The walnut stock is varnished. The major identifying feature of this model is the inside extractor. This was the only Ballard that had this feature before Marlin began to manufacture the rifle in 1875. The barrel is stamped "Ball & Williams/Worchester, Mass." and "Ballards Patent/Nov. 5, 1861." There were approximately 100 manufactured and serial numbered from 1-100.

Exc.	V.G.	Good	Fair	Poor
—	—	2500	900	400

MARLIN-BALLARD RIFLES

Commencing in 1875 the Ballard single-shot rifle was made by John Marlin for Schoverling and Daly. In 1881 the business was incorporated and became the Marlin Firearms Co. All the Ballards made from then until 1891, when they were discontinued, were produced under this banner. The only real difference in the rifles manufactured during these periods was in the markings. The earlier rifles are stamped "J.M. Marlin New Haven. Conn. U.S.A./Ballards Patent. Nov. 5, 1861"; and the post-1881 models are stamped "Marlin Firearms Co. New Haven Ct. U.S.A./Patented Feb. 9, 1875/Ballards Patent Nov. 5, 1861." The major difference between Marlin-made Ballards and the earlier models is the inside tang and the internal extractor on the Marlin-made rifles. All of the Marlin-made Ballards have an octagonal frame top, and the Marlin Firearms Co. models have grooved receiver sides. The standard finish on all these later rifles is case colored frames and blued octagonal or part-round, part-octagonal barrels. There are many variations in these rifles as to types of sights, stock, engraving, and other special order features-such as barrel lengths, weights, and contours. These rifles must be considered individually and competently appraised. There is also the fact that many of these Ballards have been rebarreled and rechambered over the years, as they were known for their shooting ability and were used quite extensively. This can seriously affect the value in a negative manner unless it can be authenticated that the work was done by the likes of Harry Pope or George Schoyen and other noted and respected gunsmiths of that era. This can add considerably to the value of the rifle. One must approach this model with caution and learn all that can be learned before purchasing.

Ballard Hunters Rifle

This model resembles the earlier Brown Manufacturing Company rifles, and it utilizes many leftover parts acquired by Marlin. It is chambered for the .32, .38, and .44 rimfire and centerfire and features John Marlin's unique reversible firing pin that allows the same gun to use both rimfire and centerfire ammunition simply by rotating the firing pin in the breechblock. This model still had the external ejector and bears the J.M. Marlin markings. There were approximately 500 manufactured in the 1 to 500 serial range. They were produced in 1875 and 1876.

Exc.	V.G.	Good	Fair	Poor
—	—	2750	950	400

Ballard No. 1 Hunters Rifle

This model bears the early J.M. Marlin marking only, as it was manufactured from 1876 until 1880 and was discontinued before the incorporation. It has a 26", 28", and 30" barrel and is chambered for the .44 rimfire or centerfire cartridge. It has the reversible firing pin and also the new internal extractor. Production figures are not available, but the serial number range is between 500 and 4000.

Exc.	V.G.	Good	Fair	Poor
—	—	3000	1000	400

Ballard No. 1-1/2 Hunters Rifle

This model is similar to the No. 1 except that it is chambered for the .45-70, .40-63, and the .40-65 cartridges and does not have the reversible firing pin. The barrel length is 30" and 32". It was manufactured between 1879 and 1883. This model is found with both early and later markings.

Photo by Lt. Col. William S. Brophy from *Marlin Firearms* with permission

Exc.	V.G.	Good	Fair	Poor
—	—	3750	1500	500

Ballard No. 1-3/4 "Far West" Hunters Rifle

This model was made by J. M. Marlin only and is similar to the 1-1/2, the difference being the addition of double-set triggers and a ring on the opening lever. It was manufactured in 1880 and 1881.

Exc.	V.G.	Good	Fair	Poor
—	—	4750	2000	600

Ballard No. 2 Sporting Rifle

This model is chambered for the .32, .38 rimfire or centerfire cartridges, and the .44 centerfire. It has the reversible firing pin and was offered in 26", 28", and 30" barrel lengths. This model features "Rocky Mountain" sights and was manufactured between 1876 and 1891. It is found with both early and late markings.

Exc.	V.G.	Good	Fair	Poor
—	—	2000	650	200

Ballard No. 3 Gallery Rifle

This model is similar to the No. 2 rifle but is chambered for the .22 rimfire cartridge and has a manually operated external extractor. The sights are the same; and a 24" barrel was offered in addition to the 26", 28", and 30". This rifle was manufactured between 1876 and 1891.

Exc.	V.G.	Good	Fair	Poor
—	—	2000	650	200

Ballard No. 3F Gallery Rifle

This is a deluxe version of the No. 3. It has a pistol-grip stock, a nickel-plated Schutzen-style buttplate, and an opening lever like a repeating rifle. It features a 26" octagonal barrel and an oil-finished stock. It was manufactured in the late 1880s and is quite scarce in today's market.

Exc.	V.G.	Good	Fair	Poor
—	—	4250	1750	500

Ballard No. 4 Perfection Rifle

This model is chambered for a number of centerfire calibers from .32-40 to .50-70. The barrel lengths are from 26" to 30", and the sights are of the "Rocky Mountain" type. This model was manufactured between 1876 and 1891.

Exc.	V.G.	Good	Fair	Poor
—	—	4250	1750	500

Ballard No. 3-1/2 Target Rifle

This model is similar to the No. 4 Perfection Rifle except that it has a checkered stock with a shotgun-style buttplate, a 30" barrel, and a tang peep sight with globe front sight. It was chambered for the .40-65 cartridge and was manufactured from 1880-1882.

Exc.	V.G.	Good	Fair	Poor
—	—	4250	1750	500

Ballard No. 4-1/2 Mid Range Rifle

This model is also a variation of the No. 4 Perfection model. It has a higher-grade checkered stock with a shotgun buttplate. It has a 30" part-round, part-octagonal barrel and is chambered for the .38-40, .40-65, and the .45-70 cartridges. It features a Vernier tang peep sight and a globe front sight. It was manufactured between 1878 and 1882.

Exc.	V.G.	Good	Fair	Poor
—	—	4500	2000	500

Ballard No. 4-1/2 A-1 Mid Range Target Rifle

This is a deluxe version of the No. 4-1/2" rifle. It features scroll engraving on the frame with "Ballard A-1" on the left and "Mid-Range" on the right. It is chambered for the .38-50 and the .40-65 cartridge and has a high-grade checkered stock with a horn forend tip. The sights are the highest-grade Vernier tang sight and a spirit lever front sight. The shotgun or rifle-style butt was optional. This model was manufactured between 1878 and 1880.

Courtesy Milwaukee Public Museum, Milwaukee, Wisconsin

Exc.	V.G.	Good	Fair	Poor
—	—	7250	3500	750

Ballard No. 5 Pacific Rifle

This model has a 30" or 32" medium to heavyweight barrel, with a ramrod mounted underneath. It is chambered for many different calibers from .38-50 to .50-70. This model features "Rocky Mountain" sights, a crescent butt, double-set triggers, and a ring-style opening lever. It was manufactured between 1876 and 1891.

Courtesy Milwaukee Public Museum, Milwaukee, Wisconsin

Exc.	V.G.	Good	Fair	Poor
—	—	4750	2000	500

Ballard No. 5-1/2 Montana Rifle

This model is similar to the Pacific Rifle, with an extra heavyweight barrel, and is chambered for the .45 Sharps cartridge only. It features a checkered steel shotgun-style buttplate. It was manufactured from 1882-1884 and has the late markings only.

Exc.	V.G.	Good	Fair	Poor
—	—	10000	5500	1250

Ballard No. 6-1/2 Off Hand Mid Range Rifle
This model is chambered for the .40-54 Everlasting cartridge only. It has a 28" or 30" part-round, part-octagonal barrel, a Schuetzen-style stock, and a plain non-engraved receiver. It was manufactured between 1880 and 1882.

Exc.	V.G.	Good	Fair	Poor
—	—	5500	2500	500

Ballard No. 6-1/2 Rigby Off Hand Mid Range Rifle
This model is chambered for the .38-50 and the .40-65 cartridges. It features the Rigby ribbed-style barrel in 26" and 28" lengths, with Vernier rear and globe front sights and a high grade, checkered walnut, Schuetzen-style stock with horn forend tip, and pistol-grip cap. The buttplate is nickel-plated, and the opening lever is of the ring type with a single trigger and extensively engraved receiver. This model was manufactured from 1880 to 1882.

Exc.	V.G.	Good	Fair	Poor
—	—	9000	5500	1250

Ballard No. 6-1/2 Off Hand Rifle
This model is chambered for the .32-40 and .38-55 cartridges and features barrel lengths of 28" and 30". It has a checkered, high-grade walnut, Schuetzen-style stock with nickel-plated buttplate. The forend tip and pistol-grip cap are of horn, and the receiver is engraved. This model has a single trigger, full-ring opening lever, Vernier tang rear sight, and spirit lever front sight. The 6-1/2 Off Hand was made by the Marlin Firearms Company between 1883 and 1891 and is found with the later markings only.

Exc.	V.G.	Good	Fair	Poor
—	—	9000	5500	1250

Ballard No. 7 "Creedmore A-1" Long Range Rifle
This model is commonly chambered for the .44-100 or the .45100 cartridges. It has a 34" part-round, part-octagonal barrel and a high grade checkered pistol-grip stock, with a horn forend tip and shotgun-style butt. The sights are a special 1,300-yard Vernier tang rear and a spirit level front. There is another sight base on the heel of the stock for mounting the rear sight for ultra long-range shooting. The opening lever is similar to a repeating rifle, and a single trigger is featured. The receiver is engraved and marked "Ballard A-1" on the left and "Long Range" on the right. This model was manufactured between 1876 and 1886 and is found with both early and late markings.

Exc.	V.G.	Good	Fair	Poor
—	—	9000	5500	1250

Ballard No. 7 Long Range Rifle
This model is similar to the "Creedmore A-1" but is slightly less deluxe. The engraving is less elaborate, and the lettering on the receiver is absent. This model was manufactured between 1883 and 1890 and is found with the later markings only.

Exc.	V.G.	Good	Fair	Poor
—	—	8000	4500	850

Ballard No. 7A-1 Long Range Rifle
This model is a higher grade version of the "Creedmore A-l," with fancier walnut and a checkered straight stock. Better sights and deluxe engraving are also featured. This model was manufactured between 1879 and 1883 and is found with both markings.

Exc.	V.G.	Good	Fair	Poor
—	—	9000	5500	1250

MARLIN HANDGUNS
The first firearm that was manufactured by John M. Marlin was actually a derringer-type single-shot that was small enough to be hidden in the palm of the hand. From this beginning evolved the company that became known for its highly accurate and dependable rifles. The Marlin Company manufactured handguns up to the turn of the century, discontinuing their last and only double-action model in 1899.

1st Model Derringer
This was the first handgun produced by Marlin. The barrel is 2-1/16" long and pivots to the side for loading. There is a plunger under the frame that is depressed to free the barrel. This device is a Ballard patent. This pistol is chambered for the .22 rimfire cartridge, and there is no extractor. The frame is brass and usually nickel-plated. It has two grooves milled beneath the blued barrel. The grips are of rosewood. The barrel is stamped "J.M. Marlin, New Haven, Ct." There were approximately 2,000 manufactured between 1863 and 1867. They are quite scarce on today's market.

Courtesy Milwaukee Public Museum, Milwaukee, Wisconsin

Exc.	V.G.	Good	Fair	Poor
—	—	750	300	100

O.K. Model Derringer
The O.K. Model is chambered for .22, .30, and .32 rimfire cartridges. The barrel is 2-1/8" or 3-1/8" on the .32. There is no extractor, and it functions as the 1st Model. The frame is plated brass with flat sides, and the barrel is found either blued or nickel-plated. The grips are rosewood. The markings are the same as on the 1st Model but are located on the right side of the barrel. The top of the barrel is marked "O.K." There were approximately 5,000 manufactured between 1863 and 1870.

Photo by Lt. Col. William S. Brophy from Marlin Firearms with permission

Exc.	V.G.	Good	Fair	Poor
—	—	750	300	100

Victor Model Derringer
This model is similar in appearance to the "O.K." Model but is larger in size and is chambered for the .38-caliber rimfire cartridge. The barrel is 2-11/16" long; and there was, for the first time, an extractor. The finish and function were unchanged. The right side of the barrel is stamped "J.M. Marlin/New Haven, Ct./Pat. April 5.1870." "Victor"

is stamped on the top of the barrel. There were approximately 4,000 manufactured between 1870 and 1881.

Courtesy Little John's Auction Service, Inc.

Exc.	V.G.	Good	Fair	Poor
—	—	1250	500	150

Nevermiss Model Derringer
This model was made in three different sizes chambered for the .22, .32, and .41 rimfire cartridges. The barrel is 2.5" long and swings sideways for loading. The frame is plated brass, and the barrels are either blued or nickel-plated. The grips are rosewood. The frame is grooved under the barrels as on the 1st model. There is an extractor on this model. The barrel markings are the same as on the "Victor," with the top of the barrel marked "Nevermiss." There were approximately 5,000 manufactured between 1870 and 1881.

.22 Caliber Model

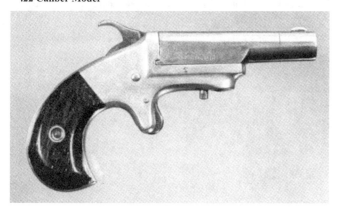

Photo by Lt. Col. William S. Brophy from *Marlin Firearms* with permission

Exc.	V.G.	Good	Fair	Poor
—	—	1150	500	100

.32 Caliber Model

Exc.	V.G.	Good	Fair	Poor
—	—	750	350	100

.41 Caliber Model

Exc.	V.G.	Good	Fair	Poor
—	—	2500	1000	400

Stonewall Model Derringer
This model is identical to the .41-caliber "Nevermiss," but the top of the barrel is marked "Stonewall." It is rarely encountered.

Exc.	V.G.	Good	Fair	Poor
—	—	4250	2000	750

O.K. Pocket Revolver
This is a solid-frame, spur-trigger, single-action revolver chambered for the .22 rimfire short. The round barrel is 2.25", and the 7-shot cylinder is unfluted. The frame is nickel-plated brass with a blue or nickel-plated barrel, and the bird's-head grips are rosewood. The cylinder pin is removable and is used to knock the empty cases out of the cylinder. The top of the barrel is marked "O.K." and "J.M. Marlin. New Haven, Conn. U.S.A." There were approximately 1,500 manufactured between 1870 and 1875.

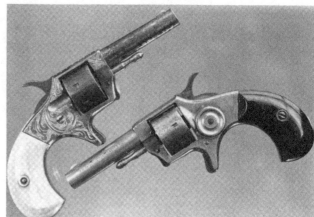

Photo by Lt. Col. William S. Brophy from *Marlin Firearms* with permission

Exc.	V.G.	Good	Fair	Poor
—	—	550	200	75

Little Joker Revolver
This model is similar in appearance to the "O.K." Model except that it features engraving and ivory or pearl grips. There were approximately 500 manufactured between 1871 and 1873.

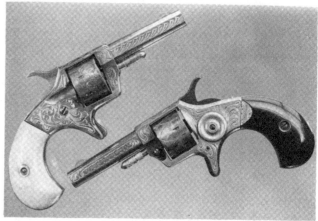

Photo by Lt. Col. William S. Brophy from *Marlin Firearms* with permission

Exc.	V.G.	Good	Fair	Poor
—	—	800	350	125

J. M. MARLIN STANDARD POCKET REVOLVERS
In 1872 Marlin began production of its Smith & Wesson look-alike. The Manhattan Firearms Company had developed a copy of the Model 1 S&W .22 cartridge revolver. In 1868 the company ceased business, and the revolvers were produced by the American Standard Tool Company until their dissolution in 1873. In 1872 Marlin had entered into an agreement with this company to manufacture these revolvers, which were no longer protected by the Rollin White patent after 1869. The Marlin revolvers are similar to those made by American Standard, the only real difference being that Marlin grips are of the bird's-head round configuration. A contoured grip frame and a patented pawl spring mechanism is utilized on the Marlin revolvers.

Marlin XXX Standard 1872 Pocket Revolver
This is the first in the series of four Standard model revolvers. It is chambered for the .30 caliber rimfire. The earlier model has an octagonal 3-1/8" barrel; and the later, a round 3" barrel. There are round and octagonal barrel variations (with unfluted cylinder) and round barrel

variations (with short and long fluted cylinders). All of the barrels are ribbed and tip up for loading. They have plated brass frames, and the barrels are nickel-plated. The bird's-head grips are of rosewood or hard rubber, bearing the monogram "M.F.A. Co." inside a star. There is a spur trigger. The markings "J.M. Marlin-New Haven Ct." appear on the earlier octagonal barreled models. "U.S.A. Pat. July 1. 1873" was added to the later round barreled models. All barrels are marked "XXX Standard 1872." There were approximately 5,000 of all types manufactured between 1872 and 1887.

Photo by Lt. Col. William S. Brophy from *Marlin Firearms* with permission

Octagon Barrel—Early Variation

Exc.	V.G.	Good	Fair	Poor
—	—	750	300	75

Round Barrel—Non-Fluted Cylinder

Exc.	V.G.	Good	Fair	Poor
—	—	700	275	75

Round Barrel—Short Fluted Cylinder

Exc.	V.G.	Good	Fair	Poor
—	—	500	200	75

Round Barrel—Long Fluted Cylinder

Exc.	V.G.	Good	Fair	Poor
—	—	450	150	75

Marlin XX Standard 1873 Pocket Revolver

This model is similar in appearance to the XXX 1872 model except that it is chambered for the .22 long rimfire and is marked "XX Standard 1873." There are three basic variations: the early octagonal barrel model with non-fluted cylinder, the round barrel model with non-fluted cylinder, and the round barrel with fluted cylinder. Function and features are the same as described for the "XXX Standard 1872" model. There were approximately 5,000 manufactured between 1873 and 1887.

Early Octagon Barrel Model

Exc.	V.G.	Good	Fair	Poor
—	—	900	400	100

Round Barrel—Fluted Cylinder

Photo by Lt. Col. William S. Brophy from *Marlin Firearms* with permission

Exc.	V.G.	Good	Fair	Poor
—	—	500	200	75

Round Barrel—Non-Fluted Cylinder

Exc.	V.G.	Good	Fair	Poor
—	—	950	450	100

Marlin No. 32 Standard 1875 Pocket Revolver

This model is also similar in appearance to the "XXX Standard 1872" model except that it is chambered for the .32 rimfire cartridge. The 3" barrel is round with a rib, and the 5-shot cylinder is fluted and is in two different lengths to accommodate either the .32 Short or Long cartridge. The finish, function, and most markings are the same as on previous models with the exception of the barrel top marking "No. 32 Standard 1875." There were approximately 8,000 manufactured between 1875 and 1887.

Photo by Lt. Col. William S. Brophy from *Marlin Firearms* with permission

Exc.	V.G.	Good	Fair	Poor
—	—	450	200	75

Marlin 38 Standard 1878 Pocket Revolver

This model is different than its predecessors in that it features a steel frame and flat bottom butt, with hard rubber monogram grips. There was still a spur trigger, and the 3.25" ribbed round barrel still tipped up for loading. This model is chambered for the .38 centerfire cartridge. The finish is full nickel plate, and the top of the barrel is marked "38 Standard 1878." There were approximately 9,000 manufactured between 1878 and 1887.

Exc.	V.G.	Good	Fair	Poor
—	—	600	250	75

EARLY PRODUCTION MARLIN RIFLES

Model 1881 Lever-Action Rifle

This was the first of the Marlin lever-action rifles and has always been regarded as a high quality rifle. It is capable of handling the large calibers and was well received by the shooting public. The rifle is chambered for the .32-40, .38-55, .40-60, .45-70, and the .45-85. The 24", 28", or 30" octagonal barrel is standard. Round barrels were offered and are scarce today. There is a tubular magazine beneath the barrel, and the rear sight is the buckhorn type with a blade on the front. This model ejects its empty cartridges from the top. The finish is blued, with a case colored hammer, lever, and buttplate. The walnut stock is varnished. There were approximately 20,000 manufactured between 1881 and 1892 but this is not easy to ascertain, as the factory records on Marlin rifles are quite incomplete.

Exc.	V.G.	Good	Fair	Poor
—	3500	2000	750	300

Lightweight Model

Thinner frame, lever, and barrel .32-40 and .38-55 caliber only-24" and 28" barrel.

Exc.	V.G.	Good	Fair	Poor
—	3000	1750	600	300

NOTE: Add 200-300 percent premium for 1st Models prior to serial number 600. Add 15 percent premium for .45-70 caliber.

Model 1888 Lever-Action Rifle

This model is chambered for the .32-20, .38-40, and the .44-40 cartridges. This is a shorter action that was designed (chiefly by Lewis Hepburn) to handle the pistol cartridges for which it was chambered. The standard barrel was octagonal, but round barrels were available as special-order items. This is a top ejecting action. It has a buckhorn rear and a blade front sight. The finish is blued with a case colored hammer, lever, and buttplate. The walnut stock is varnished. There were approximately 4,800 manufactured in 1888 and 1889. As with most of these fine old rifles, many special-order options were available that affect today's market value. Individual appraisal would be necessary for these special models, to ascertain both value and authenticity.

Exc.	V.G.	Good	Fair	Poor
—	3500	2500	600	350

NOTE: Add 40 percent premium for half octagon barrel. Add 20 percent premium for round barrel.

Model 1889 Lever-Action Rifle

This was Marlin's first side-eject, solid-top rifle. It is chambered for .25-20, .32-20, .38-40, and the .44-40 cartridges. It features either octagonal or round barrels in lengths from 24" to 32" with buckhorn rear and blade front sights. The finish is blued with a case colored hammer, lever, and buttplate. The plain walnut stock is varnished. The barrel is stamped "Marlin Fire-Arms Co. New Haven Ct. U.S.A./Patented Oct.11 1887 April 2.1889." This model features a lever latch, and many options were offered. Again one must urge individual appraisal on such variations. Values fluctuate greatly due to some seemingly insignificant variation. There were approximately 55,000 manufactured between 1889 and 1899.

Production Model
24" barrel.

Exc.	V.G.	Good	Fair	Poor
—	1500	1000	450	150

Short Carbine
15" barrel. 327 produced.

Exc.	V.G.	Good	Fair	Poor
—	5000	2250	1000	500

Carbine
20" barrel and saddle ring on left side of receiver.

Photo by Lt. Col. William S. Brophy from *Marlin Firearms* with permission

Exc.	V.G.	Good	Fair	Poor
—	2250	1250	500	250

Musket
30" barrel with full-length stock, 68 made in .4440.

Exc.	V.G.	Good	Fair	Poor
—	6500	3000	1250	650

Model 1891 Lever-Action Rifle

This was Marlin's first rifle designed to fire the .22 rimfire and the first repeating rifle to accept the .22 Short, Long, and LR cartridges interchangeably. It was also chambered for the .32 rimfire and centerfire. The 24" octagonal barrel is standard, with a buckhorn rear and blade front sight. The finish is blued with a case colored hammer, lever, and buttplate. The stock is plain walnut. The first variation is marked "Marlin Fire-Arms Co. New Haven, Ct. U.S.A./Pat'd Nov.19.1878. April 2.1889. Aug.12 1890" on the barrel, with the solid-topped frame marked "Marlin Safety." The second variation was marked the same with "March 1,1892" added. There were approximately 18,650 manufactured between 1891 and 1897.

1st Variation
.22 rimfire only, side loading, appr. 5,000.

Exc.	V.G.	Good	Fair	Poor
—	2500	1000	550	300

2nd Variation
.22 and .32 rimfire, .32 centerfire, tube loading, Model 1891 on later model tangs (3rd variation).

Exc.	V.G.	Good	Fair	Poor
—	1500	500	300	150

NOTE: Add 20 percent for .22 rifle with "1891" stamped on tang. Deduct 50 percent for .32 caliber.

Model 1892 Lever-Action Rifle

This is basically an improved version of the Model 1891 and is similar to the second variation of the 1891. The only notable exceptions were the tang marking "Model 1892" and "Model 92" on later models. The .22 rimfire was scarce in the Model 1892. There were approximately 45,000 manufactured between 1895 and 1916. There were many options, and these special-order guns must be individually appraised to ascertain value and authenticity.

Exc.	V.G.	Good	Fair	Poor
—	1250	400	250	150

NOTE: Antique (Pre-1898) add 20 percent.

.32 Rimfire and Centerfire

Exc.	V.G.	Good	Fair	Poor
—	850	350	150	100

Model 1893 Lever-Action Rifle

This model was the first rifle Marlin designed for the then new smokeless powder cartridges. It is chambered for the .25-36, .30-30, .32 Special, .32-40, and the .38-55. It was offered standard with either a round or octagonal barrel, in lengths of 24" to 32". Buckhorn rear and blade front sights were also standard. The receiver, lever, hammer, and buttplate are case colored, and the rest is blued. The stock is varnished walnut.

As with all of these early Marlins, many options were offered and, when encountered, will drastically alter the value of the particular rifle. For this reason we supply the values for the basic model and urge securing competent appraisal on non-standard specimens. The barrel on earlier guns is marked "Marlin FireArms Co. New Haven, Ct.U.S.A./ Patented Oct.11. 1887.April 2.1889.Aug.1.1893." In 1919 the markings were changed to "The Marlin Firearms Corporation/ New Haven, Conn.U.S.A.Patented." The rifles manufactured after 1904 are marked "Special Smokeless Steel" on the left side of the barrel. The upper tang is marked "Model 1893" on early guns; and "Model 93," on later specimens. There were approximately 900,000 manufactured between 1893 and 1935. Factory records are incomplete on the Model 1893.

Antique Production (Pre-1898)

Exc.	V.G.	Good	Fair	Poor
1600	1000	650	450	275

Modern Production 1899-1935

Exc.	V.G.	Good	Fair	Poor
1400	850	550	350	225

NOTE: Add 100 percent premium for musket. Deduct 50 percent for B model with blued receiver.

Model 1894 Lever-Action Rifle

This model is similar to the Model 1893, with a shorter action. It is chambered for the .25-20, .32-20, .38-40, and the .44-40. 24" to 32" round or octagonal barrels with full-length magazine tubes are standard, as are buckhorn rear and blade front sights. The finish is case colored receiver, lever, hammer, and buttplate, with the rest blued. The walnut stock is varnished. The first versions were marked "Marlin Fire-Arms Co., New Haven, Ct.U.S.A./Patented Oct.11, 1887. April 2,1889." The top of the frame is marked "Marlin Safety," and the model designation is not stamped on the tang. These early rifles were chambered for .38-40 and .44-40 only. The later rifles added the patent date "Aug. 1, 1893"; and "Model 1894" was stamped on the tang. On the latest versions this was shortened to "Model 94." There were approximately 250,000 manufactured between 1894 and 1935. This model was also produced with a great many options. Individual appraisal should be secured when confronted with these features.

Antique Production (Pre-1898)

Exc.	V.G.	Good	Fair	Poor
1700	1000	650	450	275

Modern Production (1899-1935)

Exc.	V.G.	Good	Fair	Poor
1600	850	550	350	225

NOTE: Add 100 percent premium for musket. Add 25 percent premium for saddle ring carbine. Add 30 percent premium for "Baby" carbine.

Model 1895 Lever-Action Rifle

This is a large rifle designed to fire the larger hunting cartridges. It is chambered for the .33 W.C.F., .38-56, .40-65, .40-70, .40-83, .45-70, and the .45-90. It came standard with round or octagonal barrels from 26" to 32" in length. A bull-length magazine tube was also standard, as were buckhorn rear and blade front sights. The finish is case colored receiver, lever, and hammer; the rest is blued with a varnished walnut stock. The barrel markings are the same as the Model 1894, and the top tang is marked "Model 1895." After 1896 "Special Smokeless Steel" was stamped on the barrel. There were also many options available for this model, and they have a big effect on the value. There were approximately 18,000 manufactured between 1895 and 1917.

Antique Production (Pre-1898)

Exc.	V.G.	Good	Fair	Poor
3500	2750	2000	1250	600

Modern Production (1899-1917)

Exc.	V.G.	Good	Fair	Poor
2400	1500	875	650	500

Model 336 Cowboy

This model is similar to the Model 336 CS. It is available in both .30-30 and .38-55 calibers. It is fitted with 24" tapered octagon barrel. Rear sight is Marble buckhorn. Tubular magazine holds 6 rounds. Straight grip walnut stock has a hard rubber buttplate. Weight is about 7.5 lbs. First introduced in 1999.

NIB	Exc.	V.G.	Good	Fair	Poor
650	525	—	—	—	—

Model 1894 CS Lever-Action

This model is chambered for the .38 Special and .357 Magnum cartridges. It features an 18.5" round barrel, with full-length magazine tube and two barrel bands. It holds 9 shots and has a walnut straight-grip stock. This model was manufactured between 1969 and 1984. In 1984 a hammer-block crossbolt safety was added, and the model number was changed to 1894 CS. All other specifications remained the same.

Exc.	V.G.	Good	Fair	Poor
325	250	175	125	100

Model 1894 S Lever-Action Rifle

This model was introduced in 1984. It is chambered for the .41 Magnum and the .44 Special/.44 Magnum cartridges. In 1988 the .45 Colt chambering was offered. This model has a 20" barrel and a straight-grip stock. The forend has a steel cap. This model is currently produced and features the hammer-block safety.

NIB	Exc.	V.G.	Good	Fair	Poor
350	325	250	200	175	125

Model 1894 CL (Classic) Lever-Action Rifle

This model was introduced in 1988 and is the same basic rifle chambered for the old .25-20 and .32-20 cartridges. The rifle is also chambered for the .218 Bee cartridge. The barrel is 22", and the half-length magazine tube holds 6 shots. The walnut stock has no white spacers and has a black buttplate. Discontinued in 1993.

NIB	Exc.	V.G.	Good	Fair	Poor
425	350	250	150	125	100

NOTE: Collector interest has been growing in this model since it was discontinued in 1993.

Model 1894 Century Limited

An anniversary edition of the Marlin Model 1894 is limited to 2,500 rifles chambered in .44-40 caliber. Frame engraved and case colored. It is fitted with a 24" octagon barrel with 10-round magazine tube. The stock is semi-fancy walnut with straight grip and cut checkering with brass crescent buttplate.

NIB	Exc.	V.G.	Good	Fair	Poor
950	700	425	—	—	—

Model 1894 Century Limited Employee Edition

Same as above but limited to 100 rifles. The gun has a finer grade wood and the Marlin Man on the Horse logo is inlaid in gold on the right side of the receiver.

NIB	Exc.	V.G.	Good	Fair	Poor
1500	825	—	—	—	—

Model 1894 Cowboy

Introduced in 1996 this lever-action rifle features a 24" tapered octagon barrel with a 10-round tubular magazine. It is chambered for the .45 Long Colt, a popular cartridge for "Cowboy Action Shooting." Straight-grip checkered stock with blued steel forearm cap. Weight is approximately 7.5 lbs.

NIB	Exc.	V.G.	Good	Fair	Poor
600	450	300	—	—	—

Model 1894 Cowboy 32

As above but chambered for the .32 H&R Magnum cartridge. Introduced in 2004.

NIB	Exc.	V.G.	Good	Fair	Poor
N/A	—	—	—	—	—

Model 1894 Cowboy II

Introduced in 1997 and is the same as the Model 1894 Cowboy but is chambered for several cartridges. Available in .44-40, .357 Mag., .38 Special, and .44 Mag/.44 Special.

NIB	Exc.	V.G.	Good	Fair	Poor
600	450	300	—	—	—

Model 1895 Cowboy

This rifle is chambered for the .45-70 cartridge and fitted with a 26" tapered octagon barrel. Tubular magazine has a 9-round capacity. Adjustable semi-buckhorn rear sight. American black stock with cut checkering. Hard rubber butt. Weight is about 8 lbs. Introduced in 2001.

NIB	Exc.	V.G.	Good	Fair	Poor
800	650	—	—	—	—

Model 1897 Cowboy

This .22 caliber lever-action rifle is fitted with a 24" tapered octagon barrel with adjustable Marble buckhorn sight and Marble front sight with brass bead. Full-length tubular magazine holds 26 Shorts, 21 Longs, and 19 LR cartridges. Walnut straight grip stock with hard rubber buttplate. Weight is 7.5 lbs. Introduced in 1999.

NIB	Exc.	V.G.	Good	Fair	Poor
650	525	—	—	—	—

Model 1897 Texan
Chambered for the .22 caliber cartridge and fitted with a 20" octagon barrel, this rifle has a walnut stock with straight grip. Magazine capacity is 14 to 21 cartridges depending on type. Weight is about 6 lbs. Introduced in 2002.

NIB	Exc.	V.G.	Good	Fair	Poor
725	575	—	—	—	—

MARSTON, S.W.
New York, New York

Double-Action Pepperbox
A .31 caliber double-action percussion pepperbox with a 5" barrel group and ring trigger. Blued with walnut grips. Manufactured between 1850 and 1855.

Exc.	V.G.	Good	Fair	Poor
—	—	1750	750	250

2 Barrel Pistol
A .31 or .36 revolving barrel 2-shot pistol with a ring trigger. The barrel marked "J.Cohn & S.W.Marston-New York." Blued, brass frame with walnut grips. Manufactured during the 1850s.

Exc.	V.G.	Good	Fair	Poor
—	—	2250	1000	350

MARSTON, W. W. & CO.
New York, New York

W.W. Marston & Company manufactured a variety of firearms some of which are marked only with the trade names: Union Arms Company, Phoenix Armory, Western Arms Company, Washington Arms Company, Sprague and Marston, and Marston and Knox.

Pocket Revolver
A .31 caliber percussion revolver with a 3.25" to 7.5" barrel and 6-shot cylinder. Blued with walnut grips. Approximately 13,000 were manufactured between 1857 and 1862.

Exc.	V.G.	Good	Fair	Poor
—	—	900	400	200

Navy Revolver
A .36 caliber percussion revolver with a 7.5" or 8.5" octagonal barrel and 6-shot cylinder. Blued with walnut grips. Manufactured between 1857 and 1862.

Exc.	V.G.	Good	Fair	Poor
—	—	2750	1200	400

Single-Action Pistol
A .31 or .36 caliber percussion pistol with a 4" or 6" barrel. Blued with walnut grips. Manufactured during the 1860s.

Exc.	V.G.	Good	Fair	Poor
—	—	550	225	100

3 Barreled Derringer
A .22 caliber 3-barreled spur-trigger pocket pistol with a sliding knife blade mounted on the left side of the 3" barrel group. Blued, silver-plated with walnut grips. The barrel marked "Wm. W. Marston/New York City." Approximately 1,500 were manufactured between 1858 and 1864.

Knife Bladed Model

Courtesy Milwaukee Public Museum, Milwaukee, Wisconsin

Exc.	V.G.	Good	Fair	Poor
—	—	3750	1500	400

Model Without Knife

Exc.	V.G.	Good	Fair	Poor
—	—	1750	700	200

.32 Caliber 3 Barrel Derringer
Similar to the above, but in .32 caliber with either 3" or 4" barrels and not fitted with a knife blade. Approximately 3,000 were manufactured between 1864 and 1872.

Exc.	V.G.	Good	Fair	Poor
—	—	2750	750	200

Double-Action Pepperbox
A .31 caliber double-action 6-shot percussion pepperbox with 4" or 5" barrel groups and a bar hammer. Blued, case hardened with walnut grips. Manufactured during the 1850s.

Exc.	V.G.	Good	Fair	Poor
—	—	2250	950	300

MERIDEN FIREARMS CO.
Meriden, Connecticut

Pocket Pistol
A .32 or .38 caliber double-action revolver manufactured in a variety of barrel lengths and with either an exposed or enclosed hammer. Nickel-plated with rubber grips. The barrel marked "Meriden Firearms Co. Meriden, Conn. USA." Manufactured between 1895 and 1915.

Exc.	V.G.	Good	Fair	Poor
—	400	150	75	50

Double-Barrel Shotguns
From 1905-1918 Meriden Fire Arms Co. successor to A.J. Aubrey, made 12, 16, and 20 gauge sidelock double-barrel shotguns. These were better quality hammer and hammerless side-by-sides fitted with twist, laminated, Damascus, and steel barrels in grades A to G. Some of these guns were beautifully engraved by the same artisans who worked for Parker Bros. and other Connecticut gunmakers. Prices in 1910 ranged from $40 to $250 but they represented great value for the money as they were superior to the popular Crescent guns which they closely resembled. Current values depend on model, grade, gauge, and condition. It is difficult to find examples in excellent condition as these were sold by Sears to customers who put them to hard use. In good condition their current values range from $250 for plain Janes to $3,500 or more for the top grades, of which few specimens are known.

Single-Barrel Shotguns and Rifles
Meriden Fire Arms Co. also made many single-barrel shotguns and rifles whose current values are determined by growing collector interest and condition.

MERKEL, GEBRUDER
Suhl, Germany
Importer—GSI, Inc.

An Introduction to Merkel Brother's Guns by Dan Sheil
Merkel Brothers shotgun and rifle makers began production around the turn of the century in Suhl, Germany. Merkel made a number of

different models but the company was most well known for its over-and-under shotgun. It also made bolt-action rifles, side-by-side double express rifles, falling block single-shot rifles, side-by-side shotguns, drillings, and just about anything in the way of firearms its customers desired.

Perhaps the company's greatest productive era fell between the end of World War I and the 1950s. During the 1930s most of the live pigeon shoots were won with Merkel shotguns. However, there seems to be a difference of opinion about when Merkel built its best quality guns. This is not an easy question to answer. Most shooters and collectors feel that pre-World War II guns are the best examples of Merkel craftsmanship. But, in my opinion, some of the finest Merkels I have seen were produced immediately after World War II. Outstanding examples of Merkel's quality continue to appear up to the construction of the Berlin Wall in 1961.

Another area of controversy is the high grade Merkel 300 series shotgun. Many have compared this gun to the Italian and British makers and believe it is a mass produced gun. This is not the case because all Merkel shotguns are handcrafted and as far as I know barrels will not interchange unless they are supplied with the gun from the factory. While the 100 and 200 series guns may be mass produced, the 300 series is not, and that is easy to determine by looking at the serial number together with the date stamped on the barrel. Very few 300 series guns were produced in a given period.

In terms of durability, strength, and reliability, there is not an over-and-under shotgun that is built as strong as the Merkel. It has two Kersten style locking lugs on the upper barrel that fit into the face of the receiver while the bottom has two under lugs that give the gun a rugged four position locking system. I don't think I have ever heard of a Merkel being sent back to the gunmaker or a gunsmith to have the frame tightened. It just is not necessary; the guns will not shoot loose.

With respect to value, the Merkel over-and-under guns have been sleepers in the gun industry for a number of years. Until recently they have not brought the price that they deserve. I am specifically talking about the 300 series; the 303 Luxus and the 304. Generally speaking all of the special order Merkel over-and-under shotguns have done well. I think the shooting public will begin to recognize the quality and craftsmanship built into every one of these fine guns.

One last comment regarding special order Merkels and the company's reputation for building just about anything the customer wanted. It is impossible to cover all of the variations that the company produced in its long history, but the buyer should be aware that he may encounter some different and uncataloged Merkels along the way.

In August 1993 Merkel Brothers declared bankruptcy. The assets of the company were reportedly purchased by Steyr. GSI, Inc. Trussville, Alabama currently imports Merkel guns.

NOTE: Merkel is now owned by Heckler & Koch.

Editor's Comment: The following Merkel gun prices are based on either one or two factors. First, they are no longer in production or second that the guns were built prior to the Berlin Wall, which generally bring a premium. An additional factor was introduced in 1994 when the factory began to use an alpha numeric serial number system. This new system dates the guns from 1994. The prices listed for new Merkels are influenced by the value of the dollar to the German Mark.

MERKEL SIDE-BY-SIDE SHOTGUNS

Model 8

This model has a self-cocking Deeley boxlock action side-by-side with cocking indicators. The locking mechanism is a Greener cross-bolt with double-barrel locking lug. Triggers are single-selective or double. The safety is automatic and tang mounted. This model has an extractor. Offered in 12 and 16 gauge with 28" solid rib barrels or 20 gauge with 26.75" barrels. Available with straight or pistol grip oil-finished walnut stock. Receiver is case colored with light scroll engraving. The 12 and 16 gauge guns weigh about 6.8 lbs. while the 20 gauge weighs approximately 6 lbs.

NIB	Exc.	V.G.	Good	Fair	Poor
1000	800	700	600	500	400

Model 117/117E

Offered in 12 and 16 gauge with various barrel lengths, this model featured a boxlock action with double triggers and extractors. Ejectors were available under the "E" designation. The boxlock action body was scrupled at the rear with fine line scroll engraving.

Exc.	V.G.	Good	Fair	Poor
5000	3500	1500	1000	500

Model 118/118E

Also offered in 12 and 16 gauge this model is similar to above model with slightly more engraving and better wood. This model also has some engraving coverage on the breech end of the barrels.

Exc.	V.G.	Good	Fair	Poor
6000	4000	2200	1200	650

Model 124/125

Similar to the above models but supplied with extractors for the Model 124 and ejectors for the Model 125. Both models have more engraving coverage with game scenes. Finer checkering and fancy wood is seen on this model.

Model 124

Exc.	V.G.	Good	Fair	Poor
4500	3500	2000	1500	700

Model 125

Exc.	V.G.	Good	Fair	Poor
5000	3750	3000	2000	1000

Model 170

This model was offered in 12 gauge only with automatic ejectors. The boxlock action was engraved with fine full coverage scroll.

Exc.	V.G.	Good	Fair	Poor
5000	4000	3200	2500	1200

Model 130

This was one of Merkel's highest side-by-side shotguns. It featured a sidelock action, extra fancy wood, fine line checkering, and full coverage game scene engraving.

Exc.	V.G.	Good	Fair	Poor
15000	12000	7500	4500	—

Model 126

Similar to the Model 130 but fitted with removable sidelocks.

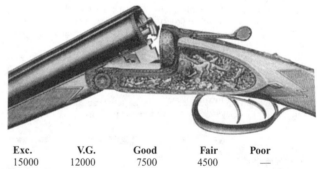

Exc.	V.G.	Good	Fair	Poor
15000	12000	7500	4500	—

Model 127

This model was Merkel's finest side-by-side shotgun. The sidelock action featured full coverage fine line scroll engraving of the best quality.

Exc.	V.G.	Good	Fair	Poor
21000	16000	12000	6000	—

Model 47E

Same as above but fitted with ejectors. Offered in 12, 16, or 20 gauge. Supplied with fitted luggage case.

NIB	Exc.	V.G.	Good	Fair	Poor
2750	2100	1500	950	—	—

Model 147
Same as Model 8 but with silver grayed receiver with fine engraved hunting scenes, engraved border, and screws. This model has been discontinued.

NIB	Exc.	V.G.	Good	Fair	Poor
2900	2500	1750	1100	600	400

Model 147E
Same as above but fitted with ejectors. Offered in 12, 16, 20, or 28 gauge. Supplied with fitted luggage case.

NIB	Exc.	V.G.	Good	Fair	Poor
3375	2500	1750	1100	—	—

Model 147EL
Similar to the Model 147E but with fancy walnut stock. Supplied with fitted luggage case.

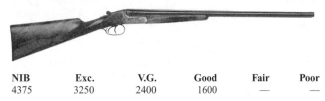

NIB	Exc.	V.G.	Good	Fair	Poor
4375	3250	2400	1600	—	—

Model 122
This model features the same specifications as the above models but has false sideplates. This model is fitted with ejectors and the receiver is silver grayed with fine engraved hunting scenes on false sideplates, engraved border, and screws.

NIB	Exc.	V.G.	Good	Fair	Poor
4900	3850	2750	1750	950	500

Model 47SL
Same as above but with scroll engraving in place of hunting scenes.

NIB	Exc.	V.G.	Good	Fair	Poor
5350	4000	2500	1750	1100	600

Model 147SL
This model features true Holland and Holland-style sidelocks with cocking indicators. Gauge and barrel lengths are as above. Stock is fancy walnut. However, 20 gauge gun weighs 6.4 lbs., 28 gauge gun weighs about 6.1 lbs.

NIB	Exc.	V.G.	Good	Fair	Poor
6950	5250	3750	2500	1500	750

Model 147SSL
Similar to the Model 147SL but fitted with removable side plates. Fancy walnut stock. Supplied with fitted luggage case.

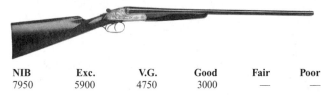

NIB	Exc.	V.G.	Good	Fair	Poor
7950	5900	4750	3000	—	—

Models 247S/347S
These models are the same as the Model 147S with the exception of the types of engraving.

Model 247S
Large scroll engraving.

NIB	Exc.	V.G.	Good	Fair	Poor
7000	5250	4000	2500	—	—

Model 347
Medium scroll engraving.

NIB	Exc.	V.G.	Good	Fair	Poor
6500	5500	4500	3500	2250	1500

Model 447SL
Small scroll engraving.

NIB	Exc.	V.G.	Good	Fair	Poor
9000	6750	5250	4000	—	—

NOTE: For wood upgrade add $1,200. For custom stock dimensions add $1,400. For left-hand stocks add $900.

Model 280
This is a boxlock gun chambered for the 28 gauge shell and fitted with 28" barrels choked Improved Cylinder and Modified. Double triggers with ejectors. Straight-grip walnut stock. Scroll engraving with case colored receiver. Weight is about 5.2 lbs.

NIB	Exc.	V.G.	Good	Fair	Poor
4195	3250	—	—	—	—

Model 280EL
This model features an Anson & Deely boxlock action with engraved hunting scenes on a silver-grayed action. Double triggers. Fancy walnut with straight grip stock. Offered in 28 gauge with 28" barrels. Fitted luggage case standard. Weight is about 5.2 lbs. First imported in 2000.

NIB	Exc.	V.G.	Good	Fair	Poor
4975	3750	—	—	—	—

Model 280SL
Similar to the Model 280EL, but with English-style scroll engraving on H&H style sidelocks with choice of pistol-grip or straight-grip fancy walnut stock. Fitted luggage case standard. First imported in 2000.

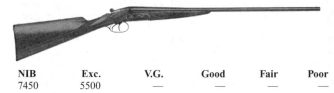

NIB	Exc.	V.G.	Good	Fair	Poor
7450	5500	—	—	—	—

Model 360
This boxlock model is the same as the Model 280 but chambered for the .410 bore. Straight grip walnut stock. Scroll engraving on case colored receiver. Barrel is 28" choke Modified and Full. Weight is about 5.2 lbs.

NIB	Exc.	V.G.	Good	Fair	Poor
4195	3250	—	—	—	—

Model 360EL
This model is the same as the Model 280EL but chambered for the .410 shell and fitted with 28" barrels. Fancy walnut and fitted case. Weight is about 5.5 lbs. First imported in 2000.

NIB	Exc.	V.G.	Good	Fair	Poor
4975	3750	—	—	—	—

Model 360SL
Same as the Model 360EL but with English-style scroll engraving on H&H style sidelocks and choice of pistol grip or straight grip stock. First imported in 2000.

NIB	Exc.	V.G.	Good	Fair	Poor
7450	5500	—	—	—	—

Model 280/360 Two-Barrel Set
This set consists of a 28 gauge 28" barrel and a .410 bore 28" barrel with scroll engraving and oil finish walnut stock. Double triggers and straight grip stock.

NIB	Exc.	V.G.	Good	Fair	Poor
6495	5000	—	—	—	—

Model 280/360EL Two Barrel Set
This set consists of a 28 gauge 28" barrel and a .410 bore 28" barrel with engraved hunting scenes and fancy walnut stock. Double triggers and straight-grip stock. First imported in 2000.

NIB	Exc.	V.G.	Good	Fair	Poor
7450	5500	—	—	—	—

Model 280/360SL Two Barrel Set
Same as above but with English-style scroll engraving and choice of pistol-grip or straight-grip stock. First imported in 2000.

NIB	Exc.	V.G.	Good	Fair	Poor
10975	8250	—	—	—	—

Model 1620
This is a boxlock side-by-side gun chambered for the 16 gauge shell. Fitted with 28" barrels with double triggers. Barrel chokes Improved Cylinder and Modified. Ejectors. Straight-grip walnut stock with oil finish. Case colored receiver finish. Light scroll engraving. Fitted luggage case. Weight is about 6.1 lbs.

NIB	Exc.	V.G.	Good	Fair	Poor
4195	3250	—	—	—	—

NOTE: For two-barrel set add $2,300. Second set is 20 gauge with 28" barrels.

Model 1620EL
As above but with high-grade walnut straight-grip stock and deeply engraved hunting scenes.

NIB	Exc.	V.G.	Good	Fair	Poor
6495	5000	—	—	—	—

NOTE: For two-barrel set add $2,900. Second set is 20 gauge with 28" barrels.

Model 1620SL
Similar to the 1620 models above but with grayed sidelocks with deeply engraved hunting scenes. High-grade walnut stock with oil finish. Weight is 6.6 lbs.

NIB	Exc.	V.G.	Good	Fair	Poor
9395	7500	—	—	—	—

NOTE: For two-barrel set add $3,800. Second set is 20 gauge with 28" barrels.

MERWIN & BRAY
Worcester, Massachusetts
This company marketed a number of firearms produced by various manufacturers under their own name.

Merwin & Bray Pocket Pistol
A .32 caliber spur trigger single-shot pistol with a 3.5" barrel. Blued, silver-plated with walnut grips. The barrel marked "Merwin & Bray New York."

Exc.	V.G.	Good	Fair	Poor
—	—	300	150	75

MERWIN HULBERT & CO.
New York, New York
By Jim Supica, Pres., Old Town Station, Ltd.

Merwin Hulbert & Co., New York City. Founder Joseph Merwin had previously been involved in Merwin & Bray. Merwin Hulbert & Co. or its principals were also involved in Phoenix Rifle, Evans Rifle Company, American Cartridge Company, and Hopkins & Allen of Norwich, CT. Most Merwin Hulbert revolvers will be marked with the Hopkins & Allen name, in addition to Merwin Hulbert. They were made for a fairly brief period, with most production apparently taking place during the 1870s & early 1880s.

There has been some confusion over a classification system for MH revolvers. The system adopted here is based on the distinctions listed in Art Phelps' book, The Story of Merwin Hulbert & Co. Firearms. We believe this is the first time the Phelps system has been adapted to a list format.

LARGE-FRAME MERWIN HULBERT SIXGUNS
There has been a marked increase in interest in Merwin Hulbert & Co. over the past decade, with many coming to recognize them as one of the pre-eminent makers of large-frame revolvers used in the American West. Total production of large-frame revolvers has been estimated at a few thousand by some sources. However, the frequency with which they are encountered suggests possibly greater production.

MH used a unique system of opening, loading & unloading their revolvers which was supposed to allow selective ejection of spent shells, leaving remaining cartridges in place. A latch on the bottom of the frame is pushed toward the rear of the gun, and the barrel and cylinder are rotated to the right (clockwise, as viewed from the rear of the revolver) 90 degrees. The barrel and cylinder are then pulled forward, far enough to allow empty brass to fall free. This system required exceptional quality machining, and some modern authorities are on record as considering the Merwin Hulbert to have the finest workmanship of all revolvers of the era.

All are .44 caliber 6-shot large-frame revolvers. Beyond that, to fully identify a large-frame Merwin Hulbert, you must specify the following:
1. **MODEL DESIGNATION** — First Model has an open top and scoop flutes, round barrel, and two small screws above the trigger guard. Second Model is similar to the first, except with only one screw above the trigger guard. Third Model has a top-strap with standard flutes and a round barrel. Fourth Model is similar to the third, except that it has a ribbed barrel. The open-top 1st and 2nd Models seem to be more sought after. The 4th Model is rare, and will bring a premium from a serious Merwin collector.
2. **FRONTIER ARMY or POCKET ARMY** — Frontier Army models have a square butt, and were made in 1st through 4th models. Pocket Army models have a bird's-head butt with a pointed extension with lanyard hole, and are found in 2nd or 3rd Model configuration. Generally, the Frontier Army will bring more than the Pocket Army.
3. **SINGLE-ACTION or DOUBLE-ACTION** — The topstrap models, 3rd and 4th, were manufactured in both single-action and double-action. The single-action models tend to bring more.
4. **BARREL LENGTH** — Standard barrel length on the Frontier Army 1st, 2nd, & 3rd Models is 7", with a 5-1/2" barrel common on the 4th Model. Standard barrel length on the Pocket Army was a more "pocket-sized" 3-1/2". However, somewhat ironically, bird's-head butt models marked "Pocket Army" were also produced with full length 7" barrels. Generally, these longer barrels will bring a bit more than the shorter ones.
5. **CALIBER** — Most common is .44-40 (designated "Winchester Calibre 1873"). Merwins were also chambered for .44 Merwin Hulbert (somewhat similar to the S&W .44 American cartridge), and .44 Russian. The less common calibers may bring a small premium from serious Merwin collectors.
6. **FOREIGN COPIES** — The Merwin Hulbert design was relatively widely copied during the period of use, particularly in Spain. It seems that much of this production may have gone to Mexico, and some found their way to the U.S. Although these Spanish copies may bear markings such as "System Merwin Hulbert" or other usage of the words "Merwin Hulbert", they generally will not be found with the Hopkins & Allen marking. Spanish firms making Merwin copies included Orbea Hermanos and Anitua y Charola. These Spanish copies may bring half or less of what an original Merwin will bring, and it can sometimes take a fairly experienced eye to tell the difference.
7. **ENGRAVING** — Special order engraving was available, and it was usually executed in a distinctive and colorful "punch dot" style, which has come to be associated with Merwins (although it is occasionally encountered on other makes of firearms). For a long time, this style was somewhat dismissed as a bit crude and lacking in artistry. However, a new appreciation of Merwin engraving has emerged, and factory engraved pieces will bring a significant premium. Often, a panel scene depicts an animal, object, or landmark. These panel scenes have an almost "folk art" quality to them, and will enhance the value further. Engraved Merwins are sometimes encountered with the engraving filled with colored enamel, quite rare, and, if original, this will bring a further premium.
8. **FINISH** — The vast majority were nickel plated. Original blued guns will bring a premium.

First Model Frontier Army, .44 open top
Two screws, square butt, 7" barrel.

Exc.	V.G.	Good	Fair	Poor
—	5500	3000	1500	500

Second Model Frontier Army, .44 open top
One screw, square butt, 7" barrel

Exc.	V.G.	Good	Fair	Poor
—	4500	2750	1000	500

Second Model Pocket Army, .44 open top
Bird's-head butt. 3-1/2" barrel standard, 7" will bring a premium.

Exc.	V.G.	Good	Fair	Poor
—	3500	2000	700	400

Third Model Frontier Army, Single-Action, .44, topstrap
Square butt, 7" barrel.

Exc.	V.G.	Good	Fair	Poor
—	3750	2250	800	450

Third Model Frontier Army, Double-Action, .44, topstrap
Square butt, 7" barrel.

Courtesy Greg Martin Auctions

Exc.	V.G.	Good	Fair	Poor
—	3250	1750	700	400

Third Model Pocket Army, Single-Action, .44 topstrap
Bird's-head butt. 3-1/2" barrel standard, 7" will bring a premium.

Exc.	V.G.	Good	Fair	Poor
—	3250	1750	700	400

Third Model Pocket Army, Double-Action, .44, topstrap
Bird's-head butt. 3-1/2" barrel standard, 7" will bring a premium.

Exc.	V.G.	Good	Fair	Poor
—	3000	1600	650	400

Fourth Model Frontier Army, Single-Action, .44, topstrap
Ribbed barrel, scarce. 5-1/2" barrel seems to be most common, also offered in 7" and 3-1/2".

Exc.	V.G.	Good	Fair	Poor
—	5000	2750	800	550

Fourth Model Frontier Army, Double-Action, .44, topstrap
Ribbed barrel. Barrel lengths as above.

Exc.	V.G.	Good	Fair	Poor
—	4750	2500	750	550

SMALL FRAME MERWIN HULBERT POCKET REVOLVERS

The .32 & .38 centerfire revolvers were manufactured with the unique Merwin Hulbert twist-open system, like the large frame revolvers. They were often advertised as chambered for the .32 MH & Co. or .38 MH & Co. cartridges, but it appears as if these cartridges may have been essentially the same as the .32 S&W and .38 S&W rounds. Of course, the Merwin Hulbert revolvers were manufactured for the original lower pressure black-powder loadings of these cartridges. Saw-handled grip frames were standard, although some were manufactured with the distinctive Pocket Army type pointed "skullcrusher" bird's-head grip frames, and these will generally bring a premium. Most common barrel length for most models is 3-1/2", with 5-1/2" barrels somewhat scarcer in most models, and 2-3/4" barrels quite scarce and worth a premium. A number of police departments purchased small frame Merwin Hulbert revolvers in the late 19th century. Department marked guns will bring a premium. Terminology alert—note that the .44 caliber "Pocket Army" model is a large-frame, and is listed in the section above. The .22 Merwin Hulbert revolver is the only one not to use the MH twist-open system. It is, instead, a tip-up revolver closely resembling the S&W Model One.

First Pocket Model Single-Action
Spur-trigger, cylinder pin exposed at front of frame, round loading aperture in recoil shield (no loading gate), five-shot .38, scarce

Exc.	V.G.	Good	Fair	Poor
—	1250	800	300	175

Second Pocket Model Single-Action
Spur-trigger, cylinder pin exposed, sliding loading gate, five-shot .38.

Exc.	V.G.	Good	Fair	Poor
—	1000	650	285	150

Third Pocket Model Single-Action Spur-Trigger
Enclosed cylinder pin, sliding loading gate, five-shot .38.

Exc.	V.G.	Good	Fair	Poor
—	950	600	225	125

Third Pocket Model Single-Action w/Trigger Guard
Five-shot .38.

Exc.	V.G.	Good	Fair	Poor
—	1000	675	285	150

Double-Action Pocket Model, medium frame
Usually .38 five shot. Scarce .32 seven shot will bring a 25 percent to 50 percent premium. Patent marked folding hammer spur will bring a small premium.

Exc.	V.G.	Good	Fair	Poor
—	900	900	225	150

Double-Action Pocket Model, small frame
.32 cal. five shot. Patent marked folding hammer spur will bring a small premium.

Exc.	V.G.	Good	Fair	Poor
—	800	550	185	125

Tip-up .22 Spur-Trigger
.22 rimfire, a S&W patent infringement, looks similar to S&W Mod. One Third Issue. Scarce. "Made by Merwin Hulbert & Co. for Smith & Wesson" marking will bring a small premium.

Exc.	V.G.	Good	Fair	Poor
—	1000	650	275	175

Merwin Hulbert Rifles
Very similar in design to Hopkins & Allen single-shot breech loaders. Advertised in .22 and .32 rimfire, as well as .32 WCF, .38 WCF, and .44 WCF. May have been offered in .32-40 and .38-55 chamberings. A 20 ga. shotgun barrel was offered separately for these rifles. Features included set trigger, rebounding hammer, pistol grip stock, & takedown. Seldom encountered, the Merwin Hulbert name on these should bring a premium over standard Hopkins & Allen single-shot rifles. A small frame "Merwin Hulbert & Co's. Junior" rifle was also offered, chambered for .22 rimfire.

METROPOLITAN ARMS CO.
New York, New York

Established in February 1864, this company manufactured copies of the Colt Model 1851 and 1861 Navy Revolvers, as well as copies of the Colt Model 1862 Police Revolver. Two of the firm's principle officers were Samuel and William Syms (formerly of Blunt & Syms) and it is believed that they were responsible for production. Curiously, although most Metropolitan pistols were produced during the 1864 to 1866 period, the company itself was not dissolved until 1920.

1851 Navy Revolver
A .36 caliber percussion revolver with a 7.5" octagonal barrel and 6-shot cylinder. Blued, case hardened with walnut grips. The barrel

marked "Metropolitan Arms Co. New York." Approximately 6,000 of these revolvers were made during the 1860s. Those bearing H.E. Dimick markings are worth considerably more than the standard marked examples.

H.E. Dimick Navy Model

Exc.	V.G.	Good	Fair	Poor
—	—	7250	2750	850

Standard Navy Model

Exc.	V.G.	Good	Fair	Poor
—	—	3750	1250	500

1861 Navy Revolver

A .36 caliber percussion revolver with a 7.5" round barrel and 6-shot cylinder. The loading lever of the rack-and-pinion type. Blued, case hardened with walnut grips. The barrel marked "Metropolitan Arms Co. New York." Approximately 50 were made in 1864 and 1865.

Exc.	V.G.	Good	Fair	Poor
—	—	7250	3000	950

Police Revolver

A .36 caliber percussion revolver with either 4.5", 5.5" or 6.5" round barrels and a fluted 5-shot cylinder. Blued, case hardened with walnut grips. The barrel normally marked "Metropolitan Arms Co. New York," although examples have been noted without any markings. Approximately 2,750 were made between 1864 and 1866.

Exc.	V.G.	Good	Fair	Poor
—	—	1500	600	250

MINNEAPOLIS F. A. CO.
Minneapolis, Minnesota

Palm Pistol

A .32 caliber radial cylinder pistol with a 1.75" barrel manufactured by the Ames Manufacturing Company (see the Ames entry). Nickel-plated with hard rubber grips. The sideplates marked "Minneapolis Firearms Co." and "The Protector." Several thousand were sold during the 1890s.

Exc.	V.G.	Good	Fair	Poor
—	2250	850	350	100

N

NAVY ARMS COMPANY
Ridgefield, New Jersey

Founded in 1957 by Val Forgett to enhance the shooting of blackpowder firearms without destroying the originals. The first replica was the Colt 1851 Navy. Thus, the name of the new company, "Navy Arms." In the early 1980s Navy Arms began importing surplus firearms from European countries. Navy Arms continues to offer both blackpowder replicas and foreign imports. For a short period of time the company imported double-barrel shotguns. This was discontinued in 1990.

SHOTGUNS

The shotguns listed were no longer imported by Navy Arms in 1990.

Model 100 Side-by-Side

A 12 or 20 gauge Magnum boxlock double-barrel shotgun with 27.5" barrels, double triggers and extractors. Blued with a walnut stock. Imported between 1985 and 1987.

Exc.	V.G.	Good	Fair	Poor
375	300	250	200	100

Model 150

As above, with automatic ejectors.

Exc.	V.G.	Good	Fair	Poor
450	350	300	225	125

REPLICA LONG GUNS

Tryon Creedmoor Rifle

This .45 caliber model features a heavy blued 33" octagonal barrel, hooded front sight, adjustable tang sight, double set triggers, sling swivels, and a walnut stock. Weighs about 9.5 lbs.

NIB	Exc.	V.G.	Good	Fair	Poor
600	525	450	400	300	150

Standard Tryon Rifle

Same as above but without target sights.

NIB	Exc.	V.G.	Good	Fair	Poor
400	350	300	250	200	100

Deluxe Tryon Rifle

Same as above but with polished and engraved lock and patch box.

NIB	Exc.	V.G.	Good	Fair	Poor
425	375	325	250	200	100

1861 Springfield Rifle

This .58 caliber replica is fitted with an 1855-style hammer. Barrel length is 40" and weight is 10 lbs. 4 oz.

NIB	Exc.	V.G.	Good	Fair	Poor
550	425	350	300	200	100

Model 1873 Springfield Officer's Trapdoor

This model features a single set trigger, case colored breechblock, deluxe walnut stock, adjustable rear peep sight with Beech front sight. Chambered for the .45-70 cartridge and fitted with a 26" round barrel. Weight is about 8 lbs. Introduced in 2003.

NIB	Exc.	V.G.	Good	Fair	Poor
1190	950	—	—	—	—

1862 C.S. Richmond Rifle
This Confederate rifle is .58 caliber and is a faithful reproduction of those produced at the Richmond Armory. Barrel length is 40". Weighs 10 lbs. 4 oz.

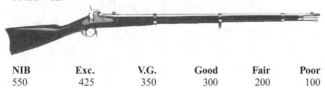

NIB	Exc.	V.G.	Good	Fair	Poor
550	425	350	300	200	100

J.P. Murray Carbine
This Confederate cavalry .58 caliber carbine has a case colored lock and brass furniture on a walnut stock. Barrel length is 23.5" and weight is 8 lbs. 5 oz.

NIB	Exc.	V.G.	Good	Fair	Poor
400	325	250	200	150	100

1863 Springfield Rifle
An exact replica of the famous Springfield Musket. Barrel is 40" with 3 barrel bands. All metal parts are finished bright. Weighs 9.5 lbs.

NIB	Exc.	V.G.	Good	Fair	Poor
550	425	350	300	200	100

1841 Mississippi Rifle
Also know as the "Yager" rifle it is offered in either .54 or .58 caliber. Barrel length is 33" and weighs 9.5 lbs.

NIB	Exc.	V.G.	Good	Fair	Poor
450	325	250	200	150	100

Zouave Rifle
This Civil War replica is a .58 caliber with polished brass hardware and blued 33" barrel. Weighs 9 lbs.

NIB	Exc.	V.G.	Good	Fair	Poor
450	325	250	200	150	100

Navy Arms Revolving Carbine
Fitted with a 20" barrel and chambered for the .357 Magnum, .44-40, or .45 Colt cartridge. This model has a revolving 6-shot cylinder. Straight-grip stock with brass buttplate and trigger guard. The action is based on the Remington Model 1874 revolver. Introduced in 1968 and discontinued in 1984.

NIB	Exc.	V.G.	Good	Fair	Poor
600	500	400	300	200	100

1859 Sharps Infantry Rifle
This is a .54 caliber copy of the three band Sharps. Barrel length is 30". Case hardened receiver and patch box. Blued barrel and walnut stock. Weight is about 8.5 lbs.

NIB	Exc.	V.G.	Good	Fair	Poor
1000	800	600	400	300	150

1859 Berdan Sharps Rifle
Similar to the 1859 Sharps above but with double set triggers.

NIB	Exc.	V.G.	Good	Fair	Poor
1075	850	650	450	325	150

1873 Sharps No. 2 Creedmore
Chambered for the .45-70 cartridge and fitted with a 30" round barrel. Polished nickel receiver. Target-grade rear tang sight and front globe sight with inserts. Checkered walnut stock with pistol grip. Weight is about 10 lbs. Introduced in 2002.

NIB	Exc.	V.G.	Good	Fair	Poor
1325	1000	—	—	—	—

Sharps #2 Silhouette Rifle
This model is identical to the standard No. 2 above but with a full octagon barrel. Weight is about 10.5 lbs. Introduced in 2003.

NIB	Exc.	V.G.	Good	Fair	Poor
1325	1000	—	—	—	—

Sharps #2 Sporting Rifle
Same as the No. 2 standard rifle but with case colored receiver. Introduced in 2003.

NIB	Exc.	V.G.	Good	Fair	Poor
1325	1000	—	—	—	—

1873 Sharps Quigley
This model is chambered for the .45-70 cartridge and fitted with a heavy 34" octagon barrel. Case hardened receiver with military patchbox. Open sights. Weight is about 13 lbs. Introduced in 2002.

NIB	Exc.	V.G.	Good	Fair	Poor
1390	1100	—	—	—	—

1874 Sharps Infantry Rifle
This model is fitted with a 30" round barrel and chambered for the .45-70 cartridge. Blued barrel with case hardened receiver. Walnut stock with 3 barrel bands. Weight is about 8.5 lbs.

NIB	Exc.	V.G.	Good	Fair	Poor
1050	750	550	—	—	—

1874 Sharps Sniper Rifle
Same as 1874 Infantry rifle but with double set triggers.

NIB	Exc.	V.G.	Good	Fair	Poor
1100	800	600	—	—	—

Sharps Cavalry Carbine
A breech-loading .54 caliber carbine with 22" blued barrel. Military-style sights, walnut stocks, and saddle bar with ring are standard. Weighs 7 lbs. 12 oz.

NIB	Exc.	V.G.	Good	Fair	Poor
925	550	500	400	300	150

Sharps Cavalry Carbine Cartridge Model
Same as above but chambered for the .45-70 Government cartridge.

NIB	Exc.	V.G.	Good	Fair	Poor
925	550	500	400	300	150

1874 Sharps Plains Rifle
This model features a case colored receiver, blued barrel, and checkered walnut stock. Offered in .44-70 or .54 caliber percussion. Barrel length is 28.5". Weight is 8 lbs. 10 oz.

NIB	Exc.	V.G.	Good	Fair	Poor
1050	800	600	400	300	150

1874 Sharps Sporting Rifle
Similar to the above model but features a full pistol grip, 32" medium weight octagonal barrel, double set triggers, and case colored frame. Weight is about 10.75 lbs.

NIB	Exc.	V.G.	Good	Fair	Poor
1090	850	650	450	350	200

1874 Sharps Buffalo Rifle
Chambered for the .45-70 or .45-90 and fitted with a 28" heavy octagon barrel. Buttstock is checkered. Weight is approximately 12 lbs.

NIB	Exc.	V.G.	Good	Fair	Poor
1090	850	650	450	350	200

1874 Sharps No. 3 Long Range Rifle
Built by Pedersoli this rifle is fitted with a 34" medium weight octagon barrel, globe target front sight and match grade rear tang sight. Double set trigger. Case hardened frame. Walnut stock. Weight is about 11 lbs.

NIB	Exc.	V.G.	Good	Fair	Poor
1725	1250	900	—	—	—

1873 Winchester Rifle
This replica features a case colored receiver, blued octagon 24" barrel, and walnut stocks. Offered in either .44-40 or .45 Long Colt. Weighs about 8 lbs. 4 oz.

NIB	Exc.	V.G.	Good	Fair	Poor
900	725	600	500	400	200

1873 Winchester Carbine
Same specifications as rifle above but fitted with a 19" round barrel, blued receiver, and saddle ring. Weighs 7 lbs. 4 oz.

NIB	Exc.	V.G.	Good	Fair	Poor
800	650	575	500	400	200

1873 Winchester Sporting Rifle
This model features a 24.25" octagonal barrel, case colored receiver, and checkered pistol grip. Offered in .44-40 or .45 Long Colt. Weighs about 8 lbs. 14 oz.

NIB	Exc.	V.G.	Good	Fair	Poor
950	750	650	525	400	200

1873 Sporting Long Range Rifle
Similar to the Sporting Rifle above but chambered for the .44-40 cartridge and fitted with a 30" octagon barrel. Long-range rear tang sight. Weight is about 7.5 lbs. Introduced in 2002.

NIB	Exc.	V.G.	Good	Fair	Poor
1075	850	—	—	—	—

1873 Border Model
Introduced in 2000 this model features a 20" blued octagon barrel with buckhorn rear sight. Magazine capacity is 10 rounds. Checkered pistol-grip stock is walnut with oil finish. Chambered for the .357 Mag., .44-40, or .45 Colt cartridge.

NIB	Exc.	V.G.	Good	Fair	Poor
975	800	700	—	—	—

1866 "Yellowboy" Rifle
This model features a brass receiver, 24" octagon barrel, and walnut stocks. Weighs 8.5 lbs.

NIB	Exc.	V.G.	Good	Fair	Poor
675	525	450	400	300	150

1866 "Yellowboy" Carbine
Same as above but fitted with a 19" round barrel and saddle ring. Weighs 7 lbs. 4 oz.

NIB	Exc.	V.G.	Good	Fair	Poor
675	525	450	400	300	150

1866 "Yellowboy" Short Rifle
Introduced in 2000 this model features a 20" barrel with buckhorn rear sight. Walnut stock with oil finish. Receiver is yellow brass. Chambered for the .38 Special, .44-40, or .45 Colt cartridge. Magazine capacity is 10 rounds.

NIB	Exc.	V.G.	Good	Fair	Poor
700	550	450	—	—	—

Iron Frame Henry
This is a replica of the famous and rare .44-40 Iron Frame Henry that features a case colored frame. Barrel length is 24" and rifle weighs 9 lbs.

NIB	Exc.	V.G.	Good	Fair	Poor
925	750	650	500	400	200

Blued Iron Frame Henry
Same as above but furnished with a highly polished blued receiver.

NIB	Exc.	V.G.	Good	Fair	Poor
925	750	650	500	400	200

Military Henry
Based on the brass frame military version of the Henry rifle this model is furnished with sling swivels mounted on the left side. The buttplate is fitted with a trap door. Caliber is .44-40 and barrel length is 24". Weighs 9 lbs. 4 oz.

NIB	Exc.	V.G.	Good	Fair	Poor
900	725	625	500	400	200

Henry Carbine
This is the brass frame carbine version and features a 22" barrel. Chambered for the .44-40 cartridge. Weighs 8 lbs. 12 oz.

NIB	Exc.	V.G.	Good	Fair	Poor
875	700	600	500	400	200

Henry Trapper
This replica is not based on an actual Henry. Fitted with a unique 16.5" barrel, this brass frame model weighs 7 lbs. 7 oz. Chambered for the .44-40 cartridge.

NIB	Exc.	V.G.	Good	Fair	Poor
875	700	600	500	400	200

1892 Rifle
This lever-action rifle is chambered for the .357 Mag., .44-40, .45 Colt, or .32-20 cartridge. Octagon barrel is 24.25". Walnut stock, crescent butt and blued or case colored receiver. Weight is about 6.25 lbs.

NIB	Exc.	V.G.	Good	Fair	Poor
525	425	350	300	250	200

1892 Short Rifle
Same as above but with 20" octagon barrel. Weight is about 6.25 lbs.

NIB	Exc.	V.G.	Good	Fair	Poor
525	425	350	300	250	200

1892 Carbine
Similar to the short rifle but fitted with a 20" round barrel and saddle ring on left side of receiver. Weight is about 5.75 lbs.

NIB	Exc.	V.G.	Good	Fair	Poor
450	350	300	250	200	150

1892 Brass Frame Carbine
Same as above but with polished brass receiver.

NIB	Exc.	V.G.	Good	Fair	Poor
450	350	300	250	200	150

1892 Brass Frame Rifle
This model is the same as the rifle but with polished brass receiver.

NIB	Exc.	V.G.	Good	Fair	Poor
525	425	350	300	250	200

No. 2 Creedmoor Target Rifle
This is a reproduction of the Remington No. 2 Creedmoor. It features a case colored receiver, tapered 30" octagonal barrel, hooded front sight, Creedmoor tang sight, and walnut stock with checkered pistol grip. Furnished in .45-70 Government. Weighs 9 lbs.

NIB	Exc.	V.G.	Good	Fair	Poor
900	725	625	500	400	200

Rolling Block Buffalo Rifle
This rifle is a replica of the Remington Buffalo rifle. It is fitted with a 26" or 30" octagonal or half octagonal barrel, case colored receiver, blade front sight, notch rear sight, brass trigger guard, with walnut stocks. Tang is drilled and tapped for tang sight.

NIB	Exc.	V.G.	Good	Fair	Poor
750	600	475	300	200	100

Half Octagon Barrel Model

NIB	Exc.	V.G.	Good	Fair	Poor
750	600	475	300	200	100

"John Bodine" Rolling Block Rifle
Chambered for the .45-70 cartridge and fitted with a 30" octagon barrel. Double set triggers. Match-grade rear tang sight. Weight is about 12 lbs. Introduced in 2002.

NIB	Exc.	V.G.	Good	Fair	Poor
1375	1050	—	—	—	—

1885 High Wall
Chambered for the .45-70 cartridge this rifle is fitted with a 30" medium heavy octagon barrel. Case colored receiver, target sights and walnut stocks. Also available with 28" round barrel.

NIB	Exc.	V.G.	Good	Fair	Poor
900	725	600	500	400	200

NOTE: Reduce price by $100 for Buckhorn sights and $60 for 28" barrel.

1873 Springfield Infantry Rifle
A copy of the Trapdoor Springfield. Chambered for .45-70 and fitted with a 32.5" barrel. Walnut stock and case hardened breechlock. Weight is approximately 8.25 lbs.

NIB	Exc.	V.G.	Good	Fair	Poor
975	800	600	500	400	200

1873 Springfield Cavalry Carbine
Same as above but with 22" barrel. Weight is about 7 lbs.

NIB	Exc.	V.G.	Good	Fair	Poor
875	700	600	500	400	200

Ithaca/Navy Hawken Rifle
Offered in either .50 or .54 caliber percussion. Features a 31.5" rust blued octagon barrel. The percussion lockplate is case colored, while the rest of the hardware is blued with the exception of the nose cap and escutcheons. Weighs about 9 lbs. 13 oz.

NIB	Exc.	V.G.	Good	Fair	Poor
350	300	250	200	150	100

Hawken Rifle
This model features a case colored lock, 28" blued octagon barrel, adjustable sights, double set triggers, and hooked breech. The polished brass furniture and patch box are mounted on a walnut stock. Weighs about 8.5 lbs.

NIB	Exc.	V.G.	Good	Fair	Poor
220	150	125	100	75	60

Hawken Hunter Rifle
Offered in .50, .54, or .58 caliber, this model features blued hardware, adjustable sights, case colored lock, and hooked breech. The walnut stock is hand checkered with a cheekpiece. Rubber recoil pad is standard. Barrel length is 28".

NIB	Exc.	V.G.	Good	Fair	Poor
240	190	150	100	75	60

Hawken Hunter Carbine
Same as above but fitted with a 22.5" barrel. Weighs about 6 lbs. 12 oz.

NIB	Exc.	V.G.	Good	Fair	Poor
240	190	150	100	75	60

Kodiak MKIV Double Rifle
Built in Europe, this model is chambered for the .45-70 cartridge and features a walnut stock with cheekpiece and hand checkering. Barrel length is 24" with adjustable sights. Engraved sideplates are polished bright. Sling swivels standard. Weighs 10.2 lbs.

NIB	Exc.	V.G.	Good	Fair	Poor
3000	2250	—	—	—	—

HANDGUNS

18th Georgia Le Mat Pistol
This 9-shot .44 caliber percussion revolver has a 7.625" blued barrel and engraved cylinder. An engraved banner on the left side of the frame reads "DEO VINDICE." Hammer and trigger are case colored. Stocks are checkered walnut. Comes with Le Mat mould and velvet draped French fitted case. Weighs 55 oz.

NIB	Exc.	V.G.	Good	Fair	Poor
795	625	500	400	300	150

Beauregard Le Mat Pistol
This is a replica of the Cavalry model. Comes cased.

NIB	Exc.	V.G.	Good	Fair	Poor
1000	800	650	550	350	200

Navy Le Mat
This model features a knurled pin barrel release and spur barrel selector.

NIB	Exc.	V.G.	Good	Fair	Poor
595	450	400	350	300	150

Army Le Mat
This model features a knurled pin barrel release and cross pin barrel selector.

NIB	Exc.	V.G.	Good	Fair	Poor
595	450	400	350	300	150

Cavalry Le Mat
This model features a lanyard ring, spur trigger, lever type barrel release, and cross pin barrel selector.

NIB	Exc.	V.G.	Good	Fair	Poor
595	450	400	350	300	150

Starr Double-Action Model 1858 Army
This model is a double-action revolver chambered for .44 caliber. Fitted with a 6" barrel. Blued finish. Weight is about 48 oz.

NIB	Exc.	V.G.	Good	Fair	Poor
350	250	200	—	—	—

Starr Single-Action Model 1863 Army
This model is fitted with an 8" barrel and is chambered for .44 caliber. Blued finish and walnut stock. Weight is about 48 oz.

NIB	Exc.	V.G.	Good	Fair	Poor
350	250	200	—	—	—

1862 New Model Police
This replica is based on the Colt .36 caliber pocket pistol of the same name. It features a half fluted and re-dated cylinder, case colored frame and loading gate, and a polished brass trigger guard and backstrap. Barrel length is 5.5" and pistol weigh 26 oz.

NIB	Exc.	V.G.	Good	Fair	Poor
290	225	175	150	100	75

1862 New Model Book-Style Cased Set

NIB	Exc.	V.G.	Good	Fair	Poor
350	250	200	150	100	75

Paterson Revolver
This replica is the five-shot .36 caliber. The cylinder is scroll engraved with a stagecoach scene. The hidden trigger drops down when the hammer is cocked. Barrel is 9" and the pistol weighs 43 oz.

NIB	Exc.	V.G.	Good	Fair	Poor
325	225	200	150	125	100

Engraved Paterson Revolver
This model features hand engraving with silver inlays.

NIB	Exc.	V.G.	Good	Fair	Poor
500	375	300	250	200	100

1851 Navy
This Colt replica is offered in either .36 or .44 caliber. A naval battle scene is engraved in the cylinder. The octagon barrel length is 7.5". The trigger guard and backstrap are polished brass. The walnut grips are hand rubbed. Weighs 32 oz.

NIB	Exc.	V.G.	Good	Fair	Poor
150	125	100	75	50	40

Single Cased Set

NIB	Exc.	V.G.	Good	Fair	Poor
275	225	175	125	100	60

Double Cased Set

NIB	Exc.	V.G.	Good	Fair	Poor
450	350	300	250	200	100

NOTE: Optional shoulder stock add $100.

1851 Navy Conversion
This is a replica of the Colt 1851 Navy cartridge conversion. Offered in 38 Special or .38 Long Colt with choice of 5.5" or 7.5" barrels. Weight is about 40 oz.

NIB	Exc.	V.G.	Good	Fair	Poor
350	275	225	—	—	—

Augusta 1851 Navy Pistol
Available with either 5" or 7.5" barrel. Engraved with "A" coverage.

NIB	Exc.	V.G.	Good	Fair	Poor
300	250	200	150	100	75

Model 1851 Navy Frontiersman
Introduced in 2003 this revolver features a 5" .36 caliber barrel. The receiver, loading lever and hammer are case colored while the barrel and cylinder are charcoal blued. Fitted with a German silver backstrap and walnut grips.

NIB	Exc.	V.G.	Good	Fair	Poor
N/A	—	—	—	—	—

Reb Model 1860 Pistol
This is a replica of the Confederate Griswold and Gunnison revolver. It features a blued round 7.5" barrel, brass frame, trigger guard and backstrap. Offered in .36 or .44 caliber. Weighs 44 oz.

NIB	Exc.	V.G.	Good	Fair	Poor
100	80	70	60	50	35

Reb 1860 Sheriff's Model
Same as above but fitted with a 5" barrel. Weighs 40 oz.

NIB	Exc.	V.G.	Good	Fair	Poor
100	80	70	60	50	35

1847 Walker Dragoon
This is a replica of the rare Colt .44 caliber revolver. The barrel and cylinder are blued while the frame and loading lever are case colored. Barrel length is 9" and pistol weighs 75 oz.

NIB	Exc.	V.G.	Good	Fair	Poor
275	225	175	150	125	100

Single Cased Set

NIB	Exc.	V.G.	Good	Fair	Poor
400	325	275	250	200	100

Single Deluxe Cased Set

NIB	Exc.	V.G.	Good	Fair	Poor
525	425	350	300	200	100

1860 Army Pistol
This .44 caliber model features a case colored frame and loading lever with blued barrel, cylinder, and backstrap. The trigger guard is brass. The cylinder is engraved with a battle scene. Barrel is 8" and pistol weighs 41 oz.

NIB	Exc.	V.G.	Good	Fair	Poor
175	150	125	100	75	45

Single Cased Set

NIB	Exc.	V.G.	Good	Fair	Poor
300	250	200	150	100	75

Double Cased Set

NIB	Exc.	V.G.	Good	Fair	Poor
490	400	325	250	200	100

1860 Army Conversion
Chambered for the .38 Special or .38 Long Colt this model is fitted with either a 5.5" or 7.5" barrel. Blued finish. Walnut grips. Weight is about 40 oz.

NIB	Exc.	V.G.	Good	Fair	Poor
350	275	225	—	—	—

1858 New Model Remington-Style Pistol
This replica has a solid frame, as did the original. The frame and 8" barrel are blued, while the trigger guard is brass. Walnut grips are standard. Weighs 40 oz.

NIB	Exc.	V.G.	Good	Fair	Poor
170	125	100	75	60	45

Single Cased Set

NIB	Exc.	V.G.	Good	Fair	Poor
290	225	175	125	100	75

Double Cased Set

NIB	Exc.	V.G.	Good	Fair	Poor
475	375	300	250	200	100

Stainless Steel 1858 New Model Army
Same as above but in stainless steel. Weighs 40 oz.

NIB	Exc.	V.G.	Good	Fair	Poor
220	180	150	125	100	80

Single Cased Set

NIB	Exc.	V.G.	Good	Fair	Poor
300	250	200	150	125	100

Double Cased Set

NIB	Exc.	V.G.	Good	Fair	Poor
525	475	400	300	200	150

Brass Framed 1858 New Model Army
This version features a highly polished brass frame. Barrel length is 7.75".

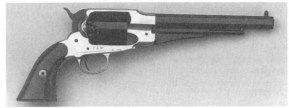

NIB	Exc.	V.G.	Good	Fair	Poor
125	100	80	60	50	35

Single Cased Set

NIB	Exc.	V.G.	Good	Fair	Poor
250	200	150	100	75	60

Double Cased Set

NIB	Exc.	V.G.	Good	Fair	Poor
395	325	300	250	200	100

1858 Target Model
Same as above but features a patridge front sight and an adjustable rear sight. Barrel length is 8".

NIB	Exc.	V.G.	Good	Fair	Poor
175	150	125	100	75	50

Deluxe 1858 New Model Army
This replica is built to the exact dimensions as the original. The barrel is 8" with adjustable front sight. The trigger guard is silver plated. The action is tuned for competition. Weighs 46 oz.

NIB	Exc.	V.G.	Good	Fair	Poor
400	325	250	200	150	100

Spiller and Burr Pistol
This is a .36 caliber pistol with 7" blued octagon barrel. The frame is brass with walnut grips. Weighs 40 oz.

NIB	Exc.	V.G.	Good	Fair	Poor
140	100	80	65	50	40

Single Cased Set

NIB	Exc.	V.G.	Good	Fair	Poor
250	200	150	100	75	60

Double Cased Set

NIB	Exc.	V.G.	Good	Fair	Poor
425	350	300	250	200	100

Rogers and Spencer
This model features a 7.5" barrel with blued frame and barrel. Offered in .44 caliber. Walnut grips. Weighs 48 oz.

NIB	Exc.	V.G.	Good	Fair	Poor
240	200	150	100	75	50

"London Gray" Rogers and Spencer Pistol
Same as above but with a burnished satin chrome finish.

NIB	Exc.	V.G.	Good	Fair	Poor
240	200	150	125	100	80

Rogers and Spencer Target Model
Same as standard model but fitted with adjustable target sights.

NIB	Exc.	V.G.	Good	Fair	Poor
275	225	175	125	100	80

1861 Navy Conversion
Replica of the cartridge conversion of the 1861 Navy. Chambered for .38 Special or .38 Long Colt. Fitted with either a 5.5" or 7.5" barrel. Weight is about 40 oz.

NIB	Exc.	V.G.	Good	Fair	Poor
350	275	225	—	—	—

1872 Colt Open Top
This model features a 5.5" or 7.5" barrel with case hardened frame, blued barrel and cylinder, and silver-plated brass trigger guard and backstrap. Walnut grips. Chambered for .38 caliber cartridge. Weight is about 40 oz.

NIB	Exc.	V.G.	Good	Fair	Poor
390	275	225	—	—	—

1873 Colt-Style Single-Action Army
This replica features a case colored frame and hammer with blued round barrel in 3", 4.75", 5.5", or 7.5" lengths. Trigger guard and cylinder are blued. Offered in .44-40, .45 Long Colt, .357 Magnum, and .32-20.

NIB	Exc.	V.G.	Good	Fair	Poor
390	325	275	200	150	100

Model 1873 SAA Stainless Gunfighter
Introduced in 2003 this model is the same as the standard 1873, but features all stainless steel construction. Offered in .45 Colt and .357 Magnum caliber with choice of 4.75", 5.5", or 7.5" barrel. Weight is about 45 oz. depending on barrel length.

NIB	Exc.	V.G.	Good	Fair	Poor
510	400	—	—	—	—

Economy Model 1873 S.A.A.
Same as above but with brass trigger guard and backstrap.

NIB	Exc.	V.G.	Good	Fair	Poor
275	250	200	150	125	100

Nickel 1873 S.A.A.

NIB	Exc.	V.G.	Good	Fair	Poor
500	400	300	225	150	100

1873 U.S. Cavalry Model
This .45 Long Colt model features U.S. arsenal stampings, case colored frame, and walnut grips. Barrel length is 7.5" and pistol weighs 45 oz.

NIB	Exc.	V.G.	Good	Fair	Poor
390	325	275	200	150	100

1873 Pinched Frame Model
This is a replica of the "pinched" frame 1873 with "U" shape rear sight notch. Chambered for .45 Colt with 7.5" barrel.

NIB	Exc.	V.G.	Good	Fair	Poor
400	325	275	225	—	—

1873 Flat Top Target
This model features a windage adjustable rear sight on a flat top frame and a spring loaded front sight. Barrel length is 7.5". Offered in .45 Colt. Weight is about 40 oz. Introduced in 1998.

NIB	Exc.	V.G.	Good	Fair	Poor
425	350	—	—	—	—

Deputy Single-Action Army
Similar to the Model 1873 but with a bird's-head grip. Barrel lengths are 3", 3.5", 4", and 4.75". Chambered for .44-40 and .45 Colt.

NIB	Exc.	V.G.	Good	Fair	Poor
400	300	250	200	—	—

Shootist Model S.A.A.
This model is a reproduction of the Colt 1873. Parts are interchangeable with the originals. Blued barrel, cylinder, trigger guard, and backstrap. Case hardened frame and hammer. Walnut grips. Offered in 4.75", 5.5", and 7.5" barrel lengths. Chambered for .357 Magnum, .44-40, or .45 Colt.

NIB	Exc.	V.G.	Good	Fair	Poor
375	275	225	—	—	—

Scout Small Frame Revolver
This model is identical to the Colt 1872 SAA but with smaller dimensions. Offered in .38 Special with choice of 4.75" or 5.5" barrel. Weight is about 30 oz. Introduced in 2003.

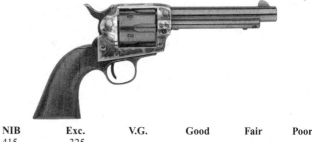

NIB	Exc.	V.G.	Good	Fair	Poor
415	325	—	—	—	—

Deluxe 1873 Colt Revolver
This model is chambered for the .32-20 cartridge and features bright charcoal blue with case colored frame and hammer. Walnut grips. Fitted with a 5.5" barrel. Limited production. Weight is about 41 oz.

NIB	Exc.	V.G.	Good	Fair	Poor
435	350	—	—	—	—

Bisley Model
This model features the famous Bisley grip. Barrel length is 4.75", 5.5", and 7.5". Chambered for .44-40 or .45 Colt.

NIB	Exc.	V.G.	Good	Fair	Poor
425	300	250	200	—	—

Bisley Flat Top Target
Similar to the Bisley but with 7.5" barrel with flat top frame with adjustable front sight and windage adjustable rear sight. Chambered for .44-40 or .45 Colt. Weight is about 40 oz.

NIB	Exc.	V.G.	Good	Fair	Poor
450	350	250	200	—	—

1895 U.S. Artillery Model
Same as Cavalry Model but fitted with a 5.5" barrel. Weighs 42 oz.

NIB	Exc.	V.G.	Good	Fair	Poor
475	375	300	250	200	100

1875 Remington-Style Revolver
The frame is case colored while all other parts are blued except for brass trigger guard. Available in .44-40 or .45 Long Colt. Furnished with walnut grips. Barrel length is 7.5". Weighs 41 oz.

NIB	Exc.	V.G.	Good	Fair	Poor
425	350	300	250	200	100

1890 Remington-Style Revolver
This is a modified version of the 1875 model that is also offered in .44-40 or .45 Long Colt. The web under the barrel has been eliminated. It has blued 5.5" steel barrel and frame. Lanyard loop is on bottom of walnut grips. Weighs 39 oz.

NIB	Exc.	V.G.	Good	Fair	Poor
445	350	300	250	200	100

TOP BREAK REVOLVERS

Model 1875 Schofield—Wells Fargo 5" barrel

NIB	Exc.	V.G.	Good	Fair	Poor
750	600	450	350	200	100

Model 1875 Schofield—Cavalry 7" barrel
A reproduction of the S&W Model 3 top break revolver in either .44-40 or .45 Long Colt. The Cavalry model has a 7" barrel while the Wells Fargo model has a 5" barrel. Weight is about 39 oz.

NIB	Exc.	V.G.	Good	Fair	Poor
750	600	450	350	200	100

Model 1875 Schofield—Deluxe
This model has a charcoal blue finish with gold inlays and "A" style hand engraving. Available in either the Cavalry or Wells Fargo model. Special order only.

NIB	Exc.	V.G.	Good	Fair	Poor
1875	1500	—	—	—	—

Model 1875 Schofield—B Engraved
Available In Cavalry or Wells Fargo Model. This grade is "B" style engraved with 35 percent coverage. Special order only.

NIB	Exc.	V.G.	Good	Fair	Poor
1550	1250	—	—	—	—

Model 1875 Schofield—C Engraved
This model is available in Cavalry or Wells Fargo with "C" style engraving with 50 percent coverage. Special order only.

NIB	Exc.	V.G.	Good	Fair	Poor
1875	1500	—	—	—	—

Model 1875 Schofield Founder's Model
Introduced in 2003 to honor Val Forgett, Sr. and Aldo Uberti. This revolver features a charcoal blued barrel and cylinder with color case hardened receiver, backstrap, trigger guard and trigger. Grip are white ivory polymer. Limited production with special serial number prefix of "VF."

NIB	Exc.	V.G.	Good	Fair	Poor
780	625	—	—	—	—

Model 1875 Schofield—Hideout
This is a short-barrel variation of the Schofield. It is fitted with a 3.5" barrel and chambered for the .44-40 or .45 Colt cartridge. Weight is about 38 oz.

NIB	Exc.	V.G.	Good	Fair	Poor
700	550	—	—	—	—

New Model Russian
Built around the single-action Smith & Wesson Model 3, this revolver is chambered for the .44 Russian cartridge. It is fitted with a 6.5" barrel. Case colored spur trigger guard, latch and hammer. Blued frame, barrel and cylinder. Walnut grips. Weight is about 40 oz. Introduced in 1999.

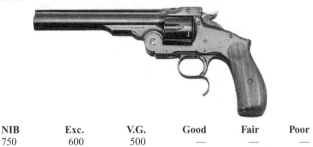

NIB	Exc.	V.G.	Good	Fair	Poor
750	600	500	—	—	—

RIFLES

Martini Target Rifle
A .444 or .45-70 caliber single-shot Martini-action rifle with a 26" or 30" octagonal barrel, tang sight, and walnut stock. Offered between 1972 and 1984.

Exc.	V.G.	Good	Fair	Poor
475	425	350	275	175

NEPPERHAN FIREARMS CO.
Yonkers, New York

Pocket Revolver
A .31 caliber percussion revolver with 3.5" to 6" barrels and a 5-shot cylinder. Blued, case hardened with walnut grips. The barrel marked "Nepperhan/Fire Arms Co" and on some additionally "Yonkers New York." The latter are worth a slight premium over the values listed. Approximately 5,000 were made during the 1860s.

Exc.	V.G.	Good	Fair	Poor
—	—	900	350	200

NOBLE
Haydenville, Massachusetts
In business between 1946 and 1971, this company manufactured a variety of plain, utilitarian firearms. In general, these arms are all worth approximately the same, that is, less than $200 in excellent condition.

SHOTGUNS

Model 420
This shotgun is a box lock design side-by-side with double triggers and offered in 12, 16, 20 gauge, as well as .410 bore. Barrel lengths are 28" for all gauges except .410 where it is 26". Lightly engraved frame. Checkered walnut stock and splinter forearm.

Exc.	V.G.	Good	Fair	Poor
300	250	200	150	100

Model 450E
This model is similar to the Model 420 with the addition of automatic ejectors and not offered in .410 bore. Checkered pistol grip stock with beavertail forearm. Produced in the late 1960s.

Exc.	V.G.	Good	Fair	Poor
350	275	225	175	125

P

PARKER BROS.
Meriden, Connecticut

Perhaps the best known of all American shotgun manufacturers. Established by Charles Parker shortly after the Civil War, this company has produced a wide variety of shotguns in a number of different styles over the years. In the early 1930s the company was purchased by Remington Arms Company.

WARNING NOTE: Parker shotguns are among the most collectible of American-made shotguns. Both the beginning and the veteran collector should be aware that originality and condition are absolutely critical in establishing such high values for these shotguns. There are numerous upgraded and refinished guns that are represented as original. Beware that such misrepresentations exist because refinished and upgraded Parker guns should sell for as much as 50 to 75 percent below the price of an original gun. Extreme caution should be exercised and we would recommend that an expert be consulted. Even the most advanced collectors may benefit from such consultations. Also, the prices indicated for guns in excellent condition may fluctuate drastically, especially in high grade or small bore guns, due to their extreme rarity.

In addition, uncommon extras such as single triggers, ventilated ribs, beavertail forearms, straight-grip stocks, and skeleton steel buttplates may add substantial value to an individual gun. Extra sets of factory barrels that were installed at the time of delivery will add an average of a 30 percent premium. This premium will increase with grade and gauge; the higher the grade and smaller the gauge the higher the premium.

NOTE: Letters of authenticity are available. These letters are a must in order for any Parker gun to attain maximum value. Contact: the Exec. Secetary Parker Gun Collectors Association, 8825 Bud Smith Road, Wake Forest, SC 27587. FAX: 919-554-8120. The letter is $25 for members of the PCGA and $40 for non-members.

Editor's Comment: We now have reliable information on the production totals of Parker gauges and grades. This information comes from the book; The Parker Story by Gunther, Mullins, Parker, Price, and Cote (1998). These totals reflect guns built with modern steel barrels only and are based on factory records. It is the editor's opinion that while production statistics are interesting it is the relative number of guns produced in each grade and bore that are the most significant.

Trojan

A 12, 16, or 20 gauge boxlock double-barrel shotgun manufactured in a variety of barrel lengths with double triggers and extractors. Only 27 Trojans were built with single triggers. Blued, case hardened receiver with a walnut stock.

*Approximately 33,000 were made: 12 gauge—21,977, 16 gauge—6,573, 20 gauge—5450, 28 gauge—only 2.

Exc.	V.G.	Good	Fair	Poor
2400	1500	1000	800	600

NOTE: 20 gauge add 40 percent, 28 gauge add 50 percent.

VH

A 12, 16, 20, 28 or .410 bore boxlock double-barrel shotgun manufactured in a variety of barrel lengths with double triggers and extractors. Blued, case hardened receiver with a walnut stock. Only 2,297 guns had single triggers. Only 3,983 guns had straight grip stocks.

*Approximately 78,659 were made: 10 gauge—20, 12 gauge—51,901, 16 gauge—14,446, 20 gauge—10,406, 28 gauge—1,417, .410 bore—469.

NOTE: Also made with automatic ejectors and known as the Model VHE. The E suffix was used on all models to denote automatic ejectors.

Exc.	V.G.	Good	Fair	Poor
3250	1800	1500	1000	700

NOTE: VHE add 40 percent, 20 gauge add 45 percent, 28 gauge add 150 percent, .410 add 400 percent.

PH

Similar to the above, but with a small amount of scroll engraving. slightly better grade of walnut.

*Approximately 1,339 were made: 10 gauge—798, 12 gauge—839, 16 gauge—208, 20 gauge—204, 28 gauge—only 5, .410 bore—only 4.

Exc.	V.G.	Good	Fair	Poor
3500	2200	1700	1200	900

NOTE: PHE add 40 percent, 20 gauge add 45 percent, 28 gauge add 150 percent.

GH

Similar to the above, with a modest amount of scroll and game scene engraving and the barrels marked "Parker Special Steel." Only about 430 G grades were built with straight grip stocks.

*Approximately 4,291 were made: 8 gauge—11, 10 gauge—63, 12 gauge—2,501, 16 gauge—607, 20 gauge—990, 28 gauge—91, .410 bore—28.

Exc.	V.G.	Good	Fair	Poor
3900	2700	2200	1400	1000

NOTE: GHE add 35 percent, 16 gauge add 15 percent, 20 gauge add 40 percent, 28 gauge add 150 percent, .410 add 400 percent.

DH

As above, but more finely finished. Engraving coverage more profuse. Most modern D grade guns were fitted with Titanic barrels. Only about 280 were built with Parker single triggers, and only about 280 were built with ventilated ribs.

*Approximately 9,346 were made: 8 gauge—10, 10 gauge—45, 12 gauge—6,330, 16 gauge—1,178, 20 gauge—1,536, 28 gauge—187, .410 bore—60.

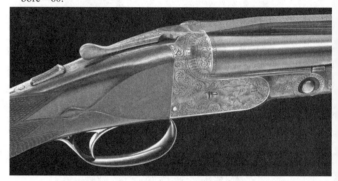

Courtesy Bonhams & Butterfields

Exc.	V.G.	Good	Fair	Poor
6500	5000	4000	2000	1500

NOTE: DHE add 35 percent, 16 gauge add 10 percent, 20 gauge add 40 percent, 28 gauge add 150 percent, .410 add 500 percent.

CH

As above, with more scroll and game scene engraving coverage. Marked with Acme steel barrels. Only about 93 C grades had straight-grip stocks.

*Approximately 697 were made: 8 gauge—only 2, 10 gauge— only 9, 12 gauge—410, 16 gauge—105, 20 gauge—149, 28 gauge—only 16, .410 bore—only 6.

Exc.	V.G.	Good	Fair	Poor
7750	5600	4300	2500	2000

NOTE: CHE add 35 percent, 16 gauge add 10 percent, 20 gauge add 40 percent, 28 gauge add 300 percent, .410 add 700 percent.

BH

As above, but offered in a variety of different styles of engraved decoration. Only about 66 guns had straight-grip stocks, 29 had beavertail forends, 20 were built with vent ribs, and 57 had single triggers.

*Approximately 512 were made: 10 gauge—only 2, 12 gauge—317, 16 gauge—71, 20 gauge—109, 28 gauge—13.

Prospective purchasers are advised to secure a qualified appraisal prior to acquisition.

Exc.	V.G.	Good	Fair	Poor
10000	7500	5000	3300	2500

NOTE: BHE add 35 percent, 16 gauge add 15 percent, 20 gauge add 50 percent, 28 gauge add 350 percent.

AH

As above, but highly engraved with finely figured walnut stocks. Most had Acme steel barrels. About 42 A grade guns were built with straight grip stocks.

*Approximately 167 were made: 10 gauge—only 1, 12 gauge—92, 16 gauge—23, 20 gauge—44, 28 gauge—only 6, .410 bore— only 1.

Due to the rarity of this grade prospective purchasers are advised to secure a qualified appraisal prior to acquisition.

Exc.	V.G.	Good	Fair	Poor
18500	13000	10000	8000	5000

NOTE: AHE add 30 percent, 16 Gauge add 25 percent, 20 gauge add 75 percent, 28 gauge add 350 percent, .410 add 600 percent.

AAH

As above, with either Whitworth or Peerless barrels and not made in .410 bore. The engraving is more extensive and of the first quality. Only one AA grade has a ventilated rib, ten were built with single trigger and 95 had straight grip stocks.

*Approximately 238 were made: 10 gauge—only 2, 12 gauge—185, 16 gauge—19, 20 gauge—27, 28 gauge—only 5.

Due to the rarity of this grade prospective purchasers are advised to secure a qualified appraisal prior to acquisition.

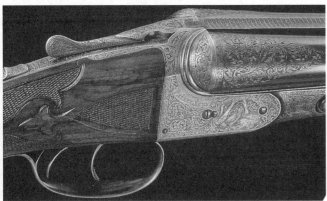

Exc.	V.G.	Good	Fair	Poor
35000	25000	18000	10000	7000

NOTE: AAHE add 30 percent, 16 gauge add 35 percent, 20 gauge add 75 percent, 28 gauge add 400 percent.

A-1 Special

As above, but made strictly on special order and not manufactured in .410 bore. Two A-1 Specials were built with ventilated rib, 7 had single triggers, 3 had beavertail forends, and 24 were built with straight-grip stocks.

*Approximately 79 were made: 12 gauge—55, 16 gauge—only 6, 20 gauge—11, and 28 gauge—only 7.

Due to the extreme rarity of this grade prospective purchasers are advised to secure a qualified appraisal prior to acquisition.

Exc.	V.G.	Good	Fair	Poor
65000	55000	42000	30000	20000

NOTE: 16 gauge add 35 percent, 20 gauge add 75 percent, 28 gauge add 500 percent.

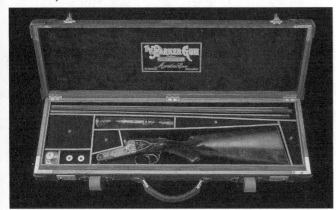

Single-Barrel Trap

A 12 gauge single-shot shotgun with a 30", 32", or 34" barrel, automatic ejector and walnut stock. Produced in a variety of grades.

Prospective purchasers are advised to secure a qualified appraisal prior to acquisition.

S.C. Grade

Exc.	V.G.	Good	Fair	Poor
3900	2500	2000	1500	1000

S.B. Grade

Exc.	V.G.	Good	Fair	Poor
4500	3700	3000	2400	1600

S.A. Grade

Exc.	V.G.	Good	Fair	Poor
7000	5500	4000	3000	2000

S.A.A. Grade

Exc.	V.G.	Good	Fair	Poor
12000	7000	5500	3800	2400

S.A-1 Special Grade

Exc.	V.G.	Good	Fair	Poor
20000	12000	8000	6000	4000

PARKER HALE LTD.
Birmingham, England

Model 640E Shotgun

A 12, 16, or 20 gauge boxlock double-barrel shotgun manufactured in a variety of barrel lengths with double triggers and extractors. Blued, French case hardened with a walnut stock. Introduced in 1986.

NIB	Exc.	V.G.	Good	Fair	Poor
575	450	400	300	250	200

Model 640A

As above, with a pistol grip, beavertail forend, and single trigger. Introduced in 1986.

NIB	Exc.	V.G.	Good	Fair	Poor
675	550	500	400	300	200

Model 645E

As above, but more finely finished and engraved.

NIB	Exc.	V.G.	Good	Fair	Poor
700	550	500	400	300	200

Model 670E

A sidelock double-barrel shotgun made on special order. Introduced in 1986.

NIB	Exc.	V.G.	Good	Fair	Poor
3000	2500	1850	1200	750	400

Model 680E—XXV

As above, with case hardened lockplates and 25" barrels.

NIB	Exc.	V.G.	Good	Fair	Poor
3000	2500	1850	1200	750	400

BLACKPOWDER REPRODUCTIONS
Imported by Gibbs Rifle Company

1853 Enfield Rifle Musket

This is a three band version in .577 caliber. Barrel length is 39". Rear sight graduated to 900 yards. Weight about 9 lbs.

NIB	Exc.	V.G.	Good	Fair	Poor
600	475	375	—	—	—

1858 Enfield Naval Pattern Rifle

This is the Naval version with two bands in .577 caliber. Barrel length is 33". Walnut stock with brass furniture. Rear sight adjustable to 1100 yards. Weight is approximately 8.5 lbs.

NIB	Exc.	V.G.	Good	Fair	Poor
550	425	325	—	—	—

1861 Enfield Artillery Carbine Musketoon
This is the Artillery version in .577 caliber with 24" barrel. Walnut stock with brass furniture. Rear sight adjustable to 600 yards. Weight is about 7.5 lbs.

NIB	Exc.	V.G.	Good	Fair	Poor
475	375	300	—	—	—

Whitworth Military Target Rifle
This model is in .451 caliber. Barrel length is 36". Weight is about 9.9 lbs.

NIB	Exc.	V.G.	Good	Fair	Poor
875	700	550	—	—	—

Whitworth Sniping Rifle
Same as above but with brass scope and mounts.

NIB	Exc.	V.G.	Good	Fair	Poor
1700	1350	950	—	—	—

Volunteer Percussion Target Rifle
This rifle is in .451 caliber and fitted with a 33" barrel. It is the two banned design with walnut stock and brass furniture. Adjustable rear sight. Weight is approximately 9.5 lbs.

NIB	Exc.	V.G.	Good	Fair	Poor
850	650	550	—	—	—

PEABODY
Providence, Rhode Island
Providence Tool Company

NOTE: For historical information, photos, and data on Peabody military rifles see the *Standard Catalog of Military Firearms, 2nd Edition*.

Peabody Rifle and Carbine
A .43 Spanish, .443, .45 Peabody, .45-70, .50 or .50-70 caliber single-shot rifle with a 33" or 20" (carbine) barrel and either a full-length or half stock. The receiver marked "Peabody's Patent July 22, 1862 / Mannf'd by Providence Tool Co. Prov. R.I." Blued, with a walnut stock. Produced in large quantities during the 1860s and 1870s.

Exc.	V.G.	Good	Fair	Poor
—	1700	750	300	100

Sporting Rifle
As above, in a sporting configuration with either 26" or 28" barrels. The frame marked, "Peabody's Patent, July 22, 1862 / Manf'd by Providence Tool Co., Prov. R.I." Blued, case hardened with a walnut stock. Manufactured from approximately 1866 to 1875.

Exc.	V.G.	Good	Fair	Poor
—	5000	2750	1000	400

PEABODY-MARTINI SPORTING RIFLES

NOTE: For historical information, photos, and data on Peabody-Martini military rifles see the *Standard Catalog of Military Firearms, 2nd Edition*.

Creedmoor
A .40-90 or .44-100 caliber Martini-action single-shot rifle with a 32" round/octagonal barrel, butt-mounted vernier rear sight, combination wind gauge and spirit level front sight. The receiver marked, "Peabody & Martini Patents" and the barrel "Manufactured by the Providence Tool Co. Providence R.I. U.S.A." Blued, case hardened with a walnut stock.

Exc.	V.G.	Good	Fair	Poor
—	7500	3500	1500	550

Creedmoor Mid-Range
Similar to the above, but in .40-70 or .40-90 caliber with a 28" round/octagonal barrel, vernier tang sight and wind gauge front sight. Blued, case hardened with a walnut stock.

Exc.	V.G.	Good	Fair	Poor
—	6000	3250	1250	400

What Cheer
The Creedmoor without a pistol grip.

Exc.	V.G.	Good	Fair	Poor
—	6000	3250	1250	400

What Cheer Mid-Range
The Mid-Range Creedmoor without a pistol grip.

Exc.	V.G.	Good	Fair	Poor
—	5000	2750	1000	300

Kill Deer
A .45-70 caliber single-shot Martini-action rifle with 28" or 30" round/octagonal barrels, adjustable tang rear sight and globe front sights. Blued, case hardened with a walnut stock.

Exc.	V.G.	Good	Fair	Poor
—	7500	4250	1500	500

PEAVY, A. J.
South Montville, Maine

Knife-Pistol
A .22 caliber single-shot knife pistol constructed of steel and brass with a folding trigger. The sideplates marked "A.J. Peavy Pat. Sept. 5, '65 & Mar. 27, '66." Produced between 1866 and 1870.

Exc.	V.G.	Good	Fair	Poor
—	—	4250	1750	500

PECARE & SMITH
New York, New York

Pepperbox
A .28 caliber 4-shot or 1-shot percussion pepperbox with a folding trigger and 4" barrel group. The barrel group enclosed within an iron casing. Blued, silver-plated frame with walnut grips. The barrel casing marked "Pecare & Smith." Manufactured during the 1840s and early 1850s.

Exc.	V.G.	Good	Fair	Poor
—	—	2750	1150	350

Ten-Shot Pepperbox (rare)

Exc.	V.G.	Good	Fair	Poor
—	—	6000	2500	600

PERRY PATENT FIREARMS CO.
Newark, New Jersey

Perry Carbine
A .54 caliber breech-loading percussion carbine with a 20.75" barrel and half-length walnut stock secured by one barrel band. Blued with a case hardened lock. Approximately 200 were made. Prospective purchasers are advised to secure a qualified appraisal prior to acquisition.

Exc.	V.G.	Good	Fair	Poor
—	—	7500	3250	1000

PERRY & GODDARD
Renwick Arms Co.
New York, New York

Derringer
A .44 caliber single-shot spur trigger pistol with a 2" octagonal barrel. Blued or silver-plated with walnut or gutta-percha grips. The barrel may be swiveled so that either end can serve as the chamber and is marked "Double Header/ E.S. Renwick." Produced in limited quantities during the 1860s. Prospective purchasers are advised to secure a qualified appraisal prior to acquisition.

Exc.	V.G.	Good	Fair	Poor
—	—	19500	8500	1500

PETTINGILL C. S.
New Haven, Connecticut
Rogers, Spencer & Co.
Willowvale, New York

Pocket Revolver
A hammerless, double-action .31 caliber percussion revolver having a 4" octagonal barrel. The frame of brass or iron. Blued barrel, the grips of oil finished walnut. The First and Second Models are marked "Pettingill's Patent 1856" as well as "T.K. Austin." The Third Model is marked "Pettengill Patent 1856", and "Raymond and Robitaille Patented 1858." Approximately 400 were manufactured in the late 1850s and early 1860s.

1st Model
Brass frame.

Exc.	V.G.	Good	Fair	Poor
—	—	2500	1000	400

2nd Model
Iron frame.

Exc.	V.G.	Good	Fair	Poor
—	—	1500	600	200

3rd Model
Iron frame and improved action.

Exc.	V.G.	Good	Fair	Poor
—	—	1250	400	200

Navy Revolver
As above but in .34 caliber with a 4.5" barrel and a 6-shot cylinder. The frame of iron, blued overall, and the grips of walnut. This model is marked "Pettingill's Patent 1856" and "Raymond & Robitaille Patented 1858." Approximately 900 were manufactured in the late 1850s and early 1860s.

Exc.	V.G.	Good	Fair	Poor
—	—	1750	700	250

Army Model Revolver
As above but of .44 caliber and fitted with a 7.5" barrel. The frame of iron that is case hardened, the octagonal barrel blued, the grips of oil finished walnut. Early production models are marked as the Navy models, while later production examples are marked "Pettingill's Patent 1856, pat'd July 22, 1856 and July 27, 1858." Some examples will be found with government inspector's marks and are worth approximately 25 percent more. It is believed that 3,400 were made in the 1860s.

Exc.	V.G.	Good	Fair	Poor
—	—	4500	1500	500

PLANT'S MANUFACTURING CO.
New Haven, Connecticut

Army Model Revolver
A large single-action revolver chambered for a .42 caliber cup-primed cartridge that loads from the front of the cylinder. Barrel length 6" and of octagonal form with a rib. The frame is made of either brass or iron. Finish is blued, with walnut or rosewood grips. Interchangeable percussion cylinders also were made for these revolvers. If present, the values would be increased approximately 30 percent. This revolver was marketed by Merwin & Bray, and there were approximately 1,500 of the 1st and 2nd Models manufactured and 10,000 of the 3rd Model in the 1860s.

1st Model Brass Frame
Marked "Plant's Mfg. Co. New Haven, Ct." on the barrel, "M & B" on the side of the frame, and "Patented July 12, 1859" on the cylinder. Approximately 100 manufactured.

Exc.	V.G.	Good	Fair	Poor
—	—	2500	950	300

1st Model Iron Frame
As above with an iron frame. Approximately 500 made.

Exc.	V.G.	Good	Fair	Poor
—	—	2500	950	300

2nd Model Rounded Brass Frame
This model is distinguished by the markings "Merwin & Bray, New York" on the frame and the patent date "July 21, 1863". Approximately 300 made.

Exc.	V.G.	Good	Fair	Poor
—	—	3250	1250	400

2nd Model Iron Frame
As above with an iron frame.

Exc.	V.G.	Good	Fair	Poor
—	—	2250	750	300

3rd Model
As above with a flat brass frame.

Exc.	V.G.	Good	Fair	Poor
—	—	1150	400	150

Pocket Revolver
Similar to the Army model described above except chambered for .30 caliber cartridges. Barrel length 3.5", five-shot cylinder. The frame normally silver plated, barrel and cylinder blued and the grips of rosewood or walnut. This model is encountered with a variety of retailer's markings: Eagle Arms Co., New York, "Reynolds, Plant & Hotchkiss, New Haven, Ct.," and Merwin & Bray Firearms Co., N.Y." Approximately 20,000 were made.

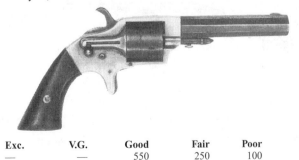

Exc.	V.G.	Good	Fair	Poor
—	—	550	250	100

POINTER
Hopkins & Allen
Norwich, Connecticut

Single-Shot Derringer

An unmarked Hopkins & Allen single-shot pistol stamped "Pointer" on the barrel. Barrel length 2.75", caliber .22, frame of nickel-plated brass. The barrel swings sideways for loading. Bird's-head walnut grips. It is believed that about 2,500 were made between 1870 and 1890.

Exc.	V.G.	Good	Fair	Poor
—	—	650	250	100

POND, LUCIUS, W.
Worcester, Massachusetts

Pocket Revolver

A single-action, spur trigger .32 caliber revolver with octagonal barrels of 4", 5", or 6" length. The barrel top strap and cylinder pivot upwards for loading. Made with either brass or iron frames. A screwdriver is fitted in the butt. As these revolvers were an infringement of Rollin White's patent, they were discontinued. Some revolvers are to be found with the inscription "Manuf'd. for Smith & Wesson Pat'd. April 5, 1855." These examples are worth approximately 20 percent more than the values listed.

Brass Framed Revolver

Exc.	V.G.	Good	Fair	Poor
—	—	800	350	100

Iron Framed Revolver

Exc.	V.G.	Good	Fair	Poor
—	—	700	300	75

PREMIER
Italy and Spain

A trade name used by various retailers on shotguns manufactured in Italy and Spain that were imported during the late 1950s and early 1960s.

Regent Side-by-Side Shotgun

A double-barrel shotgun with 26" to 30" barrels available in all standard gauges. Receiver blued, stock of walnut. Normally found with a pistol grip and beavertail forend.

Exc.	V.G.	Good	Fair	Poor
350	250	200	150	100

Regent Magnum

As above but chambered for the 3.5" 10 gauge Magnum cartridge. Barrels 32" in length and choked full and Full.

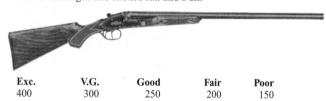

Exc.	V.G.	Good	Fair	Poor
400	300	250	200	150

Brush King

Identical to the Regent Model except that it is fitted with 22" Modified and Improved Cylinder barrels and a straight-grip English-style stock.

Exc.	V.G.	Good	Fair	Poor
400	300	250	200	150

Ambassador Model

A more ornate version of the Regent Model.

Exc.	V.G.	Good	Fair	Poor
450	350	300	250	175

Presentation Custom Grade

A custom-order shotgun with game scenes as well as gold and silver inlays.

Exc.	V.G.	Good	Fair	Poor
1500	950	600	500	400

PRESCOTT, E. A.
Worcester, Massachusetts

Percussion Pocket Revolver

A .31 caliber percussion spur trigger revolver with either 4" or 4.25" octagonal barrel and a 6-shot cylinder. The frame of brass, and the grips of walnut. It is believed that approximately 100 were manufactured during 1860 and 1861.

Exc.	V.G.	Good	Fair	Poor
—	—	2250	950	200

Pocket Revolver

A .22 or .32 spur trigger revolver with a barrel of either 3" or 4" length. The .22 caliber version has a 7-shot cylinder and the .32 caliber version a 6-shot cylinder. The standard markings are "E.A. Prescott Worcester Mass. Pat. Oct. 2, 1860." Approximately 1,000 were manufactured between 1862 and 1867.

Exc.	V.G.	Good	Fair	Poor
—	—	750	300	100

Belt Revolver

Although similar in appearance to early Smith & Wesson revolvers, the Prescott has a solid frame. Available in either .22 or .32 caliber, the .22 caliber model has a 3" barrel and the .32 caliber a 5.75" barrel. Markings are identical found on the Pocket Revolver. Approximately 300 were manufactured between 1861 and 1863.

Exc.	V.G.	Good	Fair	Poor
—	—	750	300	100

Navy Revolver

A single-action revolver fitted with a conventional trigger, chambered for .38 rimfire cartridges with a 7.25" octagonal barrel. The unfluted cylinder holds 6 shots. The frame is of either silver-plated brass or blued iron; and the barrel and the cylinder are blued, with walnut grips. The barrel marked "E.A. Prescott, Worcester, Mass. Pat. Oct. 2, 1860." It is believed that several hundred were manufactured between 1861 and 1863. The iron frame model will bring a small premium.

Exc.	V.G.	Good	Fair	Poor
—	—	1250	500	200

Army Revolver

Similar in appearance to the Navy model but with a larger frame. Chambered for .44 caliber rimfire cartridge. Fitted with a 9" octagon barrel with extractor rod and loading gate on right side of frame. Very rare.

Exc.	V.G.	Good	Fair	Poor
—	—	18000	8000	—

R

READ & WATSON
Danville, Virginia

During 1862 and 1863, Read & Watson produced approximately 900 altered Hall rifles for the State of Virginia. These arms were made from Hall rifles issued to the state prior to the Civil War. The original breech loading mechanisms were removed and a brass breech piece or receiver was secured in their place. New buttstocks were fitted and the original Hall furniture was reused. Carbines have an overall length of 42-1/8"; barrel length of 26" and are of .52 caliber. Position and style of serial numbers varies.

Prospective purchasers are strongly advised to secure a qualified appraisal prior to acquisition.

Exc.	V.G.	Good	Fair	Poor
—	—	15000	6500	1000

REEDER, GARY CUSTOM GUNS
Flagstaff, Arizona

This company offers complete guns as listed. It also offers custom options built on customer guns as well. An extensive number of custom options is available on any of these models. Prices listed reflect the standard for that particular model. Retail prices only are listed due to lack of active secondary market for these limited edition guns. Information indicates that these Gary Reeder guns hold their value well.

Black Widow
Chambered for the .44 magnum cartridge and fitted with a 4.625" barrel with black Chromix finish. Round butt with Black Cape Buffalo grips. Engraved with Black Widow on each side of the cylinder. Built on a Ruger Super Blackhawk.

NIB	Exc.	V.G.	Good	Fair	Poor
995	—	—	—	—	—

Black Widow II
Similar to the Black Widow but chambered for the .45 Long Colt cartridge. Barrel length is 4.5".

NIB	Exc.	V.G.	Good	Fair	Poor
995	—	—	—	—	—

Arizona Ranger Classic
Built on a Ruger Vaquero this model is chambered for the .45 Long Colt cartridge and fitted with a choice of a 4.5", 5.5", or 7.5" barrel. Blue or stainless steel finish. Special engraving with Stag grips.

NIB	Exc.	V.G.	Good	Fair	Poor
995	—	—	—	—	—

Badlands Classic
Built on a Ruger Vaquero and chambered for the .45 Long Colt cartridge with an extra .45 ACP cylinder. Fitted with a 4.5" barrel. Special engraving. Pearl grips.

NIB	Exc.	V.G.	Good	Fair	Poor
1095	—	—	—	—	—

Cowboy Classic
Built on a Ruger Vaquero and chambered for the .45 Long Colt with a 67.5" barrel. Stainless steel or black Chromix finish. Ivory polymer or pearlite grips. Special engraving.

NIB	Exc.	V.G.	Good	Fair	Poor
995	—	—	—	—	—

Cowtown Classic
Built on a Ruger Vaquero and chambered for the .45 Long Colt with 7.5" barrel. Special engraving. Walnut grips.

NIB	Exc.	V.G.	Good	Fair	Poor
995	—	—	—	—	—

Gamblers Classic
Built on a Ruger Vaquero and chambered for the .45 Long Colt with a 2.5" barrel. Stainless steel or black Chromix finish. Choice of black or white pearl grips. No ejector rod. Special engraving.

NIB	Exc.	V.G.	Good	Fair	Poor
995	—	—	—	—	—

Lone Star Classic
Built on a Ruger Vaquero and chambered for the .45 Long Colt cartridge with 7.5" barrel. Stainless steel finish. Special engraving and walnut grips with five notches.

NIB	Exc.	V.G.	Good	Fair	Poor
995	—	—	—	—	—

Long Rider Classic
Built on a Ruger Vaquero and chambered for the .45 Long Colt cartridge with 4.5", 5.5", or 7.5" barrel. Special engraving with black Chromix finish. Gunfighter grip with simulated pearl or ivory.

NIB	Exc.	V.G.	Good	Fair	Poor
995	—	—	—	—	—

Texas Ranger Classic
Built on a Ruger Vaquero frame and chambered for the .45 Long Colt cartridge with 4.5", 5.5", or 7.5" barrel. Stainless steel finish. Special engraving. Simulated pearl gunfighter grips.

NIB	Exc.	V.G.	Good	Fair	Poor
995	—	—	—	—	—

Trail Rider Classic
Built on a Ruger Vaquero frame and chambered for the .45 Long Colt cartridge with 7.5" barrel. Black Chromix finish. Special engraving. Simulated pearl grips.

NIB	Exc.	V.G.	Good	Fair	Poor
995	—	—	—	—	—

Tombstone Classic
Built on a Ruger Vaquero frame and chambered for the .45 Long Colt cartridge with 3.5" barrel. Black Chromix finish. Special engraving. Simulated pearl or ivory bird's-head grips.

NIB	Exc.	V.G.	Good	Fair	Poor
995	—	—	—	—	—

Doc Holliday Classic
Built on a Ruger Vaquero frame and chambered for the .45 Long Colt cartridge with 3.5" barrel. Stainless steel or black Chromix finish. Special engraving. Simulated pearl gambler grips.

NIB	Exc.	V.G.	Good	Fair	Poor
995	—	—	—	—	—

Night Rider
Built on a Ruger Vaquero frame and chambered for the .44-40 cartridge with 7.5" barrel. Black Chromix finish. Special engraving. Stag grips.

NIB	Exc.	V.G.	Good	Fair	Poor
995	—	—	—	—	—

Ultimate Vaquero
Built on a Ruger Vaquero frame and chambered for the .45 Long Colt cartridge with 4" barrel. Stainless steel or black Chromix finish. Special engraving. Simulated pearl gambler grips.

NIB	Exc.	V.G.	Good	Fair	Poor
995	—	—	—	—	—

REID, JAMES
New York, New York

Model 1 Revolver
A spur trigger .22 caliber revolver with a 3.5" octagonal barrel and 7-shot unfluted cylinder. Blued with walnut grips. The barrel marked

"J. Reid, New York." Approximately 500 were manufactured between 1862 and 1865.

Exc.	V.G.	Good	Fair	Poor
—	—	850	350	100

Model 2 Revolver
As above but in .32 caliber, the barrel marked "Address W.P. Irving, 20 Cliff Street. N.Y." or "James P. Fitch. N.Y." Approximately 1,300 were manufactured between 1862 and 1865.

Exc.	V.G.	Good	Fair	Poor
—	—	850	350	100

Model 3 Revolver
Similar to the above, but with the grip angle sharpened. Chambered for the .32 rimfire cartridge with a 4.75" barrel. The cylinder chambers are threaded so that percussion nipples can be inserted. The barrel is marked "J. Reid N.Y. City." Approximately 300 were made between 1862 and 1865.

Exc.	V.G.	Good	Fair	Poor
—	—	1250	500	200

Model 4 Revolver
As above with barrel lengths varying from 3.75" to 8". Approximately 1,600 were manufactured between 1862 and 1865.

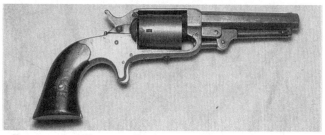

Exc.	V.G.	Good	Fair	Poor
—	—	1250	500	200

"My Friend" Knuckle Duster
A 7-shot .22 caliber revolver constructed entirely of metal and without a barrel. The frame of silver-plated brass or blued iron and marked "My Friend Patd. Dec. 26, 1865." The grip is formed with a finger hole so that the pistol can be used as a set of brass knuckles.

Brass Frame

Exc.	V.G.	Good	Fair	Poor
—	—	1200	500	200

Iron Frame

Exc.	V.G.	Good	Fair	Poor
—	—	2250	800	250

.32 Caliber Knuckle Duster
As above but .32 caliber. Approximately 3,400 were manufactured between 1869 and 1884.

Brass Frame

Exc.	V.G.	Good	Fair	Poor
—	—	1500	600	200

Iron Frame

Exc.	V.G.	Good	Fair	Poor
—	—	2250	800	250

.41 Caliber Knuckle Duster
As above but .41 caliber and marked "J. Reid's Derringer." Approximately 300 were manufactured between 1875 and 1878.

Exc.	V.G.	Good	Fair	Poor
—	—	15000	6500	1500

Model No. 1 Knuckle Duster
As above with a 3" barrel. Approximately 350 were made between 1875 and 1880.

Exc.	V.G.	Good	Fair	Poor
—	—	2750	850	250

Model No. 2 Knuckle Duster
As above with a 1.75" barrel. Approximately 150 were made between 1875 and 1880.

Exc.	V.G.	Good	Fair	Poor
—	—	3000	1250	500

Model No. 3 Derringer
A .41 caliber revolver with a 3" octagonal barrel and 5-shot fluted cylinder. The frame silver-plated and the barrel as well as cylinder blued. Approximately 75 were made between 1880 and 1884.

Exc.	V.G.	Good	Fair	Poor
—	—	2500	950	350

Model No. 4 Derringer
As above but with a brass frame and walnut grips and marked "Reid's Extra." Approximately 200 were made during 1883 and 1884.

Exc.	V.G.	Good	Fair	Poor
—	—	1500	700	250

New Model Knuckle Duster
Similar to the Model 2 with a 2" barrel and 5-shot cylinder. The barrel marked "Reid's New Model .32 My Friend." Approximately 150 were made in 1884.

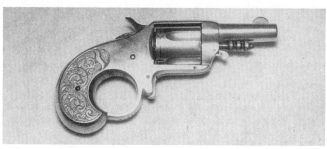

Exc.	V.G.	Good	Fair	Poor
—	—	1500	650	250

Remington. COUNTRY

REMINGTON ARMS COMPANY, INC.
Madison, North Carolina

Founded in 1816 by Eliphalet Remington, this company has the distinction of being the oldest firearms manufacturing firm in the United States. Since 1856 it has been known by four different names: between 1856 and 1888, E. Remington & Sons; 1888-1910, Remington Arms Company; 1910-1925, Remington Arms U.M.C. Company (Union Metallic Cartridge Company); and 1925 to the present, Remington Arms Company.

1st Model Remington-Beals Revolver
A .31 caliber 5-shot percussion revolver with a 3" octagonal barrel. The cylinder turning mechanism is mounted on the left outside frame. Blued, case hardened, silver-plated, brass trigger guard and gutta-percha grips. The barrel marked, " F. Beal's Patent, June 24, '56 & May 26, '57" and the frame, "Remington's Ilion, N.Y." Approximately 5,000 were manufactured in 1857 and 1858.

Exc.	V.G.	Good	Fair	Poor
—	—	1000	600	300

2nd Model Remington-Beals Revolver
A spur trigger .31 caliber 5-shot percussion revolver with a 3" octagonal barrel. Blued, case hardened with a squared gutta-percha grip. The barrel marked, "Beals Patent 1856 & 57, Manufactured by Remingtons Ilion, N.Y." Approximately 1,000 were manufactured between 1858 and 1860.

Exc.	V.G.	Good	Fair	Poor
—	—	8000	3000	1000

3rd Model Remington-Beals Revolver
A .31 caliber 5-shot percussion revolver with a 4" octagonal barrel. A loading lever mounted beneath the barrel. Blued, case hardened with gutta-percha grips. The barrel marked, "Beals Pat. 1856, 57, 58 and also "Manufactured by Remingtons, Ilion, N.Y." Approximately 1,500 were manufactured in 1859 and 1860.

Exc.	V.G.	Good	Fair	Poor
—	—	3250	1250	500

Remington-Rider Revolver
A double-action .31 caliber percussion revolver with a 3" barrel and 5-shot cylinder. Most of these revolvers were blued but a few were nickel-plated, case hardened with gutta-percha grips. This model is also encountered altered to .32 rimfire. The barrel marked, "Manufactured by Remingtons, Ilion, N.Y., Riders Pt. Aug. 17, 1858, May 3, 1859." Approximately 20,000 were manufactured between 1860 and 1873. The cartridge variation is worth approximately 20 percent less than the original percussion version.

Exc.	V.G.	Good	Fair	Poor
—	—	1150	500	200

Remington-Beals Army Revolver
A .44 caliber percussion revolver with an 8" barrel and 6-shot cylinder. Blued, case hardened with walnut grips. The barrel marked "Beals Patent Sept. 14, 1858 Manufactured by Remington's Ilion, New York." Approximately 2,500 were manufactured between 1860 and 1862. A martially marked example is extremely rare and would be worth approximately 35 percent additional.

Exc.	V.G.	Good	Fair	Poor
—	—	3750	1500	500

Remington-Beals Navy Revolver
Similar in appearance to Remington-Beals Army Revolver, but in .36 caliber with a 7.5" octagonal barrel. The first examples of this model were fitted with a loading lever that would not allow the cylinder pin to be completely removed. These examples are worth approximately 80 percent more than the standard model. Approximately 1,000 of these revolvers were purchased by the United States government and martially marked examples are worth approximately 40 percent more than the values listed. Manufactured from 1860 to 1862 with a total production of approximately 15,000.

Exc.	V.G.	Good	Fair	Poor
—	—	2500	1000	400

1861 Army Revolver
A .44 caliber percussion revolver with an 8" octagonal barrel and 6-shot cylinder. The loading lever is cut with a slot so that the cylinder pin can be drawn forward without the lever being lowered. Blued, case hardened with walnut grips. The barrel marked "Patented Dec. 17, 1861 Manufactured by Remington's, Ilion, N.Y." Some examples were converted to .46 caliber rimfire cartridge, and would be worth approximately 25 percent more than the original, martially marked, standard percussion model. Approximately 12,000 were manufactured in 1862. This model is also known as the "Old Army Model."

Courtesy Paul Goodwin

Exc.	V.G.	Good	Fair	Poor
—	—	2500	1000	500

1861 Navy Revolver
As above, but .36 caliber with a 7.25" octagonal barrel. Blued, case hardened with walnut grips. This model is also found altered to .38 metallic cartridge. Cartridge examples are worth approximately 35 percent less than the percussion versions. Approximately 8,000 were manufactured in 1862. Add 25 percent for martial.

Exc.	V.G.	Good	Fair	Poor
—	—	2250	800	400

New Model Army Revolver
A .44 caliber 6-shot percussion revolver with an 8" octagonal barrel. Blued, case hardened with walnut grips. The barrel marked "Patented Sept. 14, 1858 E. Remington & Sons, Ilion, New York, U.S.A. New Model." Approximately 132,000 were made between 1863 and 1873.

Standard Model—Military Version

Exc.	V.G.	Good	Fair	Poor
—	—	2500	1000	400

Civilian Model—No Government Inspector's Markings

Exc.	V.G.	Good	Fair	Poor
—	—	2000	800	400

.44 or .46 Cartridge Conversion

Exc.	V.G.	Good	Fair	Poor
—	—	2000	800	400

New Model Navy Revolver
As above, but .36 caliber with a 7.23" octagonal barrel. Approximately 22,000 were made between 1863 and 1875.

Military Version

Exc.	V.G.	Good	Fair	Poor
—	—	3250	1200	500

Civilian Version

Exc.	V.G.	Good	Fair	Poor
—	—	2500	1000	400

.38 Cartridge Conversion—1873 to 1888

Exc.	V.G.	Good	Fair	Poor
—	—	2000	800	400

New Model Single-Action Belt Revolver
As above, but with a 6.5" barrel. Blued or nickel-plated, case hardened with walnut grips. This model is sometimes encountered altered to .38 cartridge. Cartridge examples are worth approximately 25 percent less than the values listed. Approximately 3,000 were made between 1863 and 1873.

Exc.	V.G.	Good	Fair	Poor
—	—	1800	800	400

NOTE: Blued models will command a premium.

Remington-Rider Double-Action Belt Revolver
A double-action .36 caliber percussion revolver with a 6.5" octagonal barrel marked, "Manufactured by Remington's, Ilion, N.Y. Rider's Pt. Aug. 17, 1858, May 3, 1859." Blued or nickel-plated, case hardened with walnut grips. This model is also found altered to cartridge and such examples would be worth approximately 20 percent less than the values listed. Several hundred of this model were made with fluted cylinders and are worth a premium of about 25 percent. Approximately 5,000 were made between 1863 and 1873.

Exc.	V.G.	Good	Fair	Poor
—	—	2500	1000	400

New Model Police Revolver
A .36 caliber percussion revolver with octagonal barrels ranging from 3.5" to 6.5" and with a 5-shot cylinder. Blued or nickel-plated, case hardened with walnut grips. This model is also found altered to cartridge and such examples would be worth approximately 20 percent less than the values listed. Approximately 18,000 were manufactured between 1863 and 1873.

Exc.	V.G.	Good	Fair	Poor
—	—	1400	800	300

NOTE: Blued models will command a premium.

New Model Pocket Revolver
A .31 caliber spur trigger percussion revolver with octagonal barrels ranging from 3" to 4.5" in length and a 5-shot cylinder. Blued or nickel-plated, case hardened, walnut grips. The barrel marked, "Patented Sept. 14, 1858, March 17, 1863 E. Remington & Sons, Ilion, New York U.S.A. New Model." Approximately 25,000 were manufactured between 1863 and 1873.

1st Version
Brass frame and trigger.

Exc.	V.G.	Good	Fair	Poor
—	—	2500	1200	500

2nd Version
Iron frame, brass trigger.

Exc.	V.G.	Good	Fair	Poor
—	—	1200	800	400

3rd Version
Iron frame, iron trigger.

Exc.	V.G.	Good	Fair	Poor
—	—	1000	800	400

.32 Cartridge Conversion

Exc.	V.G.	Good	Fair	Poor
—	—	800	500	300

NOTE: Add 15 percent for blued models.

Remington-Rider Derringer
A small, silver-plated brass single-shot .17 caliber percussion pistol with a 3" round barrel. The barrel marked, "Rider's Pt. Sept. 13, 1859." Approximately 1,000 were manufactured between 1860 and 1863. Prospective purchasers are advised to secure a qualified appraisal prior to acquisition.

Exc.	V.G.	Good	Fair	Poor
—	—	6250	3000	900

Zig-Zag Derringer
A 6-shot .22 caliber revolving barrel pocket pistol with barrels 3.25" in length. The barrels are cut with zigzag grooves, which are part of the revolving mechanism. The trigger is formed as a ring that when moved forward and rearward turns the barrels and cocks the internal hammer. The barrel group marked "Elliot's Patent Aug. 17, 1858 May 29, 1860" as well as "Manufactured by Remington's Ilion, N.Y." Approximately 1,000 were manufactured in 1861 and 1862.

Exc.	V.G.	Good	Fair	Poor
—	—	3250	1500	600

Remington-Elliot Derringer
A 5-shot .22 or 4-shot .32 caliber pepperbox pistol with a revolving firing pin. Blued or nickel-plated with hard rubber grips. The barrel group marked "Manufactured by E. Remington & Sons, Ilion, N.Y. Elliot's Patents May 19, 1860 - Oct.1, 1861." Approximately 25,000 were manufactured between 1863 and 1888.

5-shot .22 caliber

Exc.	V.G.	Good	Fair	Poor
—	—	1100	400	150

4-shot .32 caliber

Exc.	V.G.	Good	Fair	Poor
—	—	950	400	150

Vest Pocket Pistol
A .22 caliber single-shot pistol with a 3.25" barrel. Blued or nickel-plated with walnut grips. The barrel marked "Remington's Ilion, N.Y. Patent Oct. 1, 1861." Early examples have been noted without any barrel markings. Approximately 25,000 were manufactured from 1865 to 1888.

Exc.	V.G.	Good	Fair	Poor
—	—	800	400	200

NOTE: Add a 35 percent premium for blued models.

Large-Bore Vest Pocket Pistol
As above, but in .30, .32, or .41 caliber with barrel lengths of either 3.5" or 4". Blued or nickel-plated with walnut or rosewood grips. The barrel markings as above except for the addition of the patent date, November 15, 1864. The smaller caliber versions are worth approximately 20 percent more than the .41 caliber. Approximately 10,000 were made from 1865 to 1888.

Exc.	V.G.	Good	Fair	Poor
—	—	1250	600	300

NOTE: Add a 35 percent premium for blued models.

Remington-Elliot Derringer
A .41 caliber single-shot pistol with a 2.5" round barrel. Blued or nickel-plated with walnut, ivory, or pearl grips. The barrel marked "Remingtons, Ilion, N.Y. Elliot Pat. Aug. 27, 1867." Approximately 10,000 were manufactured between 1867 and 1888.

Exc.	V.G.	Good	Fair	Poor
—	—	1500	700	350

NOTE: Add a 35 percent premium for blued models.

Remington Over-and-Under Derringer
A double-barrel .41 caliber pocket pistol with 3" round barrels that pivot upward for loading. There is a lock bar to release the barrels on the right side of the frame. The firing pin raises and lowers automatically to fire each respective barrel. It has a spur trigger and bird's-head grip. The finish is either blued or nickel-plated; and it is featured with walnut, rosewood, or checkered hard rubber grips. Examples with factory pearl or ivory grips would be worth a small premium. Approximately 150,000 were manufactured between 1866 and 1935.

NOTE: Add a 25 percent premium for blued models.

Early Type I
Manufactured without an extractor, this type is marked "E. Remington & Sons, Ilion, N.Y." on one side and "Elliot's Patent Dec. 12, 1865" on the other side of the barrel rib. Only a few hundred were manufactured in 1866.

Exc.	V.G.	Good	Fair	Poor
—	—	2250	800	400

Type I Mid-Production
As above, but fitted with an extractor. Manufactured in the late 1860s.

Exc.	V.G.	Good	Fair	Poor
—	—	2500	1000	500

Type I Late Production
Fitted with an automatic extractor and marked on the top of the barrel rib. Manufactured from the late 1860s to 1888.

Exc.	V.G.	Good	Fair	Poor
—	—	900	400	200

Type II
Marked "Remington Arms Co., Ilion, N.Y." on the barrel rib. Manufactured between 1888 and 1911.

Exc.	V.G.	Good	Fair	Poor
—	—	800	400	200

Type III
Marked "Remington Arms - U.M.C. Co., Ilion, N.Y." on the barrel rib. Manufactured between 1912 and 1935.

Exc.	V.G.	Good	Fair	Poor
—	—	2500	1000	500

NOTE: For Type III models, blue or nickel prices are the same.

Remington-Rider Magazine Pistol
A 5-shot .32 caliber magazine pistol with a spur trigger and 3" octagonal barrel. The magazine is located beneath the barrel and can be loaded from the front. Blued, nickel-plated or case hardened with walnut, pearl, or ivory grips. The barrel marked "E. Remington & Sons, Ilion, N.Y. Riders Pat. Aug. 15, 1871." Approximately 10,000 were manufactured between 1871 and 1888.

Exc.	V.G.	Good	Fair	Poor
—	—	1800	750	300

NOTE: For blued finish add a 50 percent premium.

Model 1865 Navy Rolling Block Pistol
A spur trigger single-shot rolling block .50 caliber rimfire cartridge pistol with an 8.5" round barrel. Blued, case hardened with walnut grips and forend. The barrel marked "Remingtons, Ilion N.Y. U.S.A. Pat. May 3d Nov. 15th, 1864 April 17th, 1866." Examples bearing military inspection marks are worth approximately 25 percent more than the values listed. Examples are also to be found altered to centerfire cartridge and these are worth approximately 10 percent less than the values listed. Approximately 6,500 were manufactured between 1866 and 1870.

Exc.	V.G.	Good	Fair	Poor
—	—	2000	1000	600

Model 1867 Navy Rolling Block Pistol
A .50 caliber single-shot rolling block pistol with a 7" round barrel. Blued, case hardened with walnut grips and forend. The majority of

these pistols were purchased by the United States government and civilian examples without inspection marks are worth approximately 30 percent more than the values listed.

Exc.	V.G.	Good	Fair	Poor
—	—	2200	1100	600

Remington Rolling Block Single-Shot Smooth Bore Pistol nfa
Also called the Remington Combination PistolShotgun, this firearm is a singleshot 20 gauge smooth bore pistol with a detachable shoulder stock, and is extremely rare. ATF advised this writer that it cannot be classified as a "curio or relic," because it is an antique firearm (manufactured in or before 1898) that fires fixed shotgun ammunition that is currently available in ordinary commercial channels. ATF classifies this firearm as a shortbarreled shotgun under the NFA, which requires payment of a $200 tax on each ownership transfer; it is unclear whether it qualifies as an "any other weapon" (and $5 transfer tax) if unaccompanied by a shoulder stock.

John B. McClernan's article, "The Remington Combination Pistol-Shotgun" (in The Canadian Journal of Arms Collecting, Vol. 5, No. 1, 1967, pages 112), contains the most published information about this firearm at this time. He reports the barrel length is 11.75", with "no rear sight nor any sign of milling or drilling for a rear sight [and] has [an] original brass pin front sight." The outside diameter at the joint with the receiver is .843" and .406" at the opposite end. The pistol's overall length is 18.25" and 27.5" with the shoulder stock attached. The receiver's left side bears the markings: Remington's Ilion, N.Y.U.S.A./Pat. May 3d Nov. 15th 1864 April 17th, 1866, which he contends "dates its production period as 18671875." Based on documented and exhaustive original research, McClernan states: "there is no way to escape the conclusion that this gun, if not experimental, is at least a rare, specialorder Remington variation."

Model 1871 Army Rolling Block Pistol
A .50 caliber rolling block single-shot pistol with an 8" round barrel. Blued, case hardened with walnut grips and forend. The distinguishing feature of this model is that it has a rearward extension at the top of the grip and a squared butt. Approximately 6,000 were made between 1872 and 1888. Engraved ivory-stocked versions, will bring considerable premiums.

Exc.	V.G.	Good	Fair	Poor
—	—	1800	800	400

Remington-Smoot No. 1 Revolver
A .30 caliber spur trigger revolver with a 2.75" octagonal barrel and 5-shot fluted cylinder. Blued or nickel-plated with walnut or hard rubber grips. The barrel rib is marked, "E. Remington & Sons, Ilion, N.Y. Pat. W. S. Smoot Oct. 21, 1873." Examples dating from the beginning of production are found with a revolving recoil shield. Such examples would command approximately a 300 percent premium over the values listed.

Exc.	V.G.	Good	Fair	Poor
—	—	1500	600	250

NOTE: For blued finish add a 50 percent premium.

Remington-Smoot No. 2 Revolver
As above, except in .32 caliber approximately 20,000 were made between 1878 and 1888.

Exc.	V.G.	Good	Fair	Poor
—	—	550	250	100

NOTE: For blued finish add a 50 percent premium.

Remington-Smoot No. 3 Revolver
Two variations of this spur trigger .38 caliber revolver exist. One with a rounded grip and no barrel rib, the other with a squared back, squared butt grip with a barrel rib. Centerfire versions are also known and they are worth approximately 10 percent more than the values listed. Blued or nickel-plated with hard rubber grips. Approximately 25,000 were made between 1878 and 1888.

Exc.	V.G.	Good	Fair	Poor
—	—	600	300	100

NOTE: For blued finish add a 50 percent premium.

No. 4 Revolver
A .38 or .41 caliber spur trigger revolver with a 2.5" barrel and no ejector rod. Blued or nickel-plated with hard rubber grips. The barrel marked "E. Remington & Sons, Ilion, N.Y." Approximately 10,000 were manufactured between 1877 and 1888.

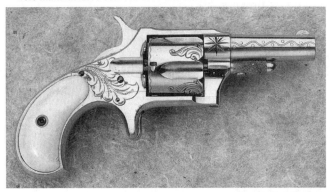
Courtesy Paul Goodwin

Exc.	V.G.	Good	Fair	Poor
—	—	450	200	100

NOTE: For blued finish add a 50 percent premium.

Remington Iroquois Revolver
A .22 caliber spur trigger revolver with a 2.25" barrel and 7-shot cylinder. Blued or nickel-plated with hard rubber grips. The barrel marked "Remington, Ilion, N.Y." and "Iroquois." Some examples of this model will be found without the Remington markings. Approximately 10,000 were manufactured between 1878 and 1888.

Exc.	V.G.	Good	Fair	Poor
—	—	750	350	150

NOTE: For blued finish add a 50 percent premium.

Model 1875 Single-Action Army
A .44 Remington or .44-40 or .45 caliber single-action revolver with a 7.5" barrel. Blued or nickel-plated, case hardened with walnut grips. Some examples are to be found fitted with a lanyard ring at the butt. The barrel marked "E. Remington & Sons Ilion, N.Y. U.S.A." Approximately 25,000 were manufactured between 1875 and 1889.

Exc.	V.G.	Good	Fair	Poor
—	—	3250	1500	600

NOTE: Blued version add 40 percent.

Model 1890 Single-Action Army
A .44-40 caliber single-action revolver with a 5.5" or 7.5" barrel and 6-shot cylinder. Blued or nickel-plated with hard rubber grips bearing the monogram "RA" at the top. The barrel marked "Remington Arms Co., Ilion, N.Y." Approximately 2,000 were made between 1891 and 1894. Prospective purchasers are advised to secure a qualified appraisal prior to acquisition.

Exc.	V.G.	Good	Fair	Poor
—	—	5500	2000	900

NOTE: Blued version add 40 percent.

Model 1891 Target Rolling Block Pistol
A .22, .25 Stevens, or .32 S&W caliber single-shot rolling block pistol with a 10" half octagonal barrel fitted with target sights. Blued, case hardened with walnut grips and forend. The barrel marked "Remington Arms Co. Ilion, N.Y.," and the frame "Remingtons Ilion N.Y. U.S.A. Pat. May 3 Nov. 15, 1864 April 17, 1866 P S." This is an extremely rare pistol, with slightly more than 100 manufactured between 1892 and 1898. Prospective purchasers are advised to secure a qualified appraisal prior to acquisition.

Exc.	V.G.	Good	Fair	Poor
—	—	2500	1100	500

Model 1901 Target Rolling Block
As above, with the exception that the bridge block thumb piece has been moved out of the line of sight and the rear sight is mounted on the frame instead of the barrel. Approximately 735 were made between 1901 and 1909. Prospective purchasers are advised to secure a qualified appraisal prior to acquisition.

Exc.	V.G.	Good	Fair	Poor
—	—	2500	1100	500

LONG ARMS

Model 1841 "Mississippi Rifle"
A .54 caliber percussion rifle with a 33" barrel and full stock secured by two barrel bands. The lock (marked Remington's Herkimer N.Y.) is case hardened, the barrel browned and the furniture of brass. The stock is fitted with a brass patch box on the right side. Approximately 20,000 were made between 1846 and 1855.

Exc.	V.G.	Good	Fair	Poor
—	—	4750	1750	750

Model 1861 U.S. Rifle Musket
A .58 caliber percussion rifle with a 40" barrel and full length stock secured by three barrel bands. The lock marked "Remington's Ilion, N.Y." Finished in the white with a walnut stock. Approximately 40,000 were made between 1864 and 1866.

Exc.	V.G.	Good	Fair	Poor
—	—	3000	1250	500

Model 1863 Zouave Rifle
A .58 caliber percussion rifle with a 33" barrel and full length stock secured by two barrel bands. The lock case hardened and marked "Remington's Ilion N.Y.", the barrel blued and the furniture of brass. Approximately 12,500 were manufactured between 1862 and 1865.

Exc.	V.G.	Good	Fair	Poor
—	—	4250	1500	500

Breech-Loading Carbine
A .46 or .50 rimfire single-shot rolling block carbine with a 20" barrel. Blued, case hardened with a walnut stock. The tang marked "Remington's Ilion, N.Y. Pat. Dec. 23, 1863 May 3 & Nov. 16, 1864." The .50 caliber version is worth approximately 15 percent more than the .46 caliber. Approximately 15,000 .50-caliber variations were made, most of which were sold to France. Approximately 5,000 carbines were made in .46 caliber. Manufactured from 1864 to 1866.

Exc.	V.G.	Good	Fair	Poor
—	—	3750	1500	500

Revolving Rifle
A .36 or .44 caliber revolving rifle with either 24" or 28" octagonal barrels with a 6-shot cylinder. The trigger guard formed with a scrolled finger extension at the rear. Blued, case hardened with a walnut stock. These rifles are also encountered altered to cartridge and would be worth approximately 20 percent less than the percussion values listed. The barrel marked "Patented Sept. 14, 1858 E. Remington & Sons, Ilion, New York, U.S.A. New Model." The .44 caliber model will bring a premium of about 15 percent and is rare. Approximately 1,000 were manufactured between 1866 and 1879.

Exc.	V.G.	Good	Fair	Poor
—	—	5000	2000	500

Remington-Beals Rifle
A .32 or .38 caliber sliding barrel single-shot rifle with octagonal barrels of 24", 26", or 28" length. The barrel can be moved forward by lowering the trigger guard/lever. This model is to be found with either frames made of brass or iron, the latter being worth approximately 20 percent more than the values listed. Walnut stock. The barrel marked "Beals Patent June 28, 1864 Jan. 30, 1866 E. Remington & Sons, Ilion, New York." Approximately 800 were manufactured between 1866 and 1888. A few examples are known to have been factory engraved. Prospective purchasers are advised to secure a qualified appraisal prior to acquisition.

Exc.	V.G.	Good	Fair	Poor
—	—	950	400	150

U.S. Navy Rolling Block Carbine

Exc.	V.G.	Good	Fair	Poor
—	—	2750	1000	350

Model 1867 Navy Cadet Rifle

Exc.	V.G.	Good	Fair	Poor
—	—	2750	1000	350

Rolling Block Military Rifles

Exc.	V.G.	Good	Fair	Poor
—	—	750	400	100

NO. 1 ROLLING BLOCK SPORTING RIFLE

Standard No. 1 Sporting Rifle
A single-shot rolling block rifle produced in a variety of calibers from .40-50 to .50-70 centerfire as well as .44 and .46 rimfire. Standard barrel lengths were either 28" or 30" and of octagonal form.

Exc.	V.G.	Good	Fair	Poor
—	—	3750	1500	500

Long-Range Creedmoor Rifle
A .44-90, .44-100, or .44-105 caliber rolling block rifle with a 34" half-octagonal barrel, long--range vernier tang sights and globe front sights. Blued, case hardened with a walnut stock and a checkered pistol grip. This rifle was available with a number of optional features and a qualified appraisal should be secured if those features are in doubt. Produced from 1873 to 1890.

Exc.	V.G.	Good	Fair	Poor
—	7500	3750	1500	500

Mid-Range Target Rifle
As above, except chambered for .40-70, .44-77, .45-70, or .50-70 caliber with 28" or 30" half-octagonal barrels. Produced from 1875 to 1890.

Exc.	V.G.	Good	Fair	Poor
—	5000	2000	750	300

Short-Range Rifle
As above, chambered for cartridges between .38 and .44 caliber with 26" or 30" round or octagonal barrels. Open rear sight with beach front sight. The walnut stock is checkered. Produced from 1875 to 1890.

Exc.	V.G.	Good	Fair	Poor
—	4000	1750	600	250

Black Hills Rifle
As above, in .45-60 caliber with a 28" round barrel fitted with open sights and a plain straight grip stock. Produced from 1877 to 1882.

Exc.	V.G.	Good	Fair	Poor
—	4000	2000	850	300

Shotgun
As above, in 16 gauge with either a 30" or 32" Damascus or fluid steel barrels. Produced from 1870 to 1892.

Exc.	V.G.	Good	Fair	Poor
—	1000	500	250	100

Baby Carbine
As above, with a 20" thin round barrel chambered for the .4440 cartridge and fitted with a saddle ring on the left side of the frame. Blued, case hardened with a walnut stock and a carbine buttplate. Manufactured from 1892 to 1902.

Exc.	V.G.	Good	Fair	Poor
—	3250	1250	600	200

Model 1-1/2 Sporting Rifle
A lightweight variation of the above using a 1.25" wide, No. 1 rolling block action. Chambered for rimfire cartridges from .22 to the .38 Extra Long, as well as centerfire cartridges from .32-20 to the .44-40. Medium weight octagonal barrels from 24" to 28" in length, with open rear and a blade-type front sight. Blued, case hardened with a walnut stock. There were several thousand manufactured between 1888 and 1897.

Courtesy Paul Goodwin

Exc.	V.G.	Good	Fair	Poor
—	2000	950	400	100

Model 2 Sporting Rifle
As above, using a No. 2 action and chambered for various cartridges from .22 to .38 caliber with 24" or 26" octagonal barrels. Blued, case hardened with a walnut stock. This model was produced with

a number of optional features that affect its value. Prospective purchasers are advised to secure a qualified appraisal prior to acquisition. Manufactured from 1873 to 1910.

Exc.	V.G.	Good	Fair	Poor
—	1500	600	250	100

No. 4 Rolling Block Rifle

Built on the lightweight No. 4 action, this rifle was available in .22, .25 Stevens, or .32 caliber, with either a 22.5" or 24" octagonal barrel. Blued, case hardened with a walnut stock. A takedown version was also made and these are worth approximately 10 percent more than the values listed. Approximately 50,000 were made between 1890 and 1933.

Exc.	V.G.	Good	Fair	Poor
—	900	400	200	75

Model No. 4 S Military Rifle

At the request of the United States Boy Scouts in 1913, the Remington Company designed a military style rifle having a 28" barrel and full length forend secured by one barrel band. A short upper hand guard was also fitted and a bayonet stud is to be found at the muzzle. In 1915 the designation of this model was changed from "Boy Scout" to "Military Model." Approximately 15,000 were made between 1913 and 1923.

Exc.	V.G.	Good	Fair	Poor
—	2250	950	400	275

No. 5 Rolling Block Rifle

Built on the No. 5 action, this rifle was designed for smokeless cartridges and was made in a variety of barrel lengths, calibers and in a carbine version. Blued, case hardened with a walnut stock.

Exc.	V.G.	Good	Fair	Poor
—	2250	800	350	100

No. 5 Sporting or Target Rifle

Chambered for the .30-30, .303 British, 7mm, .30 U.S., .32-40, .32 U.S., and the .38-55 cartridges. This rifle was offered with 28" or 30" round barrels and features a plain, straight-grip stock with a half-length forend. It has open rear sights and was available with double-set triggers that would add approximately 10 percent to the value. It was manufactured between 1898 and 1905.

Exc.	V.G.	Good	Fair	Poor
—	5750	2250	850	300

Model 1897

A 7x57mm and .30 U.S. caliber full stock rolling block rifle. The Model 1902 is of identical form except that it was fitted with an automatic ejector. Manufactured from 1897 to 1902.

Exc.	V.G.	Good	Fair	Poor
—	1250	550	250	100

Carbine

As above, fitted with a 20" round barrel and a half-length forend secured by one barrel band.

Exc.	V.G.	Good	Fair	Poor
—	1750	750	350	100

No. 6 Rolling Block Rifle

A lightweight, small rifle designed expressly to be used by young boys. It is chambered for the .22 rimfire cartridge, as well as the .32 Short or Long. It was also produced with a smoothbore barrel to be used with shot cartridges. The round barrel is 20" in length. It has a takedown action with a barrel held on by a knurled knob underneath the frame. It is a lightweight rolling block, with a thin operating knob on the breech. The finish is blued overall. Early models featured a case-colored frame, and these versions would be worth approximately 10 percent additional. It has a straight-grip walnut stock with a small forearm. Over 250,000 manufactured between 1902 and 1903.

Exc.	V.G.	Good	Fair	Poor
—	800	350	100	75

No. 7 Rolling Block Rifle

Readily identifiable by its accentuated checked pistol grip, this model was available in .22 or .25-10 Stevens caliber with 24", 26", or 28" half octagonal barrels. Fitted with a tang mounted aperture rear sight. Blued, case hardened with a walnut stock. Approximately 1,000 were made between 1903 and 1911.

Exc.	V.G.	Good	Fair	Poor
—	6500	2500	750	300

Remington-Hepburn No. 3 Rifle

A lever activated falling block single-shot rifle designed by Lewis Hepburn available in a variety of calibers from .22 Winchester centerfire to .50-90 Sharps with octagonal or round barrels of 26", 28", or 30" length. Blued, case hardened with a walnut stock. This model was available with a variety of optional features that affect the value considerably. Prospective purchasers are advised to secure a qualified appraisal prior to acquisition. Approximately 10,000 were made between 1883 and 1907.

Exc.	V.G.	Good	Fair	Poor
—	4000	1750	800	350

No. 3 Match Rifle

As above, but fitted with a high comb buttstock and a nickel-plated Schuetzen buttplate. Manufactured in various calibers from .25-20 Stevens to .40-65 with 30" half octagonal barrels. This model was made in two versions: "A Quality" with a plain stock, tang mounted rear sight and a Beach front sight, and; "B Quality" with a checkered walnut stock having a cheek rest, checkered forend, vernier rear sight and a combination wind gauge and spirit level front sight. Double set triggers were also available and these would add approximately 10 percent to the values listed. Approximately 1,000 were made between 1883 and 1907.

A Quality

Exc.	V.G.	Good	Fair	Poor
—	4500	2000	800	350

B Quality

Exc.	V.G.	Good	Fair	Poor
—	5500	2500	1200	500

No. 3 Long-Range Creedmoor Rifle

As above, in .44 caliber with a 32" or 34" half-octagonal barrel, long-range vernier rear sight, combination wind gauge and spirit level front sight, deluxe checkered walnut stock and a rubber shotgun buttplate. Produced with a number of optional features that affect the value. Prospective purchasers are advised to secure a qualified appraisal prior to acquisition. Manufactured from 1880 to 1907.

Exc.	V.G.	Good	Fair	Poor
—	7500	3500	1250	500

No. 3 Mid-Range Creedmoor Rifle

As above, but chambered for the .40-65 cartridge and fitted with a 28" barrel.

Exc.	V.G.	Good	Fair	Poor
—	5000	2250	950	350

No. 3 Long-Range Military Rifle

This is a rare variation that is chambered for the .44-20 Remington cartridge. It has a round 34" barrel and a full-length forearm held on by two barrel bands. The finish is blued and case-colored, and the stock is walnut. There are two basic versions. The plain grade has an uncheckered, straight-grip stock with military-type sights. There is also a fancy grade that features a high-grade, checkered, pistol-grip stock with a full-length, checkered forend, vernier tang sight, and wind gauge, spirit lever front sight. There were a few manufactured in the 1880s.

Plain Grade

Exc.	V.G.	Good	Fair	Poor
—	4500	2500	1200	400

Fancy Grade

Exc.	V.G.	Good	Fair	Poor
—	7500	3750	1500	600

No. 3 Schuetzen Match Rifle

As above, with the exception that instead of the side lever, the action is raised or lowered by means of the lever on the trigger guard. Chambered for various popular cartridges and offered with a 30" or 32" part-octagonal, heavy barrel. It features a vernier tang sight with a hooded front sight. It was standard with double-set triggers and a palm rest. The finish is blued and case-colored, with a high-grade checkered walnut stock and forend. It has an ornate, Swiss-type Schuetzen buttplate and is also known as the "Walker-Hepburn Rifle." There were two versions available. One, a standard breechloader with the Remington Walker-marked barrel; and the other, a muzzleloading variation that was fitted with a removable false muzzle. This version was supplied with a brass bullet starter and other accessories. Prospective purchasers are advised to secure a qualified appraisal prior to acquisition.

Breechloading Version

Courtesy Paul Goodwin

Exc.	V.G.	Good	Fair	Poor
—	27500	12500	3500	900

Muzzleloading Version

Exc.	V.G.	Good	Fair	Poor
—	42500	17500	5000	1500

No. 3 High-Power Rifle

The Model No. 3 was also made available in a variety of smokeless cartridges: .30-30, .30-40, .32 Special, .32-40 and .38-55. Standard barrel lengths were 26", 28", or 30". Produced from 1900 to 1907.

Exc.	V.G.	Good	Fair	Poor
—	4000	1750	650	250

Remington-Keene Magazine Rifle

A bolt-action rifle chambered for the .40, .43, and .45-70 centerfire cartridges with 22", 24.5", 29.25", or 32.5" barrels. It is readily identifiable by the exposed hammer at the end of the bolt. Blued, case hardened hammer and furniture, with a walnut stock. The receiver marked "E. Remington & Sons, Ilion, N.Y." together with the patent dates 1874, 1876, and 1877. The magazine on this rifle was located beneath the barrel and the receiver is fitted with a cut-off so that the rifle could be used as a single-shot. Approximately 5,000 rifles were made between 1880 and 1888 in the following variations:

Sporting Rifle
24.5" barrel.

Exc.	V.G.	Good	Fair	Poor
—	2000	750	350	150

Army Rifle
Barrel length 32.5" with a full-length stock secured by two barrel bands.

Exc.	V.G.	Good	Fair	Poor
—	—	3500	950	450

Navy Rifle
As above, with a 29.25" barrel.

Exc.	V.G.	Good	Fair	Poor
—	—	4500	1750	450

Carbine
As above, with a 22" barrel and a half-length forend secured by one barrel band.

Exc.	V.G.	Good	Fair	Poor
—	—	3250	1250	350

Frontier Model
As above, with a 24" barrel and half-length forend secured by one barrel band. Those purchased by the United States Department of the Interior for arming the Indian Police are marked "U.S.I.D." on the receiver.

Exc.	V.G.	Good	Fair	Poor
—	—	5250	2500	850

Remington-Lee Magazine Rifle

Designed by James Paris Lee, rifles of this type were originally manufactured by the Sharps Rifle Company in 1880. The Remington Company began production of this model in 1881 after the Sharps Company ceased operations. Approximately 100,000 Lee magazine rifles were made between 1880 and 1907. Their variations are as follows:

Model 1879 Sharps Mfg.

Barrel length 28" with a full-length stock secured by two barrel bands. The barrel marked "Sharps Rifle Co. Bridgeport, Conn." and "Old Reliable" in a rectangular cartouche. Approximately 300 were made prior to 1881.

Exc.	V.G.	Good	Fair	Poor
—	—	4750	2000	600

Model 1879 U.S. Navy Model

Exc.	V.G.	Good	Fair	Poor
—	—	2250	750	250

Model 1879 Sporting Rifle

Barrel length 28" or 30", .45-70 or .45-90 caliber, checkered pistol-grip stock with a sporting-style forend. Markings on the receiver as above. Approximately 450 made.

Exc.	V.G.	Good	Fair	Poor
—	—	1750	700	250

Model 1879 Military Rifle

Identical to the Navy model, except chambered for the .43 Spanish cartridge. A limited number were also produced in .45-70 caliber. The Spanish versions are worth approximately 25 percent less than the values listed. Approximately 1,000 were made. The majority of these rifles were made for export.

Exc.	V.G.	Good	Fair	Poor
—	—	1250	500	150

Model 1882 Army Contract

Exc.	V.G.	Good	Fair	Poor
—	—	2000	750	300

Model 1885 Navy Contract

Exc.	V.G.	Good	Fair	Poor
—	—	2000	750	300

Model 1882 & 1885 Military Rifles

Barrel length 32", full-length stock secured by two barrel bands, chambered for .42 Russian, .43 Spanish, .45 Gardner or .45-70 cartridges. The values for those rifles not in .45-70 caliber would be approximately 25 percent less than those listed. Approximately 10,000 Model 1882 rifles were made and 60,000 Model 1885 rifles. The two models can be differentiated by the fact that the cocking piece on the bolt of the Model 1885 is larger. The majority of these rifles were made for foreign contracts and commercial sales.

Exc.	V.G.	Good	Fair	Poor
—	—	950	400	150

Model 1882 & 1885 Sporting Rifle

As above, chambered for .45-70 and .45-90 caliber with 26" or 30" octagonal barrels and walnut sporting stocks. Approximately 200 were made.

Exc.	V.G.	Good	Fair	Poor
—	—	1750	750	200

Model 1882 & 1885 Carbine

As above, with a 24" barrel and a half-length forend secured by one barrel band. Prospective purchasers are advised to secure a qualified appraisal prior to acquisition.

Exc.	V.G.	Good	Fair	Poor
—	—	1750	750	200

Model 1899

Designed for use with smokeless and rimless cartridges, this model is marked on the receiver "Remington Arms Co. Ilion, N.Y. Patented

Aug. 26th 1884 Sept. 9th 1884 March 17th 1885 Jan 18th 1887." Produced from 1889 to 1907 in the following variations:

Military Rifle

Exc.	V.G.	Good	Fair	Poor
—	1250	500	200	100

Military Carbine

Exc.	V.G.	Good	Fair	Poor
—	1750	700	300	100

Sporting Rifle

As above, with a 24", 26", or 28" round or octagonal barrel and a half-length sporting stock with a checkered pistol grip. Approximately 7,000 were manufactured.

Courtesy Paul Goodwin

Exc.	V.G.	Good	Fair	Poor
—	1250	500	200	100

Remington Lebel Bolt-Action Rifle

Exc.	V.G.	Good	Fair	Poor
—	750	450	150	100

Remington Mosin-Nagant Bolt-Action Rifle

Exc.	V.G.	Good	Fair	Poor
—	600	300	100	75

U.S. Model 1917 Magazine Rifle

Exc.	V.G.	Good	Fair	Poor
—	1250	600	150	100

Remington-Whitmore Model 1874

A sidelock double-barrel shotgun, combination shotgun/rifle or double-barrel rifle with 28" or 30" fluid steel barrels. Also available with Damascus barrels. The barrels released by pushing forward the top lever. Blued, case hardened with a straight or semi-pistol grip walnut stock. The barrels marked "A. E. Whitmore's Patent Aug. 8, 1871, April 16, 1872." The rib between the barrels is marked "E. Remington & Sons, Ilion, N.Y." Several thousand were manufactured between 1874 and 1882.

Shotgun

Exc.	V.G.	Good	Fair	Poor
—	1750	650	250	100

Combination Gun (Rare)

Exc.	V.G.	Good	Fair	Poor
—	4250	1750	750	300

Double Rifle

Prospective purchasers are advised to secure a qualified appraisal prior to acquisition. Very rare.

Exc.	V.G.	Good	Fair	Poor
—	9000	4250	1500	500

Model 1882 Shotgun

A sidelock double-barrel 10 or 12 gauge shotgun with 28" or 30" fluid steel or Damascus barrels. Blued, case hardened with a checkered pistol grip stock and hard rubber buttplate. The barrels are marked "E. Remington & Sons, Ilion, N.Y." and the lock is marked "Remington Arms Co." This model has a conventional top lever that moves to the side. Offered with optional engraving, and such models should be individually appraised. Approximately 7,500 were manufactured between 1882 and 1889.

Exc.	V.G.	Good	Fair	Poor
—	1750	750	300	100

Model 1883 through 1889 Shotgun

A sidelock 10, 12, or 16 gauge double-barrel shotgun with fluid steel or Damascus barrels 28" to 32" in length. The models 1883, 1885, 1887, and 1889 are all somewhat alike, varying only in the form of their hammers and internal mechanisms. Blued, case hardened, checkered pistol-grip stock with a grip cap. Available in a variety of styles including highly engraved models that should be individually appraised. Approximately 30,000 were made between 1883 and 1909.

Exc.	V.G.	Good	Fair	Poor
—	1750	750	300	100

Model 1893 (No. 9)

Single-barrel hammer gun in 10, 12, 16, 20, 24, and 28 gauge. Barrel lengths from 28" to 34". Case colored frame with hard rubber buttplate.

Courtesy William F. Krause

Exc.	V.G.	Good	Fair	Poor
—	—	600	250	100

Hammerless Shotgun Model 1894

A boxlock 10, 12, or 16 gauge double shotgun with fluid steel or Damascus barrels 26" to 32" in length. Blued, case hardened with a pistol-grip stock. Available in a variety of styles and it is advised that highly engraved examples should be individually appraised.

Exc.	V.G.	Good	Fair	Poor
—	1750	750	300	100

NOTE: Fluid steel barrels add 25 percent premium.

Model 1900 Shotgun

As above, in 12 and 16 gauge only. The same cautions apply to highly engraved examples.

Exc.	V.G.	Good	Fair	Poor
—	1500	600	250	100

RENETTE, GASTINNE
Paris, France

SHOTGUNS

Model 105

An Anson & Deeley action 12 or 20 gauge double-barrel shotgun available in a variety of barrel lengths, with double triggers and automatic ejectors. Blued, case hardened with a checkered walnut stock.

Exc.	V.G.	Good	Fair	Poor
2000	1600	1250	900	500

Model 98

As above, except more finely finished.

Exc.	V.G.	Good	Fair	Poor
2750	2250	1750	1400	750

Model 202

A 12 or 20 gauge sidelock double-barrel shotgun made only on custom order. French case hardened and blued with a checkered walnut stock.

Exc.	V.G.	Good	Fair	Poor
4500	3500	2500	1750	950

Model 353

A custom manufactured double-barrel shotgun with detachable sidelocks. Highly finished.

Exc.	V.G.	Good	Fair	Poor
18000	15000	9500	4250	1500

RICHLAND ARMS CO.
Blissfield, Michigan

This company, which ceased operation in 1986, imported a variety of Spanish-made shotguns.

Model 200

An Anson & Deeley-style 12, 16, 20, 28 or .410 bore double-barrel shotgun with 22", 26" or 28" barrels, double triggers, and automatic ejectors. Blued with a checkered walnut stock.

Exc.	V.G.	Good	Fair	Poor
350	300	250	200	125

Model 202

As above, with an extra set of interchangeable barrels. Imported from 1963 to 1985.

Exc.	V.G.	Good	Fair	Poor
325	275	225	175	100

Model 711 Magnum

As above, chambered for 3" shells and fitted with 30" or 32" barrels.

Exc.	V.G.	Good	Fair	Poor
350	300	250	200	150

Model 707 Deluxe

As above, more finely finished and fitted with well figured walnut stocks.

Exc.	V.G.	Good	Fair	Poor
350	300	250	200	150

RICHMOND ARMORY
Richmond, Virginia

Carbine

This weapon was manufactured for use by the Confederate States of America and is extremely collectible. We recommend qualified individual appraisal if a transaction is contemplated. This muzzle-loading carbine is chambered for .58 caliber percussion and has a 25" round barrel and a full-length stock that is held on by two barrel bands. It was manufactured from parts that were captured at the Harper's Ferry Armory in 1861. The locks are marked "Richmond, VA" and dated from 1861 to 1865. There are sling swivels in front of the trigger guard and on the front barrel band; a third swivel is on the underside of the buttstock. The quantity manufactured is not known. They were made between 1861 and 1865.

Exc.	V.G.	Good	Fair	Poor
—	—	20000	7500	1000

Musketoon

This weapon is similar to the carbine except that the barrel is 30" in length and the front sight is also the bayonet lug. There is no sling swivel on the buttstock. This weapon was also manufactured between 1861 and 1865.

Exc.	V.G.	Good	Fair	Poor
—	—	17500	7000	1000

Rifled Musket

This model is also similar to the Carbine, with a 40" barrel and a full-length stock held on by three barrel bands. The front sling swivel is on the middle barrel band instead of on the front band. The Rifled Musket was also manufactured between 1861 and 1865.

Exc.	V.G.	Good	Fair	Poor
—	—	20000	7500	1000

RIGDON, ANSLEY & CO.
Augusta, Georgia

1851 Colt Navy Type

A .36 caliber percussion revolver with a 7.5" barrel and 6-shot cylinder. Blued with walnut grips. Initial production examples marked "Augusta, GA. C.S.A." and later models "C.S.A." Approximately 1,000 were manufactured in 1864 and 1865.

Early Production Model

Exc.	V.G.	Good	Fair	Poor
—	—	55000	25000	2000

Standard Production Model

Exc.	V.G.	Good	Fair	Poor
—	—	45000	17500	1500

ROBBINS & LAWRENCE
Windsor, Vermont

Pepperbox

A .28 or .31 caliber percussion 5 barrel pistol with the barrel groups measuring 3.5" or 4.5" in length. Ring trigger, blued iron frame with simple scroll engraving and browned barrels, which are marked "Robbins & Lawrence Co. Windsor, VT. Patent. 1849." The barrel groups for this pistol were made in two types: fluted in both calibers, and ribbed in .31 caliber only. Approximately 7,000 were made between 1851 and 1854.

Exc.	V.G.	Good	Fair	Poor
—	—	2000	600	200

ROBERTSON
Philadelphia, Pennsylvania

Pocket Pistol

A .41 caliber single-shot percussion derringer with barrels ranging in length from 3" to 4.5". The barrel marked "Robertson, Phila."

Exc.	V.G.	Good	Fair	Poor
—	—	1500	600	200

ROBINSON, S.C.
Richmond, Virginia

From December of 1862 through March 1 of 1863, S.C. Robinson produced copies of the Sharps carbine. These arms had an overall length of 38-1/2", with .52 caliber barrels 21-1/2" long. The lockplates were marked "S.C. ROBINSON/ARMS MANUFACTORY/RICHMOND VA/1862" along with the serial number. The barrels were marked forward of the rear sight "S.C. ROBINSON/ARMS MANUFACTORY," as well as "RICHMOND VA/1862" to the rear of the sight. Total number made estimated to be slightly more than 1,900.

In March of 1863, the Robinson factory was taken over by the Confederate States Government. Carbines produced after that date are only stamped with the serial number on their lockplates and "RICHMOND VA" on their barrels. Total number made in excess of 3,400. Prospective purchasers are strongly advised to secure an expert appraisal prior to acquisition.

Robinson Sharps

Exc.	V.G.	Good	Fair	Poor
—	—	27500	8500	1500

Confederate Sharps

Exc.	V.G.	Good	Fair	Poor
—	—	25000	7500	1500

ROGERS & SPENCER
Utica, New York

Army Revolver

A .44 caliber 6-shot percussion revolver with a 7.5" octagonal barrel. The barrel marked "Rogers & Spencer/Utica, N.Y." Blued, case hardened hammer with walnut grips bearing the inspector's mark "RPB." Approximately 5,800 were made between 1863 and 1865.

Exc.	V.G.	Good	Fair	Poor
—	4000	1750	750	250

RUPERTUS, JACOB
Philadelphia, Pennsylvania

Navy Revolver

This model is equally as rare as the Army model. It is chambered for .36 caliber percussion. Otherwise it is quite similar in appearance to the Army model. There were approximately 12 manufactured in 1859. Both of these revolvers were manufactured for test purposes and were not well-received by the military, so further production was not accomplished.

Exc.	V.G.	Good	Fair	Poor
—	—	10500	5000	1250

Pocket Model Revolver
This is a smaller version of the Army and Navy model, chambered for .25 caliber percussion. It has no loading lever and has a 3-1/8" octagonal barrel. There were approximately 12 manufactured in 1859.

Exc.	V.G.	Good	Fair	Poor
—	—	7500	3250	950

Double-Barrel Pocket Pistol
A .22 caliber double-barrel pistol with 3" round barrels and a spur trigger. The hammer fitted with a sliding firing pin. Blued with walnut grips.

Exc.	V.G.	Good	Fair	Poor
—	—	1750	750	200

Army Revolver
This is an extremely rare revolver chambered for .44 caliber percussion. It has a 7.25" octagon barrel with an integral loading lever that pivots to the side instead of downward. The hammer is mounted on the side, and there is a pellet priming device located on the backstrap. There is only one nipple on the breech that lines up with the top of the cylinder. The cylinder is unfluted and holds 6-shots. The finish is blued, with walnut grips; and the frame is marked "Patented April 19, 1859." There were less than 12 manufactured in 1859. It would behoove one to secure a qualified independent appraisal if a transaction were contemplated.

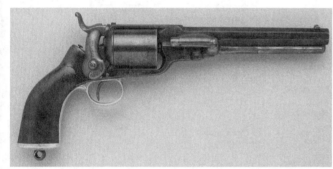

Courtesy Greg Martin Auctions

Exc.	V.G.	Good	Fair	Poor
—	—	10500	5000	1500

Single-Shot Pocket Pistol
A .22, .32, .38, or .41 rimfire single-shot pistol with half-octagonal barrels, ranging in length from 3" to 5". The barrel marked "Rupertus Pat'd. Pistol Mfg. Co. Philadelphia." Blued with walnut grips. Approximately 3,000 were made from 1870 to 1885. The .41 caliber variety is worth approximately 200 percent more than the values listed.

Exc.	V.G.	Good	Fair	Poor
—	—	500	200	75

Spur Trigger Revolver
A .22 caliber spur trigger revolver with a 2.75" round barrel and unfluted cylinder. The top strap marked "Empire Pat. Nov. 21, 71". Blued or nickel-plated with walnut grips. A .41 caliber spur trigger revolver with a 2-7/8" round barrel and a 5-shot fluted cylinder. Blued or nickel-plated with walnut grips. The top strap marked "Empire 41" and the barrel "J. Rupertus Phila. Pa." The .41 caliber variety is worth approximately 25 percent more than the values listed. Manufactured during the 1870s and 1880s.

Exc.	V.G.	Good	Fair	Poor
—	—	400	150	75

S

SKB ARMS COMPANY
Tokyo, Japan
Importer—SKB Company U.S.A.
Omaha, Nebraska

SIDE-BY-SIDE GUNS

Model 100
A boxlock 12 or 20 gauge double-barrel shotgun with 25" to 30" barrels, single-selective trigger and automatic ejectors. Blued with a walnut stock. Imported prior to 1981. Discontinued.

NIB	Exc.	V.G.	Good	Fair	Poor
500	425	375	300	200	100

Model 150
As above, with some engraving, a beavertail forearm and a figured walnut stock. Imported from 1972 to 1974.

NIB	Exc.	V.G.	Good	Fair	Poor
550	450	400	300	200	100

Model 200
As above, with a French case hardened and scalloped receiver. Discontinued.

NIB	Exc.	V.G.	Good	Fair	Poor
550	500	450	375	250	150

Model 200E
As above, with an English-style stock. Imported prior to 1989.

NIB	Exc.	V.G.	Good	Fair	Poor
800	675	600	475	275	150

Model 280
Same as Model 200 but fitted with a straight grip stock. Discontinued.

NIB	Exc.	V.G.	Good	Fair	Poor
800	675	600	475	275	150

Model 300
As above, with more engraving and a figured walnut stock. Discontinued.

NIB	Exc.	V.G.	Good	Fair	Poor
750	675	600	475	275	150

Model 385
Similar to the Model 300 but chambered for the 12, 20 or 28 gauge shell. Scroll engraved frame with semi-fancy walnut. Pistol-grip or straight-grip stock. Limited quantities imported. Weight is approximately 7 lbs. depending on barrel length and gauge. Discontinued.

NIB	Exc.	V.G.	Good	Fair	Poor
2000	1500	1000	700	450	200

Model 385 2 barrel set
Same as above but with a 20 and 28 gauge set of barrels in either 26" or 28". Discontinued.

NIB	Exc.	V.G.	Good	Fair	Poor
2900	2250	1300	—	—	—

Model 385 Sporting Clays
This model is chambered for 12, 20, or 28 gauge and fitted with a 28" barrel. Pistol-grip stock. Weight is about 7 lbs. depending on gauge. Discontinued.

NIB	Exc.	V.G.	Good	Fair	Poor
2150	1700	1150	750	500	300

NOTE: For extra set of 20 or 28 gauge barrels add $900.

Model 400E
As above, with engraved false sideplates and an English-style stock. Imported prior to 1990.

NIB	Exc.	V.G.	Good	Fair	Poor
975	875	750	600	300	150

Model 480E
As above, with a French case hardened receiver and more finely figured walnut stocks. Discontinued.

NIB	Exc.	V.G.	Good	Fair	Poor
1200	1000	850	650	350	150

Model 485
This model features an engraved sideplate boxlock action chambered for 12, 20, or 28 gauge with 26" or 28" barrels. Choke tubes. Weight is approximately 7.7 lbs. Discontinued.

NIB	Exc.	V.G.	Good	Fair	Poor
2750	2100	1500	900	650	300

Model 485 2 barrel set
Same as above but with an extra set of barrels in 20/28 gauge combinations with 26" barrels. Choice of pistol-grip or straight-grip stock. Discontinued.

NIB	Exc.	V.G.	Good	Fair	Poor
3900	3000	1850	—	—	—

SARASQUETA, J. J.
Eibar, Spain
Importer—American Arms, Inc.
Overland Park, Kansas

Model 107E
A 12, 16, or 20 gauge boxlock double-barrel shotgun with a variety of barrel lengths, double triggers and automatic ejectors. Blued with a checkered walnut stock. Discontinued in 1984.

Exc.	V.G.	Good	Fair	Poor
375	300	275	225	100

Model 119E
As above, with a more finely figured walnut stock.

Exc.	V.G.	Good	Fair	Poor
475	400	375	325	150

Model 130E
As above, but engraved.

Exc.	V.G.	Good	Fair	Poor
800	700	600	450	250

Model 131E
As above, with considerably more engraving.

Exc.	V.G.	Good	Fair	Poor
1100	900	800	650	350

Model 1882 E LUXE
As above, with a single-selective trigger and gold inlays. A silver inlaid version is sold for approximately 10 percent less.

Exc.	V.G.	Good	Fair	Poor
800	700	600	450	250

SARASQUETA, VICTOR
Eibar, Spain

Model 3
A 12, 16, or 20 gauge boxlock or sidelock double-barrel shotgun available in a variety of barrel lengths, with double triggers and automatic ejectors. Blued with a checkered straight stock. The sidelock version is worth approximately 20 percent more than the values listed. The basic Model 3 was offered in a variety of grades featuring different amounts of engraving and better quality wood. These shotguns are listed under the model designations of 4 to 12E.

Exc.	V.G.	Good	Fair	Poor
600	500	450	350	300

Model 4

Exc.	V.G.	Good	Fair	Poor
600	550	475	400	300

Model 4E (Auto-ejectors)

Exc.	V.G.	Good	Fair	Poor
675	625	550	450	350

Model 203

Exc.	V.G.	Good	Fair	Poor
650	600	525	425	325

Model 203E

Exc.	V.G.	Good	Fair	Poor
700	650	575	475	375

Model 6E

Exc.	V.G.	Good	Fair	Poor
800	750	625	525	425

Model 7E

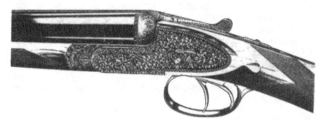

Exc.	V.G.	Good	Fair	Poor
850	800	675	575	475

Model 10E

Exc.	V.G.	Good	Fair	Poor
1750	1500	1250	950	750

Model 11E

Exc.	V.G.	Good	Fair	Poor
1850	1600	1350	1150	850

Model 12E

Exc.	V.G.	Good	Fair	Poor
2200	1850	1500	1300	1000

SAVAGE ARMS CORPORATION
Utica, New York
Westfield, Massachusetts

Established in 1894 by Arthur W. Savage, this company has manufactured a wide variety of firearms, of which its Model 99 is the best known. By 1915, Savage Arms was manufacturing centerfire and rimfire rifles, pistols, and ammunition. During World War I the company produced the Lewis machine guns. In 1920 Savage purchased J. Stevens Arms Company which was associated with Harry Pope, the famous barrel maker. Later in the decade the company acquired the Page Lewis Company, Davis-Warner, Crescent Firearms, and A.H. Fox. At one time Savage was the largest firearms manufacturing company in the free world. During World War II Savage/Stevens produced military small arms and machine guns. In 1947 the Sporting Arms division moved to Chicopee Falls, Mass., where it was incorporated into Stevens Arms Company. In 1960 the entire operation was moved to Westfield, Mass.

Model 1895
A .303 Savage caliber lever-action rifle with a 26" or 30" barrel and 5-shot rotary magazine. Identifiable by the hole in the breechbolt. The barrel marked "Savage Repeating Arms Co. Utica, N.Y. U.S.A. Pat. Feb. 7, 1893, July 25, 1893. CAL. .303." Blued with a walnut stock. Approximately 8,000 were manufactured between 1895 and 1899.

Exc.	V.G.	Good	Fair	Poor
3000	2000	1200	600	200

NOTE: 22" or 30" barrel add 10 percent.

Model 1899-A 26" Round Barrel Rifle
A .25-35, .30-30, .303 Savage, .32-40 or .38-55, .300 Savage caliber lever-action rifle with 26" barrel marked "Savage Arms Company, Utica, N.Y. Pat. Feb. 7, 1893, July 25.'93, Oct.3.'99 .CAL.30." Manufactured between 1899 and 1926/27. Blued with a walnut stock. Serial number range 10000 to 300000. Block cocking indicator on bolt to s/n 90000 then changed to pin indicator on tang.

Exc.	V.G.	Good	Fair	Poor
1200	800	500	250	100

NOTE: Add 50 percent for .25-35, .32-40, and .38-55 calibers.

Model 1899-A 22" Barrel Short Rifle
Chambered for .303, .30-30, .25-35, .32-40, .38-55. Serial number range from 10000 to 220000. Produced from 1899 to 1922. Same cocking indicator as the 1899-A rifle.

Exc.	V.G.	Good	Fair	Poor
1200	900	600	300	100

NOTE: Add 50 percent for .25-35, .32-40, and .38-55 calibers.

Model 1899-B 26" Octagon Barrel Rifle
In calibers .303, .30-30, .25-35, .32-40, .38-55. Manufactured between 1899 and 1915. Serial number range 10000 to 175000. Same cocking indicator as 1899-A rifle.

Exc.	V.G.	Good	Fair	Poor
1600	1100	700	350	150

NOTE: Add 50 percent for .25-35, .32-40, and .38-55 calibers.

Model 1899-C 26" Half Octagon Barrel Rifle
In calibers .303, .30-30, .25-35, .32-40, .38-55. Manufactured between 1899 and 1915. Serial number range 10000 to 175000. Same cocking indicator as 1899-A rifle.

Exc.	V.G.	Good	Fair	Poor
2000	1500	1000	400	150

NOTE: Add 50 percent for .25-35, .32-40, and .38-55 calibers.

Model 1899-CD Deluxe Rifle
In calibers .303, .30-30, .25-35, .32-40, .38-55. Serial number range 50000 to 175000. Built from 1905 to 1917. Same cocking indicator as the 1899-A rifle. The standard Deluxe 1899 rifle with 26" round, octagon, or half octagon barrel with pistol grip stock and checkering. Takedown barrel or short 22" barrel.

Courtesy Rock Island Auction Company

Exc.	V.G.	Good	Fair	Poor
3000	2000	1500	600	250

NOTE: Add 30 percent for .25-35, .32-40, and .38-55 calibers.

Model 1899-D Military Musket
Chambered for .303 Savage only with 28" barrel. Fitted with full military stocks. Produced from 1899 to 1915. Several hundred produced for Canadian Home Guard during WWI. These will have rack number on buttplate.

Exc.	V.G.	Good	Fair	Poor
4500	3000	1500	700	300

Model 1899-F Saddle Ring Carbine
Fitted with 20" barrel only in calibers .303, .30-30, .25-35, .32-40, .38-55. Built from 1899 to 1919 in serial number range 19000 to 200000. Same cocking indicator as 1899-A rifle. Earliest style with barrel band is rarest variation.

Exc.	V.G.	Good	Fair	Poor
1500	900	500	300	100

NOTE: Add 100 percent for .25-35, .32-40, and .38-55 calibers. Add 200 percent for barrel band carbine.

Model 1899-H Featherweight Rifle
Chambered for .303, .30-30, .25-35, and .22 HP Savage in 20" barrel. Serial number range 50000 to 220000. Built from 1905 to 1919. The revolutionary .22 HP cartridge was introduced in this model in 1912. Most 1899-Hs are found with takedown barrels.

Exc.	V.G.	Good	Fair	Poor
1600	1200	600	300	100

NOTE: Add 50 percent for .25-35, add 25 percent for .22HP.

SAVAGE SHOTGUNS

Model 411 Upland Sporter
SEE—Stevens.

Model 420
A 12, 16, or 20 gauge boxlock over-and-under shotgun with 26", 28", or 30" barrels, double triggers and extractors. Manufactured between 1937 and 1943.

Exc.	V.G.	Good	Fair	Poor
500	400	300	200	150

Model 420 with Single Trigger

Exc.	V.G.	Good	Fair	Poor
500	400	300	200	150

Model 430
As above, with a checkered walnut stock and solid barrel rib. Produced from 1937 to 1943.

Exc.	V.G.	Good	Fair	Poor
550	450	350	200	150

Model 430 with Single Trigger

Exc.	V.G.	Good	Fair	Poor
600	450	300	200	150

Model 320
This is a side-by-side model.

Exc.	V.G.	Good	Fair	Poor
800	650	500	400	300

Model 412
.410 bore adapter.

Exc.	V.G.	Good	Fair	Poor
80	60	50	40	30

Model 412F
.410 bore adapter.

Exc.	V.G.	Good	Fair	Poor
50	45	40	35	25

Model 220
A 12, 16, 20 or .410 bore boxlock single barrel shotgun with 26" to 32" barrels. Blued with a walnut stock. Manufactured between 1938 and 1965.

Exc.	V.G.	Good	Fair	Poor
100	80	70	50	35

Model 550
A 12 or 20 gauge boxlock side-by-side double-barrel shotgun with 26", 28", or 30" barrels, single triggers and automatic ejectors. Blued with a hardwood stock. Manufactured between 1971 and 1973. Barrels were built by Valmet.

Exc.	V.G.	Good	Fair	Poor
500	400	300	200	150

(SAVAGE) FOX B MODELS
The Fox Model B was introduced about 1939 by Savage for the hunter who wanted better fit and finish than offered by the Stevens brand Model 530. It was made in many variations until 1988.

Fox Model B—Utica, NY

NIB	Exc.	V.G.	Good	Fair	Poor
1000	800	600	450	400	350

Fox Model B—Chicopee Falls, Mass. (later Westfield, Mass.)

NIB	Exc.	V.G.	Good	Fair	Poor
800	750	500	400	350	300

Fox Model B—Single Trigger

NIB	Exc.	V.G.	Good	Fair	Poor
900	800	600	500	400	300

Fox Model BDL

NIB	Exc.	V.G.	Good	Fair	Poor
1000	800	700	600	400	350

Fox Model BDE

Courtesy Nick Niles, Paul Goodwin photo

NIB	Exc.	V.G.	Good	Fair	Poor
1000	800	700	600	400	350

Fox Model BST

NIB	Exc.	V.G.	Good	Fair	Poor
800	700	600	500	400	300

Fox Model BSE

NIB	Exc.	V.G.	Good	Fair	Poor
1000	750	650	550	450	350

Fox Model BE

NIB	Exc.	V.G.	Good	Fair	Poor
1000	800	600	450	400	350

SAVAGE & NORTH
Middletown, Connecticut

Figure 8 Revolver

A .36 caliber percussion revolver with a 7" octagonal barrel and 6-shot cylinder. The barrel marked "E. Savage, Middletown. CT./H.S. North. Patented June 17, 1856." The four models of this revolver are as follows: (1) With a rounded brass frame, and the mouths of the chamber fitting into the end of the barrel breech; (2) with a rounded iron frame and a modified loading lever that is marked "H.S. North, Patented April 6, 1858"; (3) with a flat-sided brass frame having a round recoil shield; (4) with an iron frame. Approximately 400 of these revolvers were manufactured between 1856 and 1859.

First Model

Courtesy Greg Martin Auctions

Exc.	V.G.	Good	Fair	Poor
—	—	15000	6500	1500

Second Model

Exc.	V.G.	Good	Fair	Poor
—	—	9000	3500	850

Third Model

Exc.	V.G.	Good	Fair	Poor
—	—	9000	3500	850

Fourth Model

Exc.	V.G.	Good	Fair	Poor
—	—	10000	4000	1000

SAVAGE REVOLVING FIREARMS CO.
Middletown, Connecticut

Navy Revolver

A .36 caliber double-action percussion revolver with a 7" octagonal barrel and 6-shot cylinder. The frame marked "Savage R.F.A. Co./H.S. North Patented June 17, 1856/Jan. 18, 1859, May 15, 1860." Approximately 20,000 were manufactured between 1861 and 1865, of which about 12,000 were purchased by the U.S. Government.

Exc.	V.G.	Good	Fair	Poor
—	—	4250	1750	700

SEMMERLING
Waco, Texas
SEE—American Derringer Corporation

SHARPS RIFLE MANUFACTURING COMPANY
Hartford, Connecticut

The first Sharps rifles to be manufactured were made by A.S. Nippes of Mill Creek, Pennsylvania. Later they were made by Robbins & Lawrence of Windsor, Vermont. It was not until 1855 that Sharps established his own factory in Hartford, Connecticut. After his death in 1874, the company was reorganized as the Sharps Rifle Company and remained in Hartford until 1876 when it moved to Bridgeport, Connecticut. It effectively ceased operations in 1880.

NOTE: Sharps rifles and carbines were produced in an almost endless variety. Collectors should note that particular features and calibers can drastically affect the value of any given Sharps. They are, therefore, strongly advised to read: Frank Sellers, Sharps Firearms (North Hollywood, California: 1978).

The following descriptions are just a brief guide and are by no means exhaustive. Be advised that single-shot rifles will have a higher value in the western U.S. than in the eastern U.S.

Model 1849

A breechloading .44 caliber percussion rifle with a 30" barrel having a wooden cleaning rod mounted beneath it. The breech is activated by the trigger guard lever, and there is an automatic disk-type capping device mounted on the right side of the receiver. The finish is blued and case colored. The stock is walnut with a brass patch box, buttplate, and forend cap. It is marked "Sharps Patent 1848." There were approximately 200 manufactured in 1849 and 1850 by the A.S. Nippes Company.

Exc.	V.G.	Good	Fair	Poor
—	—	18000	7500	1500

Model 1850

As above, with a Maynard priming mechanism mounted on the breech. Marked "Sharps Patent 1848" on the breech and the barrel "Manufactured by A.S. Nippes Mill Creek, Pa." The priming device marked "Maynard Patent 1845." There were approximately 200 manufactured in 1850. This model is also known as the 2nd Model Sharps.

Exc.	V.G.	Good	Fair	Poor
—	—	15000	6000	1200

Model 1851 Carbine

A single-shot breechloading percussion rifle in .36, .44, or .52 caliber with a 21.75" barrel and Maynard tape priming device. Blued and case hardened with a walnut stock and forearm held on by a single barrel band. The buttplate and barrel band are brass, and the military versions feature a brass patch box. The tang marked "C. Sharps Patent 1848," the barrel "Robbins & Lawrence," and the priming device "Edward Maynard Patentee 1845." Approximately 1,800 carbines and

180 rifles were manufactured by Robbins & Lawrence in Windsor, Vermont, in 1851. Those bearing U.S. inspection marks are worth approximately 75 percent more than the values listed.

Exc.	V.G.	Good	Fair	Poor
—	—	9500	4250	1000

Model 1852
Similar to the above, but with Sharps' Patent Pellet Primer. The barrel marked "Sharps Rifle Manufg. Co. Hartford, Conn." Blued, case hardened, brass furniture and a walnut stock. Manufactured in carbine, rifle, sporting rifle and shotgun form. Approximately 4,600 carbines and 600 rifles were made between 1853 and 1855.

Military Carbine
Exc.	V.G.	Good	Fair	Poor
—	—	6750	3000	750

Military Rifle
27" barrel, bayonet lug.
Exc.	V.G.	Good	Fair	Poor
—	—	9750	4000	1000

Sporting Rifle
Exc.	V.G.	Good	Fair	Poor
—	—	4250	1750	500

Shotgun
Exc.	V.G.	Good	Fair	Poor
—	—	3250	1250	500

Model 1853
As above, but without the spring retainer for the lever hinge being mounted in the forestock. Approximately 10,500 carbines and 3,000 rifles were made between 1854 and 1858.

Military Carbine
Exc.	V.G.	Good	Fair	Poor
—	—	6250	2750	750

Military Rifle
Exc.	V.G.	Good	Fair	Poor
—	—	9500	4000	1000

Sporting Rifle
Exc.	V.G.	Good	Fair	Poor
—	—	2750	1250	450

Shotgun
Exc.	V.G.	Good	Fair	Poor
—	—	2500	1000	450

Model 1855
As above, in .52 caliber and fitted with a Maynard tape primer that is marked "Edward Maynard Patentee 1845." Approximately 700 were made between 1855 and 1856.

Exc.	V.G.	Good	Fair	Poor
—	—	10500	4250	1000

Model 1855 U.S. Navy Rifle
As above, with a 28" barrel, full-length stock and bearing U.S. Navy inspection marks. Approximately 260 were made in 1855.

Exc.	V.G.	Good	Fair	Poor
—	—	10500	4000	1000

Model 1855 British Carbine
The Model 1855 with British inspection marks. Approximately 6,800 were made between 1855 and 1857.

Exc.	V.G.	Good	Fair	Poor
—	—	6250	3000	850

SHARPS STRAIGHT BREECH MODELS
Similar to the above models, but with the breech opening cut on an almost vertical angle.

Model 1859 Carbine
22" barrel, brass mountings.
Exc.	V.G.	Good	Fair	Poor
—	—	6250	2500	500

Model 1859 Carbine
Iron mountings.
Exc.	V.G.	Good	Fair	Poor
—	—	3250	1500	500

Model 1863 Carbine

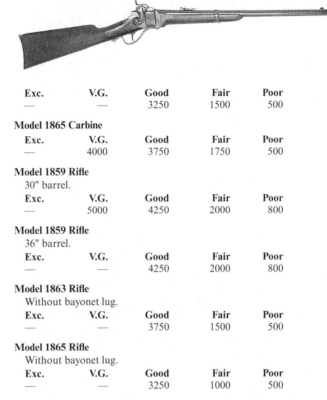

Exc.	V.G.	Good	Fair	Poor
—	—	3250	1500	500

Model 1865 Carbine
Exc.	V.G.	Good	Fair	Poor
—	4000	3750	1750	500

Model 1859 Rifle
30" barrel.
Exc.	V.G.	Good	Fair	Poor
—	5000	4250	2000	800

Model 1859 Rifle
36" barrel.
Exc.	V.G.	Good	Fair	Poor
—	—	4250	2000	800

Model 1863 Rifle
Without bayonet lug.
Exc.	V.G.	Good	Fair	Poor
—	—	3750	1500	500

Model 1865 Rifle
Without bayonet lug.
Exc.	V.G.	Good	Fair	Poor
—	—	3250	1000	500

Sporting Rifle
As above, with octagonal barrels, set triggers and finely figured walnut stocks. The Model 1853 Sporting rifle was built as a special order. About 32 were produced. The Model 1863 Sporting Rifle was also built on special order. About 16 were produced. No two of this model are alike. All reside in museums or collections.

Exc.	V.G.	Good	Fair	Poor

Too Rare To Price

Coffee-Mill Model
Some Sharps' carbines were fitted with coffee-mill style grinding devices set into their buttstocks. CAUTION: These arms are exceptionally rare and extreme caution should be exercised prior to purchase. Fakes exist.

Exc.	V.G.	Good	Fair	Poor
—	—	42500	15000	—

Metallic Cartridge Conversions
In 1867 approximately 32,000 Model 1859, 1863 and 1865 Sharps were altered to .52-70 rimfire and centerfire caliber.

Exc.	V.G.	Good	Fair	Poor
—	—	4250	2000	600

Model 1869
A .40-50 to .50-70 caliber model produced in a military form with 26", 28", or 30" barrels; as a carbine with 21" or 24" barrels and in a sporting version with various barrel lengths and a forend stock fitted with a pewter tip. Approximately 650 were made.

Carbine
.50-70, saddle ring on frame.
Exc.	V.G.	Good	Fair	Poor
—	—	4250	1750	500

Military Rifle
.50-70, 30" barrel with three barrel bands.

Exc.	V.G.	Good	Fair	Poor
—	—	5250	2000	800

Sporting Rifle
26" barrel, .44-77 and .50-70.

Exc.	V.G.	Good	Fair	Poor
—	—	6500	3000	950

Model 1870 Springfield Altered
Chambered for .50-70 caliber and fitted with a 35.5" barrel with two barrel bands, walnut stock, case hardened lock and breechlock. Buttplate stamped "US." Also built for Army trials with 22" barrel converted to centerfire.

First Type
Most common, straight breech.

Exc.	V.G.	Good	Fair	Poor
—	—	3750	1750	500

Second Type
Model 1874 action, serial #1 to 300.

Exc.	V.G.	Good	Fair	Poor
—	—	6000	2750	750

Carbine
22" barrel converted to centerfire.

Exc.	V.G.	Good	Fair	Poor
—	—	8250	5000	1250

Model 1874
This model was manufactured in a variety of calibers, barrel lengths, and stock styles. The barrel markings are of three forms: initially, "Sharps Rifle Manufg. Co. Hartford, Conn."; then, "Sharps Rifle Co. Hartford, Conn."; and finally "Sharps Rifle Co. Bridgeport, Conn." As of 1876 "Old Reliable" was stamped on the barrels. This marking is usually found on Bridgeport-marked rifles only. The major styles of this model are as follows:

Military Carbine
.50-70, 21" barrel (460 made).

Exc.	V.G.	Good	Fair	Poor
—	—	5500	2750	750

Military Rifle
In .45-70 and .50-70 centerfire caliber with a 30" barrel and full-length forend secured by three barrel bands. Approximately 1,800 made.

Exc.	V.G.	Good	Fair	Poor
—	—	5000	2250	750

Hunter's Rifle
In .40, .44, .45-70, and .50-70 caliber with 26", 28", or 30" round barrels having open sights. Approximately 600 were manufactured.

Exc.	V.G.	Good	Fair	Poor
—	—	6250	2750	800

Business Rifle
In .40-70 and .45-75 Sharps caliber with a 26", 28", or 30" round barrel, adjustable sights and double-set triggers. Approximately 1,600 manufactured.

Exc.	V.G.	Good	Fair	Poor
—	—	6000	3250	1000

Sporting Rifle
Offered in a variety of calibers, barrel lengths, barrel weights, barrel styles and stock styles. Approximately 6,000 were manufactured.

Exc.	V.G.	Good	Fair	Poor
—	—	8500	4000	1500

Creedmoor Rifle
With a checkered pistol grip stock, vernier sights, combination wind gauge and spirit level front sight, set trigger and shotgun style butt. Approximately 150 were made.

Exc.	V.G.	Good	Fair	Poor
—	—	17500	8500	2000

Mid-Range Rifle
Similar to the above, with a crescent buttplate. Approximately 180 were made.

Exc.	V.G.	Good	Fair	Poor
—	—	15000	6500	1500

Long-Range Rifle
As above with a 34" octagonal barrel. Approximately 425 were manufactured.

Exc.	V.G.	Good	Fair	Poor
—	—	16500	6000	1500

Schuetzen Rifle
Similar to the above, with a checkered pistol grip stock and forend, a large Schuetzen style buttplate, double-set triggers and a vernier tang sight. Approximately 70 were manufactured.

Courtesy Bonhams & Butterfields

Exc.	V.G.	Good	Fair	Poor
—	—	15000	6500	2000

Model 1877
Similar to the Model 1874, and in .45-70 caliber with a 34" or 36" barrel which is marked "Sharps Rifle Co. Bridgeport, Conn. Old Reliable." Approximately 100 were manufactured in 1877 and 1878.

Exc.	V.G.	Good	Fair	Poor
—	30000	10000	5000	2000

Model 1878 Sharps-Borchardt
An internal hammer breechloading rifle manufactured from 1878 to approximately 1880. The frame marked "Borchardt Patent Sharps Rifle Co. Bridgeport Conn. U.S.A."

NOTE: Be advised that the actions on Borchardt Sporting Rifles are worth a minimum of $750. Military actions are not as difficult to locate as Sporting actions. For the sake of continuity rifles in poor condition, but with usable actions, are priced at the minimum of $750.

Carbine
Approximately 385 were made in .45-70 caliber with a 24" barrel. The forend is secured by one barrel band.

Exc.	V.G.	Good	Fair	Poor
—	—	3750	1500	750

Military Rifle
Approximately 12,000 were made in .45-70 caliber with 32.25" barrels and full stocks secured by two barrel bands.

Exc.	V.G.	Good	Fair	Poor
—	3000	1250	600	750

Sporting Rifle
Approximately 1,600 were made in .45-70 caliber with 30" round or octagonal barrels.

Exc.	V.G.	Good	Fair	Poor
—	6000	2500	800	750

Hunter's Rifle
Approximately 60 were made in .40 caliber with 26" barrels and plain walnut stocks.

Exc.	V.G.	Good	Fair	Poor
—	4500	1750	700	750

Business Rifle
Approximately 90 were made with 28" barrels in .40 caliber.

Exc.	V.G.	Good	Fair	Poor
—	4500	2000	1000	750

Officer's Rifle
Approximately 50 were made in .45-70 caliber with 32" barrels and checkered walnut stocks.

Exc.	V.G.	Good	Fair	Poor
—	7500	3750	1500	750

Express Rifle
Approximately 30 were made in .45-70 caliber with 26" barrels, set triggers and checkered walnut stocks.

Exc.	V.G.	Good	Fair	Poor
—	12500	6000	2000	800

Short-Range Rifle
Approximately 155 were made in .40 caliber with 26" barrels, vernier rear sights, wind gauge front sight and a checkered walnut stock.

Exc.	V.G.	Good	Fair	Poor
—	7500	3750	1000	800

Mid-Range Rifle
Similar to the above, with a 30" barrel. Approximately 250 were manufactured.

Exc.	V.G.	Good	Fair	Poor
10000	7000	4000	2000	900

Long-Range Rifle
Similar to the above, with different sights. Approximately 230 were manufactured.

Exc.	V.G.	Good	Fair	Poor
—	16000	6500	2500	900

C. Sharps & Company and Sharps & Hankins Company Breechloading, Single-Shot Pistol
A .31, .34, or .36 caliber breechloading percussion pistol with 5" or 6.5" round barrels. Blued, case hardened with walnut stock.

Exc.	V.G.	Good	Fair	Poor
—	—	5000	2000	600

Pistol-Grip Rifle
A .31 or .38 caliber breechloading percussion rifle resembling the above. Manufactured in a variety of barrel lengths. Blued, case hardened with a walnut stock having German silver mounts.

Exc.	V.G.	Good	Fair	Poor
—	—	4750	2500	750

Percussion Revolver
A .25 caliber percussion revolver with a 3" octagonal barrel and 6-shot cylinder. Blued with walnut grips. The barrel marked "C. Sharps & Co., Phila. Pa." Approximately 2,000 were manufactured between 1857 and 1858.

Exc.	V.G.	Good	Fair	Poor
—	—	3000	1250	500

4-Shot Pepperbox Pistols
Between 1859 and 1874, these companies manufactured 4 barrel cartridge pocket pistols in a variety of calibers, barrel lengths and finishes. The barrels slide forward for loading. The major models are as follows:

Model 1
Manufactured by C. Sharps & Co. and in .22 rimfire caliber.

Exc.	V.G.	Good	Fair	Poor
—	—	600	250	100

Model 2
As above, in .30 rimfire caliber.

Exc.	V.G.	Good	Fair	Poor
—	—	600	250	100

Model 3
Manufactured by Sharps & Hankins and marked "Address Sharps & Hankins Philadelphia Penn." on the frame. Caliber. 32 short rimfire.

Exc.	V.G.	Good	Fair	Poor
—	—	750	300	150

Model 4
Similar to the above, in .32 Long rimfire and with a rounded bird's-head grip.

Exc.	V.G.	Good	Fair	Poor
—	—	750	300	150

Model 1861 Navy Rifle
A .54 Sharps & Hankins caliber breechloading single-shot rifle with a 32.75" barrel and full stock secured by three barrel bands. Blued, case hardened with a walnut stock. Approximately 700 were made in 1861 and 1862.

Exc.	V.G.	Good	Fair	Poor
—	—	5000	2000	700

Model 1862 Navy Carbine
A .54 caliber breechloading carbine with a 24" leather covered barrel. Case hardened with a walnut stock. The frame marked "Sharps & Hankins Philada." Approximately 8,000 were manufactured between 1861 and 1862.

Exc.	V.G.	Good	Fair	Poor
—	—	5000	2000	700

Short Cavalry Carbine
Similar to the above, with a 19" blued barrel. Approximately 500 were manufactured.

Exc.	V.G.	Good	Fair	Poor
—	—	5000	2000	700

Army Model
Similar to the above, with a 24" barrel that does not have a leather covering. Approximately 500 were purchased by the Army.

Exc.	V.G.	Good	Fair	Poor
—	—	4750	1750	700

SHATTUCK, C. S.
Hatfield, Massachusetts

Double-Barrel Shotguns
In addition to single-barrel shotguns, Shattuck made about 1,000 hammerless doubles.

Exc.	V.G.	Good	Fair	Poor
1000	500	400	300	200

Boom
A .22 caliber spur trigger revolver with a 2" octagonal barrel and 6-shot cylinder. Nickel-plated with rosewood or walnut grips. The barrel marked "Boom" and "Pat. Nov. 4. 1879." Manufactured during the 1880s.

Exc.	V.G.	Good	Fair	Poor
—	400	150	100	75

Pocket Revolver
A .32 caliber spur trigger revolver with a 3.5" octagonal barrel and 5-shot cylinder. Nickel-plated with hard rubber grips. The barrel marked "C. S. Shattuck Hatfield, Mass. Pat. Nov. 4, 1879." Manufactured during the 1880s.

Exc.	V.G.	Good	Fair	Poor
—	500	200	150	100

SHAW & LEDOYT
Stafford, Connecticut

Under Hammer Pistol
A .31 caliber under hammer percussion pistol with a 2.5" to 3.5" half-octagonal barrel. Blued with a brass mounted walnut grip. The frame marked "Shaw & LeDoyt/Stafford. Conn." Manufactured during the 1850s.

Exc.	V.G.	Good	Fair	Poor
—	—	1150	500	150

SHAWK & McLANAHAN
St. Louis, Missouri

Navy Revolver
A .36 caliber percussion revolver with an 8" round barrel and 6-shot cylinder. Blued with a brass frame and walnut grips. Marked "Shawk & McLanahan, St. Louis, Carondelet, Mo." Produced in limited quantities prior to 1860. Prospective purchasers are advised to secure a qualified appraisal prior to acquisition.

Exc.	V.G.	Good	Fair	Poor
—	—	10500	5000	2000

SHILOH RIFLE MFG. CO., INC.
Big Timber, Montana

Established in Farmingdale, New York, in 1976, this company moved to Big Timber, Montana, in 1983 with the name Shiloh Products. It changed its name to Shiloh Rifle Manufacturing Co. in that same year. In 1985 the company began marketing its products factory direct. In 1991 Robert, Phyllis, and Kirk Bryan purchased the company. Those interested in the Sharps reproduction rifles manufactured by this company are advised to contact them in Big Timber.

NOTE: The company will build a rifle to customers' specifications. It is therefore possible that many of these rifles have special-order features that are not reflected in the base model price.

Model 1863 Military Rifle
A .54 caliber percussion rifle with a 30" barrel, single- or double-set triggers and full-length walnut stock secured by three barrel bands.

NIB	Exc.	V.G.	Good	Fair	Poor
1750	1400	1000	—	—	—

Model 1863 Sporting Rifle
As above, with a 30" octagonal barrel, sporting sights and a half-length stock.

NIB	Exc.	V.G.	Good	Fair	Poor
1500	1200	950	—	—	—

Model 1863 Military Carbine
The Model 1863 with a 22" round barrel and carbine stock secured by one barrel band.

NIB	Exc.	V.G.	Good	Fair	Poor
1500	1200	950	—	—	—

Model 1862 Confederate Robinson
As above, with a 21.5" barrel, brass buttplate and barrel band.

NIB	Exc.	V.G.	Good	Fair	Poor
800	750	650	550	450	400

Model 1874 Creedmore Target Rifle
This model is furnished with a 32" 1/2 round, 1/2 octagon barrel. Extra-fancy wood stock with pistol grip, no cheek rest, and shotgun butt. Single trigger. No sights.

NIB	Exc.	V.G.	Good	Fair	Poor
2440	1950	1500	1000	—	—

Model 1874 Buffalo Rifle (Quigley)
Offered in .45-70 or .45-110 with 34" heavy octagon barrel. Mid-range tang sight with globe front sight. Semi buckhorn rear sight. Double-set triggers. Military buttstock with patch box. No cheek rest and straight-grip stock.

NIB	Exc.	V.G.	Good	Fair	Poor
2850	2300	1750	—	—	—

Model 1874 Long Range Express Rifle
Manufactured in a variety of calibers with a 34" octagonal barrel, double-set triggers, vernier rear sight and globe front sight.

NIB	Exc.	V.G.	Good	Fair	Poor
1600	1300	950	600	—	—

Model 1874 Montana Roughrider Rifle
As above, with either octagonal or half-octagonal barrels ranging in lengths from 24" to 34".

NIB	Exc.	V.G.	Good	Fair	Poor
1540	1200	950	600	—	—

The Saddle Rifle
As above, with a 26" barrel and shotgun butt.

NIB	Exc.	V.G.	Good	Fair	Poor
1500	1200	950	600	—	—

No. 1 Sporter Deluxe Rifle
Similar to the above, with a 30" octagonal barrel.

NIB	Exc.	V.G.	Good	Fair	Poor
1700	1350	950	700	—	—

No. 3 Standard Sporter
As above, with a military-style stock.

NIB	Exc.	V.G.	Good	Fair	Poor
1500	1200	950	600	—	—

The Business Rifle
As above, with a heavy 28" barrel.

NIB	Exc.	V.G.	Good	Fair	Poor
1500	1200	950	600	—	—

Model 1874 Military Rifle
The Model 1874 with a 30" round barrel, military sights and full-length stocks secured by three barrel bands.

NIB	Exc.	V.G.	Good	Fair	Poor
850	800	700	600	500	400

Model 1874 Carbine
Similar to the above, with a 24" round barrel.

NIB	Exc.	V.G.	Good	Fair	Poor
1500	1200	950	600	—	—

The Jaeger
The Model 1874 with a 26" half-octagonal barrel, open sights and pistol-grip stock with a shotgun butt.

NIB	Exc.	V.G.	Good	Fair	Poor
800	750	650	550	450	400

Hartford Model
A reproduction of the Sharps Hartford Model.

NIB	Exc.	V.G.	Good	Fair	Poor
1700	1350	950	600	—	—

Model 1874 Military Carbine
Similar to the Military Rifle, but with a 22" round barrel.

NIB	Exc.	V.G.	Good	Fair	Poor
1500	1100	800	600	—	—

SIMPSON, R. J.
New York, New York

Pocket Pistol
A .41 caliber single-shot percussion pocket pistol with a 2.5" barrel, German silver mounts and walnut stock. Manufactured during the 1850s and 1860s.

Exc.	V.G.	Good	Fair	Poor
—	—	1750	700	300

SIMSON & COMPANY
Suhl, Germany
SEE—Luger

NOTE: The models listed and pictured are taken from a mid-1930s Simson catalog. Because the company was Jewish-owned the Nazis took control in the mid-1930s changing the name to "Berlin Suhler Waffen." Prices are estimates.

SHOTGUNS

Model 235
Side-by-side shotgun chambered for 12 or 16 gauge with Anson & Deely action. Scalloped frame with scroll engraving. Walnut stock with pistol grip. Double triggers.

Exc.	V.G.	Good	Fair	Poor
900	700	550	400	350

Model 73
Similar to the above model but with more scroll engraving coverage.

Exc.	V.G.	Good	Fair	Poor
950	750	600	400	350

Model 74

This model features deep cut game scene engraving. Select walnut stock with fine-line checkering.

Exc.	V.G.	Good	Fair	Poor
1100	800	600	450	350

Model 74E

Same as above but with automatic ejectors.

Exc.	V.G.	Good	Fair	Poor
1200	850	650	450	350

Model 76

This side-by-side model is fitted with game scene engraved side plates and offered in 12 or 16 gauge.

Exc.	V.G.	Good	Fair	Poor
1400	1100	800	550	400

Model 76E

As above but with automatic ejectors.

Courtesy Jim Cate

Exc.	V.G.	Good	Fair	Poor
1500	1200	850	550	400

SMITH AMERICAN ARMS COMPANY
Springfield, Massachusetts

Smith Carbine

A .50 caliber breechloading percussion carbine with a 21.75" round barrel having an octagonal breech. Blued, case hardened with a walnut stock. The barrel marked "Address/Poultney & Trimble/Baltimore, USA" and the frame "Smith's Patent/June 23, 1857" as well as "American Arms Co./Chicopee Falls." Approximately 30,000 were manufactured, most of which were purchased by the United States government. The sales agents were Poultney & Trimble of Baltimore, Maryland.

Exc.	V.G.	Good	Fair	Poor
—	3500	1600	500	200

SMITH, L. C.
Syracuse, New York
Hunter Arms Company
Fulton, New York

One of the finest American-made double-barrel shotguns and very collectible in today's market. It was manufactured between 1880 and 1888 in Syracuse, New York; and between 1890 and 1945, in Fulton, New York, by the Hunter Arms Company. In 1945 Marlin Firearms Company acquired Hunter Arms, and the L.C. Smith was made until 1951. In 1968 the L.C. Smith was resurrected for five years, and production ceased totally in 1973. The values given are approximate for standard production models; and we strongly feel that competent, individual appraisals should be secured, especially on the rarer and higher grade models, if a transaction is contemplated.

The values given are for fluid steel, hammerless guns only. Damascus-barreled guns have become collectible if they are in very good or better condition, and values are approximately the same as for the fluid steel models. Damascus guns in less than good condition are worth considerably less.

Early Hammerless Shotguns

The following models were manufactured between 1890 and 1913. They are chambered for 10, 12, 16, and 20 gauge and were produced with various barrel lengths and choke combinations. They feature full sidelock actions. The difference in the models and their values is based on the degree of ornamentation and the quality of materials and workmanship utilized in their construction. The general values furnished are for 10, 12 or 16 gauge guns only. 20 gauge add 50 percent. Single-selective trigger add $250. Automatic ejectors add 30 percent.

00 Grade
60,000 manufactured.

Exc.	V.G.	Good	Fair	Poor
1500	1250	1000	650	400

0 Grade
30,000 manufactured.

Exc.	V.G.	Good	Fair	Poor
1600	1350	1050	700	450

No. 1 Grade
10,000 manufactured.

Exc.	V.G.	Good	Fair	Poor
2500	2000	1500	800	550

No. 2 Grade
13,000 manufactured.

Exc.	V.G.	Good	Fair	Poor
3000	2250	1750	900	700

No. 3 Grade
4,000 manufactured.

Exc.	V.G.	Good	Fair	Poor
3500	2750	1800	1000	750

Pigeon Grade
1,200 manufactured.

Exc.	V.G.	Good	Fair	Poor
3500	2750	1800	1000	750

No. 4 Grade
500 manufactured.

Exc.	V.G.	Good	Fair	Poor
10000	7500	5000	3000	2000

A-1 Grade
700 manufactured, all damascus, no 20 gauge.

Exc.	V.G.	Good	Fair	Poor
5000	3500	2500	1750	1000

No. 5 Grade
500 manufactured.

Exc.	V.G.	Good	Fair	Poor
8500	7000	5000	2750	2000

Monogram Grade
100 manufactured.

Exc.	V.G.	Good	Fair	Poor
11000	8500	6000	3750	2500

A-2 Grade
200 manufactured.

Exc.	V.G.	Good	Fair	Poor
15000	10000	7500	4500	3750

A-3 Grade
20 manufactured.
This is too rare to generalize a value.

Later Production Hammerless Shotguns

These were manufactured at Fulton, New York, between 1914 and 1951. They are side-by-side double-barrel shotguns chambered for 12, 16, and 20 gauge, as well as the .410. They are offered with various barrel lengths and choke combinations. They feature a full sidelock action and are available with double or single triggers, extractors, and automatic ejectors. The finishes are blued and case colored, with checkered walnut stocks that are of either straight, semi-pistolgrip, or pistolgrip configurations. The various models differ as to the degree of ornamentation and the quality of materials and workmanship utilized in their construction. These are highly collectible American shotguns. Because these guns were manufactured as late as 1951, mint original specimens and even unfired new in the box guns will be offered for sale occasionally. These guns are worth considerably more than excellent condition guns and more than ever an individual, expert authentication and appraisal is recommended if a transaction is anticipated.

The values supplied are for 12 gauge models only. For 16 gauge add 15 percent premium. For 20 gauge add 50 percent premium. For .410 bore add 200 percent premium (field grade), 300 percent to 400 percent for higher grades. Single-selective triggers add $250 premium. For automatic ejectors add 30 percent-premium.

Field Grade

Exc.	V.G.	Good	Fair	Poor
1250	1000	750	500	350

Ideal Grade

Exc.	V.G.	Good	Fair	Poor
1750	1400	1150	700	500

Trap Grade

Exc.	V.G.	Good	Fair	Poor
2200	1750	1450	900	650

Specialty Grade

Exc.	V.G.	Good	Fair	Poor
3000	2500	1750	1000	600

Skeet Special Grade

Courtesy William Hammond

Exc.	V.G.	Good	Fair	Poor
3000	2500	1750	1000	600

Premier Skeet Grade

Exc.	V.G.	Good	Fair	Poor
3000	2500	1750	1000	600

Eagle Grade

Exc.	V.G.	Good	Fair	Poor
4500	3600	2600	1500	1050

Crown Grade

With this grade, automatic ejectors became standard equipment. The .410 is extremely rare in this model and nonexistent in higher grades; there were only six manufactured, and they cannot be generally evaluated.

Exc.	V.G.	Good	Fair	Poor
6000	4500	3750	2750	2000

Monogram Grade

This version is offered standard with automatic ejectors and a single-selective trigger.

Exc.	V.G.	Good	Fair	Poor
12500	10000	7500	5000	3750

There were two higher grades offered: the Premier Grade and the Deluxe Grade. They are extremely rare, and there have not been enough transactions to generally evaluate them.

HUNTER ARMS BOXLOCKS

These shotguns have been maligned over the years being refered to as "cheap boxlocks not to be confused with the L.C. Smith." These guns, in fact, are inexpensive, high quality boxlocks built with quality equal to the Field Grade L.C. Smith. The receiver, forend iron, trigger guard and triggers are all machined from forgings. Durablity of these guns has proven to be excellent.

Fulton Model

A utility side-by-side boxlock shotgun chambered for 12, 16, 20 gauge and .410 bore. It was offered with various barrel length and choke combinations. It has double triggers and extractors with a non-selective single trigger option. Values given are for 12 and 16 gauge only.

Exc.	V.G.	Good	Fair	Poor
500	400	300	225	150

NOTE: For 20 gauge add 50 percent premium. For .410 bore add 250 percent premium. For single trigger add $150.

Fulton Special

A slightly higher grade version of the Fulton Model featuring modest engraving and pointed checkering.

Exc.	V.G.	Good	Fair	Poor
650	550	450	300	200

NOTE: For 20 gauge add 50 percent premium. For single trigger add $200.

Hunter Special

Similar to the Fulton Model but features the L.C. Smith rotary locking bolt.

Exc.	V.G.	Good	Fair	Poor
650	550	450	300	200

NOTE: For 20 gauge add 50 percent premium. For .410 bore add 300 percent premium.

Single Barrel Trap Guns

High quality, break-open, single-shot trap guns chambered for 12 gauge only. They feature 32" or 34" vent rib barrels that are full-choked. They have boxlock actions and are standard with automatic ejectors. The finish is blued and case colored, and they have a checkered walnut stock with a recoil pad. The various models differ in the amount of ornamentation and the quality of the materials and workmanship utilized in their construction. There was a total of approximately 2,650 manufactured between 1917 and 1951. Although these firearms are actually rarer and just as high a quality as their side-by-side counterparts, they are simply not as collectible as the side-by-side variations. It would still behoove the astute firearms investor to secure a qualified, individual appraisal if a transaction is contemplated.

Olympic Grade

Exc.	V.G.	Good	Fair	Poor
1500	1250	950	700	600

Specialty Grade

Exc.	V.G.	Good	Fair	Poor
2000	1750	1300	1000	800

Crown Grade

Exc.	V.G.	Good	Fair	Poor
3500	3000	2250	1500	1250

Monogram Grade

Exc.	V.G.	Good	Fair	Poor
6500	5500	3800	2600	1750

Premier Grade

Exc.	V.G.	Good	Fair	Poor
12000	10000	7000	5000	3000

Deluxe Grade

Exc.	V.G.	Good	Fair	Poor
16000	14000	10500	8000	4500

1968 Model

A side-by-side double-barrel shotgun chambered for 12 gauge with a 28" vent-rib barrel, choked Full and Modified. It features a sidelock action with double triggers and extractors. The finish is blued and case colored, with a checkered walnut stock. This shotgun was manufactured by Marlin between 1968 and 1973.

These are less desirable than earlier models because of manufacturing expedients used. Investment cast receiver rather than machined forgings were used. Cyanide case-hardening replaced bone charcoal hardening and aluminum vent ribs were used. A thin brown polymer layer was used to create the fit between the lock plates and buttstock which is a departure from traditional fitting.

Exc.	V.G.	Good	Fair	Poor
700	600	550	450	300

1968 Deluxe Model
Similar to the 1968 model but features a Simmons floating rib and a beavertail-type forearm. It was manufactured by Marlin between 1971 and 1973.

Exc.	V.G.	Good	Fair	Poor
1000	850	750	600	400

SMITH & WESSON
Springfield, Massachusetts
By Roy G. Jinks, Smith & Wesson Historian

Smith & Wesson was founded by two men who shared the dream of developing a new type of firearm – one capable of being fired repeatedly without the annoyance of having to reload it using loose powder, balls, and a primer. Their idea was to direct the firearms makers out of the era of muzzleloading, which had dominated the firearms industry since the invention of hand cannons in the 14th century.

Their dream became a reality when Horace Smith and Daniel B. Wesson formed their first partnership in 1852 to manufacture a lever-action pistol incorporating a tubular magazine and firing a fully self-contained cartridge. This new repeating pistol could be fired as rapidly as an individual could operate the lever that loaded the pistol and cocked the hammer, making it ready to be fired. The firing power of this lever-action pistol was so impressive that, in 1854 when the gun was reviewed by Scientific America, it was nicknamed the Volcanic since to the reviewer the rapid-fire sequence appeared to have the force of an erupting volcano.

The original site of the Smith & Wesson Arms Company was in Norwich, Connecticut, and the company operated in those facilities until it ran into financial difficulties in 1854. In the reorganization of the company during that year, a new investor, Oliver Winchester, provided the additional financial support to continue the manufacture of this particular type of pistol. The factory was moved to New Haven, Connecticut, the site of some of Winchester's holdings, and at this time the name was changed to Volcanic Repeating Arms Company and Smith & Wesson sold the majority of their interests. It is interesting to note that this early company continued to develop using the original Smith & Wesson patents and emerged in 1866 as the Winchester Repeating Arms Company.

Horace Smith and D.B. Wesson moved from Connecticut to Springfield, Massachusetts, and in 1856 established their company for the purpose of manufacturing a revolving pistol that would fire a small .22 caliber rimfire cartridge, patented by the partners in 1854. This new rimfire cartridge was the beginning of one of the most famous cartridges developed in the world. It was originally called the "Number One Cartridge" but today is more commonly known as the .22 rimfire. The new revolver was called the Model 1 and it gained immediate popularity because of the advantages offered by the new cartridge. In 1859, finding that demand could no longer be met in the small 25-man shop, Smith & Wesson built a new factory located on Stockbridge Street, close to the United States Armory in the center of Springfield, Massachusetts. The factory continued in a progressive manner, improving on the Model 1, and introducing a larger-frame gun more suitable to military and law enforcement use. This revolver was called the Model 2 and used a .32 rimfire cartridge.

The demand for the Smith & Wesson product was greatly accelerated in 1861 with the advent of the Civil War. In fact, by mid-1862, the demand for Smith & Wesson products had grown so great that it exceeded factory capacity, and it was necessary to close the order books and only supply products against its heavy backlog. Wartime production helped firmly establish Smith & Wesson as one of the leading firearm manufacturers in the United States. However, in the post-war depression, Smith & Wesson, like many other businesses, suffered severe business curtailments and sales dropped to only a few guns per month.

By 1867, the partners realized that a new approach was necessary. They had been experimenting with a new design but had lacked the necessary market. For this reason, in April 1867, they authorized Henry W. Hallott to negotiate contracts and establish a market in Europe, and sales agencies in England, France, and Germany. One of Hallott's first functions was to organize a display of Smith & Wesson arms at a major exposition being held in Paris. The display included the total product line as well as some of their highly engraved works of art to further illustrate the quality craftsmen employed by the firm.

The Smith & Wesson arms exhibit was extremely popular and many nations expressed interest in its products. One of the most important persons to view their product line was the Russian Grand Duke Alexis. He was so impressed with Smith & Wesson's revolvers that he purchased several small pistols for himself and his aides. This marketing approach proved highly successful and European orders helped to relieve the effects of the domestic depression. With this new marketplace and the increase in sales, Smith & Wesson introduced their first large-caliber 44 revolver called the Model 3.

The Model 3 was a totally new design known as a "top break" revolver that incorporated a fully automatic ejection system allowing rapid unloading and reloading of cartridges.

One of the first customers to receive the Model 3 was the Russian military attache, General Gorloff. He promptly sent this sample to Russia for evaluation, and it was so well received that in May 1871 the Russian government signed a contract for 20,000 Model 3s, paying Smith & Wesson in advance with gold. This contract proved to be one of many signed with the Russian government but, more significantly, it influenced the total market and soon orders poured into the factory far exceeding its ability to supply handguns. The Model 3 became extremely popular throughout the world and on our own Western frontier. One of the most interesting notes on the Model 3 appeared in an editorial in the Army/Navy Journal shortly after the Custer massacre. This article noted that if Custer and his men had been armed with Schofield's variation of the Smith & Wesson Model 3, rather than the slower-loading Colt Single-Action revolver, they might have possibly survived the Indian attack.

Smith & Wesson continued to grow and in 1880 expanded their line by introducing the first group of "double-action" revolvers, the result of more than four years of extensive research.

In 1899, Smith & Wesson developed one of its most famous revolvers, the .38 Military & Police, which was the predecessor of the Model 10. This revolver was designed to fire another first, the .38 Smith & Wesson Special.

In the summer of 1914 at the request of the British government, Smith & Wesson began development of its first side-swing revolvers in .45 caliber. As WWI was engulfing the European continent, England needed a supply of service revolvers. Smith & Wesson responded by producing more than 75,000 revolvers chambered for the .455 Mark 11 British Service cartridge in slightly more than one year, thus helping to provide the British Army with the finest revolver available in the world.

During the 1930s, Smith & Wesson introduced two more famous revolvers, the K-22 Outdoorsman for the competitive shooter and the .357 Magnum for the law enforcement officers who needed a powerful handgun to continue their fight against crime. The .357 Magnum also was significant as it was the beginning of the era of Magnum handguns —an important first in the growth of handgunning in the world.

As it had done in WWI, Smith & Wesson answered the needs of WWII's fighting forces, and by 1941 its total plant production was geared to supplying arms for the United States and all her allies. By March 1945 when WWII production was ended, Smith & Wesson had supplied 568,204 .38 military and police revolvers to its close ally Great Britain. These revolvers were produced in the British Service caliber of .38/200.

At the close of WWII, Smith & Wesson continued its progressive leadership under the management of Mr. C.R. Hellstrom, who became president in 1946 and the first person outside the Wesson family to serve in this capacity. In 1949, the company moved to a totally new facility in Springfield, Massachusetts, where it has continued to expand. It introduced the first American-made 9mm double-action pistol called the Model 39, followed by the introduction of a gun that has become a legend with sportsmen and gun enthusiasts throughout the world, the Model 29 .44 Magnum.

In 1964 Smith & Wesson entered into a completely new era as the independently owned company was purchased by Bangor Panta Corporation. Bangor Panta, recognizing an even greater potential for this giant of the firearms field, encouraged the president, W.G. Gunn, to further diversify the company. William Gunn succeeded C.R. Hellstrom as president in 1963 following the death of Mr. Hellstrom at the age of 68.

Gunn soon purchased other companies to augment Smith & Wesson's line of handgun and handcuff products to further meet the needs of the law enforcement and sporting markets. By the 1970s Smith & Wesson had increased its products to law enforcement by selling riot control equipment, police Identi-Kit identification equipment, night vision, breath-testing equipment and leather products. The sporting dealers were also now able to purchase not only Smith & Wesson handguns but ammunition, holsters and long guns, thus allowing them to sell a complete line of Smith & Wesson products.

Even with the expansion of Smith & Wesson's product line in other areas, the management in Springfield continued to concentrate on the development of new handguns. In 1965 the firm introduced the first stainless steel revolver, thus changing again the course of firearms history. The 1970s saw the continued development of stainless models and a new 15-shot 9mm autoloading pistol called the Model 59 to meet the requirement of many law enforcement agencies. Smith & Wesson opened the market of police commemorative handguns, allowing departments to purchase specially designed handguns to commemorate department history. These commemoratives helped further establish Smith & Wessons's position with law enforcement by providing the departments with a memento of their history on a fine-quality Smith & Wesson handgun.

The 1970s saw many significant improvements in Smith & Wesson: the further modernization of its manufacturing facilities in Springfield, the development of the stainless steel Model 629 .44 Magnum, the Model 547 9mm revolver using a special patented extractor system. But most important was the development of the Smith & Wesson L frame line producing the Models 581, 586, 681, and 686, which had a significant impact on both the law enforcement and sporting markets to become the most popular new revolver introduced.

With the new L frame models in the 1980s, Smith & Wesson began to consolidate its widely diversified product line by concentrating on those lines that were most profitable and beneficial to the company. Development was begun on a 9mm autoloading pistol to meet the needs of the United States military and a new .45 autoloading pistol called the Model 645.

In January 1984, Lear Siegler Corporation of Santa Monica, California, purchased Bangor Panta, thus acquiring Smith & Wesson. Lear Siegler, in their evaluation of Smith & Wesson, recognized the fact that the company's total strength was in the manufacture and sales of handguns, handcuffs, and police Identi-Kits. Under Lear's direction, Smith & Wesson divested itself of all other unrelated lines to concentrate on the product for which they were famous. This further strengthening their position in the handgun market by concentrating Smith & Wesson's efforts in providing the highest quality, most innovative designs available to handgun users of the world.

In December 1986, Lear Siegler Corporation was purchased by Forstmann Little & Company in an agreed-upon friendly takeover. However, Forstmann Little had no interest in Smith & Wesson. Their primary interest was only in Lear Siegler holdings in the automotive and aerospace industry. Therefore, they offered Smith & Wesson for sale to help finance the takeover of Lear Siegler. For the first time since 1964, Smith & Wesson was going to be offered for sale on its own merits as one of the finest handgun manufacturers in the United States.

The successful bidder for Smith & Wesson was the F.H. Tomkins p.l.c. of London, England.

NOTE: In 2001 Smith & Wesson was purchased by the Saf-T-Hammer Corporation, an American company whose executives are former S&W executives.

SMITH & WESSON ANTIQUE HANDGUNS

NOTE: A surprising number of pistols are still found in their original boxes, even for older models. This can add 100 percent to the value of the pistol.

Model 1, 1st Issue Revolver

This was the first metallic-cartridge arm produced by Smith & Wesson. It is a small revolver that weighs approximately 10 oz. and is chambered for the .22 Short rimfire cartridge. The octagonal barrel is 3.25" long. It holds 7 cartridges. The barrel and nonfluted cylinder pivot upward upon release of the under the frame. This model has a square butt with rosewood grips. The oval brass frame is silver-plated. The barrel and cylinder are blued. The barrel is stamped with the company name and address; the patent dates also appear. The sides of the frame are rounded on the 1st issue. Other characteristics which distinguish the more valuable 1st issue from later issues include a perfectly round side plate and a hinged hammer spur. Smith & Wesson manufactured approximately 11,000 of these revolvers between 1857 and 1860. Since this was the first of its kind, it is not difficult to understand the need for the number of variations within this model designation. Many small improvements were made on the way to the next model.

1st Type
Serial range 1 to low 200s, revolving recoil shield, bayonet type catch on frame.

Exc.	V.G.	Good	Fair	Poor
—	15000	10000	8000	—

NOTE: Rarity makes valuation speculative.

2nd Type
Serial range low 200s to 1130, improved recoil plate.

Exc.	V.G.	Good	Fair	Poor
—	9000	5000	2500	—

3rd Type
Serial range 1130 to low 3000s, bayonet catch dropped for spring-loaded side catch.

Courtesy Jim Supica, Old Town Station

Exc.	V.G.	Good	Fair	Poor
—	3500	2500	1500	—

4th Type
Serial range low 3000s to low 4200s, recoil shield made much smaller.

Exc.	V.G.	Good	Fair	Poor
—	3250	2000	1250	—

5th Type
Serial range low 4200s to low 5500s, has 5-groove rifling instead of 3.

Exc.	V.G.	Good	Fair	Poor
—	3250	2000	1250	—

6th Type
Serial range low 5500s to end of production 11670. A cylinder ratchet replaced the revolving recoil shield.

Exc.	V.G.	Good	Fair	Poor
—	3000	1750	1000	—

Model 1 2nd Issue

Similar in appearance to the 1st Issue this 2nd Issue variation has several notable differences that make identification rather simple. The sides of the frame on the 2nd Issue are flat not rounded as on the 1st Issue. The sideplate is irregular in shape—not round like on the 1st Issue. The barrel was 3-3/16" in length. The barrel is stamped "Smith & Wesson" while the cylinder is marked with the three patent dates: April 3, 1858, July 5 1859, and December 18, 1860. There have been 2nd Issue noted with full silver or nickel-plating. Smith & Wesson manufactured approximately 115,000 of these revolvers between 1860 and 1868. The serial numbers started around 1100 where the 1st Issue left off and continued to 126400. There were approximately 4,400 revolvers marked "2D Quality" on the barrels. These revolvers were slightly defective and were sold at a lesser price. They will bring an approximate 100 percent premium on today's market.

Exc.	V.G.	Good	Fair	Poor
—	700	400	250	—

Model 1 3rd Issue

This is a redesigned version of its forerunners. Another .22 Short rimfire, 7-shot revolver, this model has a fluted cylinder and round barrel with a raised rib. This variation was manufactured totally from wrought iron. The three patent dates are stamped on top of the ribbed barrel as is "Smith & Wesson." It features bird's-head type grips of rosewood and is either fully blued nickel-plated, or two-toned with the frame nickel and the barrel and cylinder blued. There are two barrel lengths offered: 3.25" and 2-11/16". The shorter barrel was introduced in 1872. Serial numbering began with #1 and continued to 131163. They were manufactured between 1868 and 1882. The Model 1 3rd Issue was the last of the tip-up style produced by Smith & Wesson.

Shorter Barreled Version—Rare

Exc.	V.G.	Good	Fair	Poor
—	1350	800	400	—

Longer Barreled Version—Standard

Exc.	V.G.	Good	Fair	Poor
—	500	275	200	—

Model 1-1/2 1st Issue (1-1/2 Old Model)

This model was the first of the .32-caliber Rimfire Short revolvers that S&W produced. It is a larger version of the Model 1 but is physically similar in appearance. The Model 1-1/2 was offered with a 3.5" octagonal barrel and has a 5-shot nonfluted cylinder and a square butt with rosewood grips. In 1866 a 4" barrel version was produced for a short time. It is estimated that about 200 were sold. The finish is blued or nickel-plated. The serial numbering on this model ran from serial number 1 to 26300; and, interestingly to note, S&W had most of the parts for this revolver manufactured on contract by King & Smith of Middletown, Connecticut. Smith & Wesson merely assembled and finished them. They were produced between 1865 and 1868.

Exc.	V.G.	Good	Fair	Poor
—	550	350	200	—

NOTE: Add a 50 percent premium for the 4" barrel variation.

Model 1-1/2 2nd Issue (1-1/2 New Model)

The factory referred to this model as the New Model 1-1/2 and it is an improved version of the 1st Issue. It is somewhat similar in appearance with a few notable exceptions. The barrel is 2.5" or 3.5" in length, round with a raised rib. The grip is of the bird's-head configuration, and the 5-shot cylinder is fluted and chambered for the .32 Long rimfire cartridge. The cylinder stop is located in the top frame instead of the bottom. The finish and grip material are the same as the 1st Issue. There were approximately 100,700 manufactured between 1868 and 1875.

3.5" Barrel—Standard

Exc.	V.G.	Good	Fair	Poor
—	450	275	175	—

2.5" Barrel—Rare

Exc.	V.G.	Good	Fair	Poor
—	1100	600	350	—

Model 1-1/2 Transitional Model

Approximately 650 of these were produced by fitting 1st Issue cylinders and barrels to 2nd Issue frames. They also have 1st Model octagon barrels with 2nd Model bird's-head grips. These revolvers fall into the serial number range 27200-28800.

Exc.	V.G.	Good	Fair	Poor
—	3000	1500	800	—

Model 2 Army or Old Model

Similar in appearance to the Model 1 2nd Issue, this revolver was extremely successful from a commercial standpoint. It was released just in time for the commencement of hostilities in the Civil War. Smith & Wesson had, in this revolver, the only weapon able to fire self-contained cartridges and be easily carried as a backup by soldiers going off to war. This resulted in a backlog of more than three years before the company finally stopped taking orders. This model is chambered for .32 Long rimfire cartridge and has a 6-shot nonfluted cylinder and 4", 5", or 6" barrel lengths. It has a square butt with rosewood grips and is either blued or nickel-plated. There were approximately 77,155 manufactured between 1861 and 1874.

NOTE: A slight premium for early two-pin model.

5" or 6" Barrel—Standard Barrel

Exc.	V.G.	Good	Fair	Poor
—	1500	950	450	—

4" Barrel—Rare, Use Caution

Exc.	V.G.	Good	Fair	Poor
—	5000	3000	1500	—

.32 Single-Action (Model 1-1/2 Centerfire)

This model represented the first .32 S&W centerfire caliber top-break revolver that automatically ejected the spent cartridges upon opening. It is similar in appearance to the Model 1-1/2 2nd Issue. This model has a 5-shot fluted cylinder and a bird's-head grip of wood or checkered hard rubber and was offered with barrel lengths of 3", 3.5", 6", 8", and 10". The 8" and 10" barrel are rare and were not offered until 1887. This model pivots downward on opening and features a rebounding hammer that made the weapon much safer to fully load. There were approximately 97,599 manufactured between 1878 and 1892.

Early Model w/o Strain Screw—Under #6500

Exc.	V.G.	Good	Fair	Poor
—	500	300	175	—

Later Model with Strain Screw

Exc.	V.G.	Good	Fair	Poor
—	350	250	150	—

8" or 10" Barrel—Very Rare, Use Caution

Exc.	V.G.	Good	Fair	Poor
—	3000	2000	800	—

.38 Single-Action 1st Model (Baby Russian)

This model is sometimes called the "Baby Russian." It is a top break, automatic-ejecting revolver chambered for the .38 S&W centerfire cartridge. Offered with either a 3.25" or 4" round barrel with a raised rib, has a 5-shot fluted cylinder, and finished in blue or nickel plating. A 5" barrel was added as an option a short time later. The butt is rounded, with wood or checkered hard rubber grips inlaid with the S&W medallion. It has a spur trigger. Approximately 25,548 were manufactured in 1876 and 1877, of which 16,046 were nickel and 6,502 were blued.

Exc.	V.G.	Good	Fair	Poor
—	1500	900	350	—

.38 Single-Action 2nd Model

With the exception of an improved and shortened extractor assembly and the availability of additional barrel lengths of 3.25", 4", 5", 6", 8", and 10" with the 8" and 10" barrel lengths being the most rare, this model is quite similar in appearance to the 1st Model. There were approximately 108,225 manufactured between 1877 and 1891.

Courtesy Mike Stuckslager

8" and 10" Barrel—Very Rare, Use Caution

Exc.	V.G.	Good	Fair	Poor
—	3250	2250	950	—

3.25", 4", 5", and 6" Barrel Lengths—Small Premium for 5" or 6" Lengths

Exc.	V.G.	Good	Fair	Poor
—	375	275	195	—

.38 Single-Action 3rd Model

This model differs from the first two models because it is fitted with a trigger guard. It is chambered for the .38 S&W centerfire cartridge, has a 5-shot fluted cylinder, and is a top break design with automatic ejection upon opening. The barrel lengths are 3.25", 4", and 6". The finish is blued or nickel-plated. The butt is rounded, with checkered hard rubber grips featuring S&W medallions. There were approximately 26,850 manufactured between 1891 and 1911.

Exc.	V.G.	Good	Fair	Poor
—	1700	1000	600	—

.38 Single-Action Mexican Model
This extremely rare model is quite similar in appearance to the 3rd Model Single-Action. The notable differences are the flat hammer sides with no outward flaring of the spur. The spur trigger assembly was not made integrally with the frame but is a separate part added to it. One must exercise extreme caution as S&W offered a kit that would convert the trigger guard assembly of the Third Model to the spur trigger of the Mexican Model. This, coupled with the fact that both models fall within the same serial range, can present a real identification problem. Another feature of the Mexican Model is the absence of a half cock. The exact number of Mexican Models manufactured between 1891 and 1911 is unknown but it is estimated that the number is small.

Exc.	V.G.	Good	Fair	Poor
—	3650	1500	950	—

.32 Double-Action 1st Model
This is one of the rarest of all S&W revolvers. There were only 30 manufactured. It also has a straight-sided sideplate that weakened the revolver frame. Perhaps this was the reason that so few were made. This model was the first break-open, double-action, automatic-ejecting .32 that S&W produced. It features a 3" round barrel with raised rib, a 5-shot fluted cylinder, and round butt with plain, uncheckered, black hard rubber grips. The finish is blued or nickel-plated. All 30 of these revolvers were manufactured in 1880.

Exc.	V.G.	Good	Fair	Poor
—	12000	7500	4000	—

NOTE: Rarity makes valuation speculative.

.32 Double-Action 2nd Model
This revolver is chambered for the .32 S&W cartridge and has a 3" round barrel with a raised rib. The 5-shot cylinder is fluted, and the finish is blued or nickel-plated. It is a top break design with a round butt. The grips are either checkered or floral-embossed hard rubber with the S&W monogram. This model has an oval sideplate, eliminating the weakness of the 1st Model. There were approximately 22,142 manufactured between 1880 and 1882.

Exc.	V.G.	Good	Fair	Poor
—	350	225	175	—

Model 3 American 1st Model
This model represented a number of firsts for the Smith & Wesson Company. It was the first of the top break, automatic ejection revolvers. It was also the first Smith & Wesson in a large caliber (it is chambered for the .44 S&W American cartridge as well as the .44 Henry rimfire on rare occasions). It was also known as the 1st Model American. This large revolver is offered with an 8" round barrel with a raised rib as standard. Barrel lengths of 6" and 7" were also available. It has a 6-shot fluted cylinder and a square butt with walnut grips. It is blued or nickel-plated. It is interesting to note that this model appeared three years before Colt's Single-Action Army and perhaps, more than any other model, was associated with the historic American West. There were only 8,000 manufactured between 1870 and 1872.

Courtesy Rock Island Auction Company

Standard Production Model

Exc.	V.G.	Good	Fair	Poor
—	7000	3500	1500	—

NOTE: Add 25 percent for "oil hole" variation found on approximately the first 1,500 guns. Add 50 percent for unusual barrel lengths other than standard 8". Original "Nashville Police" marked guns worth a substantial premium.

Transition Model
Serial number range 6466-6744. Shorter cylinder (1.423"), improved barrel catch.

Exc.	V.G.	Good	Fair	Poor
—	6000	3000	1500	—

U.S. Army Order
Serial number range 125-2199. One thousand (1,000) produced with "U.S." stamped on top of barrel; "OWA", on left grip.

Exc.	V.G.	Good	Fair	Poor
—	17500	7500	3000	—

.44 Rimfire Henry Model
Only 200 produced throughout serial range.

Exc.	V.G.	Good	Fair	Poor
—	12000	6000	3000	—

NOTE: Rarity makes valuation speculative.

Model 3 American 2nd Model
An improved version of the 1st Model. The most notable difference is the larger diameter trigger pivot pin and the frame protrusions above the trigger to accommodate it. The front sight blade on this model is made of steel instead of nickel silver. Several internal improvements were also incorporated into this model. This model is commonly known as the American 2nd Model. The 8" barrel length was standard on this model. There were approximately 20,735 manufactured, including 3,014 chambered for .44 rimfire Henry, between 1872 and 1874.

NOTE: There have been 5.5", 6", 6.5", and 7" barrels noted; but they are extremely scarce and would bring a 40 percent premium over the standard 8" model. Use caution when purchasing these short barrel revolvers.

.44 Henry Rimfire

Exc.	V.G.	Good	Fair	Poor
—	6500	3250	1500	—

Standard 8" Model—.44 American Centerfire

Exc.	V.G.	Good	Fair	Poor
—	5000	3000	1250	—

Model 3 Russian 1st Model
This model is quite similar in appearance to the American 1st and 2nd Model revolvers. S&W made several internal changes to this model to satisfy the Russian government. The markings on this revolver are distinct; and the caliber for which it is chambered, .44 S&W Russian, is different. There were approximately 20,000 Russian-Contract revolvers. The serial number range is 1-20000. They are marked in Russian Cyrillic letters. The Russian double-headed eagle is stamped on the rear portion of the barrel with inspector's marks underneath it. All of the contract guns have 8" barrels and lanyard swivels on the butt. These are rarely encountered, as most were shipped to Russia. The commercial run of this model numbered approximately 4,655. The barrels are stamped in English and include the words "Russian Model." Some are found with 6" and 7" barrels, as well as the standard 8". There were also 500 revolvers that were rejected from the Russian contract series and sold on the commercial market. Some of these are marked in English; some, Cyrillic. Some have the Cyrillic markings ground off and the English restamped. This model was manufactured from 1871 to 1874.

Russian Contract Model—Cyrillic Barrel Address

Exc.	V.G.	Good	Fair	Poor
—	7000	3500	2000	—

Commercial Model

Exc.	V.G.	Good	Fair	Poor
—	5000	2750	1250	—

Rejected Russian Contract Model

Exc.	V.G.	Good	Fair	Poor
—	5000	2750	1250	—

Model 3 Russian 2nd Model
This revolver was known as the "Old Model Russian." This is a complicated model to understand as there are many variations within the model designation. The serial numbering is quite complex as well, and values vary greatly due to relatively minor model differences. Before purchasing this model, it would be advisable to secure competent appraisal as well as to read reference materials solely devoted to this firearm. This model is chambered for the .44 S&W Russian, as well as the .44 Henry rimfire cartridge. It has a 7" barrel and a round butt featuring a projection on the frame that fits into the thumb web. The grips are walnut, and the finish is blue or nickel-plated. The trigger guard has a reverse curved spur on the bottom. There were approximately 85,200 manufactured between 1873 and 1878.

Commercial Model
6,200 made, .44 S&W Russian, English markings.

Exc.	V.G.	Good	Fair	Poor
—	3250	1500	850	—

.44 Rimfire Henry Model
500 made.

Exc.	V.G.	Good	Fair	Poor
—	4750	2250	1000	—

Russian Contract Model
70,000 made; rare, as most were shipped to Russia. Cyrillic markings; lanyard swivel on butt.

Exc.	V.G.	Good	Fair	Poor
—	3500	1750	950	—

1st Model Turkish Contract
.44 rimfire Henry, special rimfire frames, serial-numbered in own serial number range 1-1000.

Exc.	V.G.	Good	Fair	Poor
—	6000	3750	1750	—

2nd Model Turkish Contract
Made from altered centerfire frames from the regular commercial serial number range. 1,000 made. Use caution with this model.

Exc.	V.G.	Good	Fair	Poor
—	4500	2250	1000	—

Japanese Govt. Contract
Five thousand made between the 1-9000 serial number range. The Japanese naval insignia, an anchor over two wavy lines, found on the butt. The barrel is Japanese proofed, and the words "Jan.19, 75 REISSUE July 25, 1871" are stamped on the barrel, as well.

Exc.	V.G.	Good	Fair	Poor
—	3500	1700	950	—

Model 3 Russian 3rd Model
This revolver is also known as the "New Model Russian." The factory referred to this model as the Model of 1874 or the Cavalry Model. It is chambered for the .44 S&W Russian and the .44 Henry rimfire cartridge. The barrel is 6.5", and the round butt is the same humped-back affair as the 2nd Model. The grips are walnut; and the finish, blue or nickel-plated. The most notable differences in appearance between this model and the 2nd Model are the shorter extractor housing under the barrel and the integral front sight blade instead of the pinned-on one found on the previous models. This is another model that bears careful research before attempting to evaluate. Minor variances can greatly affect values. Secure detailed reference materials and qualified appraisal. There were approximately 60,638 manufactured between 1874 and 1878.

Commercial Model
.44 S&W Russian, marked "Russian Model" in English, 13,500 made.

Exc.	V.G.	Good	Fair	Poor
—	9000	5000	2500	—

.44 Henry Rimfire Model

Exc.	V.G.	Good	Fair	Poor
—	4500	2700	900	—

Turkish Model
Five thousand made from altered centerfire frames. Made to fire .44 Henry rimfire. "W" inspector's mark on butt. Fakes have been noted; be aware.

Exc.	V.G	Good	Fair	Poor
—	4500	2700	900	—

Japanese Contract Model
One thousand made; has the Japanese naval insignia, an anchor over two wavy lines, stamped on the butt.

Exc.	V.G	Good	Fair	Poor
—	3100	1950	850	—

Russian Contract Model
Barrel markings are in Russian Cyrillic. Approximately 41,100 were produced.

Exc.	V.G	Good	Fair	Poor
—	3100	1950	850	—

Model 3 Russian 3rd Model (Loewe & Tula Copies)
The German firm of Ludwig Loewe produced a copy of this model that is nearly identical to the S&W. This German revolver was made under Russian contract, as well as for commercial sales. The contract model has different Cyrillic markings than the S&W and the letters "HK" as inspector's marks. The commercial model has the markings in English. The Russian arsenal at Tula also produced a copy of this revolver with a different Cyrillic dated stamping on the barrel.

Courtesy Mike Stuckslager

Loewe

Exc.	V.G	Good	Fair	Poor
—	2900	1750	700	—

Tula

Exc.	V.G	Good	Fair	Poor
—	3350	2000	800	—

Model 3 Schofield 1st Model

"US" Contract
3,000 issued.

Exc.	V.G.	Good	Fair	Poor
—	8000	4250	2250	—

Civilian Model
No "US" markings, 35 made, Very Rare.
NOTE: Use Caution. UNABLE TO PRICE. At least double the military model values. Expert appraisal needed.

Model 3 Schofield 2nd Model

"US" Contract
4,000 issued.

Exc.	V.G.	Good	Fair	Poor
—	7500	4000	2250	—

Civilian Model
646 made.

Exc.	V.G.	Good	Fair	Poor
—	7000	4000	2000	—

Model 3 Schofield—Surplus Models
After the government dropped the Schofield as an issue cavalry sidearm, the remaining U.S. inventory of these revolvers was sold off as military surplus. Many were sold to National Guard units; and the remainder were sold either to Bannerman's or to Schuyler, Hartley & Graham, two large gun dealers who then resold the guns to supply the growing need for guns on the Western frontier. Schuyler, Hartley & Graham sold a number of guns to the Wells Fargo Express Co. These weapons were nickel-plated and had the barrels shortened to 5", as were many others sold during this period. Beware of fakes when contemplating purchase of the Wells Fargo revolvers.

Wells Fargo & Co. Model

Exc.	V.G.	Good	Fair	Poor
—	8000	4000	2000	—

Surplus Cut Barrel—Not Wells Fargo

Exc.	V.G.	Good	Fair	Poor
—	3500	2000	1200	—

New Model No. 3 Single-Action

Always interested in perfecting the Model 3 revolver D.B. Wesson redesigned and improved the old Model 3 in the hopes of attracting more sales. The Russian contracts were almost filled so the company decided to devote the effort necessary to improve on this design. In 1877 this project was undertaken. The extractor housing was shortened; the cylinder retention system was improved; and the shape of the grip was changed to a more streamlined and attractive configuration. This New Model has a 3.5", 4", 5", 6", 6.5", 7", 7.5", or 8" barrel length with a 6-shot fluted cylinder. The 6.5" barrel and .44 S&W Russian chambering is the most often encountered variation of this model, but the factory considered the 3-1/2" and 8" barrels as standard and these were kept in stock as well. The New Model No. 3 was also chambered for .32 S&W, .32-44 S&W, .320 S&W Rev. Rifle, .38 S&W, .38-40, .38-44 S&W, .41 S&W, .44 Henry rimfire, .44 S&W American, .44-40, .45 S&W Schofield, .450 Rev., .45 Webley, .455 MkI and .455 MkII. They are either blued or nickel-plated and have checkered hard rubber grips with the S&W logo molded into them, or walnut grips. There are many sub-variations within this model designation, and the potential collector should secure detailed reference material that deals with this model. There were approximately 35,796 of these revolvers manufactured between 1878 and 1912. Nearly 40 percent were exported to fill contracts with Japan, Australia, Argentina, England, Spain, and Cuba. There were some sent to Asia, as well. The proofmarks of these countries will establish their provenance but will not add appreciably to standard values.

Standard Model
6.5" barrel, .44 S&W Russian.

Exc.	V.G.	Good	Fair	Poor
—	3700	2000	1000	—

Japanese Naval Contract
This was the largest foreign purchaser of this model. There were more than 1,500 produced with the anchor insignia stamped on the frame.

Exc.	V.G.	Good	Fair	Poor
—	3700	2000	1000	—

Japanese Artillery Contract
This variation is numbered in the 25000 serial range. They are blued, with a 7" barrel and a lanyard swivel on the butt. Japanese characters are stamped on the extractor housing.

Exc.	V.G.	Good	Fair	Poor
—	5000	2500	1250	—

Australian Contract
This variation is nickel-plated, is chambered for the .44 S&W Russian cartridge, and is marked with the Australian Colonial Police Broad Arrow on the buff. There were 250 manufactured with 7" barrels and detachable shoulder stocks. The stock has the Broad Arrow stamped on the lower tang. There were also 30 manufactured with 6.5" barrels without the stocks. They all are numbered in the 12000-13000 serial range.

Revolver with Stock and Holsters

Exc.	V.G.	Good	Fair	Poor
—	8000	4750	2750	—

NOTE: Deduct 40 percent for no stock.

Maryland Militia Model
This variation is nickel-plated, has a 6.5" barrel, and is chambered for the .44 S&W Russian cartridge. The butt is stamped "U.S.," and the inspector's marks "HN" and "DAL" under the date 1878 appear on the revolver. There were 280 manufactured between serial-numbers 7126 and 7405.

Exc.	V.G.	Good	Fair	Poor
—	10000	6000	3000	—

NOTE: Rarity makes valuation speculative.

Argentine Model
This was essentially not a factory contract but a sale through Schuyler, Hartley and Graham. They are stamped "Ejercito/Argentino" in front of the trigger guard. The order amounted to some 2,000 revolvers between the serial numbers 50 and 3400.

Exc.	V.G.	Good	Fair	Poor
—	7000	3500	1750	—

Turkish Model
This is essentially the New Model No. 3 chambered for the .44 rimfire Henry cartridge. It is stamped with the letters "P," "U" and "AFC" on various parts of the revolver. The barrels are all 6.5"; the finish, blued with walnut grips. Lanyard swivels are found on the butt. There were 5,461 manufactured and serial numbered in their own range, starting at 1 through 5461 between 1879 and 1883.

Courtesy Mike Stuckslager

Exc.	V.G.	Good	Fair	Poor
—	7000	3500	1750	—

New Model No. 3 Target Single-Action
This revolver is similar in appearance to the standard New Model No. 3, but was the company's first production target model. It has a 6.5" round barrel with a raised rib and 6-shot fluted cylinder and is finished in blue or nickel-plated. The grips are either walnut or checkered hard rubber with the S&W logo molded into them. This model is chambered in either .32 S&W or .38 S&W. The company referred to these models as either the .32-44 Target or the .38-44 Target depending on the caliber. The designation of .44 referred to the frame size, i.e. a .32 caliber built on a .44 caliber frame. This model was offered with a detachable shoulder stock as an option. These stocks are extremely scarce on today's market. There were approximately 4,333 manufactured between 1887 and 1910.

Exc.	V.G.	Good	Fair	Poor
—	3100	1350	850	—

NOTE: Shoulder stock add 50 percent.

New Model No. 3 Frontier Single-Action
This is another model similar in appearance to the standard New Model No. 3. It has a 4", 5", or 6.5" barrel and is chambered for the .44-40 Winchester Centerfire cartridge. Because the original New Model No. 3 cylinder was 1-7/16" in length would not accommodate the longer .44-40 cartridge. The cylinder on the No. 3 Frontier was changed to 1-9/16" in length. Later the company converted 786 revolvers to .44 S&W Russian and sold them to Japan. This model is either blued or nickel-plated and has checkered grips of walnut or hard rubber. They are serial numbered in their own range from 1 through 2072 and were manufactured from 1885 until 1908. This model was designed to compete with the Colt Single-Action Army but was not successful.

.44-40—Commercial Model

Exc.	V.G.	Good	Fair	Poor
—	5000	2500	1250	—

Japanese Purchase Converted to .44 S&W Russian

Exc.	V.G.	Good	Fair	Poor
—	4000	2000	1000	—

New Model No. 3—.38 Winchester
This variation was the last of the New Model No. 3s to be introduced. It was offered in .38-40 Winchester as a separate model from 1900 until 1907. The finish is blue or nickel-plate, and the grips are checkered hard rubber or walnut. Barrel lengths of 4" or 6.5" were offered. This model was not at all popular, as only 74 were manufactured in their own serial range 1 through 74. Today's collectors are extremely interested in this extremely rare model.

Exc.	V.G.	Good	Fair	Poor
—	14000	8000	4000	—

NOTE: Rarity makes valuation speculative. A New Model #3 .38 Winchester in Good condition was offered in Old Town Station Dispatch for $6,850 in 1999.

.44 Double-Action 1st Model

This model is a top break revolver that automatically ejects the spent cartridge cases upon opening. The barrel latch is located at the top and rear of the cylinder; the pivot, in front and at the bottom. This model was also known as "The D.A. Frontier" or "The New Model Navy." The revolver is chambered for the .44 S&W Russian and was built on a modified Model 3 frame. It is also found on rare occasions chambered for the .38-40 and the .44-40 Winchester. The barrel lengths are 4", 5", 6", and 6.5", round with a raised rib. A 3-1/2" barrel was produced on this model by special request. Collectors should be aware that the barrel for this model and the New Model No. 3 were interchangeable and the factory did in fact use barrels from either model. The serial number on the rear of the barrel should match the number on the butt, cylinder and barrel latch. The cylinder holds 6 shots and is fluted. It has double sets of stop notches and long free grooves between the stops. It is serial numbered in its own range, beginning at 1. There were approximately 54,000 manufactured between 1881 and 1913.

Standard .44 S&W Russian

Exc.	V.G.	Good	Fair	Poor
—	1300	700	400	—

Model .44 Double-Action Wesson Favorite

The Favorite is basically a lightened version of the 1st Model D.A. .44. The barrel is thinner and is offered in 5" length only. There are lightening cuts in the frame between the trigger guard and the cylinder; the cylinder diameter was smaller, and there is a groove milled along the barrel rib. The Favorite is chambered for the .44 S&W Russian cartridge and has a 6-shot fluted cylinder with the same double-cylinder stop notches and free grooves as the 1st Model Double-Action .44. The company name and address, as well as the patent dates, are stamped into the edge of the cylinder instead of on the barrel rib. It is serial-numbered in the same range, between 9000 and 10100. The revolver was most often nickel-plated but was also offered blued. The grips are walnut or checkered hard rubber with the S&W logo molded in. There were approximately 1,000 manufactured in 1882 and 1883. Use caution when purchasing a blued model.

Exc.	V.G.	Good	Fair	Poor
—	9000	5000	2500	—

NOTE: Rarity makes valuation speculative.
Blued finish add 25 percent.

Model .44 Double-Action Frontier

Chambered for the .44-40 cartridge. This is a separate model from the .44 Double-Action 1st Model. It has a longer 19/16" cylinder like the later .44 double-action 1st Model's. Produced from 1886 to 1916 with their own serial number range. Approximately 15,340 built.

Exc.	V.G.	Good	Fair	Poor
—	1600	850	450	—

Model .38 Winchester Double-Action

Similar to the .44 Double-Action 1st Model except for the chamber. Fitted with long cylinder. Approximately 276 produced in their own serial number range from 1900 to 1910.

Exc.	V.G.	Good	Fair	Poor
—	5500	3000	1250	—

SNEIDER, CHARLES E.
Baltimore, Maryland

Two-Cylinder Revolver

A .22 caliber spur trigger revolver with a 2.75" octagonal barrel and twin seven-shot cylinders that can be pivoted. The barrel marked "E. Sneider Pat. March 1862." Produced in limited quantities during the 1860s. Prospective purchasers are advised to secure a qualified appraisal prior to acquisition.

Exc.	V.G.	Good	Fair	Poor
—	—	10000	5000	1250

SPALDING & FISHER
Worcester, Massachusetts

Double Barreled Pistol

A .36 caliber percussion double-barrel pocket pistol with 5.5" barrels, blued iron frame and walnut grips. The top of the barrels marked "Spalding & Fisher." Produced during the 1850s.

Exc.	V.G.	Good	Fair	Poor
—	—	850	350	100

SPANG & WALLACE
Philadelphia, Pennsylvania

Pocket Pistol

A .36 caliber percussion pocket pistol with a 2.5" to 6" barrel, German silver furniture and checkered walnut stock. The barrel marked "Spang & Wallace/Phila." Manufactured during late 1840s and early 1850s.

Exc.	V.G.	Good	Fair	Poor
—	—	1250	650	200

SPENCER
Boston, Massachusetts

Spencer Carbine

This was one of the most popular firearms used by Union forces during the Civil War. It is chambered for a metallic rimfire cartridge known as the "No. 56." It is actually a .52 caliber and was made with a copper case. The barrel is 22" in length. The finish is blued, with a carbine-length walnut stock held on by one barrel band. There is a sling swivel at the butt. There were approximately 50,000 manufactured between 1863 and 1865.

Courtesy Mike Stuckslager

Exc.	V.G.	Good	Fair	Poor
—	—	4500	1750	500

Military Rifle—Navy Model

This model is similar to the carbine, with a 30" round barrel and a full-length walnut stock held on by three barrel bands. It features an iron forend tip and sling swivels. The Civil War production consisted of two models. A Navy model was manufactured between 1862 and 1864 (there were approximately 1,000 of these so marked).

Exc.	V.G.	Good	Fair	Poor
—	—	5000	2250	600

Military Rifle—Army Model

There were approximately 11,450 produced for the Army during the Civil War. They are similar to the Navy model except that the front sight doubles as a bayonet lug. They were manufactured in 1863 and 1864.

Exc.	V.G.	Good	Fair	Poor
—	—	3750	1750	600

Springfield Armory Post-War Alteration

After the conclusion of the Civil War, approximately 11,000 carbines were refurbished and rechambered for .50 caliber rimfire. The barrels were sleeved, and a device known as the "Stabler cut-off" was added to convert the arm to single-shot function. Often they were refinished and restocked. The inspector's marks "ESA" will be found in an oval cartouche on the left side of the stock. These alterations took place in 1867 and 1868.

Exc.	V.G.	Good	Fair	Poor
—	—	3500	1500	500

Model 1865 Contract

This model was manufactured by the Burnside Rifle Company in 1865. They are similar to the Civil War-type carbine and are marked "By

Burnside Rifle Co./Model 1865." There were approximately 34,000 manufactured. Old records show that 30,500 were purchased by the United States government, and 19,000 of these had the Stabler cut-off device.

NOTE: There were a number of other variations in the Spencer line. It would behoove anyone interested in collecting this fine Civil War firearm to educate oneself on these variances and to secure individual appraisal if transactions are contemplated. This is a complex model with many subtle variations.

Exc.	V.G.	Good	Fair	Poor
—	—	3250	1250	500

SPENCER ARMS CO.
Windsor, Connecticut

From 1882 to 1889 they manufactured the first successful slide action repeating shotgun. Designed by Christopher M. Spencer who also designed the Civil War era Spencer military carbines. The shotgun came in both solid and takedown models in both 12 and 10 gauge. In 1890 Francis Bannerman & Sons of New York bought the patents and machinery and moved the operation to Brooklyn, New York. They produced what is known as the Spencer Bannerman models from 1890 to 1907. The takedown model is worth 20 percent premium and 10 gauge models are worth a 10 percent premium. The later Bannerman models are worth 20 percent less than the Spencer models.

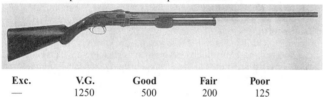

Exc.	V.G.	Good	Fair	Poor
—	1250	500	200	125

SPENCER REVOLVER
Maltby, Henley & Company
New York, New York

Safety Hammerless Revolver

A .32 caliber hammerless double-action revolver with a 3" barrel. The frame and barrel made of brass, the cylinder of steel and the grips are of walnut. The barrel is marked "Spencer Safety Hammerless Pat. Jan. 24, 1888 & Oct. 29, 1889." Manufactured by the Norwich Pistol Company circa 1890.

Exc.	V.G.	Good	Fair	Poor
—	450	200	150	100

SPILLER & BURR
Atlanta, Georgia

Navy Revolver

A .36 caliber percussion revolver with a 6" or 6.5" octagonal barrel and 6-shot cylinder. The barrel and cylinder blued, the frame of brass with walnut grips. Some pistols are marked "Spiller & Burr" while others are simply marked "C.S." Approximately 1,450 were made between 1862 and 1865. Prospective purchasers are advised to secure a qualified appraisal prior to acquisition.

Courtesy Milwaukee Public Museum, Milwaukee, Wisconsin

Exc.	V.G.	Good	Fair	Poor
—	—	40000	17500	—

SPRINGFIELD ARMORY
Springfield, Massachusetts

This was America's first federal armory. It began producing military weapons in 1795. The armory has supplied military weapons to the United States throughout its history.

NOTE: For additional Springfield Armory military firearms history, technical data, descriptions, photos, and prices see the *Standard Catalog of Military Firearms, 2nd Edition* under United States, Rifles.

Model 1841 Cadet Musket

This is a single-shot, muzzle-loading rifle chambered for .57 caliber percussion. It has a 40" round barrel with a full-length stock held on by three barrel bands. This rifle features no rear sight. It is browned and case-colored, with iron mountings. There is a steel ramrod mounted under the barrel. The lockplate is marked "Springfield" with the date of manufacture and "US" over an eagle motif. There were approximately 450 produced between 1844 and 1845.

Exc.	V.G.	Good	Fair	Poor
—	—	20000	8000	3000

Model 1842 Musket

This is a single-shot muzzleloader chambered for .69 caliber percussion. It has a 42" round barrel and a full-length stock held on by three barrel bands. The finish is white with iron mountings and a steel ramrod mounted beneath the barrel. There were a total of approximately 275,000 manufactured between 1844 and 1855 by both the Springfield Armory and the Harper's Ferry Armory. They are so marked.

Exc.	V.G.	Good	Fair	Poor
—	—	3500	1250	500

Model 1847 Artillery Musketoon

This is a single-shot muzzleloader chambered for .69 caliber percussion. It has a 26" round smooth bore barrel. The finish is white, with a full-length walnut stock held on by two barrel bands. The lock is marked "Springfield." There were approximately 3,350 manufactured between 1848 and 1859.

Exc.	V.G.	Good	Fair	Poor
—	—	6000	2500	1000

Model 1847 U.S. Sappers Musketoon

Almost identical to the Model 1847 Artillery except for a lug for sword bayonet mounted on right side of upper barrel band with twin steel guides for bayonet mounted near muzzle. A total of about 830 produced. Be aware of altered Model 1847 Artillery Muskets passed as orginal Sappers Muskets.

Exc.	V.G.	Good	Fair	Poor
—	—	6500	2750	1000

Model 1847 U.S. Cavalry Musketoon

Similar to the Model 1847 Artillery except for a button head ramrod attached with iron swivels under the muzzle. No sling swivels. As many as 6,700 were manufactured.

Exc.	V.G.	Good	Fair	Poor
—	—	7000	3000	1000

Model 1851 Percussion Cadet Musket

This single-shot muzzleloader in .57 caliber with 40" round barrel is almost identical with the Model 1841 Cadet Musket, the main difference and distinguishing feature is the use of the slightly smaller Model 1847 Musketoon lock. Markings are identical as shown for the Model 1841 Cadet Musket. These weapons were made at the Springfield Armory from 1851 to 1853, with total production of 4,000 guns.

Exc.	V.G.	Good	Fair	Poor
—	—	2500	1000	500

Model 1855 Rifle Musket

This is a single-shot muzzleloader chambered for .58 caliber percussion. It has a 40" round barrel with a full-length stock held on by three barrel bands. It has iron mountings and a ramrod mounted under the barrel. The front sight acts as a bayonet lug. The finish is white with a walnut stock. The lock is marked "U.S. Springfield." There was also a Harper's Ferry manufactured version that is so marked. There were approximately 59,000 manufactured between 1857 and 1861.

Exc.	V.G.	Good	Fair	Poor
—	—	4500	1750	750

Model 1855 Rifled Carbine

This is a single-shot muzzleloader chambered for .54 caliber percussion. It has a 22" round barrel with a 3/4-length stock held on by one barrel band. The finish is white with iron mountings and a ramrod mounted under the barrel. The lock is marked "Springfield" and dated. There were approximately 1,000 manufactured between 1855 and 1856.

Courtesy Little John's Auction Service, Inc., Paul Goodwin photo

Exc.	V.G.	Good	Fair	Poor
—	—	25000	8500	2000

Model 1858 U.S. Cadet Rifle Musket

Similar to the Model 1855 Rifled Musket but with a 38" barrel and shorter stock. The buttstock is 1" shorter than the musket and the forearm is 2" shorter. About 2,500 were built.

Exc.	V.G.	Good	Fair	Poor
—	—	5000	2250	1000

Model 1861 Percussion Rifle Musket

The Model 1861 was the standard musket in use during the Civil War. This .58 caliber single-shot muzzleloader has a 40" barrel with three barrel bands and all iron mountings; all metal parts are finished bright (some rear sights are blued) and the stock is walnut. On the lock there is an eagle motif forward of the hammer, US/SPRINGFIELD, beneath the nipple bolster, and the date at the rear section of the lock. About 256,129 of these muskets were made at the Springfield Armory, while almost 750,000 more were made under contract.

Exc.	V.G.	Good	Fair	Poor
—	—	3500	1500	800

Model 1863 Rifle Musket, Type I

This is a single-shot muzzleloader chambered for .58 caliber percussion. It has a 40" round barrel and a full-length stock held on by three barrel bands. The finish is white with iron mountings, and the lock is marked "U.S. Springfield" and dated 1863. There were approximately 275,000 manufactured in 1863.

Exc.	V.G.	Good	Fair	Poor
—	—	3500	1500	800

Model 1863 Rifle Musket, Type II, aka Model 1864

This was the last U.S. martial regulation arm of muzzleloading design, and it was widely used during the latter part of the Civil War. Produced at the Springfield Armory between 1864 and 1865, with total production of 25,540 pieces. This weapon is identical to the Type I with the exception of the dating of the lock, which is either 1864 or 1865, a single leaf rear sight, and solid barrel bands secured by flat springs mounted in the stock. The ramrod was either the tulip head type, or the new knurled and slotted design.

Exc.	V.G.	Good	Fair	Poor
—	—	3500	1500	800

SPRINGFIELD ARMS COMPANY
Springfield, Massachusetts

Belt Model

A .31 caliber percussion revolver with 4", 5", or 6" round barrels, centrally mounted hammer, and an etched 6-shot cylinder. Made with or without a loading lever. Early production versions of this revolver are marked "Jaquith's Patent 1838" on the frame and later production were marked "Springfield Arms" on the top strap. Approximately 150 were made.

Exc.	V.G.	Good	Fair	Poor
—	—	1750	800	200

Warner Model

As above, but is marked "Warner's Patent Jan. 1851." Approximately 150 of these were made.

Exc.	V.G.	Good	Fair	Poor
—	—	2500	1200	250

Double Trigger Model

As above, with two triggers, one of which locks the cylinder. Approximately 100 were made in 1851.

Exc.	V.G.	Good	Fair	Poor
—	—	2000	800	200

Pocket Model Revolver

A .28 caliber percussion revolver with 2.5" round barrel, centrally mounted hammer, no loading lever and etched 6-shot cylinder. Marked "Warner's Patent Jan. 1851" and "Springfield Arms Company." Blued, case hardened with walnut grips. Early production examples of this revolver do not have a groove on the cylinder and have a rounded frame. Approximately 525 were made in 1851.

Exc.	V.G.	Good	Fair	Poor
—	—	800	350	150

Ring Trigger Model

As above, but fitted with a ring trigger that revolved the cylinder. Approximately 150 were made in 1851.

Courtesy Milwaukee Public Museum, Milwaukee, Wisconsin

Exc.	V.G.	Good	Fair	Poor
—	—	1150	500	200

Double Trigger Model

As above, with two triggers set within a conventional trigger guard. The forward trigger revolves the cylinder. Approximately 350 were made in 1851.

Exc.	V.G.	Good	Fair	Poor
—	—	1150	500	200

Late Model Revolver

As above, except that the cylinder is automatically turned when the hammer is cocked. The top strap marked "Warner's Patent/James Warner, Springfield, Mass." Approximately 500 were made in 1851.

Exc.	V.G.	Good	Fair	Poor
—	—	800	300	100

Dragoon

A .40 caliber percussion revolver with either a 6" or 7.5" round barrel, some fitted with loading levers, others without. The top strap marked "Springfield Arms Company." Blued with walnut grips. Approximately 110 revolvers were manufactured in 1851.

Exc.	V.G.	Good	Fair	Poor
—	—	8000	3500	950

Navy Model

A .36 caliber percussion revolver with a 6" round barrel, centrally mounted hammer, and 6-shot etched cylinder. The top strap marked "Springfield Arms Company." Blued, case hardened with walnut grips. This model was manufactured in two variations, one with a single trigger and the other with a double trigger, the forward one of which locks the cylinder. Both variations had loading levers. Approximately 250 of these pistols were made in 1851.

Exc.	V.G.	Good	Fair	Poor
—	—	3750	1500	500

Double-Barrel Shotguns
The Springfield Arms Co. was bought by Stevens who used the Springfield brand name on many good quality single and double-barrel shotguns. Values range from $100 to $1,600 depending on model, gauge, and condition. See also Stevens.

SQUIBBMAN
SEE—Squires, Bingham Mfg. Co., Inc.

SQUIRES BINGHAM MFG. CO., INC.
Rizal, Philippine Islands

Firearms produced by this company are marketed under the trademark Squibbman.

Model 100D
A .38 Special caliber double-action swingout cylinder revolver with a 3", 4", or 6" ventilated-rib barrel, adjustable sights, matte black finish and walnut grips.

Exc.	V.G.	Good	Fair	Poor
200	100	80	60	40

Model 100DC
As above, without the ventilated rib.

Exc.	V.G.	Good	Fair	Poor
200	100	80	60	40

Model 100
As above, with a tapered barrel and uncheckered walnut grips.

Exc.	V.G.	Good	Fair	Poor
200	100	80	60	40

Thunder Chief
As above, but in .22 or .22 Magnum caliber with a heavier ventilated rib barrel, shrouded ejector, and ebony grips.

Exc.	V.G.	Good	Fair	Poor
225	125	100	80	60

STAFFORD, T. J.
New Haven, Connecticut

Pocket Pistol
A .22 caliber single-shot spur trigger pistol with a 3.5" octagonal barrel marked "T.J. Stafford New Haven Ct.," silver-plated brass frame and walnut or rosewood grips.

Exc.	V.G.	Good	Fair	Poor
—	—	600	250	100

Large Frame Model
As above, but in .38 rimfire caliber with a 6" barrel.

Exc.	V.G.	Good	Fair	Poor
—	—	850	400	200

STALCAP, ALEXANDER T.F.M.
Nashville, Tennessee

First in business during the 1850s, Stalcap received a contract in 1862, to modify sporting arms for military use. Overall length 50-7/8" to 51-3/4"; octagonal barrels 35-1/4" - 36" turned round at muzzle for socket bayonets; .54 caliber. Rifles assembled with sporting locks, new stocks and brass furniture. At least 102 rifles were delivered in 1862. These arms are unmarked.

Prospective purchasers are strongly advised to secure an expert appraisal prior to acquisition.

Exc.	V.G.	Good	Fair	Poor
—	—	4250	2000	1000

STANDARD ARMS CO.
Wilmington, Delaware

Model G
Chambered for .25-35, .30-30, .25 Remington, .30 Remington, and .35 Remington, with a 22" barrel, and open sights. Integral box magazine and closable gas port that allowed the rifle to be used as a slide action. Blued with a walnut stock. Produced in limited quantities, circa 1910.

Exc.	V.G.	Good	Fair	Poor
—	750	350	250	150

STAR, BONIFACIO ECHEVERRIA
Eibar, Spain
SEE—Echeverria

STARR, EBAN T.
New York, New York

Single-Shot Derringer
A .41 caliber single-shot pistol with a pivoted 2.75" round barrel. The hammer mounted on the right side of the frame and the trigger formed in the shape of a button located at the front of the frame. The frame marked "Starr's Pat's May 10, 1864." The brass frame silver-plated, the barrel blued or silver-plated with checkered walnut grips. Manufactured from 1864 to 1869.

Exc.	V.G.	Good	Fair	Poor
—	—	1750	750	200

Four Barreled Pepperbox
A .32 caliber 4 barreled pocket pistol with 2.75" to 3.25" barrels. The frame marked "Starr's Pat's May 10, 1864." Brass frames, silver-plated. The barrel is blued with plain walnut grips. This pistol was produced in six variations as follows:

First Model
Fluted breech and a barrel release mounted on the right side of the frame.

Exc.	V.G.	Good	Fair	Poor
—	—	2500	800	200

Second Model
Flat breech.

Exc.	V.G.	Good	Fair	Poor
—	—	1750	600	200

Third Model
Rounded breech with a visible firing-pin retaining spring.

Exc.	V.G.	Good	Fair	Poor
—	—	1500	500	150

Fourth Model
Rounded breech without visible springs.

Exc.	V.G.	Good	Fair	Poor
—	—	1500	500	150

Fifth Model
A larger, more angular grip.

Exc.	V.G.	Good	Fair	Poor
—	—	1250	400	150

Sixth Model
The frame length of this variation is of increased size.

Exc.	V.G.	Good	Fair	Poor
—	—	1500	500	150

STARR ARMS COMPANY
New York, New York

1858 Navy Revolver
A .36 caliber double-action percussion revolver with a 6" barrel and 6-shot cylinder. Blued, case hardened with walnut grips. The frame marked "Starr Arms Co. New York." Approximately 3,000 were made between 1858 and 1860.

Standard Model

Exc.	V.G.	Good	Fair	Poor
—	—	3250	1100	350

Martially Marked (JT)

Exc.	V.G.	Good	Fair	Poor
—	—	4250	1750	700

1858 Army Revolver
A .44 caliber double-action percussion revolver with a 6" barrel and 6-shot cylinder. Blued, case hardened with walnut grips. The frame marked "Starr Arms Co. New York." Approximately 23,000 were manufactured.

Exc.	V.G.	Good	Fair	Poor
—	—	2500	1100	300

1863 Army Revolver
Similar to the above, but single-action and with an 8" round barrel. Approximately 32,000 were manufactured between 1863 and 1865.

Exc.	V.G.	Good	Fair	Poor
—	—	3250	1500	350

Percussion Carbine
A .54 caliber breechloading percussion carbine with a 21" round barrel secured by one barrel band. Blued, case hardened with a walnut stock. The lock marked "Starr Arms Co./Yonkers, N.Y."

Exc.	V.G.	Good	Fair	Poor
—	—	2750	1250	400

Cartridge Carbine
Similar to the above, but in .52 rimfire caliber. Approximately 5,000 were manufactured.

Exc.	V.G.	Good	Fair	Poor
—	—	2500	1000	350

STEVENS, J. ARMS CO.
Chicopee Falls, Massachusetts

In 1864 this firm began doing business as J. Stevens & Company. In 1888 it was incorporated as the J. Stevens Arms & Tool Company. It operated as such until 1920, when it was taken over by the Savage Arms Company. It has operated as an independent division in this organization since. This company produced a great many firearms—most that were of an affordable nature. They are widely collected, and one interested in them should take advantage of the literature available on the subject.

Vest Pocket Pistol
This is a single-shot pocket pistol chambered for the .22 and the .30 rimfire cartridges. The .22 caliber version is rarely encountered and would be worth approximately 25 percent more than the values illustrated. It has a 2.75" part-octagonal barrel that pivots upward for loading. It has an external hammer and a spur-type trigger. The frame is nickel-plated or blued, with a blued barrel. The odd shaped flared grips are made of rosewood. The first models were marked "Vest Pocket Pistol" only. Later models have the barrels marked "J. Stevens & Co. Chicopee Falls, Mass." There were approximately 1,000 manufactured between 1864 and 1876.

Exc.	V.G.	Good	Fair	Poor
3300	2200	1650	1000	850

Pocket Pistol
This is a more conventional-appearing, single-shot pocket pistol chambered for either the .22 or the .30 rimfire cartridges. It has a 3.5" part-octagonal barrel that pivots upward for loading. It features a plated brass frame with either a blued or nickel-plated barrel and rosewood, two-piece grips. The barrel is marked "J. Stevens & Co. Chicopee Falls, Mass." There were approximately 15,000 manufactured between 1864 and 1886.

Exc.	V.G.	Good	Fair	Poor
450	325	225	125	100

Gem Pocket Pistol
This is a single-shot, derringer-type pocket pistol chambered for either the .22 or .30 rimfire cartridges. It has a 3" part-octagonal barrel that pivots to the side for loading. It has a nickel-plated brass frame with either a blued or plated barrel. It has bird's-head grips made of walnut or rosewood. The barrel is marked "Gem." The Stevens name or address does not appear on this firearm. There were approximately 4,000 manufactured between 1872 and 1890.

Exc.	V.G.	Good	Fair	Poor
1000	800	550	425	300

.41 Caliber Derringer
This is a single-shot pocket pistol chambered for the .22 or .31 caliber rimfire cartridge. It has a 4" part-octagonal barrel that pivots upward for loading. It has a spur trigger and an external hammer. The frame is plated brass with a blued barrel. It has walnut bird's-head grips. This firearm is completely unmarked except for a serial number. There were approximately 100 manufactured in 1875.

.22 Caliber

Exc.	V.G.	Good	Fair	Poor
4500	4000	3000	2100	1200

.41 Caliber

Exc.	V.G.	Good	Fair	Poor
4200	3500	2700	1900	1200

Single-Shot Pistol
This is a single-shot pistol chambered for the .22 or .30 rimfire cartridges. It has a 3.5" part-octagonal barrel that pivots upward for loading. It is quite similar in appearance to the original pocket pistol. It has a plated brass frame and either a blued or nickel-plated barrel with walnut, square-butt grips. The barrel is marked "J. Stevens A&T Co." There were approximately 10,000 manufactured between 1886 and 1896.

Exc.	V.G.	Good	Fair	Poor
450	300	225	175	125

No. 41 Pistol
This is a single-shot pocket pistol chambered for the .22 and .30 Short cartridges. It has a 3.5" part-octagonal barrel that pivots upward for loading. It features an external hammer and a spur-type trigger. It has an iron frame with the firing pin mounted in the recoil shield. It is either blued or nickel-plated, with square-butt walnut grips. There were approximately 90,000 manufactured between 1896 and 1916.

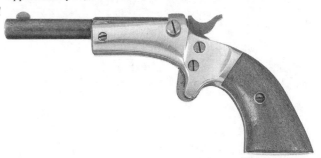

Courtesy Rock Island Auction Company

Exc.	V.G.	Good	Fair	Poor
400	350	275	225	125

Stevens Tip Up Rifles
This series of rifles was produced by Stevens beginning in the 1870s through 1895. There are a number of variations, but they are all quite similar in appearance. They feature a distinctive sloped frame made of iron and nickel-plated. Most frames are similar in size, but there is a slightly lighter frame used on the "Ladies Model" rifles. These Tip Up rifles are chambered for various calibers from the .22 rimfire to the .44 centerfire cartridges. They are offered with barrel lengths of 24", 26", 28", or 30". The actions are nickel-plated, as well as the trigger guards and the buttplates. The barrels are blued, and the two-piece stocks are of walnut. They are offered with various buttplates and sights. A shotgun version is also offered. There are a number of variations that differ only slightly, and the model numbers are not marked on the rifles. We suggest securing a qualified appraisal if in doubt. The major variations and their values are as follows:

Ladies Model
.22 or .25 rimfire only, 24" or 26" barrel

Exc.	V.G.	Good	Fair	Poor
3000	2500	1800	1200	600

Tip Up Rifle
Without forend.

Exc.	V.G.	Good	Fair	Poor
600	500	350	225	175

Tip Up Rifle
With forend, swiss-type buttplate.

Exc.	V.G.	Good	Fair	Poor
950	750	450	325	200

Tip Up Shotgun
All gauges, 30" or 32" barrel.

Exc.	V.G.	Good	Fair	Poor
350	300	200	150	100

Ideal Single-Shot Rifle

This excellent rifle was manufactured by Stevens between 1896 and 1933. It is a single-shot, falling-block type action that is activated by a trigger guard-action lever. It was produced in many popular calibers from .22 rimfire up to .30-40. It was also manufactured in a number of special Stevens calibers. It was offered with various length barrels in many different grades, from plain Spartan starter rifles up to some extremely high-grade Schuetzen-type target rifles with all available options. In 1901 Harry Pope of Hartford, Connecticut, went to work for Stevens and brought his highly respected barrel to the Stevens Company. He remained an employee for only two years, and the firearms produced during this period have the name "Stevens-Pope" stamped on the top of the barrel in addition to the other factory markings. Rifles marked in this manner and authenticated would be worth an approximate 50 percent premium if they are in very good to excellent condition. Due to numerous variations and options offered, we strongly recommend securing a qualified appraisal, especially on the higher-grade Ideal series rifles, if a transaction is contemplated.

No. 44

This version is chambered for various calibers and is offered with a 24" or 26" barrel. It has an open rear sight with a Rocky Mountain-type front sight. The finish is blued and case colored, with a walnut stock. There were approximately 100,000 manufactured between 1896 and 1933.

Exc.	V.G.	Good	Fair	Poor
1000	800	550	350	195

No. 44-1/2

This rifle is similar in appearance to the No. 44 but features an improved action. It has barrel lengths up to 34" and will be found with the Stevens-Pope barrel. It was manufactured between 1903 and 1916.

Exc.	V.G.	Good	Fair	Poor
1600	1400	1100	850	700

No. 044-1/2

This version is also known as the English Model rifle and is similar to the No. 44-1/2 except that it has a shotgun butt and a tapered barrel. There were a number of options offered that would affect the value. It was manufactured between 1903 and 1916.

Exc.	V.G.	Good	Fair	Poor
1600	1400	1100	850	700

No. 45

This version is also known as the Range Rifle. It is chambered for various calibers from the .22 rimfire to .44-40. Its identifying features are the Beach sights with an additional vernier tang sight and a Swiss-type buttstock. It is offered with a 26" or 28" part-octagonal barrel. It was manufactured between 1896 and 1916. Values for a standard version are as follows:

Exc.	V.G.	Good	Fair	Poor
1700	1500	1150	925	725

NOTE: Deduct 25 percent for .44 action.

No. 46

Same as the No. 45 but with a fancy wood stock. Manufactured from 1896 to 1902. Built in No. 44 action-only.

Exc.	V.G.	Good	Fair	Poor
2200	1900	1550	1325	1000

No. 47

This version is similar to the No. 45, with a pistol grip buttstock.

Exc.	V.G.	Good	Fair	Poor
3000	2700	2200	1600	1000

NOTE: Deduct 25 percent for .44 action.

No. 48

Same as the No. 47 but with a fancy wood checkered stock. Manufactured from 1896 to 1902. Built in a No. 44 action-only. This is a very rare model.

Exc.	V.G.	Good	Fair	Poor
4250	3750	2750	1950	1250

No. 49

This model is also known as the "Walnut Hill Rifle." It is a high grade target rifle chambered for many calibers between the .22 rimfire and the .44-40. It is offered with a 28" or 30" part-octagonal barrel that is medium- or heavy-weight. It was furnished with a globe front sight and a vernier tang sight. It is blued with a case-colored frame and has a high-grade, checkered, varnished walnut stock that has a high comb and features a pistol grip, cheekpiece, Swiss-type buttplate, and a loop-type trigger guard lever that resembles that of a lever-action rifle. The receiver is engraved, and there were a number of options available that would increase the value when present. We recommend an appraisal when in doubt. This rifle was manufactured between 1896 and 1916.

Exc.	V.G.	Good	Fair	Poor
6000	5500	3300	2100	1600

Model 50

This version is identical to the Model 49 but was offered with a higher-grade walnut stock. This is a very rare model.

Exc.	V.G.	Good	Fair	Poor
7000	6500	3900	2500	1800

Model 51

This version is known as the "Schuetzen Rifle" and is quite similar to the No. 49 except that it features double-set triggers, a higher-grade walnut stock, a wooden insert in the trigger guard action lever, and a heavy, Schuetzen-type buttplate. There were many options available on this model, and we recommend securing an appraisal when in doubt. It was manufactured between 1896 and 1916.

Exc.	V.G.	Good	Fair	Poor
10000	8000	5300	3200	2100

No. 52

This version is also known as the "Schuetzen Junior." It is similar to the No. 51 except that it features more engraving and a higher-grade walnut stock. It was manufactured between 1897 and 1916.

Exc.	V.G.	Good	Fair	Poor
9500	7400	4700	2700	1600

No. 53

This model is the same as the No. 51 except for the addition of a fancy wood stock and palm rest. Produced from 1896 to 1902 and offered only with a No. 44 action. This is a rare rifle.

Exc.	V.G.	Good	Fair	Poor
11500	8750	6000	3750	2500

No. 54

This is similar to the No. 52 except that it has double-set triggers and a palm rest, as well as a heavy, Swiss-style buttplate. It is offered with a 30" or 32" part-octagonal heavy barrel. This was Stevens' top-of-the-line rifle. It was offered with many options, and an appraisal should be secured if in doubt. It was manufactured between 1897 and 1916.

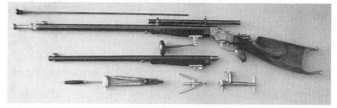

Courtesy Rock Island Auction Company

Exc.	V.G.	Good	Fair	Poor
14000	12000	8500	6000	5000

NOTE: The above prices are based on a No. 44-1/2 action. A No. 44 action will bring 20 percent less than the prices listed above.

No. 55

This version is one of the Stevens' Ideal Ladies Models. It is chambered for the smaller rimfire calibers between .22 Short and .32 Long rimfire. It features a 24" or 26" part-octagonal barrel with a vernier tang sight. The finish is blued and case-colored, with a checkered pistol grip walnut stock that features a Swiss-type buttplate. This is a lighter weight rifle that was manufactured between 1897 and 1916.

Exc.	V.G.	Good	Fair	Poor
3600	3100	1700	950	700

No. 56

This Ladies' Model rifle is similar to the No. 55 except that it is chambered for centerfire cartridges and has a higher-grade walnut stock. It was made on the improved No. 44-1/2 action. It was manufactured between 1906 and 1916.

Exc.	V.G.	Good	Fair	Poor
4000	3300	2150	1400	800

RIFLES

Beginning in 1869 the Stevens Company produced a series of single-shot, break-open target and sporting pistols that pivot upward for loading. They are chambered for the .22 and the .25 rimfire cartridges, as well as various centerfire cartridges from the .32 Short Colt to the .44 Russian. These pistols were made with various barrel lengths and have either a spur trigger or conventional trigger with a guard. They are all single-actions with exposed hammers. The finishes are nickel-plated frames with blued barrels and walnut grips. These variations and their values are as follows:

Six-inch Pocket Rifle

This version is chambered for the .22 rimfire cartridge and has a 6" part-octagonal barrel with open sights. The barrel is marked "J. Stevens & Co. Chicopee Falls, Mass." There were approximately 1,000 manufactured between 1869 and 1886.

Exc.	V.G.	Good	Fair	Poor
500	400	350	200	100

No. 36

This version is known as the Stevens-Lord pistol. It is chambered for various rimfire and centerfire calibers up to .44 Russian. It is offered with a 10" or 12" part-octagonal barrel and features a firing pin in the frame with a bushing. It has a conventional trigger with a spurred trigger guard. It features the standard Stevens barrel address. It was named after Frank Lord, a target shooter well-known at this time. There were approximately 3,500 manufactured from 1880 to 1911.

Exc.	V.G.	Good	Fair	Poor
1500	1200	900	600	350

First Issue Stevens-Conlin

This version is chambered for the .22 or .32 rimfire cartridges. It has a 10" or 12" part-octagonal barrel. It features a plated brass frame with a blued barrel and checkered walnut grips with a weighted buttcap. This version has a spur trigger either with or without a trigger guard. It was named after James Conlin, the owner of a shooting gallery located in New York City. There were approximately 500 manufactured between 1880 and 1884.

Exc.	V.G.	Good	Fair	Poor
2500	2100	1600	900	500

Second Issue Stevens-Conlin No. 38

This version is similar to the First Issue, with a conventional trigger and spurred trigger guard, as well as a fully adjustable rear sight. There were approximately 6,000 manufactured between 1884 and 1903.

Exc.	V.G.	Good	Fair	Poor
1400	1200	1000	700	400

No. 37

This version is also known as the Stevens-Gould and was named after a 19th century firearms writer. It resembles the No. 38 without the spur on the trigger guard. There were approximately 1,000 manufactured between 1889 and 1903.

Exc.	V.G.	Good	Fair	Poor
1800	1600	1200	800	400

No. 35

This version is chambered for the .22 rimfire, the .22 Stevens-Pope, and the .25 Stevens cartridges. It is offered with a 6", 8", 10", or 12.25" part-octagonal barrel. The firing pin has no bushing. It features an iron frame that is either blued or plated with a blued barrel. It has plain walnut grips with a weighted buttcap. It featured open sights. There were approximately 43,000 manufactured between 1923 and 1942.

Exc.	V.G.	Good	Fair	Poor
450	325	275	175	100

NOTE: Longer barrels worth a premium.

No. 35 Target

This version is similar to the No. 35 but has a better quality trigger guard and sights. There were approximately 35,000 manufactured between 1907 and 1916.

Exc.	V.G.	Good	Fair	Poor
500	400	325	200	100

STEVENS NO. 35 OFFHAND SHOT GUN NFA, CURIO OR RELIC

Stevens No. 35 AutoShot

The Stevens No. 35 is a .410 bore pistol manufactured by the J. Stevens Arms Co., Chicopee Falls, Massachusetts. It was available with an 8" or 12.25" smoothbore barrel, for 2.5" shells only, in two variations: the OffHand Shot Gun (1923 to 1929) and the AutoShot (1929 to 1934). Total production is unknown because the .410 and .22 rimfire variations of the No. 35 share the same serial number range. Researcher Ken Cope estimates total AutoShot production was approximately 2,000, and OffHand production at 20,000 to 25,000. Production was halted after the government ruled the .410 Stevens to be a "firearm" in the "any other weapon" category under the NFA in 1934, when its retail price was about $12. The Stevens does not possess the same collector appeal as other .410 smoothbore pistols, because (1) its relatively light weight makes it an uncomfortable shooter, and (2) the gun is not well made.

Courtesy John J. Stimson, Jr.

OffHand Shot Gun
Serial range from 1 to 43357.

Exc.	V.G.	Good	Fair	Poor
400	250	200	100	75

AutoShot

Exc.	V.G.	Good	Fair	Poor
450	300	200	125	100

NOTE: 8" barrel commands a 25 to 50 percent premium.

No. 43

This version is also called the Diamond and was produced in two distinct variations called the First Issue and the Second Issue. The First Issue has a brass frame; and the Second Issue, an iron frame and no firing pin bushing. Otherwise they are quite similar and would be valued the same. They are chambered for the .22 rimfire cartridge and are offered with either a 6" or 10" part-octagonal barrel. The frames are either nickel-plated or blued with blued barrels and square-butt walnut grips. There were approximately 95,000 manufactured between 1886 and 1916.

Exc.	V.G.	Good	Fair	Poor
400	300	250	150	75

NOTE: Add a 25 percent premium for 10" barrels.

POCKET RIFLES

This series of pistols is similar to the target and sporting pistols except that these were produced with detachable shoulder stocks that bear the same serial number as the pistol with which they were sold. They are sometimes referred to as Bicycle rifles. The collector interest in these weapons is quite high; but it would behoove one to be familiar with the provisions of the Gun Control Act of 1968 when dealing in or collecting this variation—as when the stock is attached, they can fall into the category of a short-barreled rifle. Some are considered to be curios and relics, and others have been totally declassified; but some models may still be restricted. We strongly recommend securing a qualified, individual appraisal on these highly collectible firearms if a transaction is contemplated.

NOTE: The values we supply include the matching shoulder stock. If the stock number does not match the pistol, the values would be approximately 25 percent less; and with no stock at all, 50 percent should be deducted.

Old Model Pocket Rifle

This version is chambered for the .22 rimfire cartridge and has an 8" or 10" part-octagonal barrel. It has a spur trigger and an external hammer on which the firing pin is mounted. The extractor is spring-loaded. It has a plated brass frame, blued barrel, and either walnut or rosewood grips. The shoulder stock is either nickel-plated or black. The barrel is marked "J. Stevens & Co. Chicopee Falls, Mass." There were approximately 4,000 manufactured between 1869 and 1886.

Exc.	V.G.	Good	Fair	Poor
900	700	550	325	200

Reliable Pocket Rifle

This version is chambered for the .22 rimfire cartridge and in appearance is quite similar to the Old Model. The basic difference is that the extractor operates as a part of the pivoting barrel mechanism instead of being spring-loaded. The barrel is marked "J. Stevens A&T Co." There were approximately 4,000 manufactured between 1886 and 1896.

Exc.	V.G.	Good	Fair	Poor
800	625	500	400	300

No. 42 Reliable Pocket Rifle

This version is similar to the first issue Reliable except that it has an iron frame with the firing pin mounted in it without a bushing. The shoulder stock is shaped differently. There were approximately 8,000 manufactured between 1896 and 1916.

Exc.	V.G.	Good	Fair	Poor
700	575	475	350	250

First Issue New Model Pocket Rifle

This version is the first of the medium-frame models with a frame width of 1". All of its predecessors have a 5/8" wide frame. This model is chambered for the .22 and .32 rimfire cartridges and is offered with barrel lengths of 10", 12", 15", or 18" that are part-octagonal in configuration. The external hammer has the firing pin mounted on it. It has a plated brass frame, blued barrel, and either walnut or rosewood grips. The shoulder stock is nickel-plated and fitted differently than the small-frame models in that there is a dovetail in the butt and the top leg is secured by a knurled screw. The barrel is marked "J. Stevens & Co. Chicopee Falls, Mass." There were approximately 8,000 manufactured between 1872 and 1875.

Exc.	V.G.	Good	Fair	Poor
800	700	550	400	300

Second Issue New Model Pocket Rifle

This version is similar to the First Issue except that the firing pin is mounted in the frame with a bushing. There were approximately 15,000 manufactured between 1875 and 1896.

Exc.	V.G.	Good	Fair	Poor
700	600	500	400	300

Vernier Model

This version is similar to the Second Issue except that it features a vernier tang sight located on the back strap. There were approximately 1,500 manufactured between 1884 and 1896.

Exc.	V.G.	Good	Fair	Poor
950	650	550	450	200

No. 40

This version is similar to its medium-frame predecessors except that it has a longer grip frame and a conventional trigger with trigger guard. There were approximately 15,000 manufactured between 1896 and 1916.

Courtesy Rock Island Auction Company

Exc.	V.G.	Good	Fair	Poor
700	600	500	300	200

No. 40-1/2

This version is similar to the No. 40, with a vernier tang sight mounted on the back strap. There were approximately 2,500 manufactured between 1896 and 1915.

Exc.	V.G.	Good	Fair	Poor
800	700	600	500	350

No. 34 (Hunter's Pet)

This is the first of the heavy-frame pocket rifles that featured a 1.25" wide frame. This version is also known as the "Hunter's Pet." It is chambered for many popular cartridges from the .22 rimfire to the .44-40 centerfire. It is offered with a part-octagonal 18", 20", 22", or 24" barrel. It has a nickel-plated iron frame and blued barrel. The detachable stock is nickel-plated, and the grips are walnut. There were few produced with a brass frame; and if located, these would be worth twice the value indicated. The firing pin is mounted in the frame with the bushing, and it features a spur trigger. There were approximately 4,000 manufactured between 1872 and 1900.

Exc.	V.G.	Good	Fair	Poor
950	800	500	350	250

No. 34-1/2

This version is similar to the No. 34 except that it features a vernier tang sight mounted on the back strap. There were approximately 1,200 manufactured between 1884 and 1900.

Exc.	V.G.	Good	Fair	Poor
1100	950	675	500	350

STEVENS SINGLE-SHOT SHOTGUNS

This company manufactured a number of single barrel, break-open, single-shot shotguns. They were produced chambered for various gauges with various-length barrels and chokes. They are quite similar in appearance and were designed as inexpensive, utility-grade weapons. There is little or no collector interest in them at this time, and their values are similar. We list them for reference purposes only.

Model 100	Model 125	Model 94
Model 102	Model 140	Model 944
Model 104	Model 160	Model 94A
Model 105	Model 165	Model 94C
Model 106	Model 170	Model 95
Model 107	Model 180	Model 958
Model 108	Model 89	Model 97
Model 110	Model 90	Model 970
Model 120	Model 93	

Exc.	V.G.	Good	Fair	Poor
150	100	75	50	25

Model 182

This is a single-shot, break-open shotgun chambered for 12 gauge. It is offered with a 30" or 32" trap choked barrels and features a hammerless action with an automatic ejector and a lightly engraved receiver. The finish is blued, with a checkered trap-grade stock.

Exc.	V.G.	Good	Fair	Poor
175	125	100	75	50

Model 185

This version features a half-octagonal barrel with an automatic ejector and a checkered walnut stock.

Exc.	V.G.	Good	Fair	Poor
175	125	100	75	50

NOTE: Damascus barrel deduct 25 percent.

Model 190

This is a 12-gauge hammerless gun with an automatic ejector. It is lightly engraved with a half-octagonal barrel.

Exc.	V.G.	Good	Fair	Poor
175	125	100	75	50

NOTE: Damascus barrel deduct 25 percent.

Model 195

This is another deluxe version that features engraving, a half-octagonal barrel, and a high-grade, checkered walnut stock.

Exc.	V.G.	Good	Fair	Poor
350	250	200	150	100

NOTE: Damascus barrel deduct 25 percent.

Model 240

This over-and-under model features a boxlock frame with exposed hammers.

Exc.	V.G.	Good	Fair	Poor
400	300	250	200	150

STEVENS DOUBLE-BARREL SHOTGUNS

The firm of J. Stevens and its successors produced a number of utility-grade, side-by-side double-barrel shotguns between 1877 and 1988. They are chambered for 10, 12, 16, or 20 gauge as well as the .410 bore. Stevens shotguns in 10 gauge and .410 bore will normally bring a premium as do guns with single triggers and ejectors. They have various length barrels and choke combinations. They feature double triggers and extractors except where noted. A complete list of Stevens brand models including the three in-house brands: Riverside, Springfield, and Super Value follow:

STEVENS BRAND

Model 1877—Hammer Boxlock

NIB	Exc.	V.G.	Good	Fair	Poor
1000	500	400	300	250	200

Model 250—Hammer Sidelock

NIB	Exc.	V.G.	Good	Fair	Poor
1000	500	400	300	250	200

Model 225—Hammer Boxlock

Courtesy Nick Niles, Paul Goodwin photo

NIB	Exc.	V.G.	Good	Fair	Poor
1000	500	400	300	250	200

Model 260—Hammer Sidelock

NIB	Exc.	V.G.	Good	Fair	Poor
1000	500	400	300	250	200

Model 270—Hammer Sidelock

NIB	Exc.	V.G.	Good	Fair	Poor
1000	500	400	300	250	200

Model 280—Hammer Sidelock

NIB	Exc.	V.G.	Good	Fair	Poor
1000	500	400	300	250	200

Model 325—Hammerless Boxlock

NIB	Exc.	V.G.	Good	Fair	Poor
800	400	350	300	250	200

Model 350—Hammerless Boxlock

NIB	Exc.	V.G.	Good	Fair	Poor
800	400	350	300	250	200

Model 360—Hammerless Boxlock

NIB	Exc.	V.G.	Good	Fair	Poor
800	400	350	300	250	200

Model 370—Hammerless Boxlock

NIB	Exc.	V.G.	Good	Fair	Poor
800	400	350	300	250	200

Model 380—Hammerless Boxlock

NIB	Exc.	V.G.	Good	Fair	Poor
1000	500	400	350	250	200

Model 235—Hammer Boxlock

NIB	Exc.	V.G.	Good	Fair	Poor
800	400	350	300	250	200

Model 335 (Early)—Hammerless Boxlock

NIB	Exc.	V.G.	Good	Fair	Poor
800	400	350	300	250	200

Model 335 (Late)—Hammerless Boxlock

NIB	Exc.	V.G.	Good	Fair	Poor
800	400	350	300	250	200

Model 255—Hammer Sidelock

NIB	Exc.	V.G.	Good	Fair	Poor
800	400	350	300	250	200

Model 265—Hammer Sidelock

NIB	Exc.	V.G.	Good	Fair	Poor
800	400	350	300	250	200

Model 355—Hammerless Boxlock

NIB	Exc.	V.G.	Good	Fair	Poor
1400	700	500	400	300	250

Model 365—Hammerless Boxlock

NIB	Exc.	V.G.	Good	Fair	Poor
1600	800	550	450	350	300

Model 375 (London Proofs)—Hammerless Boxlock

NIB	Exc.	V.G.	Good	Fair	Poor
2400	1200	800	600	400	350

Model 375 (U.S.)—Hammerless Boxlock

NIB	Exc.	V.G.	Good	Fair	Poor
1800	900	600	500	350	300

Model 385 (London Proofs)—Hammerless Boxlock

NIB	Exc.	V.G.	Good	Fair	Poor
2800	1400	900	600	400	350

Model 385 (U.S.)—Hammerless Boxlock

NIB	Exc.	V.G.	Good	Fair	Poor
2000	1000	750	500	400	250

Model 345—Hammerless Boxlock

NIB	Exc.	V.G.	Good	Fair	Poor
1000	500	400	300	250	200

Model 330—Hammerless Boxlock

NIB	Exc.	V.G.	Good	Fair	Poor
800	400	350	300	250	200

Model 515—Hammerless Boxlock

NIB	Exc.	V.G.	Good	Fair	Poor
1100	550	450	400	350	300

Model 515—Single Trigger Hammerless Boxlock

NIB	Exc.	V.G.	Good	Fair	Poor
1200	600	500	400	300	250

Model 500—Skeet Hammerless Boxlock

NIB	Exc.	V.G.	Good	Fair	Poor
2000	1000	800	700	600	400

Model 530—Hammerless Boxlock

NIB	Exc.	V.G.	Good	Fair	Poor
800	400	350	300	250	200

Model 530M—Tenite Hammerless Boxlock

NIB	Exc.	V.G.	Good	Fair	Poor
800	400	350	300	250	200

Model 530M—Tenite Single Trigger Hammerless Boxlock

NIB	Exc.	V.G.	Good	Fair	Poor
1200	600	500	400	350	300

Model 530A—Hammerless Boxlock

NIB	Exc.	V.G.	Good	Fair	Poor
800	400	350	300	250	200

Model 530A—Single Trigger Hammerless Boxlock

NIB	Exc.	V.G.	Good	Fair	Poor
900	450	400	350	300	250

Model 311—Tenite Hammerless Boxlock

NIB	Exc.	V.G.	Good	Fair	Poor
800	400	350	300	250	200

Model 331—Single Trigger Hammerless Boxlock

NIB	Exc.	V.G.	Good	Fair	Poor
900	450	350	300	250	200

Model 311—Tenite Single Trigger Hammerless Boxlock

NIB	Exc.	V.G.	Good	Fair	Poor
1000	500	450	400	350	300

Model 311A—Hammerless Boxlock

NIB	Exc.	V.G.	Good	Fair	Poor
800	400	350	300	250	200

Model 311C—Hammerless Boxlock

NIB	Exc.	V.G.	Good	Fair	Poor
700	350	300	250	200	150

Model 311D—Hammerless Boxlock

NIB	Exc.	V.G.	Good	Fair	Poor
800	400	350	300	250	200

Model 311E—Hammerless Boxlock

NIB	Exc.	V.G.	Good	Fair	Poor
1000	500	400	350	300	250

Model 311 F—Hammerless Boxlock

NIB	Exc.	V.G.	Good	Fair	Poor
800	400	350	300	250	200

Model 311H—Hammerless Boxlock

NIB	Exc.	V.G.	Good	Fair	Poor
800	400	350	300	250	200

Model 311H—Vent-Rib Hammerless Boxlock

NIB	Exc.	V.G.	Good	Fair	Poor
900	450	400	350	300	250

Model 311J/R—Hammerless Boxlock

NIB	Exc.	V.G.	Good	Fair	Poor
700	350	300	250	200	150

Model 311J/R—Solid Rib Hammerless Boxlock

NIB	Exc.	V.G.	Good	Fair	Poor
700	350	300	250	200	150

Model 311H—Waterfowler Hammerless Boxlock

NIB	Exc.	V.G.	Good	Fair	Poor
1200	600	500	400	300	200

Model 240—.410 Over-and-Under Hammer Tenite

NIB	Exc.	V.G.	Good	Fair	Poor
600	500	400	300	250	200

RIVERSIDE BRAND

Courtesy Nick Niles, Paul Goodwin photo

Model 215 Hammer Boxlock

NIB	Exc.	V.G.	Good	Fair	Poor
1300	650	450	350	250	200

Model 315 (Early)—Hammerless Boxlock

NIB	Exc.	V.G.	Good	Fair	Poor
1000	500	400	350	250	200

Model 315 (Late)—Hammerless Boxlock

NIB	Exc.	V.G.	Good	Fair	Poor
1000	500	400	350	250	200

SUPER VALUE BRAND

Model 511—Hammerless Boxlock

NIB	Exc.	V.G.	Good	Fair	Poor
900	450	350	300	200	150

Model 511—Sunken Rib Hammerless Boxlock

NIB	Exc.	V.G.	Good	Fair	Poor
800	400	350	300	200	150

SPRINGFIELD BRAND

Model 215—Hammer Boxlock

NIB	Exc.	V.G.	Good	Fair	Poor
1000	500	400	350	250	150

Model 311—Hammerless Boxlock

NIB	Exc.	V.G.	Good	Fair	Poor
800	400	350	300	250	150

Model 315—Hammerless Boxlock

Courtesy Nick Niles, Paul Goodwin photo

NIB	Exc.	V.G.	Good	Fair	Poor
1000	500	400	350	250	200

Model 3150—Hammerless Boxlock

NIB	Exc.	V.G.	Good	Fair	Poor
1200	600	500	350	250	200

Model 3151—Hammerless Boxlock

NIB	Exc.	V.G.	Good	Fair	Poor
1500	750	600	400	300	200

Model 3151—Single Trigger Hammerless Boxlock

NIB	Exc.	V.G.	Good	Fair	Poor
1600	800	700	500	400	300

Model 311—Single Trigger Hammerless Boxlock

NIB	Exc.	V.G.	Good	Fair	Poor
1400	700	600	500	400	200

Model 5151—Hammerless Boxlock

NIB	Exc.	V.G.	Good	Fair	Poor
1000	500	400	350	250	200

Model 5151—Single Trigger Hammerless Boxlock

NIB	Exc.	V.G.	Good	Fair	Poor
1200	600	450	350	250	200

Model 311—New Style Hammerless Boxlock

NIB	Exc.	V.G.	Good	Fair	Poor
800	350	300	250	150	100

Model 311—New Style Tenite Hammerless Boxlock

NIB	Exc.	V.G.	Good	Fair	Poor
800	400	350	300	250	150

Model 511—Sunken Rib Hammerless Boxlock

NIB	Exc.	V.G.	Good	Fair	Poor
800	400	300	250	200	150

Model 511—Hammerless Boxlock

NIB	Exc.	V.G.	Good	Fair	Poor
900	450	300	250	200	150

Model 511A—Hammerless Boxlock

NIB	Exc.	V.G.	Good	Fair	Poor
900	450	300	250	200	150

STEVENS/SAVAGE SHOTGUNS

Model 411 Upland Sporter
Introduced in 2003 this side-by-side shotgun is chambered for the 12 or 20 gauge, as well as the .410 bore. The 12 gauge is fitted with 28" barrels, while the 28 and .410 have 26" barrels. Single trigger with ejectors. False sideplates are laser engraved. European walnut stock with pistol grip and splinter forend. Weight is about 6.75 to 6.5 lbs. depending on gauge.

NIB	Exc.	V.G.	Good	Fair	Poor
395	325	—	—	—	—

NOTE: Add $35 for 20 and .410 models.

STEVENS DATE CODE
Collectors will find a date code stamped on every double-barrel shotgun in the Stevens brands produced between March 1949 and December 1968. Usually, it is behind the hinge pin or ahead of the trigger guard on the bottom of the frame. It will appear as a small circle containing a number and letter. The letters correspond to the years shown in the following table. Significance of the numbers is not known.

DATE CODES			
A-1949	B-1950	C-1951	D-1952
E-1953	F-1954	G-1955	H-1956
I-1957	J-1958	K-1959	L-1960
M-1961	N-1962	P-1963	R-1964
S-1965	T-1966	U-1967	V-1968
W-1969	X-1970		

STOCKING & CO.
Worcester, Massachusetts

Pepperbox
A .28 or .316 barreled percussion pepperbox revolver with barrel lengths from 4" to 6". The hammer is fitted with a long cocking piece at the rear and the trigger guard may or may not be made with a spur at the rear. Blued with walnut grips. The barrel group marked "Stocking & Co., Worcester." Manufactured between 1846 and 1854.

Courtesy Wallis & Wallis, Lewes, Sussex, England

Exc.	V.G.	Good	Fair	Poor
—	—	1500	600	200

Single-Shot Pistol
A .36 caliber single-shot percussion pistol of the same pattern as the pepperbox with a 4" half octagonal barrel. Marked as above. Manufactured from 1849 to 1852.

Exc.	V.G.	Good	Fair	Poor
—	—	850	350	100

STOEGER, A. F.
South Hackensack, New Jersey

SHOTGUNS

Coach Gun
This is a side-by-side gun chambered for the 12 or 20 gauge shell as well as the .410 shell. Fitted with 20" barrels with double triggers. Improved Cylinder and Modified fixed chokes. Weight is about 7 lbs.

NIB	Exc.	V.G.	Good	Fair	Poor
320	250	—	—	—	—

NOTE: Add $50 for nickel finish.

Silverado Coach Gun
Offered in 12 and 20 gauge as well as .410 bore with straight- or pistol-grip stock and matte nickel finish. Straight-stock version is offered in 12 and 20 gauge only. Weight is about 6.5 lbs.

NIB	Exc.	V.G.	Good	Fair	Poor
375	300	—	—	—	—

Coach Gun Supreme
This model is similar to the above but offered with blue, stainless, or nickel receiver. Introduced in 2004.

NIB	Exc.	V.G.	Good	Fair	Good
380	300	—	—	—	—

NOTE: Add $10 for stainless and $30 for nickel.

Uplander
This side-by-side shotgun is chambered for the 12, 16, 20, 28, and .410 bores. with choice of 26" or 28" barrels. Fixed chokes. Double triggers. Weight is about 7.25 lbs.

NIB	Exc.	V.G.	Good	Fair	Poor
325	275	—	—	—	—

Uplander Special
As above but with straight grip and oil finish stock. Offered in 12, 20, or 28 gauge. Weight is about 7.3 lbs.

NIB	Exc.	V.G.	Good	Fair	Good
375	300	—	—	—	—

Uplander Supreme
Same as above but with select wood and screw-in chokes.

NIB	Exc.	V.G.	Good	Fair	Poor
425	350	—	—	—	—

Uplander English
This variation is fitted with a straight-grip stock and chambered for the 20 gauge or .410 bore. Fitted with 24" barrels. Weight is about 7 lbs. Also available with a short stock.

NIB	Exc.	V.G.	Good	Fair	Poor
340	275	—	—	—	—

STURM, RUGER & CO.
Southport, Connecticut

In 1946 William B. Ruger applied for his first patent on a blowback operated, semi-automatic, .22 caliber pistol. In 1949 Bill Ruger and Alexander Sturm released this pistol for sale, and the Ruger dynasty began. This pistol was as perfect for the American marketplace as could be. It was accurate, reliable, and inexpensive and ensured the new company's success. In 1951 Alexander Sturm passed away, but Mr. Ruger continued forward. At this time the fledgling television industry was popularizing the early American West, and Colt had not reintroduced the Single-Action Army after WWII. Ruger decided that a Western-style six shooter would be a successful venture, and the Single Six was born. This was not a Colt copy but a new design based on the Western look. Again Ruger scored in the marketplace, and this has been pretty much the rule ever since. With few exceptions this company has shown itself to be accurate in gauging what the gun-buying public wants. They have expanded their line to include double-action revolvers, single-shots, semi-auto and bolt-action rifles, percussion revolvers, and even a semi-automatic wonder nine. They have stayed ahead of the legal profession as much as possible by introducing safety devices and comprehensive instruction manuals and generally insured their future success. For such a relatively new company, collector interest in certain models is quite keen. There are a number of factors that govern Ruger collector values. All models made in 1976 were designated "200th Year of Liberty" models and if in NIB condition will bring up to a 25 percent premium if a market is found. The newer models that have a safety warning stamped on the barrel are generally purchased only by shooters and have no collector appeal whatsoever. The astute individual must be aware of these nuances when dealing in Rugers. There are some excellent works written on the Ruger (not as many as there are on the Colt or the Smith & Wesson), and the new collector can educate himself if he so desires. We list this company's models in chronological order.

NOTE: William B. Ruger died in 2002 at the age of 86.

SINGLE-ACTION REVOLVERS

Single Six Revolver
This is a .22 rimfire, 6-shot, single-action revolver. It was first offered with a 5-1/2" barrel length and a fixed sight. In 1959 additional barrel lengths were offered for this model in 4-5/8", 61/2", and 9-1/2". It is based in appearance on the Colt Single-Action Army, but internally it is a new design that features coil springs instead of the old-style, flat leaf springs. It also features a floating firing pin and is generally a stronger action than what was previously available. The early model had a flat loading gate and was made this way from 1953-1957, when the contoured gate became standard. Early models had checkered hard rubber grips changed to smooth varnished walnut by 1962. Black eagle grip medallions were used from the beginning of production to 1971 when a silver eagle grip medallion replaced it. No "Red Eagle" single-sixes were ever produced. This model was manufactured from 1953-1972.

Flat Gate Model
60,000 produced.

NIB	Exc.	V.G.	Good	Fair	Poor
600	500	350	225	150	125

NOTE: Be aware that revolvers serial numbered under 2000 will bring a premium of 25 percent to 125 percent depending on condition, low serial number, and color of cylinder frame—bright reddish purple the most desirable.

Contoured Gate Model
Introduced 1957.

Exc.	V.G.	Good	Fair	Poor
350	225	175	150	125

NOTE: Be aware that 4-5/8" and 9-1/2" barrel lengths will bring a premium. There were 258 5-1/2" barrel factory engraved pistols in this model. Add $3,500 to $5,000 for factory engraved and cased models.

Single Six Convertible
This model is similar to the Single Six but is furnished with an extra .22 rimfire Magnum cylinder.

Exc.	V.G.	Good	Fair	Poor
350	250	200	150	125

NOTE: Barrel lengths in 4-5/8" and 9-1/2" will bring a premium.

Single Six .22 Magnum Model
This model is similar to the Single Six except that it is chambered for the .22 rimfire Magnum and the frame was so marked. It was offered in the 6.5" barrel length only and was manufactured for three years. An extra long rifle cylinder was added later in production. The serial numbers are in the 300000-340000 range.

Exc.	V.G.	Good	Fair	Poor
350	300	250	200	175

Lightweight Single Six
This model is similar to the Single Six, with an aluminum alloy frame and 4-5/8" barrel. This variation was produced between 1956 and 1958 and was in the 200000-212000 serial number range. Approximately the first 6,500 were produced with alloy cylinders with steel chamber inserts.

Silver Anodized Frame with Aluminum Cylinder Model with Martin Hardcoat Finish

Exc.	V.G.	Good	Fair	Poor
600	400	300	225	195

Black Anodized Aluminum Frame and Cylinder Model

Exc.	V.G.	Good	Fair	Poor
650	450	350	300	250

Black Anodized Frame with Blue Steel Cylinder Model

Exc.	V.G.	Good	Fair	Poor
400	350	250	225	195

Silver Anodized with Blue Steel Cylinder Model
Only a few hundred pistols in this variation were produced by the factory with an "S" suffix.

Exc.	V.G.	Good	Fair	Poor
1000	800	600	400	200

NOTE: Stamped after the serial number or on the bottom of the frame. Varieties of "S" marked lightweights exist. Individual evaluation and appraisal is recommended. These are factory seconds and are verifiable.

NOTE: For original Lightweight Single-Six boxes add 25 percent to 40 percent.

Super Single Six
Introduced in 1964, this is the Single Six with adjustable sights. Prices given are for pistols with 5-1/2" and 6-1/2" barrels.

Exc.	V.G.	Good	Fair	Poor
400	300	200	125	100

Super Single Six with 4-5/8" Barrel
200 built.

Exc.	V.G.	Good	Poor
1000	900	750	400

Super Single Six—Nickel-Plated Model
Approximately 100 built.

Exc.	V.G.	Good	Poor
2250	1600	1200	—

NOTE: The above models are factory verifiable.

Bearcat (Old Model)
This is a scaled-down version of the single-action. It is chambered for .22 rimfire and has a 4" barrel and an unfluted, roll engraved cylinder. The frame is alloy, and it has a brass colored anodized alloy trigger guard. The finish is blue, and the grips are plastic impregnated wood until 1963, thereafter walnut with eagle medallions were used. This model was manufactured from 1958-1970.

Serial Number under 30000

Exc.	V.G.	Good	Fair	Poor
400	300	225	150	125

Alphabet Model

Exc.	V.G.	Good	Fair	Poor
450	350	295	275	225

Black Anodized Trigger Guard Model
109 built.

Exc.	V.G.	Good	Fair	Poor
800	600	500	400	—

Serial Number over 30000 or with 90-prefix

Exc.	V.G.	Good	Fair	Poor
350	300	265	225	175

Super Bearcat (Old Model)
This model is similar to the with a steel frame and, on later models, a blued steel trigger guard and grip frame. The early examples still used brass. This model was manufactured from 1971 to 1974.

Exc.	V.G.	Good	Fair	Poor
450	350	250	225	175

Blackhawk Flattop—.357 Magnum
The success of the Single Six led to the production of a larger version chambered for the .357 Magnum cartridge. This model is a single-action, with a 6-shot fluted cylinder and a flat top strap with adjustable "Micro sight." The barrel length is 4-5/8", 6.5", and 10". The finish is blue with checkered hard rubber grips on the early examples and smooth walnut on later ones. There were approximately 42,600 manufactured between 1955 and 1962.

Courtesy Know Your Ruger Single-Action Revolvers 1953-63. Blacksmith Corp.

4-5/8" barrel

NIB	Exc.	V.G.	Good	Fair	Poor
800	650	500	350	250	200

6-1/2" barrel

NIB	Exc.	V.G.	Good	Fair	Poor
1000	800	600	450	350	250

10" barrel

NIB	Exc.	V.G.	Good	Fair	Poor
1500	1200	950	850	750	600

Blackhawk Flattop .44 Magnum
In 1956 the .44 Magnum was introduced, and Ruger jumped on the bandwagon. This is similar in appearance to the .357 but has a slightly heavier frame and a larger cylinder. It was available in a 6.5", 7.5", and 10" barrel. It was manufactured from 1956-1963. There were approximately 29,700 manufactured.

6-1/2" Barrel

NIB	Exc.	V.G.	Good	Fair	Poor
1000	750	600	450	350	250

7-1/2" Barrel

NIB	Exc.	V.G.	Good	Fair	Poor
1200	950	700	600	450	300

10" Barrel

NIB	Exc.	V.G.	Good	Fair	Poor
1600	1300	900	800	700	400

Blackhawk
This model is similar to the "Flattop," but the rear sight is protected by two raised protrusions—one on each side. It was available chambered for the .30 Carbine, .357 Magnum, .41 Magnum, or the .45 Colt cartridge. Barrel lengths are 4-5/8" or 6.5" in .357 Magnum and .41 Magnum. .45 Colt version has 4-5/8" and 7.5" barrel lengths. The .30 Carbine is furnished with a 7.5" barrel only. The finish is blue, and the grips are walnut with Ruger medallions. This model was produced from 1962 to 1972.

NIB	Exc.	V.G.	Good	Fair	Poor
500	400	300	200	150	125

NOTE: Add 20 percent for .41 Mag. and 50 percent for .45 Colt and 35 percent for .30 Carbine. Original verified factory brass grip frame will add at least $200 to above prices. It was available chambered for the .357 Magnum or .41 Magnum (4-5/8" or 6-1/2" barrel), or .45 Long Colt (4-5/8" or 7-1/2" barrel). The .41 Magnum with factory installed brass frame will bring $800 to $1500 depending on condition.

Blackhawk Convertible
This model is the same as the Blackhawk with an extra cylinder to change or convert calibers. The .357 Magnum has a 9mm cylinder, and the .45 Colt has a .45 ACP cylinder.

.357/9mm

NIB	Exc.	V.G.	Good	Fair	Poor
550	450	400	300	200	—

.45 L.C./.45 ACP

NIB	Exc.	V.G.	Good	Fair	Poor
800	650	500	300	200	—

NOTE: The 4-5/8" barrel will bring a slight premium. Nonprefix serial numbered .357/9mm Blackhawks will bring a premium.

Super Blackhawk
The formidable recoil of the .44 Magnum cartridge was difficult to handle in a revolver with a small grip such as found on the Blackhawk, so it was decided to produce a larger-framed revolver with increased size in the grip. The rear of the trigger guard was squared off, and the cylinder was left unfluted to increase mass. This model was offered with a 7.5" barrel; 600 6.5" barrel Super Blackhawks were produced by factory error. This model is blued and has smooth walnut grips with medallions. The first of these revolvers were offered in a fitted wood case and are rare today. The Super Blackhawk was made from 1959-1972.

NIB	Exc.	V.G.	Good	Fair	Poor
600	500	400	300	200	150

Early Model in Wood Presentation Case

NIB	Exc.	V.G.	Good	Fair	Poor
1000	850	650	475	400	300

In Fitted White Cardboard Case

NIB	Exc.	V.G.	Good	Fair	Poor
1200	1100	1000	950	875	675

Long Grip Frame in Wood Case
300 guns built.

NIB	Exc.	V.G.	Good	Fair	Poor
1500	1250	1150	1050	800	675

Factory Verified 6-1/2" Barrel
Appx. 600 guns built in the 23000-25000 serial number range.

NIB	Exc.	V.G.	Good	Fair	Poor
850	750	650	550	450	375

NOTE: For pistols with brass grip frames add $250 to above prices. For pistols with verified factory installed brass grip frame each example should be appraised.

Hawkeye Single-Shot

The shooting public wanted a small-caliber, high-velocity handgun. The Smith & Wesson Model 53, chambered for the .22 Jet, appeared in 1961; and the cartridge created extraction problems for a revolver. Ruger solved the problem with the introduction of the Hawkeye—a single-shot that looked like a six shooter. In place of the cylinder was a breech block that cammed to the side for loading. This pistol was excellent from an engineering and performance standpoint but was not a commercial success. The Hawkeye is chambered for the .256 Magnum, a bottleneck cartridge, and has an 8.5" barrel and adjustable sights. The finish is blued with walnut, medallion grips. The barrel is tapped at the factory for a 1" scope base. This pistol is quite rare as only 3,300 were produced in 1963 and 1964.

NIB	Exc.	V.G.	Good	Fair	Poor
1800	1500	1200	850	600	500

Editor's Comment: All of the above single-action Ruger pistols fitted with factory optional grips will bring a premium regardless of model. This premium applies to pistols manufactured from 1954 to 1962 only. For the following optional grips the premium is: Ivory $800, Stag $400.

NEW MODEL SERIES

The Ruger firm has always demonstrated keen perception and in 1973 completely modified their single-action lockwork to accommodate a hammer block or transfer bar. This hammer block or transfer bar prevented accidental discharge should a revolver be dropped. In doing so, the company circumvented a great deal of potential legal problems and made collectibles out of the previous models. There are many individuals who simply do not care for the "New Models," as they are called, and will not purchase them; but judging from the continued success and growth of the Ruger company, those individuals must be the exception, not the rule.

Super Single Six Convertible (New Model)

This model is similar in appearance to the old model but has the new hammer block safety system. The frame has two pins instead of three screws, and opening the loading gate frees the cylinder stop for loading. Barrel lengths are 4-5/8", 5.5", 6.5", and 9.5". The sights are adjustable; the finish is blued. The grips are walnut with a medallion, and an interchangeable .22 Magnum cylinder is supplied. This model was introduced in 1973 and is currently in production.

NIB	Exc.	V.G.	Good	Fair	Poor
315	250	200	125	100	80

Stainless Steel Single Six Convertible

The same as the standard blued model but made from stainless steel. Offered with a 4-5/8", 6-1/2", and 9-1/2" barrel.

NIB	Exc.	V.G.	Good	Fair	Poor
350	275	200	175	125	100

NOTE: Pre-Warning pistols (1973-1976) with 4-5/8" or 9-1/2" barrel will bring an additional 40 percent premium. Pistols with 4-5/8" barrels with "made in the 200th year of American Liberty" rollmark on the barrel will bring at least 100 percent premium to the NIB prices.

New Model Single-Six (.22 LR only) "Star" Model

This model was produced in blue and stainless for one year only in 4-5/8", 5-1/2", 6-1/2", and 9-1/2" barrel lengths. Very low production on this model.

Blue Variation

5.5" or 6.5" barrel

NIB	Exc.	V.G.	Good	Fair	Poor
450	400	350	300	275	—

9.5" barrel—Rare

NIB	Exc.	V.G.	Good	Fair	Poor
550	500	450	400	350	—

4.62" barrel—Very Rare

NIB	Exc.	V.G.	Good	Fair	Poor
800	750	450	400	350	—

Stainless Variation

5.5" or 6.5" barrel

NIB	Exc.	V.G.	Good	Fair	Poor
450	350	275	—	—	—

9.5" barrel

NIB	Exc.	V.G.	Good	Fair	Poor
600	500	400	—	—	—

4.62" barrel—Rare

NIB	Exc.	V.G.	Good	Fair	Poor
650	550	500	—	—	—

Fixed Sight New Model Single Six

First made as drift adjustable rear sight (500 each in 4-5/8", 51/2", and 6-1/2" blue) and now a catalogued item as a pinched frame style fixed rear sight. Barrel lengths are offered in 5-1/2" and 6-1/2" lengths. Finish is blued or glossy stainless steel. Rear sight is fixed. Weights are between 32 and 38 oz. depending on barrel length and cylinder.

Blued Finish

NIB	Exc.	V.G.	Good	Fair	Poor
300	225	200	150	125	100

Stainless Steel

NIB	Exc.	V.G.	Good	Fair	Poor
395	300	250	200	150	125

Colorado Centennial Single Six

This model had a stainless steel grip frame, and the balance is blued. It has walnut grips with medallion insert. The barrel is 6-1/2", and the revolver is furnished with a walnut case with a centennial medal insert. There were 15,000 manufactured in 1975.

NIB	Exc.	V.G.	Good	Fair	Poor
500	400	—	—	—	—

NOTE: Add 50 percent for model with Liberty marked barrel.

Model "SSM" Single Six

This is the Single Six chambered for the .32 H&R Magnum cartridge. The first 800 pistols were marked with "SSM" on the cylinder frame and will bring a slight premium. Sold from 1984 to 1997. Adjustable sights.

NIB	Exc.	V.G.	Good	Fair	Poor
450	350	200	150	125	100

New Model Single Six-Fixed Sight

Introduced in 2000 this revolver is chambered for the .32 H&R Magnum cartridge and fitted with a 4.625" barrel. Offered in blue or stainless steel. Short (1/4" shorter) simulated ivory grips. Vaquero-style frame with fixed sights.

NIB	Exc.	V.G.	Good	Fair	Poor
525	400	—	—	—	—

New Model Single Six 50th Anniversary Model
Introduced in 2003 this model features a 4.625" barrel with blued finish. Top of barrel is rollmarked "50 years of single six 1953-2003." Comes standard with both .22 LR and .22 WMR cylinders. Cocobolo grips with red Ruger medallion. Packaged in a red plastic case with special "50 Year" label. Offered only in 2003.

NIB	Exc.	V.G.	Good	Fair	Poor
425	350	—	—	—	—

New Model Super Single Six
Chambered for the .22 LR and a separate cylinder for the .22 WMR cartridge. Barrel lengths are 4.625", 5.5", 6.5", and 9.5". Rosewood grips and adjustable or fixed sights. Blued finish except for optional stainless steel on 5.5" or 6.5" revolvers. Weight is about 35 oz. depending on barrel length.

NIB	Exc.	V.G.	Good	Fair	Poor
390	325	—	—	—	—

NOTE: For stainless steel models add $80.

New Model Super Single Six, .17 HMR
As above but with 6.5" barrel and chambered for the .17 HMR cartridge. Weight is about 35 oz. Introduced in 2003.

NIB	Exc.	V.G.	Good	Fair	Poor
390	325	—	—	—	—

Buckeye Special
This model was built in 1989 and 1990. It is chambered for the .38-40 or 10mm and .32-20 or .32 H&R cartridges.

NIB	Exc.	V.G.	Good	Fair	Poor
650	500	300	250	125	—

New Model Blackhawk
This model is similar in appearance to the old model Blackhawk, offered in the same calibers and barrel lengths. It has the transfer bar safety device. It was introduced in 1973 and is currently in production.

NIB	Exc.	V.G.	Good	Fair	Poor
325	250	200	175	150	125

Stainless Steel Blackhawk (New Model)
This is simply the New Model Blackhawk made from stainless steel. To date it has been offered in .357, .44, and .45 L.C. calibers.

NIB	Exc.	V.G.	Good	Fair	Poor
400	325	275	225	175	150

Blackhawk Convertible (New Model)
This model is the same as the Blackhawk with interchangeable conversion cylinders—.357 Magnum/9mm and .45 Colt/.45 ACP. Prices are given for blued model.

NIB	Exc.	V.G.	Good	Fair	Poor
400	300	200	175	150	125

.45 ACP & .45 Long Colt convertable (1998)

NIB	Exc.	V.G.	Good	Fair	Poor
500	400	—	—	—	—

Stainless Model .357/9mm
300 guns built.

NIB	Exc.	V.G.	Good	Fair	Poor
—	700	600	500	375	250

Model SRM Blackhawk
This is the New Model Blackhawk with a 7.5" or 10.5" barrel. It was chambered for the .357 Maximum and was intended for silhouette shooting. This model experienced problems with gas erosion in the forcing cone and under the top strap and was removed from production in 1984 after approximately 9200 were manufactured.

Exc.	V.G.	Good	Fair	Poor
650	500	400	275	250

Super Blackhawk (New Model)
This model is similar in appearance to the old model but has the transfer bar safety device. It was manufactured from 1973 to the present and commenced at serial number 81-00001.

NIB	Exc.	V.G.	Good	Fair	Poor
500	400	275	225	175	125

Super Blackhawk Stainless Steel
This model is the same as the blued version but is made of stainless steel. In 1998 this model was offered in 4-5/8" or 7-1/2" barrels with hunter grip frame and laminated grip panels. Add $50 to prices for this feature.

NIB	Exc.	V.G.	Good	Fair	Poor
525	400	300	250	200	150

Super Blackhawk Hunter
Introduced in 2002 this .44 Magnum model features a 7.5" barrel with integral full-length solid rib for scope mounts. Stainless steel. Adjustable rear sight. Scope rings included. Weight is about 52 oz.

NIB	Exc.	V.G.	Good	Fair	Poor
640	500	400	—	—	—

Bisley Model
This model has the modified features found on the famous old Colt Bisley Target model—the flat top frame, fixed or adjustable sights, and the longer grip frame that has become the Bisley trademark. The Bisley is available chambered for .22 LR, .32 H&R Magnum, .357 Magnum, .41 Magnum, .44 Magnum, and .45 Long Colt. The barrel lengths are 6.5" and 7.5"; cylinders are either fluted or unfluted and roll engraved. The finish is a satin blue, and the grips are smooth Goncalo Alves with medallions. The Bisley was introduced in 1986.

.22 LR and .32 H&R Magnum

NIB	Exc.	V.G.	Good	Fair	Poor
380	305	225	200	150	125

NOTE: Add $100 for .32 Magnum Bisley.

.357 Magnum, .41 Magnum, .44 Magnum, and .45 Long Colt

NIB	Exc.	V.G.	Good	Fair	Poor
450	365	275	250	200	175

NOTE: Approximately 750 stainless grip frame .22 caliber Bisleys were made. These will demand a premium.

Shootists Bisley
Produced in 1994 for the Shootist organization in memory of Tom Ruger. Chambered for the .22 cartridge these revolvers were limited to 52 total produced. They were stainless steel and were fitted with 4-5/8" barrels. The barrels were marked, "IN MEMORY OF OUR FRIEND TOM RUGER THE SHOOTIST 1994." Some of these revolvers, but not all, have the name of the owner engraved on the backstrap.

NIB	Exc.	V.G.	Good	Fair	Poor
1500	—	—	—	—	—

Old Army Percussion Revolver
This model is a .45 caliber percussion revolver with a 7-1/2" barrel. It has a 6-shot cylinder, with a blued finish and walnut grips. For 1994 this model is offered with fixed sights. Weight is about 46 oz.

NIB	Exc.	V.G.	Good	Fair	Poor
413	325	250	100	100	100

NOTE: For pistols with original factory installed brass grip frame add $150 to above prices.

Old Army Stainless Steel
This model is the same as the blued version except that it is made of stainless steel.

NIB	Exc.	V.G.	Good	Fair	Poor
465	400	275	100	100	100

Ruger Vaquero
This single-action pistol was introduced in 1993 and was voted handgun of the year by the shooting industry. It is a fixed sight version of the New Model Blackhawk. It is available in stainless steel or blued with case-colored frame. Offered in three different barrel lengths: 4.62", 5.5", and 7.5". Chambered for the .45 Long Colt. In 1994 the .44-40 and .44 Magnum calibers were added to the Vaquero line. Capacity is 6 rounds. Weighs between 39 and 41 oz. depending on barrel length.

NIB	Exc.	V.G.	Good	Fair	Poor
495	400	300	200	150	100

NOTE: Vaqueros with 4-5/8" barrel chambered for .44 Magnum in both blue and stainless are uncatalogued, add 25 percent.

Ruger Vaquero Bird's-head
Introduced in 2001 this model features a bird's-head grip. Chambered for the .45 Long Colt cartridge and fitted with a 5.5" barrel. Offered in stainless steel and blued finish. Weight is about 40 oz.

NOTE: In 2002 this model was offered with 3.75" barrel and black Micarta grips. In 2003 this model was offered chambered for the .357 Magnum cartridge. Simulated ivory grips are also offered.

NIB	Exc.	V.G.	Good	Fair	Poor
575	450	—	—	—	—

Ruger Bisley Vaquero
Introduced in 1997 this model features a 5.5" barrel chambered for .44 Magnum or .45 Long Colt. Grips are smooth rosewood. Finish is blued with case colored frame. Blade front sight and notch rear. Weight is about 40 oz.

NIB	Exc.	V.G.	Good	Fair	Poor
425	350	—	—	—	—

New Ruger Bearcat (Super Bearcat)
The return of an old favorite was made in 1994. This new version is furnished with a .22 LR cylinder and a .22 WMR cylinder. Barrel length is 4" with fixed sights. Grips are walnut. Offered with blued finish.

Blue

NIB	Exc.	V.G.	Good	Fair	Poor
375	300	250	—	—	—

Stainless Steel

NIB	Exc.	V.G.	Good	Fair	Poor
400	325	275	—	—	—

Convertable (Recalled)

NIB	Exc.	V.G.	Good	Fair	Poor
1100	900	700	—	—	—

NOTE: There was a factory recall on the magnum cylinders. Bearcats with both cylinders are very rare.

New Model Super Bearcat
Reintroduced in 2002 this .22 caliber model features a stainless steel or blued finish, 4" barrel with fixed sights and Rosewood grips. Weight is about 24 oz.

NIB	Exc.	V.G.	Good	Fair	Poor
375	300	—	—	—	—

NOTE: Add $50 for stainless steel version.

Ruger Gold Label Side-by-Side
Introduced in 2002 this model is chambered for the 12 gauge 3" shell. Offered with 28" barrels with choke tubes. Choice of pistol or straight grip checkered walnut stock. Ejectors and single trigger. Weight is about 6.33 lbs.

NIB	Exc.	V.G.	Good	Fair	Poor
1950	1550	—	—	—	—

SUNDANCE INDUSTRIES, INC.
North Hollywood, California
This company was in business from 1989 to 2002.

Sundance Point Blank
This is an over-and-under derringer chambered for the .22 LR cartridge. It is fitted with a 3" barrel and double-action trigger. Enclosed hammer. Matte black finish. Weight is about 8 oz. Introduced in 1994.

NIB	Exc.	V.G.	Good	Fair	Poor
95	80	70	50	—	—

SUTHERLAND, S.
Richmond, Virginia

Pocket Pistol
A .41 caliber percussion single-shot pistol with round barrels of 2.5" to 4" in length, German silver mounts and a walnut stock. The lock normally marked "S. Sutherland" or "S. Sutherland/Richmond." Manufactured during the 1850s.

Exc.	V.G.	Good	Fair	Poor
—	—	2000	800	300

SYMS, J. G.
New York, New York

Pocket Pistol
A .41 caliber single-shot percussion pistol with 1.5" to 3.5" barrels, German silver mounts and a walnut stock. The lock normally marked "Syms/New York." Manufactured during the 1850s.

Exc.	V.G.	Good	Fair	Poor
—	—	2000	800	300

T

TAYLOR'S & CO., INC.
Winchester, Virginia

PISTOLS

Napoleon Le Page Pistol (Model 551)
A percussion French-style duelling pistol. Chambered for .45 caliber and fitted with a 10" octagon barrel. Walnut stock silver plated buttcap and trigger guard. Double set triggers. Made by Uberti.

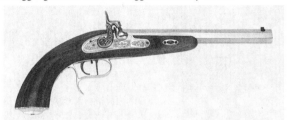

NIB	Exc.	V.G.	Good	Fair	Poor
350	275	—	—	—	—

Kentucky Pistol (Model 550)
Chambered for the .45 caliber ball and fitted with a 10" barrel. Bird's-head grip with brass ramrod thimbles and case hardened sidelock. Made by Uberti.

NIB	Exc.	V.G.	Good	Fair	Poor
185	150	—	—	—	—

Colt Model 1847 Walker (Model 500A)
Fitted with a 9" round barrel and chambered for .44 caliber. This model has a 6-round engraved cylinder. Steel frame and backstrap and brass trigger guard. One-piece walnut grips. Made by Uberti.

NIB	Exc.	V.G.	Good	Fair	Poor
370	300	—	—	—	—

Colt Model 1851 Navy
Offered with either brass or steel frame with brass backstrap and trigger guard. Chambered for .36 caliber and fitted with a 7.5" barrel. Cylinder holds 6 rounds. One-piece walnut grip. Brass frame model made by Armi San Marco. Steel frame model made by F.lli Pietta.

Brass frame (Model 210)

NIB	Exc.	V.G.	Good	Fair	Poor
135	100	—	—	—	—

Steel frame (Model 245)

NIB	Exc.	V.G.	Good	Fair	Poor
165	125	—	—	—	—

Remington Model 1858
This is a .44 caliber either a brass frame or steel frame and brass trigger guard model with 8" octagon barrel. Cylinder holds 6 rounds. Two-piece walnut grips. Brass frame made by F.lli Pietta. Steel frame made by Armi San Marco.

Brass Frame (Model 410)

NIB	Exc.	V.G.	Good	Fair	Poor
150	120	—	—	—	—

Steel Frame (Model 430)

NIB	Exc.	V.G.	Good	Fair	Poor
185	140	—	—	—	—

Colt Dragoon (Models 485A, 490A, 495A)
Offered in 1st, 2nd, and 3rd models each is fitted with a 7.5" barrel and chambered for .44 caliber. Steel frame and brass backstrap and trigger guard. The 2nd and 3rd models have a square cylinder stop. The loading lever is inverted on the 3rd model. All have one-piece walnut grip. Made by Uberti.

NIB	Exc.	V.G.	Good	Fair	Poor
295	250	—	—	—	—

NOTE: Add $15 for 3rd model.

Colt Model 1848 Baby Dragoon (Models 470, 471, 472)
Chambered for the .31 caliber and fitted with a 5-round cylinder. Barrel length is 4". Choice of blued or white steel frame. Brass backstrap and trigger guard. One-piece walnut grip. Made by Uberti.

NIB	Exc.	V.G.	Good	Fair	Poor
250	200	—	—	—	—

Starr Model 1858 (Model 510, 511)
This model is offered in either double-action or single-action. Chambered for the .44 caliber and fitted with a 6" round barrel. Made by F.lli Pietta.

NIB	Exc.	V.G.	Good	Fair	Poor
370	300	—	—	—	—

Colt Model 1860 Army
This model features an 8" round barrel except for the Sheriff's model which is 5.5". Choice of brass or steel frame with brass backstrap and trigger guard. Chambered for .44 caliber. One-piece walnut grip. Brass frame model made by Armi San Marco and steel frame by Uberti.

Brass Frame (Model 300)

NIB	Exc.	V.G.	Good	Fair	Poor
160	250	—	—	—	—

Steel Frame (Model 310, 312, 315)

NIB	Exc.	V.G.	Good	Fair	Poor
250	200	—	—	—	—

NOTE: A half-fluted cylinder model is also offered.

Colt Model 1861 Navy (Model 210)
This model is chambered for the .36 caliber and fitted with a 7.5" round barrel. Cylinder is 6 rounds. Brass frame and backstrap and trigger guard. One-piece walnut grip. Made by Uberti.

NIB	Exc.	V.G.	Good	Fair	Poor
250	200	—	—	—	—

Colt Model 1862 Police (Model 315B)
Fitted with a 6.5" round barrel and chambered for .36 caliber. Case hardened frame with brass backstrap and trigger guard. Made by Uberti.

NIB	Exc.	V.G.	Good	Fair	Poor
265	200	—	—	—	—

Colt Model 1862 Pocket (Model 315C)
Similar to the above model but fitted with a 6.5" octagonal barrel. Made by Uberti.

NIB	Exc.	V.G.	Good	Fair	Poor
235	185	—	—	—	—

Remington Model 1863 Pocket (Model 435)
This revolver is chambered for the .31 caliber ball and fitted with a 3.5" barrel. Cylinder is 5 rounds. Frame, backstrap and trigger guard are brass. Walnut grip. Made by Armi San Marco.

NIB	Exc.	V.G.	Good	Fair	Poor
150	100	—	—	—	—

Colt Model 1873 Cattleman (Models 700, 701, 702)
This famous replica is made in several different configurations. Offered in barrel lengths of 4.75", 5.5", and 7.5". Calibers are: .45 Colt, .44-40, .44 Special, .38-40, .357 Magnum, and .45 ACP. Frame is case hardened with steel backstrap. One-piece walnut grip. Made by Uberti.

NIB	Exc.	V.G.	Good	Fair	Poor
400	325	—	—	—	—

NOTE: Add $80 for dual cylinder and $80 for nickel finish.

Colt Model 1873 Bird's-head (Models 703A, 703B, 703C)
Same as above but offered with bird's-head grip.

NIB	Exc.	V.G.	Good	Fair	Poor
400	325	—	—	—	—

Colt Model 1873 "Outfitter"
Chambered for the .45 Colt or .357 Magnum cartridge and fitted with a 4.75", 5.5", or 7.5" barrel. Stainless steel finish and walnut grips.

NIB	Exc.	V.G.	Good	Fair	Poor
605	475	—	—	—	—

RIFLES

Kentucky Rifle
Offered in either flintlock or percussion this rifle is .40 caliber and fitted with a 3.5" barrel. One-piece stock with brass fixtures.

Flintlock (Model 183)

NIB	Exc.	V.G.	Good	Fair	Poor
335	250	—	—	—	—

Percussion (Model 182)

NIB	Exc.	V.G.	Good	Fair	Poor
300	240	—	—	—	—

Model 1842 U.S. Percussion Musket (Model 125)
This model is offered as a smoothbore or rifled musket with 42" .69 caliber barrel. Finish is in the white. One-piece walnut stock.

Smoothbore

NIB	Exc.	V.G.	Good	Fair	Poor
540	425	—	—	—	—

Rifled Smoothbore with Rear Sight (Model 126)

NIB	Exc.	V.G.	Good	Fair	Poor
585	450	—	—	—	—

Model 1855 U.S. Percussion Musket (Model 116)
This model has a .58 caliber 40" barrel with rear sight. One-piece walnut stock. White satin finish.

NIB	Exc.	V.G.	Good	Fair	Poor
550	425	—	—	—	—

Model 1853 3-Band Enfield Musket (Model 120)
This rifled musket has a 39" .58 caliber barrel. Blued finish. One-piece walnut stock. Brass buttplate, nosecap, and trigger guard.

NIB	Exc.	V.G.	Good	Fair	Poor
425	325	—	—	—	—

Model 1858 2-Band Enfield Musket (Model 121)
Similar to the above model but fitted with a .58 caliber 33" barrel.

NIB	Exc.	V.G.	Good	Fair	Poor
400	325	—	—	—	—

Model 1861 Springfield Musket (Model 110)
This model has a 40" .58 caliber barrel with one-piece walnut stock. White satin finish.

NIB	Exc.	V.G.	Good	Fair	Poor
475	375	—	—	—	—

Model 1862 C.S. Richmond Musket (Model 115)
This rifle is fitted with a 40" .58 caliber barrel with three barrel bands. Brass buttplate and nosecap. White satin finish. One-piece walnut stock.

NIB	Exc.	V.G.	Good	Fair	Poor
490	400	—	—	—	—

Model 1863 Remington Zouave (Model 140)
Fitted with a 33" barrel chambered for the .58 caliber ball. One-piece walnut stock with blued finish, brass buttplate, nosecap, trigger guard, patchbox, and barrel bands.

NIB	Exc.	V.G.	Good	Fair	Poor
375	300	—	—	—	—

Henry Rifle
This lever-action rifle is chambered for the .44-40 or .45 Colt cartridge. Fitted with a 24.25" octagon barrel. Walnut stock. Open sights.

Brass frame (Model 198)

NIB	Exc.	V.G.	Good	Fair	Poor
940	750	—	—	—	—

Iron Frame (Model 199)

NIB	Exc.	V.G.	Good	Fair	Poor
990	800	—	—	—	—

Winchester Model 1866 (Model 201)
This model is chambered for the .44-40 or .45 Colt cartridge. Fitted with a 24.25" octagon barrel. Brass frame. Open sights. Made by Uberti.

NIB	Exc.	V.G.	Good	Fair	Poor
830	650	—	—	—	—

Winchester Model 1866 Yellowboy Carbine (Model 202)
Same as above but with 19" round barrel and the additional .38 Special caliber. Made by Uberti.

NIB	Exc.	V.G.	Good	Fair	Poor
750	600	—	—	—	—

Winchester Model 1873 (Model 200)
This lever action model is chambered for the .44-40 or .45 Colt cartridge and fitted with a 24.25" octagon barrel. Made by Uberti.

NIB	Exc.	V.G.	Good	Fair	Poor
750	600	—	—	—	—

Winchester Model 1873 Carbine (Model 200B)
Chambered for the .45 Long Colt cartridge and fitted with a 19" barrel. Magazine capacity is 10 rounds. Walnut stock and case colored frame.

NIB	Exc.	V.G.	Good	Fair	Poor
825	650	—	—	—	—

Winchester Model 1873 Sporting Rifle (Model 200C)
Chambered for the .45 Long Colt cartridge and fitted with a 30" octagon barrel. Checkered walnut stock with pistol grip. Case colored frame and blued barrel.

NIB	Exc.	V.G.	Good	Fair	Poor
925	750	—	—	—	—

Winchester Model 1885 High Wall (Model 203)
Offered with 30" or 32" barrels chambered for the .45-70 cartridge. Walnut stock.

NIB	Exc.	V.G.	Good	Fair	Poor
800	650	—	—	—	—

Winchester Model 1885 Low Wall Sporting Rifle (Model 204)
This single-shot rifle is chambered for the .22 LR, .32-20, or .38-40 cartridge. Checkered walnut stock.

NIB	Exc.	V.G.	Good	Fair	Poor
800	650	—	—	—	—

Winchester Model 92
Introduced in 2004 this lever-action rifle is chambered for the .32-20, .32 H&R Magnum, .357 Magnum, .38 Special, .38-40, .44-40, .44 S&W, or the .45 Colt. Barrel length is 20" or 24" octagon. Takedown feature. Hardwood stock with blued barrel finish and case colored frame.

NIB	Exc.	V.G.	Good	Fair	Poor
965	750	—	—	—	—

Sharps Model 1859 Infantry (Model 151)
This rifle is fitted with a 30" round barrel and is chambered for the .54 caliber cartridge. One-piece walnut with 3 barrel bands. Adjustable rear sight.

NIB	Exc.	V.G.	Good	Fair	Poor
950	750	—	—	—	—

Sharps Model 1859 Berdan Military (Model 152)
This .54 caliber rifle is fitted with a 30" round barrel. One-piece walnut stock with 3 barrel bands. Adjustable rear sight. This model is fitted with double set triggers.

NIB	Exc.	V.G.	Good	Fair	Poor
1000	800	—	—	—	—

Sharps Model 1859 Cavalry (Model 153)
This model has a 22" round barrel with adjustable rear sight. Chambered for .54 caliber. Walnut stock is fitted with patch box.

NIB	Exc.	V.G.	Good	Fair	Poor
825	650	—	—	—	—

Sharps Model 1863 Cavalry (Model 154)
Similar to the Model 1859 Cavalry but without the patch box.

NIB	Exc.	V.G.	Good	Fair	Poor
800	650	—	—	—	—

Sharps Model 1863 Sporting Rifle (Model 131)
This .54 caliber model is offered with either 30" or 32" octagon barrel with single or double set triggers. Walnut stock.

NIB	Exc.	V.G.	Good	Fair	Poor
875	700	—	—	—	—

NOTE: Add $20 for double set trigger.

Sharps Model 1874 Sporting Rifle (Model 138)
This model is offered with a variety of features. Available in .45-70 with choice of 30" or 32" octagon barrel with a choice of single trigger or double set triggers. It is also available with Hartford-style pewter forend tip. In this configuration it is available in .45-70, .40-65, .45-90, or .45-120 calibers. Checkered stock with patch is optional.

NIB	Exc.	V.G.	Good	Fair	Poor
895	700	—	—	—	—

NOTE: Add $125 for Hartford-style forend tip. Add $250 for checkered stock with patch box.

Sharps Model 1874 Deluxe Sporting Rifle (Model 155)
This .45-70 caliber model features a hand checkered walnut stock with oil finish. Receiver is in the white with standard scroll engraving

NIB	Exc.	V.G.	Good	Fair	Poor
1800	1350	—	—	—	—

NOTE: For Deluxe Model 1874 with gold inlay add $800.

Sharps Model 1874 Infantry Rifle (Model 157)
This .45-70 caliber model features a 30" round barrel with 3 barrel bands. One-piece walnut stock. Adjustable rear sight. Single trigger. Patch box in stock.

NIB	Exc.	V.G.	Good	Fair	Poor
1000	800	—	—	—	—

Sharps Model 1874 Berdan Rifle (Model 158)
Similar to the above model but with a double set trigger.

NIB	Exc.	V.G.	Good	Fair	Poor
1050	825	—	—	—	—

Sharps Model 1874 Cavalry (Model 159)
This .45-70 caliber model is fitted with a 22" round barrel. Adjustable rear sight.

NIB	Exc.	V.G.	Good	Fair	Poor
875	700	—	—	—	—

Spencer Model 1865 Carbine (Model 160)
This lever-action model is chambered in a choice of calibers: .56-50, .44 Russian, or .45 Schofield. Fitted with a 20" round barrel. Walnut stock. Case hardened receiver and blued barrel. Made by Armi Sport.

NIB	Exc.	V.G.	Good	Fair	Poor
1200	950	—	—	—	—

TAYLOR, L.B.
Chicopee, Massachusetts

Pocket Pistol
A .32 caliber spur trigger single-shot pocket pistol with a 3.5" octagonal barrel marked "L. B. Taylor & Co. Chicopee Mass." Silver-plated brass frame, blued barrel and walnut grips. Manufactured during the late 1860s and early 1870s.

Exc.	V.G.	Good	Fair	Poor
—	—	800	350	100

TERRIER ONE
Importer—Southern Gun Distributors
Miami, Florida

Terrier One
A .32 caliber double-action swing-out cylinder revolver with a 2.25" barrel and 5-shot cylinder. Nickel-plated with checkered walnut grips. Manufactured from 1984 to 1987.

Exc.	V.G.	Good	Fair	Poor
100	75	50	30	25

TERRY, J. C.
New York City, New York

Pocket Pistol
A .22 caliber spur trigger single-shot pocket pistol with a 3.75" round barrel. The back strap marked "J.C. Terry/Patent Pending." Silver-plated brass frame, blued barrel and rosewood or walnut grips. Manufactured in the late 1860s.

Exc.	V.G.	Good	Fair	Poor
—	—	950	475	100

TEXAS CONTRACT RIFLES
Three contractors produced rifles for the State of Texas during 1862 and 1863. One of these patterns has a sporting back-action lock, Enfield barrel bands, an overall length of 47-3/8", heavy 32" long barrel of .58 caliber. Total deliveries by all contractors amounted to 1,464 rifles. Quality of these arms was decidedly inferior and often complained about.

Prospective purchasers are strongly advised to secure an expert appraisal prior to acquisition.

TEXAS GUNFIGHTERS
Ponte Zanano, Italy
Importer—Texas Gunfighters
Irving, Texas

Shootist Single-Action
A .45 Long Colt caliber single-action revolver with a 4.75" barrel. Nickel-plated with one-piece walnut grips. This model is made by Aldo Uberti. Introduced in 1988.

NIB	Exc.	V.G.	Good	Fair	Poor
600	550	500	400	350	200

1-of-100 Edition
As above, with one-piece mother-of-pearl grips fitted in a case with an additional set of walnut grips. 100 were made in 1988.

NIB	Exc.	V.G.	Good	Fair	Poor
1250	1000	850	700	600	300

TEXAS LONGHORN ARMS, INC.
Richmond, Texas

NOTE: As of 1998 this company had suspended operations.

Texas Border Special
A .44 Special or .45 Colt caliber single-action revolver with a 3.5" barrel and Pope-style rifling. Blued, case hardened with one-piece walnut grips.

NIB	Exc.	V.G.	Good	Fair	Poor
1500	1250	1000	800	600	300

Mason Commemorative
As above, in .45 Colt with a 4.75" barrel and the Mason's insignia. Gold inlaid. Introduced in 1987.

NIB	Exc.	V.G.	Good	Fair	Poor
1500	1250	1000	800	600	300

South Texas Army
As above, but with a 4.75" barrel also chambered for the .357 Magnum cartridge and fitted with conventional one-piece walnut grips.

NIB	Exc.	V.G.	Good	Fair	Poor
1500	1250	1000	800	600	300

West Texas Target
As above, with a 7.5" barrel, flat top frame and in .32-20 caliber in addition to the calibers noted above.

NIB	Exc.	V.G.	Good	Fair	Poor
1500	1250	1000	800	600	300

Grover's Improved Number Five
Similar to the above, in .44 Magnum with a 5.5" barrel. Serial Numbered K1 to K1200. Introduced in 1988.

NIB	Exc.	V.G.	Good	Fair	Poor
1000	800	700	600	500	250

Texas Sesquicentennial Commemorative
As above, engraved in the style of Louis D. Nimschke with one-piece ivory grips and a fitted case.

NIB	Exc.	V.G.	Good	Fair	Poor
2500	2000	1500	900	750	400

THAMES ARMS CO.
Norwich, Connecticut

A .22, .32, or .38 caliber double-action top break revolver with varying length barrels normally marked "Automatic Revolver", which refers to the cartridge ejector. Nickel-plated with walnut grips.

Exc.	V.G.	Good	Fair	Poor
500	200	100	75	50

TRADITIONS
Old Saybrook, Connecticut

SIDE-BY-SIDE SHOTGUNS
NOTE: These side-by-side guns are imported from the Italian firm of Fausti Stanfano.

Elite I DT
This model is offered in 12, 20, and 28 gauge as well as .410 bore. All gauges are fitted wtih 26" barrels with fixed chokes. Double triggers and extractors. Walnut stock. Weight about 6 lbs.

NIB	Exc.	V.G.	Good	Fair	Poor
750	600	—	—	—	—

NOTE: Add $60 for 28 and .410 models.

Elite I ST
Same as above but with single-selective trigger.

NIB	Exc.	V.G.	Good	Fair	Poor
890	700	—	—	—	—

Elite Hunter
Introduced in 2001 this model features either a 12 or 20 gauge gun with 26" barrels with screw-in chokes. Walnut stock with beavertail forend. Single non-selective trigger. Weight is about 6.5 lbs.

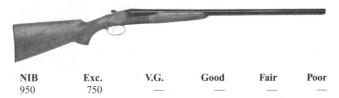

NIB	Exc.	V.G.	Good	Fair	Poor
950	750	—	—	—	—

Elite Field III ST
Introduced in 2001 this model is offered in either 28 or .410 bore with 26" barrels. High grade walnut stock with straight grip. Fixed chokes. Engraved receiver with gold. Weight is about 6.25 lbs.

NIB	Exc.	V.G.	Good	Fair	Poor
2000	1500	—	—	—	—

Uplander II Silver
Chambererd for the 12 gauge with 28" barrels or 20 gauge with 26" barrels. Choke tubes. Silver receiver with light scroll engraving. Checkered stock with high grade walnut. Straight grip. Single trigger and auto ejectors. Weight is about 6.75 lbs.

NIB	Exc.	V.G.	Good	Fair	Poor
2130	1575	—	—	—	—

Uplander III Silver
As above but with more extensive engraving with gold inlays.

NIB	Exc.	V.G.	Good	Fair	Poor
2890	2150	—	—	—	—

Uplander V Silver
As above but with sideplates, extensive engraving and gold inlays.

NIB	Exc.	V.G.	Good	Fair	Poor
3440	2550	—	—	—	—

TRANTER, WILLIAM
Birmingham, England

William Tranter produced a variety of revolvers on his own and a number of other makers produced revolvers based upon his designs. Consequently, "Tranter's Patent" is to be found on revolvers made by such firms as Deane, Adams and Deane, etc.

Model 1872
A .38 caliber double-action revolver with a 6" octagonal barrel and 6-shot cylinder. Blued with walnut grips.

Exc.	V.G.	Good	Fair	Poor
—	1000	500	300	200

Model 1878
A .450 caliber double-action revolver with a 6" octagonal barrel. Blued with a walnut grip. Manufactured from 1878 to 1887.

Exc.	V.G.	Good	Fair	Poor
—	1200	500	275	175

TRIPPLET & SCOTT
MERIDAN MANUFACTURING COMPANY
Meridan, Connecticut

Repeating Carbine
A .50 caliber carbine with either a 22" or 30" round barrel and a 7-shot magazine located in the butt. This model is loaded by turning the barrel until it comes in line with the magazine. Blued, case hardened with a walnut stock. Approximately 5,000 were made in 1864 and 1865.

Exc.	V.G.	Good	Fair	Poor
—	3500	1500	500	200

TRISTAR SPORTING ARMS
N. Kansas City, Missouri

Tristar 300 series over-and-under guns are imported from Turkey. Tristar Nova series are imported from Italy.

NOTE: In 2000 Tristar bought American Arms. American Arms no longer exists but some of its models will appear under the Tristar name. For American Arms firearms built prior to the sale see that section.

BASQUE SERIES
This series of side-by-side shotguns was introduced in 2003. They are produced in Spain by Zabala.

Brittany Sporting
Offered in 12 and 20 gauge with 28" barrels with 3" chambers and choke tubes. The action is box lock with sideplates scroll engraved with

case coloring. Semi-fancy checkered walnut stock with oil finish and pistol grip. Semi beavertail forend. Single-selective trigger and ejectors. Weight is around 6.75 lbs.

NIB	Exc.	V.G.	Good	Fair	Poor
865	675	—	—	—	—

Brittany

This model features a boxlock action with case colored frame with scroll engraving. Walnut stock with straight grip. Offered in 12 or 20 gauge with 26" barrels with choke tubes. Single-selective trigger and ejectors. Weight is about 6.5 lbs. depending on gauge.

NIB	Exc.	V.G.	Good	Fair	Poor
750	600	—	—	—	—

Gentry/Gentry Coach

This model is offered in 12, 16, 20 or 28 gauge and .410 bore in the Gentry and 12 and 20 gauge in the Gentry Coach. Barrel length are 28" for the Gentry (26" for 28 and .410) and 20" for the Gentry Coach. Boxlock action with engraved antique silver finish. Walnut stock with pistol grip. Choke tubes. Single-selective trigger. Weight is about 6.5 lbs. for Gentry and Gentry Coach depending on gauge.

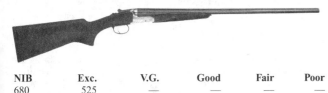

NIB	Exc.	V.G.	Good	Fair	Poor
680	525	—	—	—	—

Derby Classic

This model features a sidelock frame and action that is engraved and case colored. Offered in 12 gauge with fixed chokes in modified and full. Fitted with 28" barrel. Double trigger and automatic ejectors. Weight is approximately 7.75 lbs.

NIB	Exc.	V.G.	Good	Fair	Poor
1240	975	—	—	—	—

411 SERIES

These shotguns are made in Italy by R.F.M. Luciano Rota.

Model 411

This side-by-side double is imported from Italy and introduced in 1998. Chambered for 12, 20, and .410 bore with choice of 26" or 28" barrels with choke tubes or fixed chokes. Boxlock action with engraving and case coloring. Double triggers and extractors. Standard walnut stock with pistol grip and splinter forearm. Weight is between 6 and 6.5 lbs.

NIB	Exc.	V.G.	Good	Fair	Poor
850	675	—	—	—	—

Model 411D

This model is similar to the Model 411 but with engraved case, colored finish on the receiver, auto ejectors, single trigger, and straight grip stock. Weight for 28 gauge is about 6.25 lbs. and for the 12 gauge about 7 lbs.

NIB	Exc.	V.G.	Good	Fair	Poor
1100	850	—	—	—	—

Model 411F

Same as the Model 411D but with silver engraved receiver.

NIB	Exc.	V.G.	Good	Fair	Poor
1600	1200	—	—	—	—

Model 411R

Offered in 12 or 20 gauge with 20" barrel with fixed cylinder chokes. Extractors. Weight is about 6.5 lbs. for 12 gauge and 6 lbs. for 20 gauge.

NIB	Exc.	V.G.	Good	Fair	Poor
750	600	—	—	—	—

CD DIANA SERIES

These shotguns are made in Turkey by Eqsilah. This line has replaced the Phantom Series and was first imported by Tristar in 2003.

Model 1887

This is a reproduction of the Winchester Model 1887 lever action shotgun. Offered in 12 gauge only with 22" Cylinder choked barrel. Walnut stock. Five-round magazine. Weight is about 8.75 lbs. Made in Australia by ADI, Limited, Lithgow.

NIB	Exc.	V.G.	Good	Fair	Poor
1195	900	750	—	—	—

TROCAOLA
Eibar, Spain

This maker produced a variety of .32, .38, and .44 caliber top break revolvers between approximately 1900 and 1936. These pistols can be identified by the monogram "TAC" stamped on the left side of the frame. The value of all these revolvers is as follows:

Exc.	V.G.	Good	Fair	Poor
200	125	100	75	50

TRYON, EDWARD K. & COMPANY
Philadelphia, Pennsylvania

Pocket Pistol

A .41 caliber single-shot percussion pocket pistol with a 2" or 4" barrel, German silver mounts and a walnut stock. The lock marked "Tryon/Philada." Manufactured during the 1860s and 1870s.

Exc.	V.G.	Good	Fair	Poor
—	—	1900	750	200

TUCKER SHERARD & COMPANY
Lancaster, Texas

Dragoon

A .44 caliber percussion revolver with a 7.75" round barrel fitted with a loading lever and a 6-shot cylinder. The barrel marked "Clark, Sherard & Co., Lancaster, Texas," and the cylinder etched in two panels with crossed cannons and the legend "Texas Arms." Approximately 400 revolvers of this type were made between 1862 and 1867. Prospective purchasers are advised to secure a qualified appraisal prior to acquisition.

Exc.	V.G.	Good	Fair	Poor
—	—	50000	20000	—

TUFTS & COLLEY
New York, New York

Pocket Pistol

A .44 caliber single-shot percussion pocket pistol with a 3.5" barrel, German silver mounts and walnut stock. The lock marked "Tufts & Colley" and the barrel "Deringer/Pattn." Manufactured during the 1860s.

Exc.	V.G.	Good	Fair	Poor
—	—	1750	750	200

TURBIAUX, JACQUES
Paris, France
SEE—Ames

TURNER, THOMAS
Redding, England

Pepperbox

A .476 double-action percussion pepperbox having 6 barrels. Blued, case hardened with walnut grips. The left side of the frame is engraved in an oval "Thomas Turner, Redding."

Exc.	V.G.	Good	Fair	Poor
—	5000	1750	900	400

U

UBERTI U.S.A.
Lakeville, Connecticut

The prices listed represent the Uberti line as imported into the United States. Uberti offeres a number of options that will affect price. Many of these options are special finishes and grips. It is strongly suggested that before a sale that expert opinion is sought.

Patterson Revolver
This is an exact copy of the famous and rare Colt pistol. Offered in .36 caliber with engraved 5-shot cylinder, the barrel is 7.5" long and octagonal forward of the lug. The frame is case hardened steel as is the backstrap. Grips are one-piece walnut. Overall length is 11.5" and weight is about 2.5 lbs.

NIB	Exc.	V.G.	Good	Fair	Poor
375	300	200	125	100	75

Walker Colt Revolver
This is a faithful reproduction of the famous and highly sought-after Colts. Caliber is .44 and the round barrel is 9" in length. The frame is case hardened steel and the trigger guard is brass. The 6-shot cylinder is engraved with fighting dragoons scene. Grip is one-piece walnut. Overall length is 15.75" and weight is a hefty 70 oz.

NIB	Exc.	V.G.	Good	Fair	Poor
350	300	200	125	100	75

Colt Whitneyville Dragoon
This was the transition Walker. A reduced version of the Model 1847 Walker. Fitted with a 7.5" barrel and chambered for the .44 caliber.

NIB	Exc.	V.G.	Good	Fair	Poor
330	275	200	125	100	75

Colt 1st Model Dragoon Revolver
This was a shorter version of the Walker and evolved directly from that original design. This model is a 6-shot .44 caliber with a 7.5" barrel. The frame is color case hardened steel while the backstrap and trigger guard are brass. Grips are one-piece walnut. Overall length is 13.5" and weight is about 63 oz.

NIB	Exc.	V.G.	Good	Fair	Poor
300	200	175	125	100	75

Colt 2nd Model Dragoon Revolver
This differs from the 1st model in that the cylinder bolt slot is square instead of oval.

NIB	Exc.	V.G.	Good	Fair	Poor
300	200	175	125	100	75

Colt 3rd Model Dragoon Revolver
This model varies from the 2nd model as follows:
- a: Loading lever taper is inverted.
- b: Loading lever latch hook is different shape.
- c: Loading lever latch.
- d: Backstrap is steel and trigger guard is brass oval.
- e: Frame is cut for a shoulder stock.

NIB	Exc.	V.G.	Good	Fair	Poor
300	225	175	125	100	75

Colt Model 1849 Wells Fargo
This model has no loading lever. Chambered for .31 caliber cartridge. The barrel is octagonal. The frame is case colored and hardened steel while the backstrap and trigger guard are brass. Cylinder is engraved and holds 5 rounds. Grip is one-piece walnut. Overall length is 9.5" and weight is 34 oz.

NIB	Exc.	V.G.	Good	Fair	Poor
275	200	150	125	100	75

Colt Model 1849 Pocket Revolver
Same as the Wells Fargo with the addition of a loading lever.

NIB	Exc.	V.G.	Good	Fair	Poor
265	200	150	125	100	75

Colt Model 1848 Baby Dragoon
Similar is appearance to the Model 1849 but with a 4" tapered octagonal barrel and a square back trigger guard. No loading lever. Weight is about 23 oz.

NIB	Exc.	V.G.	Good	Fair	Poor
275	200	150	125	100	75

Colt Model 1851 Navy
Chambered for .36 caliber with an engraved 6-shot cylinder. The tapered octagonal barrel is 7.5". The frame is case colored steel and the backstrap and oval trigger guard are brass. Grips are one-piece walnut. Overall length is 13" and weight is about 44 oz.

NIB	Exc.	V.G.	Good	Fair	Poor
250	175	150	125	100	75

Colt Model 1861 Navy
Sometimes referred to as the "New Navy" this model is similar in appearance to the Model 1851. Offered in two variations. The military version has a steel backstrap and trigger guard and is cut for a shoulder stock. The civilian version has a brass backstrap and trigger guard and is not cut for a shoulder stock.

Military Model

NIB	Exc.	V.G.	Good	Fair	Poor
250	200	150	125	100	75

Civilian Model

NIB	Exc.	V.G.	Good	Fair	Poor
250	200	150	125	100	75

Colt Model 1860 Army
Chambered for the .44 caliber ball and fitted with a round tapered 8" barrel, this revolver has a 6-shot engraved cylinder. Grips are one-piece walnut. Overall length is 13.75" and weight is approximately 42 oz.

Military
Steel backstrap and brass trigger guard and is cut for a shoulder stock.

NIB	Exc.	V.G.	Good	Fair	Poor
250	200	150	125	100	75

Civilian
Brass backstrap and trigger guard and is not cut for a shoulder stock.

NIB	Exc.	V.G.	Good	Fair	Poor
250	200	150	125	100	75

Fluted Cylinder

Military

NIB	Exc.	V.G.	Good	Fair	Poor
260	200	160	125	100	75

Civilian

NIB	Exc.	V.G.	Good	Fair	Poor
250	200	150	125	100	75

Colt Model 1862 Police Revolvers
Chambered for .36 caliber and fitted with a round tapered barrel in 4.5", 5.5", or 6.5" barrel. The 5-shot cylinder is fluted, the frame color case hardened, and the backstrap and trigger guard are brass. Grips are one-piece walnut. Weight is about 25 oz.

NIB	Exc.	V.G.	Good	Fair	Poor
275	200	175	150	125	100

Colt Model 1862 Pocket Navy Revolver
Similar to the Model 1862 Police model but fitted with a 5-shot engraved nonfluted cylinder. Barrel lengths are 4.5", 5.5", and 6.5". Weight is about 27 oz.

NIB	Exc.	V.G.	Good	Fair	Poor
225	200	175	150	125	100

Colt Model 1868 Army Thuer Conversion

NIB	Exc.	V.G.	Good	Fair	Poor
400	325	225	175	150	100

Remington Model 1858 New Army .44 Caliber
Chambered for .44 caliber and fitted with a tapered octagonal 8" barrel. Cylinder holds 6 shots and the frame is blued steel. trigger guard is brass. Grips are two-piece walnut. Overall length is 13.75" and weight is about 42 oz.

NIB	Exc.	V.G.	Good	Fair	Poor
250	200	150	125	100	75

Remington Model 1858 New Army .36 Caliber
Similar to above model but fitted with a 7-3/8" tapered octagonal barrel. Weight is approximately 40 oz.

NIB	Exc.	V.G.	Good	Fair	Poor
250	200	150	125	100	75

Remington Model 1858 New Army .44 Caliber Target
This version is fitted with a fully adjustable rear sight and ramp front sight.

NIB	Exc.	V.G.	Good	Fair	Poor
275	225	175	150	100	75

Remington Model 1858 New Army .44 Caliber Stainless Steel
All parts are stainless steel.

NIB	Exc.	V.G.	Good	Fair	Poor
350	275	225	150	100	75

Remington Model 1858 New Army .44 Cal. SS Target
Same as Target Model but all parts are stainless steel.

NIB	Exc.	V.G.	Good	Fair	Poor
375	300	225	175	100	75

Remington Model 1858 Target Revolving Carbine
Chambered for .44 caliber and fitted with an 18" octagon barrel. The frame is blued steel and the trigger guard is brass. Stock is select walnut. Overall length is 35" and weight is about 4.4 lbs.

NIB	Exc.	V.G.	Good	Fair	Poor
400	300	200	150	100	75

1875 Remington "Outlaw"
This is a replica of the original Remington cartridge pistol chambered for .357 Magnum, .44-40, .45 ACP, .45 ACP/.45 L.C. conversion, and .45 Colt. The frame is case colored steel and the trigger guard is brass. It is offered with a 7.5" round barrel and is either blued or nickel-plated, with two-piece walnut grips. Overall length is 13.75" and weight is about 44 oz.

NIB	Exc.	V.G.	Good	Fair	Poor
475	350	275	225	175	125

Remington Model 1890 Police
This is a 5.5"-barreled replica of the original Remington Pistol. It is chambered for .357 Magnum, .44-40, .45 ACP, .45 ACP/.45 L.C. conversion, and .45 Colt. The frame is case colored steel and the trigger guard is brass. It was available in either blued or nickel-plate. Grips are two-piece walnut and are fitted with a grip ring. Overall length is 11.75" and weight is about 41 oz.

NIB	Exc.	V.G.	Good	Fair	Poor
475	350	300	275	225	175

Model 1871 Rolling Block Pistol
This is a single-shot target pistol chambered for .22 LR, .22 Magnum, .22 Hornet, .222 Rem., 223 Rem., .45 Long Colt, or .357 Magnum. It has a 9.5" half-octagonal, half-round barrel and is blued, with a case colored receiver and walnut grip and forearm. The trigger guard is brass. Overall length is 14" and weight is about 44 oz.

NIB	Exc.	V.G.	Good	Fair	Poor
400	300	225	200	150	100

Model 1871 Rolling Block Carbine
This model is similar to the pistol, with a 22.5" half-octagonal, half-round barrel and a full-length walnut stock. trigger guard and buttplate are brass. Overall length is 35.5" and weight is approximately 4.8 lbs.

NIB	Exc.	V.G.	Good	Fair	Poor
475	350	275	225	175	125

Henry Rifle
This is a brass-framed reproduction of the famous Winchester/Henry Rifle. It is chambered for the .44-40 cartridge, and this is basically the only departure from being a true and faithful copy. The octagonal barrel is 24.25" on the rifle model and 22.25" on the carbine model. There are also two Trapper models offered: an 18.5" barrel and a 16.5" version. This is a high-quality rifle and amazingly close to the original in configuration. There are three grades of engraving also available. Weights are as follows: rifle 9.2 lbs., carbine 9 lbs., 18.5" trapper 7.9 lbs., 16.5" trapper 7.4 lbs. Finish can be steel, standard blued or charcoal blue.

NIB	Exc.	V.G.	Good	Fair	Poor
900	700	550	450	350	200

NOTE: Grade A add $350. Grade B add $450. Grade C add $600.

Winchester Model 1866
This is a faithful replica of the Winchester 1866. It is chambered for .22 LR, .22 Magnum, .38 Special, and .44-40, and .45 Long Colt. The rifle version has a brass frame and a 24.25" tapered octagon barrel. The frame finish is brass, with a walnut stock. Weight is about 8 lbs.

NIB	Exc.	V.G.	Good	Fair	Poor
800	650	550	450	350	200

1866 Yellowboy Carbine
This model is similar to the standard rifle, but is offered with a 19" round tapered barrel.

NIB	Exc.	V.G.	Good	Fair	Poor
700	600	500	450	350	200

Winchester Model 1873 Carbine
This is a reproduction of the Winchester 1873 chambered for .357 Magnum, .45 Long Colt, and .44-40. It has a case colored steel receiver and a 19" round tapered barrel. The lever is also case colored. The stock and forearm are walnut. Overall length is 38.25" and weight is about 7.4 lbs.

NIB	Exc.	V.G.	Good	Fair	Poor
900	700	500	450	350	200

Winchester Model 1873 Rifle
This model is similar to the Carbine, with a 24.25" octagonal barrel. Overall length is 43.25" and weight is approximately 8.2 lbs.

NIB	Exc.	V.G.	Good	Fair	Poor
950	750	600	450	350	200

NOTE: Extra barrel lengths from 30" to 20" in .45 L.C. and .4440 are also offered at extra cost.

Winchester 1873 Short Sporting Rifle
As above but fitted with a 20" octagon barrel.

NIB	Exc.	V.G.	Good	Fair	Poor
950	750	—	—	—	—

Winchester 1873 Half-Octagon Rifle
Same as above but with 24.25" half octagon barrel. Stock has a checkered pistol grip.

NIB	Exc.	V.G.	Good	Fair	Poor
1000	800	600	450	350	200

Winchester 1873 Musket
Chambered for the .44-40 or .45 Long Colt cartridge and fitted with a 30" barrel with full stock and three barrel bands. Magazine capacity is 14 rounds. Weight is about 9 lbs.

NIB	Exc.	V.G.	Good	Fair	Poor
1000	800	600	450	350	200

Model 1885 High Wall Single-Shot Carbine
Chambered for .38-55, .30-30, .44-40, .45 Colt, .40-65, or .45-70 with 28" barrel. Walnut stock.

NIB	Exc.	V.G.	Good	Fair	Poor
825	600	450	350	250	—

Model 1885 High Wall Single-Shot Rifle
Same as above but with 30" barrel.

NIB	Exc.	V.G.	Good	Fair	Poor
900	675	500	400	300	—

Model 1885 High Wall Single-Shot Rifle Pistol Grip
Fittted with a 30" or 32" barrel and checkered pistol-grip stock. Same calibers as above.

NIB	Exc.	V.G.	Good	Fair	Poor
1000	800	600	450	350	—

Winchester 1885 Low Wall Sporting Rifle
This version of the Low Wall Winchester is chambered for the .22 Hornet, .30-30, .44 Mag, or .45 Colt cartridges. Fitted with a 30" octagon barrel. Walnut stock with pistol grip. Weight is about 7.5 lbs. Introduced in 2004.

NIB	Exc.	V.G.	Good	Fair	Poor
950	—	—	—	—	—

Winchester 1885 Low Wall Schuetzen
As above but chambered for the .45 Colt cartridge and fitted with a palm rest and Swiss butt. Weight is about 7.75 lbs. Introduced in 2004.

NIB	Exc.	V.G.	Good	Fair	Poor
1100	—	—	—	—	—

Hawken Santa Fe
Based on the famous original rifle this reproduction is bored for .54 caliber and fitted with a 32" octagon barrel. A double set trigger and case hardened lock plate are standard. The stock ferrule and wedge plates are German silver. The stock is walnut with cheekpiece. Overall length is 50" and weight is about 9.5 lbs. Also available in kit form.

NIB	Exc.	V.G.	Good	Fair	Poor
350	300	250	200	150	100

Cattleman
This is a single-action revolver patterned closely after the Colt Single-Action Army. It is chambered in various popular calibers: .357 Magnum, .44-40, .44 Special, .45 ACP, .45 L.C./.45 ACP convertible, and .45 Colt. It is offered with barrel lengths of 4.75", 5.5", and 7.5". It is offered with either a modern or black powder-type frame and brass or steel backstraps. The finish is blued, with walnut grips. A Sheriff's Model with a 3" barrel and no ejector rod chambered for .44-40 and .45 Colt is also available and is valued the same. Weight is approximately 38 oz. for 5.5" barrel gun.

NIB	Exc.	V.G.	Good	Fair	Poor
325	275	250	200	150	100

Cattleman Flattop Target Model
This model is similar to the standard Cattleman, with an adjustable rear sight.

NIB	Exc.	V.G.	Good	Fair	Poor
435	350	275	225	175	125

New Thunderer Model
Designed and imported exclusively by Cimarron Arms for single-action shooting competition. Fitted with bird's-head grip with hard rubber, this model is chambered for the .357 Magnum, .44 Special, .44 WCF, and .45 Colt. Offered in barrel lengths of 3.5" and 4.75". Finish in nickel or blued with case colored frame.

NIB	Exc.	V.G.	Good	Fair	Poor
450	350	300	250	200	100

Bisley
Chambered for the .32-20, .38 Special, .357 Mag, .38-40, .44-40, and .44 Special and fitted with either 4.75", 5.5", or 7.5" barrel. Case hardened frame with two-piece walnut grips.

NIB	Exc.	V.G.	Good	Fair	Poor
435	350	275	225	175	125

Bisley Flattop
As above but with adjustable rear sight.

NIB	Exc.	V.G.	Good	Fair	Poor
435	350	275	225	175	125

Buckhorn Buntline
This version is chambered for the .44 Magnum. It has an 18" round barrel, and it is cut for attaching a shoulder stock. Steel backstrap and trigger guard. Overall length is 23" and weight is about 57 oz.

NIB	Exc.	V.G.	Good	Fair	Poor
400	325	300	250	200	100

NOTE: Detachable shoulder stock add 25 percent.

Buckhorn Target
Same as above but fitted with an adjustable rear sight and ramp front sight. Has a flat upper frame.

NIB	Exc.	V.G.	Good	Fair	Poor
450	350	300	250	200	100

Phantom
Similar to the Buckhorn, but chambered for the .44 Magnum and the .357 Magnum. The barrel is a round 10.5" and the frame is blued with blued steel backstrap. One-piece walnut grips with anatomic profile. Adjustable sight. Weight is approximately 53 oz.

NIB	Exc.	V.G.	Good	Fair	Poor
350	325	300	250	200	100

Buntline Carbine
This version has the 18" barrel but is fitted with a permanently mounted shoulder stock with a brass buttplate and sling swivel. Chambered for .44-40, .45 Long Colt, .357 Magnum, and .44 Magnum. Offered with fixed or adjustable sights.

NIB	Exc.	V.G.	Good	Fair	Poor
450	400	350	300	250	200

Tornado
This 6-shot revolver is chambered for the .454 Casull and fitted with a 4.75", 5.5" or 7.5" with ported barrel. Sandblasted nickel finish. Weight is about 47 oz.

NIB	Exc.	V.G.	Good	Fair	Poor
750	600	500	—	—	—

1873 Stallion
This is a scaled-down version, chambered for .22 LR/.22 Magnum. It is blued with a case colored frame and features one-piece walnut grips.

NIB	Exc.	V.G.	Good	Fair	Poor
325	275	250	200	150	100

Schofield Revolver
Patterned after the original S&W revolver this model is chambered for the .44-40 or .45 Colt cartridge. It is fitted with a 7", 5", or 3.5" barrel. Weight with 7" barrel is approximately 40 oz.

NIB	Exc.	V.G.	Good	Fair	Poor
750	550	400	300	—	—

Model 1874 Russian
Chambered for the .44 Russian cartridge and fitted with a 6" or 7" barrel.

NIB	Exc.	V.G.	Good	Fair	Poor
800	650	450	350	—	—

Inspector Model
This is a double-action revolver built on the same general lines as the Colt Detective model. Cylinder holds six cartridges and is chambered for the .38 Special. Offered in the following barrel lengths with fixed sights: 2", 2.125", 2.5", 3", 4", 6" and also offered in 4" and 6" barrel lengths with adjustable sights. Grips are walnut and finish is blued or chrome. With the 3" barrel the weight is about 24 oz.

NIB	Exc.	V.G.	Good	Fair	Poor
250	200	150	125	100	75

UHLINGER, WILLIAM P.
Philadelphia, Pennsylvania

Pocket Revolver
A .32 caliber spur trigger revolver with a 2.75" or 3" octagonal barrel and an unfluted 6-shot cylinder. Blued with rosewood or walnut grips. Manufactured during the late 1860s and early 1870s.
NOTE: Uhlinger-manufactured pistols will often be found with retailer's names on them, such as: D.D. Cone, Washington, D.C.; J.P. Lower; and W.L. Grant.

Long Cylinder (1-3/16")

Exc.	V.G.	Good	Fair	Poor
—	—	500	250	100

Short Cylinder (1")

Exc.	V.G.	Good	Fair	Poor
—	—	375	175	75

.32 Rimfire Model (5", 6", or 7" Barrel)

Exc.	V.G.	Good	Fair	Poor
—	—	600	250	100

UNION FIRE ARMS COMPANY
Toledo, Ohio

This company was incorporated in 1902 and used the names of Union Fire Arms, Union Arms Company, Illinois Arms Company (made for Sears) and Bee Be Arms Company. In 1917 the company was either bought up or absorbed by Ithaca Gun Company.

Double Barrel Shotguns
Union's predecessor, Colton Manufacturing Co. (1894-1902) made a double for Sears. It was cleverly designed with coil mainspring striker locks set into sideplates. The Union double in 12 and 16 gauge with steel or Damascus barrels derived from it, but was a traditional hammerless sidelock side-by-side well-made gun (1902-1913) and also sold by Sears. Values depend on grade and condition.

Union also offered, about 1905, an unusual boxlock hammer gun, the Model 25 in 12 gauge only. It employs external hammers but they are mounted within the frame and the spurs protrude in front of the topsnap opener. These guns are hard to find and values range from $300 to $1,200 depending on condition. They are produced with steel, twist, or Damascus barrels but only in a plain grade.

Exc.	V.G.	Good	Fair	Poor
1250	500	400	300	200

Model 24
Slide action, Model 25 Peerless that was a fancy version of the Model 24 and the Model 25A, which was a trap model, were manufactured from 1902 to 1913 in 12 or 16 gauge with 24", 26", 28", or 32" steel or Damascus barrels. This gun had a unique double trigger. The front trigger cocked and decocked an internal firing pin and the back trigger fired the gun. The gun is marked on the left side of the frame and the pump release is on the right side. This model had one serious drawback, in that the slide that extracted a spent shell extended back over the comb of the stock. This often hit the shooter's thumb knuckle and caused injury. In 1907 Union redesigned their slide by reducing its length and shielding it behind a steel plate that covered the rear half of the opening. These are the Model 24, 25, and 25A improved versions. Approximately 17,000 of all models combined were made.

Exc.	V.G.	Good	Fair	Poor
—	750	300	200	100

Model 50
Manufactured 1911 to 1913. This was basically a redesign of the Model 24. The main distinguishing feature of the Model 50 was that the frame sloped down to meet the comb of the stock and the double trigger system was replaced by a single trigger. It came in 12 or 16 gauge with a 26", 28", 30", or 32" Krupp steel barrel. Fewer than 3,000 were made.

Exc.	V.G.	Good	Fair	Poor
—	850	400	300	200

Model 23
Hammerless double, manufactured between 1902 and 1913 with or without automatic ejectors. With some engraving, it came in both single and double trigger models; this was their top grade gun. Came in 12 and 16 gauge with 28", 30", or 32" steel, twist, or Damascus barrels.

Exc.	V.G.	Good	Fair	Poor
—	450	150	125	100

Model 22
This was essentially a no frills Model 23. It had the same barrel length and steel options, but it had a plain walnut stock and no engraving. There were fewer than 10,000 Model 22 and 23s made.

Exc.	V.G.	Good	Fair	Poor
—	300	100	75	50

Model 18
Single-shot, manufactured 1906 to 1913 came in 12 or 16 gauge. 30", 32", 34", or 36" steel barrel. A plain single-shot. Very few made.

Exc.	V.G.	Good	Fair	Poor
—	200	75	50	25

Reifngraber
A .32 or .38 S&W caliber gas operated semi-automatic pistol, with a 3" barrel. Blued with walnut grips, approximately 100 of these pistols were manufactured.

Exc.	V.G.	Good	Fair	Poor
—	2250	1100	500	350

Automatic Revolver
.32 S&W caliber, similar to the Webley Fosbery semi-automatic revolver with a 3" barrel. Blued with either walnut or hard rubber grips. The cylinder has zigzag grooves.

Exc.	V.G.	Good	Fair	Poor
—	3250	1250	500	250

UNITED SPORTING ARMS, INC.
Tucson, Arizona
THE HISTORY OF SEVILLE AND EL DORADO REVOLVERS
by J.C. Munnell

The history of United Sporting Arms, its related companies, and the Seville and El Dorado line of single-action revolvers is a long and torturous one. It actually begins in 1973 or 1974, with the formation of United States Arms in Riverhead, New York, by three individuals. Before any but a few prototype guns were made, the partners split up, with one remaining as United States Arms, and the other two forming United Sporting Arms in nearby Hauppauge, New York.

United States Arms produced the Abilene revolver, intended to compete head-on price-wise with the Ruger Blackhawk, while United Sporting Arms, intending to make a superior (and higher-priced) product, initially produced the Seville in chrome moly steel, and slightly later, the El Dorado revolver out of stainless steel.

The Abilene was manufactured in Riverhead until 1979 or 1980 in calibers .357 and .44 magnum, and possibly the .45 Colt, all in blued steel. The assets of this company were eventually sold to A.I.G., Inc., which was a division of Mossberg. A.I.G. assembled guns from existing parts until 1983, at which time the Abilene production ended. These guns bore a North Haven, CT address, and utilized a distinctive hammer-nose safety device instead of the former transfer bar system. Calibers were the same, and all guns were made from carbon steel. Some guns had a Magnaloy finish, thereby giving rise to the misconception that some Abilenes were made from stainless steel, none were.

Meanwhile, the two remaining original partners began production of the United Sporting Arms Seville revolver in 1977. By late in that year, this company had accomplished several firearms "firsts" with production of the stainless steel El Dorado revolver. This was the first use of 17-4 pH stainless for a revolver frame, far pre-dating Freedom Arms, and was made at a time when Sturm Ruger engineering department was sending lengthy letters explaining why stainless steel was totally unsuitable for guns chambered for the .44 magnum cartridge. It would be years until the rest of the firearms industry caught up to this fledgling company

In 1979, one of the remaining partners established a second production facility in Tombstone, Arizona, under the name of United Sporting Arms of Arizona, Inc. Guns made in this plant still utilized frames made in New York, and therefore bore the Hauppauge, N.Y., frame inscription. However, Tombstone-built guns will contain the letter "T" as a suffix to the serial number. In Tombstone, the Silver Seville was born, having a highly-polished stainless grip frame on an otherwise blued gun. This is a striking combination, and has become quite popular on custom guns as well as some limited production runs from other makers. (Neither the guns themselves, nor the official company records reflect this designation, only the boxes for the guns do.) Here, to the .41 magnum and .45 Colt calibers were added to the Seville line. No stainless steel guns were made in Tombstone, Arizona.

Later in 1979, the Arizona facility was relocated to the town of Bisbee, Arizona. Less than 200 guns were made with the Bisbee address. These were all made from blued steel, and were all in .45 Colt or .44 Magnum, except as noted. Oddly enough, in the short time the company was at this location, three very distinct models were produced.

First was the Tombstone Commemorative. Although 200 were commissioned by the city of Tombstone, only about 60 were ever completed. These guns had blued frames, and stainless steel cylinders, barrels and grip frames. Some engraving was present on the cylinder and barrel, and the legend "Tombstone, Arizona 100 years of history 1879-1979" appears in three lines on the barrel. The guns came in a wooden case, and serial numbers began with TC-1. All were in .44-40 WCF caliber.

The second Bisbee gun was the Helldorado. Originally designed for the Old Tucson stunt man group "The Fall Guys," the gun had a flat-top frame with no sights, and was intended for blanks only. Only 4 were made. The final Bisbee introduction, and the only one to survive the next location change, was the Quik Kit. This was an ingenious multi-caliber system of interchangeable barrels and cylinders; invented by Ray Herriott of Centaur Systems. Only about 30 such guns were produced in Bisbee, some in blue and some in stainless. All bore the Centaur logo on the frame and all had the serial number prefix of "QK."

In late 1979, the company moved once again, this time to Tucson, Arizona. By now, the split from the New York concern was completed legally as well as physically, new guns were in blue and stainless, but all were called Sevilles. (The New York operation retained exclusive rights to the El Dorado name.) Also at this time, the frame marking on the guns simply read "Sporting Arms, Inc."

Between late 1979 and the end of 1981, several new variations of the Seville revolver were introduced. Shortly after Ruger announced the Blackhawk SRM in .357 Maximum caliber, United Sporting Arms offered a lengthened-frame stainless steel gun in this caliber. This gun did not suffer from the various maladies which eventually doomed the Ruger version, and was winning silhouette matches long after the demise of the Blackhawk SRM. This model also spawned the awesome .375 USA Seville—the same caliber later renamed the .375 Super Magnum by Dan Wesson. Although only two prototypes of this caliber were made before the next company change, several hundred guns were made in .357 Maximum.

Also during this period the Sherrifs' Model with 3-1/2" barrel was introduced. Most of these guns were produced in chrome moly steel, and most were shipped with a distinctive round-butt "bird's-head" grip frame. This proved very popular, and these guns became a mainstay of the company's line right until the end. Most of these Sherrifs' Models had fully adjustable sights, but at least three were made with Colt-like fixed sights, all of which, oddly, were convertibles in .45 Colt and .45 ACP.

Guns were produced in calibers 9mm Winchester Magnum, and .45 Winchester Magnum, primarily for export to Europe. A few guns were made in .44-40 and .44 Special. Also introduced was the Hunter Finish, a bead-blasted stainless steel, and the Rawhide finish, with the same treatment to a blued gun. A very few blued guns were made with a brass grip frame, as well as the "Silver Seville" configuration.

In early February of 1982, the company again changed ownership. The company name, and the frame marking on the guns, returned to United Sporting Arms, Inc. About half of the production was devoted to the so-called long-frame guns—.357 Maximum and .375 USA—and about half of these were silhouette guns with 10-1/2" barrels. The .454 magnum (.454 Casull) was added to the line. However, only 30 of these guns were ever made. (Note: perhaps as many as 50 guns in this chambering were made and marked "Sporting Arms, Inc." These guns were NOT made in any United Sporting Arms factory, and are very definitely of sub-standard quality.) These guns were made on a special frame, different from all other caliber guns.

Prototype guns were made—usually two in each caliber. Produced were .41 Super Magnum and .44 Super Magnum (long before Dan Wesson made guns available in .445 and .414 Super Magnums), as well as .375 Special, and, oddly enough, .218 Mashburn Bee. None of these went into regular; production.

Normal production guns were, as to be expected, with blued, stainless steel, "silver" and brass grip-frame guns were all produced. Quite a few bird's-head grip guns were made, not only in the Sherrif's Model configuration. Guns in heavy-recoiling calibers are particularly comfortable to shoot two-handed with this grip configuration. The author has a .454 Magnum Seville with a 6-1/2" barrel and the bird's-head grip frame, and it is by far the most comfortable gun I've ever shot, even with 325 grain bullets at over 1700 fps!

In November of 1985, the company was again sold, and this time it was moved to Post Fails, Idaho. Problems developed almost immediately, and even though it would be three years until the assets were sold (to the previous owners from Tucson), very few guns were ever made; less than 200. The only new product introduced in Idaho was the .32 H&R magnum chambering.

Caution: Several hundred frames "disappeared" from the Idaho plant right before the bankruptcy sale, and several bootleg guns have turned up. These guns are of distinctly dubious quality, as are many of the Idaho-marked guns. Supposedly, the BATF is aware of the situation, and arrests may yet happen.

When the assets of the Idaho plant were sold to the former owners, they had no desire to resume the firearm-manufacturing business, so they shipped the remaining parts, tooling and moulds to Chimney Rock, North Carolina. In a moment you'll see why.

While all this changing of location and ownership was going on, the remaining original partner in Hauppauge, N.Y. had reorganized as El Dorado Arms, Inc., and had been in continuous production of the El Dorado revolver (although on a very limited basis) since 1979. Until the mid-1980s, all El Dorados were made from 17-4 pH stainless steel, and nearly all were chambered for the .44 magnum cartridge.

In 1985, El Dorado Arms relocated to Chimney Rock, N.C., where production continued, and the model line was expanded to include the Laredo in blued steel, and the fixed-sight Rebel in both blued and stainless steel. Also introduced at this time (although at least two prototype guns so chambered had been made in New York) was the .22 long rifle chambering, complete with match chambers, specifically for the silhouette market. Eventually .22 rimfire magnum guns were added.

The only thing lacking from the North Carolina lineup was a long-frame revolver for the Super Magnum calibers. When the remaining Idaho assets were received in North Carolina, not only were there parts for the long-frame gun, but also the molds to produce more parts for these guns. In fact quite a few El Dorado .357 and .375 Super Magnum-chambered guns found their way into the silhouette winner's circle, alongside their smaller brothers.

Ironically, it had taken nine years, but all the components of United Sporting Arms had came full circle, and were reunited under one roof. And this was under the ownership of one of the founders of the original United States Arms!

Production of El Dorado revolvers always was very limited, and it finally ceased for good in 1997 or 1998.

Altogether, only about 6,000 or 7,000 guns were produced by all of the United Sporting Arms/El Dorado Arms companies. (Total production of the Abilene revolver by either United States Arms or A.I.G. is not available). However, even forgetting the eight different frame inscriptions, barrel lengths between 3-1/2" and 10-1/2" were made; there were all-blue, all stainless, blue and stainless, and blue and brass guns, standard finish, "hunter" and "rawhide" finishes as well as high-polish stainless; standard and bird's-head grip frame guns; Quik-Kits, convertibles and Tombstone Commemoratives; long-frame, short-frame and .454-frame guns. There were also at least 21 different chamberings. Thus, the variations are practically endless.

Quality, except for the very few noted instances, was always very high. An informal United Sporting Arms slogan was that a Seville was what a Super Blackhawk could be if Ruger had a custom shop. Given the truth of this statement, it must be admitted that an El Dorado Arms gun as what a custom Seville could have been.

Advertised prices for Sevilles and El Dorados run the full gamut from bargain "orphaned" gun prices to those reflecting the semi-custom nature of these guns For the most part, what price stability does exist is on the higher end. and this is as it should be.

For most of the production of United Sporting Arms guns, and some of the El Dorado Arms guns, copies of original factory records are available. For a letter of verification for any particular gun (refunded if no records are available, send $20 to J.C. Munnell, 633 Long Run Rd, McKeesport, PA 15132. Phone information is not available.

These two United Sporting Arms, Inc. of Bisbee, Arizona, revolvers are the sightless Heldorados.

Blued Guns

NIB	Exc.	V.G.	Good	Fair	Poor
N/A	500	450	350	N/A	N/A

Blue Silhouette (10.5" barrels)

NIB	Exc.	V.G.	Good	Fair	Poor
N/A	600	550	500	N/A	N/A

NOTE: Add $100 for stainless, $250 for stainless long-frame models (calibers .357 Maximum/Super Mag. and .357 USA/Super Mag)

Silver Sevilles

NIB	Exc.	V.G.	Good	Fair	Poor
N/A	550	475	400	N/A	N/A

Stainless Steel Guns

NIB	Exc.	V.G.	Good	Fair	Poor
N/A	600	525	450	N/A	N/A

Tombstone Commemorative

NIB	Exc.	V.G.	Good	Fair	Poor
1000	750	N/A	N/A	N/A	N/A

Quik-Kit Stainless Steel

NIB	Exc.	V.G.	Good	Fair	Poor
1500	1250	N/A	N/A	N/A	N/A

Quik-Kit Blued

NIB	Exc.	V.G.	Good	Fair	Poor
1200	1000	N/A	N/A	N/A	N/A

NOTE: For Quik-Kit guns with extra barrel and cylinder add $200 for each barrel and cylinder. Deduct 10 percent if United Sporting Arms, Hauppauge, N.Y. Deduct 20 percent if United Sporting Arms, Post Falls, ID. Add 20 percent if El Dorado Arms (either N.Y. or N.C.) Add 10 percent for 1-1/2" barrel Sheriff's Model. Add 20 percent for 10-1/2" barrel. Add 20 percent for bird's-head grip frame. Add 20 percent if brass grip frame.

UNITED STATES ARMS
Otis A. Smith Company
Rockfall, Connecticut

Single-Action Revolver

A .44 rimfire and centerfire single-action revolver with a 7" barrel and integral ejector. The hammer nose is fitted with two firing pins so that rimfire or centerfire cartridges can be used interchangeably. The barrel marked "United States Arms Company - New York", the top strap "No. 44." Blued with either hard rubber or rosewood grips. Manufactured in limited quantities. Circa 1870 to 1875.

Exc.	V.G.	Good	Fair	Poor
—	—	3250	1250	500

UNITED STATES HISTORICAL SOCIETY
Richmond, Virginia

The following arms are manufactured by the Williamsburg Firearms Manufactory and the Virginia Firearms Manufactory. This company ceased business under this name in 1994 and resumed business under the name of America Remembers in Mechanicsville, Va. No current prices are given for these models due to the lack of an active secondary market. Issue prices only are given.

George Washington

A reproduction of a flintlock pistol originally owned by George Washington. A total of 975 were made and were issued at a price of $3,000.

Thomas Jefferson

A reproduction of a flintlock pistol originally owned by Thomas Jefferson. A total of 1,000 were made and were issued at a price of $1,900.

Hamilton-Burr Dueling Pistols

Reproductions of the flintlock pistols used in the Hamilton-Burr duel. A total of 1,200 sets were made and sold at an issue price of $2,995.

Stonewall Jackson Pistol

A reproduction of a Colt Model 1851 Navy cased with accessories. Total of 2,500 were made in 1988. Issue Price was $2,100.

Texas Paterson Edition

A reproduction of a Colt Paterson revolver cased with accessories. Total of 1,000 were made in 1988. Issue price was $2,500.

Buffalo Bill Centennial

A reproduction of a Colt Model 1860 Army revolver with acid-etched scenes inlaid in gold, cased with accessories. Total of 2,500 were made in 1983 and issued at a price of $1,950.

U.S. Cavalry Model

A reproduction of a Colt Model 1860 Army revolver with a gold-plated cylinder and stag grips, cased with a brass belt buckle. Total of 975 were made beginning in 1988. Issue price was $1,450.

Sam Houston Model

Reproduction of a Colt Model 1847 Army revolver with etched and gilt additions. Total of 2,500 were made. Issue price was $2,300.

Robert E. Lee Model
Reproduction of the Colt Model 1851 Navy revolver with gilt additions and cased with accessories. A total of 2,500 were made. Issue price was $2,100.

H. Deringer Set
Cased pair of reproduction .41 caliber Henry Deringer percussion pocket pistols available in three grades as follows:

Silver Mounted: 1,000
Issue Price $1,900.

14 Kt. Gold Mounted: 100
Issue Price $2,700.

18 Kt. Mounted with Gemstone: 5
Issue Price-$25,000.

UNITED STATES PATENT FIREARMS MANUFACTURING COMPANY
Hartford, Connecticut

This company began business in 1992. The company uses parts manufactured in the U.S. and fits, finishes, and assembles the gun in Hartford. Produces only reproductions of Colt revolvers and rifles.

Single-Action Army Revolver
Offered in a wide variety of calibers including .22 rimfire, .32 WCF, .38 S&W, .357 Magnum, .38-40, .41 Colt, .44 Russian, .44-40, .45 Colt, and .45 ACP. Barrel lengths are 4.75", 5.5", and 7.5" with or without ejector. A modern cross pin frame is available for an additional $10. Prices listed are for standard grips and finish, Armory bone case finish, and Dome blue finish.

NIB	Exc.	V.G.	Good	Fair	Poor
1250	975	—	—	—	—

Single-Action Army Revolver Pre-War
As above but with pre-war "P" frame.

NIB	Exc.	V.G.	Good	Fair	Poor
1525	1100	—	—	—	—

Flattop Target Model
This model is offered with the same calibers as the Single-Action Army above. Barrel lengths are 4.75", 5.5", and 7.5". Grips are two-piece hard rubber. Prices listed are given for standard finish. Introduced in 1997.

NIB	Exc.	V.G.	Good	Fair	Poor
1000	725	575	—	—	—

Rodeo
This single-action revolver is offered in .45 Colt, .44-40 and .38 Special calibers with a choice of 4.75" or 5.50" barrel. Satin blue finish with bone case hammer. "US" hard rubber grips are standard.

NIB	Exc.	V.G.	Good	Fair	Poor
550	450	—	—	—	—

Model 1873 Cut Away
Chambered for the .45 Colt cartridge but not to be fired. Fitted with a 7.5" barrel and brushed steel finish. Parts cut away for display. Discontinued.

NIB	Exc.	V.G.	Good	Fair	Poor
N/A	—	—	—	—	—

Buntline
This model features an all blued finish with 16" barrel. Chambered for the .45 Colt cartridge.

NIB	Exc.	V.G.	Good	Fair	Poor
2300	1750	—	—	—	—

Buntline Special
Fitted with a 16" barrel and chambered for the .45 Colt cartridge. Supplied with nickel stock. Limited edition. Cased.

NIB	Exc.	V.G.	Good	Fair	Poor
2895	2250	—	—	—	—

Henry Nettleton Revolver
This is an exact reproduction of the U.S. Government inspector model produced in the Springfield Armory. Offered in 7.5" and 5.5" models. Introduced in 1997. Discontinued.

NIB	Exc.	V.G.	Good	Fair	Poor
1100	800	600	—	—	—

Sheriff's Model
Chambered for a wide variety of calibers from the .45 Colt to the .32 WCF. Choice of 2.5", 3", 3.5", or 4" barrel. No ejector.

NIB	Exc.	V.G.	Good	Fair	Poor
950	700	—	—	—	—

NOTE: Add $250 for nickel finish.

China Camp Cowboy Action Gun
Chambered for .45 Colt cartridge but other calibers also available from .32 WCF to .44 WCF. Barrel lengths are 4.75", 5.5", and 7.5". Special action job. Two-piece hard rubber grips standard. Finish is silver steel.

NIB	Exc.	V.G.	Good	Fair	Poor
1200	950	750	—	—	—

The Plinker
Chambered for the .22 cartridge and fitted with a choice of barrel lengths of 4.75", 5.5", or 7.5". An extra .22 WMR cylinder is included.

NIB	Exc.	V.G.	Good	Fair	Poor
950	700	—	—	—	—

The .22 Target
As above but with adjustable rear sight and replaceable front sight blade.

NIB	Exc.	V.G.	Good	Fair	Poor
990	750	—	—	—	—

The Hunter
This revolver is chambered for the .17 HMR cartridge and fitted with a 7.5" barrel with adjustable rear sight and replaceable front sight blade. Finish is matte blue.

NIB	Exc.	V.G.	Good	Fair	Poor
840	600	—	—	—	—

Omni-Potent Bird's-Head Model
Chambered for the .45 Colt, .45 ACP, .44 Special, .44 WCF, .38 Special, .38 WCF, or the .32 WCF cartridges. Offered with bird's-head grips and available with 3.5", 4", or 4.75" barrel lengths.

NIB	Exc.	V.G.	Good	Fair	Poor
1250	925	700	—	—	—

Omni-Potent Subnose
As above but with 2", 3", or 4" barrel without ejector.

NIB	Exc.	V.G.	Good	Fair	Poor
940	700	—	—	—	—

Omni-Potent Target
Choice of 4.75", 5.5", or 7.5" barrel with adjustable rear sight and replaceable front blade sight.

NIB	Exc.	V.G.	Good	Fair	Poor
1325	975	—	—	—	—

Bisley Model
Based on the famous Bisley model this reproduction features barrel lengths of 4.75", 5.5", 7.5", and 10". The .45 Colt caliber is standard but .32 WCF, .38 S&W, .44 S&W, .41 Colt, .38 WCF, .44 WCF are optional. Add $60 for 10" models. Introduced in 1997. Discontinued.

NIB	Exc.	V.G.	Good	Fair	Poor
1100	800	600	—	—	—

Bisley Target
As above but with adjustable rear sight and replaceable blade front sight.

NIB	Exc.	V.G.	Good	Fair	Poor
1225	900	—	—	—	—

Pony Express
This model features a 5.50" barrel with special finish and engraved frame and barrel. Ivory grips are etched with pony express rider. Custom gun.

NIB	Exc.	V.G.	Good	Fair	Poor
3895	—	—	—	—	—

Sears 1902 Colt
This model is a replica of the Sears 1902 Colt SAA. Fitted with a 5.50" barrel, pearl grips, and full coverage engraving with gold line work on the cylinder and barrel. Custom gun.

NIB	Exc.	V.G.	Good	Fair	Poor
8995	—	—	—	—	—

NOTE: This company offers a wide variety of special order options on its revolvers, from special bluing to grips to engraving. These special order options will affect price to a significant degree. Seek qualified assistance prior to a sale.

RIFLES

Cowboy Action Lightning
This is a copy of the Colt Lightning rifle chambered for the .44-40, .45 Colt, or the .38 WCF cartridge. Fitted with a 26" round barrel and walnut stock with crescent butt. Magazine capacity is 15 rounds. Introduced in the fall of 2003.

NIB	Exc.	V.G.	Good	Fair	Poor
995	725	—	—	—	—

Cowboy Action Carbine
As above but with 20" round barrel. Magazine capacity is 12 rounds.

NIB	Exc.	V.G.	Good	Fair	Poor
995	725	—	—	—	—

Lightning Magazine Rifle
This model is a premium version of the Cowboy Action Lightning and features a choice of 26" round, half round, or octagon barrel. Checkered American walnut forearm with non-checkered stock with oil finish. Many extra cost options are offered for this model.

NIB	Exc.	V.G.	Good	Fair	Poor
1295	950	—	—	—	—

NOTE: Add $200 for half round barrel. Fancy wood, pistol grip, finish and engraving offered for this rifle.

Lightning Magazine Carbine
As above but with 20" round barrel.

NIB	Exc.	V.G.	Good	Fair	Poor
1295	950	—	—	—	—

Lightning Baby Carbine
This model is fitted with a 20" special round tapered barrel. Lightweight carbine forearm with border line.

NIB	Exc.	V.G.	Good	Fair	Poor
1690	1200	—	—	—	—

W

WALCH, JOHN
New York, New York

Navy Revolver
A .36 caliber superimposed load percussion revolver with a 6" octagonal barrel and a 6-shot cylinder fitted with 12 nipples, two hammers, and two triggers. The barrel marked "Walch Firearms Co. NY." and "Patented Feb. 8, 1859." Blued with walnut grips.

Exc.	V.G.	Good	Fair	Poor
—	—	9000	4000	950

Pocket Revolver
A spur trigger .31 caliber 10-shot percussion revolver with either a brass or iron frame and walnut grips. The iron frame version is worth approximately 50 percent more than the brass variety.

Exc.	V.G.	Good	Fair	Poor
—	—	2750	1000	300

WALLIS & BIRCH
Philadelphia, Pennsylvania

Pocket Pistol
A .41 caliber single-shot percussion pocket pistol with a 2.5" or 3" barrel, German silver furniture and walnut stock. The barrels marked "Wallis & Birch Phila." Produced during the 1850s.

Exc.	V.G.	Good	Fair	Poor
—	—	2250	800	250

WARNER, CHAS.
Windsor Locks, Connecticut

Pocket Revolver
A .31 caliber percussion revolver with a 3" round barrel and 6-shot unfluted cylinder. The cylinder marked "Charles Warner. Windsor Locks, Conn." Blued with walnut grips. Approximately 600 were made between 1857 and 1860.

Exc.	V.G.	Good	Fair	Poor
—	—	1150	450	100

WARNER, JAMES
Springfield, Massachusetts

Revolving Carbines
A variety of revolving carbines were made by this maker, nearly all of which are of .40 caliber, with octagonal barrels measuring 20" to 24" in length. The most commonly encountered variations are listed.

Manually Revolved Grooved Cylinder
This model is fitted with two triggers, one of which is a release so that the cylinder can be manually turned. Not fitted with a loading lever. The top strap marked "James Warner/Springfield, Mass." Approximately 75 were made in 1849.

Exc.	V.G.	Good	Fair	Poor
—	—	4250	2000	500

Retractable Cylinder Model
This version has a cylinder that fits over the breech, and it must be retracted before it can be manually rotated. The cylinder release is a button located in front of the trigger. It is marked "James Warner/Springfield Mass" and with an eagle over the letters "U.S." The cylinder is etched, and there is no loading lever. It also has a walnut stock with patch box and no forearm. There were approximately 25 manufactured in 1849.

Exc.	V.G.	Good	Fair	Poor
—	—	6250	2750	800

Automatic Revolving Cylinder
The cylinder is automatically turned when the hammer is cocked. This model is fitted with a loading lever and is marked "Warner's Patent/

Jan. 1851" and "Springfield Arms Co." Approximately 200 were made during the 1850s.

Exc.	V.G.	Good	Fair	Poor
—	—	4250	1750	500

Belt Revolver
A .31 caliber double-action percussion revolver with a 4" or 5" round barrel and 6-shot etched cylinder. Blued with walnut grips. No markings appear on this model except for the serial number. Manufactured in 1851.

Exc.	V.G.	Good	Fair	Poor
—	—	1500	600	100

Pocket Revolver
A .28 caliber percussion revolver with a 3" octagonal barrel marked "James Warner, Springfield, Mass., USA" and a 6-shot cylinder. Blued with walnut grips. Approximately 500 were made.

Exc.	V.G.	Good	Fair	Poor
—	—	650	250	100

Second Model
As above, with either a 3" or 4" barrel and marked "Warner's Patent 1857."

Exc.	V.G.	Good	Fair	Poor
—	—	650	300	100

Third Model
As above, but in .31 caliber.

Exc.	V.G.	Good	Fair	Poor
—	—	600	275	100

Single-Shot Derringer
A .41 caliber rimfire single-shot pocket pistol with a 2.75" round barrel, brass frame and walnut grips. As this model is unmarked, it can only be identified by the large breechblock which lifts upward and to the left for loading.

Exc.	V.G.	Good	Fair	Poor
—	—	17500	6500	1000

Pocket Revolver
A .30 caliber rimfire revolver with a 3" barrel marked "Warner's Patent 1857" and 5-shot cylinder. Blued or nickel-plated with walnut grips. Approximately 1,000 were made during the late 1860s.

Exc.	V.G.	Good	Fair	Poor
—	—	550	150	75

WEBLEY & SCOTT, LTD.
Birmingham, England
SEE ALSO—British Double Guns

Established in 1860, this firm has produced a wide variety of firearms over the years and has been known as Webley & Scott, Ltd. since 1906. **NOTE:** For all Webley .455 revolvers deduct 35 percent if converted to .45 ACP/.45 Auto Rim.

Model 1872 Royal Irish Constabulary
A .450 double-action revolver with a 3.25" barrel, 5-shot cylinder and rotating ejector. This model was also offered with 2.5" and 3.5" barrels. Blued with checkered walnut grips.

Exc.	V.G.	Good	Fair	Poor
650	400	250	200	150

Model 1880 Metropolitan Police
As above, with a 2.5" barrel and 6-shot cylinder.

Exc.	V.G.	Good	Fair	Poor
400	325	250	200	150

Model 1878 Webley-Pryse
Chambered for the .455 and .476 Eley cartridge.

Exc.	V.G.	Good	Fair	Poor
1100	900	750	550	300

NOTE: Add 200 percent premium for revolvers chambered for .577. Deduct 50 percent for revolvers chambered for cartridges below .442.

New Model 1883 R.I.C.
Similar to the Model 1880, but in .455 caliber with a 4.5" barrel. Also made with a 2.5" barrel.

Exc.	V.G.	Good	Fair	Poor
550	400	300	200	100

Model 1884 R.I.C. Naval
As above, with a brass frame and oxidized finish. Barrel length 2.75" and of octagonal form.

Exc.	V.G.	Good	Fair	Poor
1000	800	700	600	500

British Bulldog
Similar to the new Model 1883 R.I.C. blued, checkered walnut grips. Those engraved on the back strap "W.R.A. Co." were sold through the Winchester Repeating Arms Company's New York sales agency and are worth a considerable premium over the values listed. Manufactured from 1878 to 1914.

Exc.	V.G.	Good	Fair	Poor
350	300	250	200	150

NOTE: Add a premium for U.S. dealer markings, see above.

Model 1878 Army Express Revolver
A .455 caliber double-action revolver with a 6" barrel and integral ejector. Blued with one-piece walnut grips.

Exc.	V.G.	Good	Fair	Poor
1300	1000	750	500	350

NOTE: Add 100 percent premium for single-action version. Add 25 percent for .450 Long (.45 Colt) markings.

Webley Kaufmann Model 1880
A top break, hinged-frame double-action revolver chambered for the .450 centerfire cartridge, with a 5.75" barrel and a curved bird's-head butt. Blued, with walnut grips.

Exc.	V.G.	Good	Fair	Poor
1200	1000	800	—	—

Webley-Green Model
A double-action, top break revolver chambered for the .455 cartridge, with a 6" ribbed barrel and a 6-shot cylinder. The cylinder flutes on this model are angular and not rounded in shape. Blued, with checkered walnut, squared butt grips with a lanyard ring on the butt. Introduced in 1882 and manufactured until 1896.

Exc.	V.G.	Good	Fair	Poor
1000	800	600	—	—

Mark I
A .442, .455, or .476 double-action top break revolver with a 4" barrel and 6-shot cylinder. Blued with checkered walnut grips. Manufactured from 1887 to 1894.

Exc.	V.G.	Good	Fair	Poor
600	500	350	250	150

Mark II
As above, with a larger hammer spur and improved barrel catch. Manufactured from 1894 to 1897.

Exc.	V.G.	Good	Fair	Poor
550	450	300	200	100

Mark III

As above, with internal improvements. Introduced in 1897.

Exc.	V.G.	Good	Fair	Poor
400	325	225	150	75

Mark IV

As above, with a .455 caliber 3", 4", 5", or 6" barrel. This model was also available in .22 caliber with 6" barrel, .32 caliber with 3" barrel, and .38 caliber with 3", 4", or 5" barrel.

Exc.	V.G.	Good	Fair	Poor
400	325	225	150	75

WESSON, FRANK
Worcester, Massachusetts
Springfield, Massachusetts

Manual Extractor Model

A .22 caliber spur trigger single-shot pistol with a 4" octagonal barrel and thin brass frame. The barrel release is located in the front of the trigger. No markings. Approximately 200 were made in 1856 and 1857.

Exc.	V.G.	Good	Fair	Poor
—	—	900	400	100

First Model Small Frame

As above, with a 3", 3.5", or 6" half-octagonal barrel. Blued with rosewood or walnut grips. The barrel marked "Frank Wesson Worcester Mass/Pat'd Oct. 25, 1859 & Nov. 11, 1862." Serial numbered from 1 to 2500.

Exc.	V.G.	Good	Fair	Poor
—	—	550	200	75

Second Type

As above, with a flat sighted frame and a circular sideplate.

Exc.	V.G.	Good	Fair	Poor
—	—	500	175	75

First Model Medium Frame

As above, in .30 or .32 rimfire with a 4" half-octagonal barrel and an iron frame. Approximately 1,000 were made between 1859 and 1862.

Exc.	V.G.	Good	Fair	Poor
—	—	550	200	75

Medium Frame Second Model

As above, with a longer spur trigger and a slightly wider frame at the barrel hinge. Manufactured from 1862 to 1870.

Exc.	V.G.	Good	Fair	Poor
—	—	550	200	75

Small Frame Pocket Rifle

A .22 caliber spur trigger single-shot pistol with a 6" half octagonal barrel and narrow brass frame. This model is adopted for use with a detachable skeleton shoulder stock. The barrel marked "Frank Wesson Worcester, Mass." Manufactured from 1865 to 1875 with approximately 5,000 made.

Pistol Only

Exc.	V.G.	Good	Fair	Poor
—	—	850	300	100

NOTE: Matching shoulder stock add 100 percent.

Medium Frame Pocket Rifle

As above, in .22, .30, or .32 rimfire with a 10" or 12" half octagonal barrel. Approximately 1,000 were made from 1862 to 1870.

Pistol Only

Exc.	V.G.	Good	Fair	Poor
—	—	500	200	75

NOTE: Matching shoulder stock add 100 percent.

Model 1870 Small Frame Pocket Rifle

As above, in .22 caliber with a 10", 12", 15", or 18" or 20" half octagonal barrel that rotates to the side for loading. This model was made with either a brass or iron frame. It has a half cocked notch on the hammer.

Pistol Only

Exc.	V.G.	Good	Fair	Poor
—	—	550	200	75

NOTE: Matching shoulder stock add 100 percent.

1870 Medium Frame Pocket Rifle First Type

As above, but with a slightly larger frame chambered for .32 rimfire. Approximately 5,000 were made from 1870 to 1893.

Pistol Only

Exc.	V.G.	Good	Fair	Poor
—	—	500	175	75

NOTE: Match shoulder stock add 100 percent.

1870 Medium Frame Pocket Rifle Second Type

As above, with an iron frame and a push-button half cocked safety.

Pistol Only

Exc.	V.G.	Good	Fair	Poor
—	—	475	175	75

NOTE: Match shoulder stock add 100 percent.

1870 Medium Frame Pocket Rifle Third Type

As above, with three screws on the left side of the frame.

Pistol Only

Exc.	V.G.	Good	Fair	Poor
—	—	475	175	75

NOTE: Matching shoulder stock add 100 percent.

1870 Large Frame Pocket Rifle First Type

As above, in .32, .38, .42, or .44 rimfire with an octagonal barrel from 15" to 24" in length. The barrel marked "Frank Wesson Worcester, Mass Patented May 31, 1870." Fewer than 250 of these rifles were made between 1870 and 1880.

Pistol Only

Exc.	V.G.	Good	Fair	Poor
—	—	1500	550	200

NOTE: Matching shoulder stock add 100 percent.

1870 Large Frame Pocket Rifle Second Type

As above, with a sliding extractor.

Pistol Only

Exc.	V.G.	Good	Fair	Poor
—	—	1500	550	200

NOTE: Matching shoulder stock add 100 percent.

Small Frame Superposed Pistol

A .22 caliber spur trigger over/under pocket pistol with 2" or 2.5" octagonal barrels that revolve. Approximately 3,500 were made between 1868 and 1880. On occasion. this pistol is found with a sliding knife blade mounted on the side of the barrels. The presence of this feature would add approximately 25 percent to the values listed.

Exc.	V.G.	Good	Fair	Poor
—	—	1750	850	250

Medium Frame Superposed Pistol

As above, in .32 rimfire with 2.5" or 3.5" barrels. As with the smaller version, this pistol is occasionally found with a sliding knife blade mounted on the barrels that would add 25 percent to the values listed. Manufactured from 1868 to 1880.

First Type Marked "Patent Applied For"

Exc.	V.G.	Good	Fair	Poor
—	—	1250	400	100

Second Type Marked "Patent December 15, 1868"

Exc.	V.G.	Good	Fair	Poor
—	—	1200	400	100

Third Type Full-Length Fluted Barrels

Exc.	V.G.	Good	Fair	Poor
—	—	1500	450	150

Large Frame Superposed Pistol

As above, in .41 rimfire with a 3" octagonal barrel fitted with a sliding knife blade. Approximately 2,000 were made from 1868 to 1880.

Exc.	V.G.	Good	Fair	Poor
—	—	2750	1250	400

No. 1 Long Range Rifle
A .44-100 or .45-100 caliber single-shot dropping block rifle with a 34" octagonal barrel. Blued with a checkered walnut stock. The barrel marked "F. Wesson Mfr. Worcester, Mass. Long Range Rifle Creedmoor." Manufactured in 1876.

Exc.	V.G.	Good	Fair	Poor
—	12500	4500	2000	500

No. 2 Mid-Range or Hunting Rifle
Similar to the above, with the firing pin located in a bolster on the right side of the receiver. The trigger guard has a rear finger loop. Standard barrel length 28", 32", and 34" and marked "F. Wesson Maker Worcester, Mass." The 32" and 34" barrels are occasionally marked "Long Range Rifle Creedmoor." Approximately 100 were made.

Courtesy Buffalo Bill Historical Center, Cody, Wyoming

Exc.	V.G.	Good	Fair	Poor
—	7250	3750	1750	500

No. 2 Sporting Rifle
A .38-100, .40-100, or .45-100 caliber single-shot dropping-barrel-action rifle with barrels ranging from 28" to 34" in length. Approximately 25 were made.

Exc.	V.G.	Good	Fair	Poor
—	8250	3750	1750	500

Military Carbine
Fitted with a 24" barrel with sling swivels and chambered for the .44 caliber rimfire cartridge. Approximately 4,500 were manufactured.

Exc.	V.G.	Good	Fair	Poor
—	—	2500	1100	500

NOTE: Add 100 percent for martially marked examples.

WESSON & LEAVITT
MASSACHUSETTS ARMS COMPANY
Chicopee Falls, Massachusetts

Revolving Rifle
A .40 caliber percussion revolving rifle with a 16" to 24" round barrel and 6-shot cylinder. Blued with a walnut stock. Approximately 25 were made in 1849.

Exc.	V.G.	Good	Fair	Poor
—	—	7500	3500	950

Dragoon
A .40 caliber percussion revolver with a 6.25" or 7" round barrel and 6-shot cylinder. These pistols are marked "Mass. Arms Co./Chicopee Falls." Approximately 30 were made with the 6.25" barrel and 750 with the 7" barrel. Manufactured in 1850 and 1851.

Exc.	V.G.	Good	Fair	Poor
—	—	4750	2000	500

WESTERN ARMS
SEE—Bacon

WESTERN ARMS CORPORATION
SEE—Ithaca

WESTERN FIELD
Montgomery Ward
"Western Field" is the trade name used by Montgomery Ward & Company on arms that they retail. See Firearms Trade Names List at the end of this book.

WESTLEY RICHARDS & CO., LTD.
Birmingham, England
SEE—British Double Guns
A wide variety of firearms have been produced by this company since its founding. Presently, it produces boxlock and sidelock double-barrel shotguns of both side-by-side and over/under form, bolt-action rifles and double-barrel rifles. Prospective purchasers are advised to secure individual appraisals prior to acquisition.

ROBERT WHEELER
SEE—English Military Firearms

WHITE, ROLLIN
Lowell, Massachusetts

Pocket Pistol
A .32 or .38 rimfire spur trigger single-shot pistol with a 3" or 5" octagonal barrel. Brass or iron frames with walnut grips. The .38 caliber version with the 5" barrel was not produced in large quantities and therefore is worth approximately 25 percent more than the values listed. The barrels are marked "Rollin White Arms Co., Lowell, Mass."

Exc.	V.G.	Good	Fair	Poor
—	—	750	350	150

Pocket Revolver
A .22 caliber spur trigger revolver with a 3.25" octagonal barrel and 7-shot cylinder. The brass frame silver-plated, barrel blued and grips of walnut. This revolver was marked in a variety of ways including "Rollin White Arms Co., Lowell, Mass.," "Lowell Arms Co., Lowell, Mass.," or "Made for Smith & Wesson by Rollin White Arms Co., Lowell, Mass." Approximately 10,000 were made during the late 1860s.

Exc.	V.G.	Good	Fair	Poor
—	—	600	250	75

WHITNEY ARMS COMPANY
INCLUDING
ELI WHITNEY, SR. / P. & E.W. BLAKE /
ELI WHITNEY, JR.

As the United States' first major commercial arms maker, Eli Whitney's New Haven plant, which began production in 1798 and continued under family control for the next 90 years, was one of the more important American arms manufactories of the 19th century. Its products, accordingly, are eminently collectible. Moreover, during its 90 years of operation, the Whitney clan produced a number of unusual arms, some exact copies of regulation U.S. martial longarms, others variations and derivatives of U.S. and foreign longarms, a variety of percussion revolvers, and finally a variety of single-shot and repeating breechloading rifles in an attempt to capture a portion of the burgeoning market in these cartridge arms during the post-Civil War period. Contrary to the prevailing myth, Eli Whitney, Sr., who also invented the cotton gin, did NOT perfect a system of interchangeability of parts in the arms industry. His contributions in this line were more as a propagandist for the concept that was brought to fruition by others, notably Simeon North and John Hall.

Eli Whitney, Sr. Armory Muskets, 1798-1824.
1798 U.S. Contract Muskets, Types I-IV
On 14 January 1798, Eli Whitney, Sr., having convinced the U.S. War Department that he could mass-produce interchangeable parts muskets, was awarded a contract for 10,000 muskets following the "Charlesville" (French M1766) pattern, then also being copied at the newly opened Springfield Armory and most of the U.S. musket contractors. Whitney's 1798 contract muskets measure between 58-7/8" and 57-3/4" in overall length, with the longer arms delivered earlier. The .69-caliber smoothbore barrels measure approximately 44", though most are shy of that length by anywhere from 1/16" to a maximum of 1-1/4". Lockplates are flat with a beveled edge and are marked "U.STATES" in a curve on the pointed tail and with a perched eagle with down folded wings over "NEW HAVEN" forward of the cock. Four differences in the material and manner of attachment of the pan distinguish the subtypes. The first deliver of 500 muskets in September of 1801 had an integral, faceted iron pan (Type I); the second delivery of 500 muskets in June of 1802 also had faceted iron pans, but were detachable (Type II). The 1,000 muskets delivered in September of 1802 and March of 1803 had faceted, detachable pans, but these were made of brass instead of iron (Type III). The final 8,000 muskets, delivered between 1803 and 1809, had detachable brass pans with a rounded

bottom that Whitney copied from the French M1777 musket (Type IV) and a rounded cock, also copied from the French M1777 musket. Generally speaking, due to the limited production of Types I - III, they should command a higher price; prices are given for the more common Type IV 1798 contract musket. It should be noted however, that about 1804 Whitney delivered 112 Type IV muskets to Connecticut's "1st Company of Governor's Foot Guards." Although similar to the Type IV musket, these 112 arms are distinguished by the absence of the "U.STATES" on the tail of the lock and the addition of the name "CONNECTICUT" to the left side plate. Such an arm should demand a considerable premium over the usual Type IV musket.

Exc.	V.G.	Good	Fair	Poor
—	—	4500	2000	500

Whitney Connecticut, New York, and U.S. 1812 Contract Muskets

In 1808, Whitney received a contract from the state of New York for 2,000 muskets. In 1810, he received a second contract from the same source for an additional 2,000 muskets, all of which were eventually delivered by mid-1813. In the interim, in 1809, the state of Connecticut contracted with Whitney to deliver 700 muskets per year over the next three years. With the outbreak of the War of 1812, in July of 1812, a contract was let to Eli Whitney for 15,000 muskets (later extended by another 3,000 muskets), conforming to the pattern he had made for the state of New York, but with 42"-long barrels. All of these contract muskets shared most of the same features. Overall length was 58". The .69-caliber smoothbore barrel was nominally 42", though the two state contracts did not rigidly enforce that dimension. The lockplate of these muskets bore the inscription "NEW HAVEN" within a curving scroll forward of the cock. Like the Type III 1798 U.S. contract muskets, the lockplates incorporated a detachable round-bottomed brass pan and a round faced cock. The stock was distinguished by having a low, virtually nonexistent comb similar to that of the 1816 musket pattern. The New York state contract muskets are distinguished by having the state ownership mark "SNY" on the axis of the barrel near the breech. (It should be noted that the first 1,000 muskets delivered under the U.S. 1812 contract were also delivered to New York, but these have the mark across the breech at right angles to the axis of the barrel.) The Connecticut contract muskets are distinguishable by having the state-ownership mark "S.C." (for "state of Connecticut" on the barrel and the top of the comb of the stock. On Connecticut muskets in better condition, the Connecticut coat of arms (a shield with three clusters of grape vines) should also be visible struck into the wood on the left side of the musket opposite the lock. Verifiable Connecticut and New York contract muskets should bring a premium over the U.S. contract muskets.

Exc.	V.G.	Good	Fair	Poor
—	—	3250	1500	500

Whitney Armory Muskets, 1825-1842

Eli Whitney died in 1825. Although he had a son destined to take over the family business, Eli Whitney, Jr. was only 5 years old when his father passed away and could not assume legal possession until he turned 21 in 1842. In the interim, the company was administered by the senior Whitney's trustees, Henry Edwards and James Goodrich, while the plant itself was run by Whitney's nephews, Philo and Eli Whitney Blake. During their control of the factory, three contracts were fulfilled for the U.S. government, one awarded in August of 1822 for 15,000 muskets (delivered between 1826 and 1830), a second awarded in March of 1830 for 8,750 muskets (delivered between 1831 and 1836) and a final contract in January of 1840 for 3,000 muskets (delivered between 1840 and 1842). An additional 6,750 were delivered under annual allotments granted by the War Department between 1835 and 1839 over and above the contracts for distribution to the states under the 1808 Militia Act. Although the 1840 contract had originally called for U.S. M1840 muskets, in April of that year, the contract was altered so that Whitney's plant could continue to deliver what it had delivered consistently from 1824, the U.S. M1816/1822 flintlock musket.

Whitney (and P. & E.W. Blake) U.S. M1816/1822 Contract Muskets

The U.S. M1816/1822 muskets manufactured at Whitney's Armory were identical to those produced at the U.S. Armories at Springfield and Harpers Ferry. The overall length was 57-3/4". The 42"-long, .69-caliber smoothbore barrels were finished with a browning solution until 1831; after that date the metal was left in the polished "bright." The stock and the lock reflect Whitney's earlier attempts impart his design elements into the U.S. patterns. The stock had the low comb of his M1812 musket and the lock incorporated the rounded cock and round bottomed brass pan that he had championed from the French M1777 musket. The lock markings varied during the period that the arm was produced, though all were marked on the pointed tail with the vertical stamp: "NEW HAVEN" arced around the date (1825-1830), or in three vertical lines: "NEW / HAVEN / (date: 1831-1842)." Those made between 1825 and 1830 under the direct supervision of Whitney's nephews bore the two line mark "U.S. / P. & E.W. BLAKE" forward of the cock; those made from 1830 to 1837 bear the "U.S" over "E. WHITNEY" with a crossed arrow and olive branch between; after 1837 the crossed arrow and olive branch motif was eliminated in favor of the simple two lines. In addition to the Whitney Armory's federal contracts, Whitney executed at least one contract with the state of South Carolina in the mid-1830s for an estimated 800 to 2,000 muskets. Basically identical in configuration to the federal contract muskets, the South Carolina muskets were distinguished by the substitution of "S.C." for "U.S." over the "E. WHITNEY" stamp of the lockplate. They also bear the state ownership mark "So. CAROLINA" on the top of the barrel. Due to their relative rarity and Confederate usage (especially if altered to percussion by means of a brazed bolster), the South Carolina contract arms should bring a considerable premium.

Exc.	V.G.	Good	Fair	Poor
—	—	3500	1500	500

Whitney Armory U.S. M1816/M1822 Muskets, Altered to Percussion

From 1850 through 1856, many of the contract muskets in store at the U.S. arsenals were altered from flintlock to percussion by means of the "Belgian" or "cone-in barrel" method. The system of alteration involved the removal of the flintlock battery from the lock, filing in the screw holes from those parts, substituting a percussion hammer for the cock, plugging the vent, removing the breech plug so as to "upset" the upper, right-hand side top of the barrel, drilling and threading the "upset" section for a cone, reinserting the breech plug, and screwing in a new percussion cone. The percussioned musket was effective but the barrel was considerably weakened by the process, and while some were rifled during the American Civil War, most saw service in that conflict as smoothbores. As a general rule, the muskets so altered generally command about one-third the price of the arm in original flintlock. Exceptions are those with state ownership marks (eg. "OHIO" in the stock), with regimental marks, or with the so-called "Sea Fencible" buttplate.

Whitney Armory U.S. M1816/M1822 Muskets, Flintlock or Altered to Percussion and Adapted with "Sea Fencible" Heavy Buttplates

A number of the Whitney U.S. M1816/M1822 muskets were delivered to the Commonwealth of Massachusetts under the terms of the 1808 Militia Act. Many of these were subsequently altered to percussion at the Watertown Arsenal near Boston for the state after 1850. At some time in their career both some of the flintlock arms and those that had been altered to percussion were adapted to a heavy brass buttplate with a peculiar knob at its heel. In the process the buttstock was usually narrowed to conform to the width of the new buttplate. Because many of the muskets encountered with this buttplate bore the inspection mark of Samuel Fuller ("SF/V" within a lozenge), these arms were initially considered to have been made for the Massachusetts "Sea Fencible" organizations formed during and after the War of 1812. That appellation, however, has been dismissed, although the exact purpose of the new buttplate and the date of its application are not known. These butt-plates are usually (but not necessarily) found on Whitney contract muskets and invariably are marked with the Massachusetts state ownership mark "MS" on the barrel as well as rack numbers on the tang of the buttplate itself. Despite the unknown purpose of these arms, they command a considerable premium over standard flintlock or altered to percussion Whitney muskets.

Exc.	V.G.	Good	Fair	Poor
—	—	3500	1250	400

Eli Whitney Jr. Armory Rifles and Rifle-Muskets, 1842-1865

Upon reaching the age of 21 in 1842, Eli Whitney, Jr. assumed command of his late father's gun making empire. Although he realized that the armory required updating to meet the improved tolerances adopted by the U.S. War Department, he also realized that a profit might be made in turning out arms of lesser standards for independent sale to the militia or the states. As a result, the younger Whitney's product line included not only several of the regulation U.S. longarms, but also a number of "good and serviceable" militia arms, including:

Whitney U.S. M1841 Contract Rifle (unaltered)

Between 1842 and 1855 Eli Whitney, Jr. received five contracts from the U.S. War Department to manufacture the newly adopted U.S. M1841 percussion rifle: 7,500 on October of 1842 (delivered between 1844 and 1847), 7,500 in March of 1848, subsequently extended to 10,000 in January of 1849 (delivered between 1849 and 1853) 5,000 (previously contracted for by Edward K. Tryon) in October of 1848 (delivered contiguous with the 1848 contract for 10,000), 5,000 in 1853 (delivered between 1853 and 1855), and 100 in 1855 (delivered that year). All except the final 1,100 delivered in 1855 conformed to the model made at Harpers Ferry, and of those 1,100, the only difference of 500 of them was the ramrod. This rifle was 49" in length, overall, having a 33" long browned barrel with .54 caliber rifled (7 groove) bore. The barrel bears the stamp of inspection at the breech, usually "U S /(inspectors' initials) / P", while the left flat (after mid-1848 for Whitney rifles) should also bear the stamping "STEEL" to indicate that the barrel had been rolled from "cast steel." Furniture is brass, the buttplate bearing the stamped letters, "U S." The lockplate is flat with a beveled edge and bears the horizontal two line inscription "E. WHITNEY" / "U S" forward of the hammer and the vertical, two line inscription "N. HAVEN" / (date) on the tail. (The date also appears on the breech plug tang). As originally made, the M1841 rifle was not adapted for a bayonet, though several modifications were made to the rifle between 1855 and 1862 to effect that adaptation.

Exc.	V.G.	Good	Fair	Poor
—	—	4750	1750	500

Whitney U.S. M1841/1855 Contract Rifle, Adapted to Saber Bayonet and Long Range Sights

Before the final 600 rifles (of the 2,600 made in 1855) left the factory, the U.S. War Department contracted with Whitney to bring them up to the standards of the modified U.S. M1841 rifle then being produced or adapted at the Harpers Ferry Armory. The adaptation was two fold. First, a long range rear "ladder" style rear sight, having a 2-1/4" base was soldered to the top of the barrel; then a 1/2" long bayonet lug with 1" guide was brazed to the right side of the barrel, 2-1/2" from the muzzle. To permit disassembly, the old front band was removed and replaced with a shortened version. A new ramrod (also applied to 500 rifles without this adaptation), having an integral iron head cupped for the newly adopted "Minie ball" replaced the flat brass headed ramrod to complete the process; the rifle remained in .54 caliber with 7 grooves. Neither was the front sight modified. Bayonets were furnished by the Ames Manufacturing Company on a separate contract. Rifles so adapted at the Whitney Armory are among the rarer variants of the U.S. M1841 line and prices reflect that rarity.

Exc.	V.G.	Good	Fair	Poor
—	—	4750	1750	650

Whitney U.S. M1841 Contract Rifles, Adapted to Saber Bayonets and Long Range Rear Sights (Colt 1862 Adaptation)

A large number of unaltered U.S. M1841 rifles remained on hand in U.S. Arsenals when the Civil War broke out, primarily those of Whitney's and Robbins & Lawrence's manufacture. To upgrade these rifles, revolver maker, Samuel Colt arranged to purchase 10,500 and adapt them to bayonets and long-range sights. The sight that he affixed consisted of a two leaf rear sight he had been using on his revolving rifles, with one leaf flopping forward and one flopping backward from the 100 yard block. The saber bayonet lug he attached consisted of a blued clamping ring with integral 1/2"-long lug attached that could fastened to the barrel so that the lug projected from the right side. These lugs were numbered both to the bayonet and the rifle's barrel, the number appearing on the lower surface of the barrel just behind the location of the clamping ring. Colt also bored the rifles up to .58 caliber, leaving some with 7 grooves but rerifling others with 3 wide grooves. An estimated half of the 10,200 rifles so modified by Colt were of Whitney's earlier production. Due to the Colt association, rifles so modified usually command slightly higher prices than other Civil War adaptations for saber or socket bayonets.

Exc.	V.G.	Good	Fair	Poor
—	—	4750	1750	650

Whitney South Carolina Contract M1841 Rifle

To meet the perceived needs of South Carolina during the anti-slavery debates following the Mexican War Annexation, Whitney produced a variant of the U.S. M1841 rifle for that state, delivering only 274 in 1849. The marking of this rifle differed only in having the letters "S C" on the plate beneath the "E. WHITNEY" stamp. Because South Carolina had previously contracted for 1,000 variant M1841 rifles from William Glaze & Co. in 1853 which accepted a socket bayonet, Whitney provided the 274 1849 dated rifles with that provision also, although the lug was located under the barrel instead of atop it. Because the socket bayonet dominated the forward 3" of the barrel, the front sight was relocated to the top of the upper strap of the front band. Rifles from this contract are exceedingly rare.

Exc.	V.G.	Good	Fair	Poor
—	—	6500	3250	950

Whitney "Good & Serviceable" M1841 Derivatives

From parts or entire rifles rejected for his federal contracts for U.S. M1841 rifles, between 1848 and 1860, Eli Whitney, Jr. assembled a number of rifles similar in overall characteristics to the federal contract rifles but differing both in quality and in a number of minor details. At least four variants were produced between 1855 and 1862 and sold to various states or independent militia companies. Distinguishing characteristics of these four are:

Type I. M1841 rifle adapted to saber bayonet but not to long range sights.

A 1/2"-long saber bayonet lug (either with or without the 1" guide) brazed to the right side of the barrel; long front band replaced with short double strapped band left over from 1855 contract. Some of this type (without 1" guide) are known with "OHIO" state ownership marks and are thought to be from among the 420 purchased by the state in 1861 from Schuyler, Hartley & Graham. Examples are known with the lockplate dated 1855 and without any date or "US" stamp below "E. WHITNEY."

Type II. M1841 rifle adapted to saber bayonet and Sharps long range sight.

These rifles also bear the 1/2" brazed saber bayonet lug (with the 1" guide) and the short front band, but they also have a Sharps M1853 "ladder" rear sight added in lieu of the standard notched iron block. Moreover, rifles in this configuration lack the brass patchbox lid and its underlying cavity for implements and greased patches.

Type III. M1841 rifle adapted to socket bayonet and Sharps long-range sight.

These late-production (1859-1860) derivatives of the M1841 rifle are adapted to the Sharps long-range sight used on the Type II. rifles but have a patch box. Unlike standard production, however, it is covered with an iron lid and hingle. The trigger guard strap is also iron. Lock plates delete both the date from the tail and the "US" under "E. WHITNEY." An iron stud is added below the barrel near the muzzle for a socket bayonet, necessitating the relocation of the brass blade front sight to the upper strap of the forward band. Probably fewer than 100 of this configuration were made, making it the most desirable of the derivative M1841 rifles.

Type IV. M1841 rifle unadapted using modified parts.

Rifles of this configuration use the same markings as the type III rifles but delete entirely the patch box and its lid (like the type II rifles). The trigger guard strap is iron and the lock screws seem to be the same as Whitney used for his Whitney short Enfield derivative rifles. It is suspected that these rifles were purchased from New York dealers and sold to Georgia during the secession crisis of 1860-1861, thereby enhancing their collector's value, though in general Whitney M1841 derivative rifles are equal in pricing:

Exc.	V.G.	Good	Fair	Poor
—	—	3250	1250	500

Whitney M1842 Rifled Musket Derivative

Using rejected U.S. M1842 barrels sold at auction by the Springfield Armory, Whitney assembled approximately 2,000 .69 caliber rifled muskets that he exchanged with the state of New Hampshire in 1858 for a number of old flintlock muskets owned by that state. These rifled muskets exhibit a number of anomalies from the U.S. M1842 musket, although overall length (57-3/4") and the barrel length (42") remain the same as that musket, the bores are rifles with 7 narrow grooves, and in addition to the dates and inspection marks placed at Springfield usually bear the state ownership mark "NEW HAMPSHIRE" on the top of the barrel. In finishing these rifled muskets, Whitney utilized a number of parts from other gun makers, including Sharps M1853 "ladder" style carbine rear sights, bands from the Robbins & Lawrence P1853 Enfield rifle-musket contract, and internal lock parts remaining from his M1841 rifles. Parts that are unique to these arms include the iron nosecap and the flat lockplate. The lockplates are unmarked, but the barrels usually show a letter/number code common to Whitney's production during this period. Despite a production of approximately 2,000 muskets, the survival rate for this type of arm is quite low.

Exc.	V.G.	Good	Fair	Poor
—	—	3250	1250	400

Whitney P1853 "Long Enfield" Rifle-Musket Derivative
Having secured a number of bands and other furniture from the Robbins & Lawrence contract for P1853 Enfield rifle-muskets, about 1859 Whitney developed a derivative of that arm that combined those bands with a 40"-barrel .58 caliber, rifled with 7 grooves that basically resembled the configuration of the U.S. M1855 rifle-musket, a copy of which Whitney was also making. The 56"-long rifle-musket that resulted was sold to state militia companies and two states, Maryland purchasing 2,000 and Georgia contracting for 1,700 (of which 1,225 were delivered). Although several of the components of the furniture were from the Robbins & Lawrence contract, the nosecap was pewter (Enfield style), and the iron buttplate and brass trigger guard bow/iron strap were of a style peculiar to Whitney's Enfield series. The rear sight resembled the ladder pattern of the U.S. M1855 rifle musket. The unique flat, unbeveled lockplate simply bears the one line stamp, "E. WHITNEY" forward of the hammer.

Exc.	V.G.	Good	Fair	Poor
—	—	3250	1250	600

Whitney P1853 "Short Enfield" Rifle Derivative
At the same time that Whitney developed his "Long Enfield" Derivative Rifle-Musket, he also prepared a short version of it similar to the British P1856 sergeant's rifle. Having an overall length of 49", the rifle version had a 33"-long barrel in .58 caliber and rifled with 7 grooves like the rifle-musket. The furniture was basically the same as the rifle-musket as well, with a pewter nosecap, iron buttplate, and combination brass bow and iron strap trigger guard (although some variants are known with all brass P1853 trigger guards). The two iron bands were from the Robbins & Lawrence contract salvage, as were the brass lock screw washers. The flat, unbeveled lockplate is the same style as used in the Long Enfield derivative rifle-muskets and is similarly marked "E. WHITNEY" forward of the hammer. In the manufacture of the rifle, four variants evolved.
Type I. Buttstock incorporated an oval iron patch box; front and rear sights were of standard U.S. M1841 configuration and no provision was made for a saber bayonet.
Type II. Buttstock continued to incorporate an oval iron patch box; rear sight was now the long range "ladder" type on a 25/16" base as used on the long Enfield rifle-musket derivative. Front sight was an iron block with integral blade. A 1/2" long saber bayonet lug was added to the right side of the barrel.
Type III. The oval iron patchbox was deleted from the buttstock. Front and rear sights remain as in Type II, as does bayonet lug.
Type IV. Identical to Type III but with a new single leaf rear sight on a 1-1/4" long base.
Total production of these rifles is estimated to have been between 800 and 1,000, with approximately half of the number going to southern states. Prices should not vary between the four types; however, confirmed Confederate usage will increase the value significantly.

Exc.	V.G.	Good	Fair	Poor
—	—	4250	2000	600

Whitney M1855 Rifle Derivative
At the same time that Whitney advertised his Enfield derivative series of rifle-muskets and rifles, he also indicated the availability of a short rifle with saber bayonet. This rifle combined rejected barrels made at Harpers Ferry in 1858 for the U.S. M1855 rifles with rejected, unmilled Maynard tape primer lockplates that had been shaved of their top "hump", marked forward of the hammer with the single line stamp, "E. WHITNEY." The buttplate and the trigger guard also conform to that of the U.S. M1855 rifle, but the bands are brass, remaining from Whitney's M1841/1855 rifle contract. Early in production these rifles used round brass lock screw washers following the M1855 pattern; later production used the winged brass lock screw washers that Whitney inherited from the Robbins & Lawrence P1853 rifle-musket contract and which he used on his Enfield series derivatives. At least two patterns of saber bayonet were used on this rifle.

Exc.	V.G.	Good	Fair	Poor
—	—	3500	1250	500

Whitney M1855 Rifle-Musket Derivative
In 1861, Whitney accepted a U.S. contract to produce 40,000 U.S. "M1855" rifle-muskets. What Whitney had in mind under this contract and what the War Department demanded were two different arms. Whitney's product was similar to the U.S. M1855 rifle-musket but differed in a number of respects. The 40" barrel was .58 caliber but was rifled with 7 rather than 3 grooves and was adapted to the English P1853 socket bayonet he had been using on his Enfield derivative rifle-muskets. The initial rear sight, while similar to the U.S. M1855 type, was slightly shorter, having a 2-5/16" base. (On later production, Whitney substituted a shorter, 1-1/4"-long base with a single, pierced leaf sight.) The nosecap, moreover, was made of pewter and followed the Enfield pattern rather than being malleable iron of the U.S. M1855 pattern. On later production, Whitney also substituted brass winged lock screw washers from his Enfield derivative series. The lockplates for these arms were drawn from complete Maynard locks made at the federal armories in 1858 and 1859 but later rejected for flaws. Upon these plates Whitney stamped "E. WHITNEY / N. HAVEN," as on his early Connecticut contract M1861 derivative rifle-muskets. Except for the letter/number code, the barrels are unmarked. Examples are known whose stocks bear indications of issue to the 8th Connecticut Infantry during the Civil War, suggesting Whitney may have sold the few made to Connecticut under his first state contract. Arms with these regimental marks should command a premium over unmarked arms.

Exc.	V.G.	Good	Fair	Poor
—	—	3500	1250	500

Whitney M1861 Connecticut Contract Rifle-Musket Derivative
In 1861 and 1862, Eli Whitney, Jr. entered into two contracts with his home state of Connecticut for respectively 6,000 and 8,000 rifle-muskets generally conforming to the U.S. M1861 rifle musket. A number of exceptions to the U.S. model, however, were permitted. On the first contract, the 40" barrels were in .58 caliber but were made with 7 groove rifling instead of 3 groove; on the second contract, the arms were made with 3-groove rifling. Nosecaps for both contracts were of the U.S. M1855/1861 pattern but were cast in pewter instead of malleable iron. An exception was also permitted in the rear sights, which initially were the same 1-1/4" long base with pierced single leaf that Whitney had used on his Type IV short Enfield derivative rifles, though later the base was changed to conform to the pattern adopted for the U.S. M1861 rifle-musket but still retaining the single leaf. Lockplates were M1861-style, marked forward of the hammer "E. WHITNEY / N. HAVEN" on early production and with an eagle surmounting a panoply of flags and trophies over "WHITNEYVILLE" on later production. The barrels bore the typical Whitney letter/number code and were adapted to the Enfield pattern socket bayonets rather than the U.S. M1855 socket bayonets. Later production occasionally bears the inspection letters "G.W.Q."

Exc.	V.G.	Good	Fair	Poor
—	—	2750	1150	400

Whitney "High Humpback" Lockplate M1861 Rifle-Musket Derivative
With the completion of his Connecticut contracts, Whitney combined the excess parts from its production with some of the unmilled and unshaved lockplates that he still had on hand from his M1855 Rifle Derivatives. The 56"-long rifle-muskets that resulted have 40" barrels in .58 caliber with 3-groove rifling and a rear sight that conforms to the U.S. M1861 pattern that Whitney began making in 1863. The flat, beveled unmilled lockplates bear the two line stamp "E. WHITNEY / N. HAVEN" that Whitney had used on his M1855 rifle-musket derivative and on the early M1861 Connecticut contract rifle-muskets, but

showing considerable wear, to the extent that the second line is often incomplete or missing entirely. Photograph evidence indicates that the 21st Connecticut Infantry received some of these rifle-muskets. They are often mistaken as a southern purchase, which artificially raises the asking prices.

Exc.	V.G.	Good	Fair	Poor
—	—	3250	1250	500

Whitney "Manton" M1861 Rifle-Musket Derivative
In order to dispose of some of his inferior arms from the second Connecticut state contract, Whitney assembled at least 1,300 bearing a fictitious Old English lock stamp "Manton" forward of the hammer and the date "1862" on its tail. In most respects this arm resembled the U.S. M1861 rifle musket, complete with 3-groove rifling in its .58-caliber, 40" barrel with typical Whitney letter/number code near the muzzle (and often also marked "G.W.Q. on its left flat). Nosecaps, in typical Whitney style, were case from pewter instead of being formed from malleable iron. The rear sight closely follows the M1861 pattern but lacks the step on its side walls since it utilized a simple pierced leaf instead of the compound double leaf of the M1861 rifle-musket. These arms were disposed of in the New York City market after the 1863 Draft Riot and issued to the New York National Guard.

Exc.	V.G.	Good	Fair	Poor
—	—	4250	2000	600

Whitney "Direct Vent" M1861 Rifle-Musket Derivatives
In his continued efforts to dispose of surplus and rejected parts from his Connecticut and federal contracts, Whitney devised in 1863 a rifle-musket generally conforming to the M1861 rifle-musket except in two notable features. The bolster, instead of projecting considerably away from the barrel and having a clean-out screw was relatively short and flat faced. The process of making this bolster eliminated one production sequence, since it was not possible to drill the hole for the cone directly to the barrel. To accommodate the new cone position, the lockplates were made flat, without the bevel, and inletted flush with the stock. Lockplates bear the eagle surmounting the panoply of flags and trophies over "WHITNEYVILLE" stamp forward of the hammer, and are known with "1863" on the tail or without any date. The rear sight is the same as used on the "Manton" rifle-musket derivative. Arms with barrels than 40", 39", and 30" exist, all in .58 caliber with 3-groove rifling; however, the shortest of these may be postwar modifications for cadet use. Quantities made are not known, but surviving examples suggest limited production, probably to use faulty parts from the 1863 federal contract.

Exc.	V.G.	Good	Fair	Poor
—	—	3250	1250	400

Whitney U.S. M1861 Contract Rifle-Musket
In October of 1863, Whitney secured a contract with the U.S. War Department to produce 15,000 U.S. M1861 rifle-muskets. The arms manufactured under this contract conform in all respects to the Springfield Model adopted in 1861. The 40" barrel is in .58 caliber and rifled with 3 grooves; its rear sight conforms to the two-leaf model with stepped side walls. Nosecap is M1861 style and made of malleable iron. Socket bayonets furnished with them conform to the U.S. M1855/M1861 pattern. Marks include "US" on buttplate and standard inspection marks on barrel and stock. Lockplate marked with eagle surmounting letters "US" forward of the hammer and "WHITNEYVILLE" on the forward projection of the plate; date, "1863" or "1864" stamped on tail of the plate.

Exc.	V.G.	Good	Fair	Poor
—	—	3250	1250	400

Whitney U.S. Navy Contract Rifle
In July of 1861, Whitney entered a contact with the U.S. Navy to produce 10,000 rifles of the "Plymouth Pattern." So called after the U.S. Navy warship whereupon the first Harpers Ferry trial rifles had been developed, the new Navy rifle borrowed many of its characteristics from the French M1846 "carbine a tige." Overall length was 50" with a 34"-long barrel bearing a saber bayonet lug with guide extending nearly to the muzzle on its right side. The bore was .69 caliber, rifled with three broad lands and grooves. The rear sight copied the French M1846 and M1859 styles, i.e. it has an elevating ladder but no sidewalls. On early production the sights are serially numbered to the rifle's serial number (appearing on the breech plug tang). Barrels bear the standard U.S. inspection marks on the left quarter flat and the production date ("1863" or "1864") on the top of the barrel near the breech. Two lock markings have been encountered. The earlier production uses flat beveled plate marked with the date "1863" on its tail and an eagle surmounting a panoply of flags and trophies over the name "WHITNEYVILLE." In later (after serial no. 3,000) the lock's tail is marked "1864" and the stamping forward of the hammer matches that on the U.S. M1861 Whitney contract rifle-muskets, i.e. a small eagle over "U S" and "WHITNEYVILLE" in the forward projection of the plate. Inspector's initials (F.C.W.) appear on the barrel and in a cartouche on the stock.

Exc.	V.G.	Good	Fair	Poor
—	—	4250	1750	600

The Whitney Arms Company, 1865-1888
With the close of the American Civil War, Eli Whitney, Jr. again turned his eyes to the manufacture of inexpensive arms from parts remaining on hand from his Civil War contracts. Extra barrels were turned into inexpensive muzzleloading shotguns, and a few breechloading designs were toyed with. Following Remington's example, Whitney soon realized that a substantial profit could be made in the production of single-shot martial arms for foreign governments. The result was a series of breechloading arms that copied many salient features of the Remington line, including a direct copy after the expiration of the Remington patent for the "rolling block" mechanism. Not until the late 1870s did Whitney acquire the rights to several patents that led to the production of a lever-action repeating rifle. During the postwar period, revolver production, which had begun with evasions of Colt's patents in the decade prior to the Civil War, mushroomed with the production of small spur-trigger rimfire cartridge revolvers. Despite the variety of arms produced, by 1883 Whitney was considering the sale of his company. Business reverses over the next five years necessitated the sale of the firm to Winchester in 1888. Primarily interested securing in the patent rights for Whitney's lever-action series of rifles, Winchester closed the plant and moved its machinery to New Haven. After 90 years of production, the Whitneyville Armory ceased to exist.

Single Barreled Percussion Shotgun
This firearm was manufactured by Whitney out of surplus .58 caliber rifle barrels that were opened up and converted to smoothbore .60-caliber shotgun barrels. They are offered in lengths of 28" to 36" and are marked "Whitney Arms Co., Whitneyville, Conn. Homogeneous Wrought Steel." The finish is blued, with varnished walnut stocks that are crudely checkered. There were approximately 2,000 manufactured between 1866 and 1869. These guns are rarely encountered on today's market.

Exc.	V.G.	Good	Fair	Poor
—	—	950	400	150

Double-Barreled Percussion Shotgun
The specifications for this version are similar to that of the single barrel except that there are two side-by-side barrels with double locks and hammers and double triggers. They are slightly more common than the single barreled version.

Exc.	V.G.	Good	Fair	Poor
—	—	950	400	150

Swing-Breech Carbine
This is a single-shot breechloading carbine chambered for the .46-caliber rimfire cartridge. It has a 22" round barrel with a button-released breechblock that swings to the side for loading. The finish is blued, with a walnut stock. There were fewer than 50 manufactured in 1866.

Exc.	V.G.	Good	Fair	Poor
—	—	3250	1750	600

Whitney-Cochran Carbine
This is a single-shot breechloading carbine chambered for the .44 rimfire cartridge. It has a 28" round barrel with a lever-activated breechblock that raises upward for loading. It was manufactured under license from J.W. Cochran. The finish is blued, with a walnut stock. There is a saddle ring on the left side of the frame. It is marked "Whitney Arms Co. - Whitneyville, Conn." This gun was produced for the 1867 Government Carbine Trials. There were fewer than 50 manufactured in 1866 and 1867.

Exc.	V.G.	Good	Fair	Poor
—	—	3500	1500	600

Excelsior

This is a single-shot rifle chambered for the .38, .44, or .50 rimfire cartridges. It is found with various-length octagonal or round barrels. The finish is blued, with a walnut stock and forearm held on by one barrel band. The breechblock pivots downward for loading. There is a center-mounted hammer. It is marked "Whitney Arms Co. Whitneyville Conn." The shorter barreled carbine versions have a saddle ring on the frame. There were approximately 200 manufactured between 1866 and 1870.

Exc.	V.G.	Good	Fair	Poor
—	—	2750	1150	400

Whitney-Howard Lever Action

This is a single-shot breechloader that is chambered for the .44 rimfire cartridge. It has also been noted as a shotgun chambered for 20 gauge smoothbore with barrels from 30" to 40" in length. The rifle version has barrel lengths from 22" to 28". The breechblock is opened by means of a combination lever and trigger guard. There is also a carbine version with barrel lengths of 18.5" or 19". There were approximately 2,000 manufactured totally between 1866 and 1870. Values are as follows:

Shotgun
Exc.	V.G.	Good	Fair	Poor
—	—	650	300	100

Rifle
Exc.	V.G.	Good	Fair	Poor
—	—	900	450	150

Carbine
Exc.	V.G.	Good	Fair	Poor
—	—	1250	500	200

Whitney Phoenix

There is little known about the origin of this model. It is built on a patent issued to Whitney in 1874. There are a number of variations that are all marked "Phoenix, Patent May 24, 74." The Whitney name is not marked on any of the versions. They are all single-shot breechloaders with a breechblock that lifts to the right side and upward for loading. The barrels are all blued, with either case colored or blued receivers and walnut stocks. There were approximately 25,000 total manufactured between 1867 and 1881. The models and values are as follows:

Gallery Rifle
This version is chambered for the .22 rimfire caliber and has a 24" half-octagonal barrel. Its production was quite limited.

Exc.	V.G.	Good	Fair	Poor
—	—	1500	600	200

Shotgun
This is a smoothbore version chambered for 10, 12, 14, 16, or 22 gauge. It has smoothbore barrels between 26" and 32" in length. There were approximately 5,000 manufactured.

Exc.	V.G.	Good	Fair	Poor
—	—	600	250	100

Military Rifle
This version is chambered for the .433, .45, or .50 caliber centerfire cartridges. It has a 35" round barrel with a full-length, two-piece walnut stock held on by three barrel bands. There were approximately 15,000 manufactured. Many were sent to Central or South America.

Exc.	V.G.	Good	Fair	Poor
—	—	3000	1250	400

Schuetzen Rifle
This is a target-shooting version chambered for the .38, .40, or .44 centerfire cartridges. It has either a 30" or 32" octagonal barrel with a Schuetzen-type walnut stock and forearm that features hand checkering. It has a nickel-plated, Swiss-style buttplate and adjustable sights with a spirit level. This model has been noted with double-set triggers. There were few manufactured.

Exc.	V.G.	Good	Fair	Poor
—	—	3250	1250	400

Civilian Carbine
This version is chambered for the .44 caliber centerfire and has a 24" round barrel. The finish is blued, with a case colored frame and a walnut stock and forearm held on by one barrel band. It has military-type sights, buttplate, and a saddle ring mounted on the frame. There were approximately 500 manufactured.

Exc.	V.G.	Good	Fair	Poor
—	—	2500	850	400

Military Carbine
This version is chambered for the .433, .45, or .50 centerfire cartridges. It has a 20.5" round barrel and was manufactured for Central and South America. It is very rarely encountered on today's market.

Exc.	V.G.	Good	Fair	Poor
—	—	2750	1000	400

Whitney-Laidley Model I Rolling Block

Whitney acquired manufacturing rights for this model from the inventors T. Laidley and C.A. Emery, who had received the patent in 1866. Whitney immediately started to modify the action to become competitive with the Remington Rolling Block. There were approximately 50,000 manufactured total between 1871 and 1881. There are a number of variations of this model as follows:

Military Carbine
There were approximately 5,000 manufactured chambered for the .433, .45, or .50 centerfire cartridges. It has a 20.5" round barrel with military-type sights and a saddle ring on the receiver. The finish is blued, with a case colored frame and a walnut stock. Most of them were shipped to Central or South America.

Exc.	V.G.	Good	Fair	Poor
—	—	1750	700	250

Civilian Carbine
This version is chambered for .44 rimfire or centerfire and .46 rimfire. It has either an 18.5" or 19.5" barrel. It is blued, with a case colored frame. The stock is walnut. A nickel-plated version is also available. There were approximately 1,000 of this version manufactured.

Exc.	V.G.	Good	Fair	Poor
—	—	1750	700	250

Military Rifle
This version is chambered the same as the Military Carbine but has either a 32.5" or 35" round barrel with a full-length two-piece stock held on by three barrel bands. The finish is blued, with a case colored receiver and a walnut stock. There were approximately 30,000 manufactured. Most were shipped to Central or South America.

Courtesy Milwaukee Public Museum, Milwaukee, Wisconsin

Exc.	V.G.	Good	Fair	Poor
—	—	2000	800	300

Gallery Rifle
This is a .22 caliber sporting-rifle version with a 24" octagonal barrel. The finish is similar to the Military Rifle. There were approximately 500 manufactured.

Exc.	V.G.	Good	Fair	Poor
—	—	1750	700	250

Sporting Rifle
This version is chambered for .38, .40, .44, .45, or .50 centerfire, as well as .32, .38, or .44 rimfire. It features barrel lengths from 24" to 30" in either round or octagonal configurations. The finish is similar to the Military Rifle, and there were approximately 5,000 manufactured.

Exc.	V.G.	Good	Fair	Poor
—	—	2000	750	300

Creedmoor No. 1 Rifle
This version is chambered for the .44 caliber cartridge and has a 32" or 34" barrel that is either round or octagonal in configuration. It has a blued finish with case colored frame and a hand checkered, select walnut stock and forearm. It features vernier adjustable sights with a spirit level. It is marked "Whitney Creedmoor." There were fewer than 100 manufactured.

Exc.	V.G.	Good	Fair	Poor
—	—	6250	2750	850

Creedmoor No. 2 Rifle
This version is similar to the No. 1 Rifle except that it is chambered for the .40 caliber cartridge with either a 30" or 32" barrel.

Exc.	V.G.	Good	Fair	Poor
—	—	4250	1750	500

Whitney-Remington Model 2 Rolling Block
When Remington's patent for the Rolling Block action expired, Whitney was quick to reproduce the action, labeling it his "New Improved System." It is essentially quite similar to Remington's Rolling Block and is easily recognized when compared with the Model 1 because it has only two parts — the hammer and the breechblock. The frame is also rounded. The tang on this model is marked "Whitney Arms Company, New Haven Ct USA." There were approximately 50,000 total manufactured between 1881 and 1888. There are a number of variations as follows:

Shotgun
This is a smoothbore version chambered for 12, 14, 16, or 20 gauge. It is offered with barrel lengths between 26" and 30". Twenty inch barrels have also been noted.

Exc.	V.G.	Good	Fair	Poor
—	—	650	250	100

Military Carbine
This version is chambered for the .433 and .45 centerfire cartridges. It has a 20.5" barrel and is blued, with a case colored receiver and walnut stock. There were approximately 5,000 manufactured. Most were sent to South or Central America.

Exc.	V.G.	Good	Fair	Poor
—	—	1750	700	300

Civilian Carbine
This version is chambered for the .44 rimfire or centerfire cartridge with an 18.5" round barrel. The finish is similar to the Military Carbine. There were approximately 2,000 manufactured.

Exc.	V.G.	Good	Fair	Poor
—	—	1600	600	250

Military Rifle
This version is chambered for the .433, .45, or .50 centerfire cartridge. It has a 32.5" or 35" barrel. It is finished similarly to the Military Carbine. There were approximately 39,000 manufactured.

Exc.	V.G.	Good	Fair	Poor
—	—	2000	750	300

No. 1 Sporting Rifle
This version is chambered for various popular sporting cartridges and is offered with barrel lengths from 26" to 30", either round or octagonal in configuration. The finish is blued, with a case colored receiver and a varnished walnut stock. There were many options available that could radically affect the value, and a qualified appraisal would be advisable. There were approximately 3,000 manufactured.

Exc.	V.G.	Good	Fair	Poor
—	—	2500	1000	400

No. 2 Sporting Rifle
This is a smaller version of the No. 1 Rifle, chambered for the .22 rimfire, .32, .38, and .44-40 centerfire cartridges. Again, a qualified appraisal would be helpful, as many options can affect the value.

Exc.	V.G.	Good	Fair	Poor
—	—	1750	700	250

Whitney-Burgess-Morse Rifle
This is a lever action repeating rifle chambered for the .45-70 Government cartridge. There are three variations. All have a magazine tube mounted beneath the barrel with blued finishes and walnut stocks. The barrels are marked "G. W. Morse Patented Oct. 28th 1856." The tang is marked "A. Burgess Patented Jan. 7th, 1873, Patented Oct 19th 1873." There were approximately 3,000 total manufactured between 1878 and 1882. The variations areas follows:

Sporting Rife
This version has a 28" octagonal or round barrel. The magazine tube holds 9 rounds. There are a number of options available that can increase the value drastically; and we recommend competent, individual appraisal. Value given is for a standard model.

Exc.	V.G.	Good	Fair	Poor
—	—	3250	1250	400

Military Rifle
This version has a 33" round barrel with a full-length forearm held on by two barrel bands. It features military sights and has an 11-round tubular magazine. It has a bayonet lug and sling swivels. This variation is also found chambered for the .43 Spanish and .42 Russian cartridges. There were approximately 1,000 manufactured.

Exc.	V.G.	Good	Fair	Poor
—	—	4250	2000	700

Carbine
This version has a 22" round barrel with a full-length forearm held on by one barrel band. It has a 7-round tubular magazine and a saddle ring attached to the frame. There were approximately 500 manufactured.

Exc.	V.G.	Good	Fair	Poor
—	—	4750	2250	750

Whitney-Kennedy Rifle
This is a lever action repeating rifle that was manufactured in two sizes. It has a magazine tube mounted under the barrel and a blued finish with a case colored lever. The stock is walnut. The barrel is marked "Whitney Arms Co New Haven, Conn. U.S.A." Occasionally, the word "Kennedy" is marked after the Whitney name. There are two major variations. One features a standard-type action lever; and the other, the same "S"-shaped lever that is found on the Burgess model. This version would be worth approximately 10 percent additional. As with many of the rifles of this era, there were many options available that will affect the values. We strongly recommend securing a qualified appraisal for all but the standard models if a transaction is contemplated. There were approximately 15,000 manufactured between 1879 and 1886. The variations of the Whitney-Kennedy and their values are listed.

Small Frame Sporting Rifle
This version is chambered for the .32-20, .38-40, and the .40-40 cartridges. It has a 24" barrel that is either round or octagonal in configuration. Examples will be noted with either a full-length or half-length tubular magazine.

Exc.	V.G.	Good	Fair	Poor
—	—	2750	1200	500

Large Frame Sporting Rifle
This version is chambered for the .40-60, .45-60, .45-75, and the .50-90 cartridges. The .50-caliber version is uncommon and will bring a 20 percent premium. The barrel lengths offered are 26" or 28".

Exc.	V.G.	Good	Fair	Poor
—	—	3000	1350	500

Military Rifle
This is a large-frame model, chambered for the .40-.60, .44-.40, and the .45-60 cartridges. It has a 32.25" round barrel and either an 11- or 16-round tubular magazine. It has a full-length walnut forend held on by two barrel bands and features a bayonet lug and sling swivels. There were approximately 1,000 manufactured. Most were shipped to Central or South America.

Exc.	V.G.	Good	Fair	Poor
—	—	3750	1750	550

Military Carbine
This is built on either the small-frame or large-frame action and is chambered for the .38-40, .44-40, .40-60, or .45-60 cartridges. It has either a 20" or 22" round barrel and a 9- or 12-round tubular magazine, depending on the caliber. It has a short forend held on by a single barrel band. There were approximately 1,000 manufactured. Most were sent to Central or South America.

Exc.	V.G.	Good	Fair	Poor
—	—	3750	1750	550

Hooded Cylinder Pocket Revolver
This is an unusual revolver that is chambered for .28 caliber percussion. It has a manually rotated, 6-shot hooded cylinder that has etched decorations. The octagonal barrel is offered in lengths of 3" to 6". There is a button at the back of the frame that unlocks the cylinder so that it can be rotated. The finish is blued, with a brass frame and two-piece rounded walnut grips. It is marked "E. Whitney N. Haven Ct." There were approximately 200 manufactured between 1850 and 1853.

Exc.	V.G.	Good	Fair	Poor
—	—	3250	1500	600

Two Trigger Pocket Revolver

This is a conventional-appearing pocket revolver with a manually rotated cylinder. There is a second trigger located in front of the conventional trigger guard that releases the cylinder so that it can be turned. It is chambered for .32 caliber percussion and has an octagonal barrel from 3" to 6" in length. It has a 5-shot unfluted cylinder that is etched and a brass frame. The remainder is blued, with squared walnut two-piece grips. An iron-frame version is also available, but only 50 were produced. It would bring approximately 60 percent additional. There were approximately 650 total manufactured between 1852 and 1854.

Exc.	V.G.	Good	Fair	Poor
—	—	2000	850	300

Whitney-Beals Patent Revolver

This was an unusual, ring-trigger pocket pistol that was made in three basic variations.

First Model

This version is chambered for .31-caliber percussion and has barrels of octagonal configuration from 2" to 6" in length. It has a brass frame and a 6-shot cylinder. It is marked "F. Beals/New Haven, Ct." There were only 50 manufactured.

Exc.	V.G.	Good	Fair	Poor
—	—	3500	1500	450

.31 Caliber Model

This version has an iron frame and a 7-shot cylinder. The octagonal barrels are from 2" to 6" in length. It is marked "Address E. Whitney/Whitneyville, Ct." There were approximately 2,300 manufactured.

Exc.	V.G.	Good	Fair	Poor
—	—	1500	600	200

.28 Caliber Model

Except for the caliber, this model is similar to the .31 Caliber Model. There were approximately 850 manufactured.

Exc.	V.G.	Good	Fair	Poor
—	—	1750	700	300

Whitney 1851 Navy

This is a faithful copy of the 1851 Colt Revolver. It is virtually identical. There is a possibility that surplus Colt parts were utilized in the construction of this revolver. There were approximately 400 manufactured in 1857 and 1858.

Exc.	V.G.	Good	Fair	Poor
—	—	4250	1750	650

Whitney Navy Revolver

This is a single-action revolver chambered for .36 caliber percussion. It has a standard octagonal barrel length of 7.5". It has an iron frame and a 6-shot unfluted cylinder that is roll engraved. The finish is blued, with a case colored loading lever and two-piece walnut grips. The barrel is marked either "E. Whitney/N. Haven" or "Eagle Co." There are a number of minor variations on this revolver, and we strongly urge competent appraisal if contemplating a transaction. There were 33,000 total manufactured between 1858 and 1862.

First Model

Nearly the entire production of the First Model is marked "Eagle Co." The reason for this marking is unknown. There are four distinct variations of this model. They are as follows:

First Variation

This model has no integral loading-lever assembly and has a thin top strap. There were only 100 manufactured.

Exc.	V.G.	Good	Fair	Poor
—	—	3750	1500	550

Second Variation

This version is similar to the First Variation, with an integral loading lever. There were approximately 200 manufactured.

Exc.	V.G.	Good	Fair	Poor
—	—	3000	1200	400

Third Variation

This is similar to the Second, with a three-screw frame instead of four screws. The loading lever is also modified. There were approximately 500 manufactured.

Exc.	V.G.	Good	Fair	Poor
—	—	2500	1000	300

Fourth Variation

This version has a rounded frame and a safety notch between the nipples on the rear of the cylinder. There have been examples noted marked "E. Whitney/N. Haven." There were approximately 700 manufactured.

Exc.	V.G.	Good	Fair	Poor
—	—	2500	1000	300

Second Model

First Variation

This version features a more robust frame with a brass trigger guard. The barrel is marked "E. Whitney/N. Haven." The cylinder pin is secured by a wing nut, and there is an integral loading lever. There were approximately 1,200 manufactured.

Exc.	V.G.	Good	Fair	Poor
—	—	2000	900	300

Second Variation

This version has six improved safety notches on the rear of the cylinder. There were approximately 10,000 manufactured.

Exc.	V.G.	Good	Fair	Poor
—	—	1750	750	250

Third Variation

This version has an improved, Colt-type loading-lever latch. There were approximately 2,000 manufactured.

Exc.	V.G.	Good	Fair	Poor
—	—	1750	750	250

Fourth Variation

This is similar to the Third except the cylinder is marked "Whitneyville." There were approximately 10,000 manufactured.

Exc.	V.G.	Good	Fair	Poor
—	—	1750	750	250

Fifth Variation

This version has a larger trigger guard. There were approximately 4,000 manufactured.

Exc.	V.G.	Good	Fair	Poor
—	—	1750	750	250

Sixth Variation

This version has the larger trigger guard and five-groove rifling instead of the usual seven-groove. There were approximately 2,500 manufactured.

Exc.	V.G.	Good	Fair	Poor
—	—	1750	750	250

Whitney Pocket Revolver

This is a single-action revolver chambered for .31 caliber percussion. It has octagonal barrels between 3" and 6" in length. It has a 5-shot unfluted cylinder that is roll engraved and marked "Whitneyville". The frame is iron with a blued finish and a case colored integral loading lever. The grips are two-piece walnut. The development of this model, as far as models and variations go, is identical to that which we described in the Navy Model designation. The values are different, and we list them for reference. Again, we recommend securing qualified appraisal if a transaction is contemplated. There were approximately 32,500 manufactured from 1858 to 1862.

First Model

First Variation

Exc.	V.G.	Good	Fair	Poor
—	—	2000	900	300

Second Variation

Exc.	V.G.	Good	Fair	Poor
—	—	1250	500	200

Third Variation

Exc.	V.G.	Good	Fair	Poor
—	—	1000	400	150

Fourth Variation

Exc.	V.G.	Good	Fair	Poor
—	—	1000	400	150

Fifth Variation

Exc.	V.G.	Good	Fair	Poor
—	—	1000	400	150

Second Model

First Variation

Exc.	V.G.	Good	Fair	Poor
—	—	900	400	100

Second Variation

Exc.	V.G.	Good	Fair	Poor
—	—	900	400	100

Third Variation

Exc.	V.G.	Good	Fair	Poor
—	—	900	400	100

Fourth Variation

Exc.	V.G.	Good	Fair	Poor
—	—	1000	425	125

New Model Pocket Revolver

This is a single-action, spur-triggered pocket revolver chambered for .28-caliber percussion. It has a 3.5" octagonal barrel and a 6-shot roll engraved cylinder. It features an iron frame with a blued finish and two-piece walnut grips. The barrel is marked "E. Whitney/N. Haven." There were approximately 2,000 manufactured between 1860 and 1867.

Exc.	V.G.	Good	Fair	Poor
—	—	1250	500	200

Rimfire Pocket Revolver

This is a spur-trigger, single-action, solid-frame pocket revolver that was produced in three frame sizes, depending on the caliber. It is chambered for the .22, .32, and .38 rimfire cartridges. The frame is brass, and it is found in a variety of finishes- nickel-plated or blued, or a combination thereof. The bird's-head grips are rosewood or hard rubber; ivory or pearl grips are sometimes encountered and will bring a slight premium in value. The barrels are octagonal and from 1.5" to 5" in length. The barrels are marked "Whitneyville Armory Ct. USA." They have also been noted with the trade names "Monitor," "Defender," or "Eagle." They were commonly referred to as the Model No. 1, No. 1.5, Model 2, or Model 2.5. The values for all are quite similar. There were approximately 30,000 manufactured of all types between 1871 and 1879.

Exc.	V.G.	Good	Fair	Poor
—	—	500	200	75

WINCHESTER REPEATING ARMS COMPANY
New Haven, Connecticut

Winchester is a name that is identified with the Old West and the frontier days of America. Winchester rifles and shotguns are prized for their historical significance as well as their collectiblity. The Winchester Repeating Arms Company was formally established by Oliver F. Winchester on February 20, 1866, and the first model to bear the name of the company was the Model 1866 lever-action rifle chambered for the .44 caliber rimfire cartridge. As with any enterprise it is helpful to study the background and beginnings of the Winchester company so as to better understand the chronological sequence of various rifles and pistols that preceded the Winchester Model 1866.

The story begins with Walter Hunt of New York City who, in 1848, developed the Rocket Ball and Volition Repeater, a unique lever-action, breechloading, under barrel magazine tube repeater. This rifle was the origin for future concepts. Hunt's business partner, George Arrowsmith, had as his machinist a man named Lewis Jennings, who improved and simplified Walter Hunt's original concept. Jennings' improvements were granted a U.S. patent in 1849.

The prices given here are for the most part standard guns without optional features that were so often furnished by the factory. These optional or extra-cost features are too numerous to list and can affect the price of a shotgun or rifle to an enormous degree. In some cases these options are one of a kind. Collectors and those interested in Winchester firearms have the benefit of some of the original factory records. These records are now stored in the Cody Firearms Museum, Buffalo Bill Historical Center, P.O. Box 1000, Cody, Wyoming (307) 587-4771. For a $25 fee the museum will provide factory letters containing the original specifications of certain Winchester models using the original factory records.

CAUTION: Buyers should confirm by Cody letter any special-order feature on any Winchester within the Cody record range before paying a premium for a scarce feature.

Hunt Repeating Rifle

Walter Hunt described his repeating rifle as the Volition Repeater. Hunt was granted U.S. patent number 6663 in August 1849 for his repeating rifle that was to pave the way for future generations of Winchester repeating rifles. Hunt's rifle design was unique and innovative as was his patent number 5701 for a conical lead bullet that was to be fired in his rifle. This ingenious bullet had a hole in its base filled with powder and closed by a disc with an opening in the middle to expel the ignition from an independent priming source that used priming pellets made of fulminate of mercury. The rifle actually worked but only the patent model was built; it is now in the Cody Firearms Museum.

Jennings

Second in the evolutionary line of Winchester rifles is the Jennings. Made by Robbins & Lawrence of Windsor, Vermont, this rifle incorporated the original concept of the Hunt design with the additional improvements utilized by Lewis Jennings. The Jennings rifle is important not only as a link in the chain of repeating-rifle development but also because it introduced Benjamin Henry Tyler to the concept of the tubular magazine lever-action repeating rifle. The Jennings rifle was built in three separate and distinct models. While total production of the three types was contracted for 5,000 guns, it is probable that only about 1,000 were actually produced.

First Model

The First Model Jennings was built in a .54 caliber, breech-loading, single-shot configuration with a ring trigger, oval trigger guard, and 26" barrel. A ramrod was fixed to the underside of the barrel as well. This variation was made from 1850 to 1851.

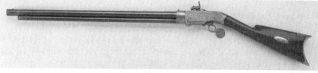

Courtesy Little John's Auction Service, Inc.

Exc.	V.G.	Good	Fair	Poor
—	—	4000	1750	700

Second Model

The Second Model Jennings was produced adopting the improvements made by Horace Smith. This Second Model is a breech-loading repeating rifle with an under barrel magazine tube and a 26" barrel. The frame is sculptured, unlike the First Model. The ring trigger is still present, but the trigger guard was removed as part of the design change. The caliber remained a .54, and the rifle was fitted with a 25" barrel. The Second Model was produced in 1851 and 1852.

Exc.	V.G.	Good	Fair	Poor
—	—	8000	4000	1500

Third Model

The Third Model represents an attempt by investors to use the remaining parts and close out production. The .54 caliber Third Model was a muzzleloading rifle with a ramrod mounted under the barrel and a 26-1/2" barrel. The frame was the same as that used on the First Model, but the trigger was more of the conventional type. The trigger guard had a bow in the middle giving this model a distinctive appearance. This variation was produced in 1852 and marks the end of the early conceptual period in repeating rifle development.

Exc.	V.G.	Good	Fair	Poor
—	—	9500	4500	1500

Smith & Wesson Volcanic Firearms

An interesting connection in the evolution of the lever-action repeating firearm is found in the production of a small group of pistols and rifles built in Norwich, Connecticut, by Horace Smith and Daniel Wesson under the firm name of Smith & Wesson. The company built two types of Volcanic pistols. One was a large-frame model with an 8" barrel and chambered in .41 caliber. About 500 of these large frames were produced. The other pistol was a small-frame version with a 4" barrel chambered in .31 caliber. Slightly more of these small-frame pistols were built, about 700, than the large-frame version. In both variations the barrel, magazine, and frame were blued. Smith & Wesson also produced a lever-action repeating rifle. These rifles are exceedingly rare with fewer than 10 having been built. They were chambered for the .528 caliber and were fitted with 23" barrels. Because of the small number of rifles built, no value is offered.

4" Pistol
Exc.	V.G.	Good	Fair	Poor
—	—	11000	4000	1000

8" Pistol
Exc.	V.G.	Good	Fair	Poor
—	—	13000	6000	1500

Volcanic Firearms (Volcanic Repeating Arms Company)

With the incorporation of the Volcanic Repeating Arms Company, a new and important individual was introduced who would have an impact on the American arms industry for the next 100 years: Oliver F. Winchester. This new company introduced the Volcanic pistol using the improvements made by Horace Smith and Daniel Wesson. Volcanic firearms are marked on the barrel, "THE VOLCANIC REPEATING ARMS CO. PATENT NEW HAVEN, CONN. FEB. 14, 1854." The Volcanic was offered as a .38 caliber breechloading tubular magazine repeater with blued barrel and bronze frame. These pistols were available in three barrel lengths.

6" Barrel
Exc.	V.G.	Good	Fair	Poor
—	—	7000	3500	1500

8" Barrel
Exc.	V.G.	Good	Fair	Poor
—	—	7000	3500	1500

16" Barrel
Exc.	V.G.	Good	Fair	Poor
—	—	14000	5500	2500

NOTE: A few Volcanic pistols were produced with detachable shoulder stocks. These are considered quite rare. For original guns with this option, the above prices should be increased by 25 percent.

Volcanic Firearms (New Haven Arms Company)

In 1857 the New Haven Arms Company was formed to continue the production of the former Volcanic Repeating Arms Company. Volcanic firearms continued to be built but were now marked on the barrel, "NEW HAVEN, CONN. PATENT FEB. 14, 1854." The Volcanic pistols produced by the New Haven Arms Company were built in .30 caliber and used the same basic frame as the original Volcanic. These pistols were produced in 3-1/2" and 6" barrel lengths.

3-1/2" Barrel
Exc.	V.G.	Good	Fair	Poor
—	—	5000	2500	1500

6" Barrel
Exc.	V.G.	Good	Fair	Poor
—	—	5750	3000	1500

Lever Action Carbine

New Haven Arms introduced, for the first time, a Volcanic rifle that featured a full-length slotted magazine tube with a spring-activated thumbpiece follower that moved along the entire length of the magazine tube. These rifles were chambered for .38 caliber cartridge and were offered in three barrel lengths: 16", 20", and 24".

16" Barrel
Exc.	V.G.	Good	Fair	Poor
—	—	15000	6000	2000

20" Barrel
Exc.	V.G.	Good	Fair	Poor
—	—	18000	8000	3000

24" Barrel
Exc.	V.G.	Good	Fair	Poor
—	—	22500	10000	3000

Henry Rifle

With the development of B. Tyler Henry's improvements in the metallic rimfire cartridge and his additional improvements in the Volcanic frame, the direct predecessor to the Winchester lever-action repeater was born. The new cartridge was the .44 caliber rimfire, and the Henry rifle featured a 24" octagon barrel with a tubular magazine holding 15 shells. The rifle had no forearm, but was furnished with a walnut buttstock with two styles of buttplates: an early rounded heel crescent shape seen on guns produced from 1860 to 1862 and the later sharper heel crescent butt found on guns built from 1863 to 1866. The early models, produced from 1860 to 1861, were fitted with an iron frame, and the later models, built from 1861 to 1866, were fitted with brass frames. About 14,000 Henry rifles were made during the entire production period; only about 300 were iron frame rifles.

Iron Frame Rifle
Exc.	V.G.	Good	Fair	Poor
—	—	85000	30000	—

Brass Frame Rifle

Courtesy Little John's Auction Service, Inc.

Exc.	V.G.	Good	Fair	Poor
—	—	37500	17500	9000

Martially Inspected Henry Rifles

Beginning in 1863 the Federal Government ordered 1,730 Henry Rifles for use in the Civil War. Most of these government-inspected rifles fall into serial number range 3000 to 4000 while the balance are close to this serial-number range. They are marked "C.G.C." for Charles G. Chapman, the government inspector. These Henry rifles were used under actual combat conditions and for that reason it is doubtful that there are any rifles that would fall into the excellent condition category. Therefore no price is given.

NOTE: There are many counterfeit examples of these rifles. It is strongly advised that an expert in this field be consulted prior to a sale.

Exc.	V.G.	Good	Fair	Poor
—	—	60000	25000	12000

Winchester's Improvement Carbine

Overall length 43-1/2"; barrel length 24"; caliber .44 rimfire. Walnut stock with a brass buttplate; the receiver and magazine cover/forend of brass; the barrel and magazine tube blued. The magazine loading port is exposed by sliding the forend forward. This design was protected by O.F. Winchester's British Patent Number 3285 issued December 19, 1865. Unmarked except for internally located serial numbers. Approximately 700 manufactured in December of 1865 and early 1866, the majority of which were sold to Maximilian of Mexico. Prospective purchasers are strongly advised to secure an expert appraisal prior to acquisition.

Exc.	V.G.	Good	Fair	Poor
—	—	35000	12500	9000

Model 1866

In 1866 the New Haven Arms Company changed its name to the Winchester Repeating Arms Company. The first firearm to be built under the Winchester name was the Model 1866. This first Winchester was a much-improved version of the Henry. A new magazine tube developed by Nelson King, Winchester's plant superintendent, was a vast improvement over the slotted magazine tube used on the Henry and its predecessor. The old tube allowed dirt to enter through the slots and was weakened because of it. King's patent, assigned to Winchester, featured a solid tube that was much stronger and reliable. His patent also dealt with an improved loading system for the rifle. The rifle now featured a loading port on the right side of the receiver with a spring-loaded cover. The frame continued to be made from brass. The Model

1866 was chambered for the .44 caliber Flat Rimfire or the .44 caliber Pointed Rimfire. Both cartridges could be used interchangeably. The barrel on the Model 1866 was marked with two different markings. The first, which is seen on early guns up to serial number 23000, reads "HENRY'S PATENT-OCT. 16, 1860 KING'S PATENT-MARCH 29, 1866." The second marking reads, "WINCHESTER'S-REPEATING-ARMS.NEW HAVEN, CT. KING'S-IMPROVEMENT-PATENTED MARCH 29, 1866 OCTOBER 16, 1860." There are three basic variations of the Model 1866:

1. Sporting Rifle round or octagon barrel. Approximately 28,000 were produced.
2. Carbine round barrel. Approximately 127,000 were produced.
3. Musket round barrel. Approximately 14,000 were produced.

The rifle and musket held 17 cartridges, and the carbine had a capacity of 13 cartridges. Unlike the Henry, Model 1866s were fitted with a walnut forearm. The Model 1866 was discontinued in 1898 with approximately 170,000 guns produced. The Model 1866 was sold in various special order configurations, such as barrels longer or shorter than standard, including engraved guns. The prices listed represent only standard-model 1866s. For guns with special-order features, an independent appraisal from an expert is highly recommended.

First Model
This first style has both the Henry and King patent dates stamped on the barrel, a flat-loading port cover, and a two-screw upper tang. Perhaps the most distinctive feature of the First Model is the rapid drop at the top rear of the receiver near the hammer. This is often referred to as the "Henry Drop," a reference to the same receiver drop found on the Henry rifle. First Models will be seen up through the 15000 serial number range.

Rifle

Exc.	V.G.	Good	Fair	Poor
—	27500	17500	8500	4000

Carbine

Exc.	V.G.	Good	Fair	Poor
—	25000	14000	7500	5000

Second Model
The second style differs from the first most noticeably in its single screw upper tang and a flare at the front of the receiver to meet the forearm. The Second Model also has a more gradual drop at the rear of the receiver than the First Model. The Second Style Model 1866 appears through serial number 25000.

Rifle

Exc.	V.G.	Good	Fair	Poor
—	22500	12500	7000	4000

Carbine

Exc.	V.G.	Good	Fair	Poor
—	17500	12000	8500	3500

Third Model
The third style's most noticeable characteristic is the more moderately curved receiver shape at the rear of the frame. The serial number is now stamped in block numerals behind the trigger, thus allowing the numbers to be seen for the first time without removing the stock. The barrel marking is stamped with the Winchester address. The Third Model is found between serial numbers 25000 and 149000. For the first time, a musket version was produced in this serial-number range.

Rifle

Courtesy Little John's Auction Service, Inc.

Exc.	V.G.	Good	Fair	Poor
—	16000	11000	6000	3500

Carbine

Exc.	V.G.	Good	Fair	Poor
—	12000	9500	5500	3500

Musket

Exc.	V.G.	Good	Fair	Poor
—	11000	8000	3500	2500

Fourth Model
The fourth style has an even less pronounced drop at the top rear of the frame, and the serial number is stamped in script on the lower tang under the lever. The Fourth Model is seen between serial number 149000 and 170100 with the late guns having an iron buttplate instead of brass.

Iron

Exc.	V.G.	Good	Fair	Poor
—	14000	8500	5000	3500

Carbine

Exc.	V.G.	Good	Fair	Poor
—	11000	9000	3500	2500

Musket

Exc.	V.G.	Good	Fair	Poor
—	12000	9000	3500	2500

Model 1866 Iron Frame Rifle Musket
Overall length 54-1/2"; barrel length 33-1/4"; caliber .45 centerfire. Walnut stock with case hardened furniture, barrel burnished bright, the receiver case hardened. The finger lever catch mounted within a large bolster at the rear of the lever. Unmarked except for serial numbers that appear externally on the receiver and often the buttplate tang. Approximately 25 made during the early autumn of 1866. Prospective purchasers are strongly advised to secure an expert appraisal prior to acquisition. Due to the recent identification of this model pricing schedules have yet to be established.

Model 1866 Iron Frame Swiss Sharpshooters Rifle
As above, but in .41 Swiss caliber and fitted with a Scheutzen style stock supplied by the firm of Weber Ruesch in Zurich. Marked Weber Ruesch, Zurich on the barrel and serial numbered externally. Approximately 400 to 450 manufactured in 1866 and 1867. Prospective purchasers are strongly advised to secure an expert appraisal prior to acquisition. Due to the recent identification of this model pricing schedules have yet to be established.

Model 1867 Iron Frame Carbine
Overall length 39-1/4"; barrel length 20"; caliber .44 rimfire. Walnut stock with case hardened furniture; the barrel and magazine tube blued; the receiver case hardened. The finger lever catch mounted within the rear curl of the lever. Unmarked except for serial numbers that appear externally on the receiver and often the buttplate tang. Approximately 20 manufactured. Prospective purchasers are strongly advised to secure an expert appraisal prior to acquisition. Due to the recent identification of this model pricing schedules have yet to be established.

Model 1868 Iron Frame Rifle Musket
Overall length 49-1/2" (.455 cal.), 50-1/2" or 53" (.45 and .47 cal.); barrel length 29-1/2" (.455 cal.) and 30-1/4" or 33" (.45 and .47 cal.); calibers .45, .455, and .47 centerfire. Walnut stock with case hardened or burnished bright (.45 and .47 cal.) furniture; the barrel burnished bright; the receiver case hardened or burnished bright (.45 and .47 cal.). The finger lever catch mounted on the lower receiver tang. The rear of the finger lever machined with a long flat extension on its upper surface. Unmarked except for serial number. Approximately 30 examples made in .45 and .455 caliber and 250 in .47 caliber. Prospective purchasers are strongly advised to secure an expert appraisal prior to acquisition. Due to the recent identification of this model pricing schedules have yet to be established.

Model 1868 Iron Frame Carbine
Overall length 40"; barrel length 20"; caliber .44 centerfire. Walnut stock with case hardened furniture; barrel and magazine tube blued; the receiver case hardened. The finger lever catch as above. Unmarked except for serial numbers (receiver and buttplate tang). Approximately 25 manufactured. Prospective purchasers are strongly advised to secure an expert appraisal prior to acquisition. Due to the recent identification of this model pricing schedules have yet to be established.

Model 1873

This Winchester rifle was one of the most popular lever-actions the company ever produced. This is the "gun that won the West" and with good reason. It was chambered for the more powerful centerfire cartridge, the .44-40. Compared to the .44 Henry, this cartridge was twice as good. With the introduction of the single-action Colt pistol in 1878, chambered for the same cartridge, the individual had the convenience of a pistol for protection and the accuracy of the Winchester for food and protection. The .44-40 was the standard cartridge for the Model 1873. Three additional cartridges were offered but were not as popular as the .44. The .38-40 was first offered in 1879 and the .32-20 was introduced in 1882. In 1884 the Model 1873 was offered in .22 caliber rimfire, with a few special order guns built in .22 extra long rimfire. Approximately 19,552 .22 caliber Model 1873s were produced.

Early Model 1873s were fitted with an iron receiver until 1884, when a steel receiver was introduced. The Model 1873 was offered in three styles:

1. Sporting Rifle, 24" round, octagon, or half-octagon barrel. Equipped standard with a crescent iron buttplate, straight-grip stock and capped forearm.
2. Carbine, 20" round barrel. Furnished standard with a rounded iron buttplate, straight-grip stock, and carbine style forend fastened to the barrel with a single barrel band.
3. Musket, 30" round barrel. Standard musket is furnished with a nearly full-length forearm fastened to the barrel with three barrel bands. The buttstock has a rounded buttplate.

The upper tang was marked with the model designation and the serial number was stamped on the lower tang. Caliber stampings on the Model 1873 are found on the bottom of the frame and on the breech end of the barrel. Winchester discontinued the Model 1873 in 1919, after producing about 720,000 guns.

Courtesy Greg Martin Auctions

The Winchester Model 1873 was offered with a large number of extra-cost options that greatly affect the value of the gun. For example, Winchester built two sets of special Model 1873s: the 1-of-100 and the 1-of-1000. Winchester sold only eight 1-of-100 Model 1873s, and 136 of the 1-of-1000 guns that were built. In 1991 a few of these special guns were sold at auction and brought prices exceeding $75,000. The prices listed here are for standard guns only. For Model 1873 with special features, it is best to secure an expert appraisal. Model 1873s with case colored receivers will bring a premium.

First Model

The primary difference between the various styles of the Model 1873 is found in the appearance and construction of the dust cover. The First Model has a dust cover held in place with grooved guides on either side. A checkered oval finger grip is found on top of the dust cover. The latch that holds the lever firmly in place is anchored into the lower tang with visible threads. On later First Models, these threads are not visible. First Models appear from serial number 1 to about 31000.

Rifle

Exc.	V.G.	Good	Fair	Poor
17500	9000	4750	3000	1400

Carbine

Exc.	V.G.	Good	Fair	Poor
25000	17500	9000	4000	2500

Musket

Exc.	V.G.	Good	Fair	Poor
—	4750	2500	1800	1000

Second Model

The dust cover on the Second Model operates on one central guide secured to the receiver with two screws. The checkered oval finger grip is still used, but on later Second Models this is changed to a serrated finger grip on the rear of the dust cover. Second Models are found in the 31000 to 90000 serial number range.

Rifle

Exc.	V.G.	Good	Fair	Poor
16000	8500	4000	3000	1250

Carbine

Exc.	V.G.	Good	Fair	Poor
17000	9000	6000	3000	1000

Musket

Exc.	V.G.	Good	Fair	Poor
7500	4000	2000	1250	900

Third Model

The central guide rail is still present on the Third Model, but it is now integrally machined as part of the receiver. The serrated rear edges of the dust cover are still present on the Third Model.

Rifle

Exc.	V.G.	Good	Fair	Poor
11500	7500	4000	2000	750

Carbine

Exc.	V.G.	Good	Fair	Poor
14000	9000	5000	2000	800

Musket

Courtesy Rock Island Auction Company

Exc.	V.G.	Good	Fair	Poor
6000	3500	1250	850	500

Model 1873 .22 Rimfire Rifle

Winchester's first .22 caliber rifle and the first .22 caliber repeating rifle made in America was introduced in 1884 and discontinued in 1904. Its drawback was the small caliber. The general preference during this period of time was for the larger-caliber rifles. Winchester sold a little more than 19,000 .22 caliber Model 1873s.

Exc.	V.G.	Good	Fair	Poor
12500	6500	3000	1700	750

Model 1876

Winchester's Model 1876, sometimes referred to as the Centennial Model, was the company's response to the public's demand for a repeater rifle capable of handling larger and more potent calibers. Many single-shot rifles were available at this time to shoot more powerful cartridges, and Winchester redesigned the earlier Model 1873 to answer this need. The principal changes made to the Model 1873 were a larger and stronger receiver to handle more powerful cartridges. Both the carbine and the musket had their forearms extended to cover the full length of the magazine tube. The carbine barrel was increased in length from 20" to 22", and the musket barrel length was increased from 30 to 32". The Model 1876 was the first Winchester to be offered with a pistol-grip stock on its special Sporting Rifle. The Model 1876 was available in the following calibers: .45-77 W.C.F., .50-95 Express, .45-60 W.C.F., .40-60 W.C.F. The Model 1876 was offered in four different styles:

1. Sporting Rifle, 28" round, octagon, or half-octagon barrel. This rifle was fitted with a straight-grip stock with crescent iron buttplate. A special sporting rifle was offered with a pistol-grip stock.
2. Express Rifle, 26" round, octagon, or half-octagon barrel. The same sporting rifle stock was used.
3. Carbine, 22" round barrel with full length forearm secured by one barrel band and straight-grip stock.
4. Musket, 32" round barrel with full-length forearm secured by one barrel band and straight-grip stock. Stamped on the barrel is the Winchester address with King's patent date. The caliber marking is stamped on the bottom of the receiver near the magazine tube and the breech end of the barrel. Winchester also furnished the Model 1876 in 1-of-100 and 1-of-1000 special guns. Only 8 1-of-100 Model 1876s were built and 54 1-of-1000 76s were built. As with their Model 1873 counterparts, these rare guns

often sell in the $75,000 range or more. Approximately 64,000 Model 1876s were built by Winchester between 1876 and 1897. As with other Winchesters, the prices given are for standard guns.

First Model
As with the Model 1873, the primary difference in model types lies in the dust cover. The First Model has no dust cover and is seen between serial number 1 and 3000.

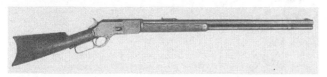

Rifle

Exc.	V.G.	Good	Fair	Poor
12000	8500	4500	2750	1000

Carbine

Exc.	V.G.	Good	Fair	Poor
10000	7500	5000	2500	1000

Musket

Exc.	V.G.	Good	Fair	Poor
15000	12000	6500	3000	1500

Second Model
The Second Model has a dust cover with guide rail attached to the receiver with two screws. On the early Second Model an oval finger guide is stamped on top of the dust cover while later models have a serrated finger guide along the rear edge of the dust cover. Second Models range from serial numbers 3000 to 30000.

Rifle

Exc.	V.G.	Good	Fair	Poor
11000	7500	4000	2000	1000

Carbine

Exc.	V.G.	Good	Fair	Poor
9000	6000	4250	2000	1200

Musket

Exc.	V.G.	Good	Fair	Poor
18000	9000	5000	1750	1000

Northwest Mounted Police Carbine
The folding rear sight is graduated in meters instead of yards.

Courtesy Little John's Auction Service, Inc.

Exc.	V.G.	Good	Fair	Poor
15000	9000	4500	2000	1250

NOTE: Deduct 50 percent from prices if factory records do not confirm NPW use. A Model 1876 NWP in excellent condition is very rare. Proceed with caution.

Third Model
The dust cover guide rail on Third Model 76s is integrally machined as part of the receiver with a serrated rear edge on the dust cover. Third Model will be seen from serial numbers 30000 to 64000.

Rifle

Exc.	V.G.	Good	Fair	Poor
10000	6500	3250	1500	750

Carbine

Exc.	V.G.	Good	Fair	Poor
10000	6500	3000	2000	1250

Musket

Exc.	V.G.	Good	Fair	Poor
9500	4750	3000	1250	1000

Model 1885 (Single-Shot)
The Model 1885 marks an important development between Winchester and John M. Browning. The Single-Shot rifle was the first of many Browning patents that Winchester would purchase and provided the company with the opportunity to diversify its firearms line. The Model 1885 was the first single-shot rifle built by Winchester. The company offered more calibers in this model than any other. A total of 45 centerfire calibers were offered from the .22 extra long to the 50-110 Express, as well as 14 rimfire caliber from .22 B.B. cap to the .44 Flat Henry. Numerous barrel lengths, shapes, and weights were available as were stock configurations, sights, and finishes. These rifles were also available in solid frame and takedown styles. One could almost argue that each of the 139,725 Model 1885s built are unique. Many collectors of the Winchester Single-Shot specialize in nothing else. For this reason it is difficult to provide pricing that will cover most of the Model 1885s that the collector will encounter. However the prices given here are for standard guns in standard configurations.

The Model 1885 was offered in two basic frame types:
A. The High Wall was the first frame type produced and is so called because the frame covers the breech and hammer except for the hammer spur.
B. The breech and hammer are visible on the Low Wall frame with its low sides. This frame type was first introduced around the 5000 serial number range.

Both the High Wall and the Low Wall were available in two type frame profiles; the Thickside and the Thinside. The Thickside frame has flat sides that do not widen out to meet the stock. The Thickside is more common on the low wall rifle and rare on the High Walls.

The Thinside frame has shallow milled sides that widen out to meet the stock. Thinside frames are common on High Wall guns and rare on Low Wall rifles.

1. The standard High Wall rifle was available with octagon or round barrel with length determined by caliber. The butt stock and forearm were plain walnut with crescent buttplate and blued frame.
2. The standard Low Wall featured a round or octagon barrel with length determined by caliber and a plain walnut stock and forearm with crescent buttplate.
3. The High Wall musket most often had a 26" round barrel chambered for the .22 caliber cartridge. Larger calibers were available as were different barrel lengths. The High Wall Musket featured an almost full length forearm fastened to the barrel with a single barrel band and rounded buttplate.
4. The Low Wall musket is most often referred to as the Winder Musket named after the distinguished marksman, Colonel C.B. Winder. This model features a Lyman receiver sight and was made in .22 caliber.
5. The High Wall Schuetzen rifle was designed for serious target shooting and was available with numerous extras including a 30" octagon barrel medium weight without rear sight seat; fancy walnut checkered pistol grip Schuetzen-style cheekpiece; Schuetzen-style buttplate; checkered forearm; double set triggers; spur finger lever, and adjustable palm rest.
6. The Low Wall carbine was available in 15", 16", 18", and 20" round barrels. The carbine featured a saddle ring on the left side of the frame and a rounded buttplate.
7. The Model 1885 was also available in a High Wall shotgun in 20 gauge with 26" round barrel and straight-grip stock with shotgun style rubber buttplate. The Model 1885 was manufactured between 1885 and 1920 with a total production of about 140,000 guns.

Standard High Wall Rifle

Exc.	V.G.	Good	Fair	Poor
6500	4000	3250	1500	950

Standard Low Wall Rifle

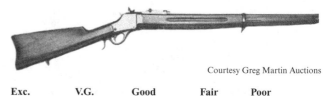

Courtesy Greg Martin Auctions

Exc.	V.G.	Good	Fair	Poor
5000	3500	2250	1400	900

High Wall Musket

Courtesy Greg Martin Auctions

Exc.	V.G.	Good	Fair	Poor
4000	3000	2000	1500	900

Low Wall Musket (Winder Musket)

Exc.	V.G.	Good	Fair	Poor
3500	2000	1200	750	400

High Wall Schuetzen Rifle

Exc.	V.G.	Good	Fair	Poor
17500	1200	6000	4000	2500

Low Wall Carbine

Courtesy Greg Martin Auctions

Exc.	V.G.	Good	Fair	Poor
17500	10000	7000	3000	1500

High Wall Shotgun

Exc.	V.G.	Good	Fair	Poor
4500	3000	2250	1250	850

NOTE: Model 1885s with case colored frames bring a premium of 25 percent over guns with blued frames. Model 1885s in calibers .50-110 and .50-100 will bring a premium depending on style and configuration.

Model 1886

Based on a John Browning patent, the Model 1886 was one of the finest and strongest lever-actions ever utilized in a Winchester rifle. Winchester introduced the Model 1886 in order to take advantage of the more powerful centerfire cartridges of the time.

Model 1886 rifles and carbines were furnished with walnut stocks, case hardened frames, and blued barrels and magazine tubes. In 1901 Winchester discontinued the use of case hardened frames on all its rifles and used blued frames instead. For this reason, case hardened Model 1886 rifles will bring a premium. Winchester provided a large selection of extra cost options on the Model 1886, and for rifles with these options, a separate valuation should be made by a reliable source. The Model 1886 was produced from 1886 to 1935 with about 160,000 in production.

The rifle was available in 10 different chambers:

.45-70 U.S. Government .50-110 Express
.45-90 W.C.F. .40-70 W.C.F.
.40-82 W.C.F. .38-70 W.C.F.
.40-65 W.C.F. .50-100-450
.38-56 W.C.F. .33 W.C.F.

The most popular caliber was the .45-70 Government. Prices of the Model 1886 are influenced by caliber, with the larger calibers bringing a premium. The 1886 was available in several different configurations.

1. Sporting Rifle, 26", round, octagon, or half-octagon barrel, full or half magazine and straight-grip stock with plain forearm.
2. Fancy Sporting Rifle, 26", round or octagon barrel, full or half magazine and fancy checkered walnut pistol-grip stock with checkered forearm.
3. Takedown Rifle, 24" round barrel, full or half magazine with straight-grip stock fitted with shotgun rubber buttplate and plain forearm.
4. Extra Lightweight Takedown Rifle, 22" round barrel, full or half magazine with straight-grip stock fitted with shotgun rubber buttplate and plain forearm.
5. Extra Lightweight Rifle, 22" round barrel, full or half magazine with straight-grip stock fitted with a shotgun rubber butt-plate and plain forearm.
6. Carbine, 22" round barrel, full or half magazine, with straight-grip stock and plain forearm.
7. Musket, 30" round barrel, musket-style forearm with one barrel band. Military-style sights. About 350 Model 1886 Muskets were produced.

Sporting Rifle

Courtesy Rock Island Auction Company

Exc.	V.G.	Good	Fair	Poor
15000	10000	7500	5000	2500

Fancy Sporting Rifle

Exc.	V.G.	Good	Fair	Poor
25000	14000	8000	6000	3000

Takedown Rifle—Standard

Exc.	V.G.	Good	Fair	Poor
12500	8500	4200	2000	700

Extra Lightweight Takedown Rifle—.33 caliber

Exc.	V.G.	Good	Fair	Poor
4500	3000	1500	750	400

Extra Lightweight Takedown Rifle—Other Calibers

Exc.	V.G.	Good	Fair	Poor
7750	5500	1800	1250	500

Extra Lightweight Rifle—.33 caliber

Exc.	V.G.	Good	Fair	Poor
5000	3500	1800	1000	500

Extra Lightweight Rifle—Other Calibers

Exc.	V.G.	Good	Fair	Poor
7750	5500	2250	950	500

Carbine

Model 1886 carbine barrels are 22". A few were Trappers with 20" barrels. Add 50 percent if Trapper.

Courtesy Bonhams & Butterfields

Exc.	V.G.	Good	Fair	Poor
25000	15000	9000	4500	2000

Musket

Exc.	V.G.	Good	Fair	Poor
—	18000	9000	3500	1500

NOTE: For .50 Express add a premium of 20 percent. Case colored Model 1886s will bring a premium of 20 percent.

Model 71

When Winchester dropped the Model 1886 from its line in 1935, the company replaced its large-bore lever-action rifle with the Model 71 chambered for the .348 caliber. The Model 71 is similar in appearance to the Model 1886 with some internal parts strengthened to handle the powerful .348 cartridge. The rifle was available in three basic configurations:

1. Standard Rifle, 24" round barrel, 3/4 magazine, plain walnut pistol-grip stock and semi-beavertail forearm.
2. Standard Rifle (Carbine), 20" round barrel, 3/4 magazine, plain walnut pistol-grip stock and semi-beavertail forearm.
3. Deluxe Rifle, 24" round barrel, 3/4 magazine, checkered walnut pistol-grip stock and checkered semi-beavertail forearm. The frames and barrels were blued on all models of this rifle.
4. Deluxe Rifle (Carbine), 20" round barrel, 3/4 magazine, checkered walnut pistol-grip stock and checkered semi-beavertail forearm. The frames and barrels were blued on all models of this rifle.

The Model 71 was produced from 1935 to 1957 with about 47,000 built.

Standard Rifle
24" barrel.

Exc.	V.G.	Good	Fair	Poor
1400	1000	800	400	300

Standard Rifle (Carbine)
20" barrel.

Exc.	V.G.	Good	Fair	Poor
3250	2000	1600	1200	650

Deluxe Rifle
24" barrel.

Exc.	V.G.	Good	Fair	Poor
2500	1800	800	525	425

Deluxe Rifle (Carbine)
20" barrel.

Exc.	V.G.	Good	Fair	Poor
3750	3000	2000	1250	700

NOTE: For prewar Model 71s add a premium of 20 percent. The prewar Model 71 has a longer tang than its post-war predecessor. for a bolt peep sight add 10 percent.

Model 1892

The Model 1892 was an updated successor to the Model 1873 using a scaled down version of the Model 1886 action. The rifle was chambered for the popular smaller cartridges of the day, namely the .25-20, .32-20, .38-40, .44-40, and the rare .218 Bee. The rifle was available in several different configurations:
1. Sporting Rifle, solid frame or takedown (worth an extra premium of about 20 percent), 24" round, octagon, or half-octagon barrel with 1/2, 2/3, or full magazines. Plain straight-grip walnut stock with capped forearm.
2. Fancy Sporting Rifle, solid frame or takedown (worth 20 percent premium), 24" round, octagon, or half-octagon barrel with 1/2, 2/3, or full magazine. Checkered walnut pistol-grip stock with checkered capped forearm.
3. Carbine, 20" round barrel, full or half magazine, plain walnut straight-grip stock with one barrel band forearm. Carbines were offered only with solid frames.
4. Trapper's Carbine, 18", 16", 15", or 14" round barrel with the same dimensions of standard carbine. Federal law prohibits the possession of rifles with barrel lengths shorter than 16". The Model 1892 Trapper's Carbine can be exempted from this law as a curio and relic with a federal permit providing the trapper is an original trapper and left the factory with the short trapper barrel.
5. Musket, 30" round barrel with full magazine. Almost full-length forearm held by two barrel bands. Buttstock is plain walnut with straight grip.

The Model 1892 was built between 1892 and 1932 with slightly more than 1 million sold. The Model 1892 carbine continued to be offered for sale until 1941.

NOTE: Antique Winchester Model 1892s (pre-1898 manufacture) will bring a premium of 10 percent.

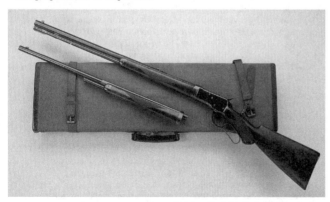

Courtesy Little John's Auction Service, Inc.

Sporting Rifle

Exc.	V.G.	Good	Fair	Poor
5000	3500	1250	700	350

Fancy Sporting Rifle

Exc.	V.G.	Good	Fair	Poor
12000	7500	4000	2500	1000

Carbine

Courtesy Bonhams & Butterfields

Exc.	V.G.	Good	Fair	Poor
5000	4000	2000	1200	600

Trapper's Carbine

Exc.	V.G.	Good	Fair	Poor
12000	8500	4000	2500	1250

NOTE: Add 20 percent for 15" barrel. Add 50 percent for carbines chambered for .25-20 cartridge.

Musket

Exc.	V.G.	Good	Fair	Poor
—	9500	4500	2500	1500

Model 1894

Based on a John M. Browning patent, the Model 1894 was the most successful centerfire rifle Winchester ever produced. This model is still in production, and the values given here reflect those rifles produced before 1964, or around serial number 2550000. The Model 1894 was the first Winchester developed especially for smokeless powder and was chambered for the following cartridges: .32-40, .38-55, .25-35 Winchester, .30-30 Winchester, and the .32 Winchester Special. The rifle was available in several different configurations:
1. Sporting Rifle, 26" round, octagon, or half-octagon barrel, in solid frame or takedown. Full, 2/3 or 1/2 magazines were available. Plain walnut straight or pistol-grip stock with crescent buttplate and plain capped forearm.
2. Fancy Sporting Rifle, 26" round, octagon, or half-octagon barrel, in solid frame or takedown. Full, 2/3, or 1/2 magazines were available. Fancy walnut checkered straight or pistol-grip stock with crescent buttplate and checkered fancy capped forearm.
3. Extra lightweight Rifle, 22" or 26" round barrel with half magazine. Plain walnut straight-grip stock with shotgun buttplate and plain capped forearm.
4. Carbine, 20" round barrel, plain walnut straight-grip stock with carbine style buttplate. Forearm was plain walnut uncapped with one barrel band. Carbines were available with solid frame only. Carbines made prior to 1925 were fitted with a saddle ring on the left side of receiver and worth a premium over carbines without saddle ring.
5. Trapper's Carbine, 18", 16", 15", or 14". Buttstock, forearm, and saddle ring specifications same as standard carbine.
All Model 1894s were furnished with blued frames and barrels, although case hardened frames were available as an extra-cost option. Case colored Model 1894s are rare and worth a considerable premium, perhaps as much as 1,000 percent. Guns with extra-cost options should be evaluated by an expert to determine proper value. Between 1894 and 1963, approximately 2,550,000 Model 1894s were sold.

NOTE: Antique Winchester Model 1894s (pre-1898 manufacture) will bring a premium of 10 percent. First year production guns, October 1894 to December 1894, documented by the Cody Museum will command a 100 percent premium.

First Model Sporting Rifle
Very early model that incorporates a screw entering the receiver over the loading port from the outside. Rare.

Exc.	V.G.	Good	Fair	Poor
8500	4000	2000	1250	500

Sporting Rifle

Exc.	V.G.	Good	Fair	Poor
4000	3000	1500	850	450

NOTE: Takedown versions are worth approximately 20 percent more.

Fancy Sporting Rifle

Exc.	V.G.	Good	Fair	Poor
12000	7500	3500	2000	900

NOTE: Takedown versions are worth approximately 20 percent more. Fancy Sporting Rifles were also engraved at the customer's request. Check factory where possible and proceed with caution. Factory engraved Model 1894s are extremely valuable.

Extra Lightweight Rifle

Exc.	V.G.	Good	Fair	Poor
5500	4000	1500	1000	450

Carbine

Exc.	V.G.	Good	Fair	Poor
3000	2000	600	400	200

NOTE: Above values are for guns with saddle rings. For carbines without saddle rings deduct 35 percent. Add 25 percent for carbines chambered for .25-35 or .38-55 cartridge.

Trappers Carbine

Exc.	V.G.	Good	Fair	Poor
6500	4250	2500	1500	700

NOTE: Add 30 percent for carbines chambered for .25-35 or .38-55 calibers.

Model 53

This model was in fact a slightly more modern version of the Model 1892 offered in the following calibers: .25-20, .32-20, and the .44-40. It was available in only one style: the Sporting Rifle, 22" round barrel, half magazine, straight- or pistol-grip plain walnut stock with shotgun butt. It was available in solid frame or takedown with blued frame and barrel. The Model 53 was produced from 1924 to 1932 with about 25,000 built.

Sporting Rifle

Exc.	V.G.	Good	Fair	Poor
3500	2500	1000	500	300

NOTE: Add 10 percent for takedown model. Add 40 percent for rifles chambered for .44-40 cartridge. A few of these rifles were fitted with stainless steel barrel in the early 1930s. If the black paint on these barrels is in good condition, they will bring a substantial premium.

Model 55

This model was a continuation of the Model 1894 except in a simplified version. Available in the same calibers as the Model 1894, this rifle could be ordered only with a 24" round barrel, plain walnut straight-grip stock with plain forend and shotgun butt. Frame and barrel were blued with solid or takedown features. This model was produced between 1924 and 1932 with about 21,000 sold. Serial numbers for the Model 55 were numbered separately until about serial number 4500; then the guns were numbered in the Model 1894 sequence.

Standard Rifle

Exc.	V.G.	Good	Fair	Poor
1500	1000	650	450	200

NOTE: .25-35 caliber will bring about a 60 percent premium. Add 10 percent for models with solid frame.

Model 64

An improved version of the Model 55, this gun featured a larger magazine, pistol-grip stock, and forged front sight ramp. The trigger pull was also improved. Frame and barrel were blued. Chambered for the .25-35 Win., .30-30 Win., .32 Win. Special, and the .219 zipper added in 1938 (and discontinued in the Model 64 in 1941). Serial number of the Model 64 was concurrent with the Model 1894. Built between 1933 and 1957, approximately 67,000 were sold. This model was reintroduced in 1972 and discontinued in 1973. The values listed are for the early version only.

Standard Rifle

Exc.	V.G.	Good	Fair	Poor
1200	900	500	300	200

Carbine—20" Barrel

Exc.	V.G.	Good	Fair	Poor
1550	1000	650	500	250

NOTE: For Deluxe model add 50 percent to above prices. For Carbine model add 50 percent to above prices. For rifles chambered for the .219 Zipper and .25-35 cartridges add 50 percent. Add 10 percent for bolt peep sight. Model 64s in .219 Zipper left the factory with bolt peep sights as original equipment.

Model 65

This model was a continuation of the Model 53 and was offered in three calibers: .25-20, .32-20, and .218 Bee. It had several improvements over the Model 53, namely the magazine capacity was increased to seven cartridges, forged ramp for front sight, and a lighter trigger pull. The Model 65 was available only in solid blued frame with blued barrel and pistol grip with plain walnut stock. Only about 5,700 of these rifles were built between 1933 and 1947.

Standard Rifle

Courtesy Rock Island Auction Company

Exc.	V.G.	Good	Fair	Poor
3500	2500	1000	550	250

NOTE: Add 10 percent for bolt peep sight. Model 65s in .218 Bee left the factory with bolt peep sights as original equipment.

Model 1895

The Model 1895 was the first nondetachable box magazine rifle offered by Winchester. Built on a John M. Browning patent, this rifle was introduced by Winchester to meet the demand for a rifle that could handle the new high-power, smokeless hunting cartridges of the period. The Model 1895 was available in the following calibers: .30-40 Krag, .38-72 Winchester, .40-72 Winchester, .303 British, .35 Winchester, .405 Government, 7.62 Russian, .30-03, and .30-06. The rifle gained fame as a favorite hunting rifle of Theodore Roosevelt. Because of its box magazine, the Model 1895 has a distinctive look like no other Winchester lever-action rifle. The rifle was available in several different configurations:

1. Sporting Rifle, 28" or 24" (depending on caliber) round barrel, plain walnut straight-grip stock with plain forend. The first 5,000 rifles were manufactured with flat-sided receivers, and the balance of production were built with the receiver sides contoured. After serial-number 60000, a takedown version was available.
2. Fancy Sporting Rifle, 28" round barrel, fancy walnut checkered straight-grip stock and fancy walnut checkered forearm.
   Rifles with serial numbers below 5000 had flat sided frames.
3. Carbine, 22" round barrel, plain walnut straight-grip stock with military-style hand guard forend. Some carbines are furnished with saddle rings on left side of receiver.
4. Musket:
   A. Standard Musket, 28" round, plain walnut straight-grip stock with musket style forend with two barrel bands.
   B. U.S. Army N.R.A. Musket, 30" round barrel, Model 1901 Krag-Jorgensen rear sight. Stock similar to the standard musket. This musket could be used for "Any Military Arm" matches under the rules of the National Rifle Association.

Courtesy Little John's Auction Service, Inc.

C. N.R.A. Musket, Models 1903 and 1906, 24" round barrel with special buttplate. Also eligible for all matches under

"Any Military Arm" sponsored by the NRA. This musket was fitted with the same stock as listed above.

D. U.S. Army Musket, 28" round barrel chambered for the .30-40 Krag. Came equipped with or without knife bayonet. These muskets were furnished to the U.S. Army for use during the Spanish-American War and are "US" marked on the receiver.

E. Russian Musket, similar to standard musket but fitted with clip guides in the top of the receiver and with bayonet. Approximately 294,000 Model 1895 Muskets were sold to the Imperial Russian Government between 1915 and 1916. The first 15,000 Russian Muskets had 8" knife bayonets, and the rest were fitted with 16" bayonets.

The Model 1895 was produced from 1895 to 1931 with about 426,000 sold.

NOTE: Add a 10 percent premium for rifles built before 1898.

Sporting Rifle

Exc.	V.G.	Good	Fair	Poor
5000	3000	1200	700	300

NOTE: Flat-side rifles will bring a premium of 100 percent. Takedown rifles will add an additional 15 percent.

Fancy Sporting Rifles

Exc.	V.G.	Good	Fair	Poor
6500	4500	1500	1100	500

NOTE: Flat-side rifles will bring a premium of 100 percent. Takedown rifles will add an additional 15 percent.

Carbine

Exc.	V.G.	Good	Fair	Poor
3000	1750	1050	600	300

Standard Musket

Exc.	V.G.	Good	Fair	Poor
3000	1750	1050	600	300

U.S. Army N.R.A. Musket

Exc.	V.G.	Good	Fair	Poor
4500	2000	1200	800	400

N.R.A. Musket, Model 1903 and 1906

Exc.	V.G.	Good	Fair	Poor
5500	2500	1200	800	400

U.S. Army Musket

Exc.	V.G.	Good	Fair	Poor
—	3000	1500	850	450

Russian Musket

Exc.	V.G.	Good	Fair	Poor
4000	2500	1000	500	250

Breechloading Double-Barrel Shotgun

Winchester imported an English-made shotgun sold under the Winchester name between 1879 and 1884. The gun was available in 10 and 12 gauge with 30" or 32" Damascus barrels. It was sold in five separate grades referred to as "classes." The lowest grade was the "D" and the best grade was called the "Match Grade." These were marked on the sidelocks. The center rib was stamped "Winchester Repeating Arms Co., New Haven, Connecticut, U.S.A." About 10,000 of these guns were imported by Winchester.

Class A, B, C, and D

Exc.	V.G.	Good	Fair	Poor
2500	2250	1250	850	500

Match Gun

Exc.	V.G.	Good	Fair	Poor
2500	2250	1250	850	500

Model 1887 Shotgun

Winchester enjoyed a great deal of success with its imported English shotgun, and the company decided to manufacture a shotgun of its own. In 1885 it purchased the patent for a lever-action shotgun designed by John M. Browning. By 1887 Winchester had delivered the first model 1887 in 12 gauge and shortly after offered the gun in 10 gauge. Both gauges were offered with 30" or 32" Full choked barrels, with the 30" standard on the 12 gauge and 32" standard on the 10 gauge. A Riot Gun was offered in 1898 both in 10, and 12 gauge with 20" barrels choked cylinder. Both variations of the Model 1887 were offered with plain walnut pistol-grip stocks with plain forend. The frame was case hardened and the barrel blued. Between 1887 and 1901 Winchester sold approximately 65,000 Model 1887 shotguns.

Standard Shotgun

Exc.	V.G.	Good	Fair	Poor
2500	1500	850	500	300

Riot Shotgun

Courtesy Bonhams & Butterfields

Exc.	V.G.	Good	Fair	Poor
3000	2000	950	600	400

Model 1901 Shotgun

This model is a redesign of the Model 1887 shotgun and was offered in 10 gauge only with a 32" barrel choked Full, Modified, or Cylinder. The barrel was reinforced to withstand the new smokeless powder loads and the frame was blued instead of case hardened. The stock was of plain walnut with a modified pistol and plain forearm. The Model 1901 was built between 1901 and 1920 with about 65,000 guns sold.

Standard Shotgun

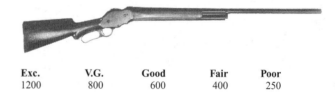

Exc.	V.G.	Good	Fair	Poor
1200	800	600	400	250

Model 1893

This was the first slide-action repeating shotgun built by Winchester. It featured an exposed hammer and side ejection. Based on a John M. Browning patent, this model was not altogether satisfactory. The action proved to be too weak to handle smokeless loads, even though the gun was designed for black powder. The gun was offered in 12 gauge with 30" or 32" barrels choked Full. Other chokes were available on special order and will command a premium. The stock was plain walnut with a modified pistol grip, grooved slide handle, and hard rubber buttplate. The receiver and barrel were blued. Winchester produced the Model 1893 between 1893 and 1897, selling about 31000 guns.

Standard Shotgun

Courtesy Bonhams & Butterfields

Exc.	V.G.	Good	Fair	Poor
1000	700	600	325	250

Model 1897

The Model 1897 replaced the Model 1893, and while similar to the Model 1893, the new model had several improvements such as a stronger frame, chamber made longer to handle 2-3/4" shells, frame top was covered to force complete side ejection, the stock was made longer and with less drop. The Model 1897 was available in 12 or 16 gauge with the 12 gauge offered either in solid or takedown styles and the 16 gauge available in takedown only. The Model 1897 was available with barrel lengths of 20", 26", 28", 30", and 32" and in practically all choke options from full to cylinder. The shotgun could be ordered in several different configurations:

1. Standard Gun, 12 or 16 gauge, 30" barrel in 12 gauge and 28" barrel in 16 gauge, with plain walnut modified pistol-grip stock and grooved slide handle. Steel buttplate standard.
2. Trap Gun 12 or 16 gauge, 30" barrel in 12 gauge and 28" barrel in 16 gauge, fancy walnut stock with oil finish checkered pistol-grip or straight-grip stock with checkered slide handle. Marked "TRAP" on bottom of frame.
3. Pigeon Gun, 12 or 16 gauge, 28" barrel on both 12 and 16 gauge, straight- or pistol-grip stock same as Trap gun, receiver hand engraved.
4. Tournament Gun, 12 gauge only with 30" barrel, select walnut checkered straight-grip stock and checkered slide handle, top of receiver is matted to reduce glare.
5. Brush Gun, 12 or 16 gauge, 26" barrel, Cylinder choke, has a slightly shorter magazine tube than standard gun, plain walnut modified pistol-grip stock with grooved slide handle.
6. Brush Gun, Takedown, same as above with takedown feature and standard length magazine tube.
7. Riot Gun, 12 gauge, 20" barrel bored to shoot buckshot, plain walnut modified pistol-grip stock with grooved slide handle. Solid frame or takedown.
8. Trench Gun, same as Riot Gun but fitted with barrel hand guard and bayonet.

The Winchester Model 1897 was a great seller for Winchester. During its 60-year production span, 1,025,000 guns were sold.

Standard Gun

Exc.	V.G.	Good	Fair	Poor
800	650	450	300	200

Trap Gun

Exc.	V.G.	Good	Fair	Poor
1050	900	600	500	400

Pigeon Gun

Exc.	V.G.	Good	Fair	Poor
3000	2500	1600	1250	1000

Tournament Gun

Exc.	V.G.	Good	Fair	Poor
1100	900	700	500	400

Brush Gun

Exc.	V.G	Good	Fair	Poor
950	750	600	500	400

Riot Gun

Courtesy Bonhams & Butterfields

Exc.	V.G.	Good	Fair	Poor
850	600	500	350	200

Trench Gun

Exc.	V.G.	Good	Fair	Poor
2750	2000	1000	500	300

NOTE: Add 25 percent for 16 gauge guns in excellent, very good, and good condition.

Model 21

The Model 21 was Winchester's finest effort with regard to quality, reliability, and strength. Developed in the late 1920s the introduction of this fine side-by-side shotgun was delayed by the company's financial troubles. When Winchester was purchased by the Olin family, the Model 21 was assured the attention it richly deserved due to John M. Olin's love for the gun. Despite the Model 21 being offered as a production gun it was, in fact, a hand-built custom-made shotgun. Almost each Model 21 built has a personality of its own because each shotgun is slightly different with regard to chokes, barrel lengths, stock dimensions, and embellishments. The gun was introduced in 1931. From 1931 to 1959 the Model 21 was considered a production line gun and about 30,000 were sold. In 1960, when the Custom Shop was opened, the Model 21 was built there using the same procedures. Sales during the Custom Shop era were about 1,000 guns. Winchester changed the name of some of the Model 21 styles but the production methods stayed the same. In 1981 Winchester sold its firearms division to U.S. Repeating Arms Company including the right to build the Model 21. Again the production procedures stayed the same as did many of the former employees. U.S. Repeating Arms expanded and changed some of the style designations for the Model 21. Production was discontinued in about 1991. No sales figures are available for this time period. Collectors and shooters will be given the price breakdown for all three eras of production separately.

Model 21—1931 to 1959

The Model 21 was available in several different styles and configurations:
1. Standard Grade, chambered in 12, 16, and 20 gauge with barrel length from 26", 28", 30", and 32" with matted rib or ventilated rib, select walnut checkered pistol- or straight-grip stock with checkered beavertail forend. Built from 1931 to 1959.
2. Tournament Grade, same as above with special dimension stock. Marked "TOURNAMENT" on bottom of trigger plate. Built from 1933 to 1934.
3. Trap Grade, same as above with slightly better-grade wood and stock made to customers' dimensions. Marked "TRAP" on trigger plate. Built from 1932 to 1959.
4. Skeet Grade, same as above with the addition of the 28 gauge, stock furnished with checkered butt. Marked "SKEET" on trigger plate. Built from 1936 to 1959.
5. Duck Gun, chambered for 12 gauge 3" magnum shells, 30" or 32" barrels, Standard Grade stock except for shorter length of pull. Marked "DUCK" on trigger plate. Built from 1940 to 1952.
6. Magnum Gun, chambered for 3" 12 or 20 gauge, same stock as Duck Gun. Not marked on trigger plate. Built from 1953 to 1959.
7. Custom Built/Deluxe Grade, chambered for 12, 16, 20, 28, and .410, barrel lengths from 26" to 32", stock built to customer's specifications using fancy walnut. Marked "CUSTOM BUILT" on top of rib or "DELUXE" on trigger plate. These grades are frequently but not always engraved. Built from 1933 to 1959.

NOTE: Some early Model 21s were furnished with double triggers, extractors, and splinter forends. This combination reduces the price of the gun regardless of grade. Deduct about 25 percent.

Standard Grade

	Exc.	V.G.	Good	Fair	Poor
12 gauge	5200	4600	3800	3300	3000
16 gauge	6500	6000	5400	4700	4200
20 gauge	6800	6300	5700	5100	4700

Tournament Grade

	Exc.	V.G.	Good	Fair	Poor
12 gauge	5300	4700	3900	3500	3300
16 gauge	6900	6400	5800	5000	4500
20 gauge	7000	6600	6000	5400	4800

Trap Grade

	Exc.	V.G.	Good	Fair	Poor
12 gauge	5500	4800	4000	3800	3600
16 gauge	7200	6500	5900	5300	4900
20 gauge	7500	6900	6300	5800	5300

Skeet Grade

	Exc.	V.G.	Good	Fair	Poor
12 gauge	5200	4300	3700	3400	3200
16 gauge	6500	5600	5200	4900	4400
20 gauge	6500	5700	5200	4800	4200

Duck/Magnum Gun

Exc.	V.G.	Good	Fair	Poor
5300	4600	4200	4000	3800

NOTE: Add 30 percent for 20 gauge Magnum. Factory ventilated ribs command a premium of about $1,800 on 12 gauge guns and $2,500 on

20 and 16 gauge guns. Models 21s with factory furnished extra barrels will bring an additional premium of about $2,500. Refinished and restored Model 21s are in a somewhat unique category of American-made collectible shotguns. A gun that has been professionally refinished by a master craftsman will approximate 90 percent of the value of factory original guns.

Custom Built/Deluxe Grade
The prices paid for guns of this grade are determined by gauge, barrel and choke combinations, rib type, stock specifications, and engraving.

	Exc.	V.G.	Good	Fair	Poor
12 gauge	7000	6500	5500	4500	4000
16 gauge	8000	7500	6500	5500	4500
20 gauge	8500	8000	7000	6000	5000

It is best to secure a factory letter from the Cody Firearms Museum. With respect to such letter, it is important to note that these records are incomplete and may be inaccurate in a few cases. Records for Model 21s built during the 1930s may be missing. Special-order guns may have incomplete records. In such cases, a written appraisal from an authoritative collector or dealer may be helpful.

Custom Built .410 Bore

Exc.	V.G.	Good	Fair	Poor
45000	35000	30000	26000	22000

NOTE: Fewer than 50 .410 Model 21s were built between 1931 and 1959 in all grades. The number of 28 gauge Model 21s built is unknown but the number is probably no greater than the .410 bore.

Custom Shop Model 21s—1960 to 1981
When Winchester moved the production of the Model 21 into the Custom Shop, the number of styles was greatly reduced. There were now three distinct styles:
1. Custom Grade, chambered in 12, 16, 20, 28 gauge, and .410 bore in barrel lengths from 26" to 32". Matted rib, fancy walnut checkered pistol- or straight-grip stock with checkered forend. Guns with pistol grips furnished with steel grip cap. A small amount of scroll engraving was provided on the frame of this grade.
2. Pigeon Grade, same chambers and barrel lengths as above with the addition of choice of matted or ventilated-rib, leather-covered recoil pad, style "A" carving on stock and forend, and gold engraved pistol grip cap. The frame was engraved with the 21-6 engraving pattern.
3. Grand American Grade, same chambers and barrel lengths as Pigeon Grade with the addition of "B" carving on the stock and forend, 21-6 engraving with gold inlays, extra set of interchangeable barrels with extra forend. All of this was enclosed in a leather trunk case.

Custom Grade—12 Gauge

Exc.	V.G.	Good	Fair	Poor
9500	7500	6800	6000	5200

NOTE: Add $4,000 for 16 gauge. Add $3,000 for 20 gauge.

Pigeon Grade—12 Gauge

Exc.	V.G.	Good	Fair	Poor
18000	15000	12000	10000	8000

NOTE: Add $6,000 for 16 gauge. Add $5,000 for 20 gauge.

Grand American—12 Gauge

Exc.	V.G.	Good	Fair	Poor
25000	20000	16000	14000	13000

NOTE: Add $15,000 for 16 gauge (extremely rare). Add $5,000 for 20 gauge.

Editor's Comment: There were eight 28 gauge Model 21s built during this period and five .410 bores built. These guns obviously command a large premium. Factory letters are available on these guns.

ENGRAVED MODEL 21S
Winchester catalogued a number of special-order engraving patterns which ranged from a small amount of scroll (#1) to full-coverage game scene and scroll (#6). In addition, there were a few guns engraved on special order to the customer's request. Engraved guns are extremely rare, and the value added will vary with the rarity of the gauge and the date of manufacture. The following table represents the value added for various standard engraving patterns on 12 gauge guns for the "Custom Shop" (1960-1982) and "Pre-Custom Shop" (1932-1959) periods. However, it is advisable to seek the opinion of an authorative collector or dealer prior to a sale.

Engraving Pattern	Pre-Custom Shop	Custom Shop
#1	30 percent	20 percent
#2	40 percent	30 percent
#3	60 percent	45 percent
#4	70 percent	50 percent
#5	90 percent	70 percent
#6	100 percent	80 percent

Custom Shop Model 21s—1982 to Present
When U.S. Repeating Arms Company took over the production of the Model 21, the Pigeon Grade was dropped from the line. The Grand American Grade was retained with all the features of its predecessor but with the addition of a small-bore set featuring a 28 gauge and .410 bore set of barrels. Two new grades were introduced in 1983: the Standard Custom Grade and the Special Custom Grade. In addition to these grades, the factory would undertake to build for its customers whatever was desired. Due to the unique nature of these guns, it is advised that an expert appraisal be sought to establish a value. While the change-over from Winchester to U.S. Repeating Arms was a transfer of business assets and the craftsmen and personnel remained the same, collectors are reluctant to assign the same values to U.S. Repeating Arms Model 21s as those produced by Winchester. No official production figures are available for U.S.R.A. Model 21s, but the number is most likely small; perhaps around 200 guns.

Standard Custom Built

NIB	Exc.	V.G	Good	Fair	Poor
8000	6500	5500	5000	4500	4000

Grand American

NIB	Exc.	V.G.	Good	Fair	Poor
18000	13000	10000	8500	6000	5000

Grand American Small Gauge Set—28 or .410 bore

NIB	Exc.	V.G.	Good	Fair	Poor
60000	45000	35000	27000	22000	20000

Model 24
The Model 24 was Winchester's attempt to develop a medium-priced double-barrel shotgun. Like the Model 21, it was a top lever breakdown model that was available in 12, 16, and 20 gauge in various barrel lengths from 26" to 30". Offered in a Standard model only with double triggers, raised matted rib, plain walnut pistol- or straight-grip stock with semi-beavertail forend, the Model 24 was introduced in 1939 and was discontinued in 1957 with about 116,000 guns sold.

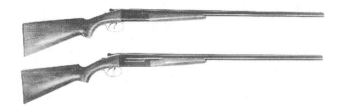

Top: Model 24 Standard. Bottom: Model 24 Improved.

Exc.	V.G.	Good	Fair	Poor
650	500	400	250	200

NOTE: Add 10 percent for 16 gauge. Add 25 percent for 20 gauge.

POST-1963 RIFLES AND SHOTGUNS

RIFLES

Model 94 Centennial Limited Editions
Introduced in 1994 these models celebrate the 100-year anniversary of the Winchester Model 1894. Offered in three grades, these models are of limited production. The Grade I is limited to 12,000 rifles while the High Grade is limited to 3,000 rifles. Only 94 of the Custom Limited

model were produced. Each Limited model has different grades of select walnut and engraving coverage. All are chambered for the .30-30 Winchester cartridge.

Grade I

NIB	Exc.	V.G.	Good	Fair	Poor
750	700	600	450	300	200

High Grade

NIB	Exc.	V.G.	Good	Fair	Poor
1200	950	700	500	300	200

Custom High Grade

NIB	Exc.	V.G.	Good	Fair	Poor
4500	3900	2500	1000	750	450

Model 94 Trapper

16" barrel. Chambered for the .30-30, .357 Mag., .44 Mag, or .45 Colt cartridge. In 2003 a top-tang safety was installed.

NIB	Exc.	V.G.	Good	Fair	Poor
450	350	250	150	100	75

Model 94 Heritage—Limited 1 of 1000

Introduced in 2002 and limited to 1,000 rifles. Fitted with half round/half octagon 26" barrel. Engraved with #3 pattern with gold plate. Fancy walnut stock. Chambered for the .38-55 cartridge.

NIB	Exc.	V.G.	Good	Fair	Poor
1885	1500	—	—	—	—

Model 94 Heritage—Custom 1 of 100

Similar to the above model but with finer wood and engraved with #2 pattern with gold. Limited to 100 rifles. Introduced in 2002.

NIB	Exc.	V.G.	Good	Fair	Poor
N/A	—	—	—	—	—

Model 94 Trails End

This model is chambered for the .357 Mag., .44 Mag., and .45 Colt. Offered with standard-size loop lever or Wrangler-style loop. Introduced in 1997.

NIB	Exc.	V.G.	Good	Fair	Poor
475	350	250	—	—	—

Model 9410

Introduced in 2001 this model features a .410 shotgun in a lever-action configuration. Barrel length is 24" and is smoothbore with Cylinder choke. Chambered is 2.5". Magazine capacity is nine rounds. Tru-glo front sight. Weight is about 6.75 lbs. In 2003 a top-tang safety was installed.

NIB	Exc.	V.G.	Good	Fair	Poor
550	400	—	—	—	—

Model 9410 Semi-Fancy

As above but with semi-fancy walnut stock with checkering. Introduced in 2004.

NIB	Exc.	V.G.	Good	Fair	Poor
790	625	—	—	—	—

Model 9410 Packer

Introduced in 2002 this model features a 20" barrel with 3/4 magazine and pistol-grip stock. Weight is about 6.5 lbs.

NIB	Exc.	V.G.	Good	Fair	Poor
575	425	—	—	—	—

Model 9410 Packer Compact

Introduced in 2003 this model features a reduced length of pull to 12-1/2". Fitted with Invector chokes. Weight is about 6.25 lbs.

NIB	Exc.	V.G.	Good	Fair	Poor
655	525	—	—	—	—

Model 9410 Ranger

This version is the same as the standard or traditional Model 9410 but hardwood stock without checkering. Weight is about 6.75 lbs. Fitted with top-tang safety. Introduced in 2003.

NIB	Exc.	V.G.	Good	Fair	Poor
540	425	—	—	—	—

Model 9422

Introduced in 1972 this model is chambered for the .22 rimfire and .22 Magnum rimfire cartridges. It was fitted with a 20.5" barrel, front ramp sight with hood, and adjustable semi-buckhorn rear sight. Tubular magazine holds 21 Shorts, 17 Longs, and 15 LR cartridges. The Magnum version holds 11 cartridges. Weight is about 6.25 lbs. Two-piece American walnut stock with no checkering. Between 1972 and 1992 approximately 750,000 Model 9422s were produced.

NIB	Exc.	V.G.	Good	Fair	Poor
470	375	250	200	150	100

Model 9422 XTR

This is a deluxe lever-action rifle chambered for the .22 rimfire cartridge. It is a takedown rifle with a 20.5", round barrel and a tubular magazine. The finish is blued with a checkered, high-gloss, straight-grip walnut stock. It was introduced in 1978. A .22 Magnum version is also available and would be worth approximately $10 additional.

NIB	Exc.	V.G.	Good	Fair	Poor
350	300	250	200	125	100

Model 9422 XTR Classic

This version is similar to the standard Model 9422 XTR except that it features a 22.5" barrel and a satin-finished, plain, pistol-grip walnut stock. It was manufactured between 1985 and 1987.

NIB	Exc.	V.G.	Good	Fair	Poor
650	550	350	250	200	125

Model 9422 WinTuff

This model features an uncheckered laminated wood stock that is brown in color. Chambered for both the .22 Rimfire and the .22 Winchester Magnum Rimfire. Weighs 6.25 lbs. Other features are the same as the standard Model 9422.

NIB	Exc.	V.G.	Good	Fair	Poor
325	275	225	165	100	75

Model 9422 WinCam

This model is chambered only for the .22 Winchester Magnum Rimfire. The laminated stock is a green color. Weighs 6.25 lbs.

NIB	Exc.	V.G.	Good	Fair	Poor
350	280	225	165	100	75

Model 9422 Trapper

Introduced in 1996 this model features a 16.5" barrel. It has an overall length of 33". Weight is 5.5 lbs.

NIB	Exc.	V.G.	Good	Fair	Poor
350	300	250	200	150	100

Model 9422 High Grade
This variation of the Model 9422 series features a specially engraved receiver and fancy wood stock. Barrel length is 20.5". Weight is about 6 lbs.

NIB	Exc.	V.G.	Good	Fair	Poor
450	400	300	250	175	125

Model 9422 25th Anniversary Rifle
Introduced in 1997 this model features 20.5" barrel. Limited quantities.

Grade I
Engraved receiver.

NIB	Exc.	V.G.	Good	Fair	Poor
600	475	—	—	—	—

High Grade
Engraved receiver with silver border.

NIB	Exc.	V.G.	Good	Fair	Poor
1350	1100	—	—	—	—

Model 9422 Legacy
This model has a semi-pistol-grip stock of checkered walnut. Will shoot .22 caliber LR, L, or S cartridges. Fitted with a 16" barrel. Weight is about 6 lbs. Introduced in 1998.

NIB	Exc.	V.G.	Good	Fair	Poor
500	400	325	250	—	—

Model 9422 Large Loop & Walnut
Introduced in 1998 this model features a walnut stock with large loop lever. Large loop offered on .22 LR, L, or S model. Standard lever on .22 WMR version. Fitted with 16" barrel. Weight is about 6 lbs.

NIB	Exc.	V.G.	Good	Fair	Poor
400	300	—	—	—	—

Model 9422 High Grade Series II
This model features a high-grade walnut stock with cut checkering. Receiver engraved with dogs and squirrels. Fitted with 16" barrel. Weight is about 6 lbs. Introduced in 1998.

NIB	Exc.	V.G.	Good	Fair	Poor
500	400	—	—	—	—

Model 9417 Traditional
Introduced in 2003 this model is chambered for the .17 HMR cartridge and fitted with a 20.5" barrel. Adjustable sights. Checkered walnut stock with straight grip. Weight is about 6 lbs.

NIB	Exc.	V.G.	Good	Fair	Poor
500	400	—	—	—	—

Model 9417 Legacy
Similar to the model above but fitted with a 22.5" barrel and checkered walnut with pistol grip. Weight is about 6 lbs. Introduced in 2003.

NIB	Exc.	V.G.	Good	Fair	Poor
535	425	—	—	—	—

Model 1885 Low Wall Classic
This single-shot rifle is chambered for the .17 HMR cartridge and fitted with a 24" octagon barrel. Checkered walnut stock with straight grip and schnabel forend. Adjustable sights. Weight is about 8 lbs. Introduced in 2003.

NIB	Exc.	V.G.	Good	Fair	Poor
935	750	—	—	—	—

Model 1885 Low Wall
Introduced in fall of 1999 this single-shot model is chambered for the .22 LR cartridge. It is fitted with a 24.5" half octagon barrel with leaf rear sight. Drilled and tapped for a tang sight. Crescent steel buttplate. Walnut stock. Weight is about 8 lbs. Limited to 2,400 rifles.

Grade I

NIB	Exc.	V.G.	Good	Fair	Poor
750	600	—	—	—	—

High Grade

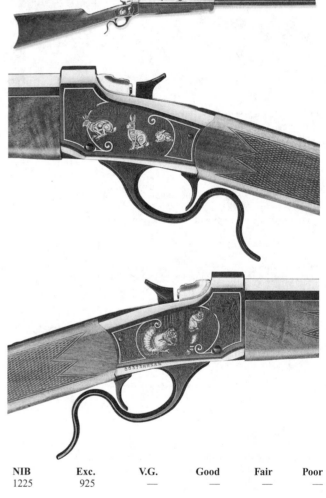

NIB	Exc.	V.G.	Good	Fair	Poor
1225	925	—	—	—	—

Model 1892
Introduced in mid-1997 this model is chambered for the .45 Colt cartridge. It features a straight grip, full magazine, and crescent buttplate.

Grade I
2,500 rifles with engraved receiver.

NIB	Exc.	V.G.	Good	Fair	Poor
725	575	—	—	—	—

High Grade
1,000 rifle with gold accents.

NIB	Exc.	V.G.	Good	Fair	Poor
1275	1050	—	—	—	—

Model 1892 Short Rifle
This model is fitted with a 20" barrel and chambered for the .45 Colt, .357 Magnum, .44 Magnum, and .44-40 cartridges. Walnut stock and blued barrel and receiver. Weight is about 6.25 lbs. Introduced in 1999.

NIB	Exc.	V.G.	Good	Fair	Poor
740	575	—	—	—	—

Model 1886
Introduced to the Winchester line in 1997 this was a noncatalogued item. This model features a 26" octagon barrel, semi-pistol grip, and crescent buttplate.

Grade I
2,500 rifles blued receiver.

NIB	Exc.	V.G.	Good	Fair	Poor
1000	800	—	—	—	—

High Grade
1,000 rifles with gold accents on receiver.

NIB	Exc.	V.G.	Good	Fair	Poor
1575	1300	—	—	—	—

Model 1886 Take Down Classic
Introduced in 1999 this model is chambered for the .45-70 cartridge and features a 26" barrel with takedown feature. Walnut stock with pistol grip and crescent butt. Magazine capacity is 8 rounds. Weight is about 9.25 lbs.

NIB	Exc.	V.G.	Good	Fair	Poor
1140	900	—	—	—	—

Model 1886 Extra Light
This model is similar to the Model 1886 Classic but fitted with a 22" round tapered barrel and half magazine. Chambered for the .45-70 cartridge. Shotgun butt. Weight is about 7.25 lbs. Limited edition. Introduced in 2000.

Grade I
3,500 manufactured.

NIB	Exc.	V.G.	Good	Fair	Poor
1150	850	—	—	—	—

High Grade
1,000 manufactured.

NIB	Exc.	V.G.	Good	Fair	Poor
1450	1050	—	—	—	—

Model 1895 Limited Edition
Introduced in 1995 this reproduction of the famous Model 1895 is offered in .30-06 caliber with 24" barrel. Magazine capacity is 4 rounds. Weight is approximately 8 lbs. Available in two grades, each limited to 4,000 rifles.

Grade I

NIB	Exc.	V.G.	Good	Fair	Poor
800	700	—	—	—	—

High Grade

NIB	Exc.	V.G.	Good	Fair	Poor
1300	1000	—	—	—	—

Model 1895—Limited Edition for the year 2000
Same as above but chambered for the .405 Win. cartridge. Introduced in 2000.

Grade I

NIB	Exc.	V.G.	Good	Fair	Poor
1150	800	—	—	—	—

High Grade

NIB	Exc.	V.G.	Good	Fair	Poor
1550	1150	—	—	—	—

Model 52B Sporting Rifle
A 1993 limited-edition rifle (6,000 guns) that is a faithful reproduction of the famous Winchester Model 52 Sporter. Equipped with a 24" barrel, adjustable trigger, and "B" style cheekpiece. This model was reissued in 1997 and limited to 3,000 rifles.

NIB	Exc.	V.G.	Good	Fair	Poor
575	500	450	325	225	100

MODEL 23 SERIES

Model 23 XTR
This is a side-by-side, double-barrel shotgun chambered for 12 or 20 gauge. It is offered with 25.5", 26", 28", or 30" vent-rib barrels with 3" chambers and various choke combinations. It is a boxlock gun that features a single trigger and automatic ejectors. It is scroll-engraved with a coin-finished receiver, blued barrels, and a checkered, select walnut stock. It was introduced in 1978. This model is available in a number of configurations that differ in the amount of ornamentation and the quality of materials and workmanship utilized in their construction. These models and their values are as follows:

Grade I
Discontinued.

Exc.	V.G.	Good	Fair	Poor
1325	1100	900	725	450

Pigeon Grade
With WinChokes.

Exc.	V.G.	Good	Fair	Poor
1450	1200	1075	900	550

Pigeon Grade Lightweight
Straight stock.

Exc.	V.G.	Good	Fair	Poor
1850	1450	1250	950	650

Golden Quail
This series was available in 28 gauge and .410, as well as 12 or 20 gauge. It features 25.5" barrels that are choked improved cylinder/modified. It features a straight-grip, English-style stock with a recoil pad. The .410 version would be worth approximately 10 percent more than the values given. This series was discontinued in 1987.

Exc.	V.G.	Good	Fair	Poor
2150	1800	1500	1100	850

Model 23 Light Duck
This version is chambered for 20 gauge and was offered with a 28" Full and Full-choked barrel. There were 500 manufactured in 1985.

Exc.	V.G.	Good	Fair	Poor
1500	1250	1100	850	750

Model 23 Heavy Duck
This version is chambered for 12 gauge with 30" Full and Full-choked barrels. There were 500 manufactured in 1984.

Exc.	V.G.	Good	Fair	Poor
1500	1250	1100	850	750

WINCHESTER COMMEMORATIVE RIFLES

Since the early 1960s, Winchester has produced a number of special Model 1894 rifles and carbines that commemorated certain historic events, places, or individuals. In some cases they are slightly embellished and in others are quite ornate. The general liquidity of these commemoratives has not been as good as would be expected. In some cases they were produced in excessive amounts and could not, in all honesty, be considered limited-production items. In any case, in our opinion one should purchase weapons of this nature for their enjoyment factor as the investment potential is not sufficient reason for their purchase. As with all commemoratives, in order to realize the collector potential they must be NIB with all supplied materials including, in the case of Winchester, the colorful outer sleeve that encased the factory carton. If a Winchester commemorative rifle has been cocked leaving a line on the hammer or the lever, many collectors will show little or no interest in its acquisition. If they have been fired, they will realize little premium over a standard, Post-1964 Model 94. A number of commemoratives have been ordered by outside concerns and are technically not factory issues. Most have less collectibility than factory-issued models. There are a number of concerns that specialize in marketing the total range of Winchester commmemorative rifles. We list the factory-issue commemoratives with their current value, their issue price, and the number manufactured.

1964 Wyoming Diamond Jubilee—Carbine
NIB	Issue	Amt. Mfg.
1295	100	1,500

1966 Centennial—Rifle
NIB	Issue	Amt. Mfg.
450	125	102,309

1966 Centennial—Carbine
NIB	Issue	Amt. Mfg.
425	125	102,309

1966 Nebraska Centennial—Rifle
NIB	Issue	Amt. Mfg.
1195	100	2,500

1967 Canadian Centennial—Rifle
NIB	Issue	Amt. Mfg.
450	125	—

1967 Canadian Centennial—Carbine
NIB	Issue	Amt. Mfg.
425	125	90,301

1967 Alaskan Purchase Centennial—Carbine
NIB	Issue	Amt. Mfg.
1495	125	1,500

1968 Illinois Sesquicentennial—Carbine
NIB	Issue	Amt. Mfg.
395	110	37,648

1968 Buffalo Bill—Carbine
NIB	Issue	Amt. Mfg.
425	130	112,923

1968 Buffalo Bill—Rifle
NIB	Issue	Amt. Mfg.
450	130	—

1968 Buffalo Bill "1 of 300"—Rifle
NIB	Issue	Amt. Mfg.
2650	1000	300

1969 Theodore Roosevelt—Rifle
NIB	Issue	Amt. Mfg.
450	135	—

1969 Theodore Roosevelt—Carbine
NIB	Issue	Amt. Mfg.
425	135	52,386

1969 Golden Spike Carbine
NIB	Issue	Amt. Mfg.
495	120	69,996

1970 Cowboy Commemorative Carbine
NIB	Issue	Amt. Mfg.
450	125	27,549

1970 Cowboy Carbine "1 of 300"
NIB	Issue	Amt. Mfg.
2650	1000	300

1970 Northwest Territories (Canadian)
NIB	Issue	Amt. Mfg.
850	150	2,500

1970 Northwest Territories Deluxe (Canadian)
NIB	Issue	Amt. Mfg.
1100	250	500

1970 Lone Star—Rifle
NIB	Issue	Amt. Mfg.
450	140	—

1970 Lone Star—Carbine
NIB	Issue	Amt. Mfg.
425	140	38,385

1971 NRA Centennial—Rifle
NIB	Issue	Amt. Mfg.
425	150	21,000

1971 NRA Centennial—Musket
NIB	Issue	Amt. Mfg.
425	150	23,400

1971 Yellow Boy (European)
NIB	Issue	Amt. Mfg.
1150	250	500

1971 Royal Canadian Mounted Police (Canadian)
NIB	Issue	Amt. Mfg.
795	190	9,500

1971 Mounted Police (Canadian)
NIB	Issue	Amt. Mfg.
795	190	5,100

1971 Mounted Police, Presentation
NIB	Issue	Amt. Mfg.
9995	—	10

1974 Texas Ranger—Carbine
NIB	Issue	Amt. Mfg.
695	135	4,850

1974 Texas Ranger Presentation Model
NIB	Issue	Amt. Mfg.
2650	1000	150

1974 Apache (Canadian)
NIB	Issue	Amt. Mfg.
795	150	8,600

1974 Commanche (Canadian)
NIB	Issue	Amt. Mfg.
795	230	11,500

1974 Klondike Gold Rush (Canadian)
NIB	Issue	Amt. Mfg.
795	240	10,500

1975 Klondike Gold Rush—Dawson City Issue (Canadian)
NIB	Issue	Amt. Mfg.
8500	—	25

1976 Sioux (Canadian)
NIB	Issue	Amt. Mfg.
795	280	10,000

1976 Little Bighorn (Canadian)
NIB	Issue	Amt. Mfg.
795	300	11,000

1976 U.S. Bicentennial Carbine
NIB	Issue	Amt. Mfg.
595	325	19,999

1977 Wells Fargo
NIB	Issue	Amt. Mfg.
495	350	19,999

1977 Legendary Lawman
NIB	Issue	Amt. Mfg.
495	375	19,999

1977 Limited Edition I
NIB	Issue	Amt. Mfg.
1395	1500	1,500

1977 Cheyenne—.22 Cal. (Canadian)
NIB	Issue	Amt. Mfg.
695	320	5,000

1977 Cheyenne—.44-40 Cal. (Canadian)
NIB	Issue	Amt. Mfg.
795	300	11,225

1977 Cherokee—.22 Cal. (Canadian)
NIB	Issue	Amt. Mfg.
695	385	3,950

1977 Cherokee—.30-30 Cal. (Canadian)
NIB	Issue	Amt. Mfg.
795	385	9,000

1978 "One of One Thousand" (European)
NIB	Issue	Amt. Mfg.
7500	5000	250

1978 Antler Game Carbine
NIB	Issue	Amt. Mfg.
550	375	19,999

1979 Limited Edition II
NIB	Issue	Amt. Mfg.
1395	1500	1,500

1979 Legendary Frontiersman Rifle
NIB	Issue	Amt. Mfg.
550	425	19,999

1979 Matched Set of 1,000
NIB	Issue	Amt. Mfg.
2250	3000	1,000

1979 Bat Masterson (Canadian)
NIB	Issue	Amt. Mfg.
795	650	8,000

1980 Alberta Diamond Jubilee (Canadian)
NIB	Issue	Amt. Mfg.
795	650	2,700

1980 Alberta Diamond Jubilee Deluxe (Canadian)
NIB	Issue	Amt. Mfg.
1495	1900	300

1980 Saskatchewan Diamond Jubilee (Canadian)
NIB	Issue	Amt. Mfg.
795	695	2,700

1980 Saskatchewan Diamond Jubilee Deluxe (Canadian)
NIB	Issue	Amt. Mfg.
1495	1995	300

1980 Oliver Winchester
NIB	Issue	Amt. Mfg.
695	375	19,999

1981 U.S. Border Patrol
NIB	Issue	Amt. Mfg.
595	1195	1,000

1981 U.S. Border Patrol—Member's Model
NIB	Issue	Amt. Mfg.
595	695	800

1981 Calgary Stampede (Canadian)
NIB	Issue	Amt. Mfg.
1250	2200	1,000

1981 Canadian Pacific Centennial (Canadian)
NIB	Issue	Amt. Mfg.
550	800	2,000

1981 Canadian Pacific Centennial Presentation (Canadian)
NIB	Issue	Amt. Mfg.
1100	2200	300

1981 Canadian Pacific Employee's Model (Canadian)
NIB	Issue	Amt. Mfg.
550	800	2,000

1981 John Wayne (Canadian)
NIB	Issue	Amt. Mfg.
1195	995	1,000

1981 John Wayne
NIB	Issue	Amt. Mfg.
995	600	49,000

1981 Duke
NIB	Issue	Amt. Mfg.
2950	2250	1,000

1981 John Wayne "1 of 300" Set
NIB	Issue	Amt. Mfg.
6500	10000	300

1982 Great Western Artist I
NIB	Issue	Amt. Mfg.
1195	2200	999

1982 Great Western Artist II
NIB	Issue	Amt. Mfg.
1195	2200	999

1982 Annie Oakley
NIB	Issue	Amt. Mfg.
695	699	6,000

1983 Chief Crazy Horse
NIB	Issue	Amt. Mfg.
595	600	19,999

1983 American Bald Eagle
NIB	Issue	Amt. Mfg.
595	895	2,800

1983 American Bald Eagle—Deluxe
NIB	Issue	Amt. Mfg.
3000	2995	200

1983 Oklahoma Diamond Jubilee
NIB	Issue	Amt. Mfg.
1395	2250	1,001

1984 Winchester—Colt Commemorative Set
NIB	Issue	Amt. Mfg.
2250	3995	2,300

1985 Boy Scout 75th Anniversary .22 Cal.
NIB	Issue	Amt. Mfg.
595	615	15,000

1985 Boy Scout 75th Anniversary—Eagle Scout
NIB	Issue	Amt. Mfg.
3000	2140	1,000

Texas Sesquicentennial Model—Rifle .38-55 Cal.
NIB	Issue	Amt. Mfg.
2400	2995	1,500

Texas Sesquicentennial Model—Carbine .38-55 Cal.
NIB	Issue	Amt. Mfg.
695	695	15,000

Texas Sesquicentennial Model Set with Bowie Knife
NIB	Issue	Amt. Mfg.
6250	7995	150

1986 Model 94 Ducks Unlimited
NIB	Issue	Amt. Mfg.
650	—	2,800

1986 Statue of Liberty
NIB	Issue	Amt. Mfg.
7000	6500	100

1986 120th Anniversary Model—Carbine .44-40 Cal.
NIB	Issue	Amt. Mfg.
895	995	1,000

1986 European 1 of 1,000 Second Series (European)
NIB	Issue	Amt. Mfg.
7000	6000	150

1987 U.S. Constitution 200th Anniversary 44-40
NIB	Issue	Amt. Mfg.
13500	12000	17

1990 Wyoming Centennial-30-30
NIB	Issue	Amt. Mfg.
1095	895	500

1991 Winchester 125th Anniversary
NIB	Issue	Amt. Mfg.
5500	4995	61

1992 Arapaho—30-30
NIB	Issue	Amt. Mfg.
1095	895	500

1992 Ontario Conservation-30-30
NIB	Issue	Amt. Mfg.
1195	1195	400

1992 Kentucky Bicentennial-30-30
NIB	Issue	Amt. Mfg.
1095	995	500

1993 Nez Perce—30-30
NIB	Issue	Amt. Mfg.
1095	995	600

1995 Florida Sesquicentennial Carbine
NIB	Issue	Amt. Mfg.
1195	1195	360

1996 Wild Bill Hickok Carbine
NIB	Issue	Amt. Mfg.
1195	1195	350

Winchester Serial Numbers

Records at the factory indicate the following serial numbers were assigned to guns at the end of the calendar year.

MODEL 100

Year	Serial	Year	Serial
1961 —	1 to 32189	1968 —	210053
62 —	60760	69 —	A210999
63 —	78863	70 —	229995
64 —	92016	71 —	242999
65 —	135388	72 —	A258001
66 —	145239	73 —	A262833
67 —	209498		

Records at the factory indicate the following serial numbers were assigned to guns at the end of the calendar year.

MODEL 88

Year	Serial	Year	Serial
1955 —	1 to 18378	1965 —	162699
56 —	36756	66 —	192595
57 —	55134	67 —	212416
58 —	73512	68 —	230199
59 —	91890	69 —	H239899
60 —	110268	70 —	H258229
61 —	128651	71 —	H266784
62 —	139838	72 —	H279014
63 —	148858	73 —	H283718
64 —	160307		

Records at the factory indicate the following serial numbers were assigned to guns at the end of the calendar year.

MODE\L 74

Year	Serial	Year	Serial
1939 —	1 to 30890	1948 —	223788
40 —	67085	49 —	249900
41 —	114355	50 —	276012
42 —	128293	51 —	302124
43 —	None	52 —	328236
44 —	128295	53 —	354348
45 —	128878	54 —	380460
46 —	145168	55 —	406574
47 —	173524		

Records at the factory indicate the following serial numbers were assigned to guns at the end of the calendar year.

MODEL 71

Year	Serial	Year	Serial
1935 —	1 to 4	1947 —	25758
36 —	7821	48 —	27900
37 —	12988	49 —	29675
38 —	14690	50 —	31450
39 —	16155	51 —	33225
40 —	18267	52 —	35000
41 —	20810	53 —	37500
42 —	21959	54 —	40770
43 —	22048	55 —	43306
44 —	22051	56 —	45843
45 —	22224	57 —	47254
46 —	23534		

Records at the factory indicate the following serial numbers were assigned to guns at the end of the calendar year.

MODEL 70

Year	Serial	Year	Serial
1935 —	1 to 19	1950 —	173150
36 —	2238	51 —	206625
37 —	11573	52 —	238820
38 —	17844	53 —	282735
39 —	23991	54 —	323530
40 —	31675	55 —	361025
41 —	41753	56 —	393595
42 —	49206	57 —	425283
43 —	49983	58 —	440792

44 —	49997	59 —	465040
45 —	50921	60 —	504257
46 —	58382	61 —	545446
47 —	75675	62 —	565592
48 —	101680	63 —	581471
49 —	131580		

All post-1964 Model 70s began with the serial number 700000

1964 —	740599	1973 —	G1128731
65 —	809177	74 —	G1175000
66 —	833795	75 —	G1218700
67 —	869000	76 —	G1266000
68 —	925908	77 —	G1350000
69 —	G941900	78 —	G1410000
70 —	G957995	79 —	G1447000
71 —	G1018991	80 —	G1490709
72 —	G1099257	81 —	G1537134

Records at the factory indicate the following serial numbers were assigned to guns at the end of the calendar year.

MODEL 63

1933 —	1 to 2667	1946 —	61607
34 —	5361	47 —	71714
35 —	9830	48 —	80519
36 —	16781	49 —	88889
37 —	25435	50 —	97259
38 —	30934	51 —	105629
39 —	36055	52 —	114000
40 —	41456	53 —	120500
41 —	47708	54 —	127000
42 —	51258	55 —	138000
43 —	51631	56 —	150000
44 —	51656	57 —	162345
45 —	53853	58 —	174692

Records at the factory indicate the following serial numbers were assigned to guns at the end of the calendar year.

MODEL 62

1932 —	1 to 7643	1946 —	183756
33 —	10695	47 —	219085
34 —	14090	48 —	252298
35 —	23924	49 —	262473
36 —	42759	50 —	272648
37 —	66059	51 —	282823
38 —	80205	52 —	293000
39 —	96534	53 —	310500
40 —	116393	54 —	328000
41 —	137379	55 —	342776
42 —	155152	56 —	357551
43 —	155422	57 —	383513
44 —	155425	58 —	409475
45 —	156073		

Records at the factory indicate the following serial numbers were assigned to guns at the end of the calendar year.

MODEL 61

1932 —	1 to 3532	1948 —	115281
33 —	6008	49 —	125461
34 —	8554	50 —	135641
35 —	12379	51 —	145821
36 —	20615	52 —	156000
37 —	30334	53 —	171000
38 —	36326	54 —	186000
39 —	42610	55 —	200962
40 —	49270	56 —	215923
41 —	57493	57 —	229457
42 —	59871	58 —	242992
43 —	59872	59 —	262793
44 —	59879	60 —	282594
45 —	60512	61 —	302395
46 —	71629	62 —	322196
47 —	92297	63 —	342001

This model was discontinued in 1963. For some unknown reason there are no actual records available from 1949 through 1963. The serial number figures for these years are arrived at by taking the total production figure of 342,001, subtracting the last known number of 115281, and dividing the difference equally by the number of remaining years available, (15).

Records at the factory indicate the following serial numbers were assigned to guns at the end of the calendar year.

MODEL 55 CENTERFIRE

1924 —	1 to 836	1929 —	12258
25 —	2783	30 —	17393
26 —	4957	31 —	18198
27 —	8021	32 —	19204
28 —	10467	33 —	Clean-up 20580

Records at the factory indicate the following serial numbers were assigned to guns at the end of the calendar year.

MODEL 54

1925 —	1 to 3140	1931 —	36731
26 —	8051	32 —	38543
27 —	14176	33 —	40722
28 —	19587	34 —	43466
29 —	29104	35 —	47125
30 —	32499	36 —	50145

Records at the factory indicate the following serial numbers were assigned to guns at the end of the calendar year.

MODEL 53

In the case of the Model 53 the following list pertains to the number of guns produced each year rather than a serial number list.
The Model 53 was serially numbered concurrently with the Model 92.

MODEL 53s PRODUCED

1924 —	1488	1929 —	1733
25 —	2861	30 —	920
26 —	2531	31 —	621
27 —	2297	32 —	206
28 —	1958		

This model was discontinued in 1932, however, a clean-up of production continued for nine more years with an additional 486 guns.
TOTAL PRODUCTION APPROXIMATELY—15,100

Records at the factory indicate the following serial numbers were assigned to guns at the end of the calendar year.

1920 —	None indicated	1950 —	70766
21 —	397	51 —	73385
22 —	745	52 —	76000
23 —	1394	53 —	79500
24 —	2361	54 —	80693
25 —	3513	55 —	81831
26 —	6383	56 —	96869
27 —	9436	57 —	97869
28 —	12082	58 —	98599
29 —	14594	59 —	98899
30 —	17253	60 —	102200
31 —	21954	61 —	106986
32 —	24951	62 —	108718
33 —	26725	63 —	113583
34 —	29030	64 —	118447
35 —	32448	65 —	120992
36 —	36632	66 —	123537
37 —	40419	67 —	123727
38 —	43632	68 —	123917
39 —	45460	69 —	E124107
40 —	47519	70 —	E124297
41 —	50317	71 —	E124489
42 —	52129	72 —	E124574
43 —	52553	73 —	E124659
44 —	52560	74 —	E124744
45 —	52718	75 —	E124828

46 —		56080	76 —	E125019	33 —	664544	59 —	1795500
47 —		60158	77 —	E125211	34 —	673994	60 —	1800000
48 —		64265	78 —	E125315	35 —	686978	61 —	1930029
49 —		68149			36 —	720316	62 —	1956990
					37 —	754250	63 —	1962001

This model was discontinued in 1978. A small clean-up of production was completed in 1979 with a total of 125,419.

Records at the factory indicate the following serial numbers were assigned to guns at the end of the calendar year.

MODEL 50

1954 —	1 to 24550	1958 —	122750
55 —	49100	59 —	147300
56 —	73650	60 —	171850
57 —	98200	61 —	196400

Records at the factory indicate the following serial numbers were assigned to guns at the end of the calendar year.

MODEL 42

1933 —	1 to 9398	1949 —	81107
34 —	13963	50 —	87071
35 —	17728	51 —	93038
36 —	24849	52 —	99000
37 —	30900	53 —	108201
38 —	34659	54 —	117200
39 —	38967	55 —	121883
40 —	43348	56 —	126566
41 —	48203	57 —	131249
42 —	50818	58 —	135932
43 —	50822	59 —	140615
44 —	50828	60 —	145298
45 —	51168	61 —	149981
46 —	54256	62 —	154664
47 —	64853	63 —	159353
48 —	75142		

Records at the factory indicate the following serial numbers were assigned to guns at the end of the calendar year.

MODEL 24

1939 —	1 to 8118	1944 —	33683
40 —	21382	45 —	34965
41 —	27045	46 —	45250
42 —	33670	47 —	58940
43 —	None recorded	48 —	64417

There were no records kept on this model from 1949 until its discontinuance in 1958. The total production was approximately 116,280.

Records at the factory indicate the following serial numbers were assigned to guns at the end of the calendar year.

MODEL 12

1912 —	5308	1938 —	779455
13 —	32418	39 —	814121
14 —	79765	40 —	856499
15 —	109515	41 —	907431
16 —	136412	42 —	958303
17 —	159391	43 —	975640
18 —	183461	44 —	975727
19 —	219457	45 —	990004
20 —	247458	46 —	1029152
21 —	267253	47 —	1102371
22 —	304314	48 —	1176055
23 —	346319	49 —	1214041
24 —	385196	50 —	1252028
25 —	423056	51 —	1290015
26 —	464564	52 —	1328002
27 —	510693	53 —	1399996
28 —	557850	54 —	1471990
29 —	600834	55 —	1541929
30 —	626996	56 —	1611868
31 —	651255	57 —	1651435
32 —	660110	58 —	1690999

A clean-up of production took place from 1964 through 1966 with the ending serial number 70875

NEW STYLE MODEL 12

1972 —	Y2000100-Y2006396
73 —	Y2015662
74 —	Y2022061
75 —	Y2024478
76 —	Y2025482
77 —	Y2025874
78 —	Y2026156
79 —	Y2026399

Records at the factory indicate the following serial numbers were assigned to guns at the end of the calendar year.

MODEL 1911 S.L.

1911 —	1 to 3819	1919 —	57337
12 —	27659	20 —	60719
13 —	36677	21 —	64109
14 —	40105	22 —	69132
15 —	43284	23 —	73186
16 —	45391	24 —	76199
17 —	49893	25 —	78611
18 —	52895		

The model 1911 was discontinued in 1925. However, guns were produced for three years after that date to clean up production and excess parts. When this practice ceased there were approximately 82,774 guns produced.

Records at the factory indicate the following serial numbers were assigned to guns at the end of the calendar year.

MODEL 1910

1910 —	1 to 4766	1924 —	17030
11 —	7695	25 —	17281
12 —	9712	26 —	17696
13 —	11487	27 —	18182
14 —	12311	28 —	18469
15 —	13233	29 —	18893
16 —	13788	30 —	19065
17 —	14255	31 —	19172
18 —	14625	32 —	19232
19 —	15665	33 —	19281
20 —	Not Available	34 —	19338
21 —	15845	35 —	19388
22 —	16347	36 —	19445
23 —	16637		

A clean-up of production continued into 1937 when the total of the guns were completed at approximately 20786.

Records at the factory indicate the following serial numbers were assigned to guns at the end of the calendar year.

MODEL 1907

1907 —	1 to 8657	1933 —	44806
08 —	14486	34 —	44990
09 —	19707	35 —	45203
10 —	23230	36 —	45482
11 —	25523	37 —	45920
12 —	27724	38 —	46419
13 —	29607	39 —	46758
14 —	30872	40 —	47296
15 —	32272	41 —	47957
16 —	36215	42 —	48275
17 —	38235	43 —	None
18 —	39172	44 —	None
19 —	40448	45 —	48281

20 —	Not Available	46 —	48395
21 —	40784	47 —	48996
22 —	41289	48 —	49684
23 —	41658	**49 —	50662
24 —	42029	**50 —	51640
25 —	42360	**51 —	52618
26 —	42688	**52 —	53596
27 —	43226	**53 —	54574
28 —	43685	**54 —	55552
29 —	44046	**55 —	56530
30 —	44357	**56 —	57508
31 —	44572	**57 —	58486
32 —	44683		

Actual records on serial numbers stops in 1948. The serial numbers ending each year from 1948 to 1957 were derived at by taking the last serial number recorded (58486) and the last number from 1948, (49684) and dividing the years of production, (9), which relates to 978 guns each year for the nine year period.

Records at the factory indicate the following serial numbers were assigned to guns at the end of the calendar year.

MODEL 1906

1906 —	1 to 52278	1920 —	None
07 —	89147	21 —	598691
08 —	114138	22 —	608011
09 —	165068	23 —	622601
10 —	221189	24 —	636163
11 —	273355	25 —	649952
12 —	327955	26 —	665484
13 —	381922	27 —	679692
14 —	422734	28 —	695915
15 —	453880	29 —	711202
16 —	483805	30 —	720116
17 —	517743	31 —	725978
18 —	535540	32 —	727353
19 —	593917		

A clean-up of production took place for the next few years with a record of production reaching approximately 729,305.

Records at the factory indicate the following serial numbers were assigned to guns at the end of the calendar year.

MODEL 1905

1905 —	1 to 5659	1913 —	25559
06 —	15288	14 —	26110
07 —	19194	15 —	26561
08 —	20385	16 —	26910
09 —	21280	17 —	27297
10 —	22423	18 —	27585
11 —	23503	19 —	28287
12 —	24602	20 —	29113

Records at the factory indicate the following serial numbers were assigned to guns at the end of the calendar year.

MODEL 1903

1903 —	Not Available	1918 —	92617
04 —	6944	19 —	96565
05 —	14865	20 —	Not Available
06 —	23097	21 —	97650
07 —	31852	22 —	99011
08 —	39105	23 —	100452
09 —	46496	24 —	101688
10 —	54298	25 —	103075
11 —	61679	26 —	104230
12 —	69586	27 —	105537
13 —	76732	28 —	107157
14 —	81776	29 —	109414
15 —	84563	30 —	111276
16 —	87148	31 —	112533
17 —	89501	32 —	112992

This model was discontinued in 1932, however, a clean up of parts was used for further production of approximately 2,000 guns. Total production was stopped at serial number 114962 in 1936.

Records at the factory indicate the following serial numbers were assigned to guns at the end of the calendar year.

MODEL 1901 SHOTGUN

1904 —	64856 to 64860	1913 —	72764
05 —	66483	14 —	73202
06 —	67486	15 —	73509
07 —	68424	16 —	73770
08 —	69197	17 —	74027
09 —	70009	18 —	74311
10 —	70753	19 —	74872
11 —	71441	20 —	77000
12 —	72167		

Records at the factory indicate the following serial numbers were assigned to guns at the end of the calendar year.

MODEL 1897

1897 —	to 32335	1928 —	796806
98 —	64668	29 —	807321
99 —	96999	30 —	812729
1900 —	129332	31 —	830721
01 —	161665	32 —	833926
02 —	193998	33 —	835637
03 —	226331	34 —	837364
04 —	258664	35 —	839728
05 —	296037	36 —	848684
06 —	334059	37 —	856729
07 —	377999	38 —	860725
08 —	413618	39 —	866938
09 —	446888	40 —	875945
10 —	481062	41 —	891190
11 —	512632	42 —	910072
12 —	544313	43 —	912265
13 —	575213	44 —	912327
14 —	592732	45 —	916472
15 —	607673	46 —	926409
16 —	624537	47 —	936682
17 —	646124	48 —	944085
18 —	668383	49 —	953042
19 —	691943	50 —	961999
20 —	696183	51 —	970956
21 —	700428	52 —	979913
22 —	715902	53 —	988860
23 —	732060	54 —	997827
24 —	744942	55 —	1006784
25 —	757629	56 —	1015741
26 —	770527	57 —	1024700
27 —	783574		

Records on this model are incomplete. The above serial numbers are estimated from 1897 through 1903 and again from 1949 through 1957. The actual records are in existence from 1904 through 1949.

Records at the factory indicate the following serial numbers were assigned to guns at the end of the calendar year.

MODEL 1895

1895 —	1 to 287	1914 —	72082
96 —	5715	15 —	174233
97 —	7814	16 —	377411
98 —	19871	17 —	389106
99 —	26434	18 —	392731
1900 —	29817	19 —	397250
01 —	31584	20 —	400463
02 —	35601	21 —	404075
03 —	42514	22 —	407200
04 —	47805	23 —	410289
05 —	54783	24 —	413276

06 —	55011	25 —	417402
07 —	57351	26 —	419533
08 —	60002	27 —	421584
09 —	60951	28 —	422676
10 —	63771	29 —	423680
11 —	65017	30 —	424181
12 —	67331	31 —	425132
13 —	70823	32 —	425825

Records at the factory indicate the following serial numbers were assigned to guns at the end of the calendar year.

MODEL 94

1894 —	1 to 14579	1939 —	1101051
95 —	44359	40 —	1142423
96 —	76464	41 —	1191307
97 —	111453	42 —	1221289
98 —	147684	43 —	No Record Avail.
99 —	183371	44 —	No Record Avail.
1900 —	204427	45 —	No Record Avail.
01 —	233975	46 —	No Record Avail.
02 —	273854	47 —	No Record Avail.
03 —	291506	48 —	1500000
04 —	311363	49 —	1626100
05 —	337557	50 —	1724295
06 —	378878	51 —	1819800
07 —	430985	52 —	1910000
08 —	474241	53 —	2000000
09 —	505831	54 —	2071100
10 —	553062	55 —	2145296
11 —	599263	56 —	2225000
12 —	646114	57 —	2290296
13 —	703701	58 —	2365887
14 —	756066	59 —	2410555
15 —	784052	60 —	2469821
16 —	807741	61 —	2500000
17 —	821972	62 —	2551921
18 —	838175	63 —	2586000
19 —	870762	*1964 —	2700000
20 —	880627	64 —	2797428
21 —	908318	65 —	2894428
22 —	919583	66 —	2991927
23 —	938539	67 —	3088458
24 —	953198	68 —	3185691
25 —	978523	69 —	3284570
26 —	997603	70 —	3381299
27 —	1027571	71 —	3557385
28 —	1054465	72 —	3806499
29 —	1077097	73 —	3929364
30 —	1081755	74 —	4111426
31 —	1084156	75 —	4277926
32 —	1087836	76 —	4463553
33 —	1089270	77 —	4565925
34 —	1091190	78 —	4662210
35 —	1099605	79 —	4826596
36 —	1100065	80 —	4892951
37 —	1100679	81 —	5024957
38 —	1100915	62 —	5103248

*The post-1964 Model 94 began with serial number 2700000.

Serial number 1000000 was presented to President Calvin Coolidge in 1927.

Serial number 1500000 was presented to President Harry S. Truman in 1948.

Serial number 2000000 was presented to President Dwight D. Eisenhower in 1953.

Serial numbers 2500000 and 3000000 were presented to the Winchester Gun Museum, now located in Cody, Wyoming.

Serial number 3500000 was not constructed until 1979 and was sold at auction in Las Vegas, Nevada. Serial number 4000000—whereabouts unknown at this time.

Serial number 4500000—shipped to Italy by Olin in 1978. Whereabouts unknown.

Serial number 5000000—in New Haven, not constructed as of March 1983.

Records at the factory indicate the following serial numbers were assigned to guns at the end of the calendar year.

MODEL 1892

1892 —	1 to 23701	1913 —	742675
93 —	35987	14 —	771444
94 —	73508	15 —	804622
95 —	106721	16 —	830031
96 —	144935	17 —	853819
97 —	159312	18 —	870942
98 —	165431	19 —	903649
99 —	171820	20 —	906754
1900 —	183411	21 —	910476
01 —	191787	22 —	917300
02 —	208871	23 —	926329
03 —	253935	24 —	938641
04 —	278546	25 —	954997
05 —	315425	26 —	973896
06 —	376496	27 —	990883
07 —	437919	28 —	996517
08 —	476540	29 —	999238
09 —	522162	30 —	999730
10 —	586996	31 —	1000727
11 —	643483	32 —	1001324
12 —	694752		

Records on the Model 1890 are somewhat incomplete. Our records indicate the following serial numbers were assigned to guns at the end of the calendar year beginning with 1908. Actual records on the firearms that were manufactured between 1890 and 1907 will be available from the "Winchester Museum," located at The "Buffalo Bill Historical Center", P.O. Box 1020, Cody, WY 82414

MODEL 1890

1908 —	330000 to 363850	1920 —	None
		21 —	634783
09 —	393427	22 —	643304
10 —	423567	23 —	654837
11 —	451264	24 —	664613
12 —	478595	25 —	675774
13 —	506936	26 —	687049
14 —	531019	27 —	698987
15 —	551290	28 —	711354
16 —	570497	29 —	722125
17 —	589204	30 —	729015
18 —	603438	31 —	733178
19 —	630801	32 —	734454

The Model 1890 was discontinued in 1932, however, a clean-up of the production run lasted another 8+ years and included another 14,000 to 15,000 guns. Our figures indicate approximately 749,000 guns were made.

Records at the factory indicate the following serial numbers were assigned to guns at the end of the calendar year.

MODEL 1887

1887 —	1 to 7431	1993 —	54367
88 —	22408	94 —	56849
89 —	25673	95 —	58289
90 —	29105	96 —	60175
91 —	38541	97 —	63952
92 —	49763	98 —	64855

According to these records no guns were produced during the last few years of this model and it was therefore discontinued in 1901.

Records at the factory indicate the following serial numbers were assigned to guns at the end of the calendar year.

MODEL 1886

1886 —	1 to 3211	1905 —	138838
87 —	14728	06 —	142249
88 —	28577	07 —	145119

Year	Serial	Year	Serial
89 —	38401	08 —	147322
90 —	49723	09 —	148237
91 —	63601	10 —	150129
92 —	73816	11 —	151622
93 —	83261	12 —	152943
94 —	94543	13 —	152947
95 —	103708	14 —	153859
96 —	109670	15 —	154452
97 —	113997	16 —	154979
98 —	119192	17 —	155387
99 —	120571	18 —	156219
1900 —	122834	19 —	156930
01 —	125630	20 —	158716
02 —	128942	21 —	159108
03 —	132213	22 —	159337
04 —	135524		

No further serial numbers were recorded until the discontinuance of the model, which was in 1935 at 159994.

Records at the factory indicate the following serial numbers were assigned to guns at the end of the calendar year.

MODEL 1885 SINGLE-SHOT

Year	Serial	Year	Serial
1885 —	1 to 375	1900 —	88501
86 —	6841	01 —	90424
87 —	18328	02 —	92031
88 —	30571	03 —	92359
89 —	45019	04 —	92785
90 —	None	05 —	93611
91 —	53700	06 —	94208
92 —	60371	07 —	95743
93 —	69534	08 —	96819
94 —	None	09 —	98097
95 —	73771	10 —	98506
96 —	78253	11 —	99012
97 —	78815	12 —	None
98 —	84700	13 —	100352
99 —	85086		

No further serial numbers were recorded until the end of 1923. The last number recorded was 139700.

Records at the factory indicate the following serial numbers were assigned to guns at the end of the calendar year.

MODEL 1876

Year	Serial	Year	Serial
1876 —	1 to 1429	1988 —	63539
77 —	3579	89 —	None
78 —	7967	90 —	None
79 —	8971	91 —	None
80 —	14700	92 —	63561
81 —	21759	93 —	63670
82 —	32407	94 —	63678
83 —	42410	95 —	None
84 —	54666	96 —	63702
85 —	58714	97 —	63869
86 —	60397	98 —	63871
87 —	62420		

Records at the factory indicate the following serial numbers were assigned to guns at the end of the calendar year.

MODEL 1873

Year	Serial	Year	Serial
1873 —	1 to 126	1897 —	513421
74 —	2726	98 —	525922
75 —	11325	99 —	541328
76 —	23151	1900 —	554128
77 —	23628	01 —	557236
78 —	27501	02 —	564557
79 —	41525	03 —	573957
80 —	63537	04 —	588953
81 —	81620	05 —	602557
82 —	109507	06 —	613780

Year	Serial	Year	Serial
83 —	145503	07 —	None
84 —	175126	08 —	None
85 —	196221	09 —	630385
86 —	222937	10 —	656101
87 —	225922	11 —	669324
88 —	284529	12 —	678527
89 —	323956	13 —	684419
90 —	363220	14 —	686510
91 —	405026	15 —	688431
92 —	441625	16 —	694020
93 —	466641	17 —	698617
94 —	481826	18 —	700734
95 —	499308	19 —	702042
96 —	507545		

No last number available: 1920, 21, 22, 23—720609.

Records at the factory indicate the following serial numbers were assigned to guns at the end of the calendar year.

MODEL 1866

Year	Serial	Year	Serial
1866 —	12476 to 14813	1883 —	162376
67 —	15578	84 —	163649
68 —	19768	85 —	163664
69 —	29516	86 —	165071
70 —	52527	87 —	165912
71 —	88184	88 —	167155
72 —	109784	89 —	167401
73 —	118401	90 —	167702
74 —	125038	91 —	169003
75 —	125965	92 —	None
76 —	131907	93 —	169007
77 —	148207	94 —	169011
78 —	150493	95 —	None
79 —	152201	96 —	None
80 —	154379	97 —	169015
81 —	156107	98 —	170100
82 —	159513	99 —	Discontinued

X

XL HOPKINS & ALLEN
Norwich, Connecticut

Derringer

A .41 caliber spur trigger single-shot pistol with a 2.75" octagonal barrel and either iron or brass frame. Blued, nickel-plated with rosewood grips. The barrel marked "XL Derringer." Manufactured during the 1870s.

Exc.	V.G.	Good	Fair	Poor
—	—	950	400	150

Vest Pocket Derringer

As above, in .22 caliber with a 2.25" round barrel and normally full nickel-plated. The barrel marked "XL Vest Pocket." Manufactured from 1870s to 1890s.

Exc.	V.G.	Good	Fair	Poor
—	—	600	275	75

XPERT HOPKINS & ALLEN
Norwich, Connecticut

Xpert Derringer

A .22 or .30 caliber spur trigger single-shot pistol with round barrels, 2.25" to 6" in length and a nickel-plated finish with rosewood grips. The breechblock pivots to the left side for loading. The barrel marked "Xpert-Pat. Sep. 23. 1878." Manufactured during the 1870s.

Exc.	V.G.	Good	Fair	Poor
—	—	750	300	75

Xpert Pocket Rifle

Similar to the derringer with the same size frame but fitted with a 7.5" barrel and chambered for the .22 cartridge, as well as the .30 caliber rimfire. Supplied with wire stock. Values are for gun with stock. Produced from about 1870 to 1890s.

Exc.	V.G.	Good	Fair	Poor
—	—	900	400	100

Z

ZOLI, ANTONIO
Brescia, Italy

Silver Hawk

A 12 or 20 gauge boxlock double-barrel shotgun produced in a variety of barrel lengths and chokes with a double trigger. Engraved, blued with walnut stock.

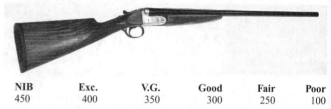

NIB	Exc.	V.G.	Good	Fair	Poor
450	400	350	300	250	100

Ariete M2

A 12 gauge boxlock double-barrel shotgun with 26" or 28" barrels, non-selective single trigger and automatic ejectors. Engraved, blued with a walnut stock.

NIB	Exc.	V.G.	Good	Fair	Poor
600	500	450	400	350	200

Empire

As above, in 12 or 20 gauge with 27" or 28" barrels. Engraved, French case hardened, blued with a walnut stock.

NIB	Exc.	V.G.	Good	Fair	Poor
1650	1450	1200	950	750	400

Volcano Record

A 12 gauge sidelock double-barrel shotgun with 28" barrels available in a variety of chokes, single-selective trigger and automatic ejectors. Engraved, French case hardened, blued with a walnut stock.

NIB	Exc.	V.G.	Good	Fair	Poor
5500	5000	4000	3000	2000	1000

SASS-Affiliated Clubs

The following information was taken from the official SASS website (sassnet.com)

 Denoted Mounted Shooting Event

ALABAMA

Club Name	When They Meet	Where They Meet	Contact	Phone Number
North Alabama Regulators	1st Sun	Scottsboro, AL	Six String	256-582-3621
Alabama Rangers	2nd Sun	Brierfield, AL	Major Dundee	205-988-3735
Vulcan Long Rifles	3rd Sat	Hoover, AL	Havana Jim	205-822-1799
Cahaba Cowboys	3rd Sun	Birmingham, AL	Fast Gun	205-980-0115
Old York Shootist	4th Sun	Oakman, AL	Pistoleer	205-680-1001

Photos courtesy North Alabama Regulators

ALASKA

Club Name	When They Meet	Where They Meet	Contact	Phone Number
Alaska 49er's	1st Sat, 3rd Sun	Anchorage, AK	David Cook	907-243-0181
Golden Heard Shootist Society	2nd Sat, Last Sun	Fairbanks, AK	Poco Loco Louie	907-488-7660
Juneau Gold Miners Posse	3rd Sat	Juneau, AK	C.W. Knight	907-789-2456

ARIZONA

Club Name	When They Meet	Where They Meet	Contact	Phone Number
Rio Salado Cowboy Action Shooters	1st Sat	Arizona Mesa, AZ	Lightning Jack	480-820-7372
Cochise Gunfighters	1st Sat	Sierra Vista, AZ	I.B. Good	520-366-5401
Cowtown Cowboy Shooters Assoc.	1st Sun	Cowtown, AZ	Barbwire	480-488-3064
Arizona Cowboy Shooting Assoc., Inc.	2nd Sat	Phoenix, AZ	Silver Hammers	480-595-8400
Pima Pistoleros Cowboy Action Shooter	2nd Sat	Tucson, AZ	Wander N. Star	520-744-3869
Dusty Bunch Old Western Shooters	2nd Sun	Casa Grande, AZ	Tom Thoresz	520-568-2852
Colorado River Regulators	2nd Sun	Lake Havasu City, AZ	Crowheart	928-855-2893
White Mountain Old West Shootists	3rd Sat	Snowflake, AZ	Timber Kid	928-368-8985
Altar Valley Pistoleros	3rd Sun	Tucson, AZ	Swift Water	520-883-1217
Mohave Marshalls	3rd Sun	Kingman, AZ	Mizkiz	805-399-0142
Tombstone Buscaderos	4th Sat	Tombstone, AZ	SixPak	520-743-0179
Colorado River Shootists	4th Sun	Yuma, AZ	Leon Wilmot	928-726-7727

ARKANSAS

Club Name	When They Meet	Where They Meet	Contact	Phone Number
Judge Parker's Marshals	1st Sat	Fort Smith, AR	Larry Duffy	918-647-9704
Mountain Valley Vigilantes	1st Sat	Hot Springs, AR	Christmas Kid	501-525-3451
Running W Regulators	1st Sat & 3rd Sun	Lincoln, AR	Arkansaw Mule Skinner	479-824-2590
Northwest Arkansas Range Riders Mounted	1st Sat & 3rd Sun	Lincoln, AR	Lester Whitney	479-824-2590
Critter Creek Citizens Vigilance Committee	1st Sun	Fouke, AR	Critter Creek Undertaker	903-838-8944
Peach Orchard Pistoleros	2nd Sat, 4th Sun	Bentonville, AR	Doc Sorebones	479-855-8793
South Fork River Regulators	3rd Sat	Salem, AR	Standing Eagle	870-895-2677
True Grit Single Action Shooters Club	4th Sun	Belleville, AR	Cathy Fulmer	479-968-7129
Bordertown, Inc.	State Championship	Tuscon, AZ	Mick Thames	520-883-1217

CALIFORNIA

Club Name	When They Meet	Where They Meet	Contact	Phone Number
Escondido Bandidos	1st Sat	Escondido, CA	J.W. Bass	760-789-5828
Lassen Regulators	1st Sat	Susanville, CA	Marshel Hankins	530-257-8958
California Range Riders–Mounted Shooters	1st Sat & 3rd Sun	Gilroy, CA	Old Buckaroo	408-710-1616
West End Gun Club	1st Sat & 3rd Sat	Lytle Creek, CA	Justin O. Sheriff	909-982-8162
5 Dogs Creek	1st Sun	Bakersfield, CA	Almost Dangerous	760-376-4493
The Hole In The Wall Gang	1st Sun	Piru, CA	Gun Hawk	818-761-0512
LC Cowboys	1st Sun	Winchester, CA	L.C. Smith	909-926-0070
Mother Lode Shootist Society	1st Sun	Jamestown, CA	Al Compasso	209-728-2226
River City Regulators	1st Sun	Davis, CA	J.C. Boggs	530-887-8646
Cajon Cowboys	2nd Sat & 4th Sat	Devore, CA	Bojack	760-956-5044
California Rangers	2nd Sat	Fair Oaks, CA	Mevin P. Thorpe	916-984-9770
Dulzura Desporado's	2nd Sat	Dulzura, CA	Tecolote Jack	619-987-9096
Palm Springs Gun Club	2nd Sat	Palm Springs, CA	Dick Folkers	760-340-0828
Shasta Regulators	2nd Sat	Burney, CA	Dave Boddy	530-275-3158
Roy Rogers Rangers Mounted	2nd Sat	Menifee, CA	Wildcat Kate	909-928-4601
Burro Canyon Gunslingers	2nd Sun	Orange, CA	Dennis Richardson	714-639-8723
Chorro Valley Regulators	2nd & 5th Sun	San Luis Obispo, CA	Fillmore Coffins	805-528-6705
Double R Bar Regulators	2nd Sun	Lucerne Valley, CA	Kentucky Gal	760-868-3685
Richmond Roughriders	2nd Sun	Richmond, CA	Buff Porcine	650-994-9412
Gold Field Monitors	3rd Sat	Oroville, CA	Darell Chenault	530-534-8359
NCSA Saddle Tramps	3rd Sat	Pala Reservation, CA	Harold Itchkawich	760-727-9160
Robbers Roost Vigilantes	3rd Sat	Ridgecrest, CA	Coso Kid	760-375-9519
Shasta Regulators	3rd Sat	Redding, CA	Silver Vern Garrett	530-474-3194

CALIFORNIA (cont.)

Photos courtesy Coyote Valley Regulators Mounted

Club Name	When They Meet	Where They Meet	Contact	Phone Number
Coyote Valley Regulators Mounted	3rd Sat	Gilroy, CA	Leroy P. Justice	408-842-6694
High Desert Cowboys	3rd Sun	Acton, CA	Michael Bossoni	661-948-2543
Kings River Regulators	3rd Sun	Clovis, CA	Slick Rock Rooster	559-299-8669
Murieta Posse	3rd Sun	Rancho Murieta, CA	Black Jack Traven	530-677-0368
Panorama Sportsman Club	3rd Sun	Sylmar, CA	Desperado	818-341-7255
Ukiah Gun Club	3rd Sun	Ukiah, CA	Will Bonner	707-462-1466
Hat Creek Rangers Mounted	4th Sat	Aguanga, CA	James Bell	909-763-1168
Brimstone Pistoleros	4th Sat	Devore, CA	Rowdy Yates	714-532-2922
Mad River Rangers	4th Sat	Blue Lake, CA	Kid Kneestone	707-445-1981
Fault Line Shootist Society	4th Sun	Gonzales, CA	Tie Long	408-226-8181
Fresno Stage Robbers	4th Sun	Fresno, CA	Steven Tiller	559-846-6341
The Cowboys	4th Sun	Norco, CA	Captain Jake	714-536-2635
The Range	4th Sun	Grass Valley, CA	Jerod Johnson	530-273-4440
Two Rivers Posse	4th Sun	Manteca, CA	David Barnes	209-477-8883
Malibu Desperados	As Scheduled	Malibu, CA	Doc Snakeoil Schulze	310-589-2111
California Desperados Mounted Shooters	As Scheduled	Acton, CA	Gentleman Joe	661-538-9826
Ghost Town Riders Mounted Shooters	As Scheduled	Norco, CA	Buck Cantrel	714-970-5767
San Juaquin Valley Rangers Mounted	As Scheduled	Stockton, CA	Jim Wild	209-941-4655
Way Out West Bunch	As Scheduled	Red Bluff, CA	Jeb Mcfoo	530-865-9586

COLORADO

Club Name	When They Meet	Where They Meet	Contact	Phone Number
Colorado Cowboys	1st Sat	Lake George, CO	Mule Creek	719-748-3398

COLORADO (cont.)

Photos courtesy Windy Gap Regulators

Club Name	When They Meet	Where They Meet	Contact	Phone Number
Windy Gap Regulators	1st Sat	Cortez, CO	Piedra Kid	970-565-9228
Colorado Shaketails	1st Sun	Ramah, CO	Yaro	303-646-3777
Castle Peak Wild Shots	1st Sun	Gypsum, CO	Old Squinteye	970-524-9348
San Juan Rangers	1st Sun	Montrose, CO	Sapinero	970-323-6566
Rifle Creek Rangers	2nd Sun	Rifle, CO	Charles Bolton	970-625-3710
Colorado Cowboys Mounted	2nd Sun	Lake George, CO	Mule Creek	719-748-3398
Four Corners Rifle and Pistol Club	2nd Sun	Cortez, CO	Mike Kelso	970-565-8960
Montrose Marshals	2nd Sun	Montrose, CO	Bob Eakin	970-249-7701
Mt. Princeton Outriders	3rd Sat	Nathrop, CO	Chuckwagon Chuck	719-539-4623
Pawnee Station	3rd Sat	Ft Collins, CO	Bob Reed	970-482-6165
Thunder Mountain Shootists	3rd Sat & 3rd Sun	Whitewater, CO	Pat Schutz	970-464-7118
Four Corners Gunslingers	3rd Sun	Durango, CO	Ruff Cobb	970-247-4386
Northwest Colorado Rangers	4th Sat	Craig, CO	Sagebrush Burns	970-824-8407
Shootists Society of Pawnee Sportsmens Center	4th Sat	Briggsdale, CO	General Mercantile	970-484-3789
Black Canyon Ghost Riders	4th Sun	Hotchkiss, CO	Double Bit	970-874-8745
Sand Creek Shadow Riders	As Scheduled	Byers, CO	Wildkat Mike	303-257-9565
Revengers of Montezuma Mounted	As Scheduled	Cortez, CO	Piedra Kidd	970-565-9228

CONNECTICUT

Club Name	When They Meet	Where They Meet	Contact	Phone Number
Congress of Rough Riders	1st Sun	Naugatuck, CT	Snake Eyes/Frank Tanner	203-386-9431
Bluffhead Bushwackers	2nd Sun	Guilford, CT	Glenn Johnson	860-663-1456

Photos courtesy Homesteaders Shooting Club

Homesteaders Shooting Club	3rd Sun	Ledyard, CT	Ken Sylvia	860-848-8451

DELAWARE

Club Name	When They Meet	Where They Meet	Contact	Phone Number
Padens Posse	3rd Sun	Seaford, DE	Deacon Will	302-422-6534

FLORIDA

Club Name	When They Meet	Where They Meet	Contact	Phone Number
Big River Rangers	1st Sat	Grand Ridge, FL	Nimrod Long	850-592-5665

Photos courtesy Gold Coast Gunslingers

Gold Coast Gunslingers	1st Sat	Ft. Lauderdale, FL	L.Topay	305-233-5756
The Polk County Crackers	1st Sat	Lakeland, FL	Dutch Wanigan	863-294-1589
Hernando County Regulators	1st Sun	Brooksville, FL	Yancy Jack Derringer	352-344-0912
The Hatbill Gang	1st Sun	Titusville, FL	Hoss McCabe	321-636-7099
Fort White Cowboy Cavalry	2nd Sat	Fort White, FL	Delta Glen	352-317-2357

Photos courtesy Okeechobee Marshals

Okeechobee Marshals	2nd Sat & 4th Sun	Okeechobee, FL	Black Hills Blacky	561-637-0349
Tater Hill Gunfighters	2nd Sun	Arcadia, FL	Judge JD Justice	941-743-4043
Weewahootee Vigilance Committee	2nd Sun	Orlando, FL	Weewahootee	407-857-1107

FLORIDA (cont.)

Club Name	When They Meet	Where They Meet	Contact	Phone Number
Lake County Pistoleros	3rd Sat	Tavares, FL	Brocky Jack Norton	352-253-2547
Martin County Marshals	3rd Sat	Palm City, FL	Papa Dave	561-747-7588
Miakka Misfits	3rd Sun	Myakka City, FL	Keokotah	941-748-5357
Southwest Florida Gunslingers	3rd Sun	Naples, FL	Carbon Steel	239-455-9452
Indian River Regulators	4th Sat	Palm Bay, FL	Burt Blade	321-242-8163
Panhandle Cattle Co.	4th Sat	Port St. Joe	Jack Hammer	850-785-6535
Cowford Regulators	4th Sun	Jacksonville, FL	Deadwood Jake	904-724-7012
Doodle Hill Regulators	4th Sun	Ruskin, FL	Dave Smith	813-645-3828
Five County Regulators	4th Sun	Punta Gorda, FL	Dead Shot Scott	239-261-2892
The Withlacoochee Renegades	Last Sat	Pinetta, FL	Hungry Bear	850-929-2406

GEORGIA

Club Name	When They Meet	Where They Meet	Contact	Phone Number
American Old West Cowboys	1st Sat	Flintstone, GA	Josey Buckhorn	423-236-5281
River Bend Rough Riders	1st Sat	Dawson County, GA	Jim Whitaker	770-442-8630
Lonesome Valley Regulators, Inc.	1st Sun	Macon, GA	Wishbone Hooper	478-922-9384
Keg Creek Renegades	2nd Sat	Sharpsburg, GA	Nooga Kid	770-460-0752
Pale Riders	2nd Sat	Mauk, GA	Injun John Irontree	229-649-6753
Valdosta Vigilance Committee	2nd Sat	Valdosta, GA	Big Boyd	229-244-3161
Bitter Creek Rangers	3rd Sat	Ft. Oglethorpe, GA	Cherokee Maddog	423-326-3759
Mule Camp Cowboys	3rd Sat	Covington, GA	San Quinton	706-335-7302
Doc Holliday's Immortals	4th Sat	Jonesboro, GA	Alabama Southpaw	770-631-0534
Cherokee Cowboys	4th Sat	Gainesville, GA	Southern Breeze	770-889-2434

HAWAII

Club Name	When They Meet	Where They Meet	Contact	Phone Number
Maui Marshals	1st Sat	Maui, HI	Bad Burt	808-875-9085
Big Island Cowboys	2nd Sat	Kona, HI	Cowboy Two Guns	808-325-2070
Maui Marshals	3rd Sat	Maui, HI	Bad Burt	808-875-9085
Single Action Shooters of Hawaii	4th Sun	Honolulu, HI	Clell Miller	808-923-9051

IDAHO

Club Name	When They Meet	Where They Meet	Contact	Phone Number
Panhandle Regulators	1st Sun & 3rd Sun	Bayview, ID	Rusty Buckets	208-687-0369
Squaw Butte Regulators	1st Sun & 2nd Sat	Emmett, ID	Acequia Kidd	208-365-4551
Northwest Shadow Riders	2nd Sat	Lewiston, ID	Silverado Belle	208-743-5765
Southern Idaho Rangers	2nd Sat	Pocatello, ID	Rattlesnake Jack Johnson	208-237-8782
Oregon Trail Rough Riders	2nd Sun & 3rd Sat	Kuna, ID	Pinkeye Pinkerton	208-658-0483
Twin Butte Bunch	3rd Sat	Rigby, ID	Judge M. Quick	208-745-0703
Snake River Western Shooting Society	4th Sat	Jerome, ID	P.G. Taylor	208-734-5011

IDAHO (cont.)

Club Name	When They Meet	Where They Meet	Contact	Phone Number
The Leesburg Vigilantes	4th Sun	Salmon, ID	Col. Wilbur Fisk Sanders	208-756-8037
Idaho Regulators	4th Sun	Gooding, ID	My Name Is Nobody	208-536-2641
Northwest Mounted Shooters	Sat	Cocolalla Creek, ID	Mrs. Remuda	208-773-7970

ILLINOIS

Club Name	When They Meet	Where They Meet	Contact	Phone Number
Rangeless Riders	1st Sat	Highland, IL	Inspector 'The'	618-345-5048
The Lakewood Marshals	1st Sat	Cisne, IL	Pine Ridge Jack	618-673-2568

Photos courtesy Boneyard Creek Regulators

Boneyard Creek Regulators	1st Sun	Murdock, IL	Kiowa	217-834-3774
Kishwaukee Valley Regulators	1st Sun	Sycamore, IL	Montana Mountain Man Mike	815-899-0046
Shady Creek Shootists	1st Sun & 4th Sun	Monmouth, IL	Dapper Dan Porter	309-734-2324
Effingham County Sportsman's Club	2nd Sat	Effingham, IL	Fossil Creek Bob	618-238-4222

Photos courtesy Illinois River City Regulators and Chillicothe Sportsmen's Club

Illinois River City Regulators	2nd Sun	East Peoria, IL	Chillicothe Outlaw	309-579-2443
Vermilion River Long Riders	2nd Sun	Streator, IL	Cole Blackheart	815-699-7056
McLean County Peacemakers	3rd Sat	Bloomington, IL	Marshal RD	309-379-4330
Nason Mining Company Regulators	3rd Sat	Nason, IL	Lowdown Highwall	618-279-3500
Illowa Irregulers	3rd Sun	Reynolds, IL	Sassparilla Ken	309-792-0111
Oak Park Sportsmen's Club	3rd Sun	Plainfield, IL	Lindsay Wales	815-744-4110
Marion County Renegades	4th Sat	Sandoval, IL	Shell Stuffer	618-822-6952

ILLINOIS (cont.)

Club Name	When They Meet	Where They Meet	Contact	Phone Number
Long Nine	4th Sun	Springfield, IL	Black Jack McGinnis	217-787-2834
Dewmaine Drifters	As Scheduled	Carterville, IL	Wounded Knees	618-997-4261
Midwest Firearms Association Mounted	As Scheduled	Quincy, IL	Cockrum	217-964-2433
Midwest Rangers, Inc. Mounted	As Scheuled	Rockford, IL	Thunderbird Kid	815-509-6375
Rock River Mounted Regulators	As Scheduled	Beloit, IL	Easy Pickens	608-676-2518

INDIANA

Club Name	When They Meet	Where They Meet	Contact	Phone Number
Cutter's Raiders	1st Sat	Warsaw, IN	Midnite Desperado	574-893-7214
Indiana Rough Riders Mounted	1st Sat	Rushville, IN	Marshal Cahill	812-438-4443
Thunder Valley	1st Sat & 3rd Sat	Campbellsburg, IN	Redneck Rebel	812-755-4237
Daleville Desperados	2nd Sat & 4th Sat	Daleville, IN	Swifty Smoothbore	765-378-5122
Schuster's Rangers	2nd Sun	Chesterton, IN	Coal Car Kid	219-759-3498
Indian Trail Ambush	3rd Sat	Modoc, IN	42044	765-853-1266
10 O'Clock Line Shootist Club	3rd Sun	Cayuga, IN	Bunsen Rose	765-832-6620
Big Rock SASS	4th Sat	Lexington, IN	South Paw Too	812-866-2406
Deer Creek Conservation Club	4th Sun	Jonesboro, IN	C. Bubba McCoy	765-948-4487
Wildwood Wranglers	4th Sun	Michigan City, IN	VOODOOMAN	219-872-2721
Circle C Cowboys	As Scheduled	Indianapolis, IN	Marshal J.J.Montana	317-842-7316
Red Brush Raiders	As Scheduled	Newburgh, IN	Nine Fingers Cosby	812-490-1009

IOWA

Club Name	When They Meet	Where They Meet	Contact	Phone Number
Iowa South West Shootist	1st Sun	Glenwood, IA	Robert Hall	402-291-2053
Iowa Frontier Cowboy Action Shootists	2nd Sun	Eddyville, IA	Hiram	641-673-8720
Zen Shootists	2nd Sun	Colfax, IA	Rhett Maverick	515-270-8654
Turkey Foot Cowboys	3rd Sat	Cedar Falls, IA	Cedar Falls Kid	319-266-5259

KANSAS

Club Name	When They Meet	Where They Meet	Contact	Phone Number
Butterfield Gulch Gang	1st Sun	Chapman, KS	Shylock	785-823-1333
Powder Creek Cowboys	2nd Sat	Lenexa, KS	Platte County Kid	816-505-9002
Millbrook Wranglers	2nd Sun	Hill City, KS	Glacier Grizz	785-421-3329
Sand Hills Regulators	3rd Sat	Hutchinson, KS	Sierra Joe	316-722-7896
Free State Rangers	3rd Sun	Parker, KS	O.D. Cleaver	913-541-9020
Capital City Cowboys	4th Sun	Topeka, KS	Kant Kount	785-266-6408

KENTUCKY

Club Name	When They Meet	Where They Meet	Contact	Phone Number
Hooten Old Town Regulators	1st Sat	Mckee, KY	Cherokee Big Dawg	606-633-7688
Kentucky Regulators Cowboy Action Shooters	1st Sat	Boaz, KY	Kentucky Drover	270-658-3247
Knob Creek Gunfighters Guild	1st Sun & 3rd Sat	Louisville, KY	Ranger W. B. "Tex" Bowdrie	270-828-4251
Crab Orchard Cowboy Shootist	2nd Sat	Clay KY	Rowdy Fulcher	270-389-9402
Kentucky Longrifles Cowboys	2nd Sat	Morehead KY	Hoss Lytle	606-784-0067
Ohio River Rangers	3rd Sat	Paducah KY	Jim Spears	270-443-5216
Lonesome Pine Pistoleros	3rd Sun	Blackey KY	Isom Kid	606-633-4465
Highland Regulators, Inc.	3rd & 4th Wknd (Sat & Sun)	Stearns, KY	Double Barrel Anderson	606-376-5836
Fox Bend Peacemakers	4th Sun	Lexington KY	Tioga Kid	859-377-9693

LOUISIANA

Club Name	When They Meet	Where They Meet	Contact	Phone Number
Up The Creek Gang	2nd Sat, 4th Sat	Lake Charles, LA	Slugs	337-439-4579
Bayou Bounty Hunters	2nd Sat	Covington, LA	Soiled Dove	985-796-9698
Cajun Cowboy Shooters Society	2nd Sun	Baton Rouge, LA	Steeleye Kid Shelleen	225-766-6111
Cypress Creek Cowboys LLC	2nd Wknd	Calhoun, LA	Trashy Tracy	318-644-5179
Deadwood Marshals	3rd Wknd	Sorrento, LA	Cajun Dove	225-751-8552

MAINE

Club Name	When They Meet	Where They Meet	Contact	Phone Number
Hurricane Valley Rangers	2nd Sun	Falmouth, ME	Garrett Slowhand Wade	207-786-8929
Capitol City Vigilance Committee	As Scheduled	Augusta, ME	Mark Lake	207-622-9400

MARYLAND

Club Name	When They Meet	Where They Meet	Contact	Phone Number
Thurmont Rangers	1st Sun	Thurmont, MD	Cody Conagher	301-624-4348
St. Charles Sportman's Club	2nd Sat	Waldorf, MD	Corn Dodger	301-423-7232
The Damascus Wildlife Rangers	4th Sat	Damascus, MD	Chuckaroo	301-831-9666
Potomac Rangers at SCSC	As Scheduled	Waldorf, MD	Baltimore Kid 'The'	410-257-3360

MASSACHUSETTS

Club Name	When They Meet	Where They Meet	Contact	Phone Number
Nashoba Valley Regulators	1st Sun	Harvard, MA	Texas Jack Black	978-874-6220
Gunnysackers	As Scheduled	Scituate, MA	Nantucket Dawn	781-749-6951
Mansfield Marauders	As Scheduled	Mansfield, MA	Mohawk Mac	508-761-5897
Shawsheen River Rangers	As Scheduled	Bedford, MA	Bill Batty	978-667-2219

MICHIGAN

Club Name	When They Meet	Where They Meet	Contact	Phone Number

Photos courtesy Rockford Regulators and Rockford Sportsman's Club, Ron Parker, Photographer

Club Name	When They Meet	Where They Meet	Contact	Phone Number
Rockford Regulators	1st Sat	Rockford, MI	Diewalker	616-837-0428
River Bend Rangers	2nd Sat	Buchanan, MI	Jonathan Slim Chance	574-277-9712
Sucker Creek Saddle & Gun Club	2nd Sat	Midland, MI	Rodeo Road	989-205-0096
Timber Town Marshals	3rd Sat	Midland, MI	Grizzly Bear Pete	989-631-6658
Hidden Valley Cowboys	3rd Sun	Sturgis, MI	Triple Creek Shorty	269-273-8334
Rocky River Regulators	3rd Sun	Utica, MI	MacKinaw Kid	248-852-0351
Eagleville Cowboys	4th Sat	Central Lake, MI	Kewadin Kid	231-264-8633
Johnson Creek Regulators	As Scheduled	Plymouth, MI	Cheyenne Raider	734-564-8391
Michigan Pistoleros	As Scheduled	Davison, MI	Dakota Doc	810-733-8454
The Double Barrel Gang	As Scheduled	Hastings, MI	Nitro Nellie	616-527-1531
Lapeer County Sportsmans Club Wranglers	As Scheduled	Lapeer, MI	Ricochet Bill	810-793-2376
Wolverine Rangers	As Scheduled	Port Huron, MI	No Cattle	616-361-6720
Saginaw Six-Shooters	As Scheduled	Saginaw, MI	Bad River Marty	989-585-3292

MINNESOTA

Club Name	When They Meet	Where They Meet	Contact	Phone Number
Crow River Rangers	1st Sun	Howard Lake, MN	Cantankerous Jeb	763-682-3710
Cedar Valley Vigilantes	3rd Sat	Morristown, MN	Mogollon Drifter	507-838-7334
Lookout Mountain Gunsmoke Society	3rd Sat	Virginia, MN	Wagonmaster	218-744-4694
East Grand Forks Rod & Gun Club	3rd Sun	East Grand Forks, MN	BB Gunner	218-779-8555
Ike's Clantons	4th Sun	New Ulm, MN	H.B. Lovett	507-354-1270

The Gun Digest® Book of Cowboy Action Shooting

MISSISSIPPI

Club Name	When They Meet	Where They Meet	Contact	Phone Number
Natchez Six Gunners	1st Sat	Natchez, MS	Winchester	601-445-5223
Mississippi Peacemakers	3rd Sat	Mendenhall, MS	Squinter	601-825-8640
Mississippi Regulators	4th Sat	McComb, MS	Lone Yankee	601-249-3315
Mississippi River Rangers	4th & 5th Sat	Byhalia, MS	Easy Lee	662-838-7451

MISSOURI

Club Name	When They Meet	Where They Meet	Contact	Phone Number
Moniteau Creek River Raiders	1st Sun	Fayette, MO	Monitor Creek	660-248-1816

Photos courtesy Rocky Branch Rangers

Club Name	When They Meet	Where They Meet	Contact	Phone Number
Rocky Branch Rangers	1st Sun	Higginsville, MO	Iza Littleoff	816-524-1462
Green Valley Raiders	2nd Sun	Hallsville, MO	T.J. Casino	573-696-3738
Gateway Shootist Society	3rd Sun	Louis, MO	Bounty Seeker	636-464-6569
Central Ozarks Western Shooters	3rd Sun	St. Robert, MO	X S Chance	573-765-5483
Southern Missouri Rangers	4th Wknd	Willard, MO	Smokie	417-759-9114

MONTANA

Club Name	When They Meet	Where They Meet	Contact	Phone Number
Sun River Rangers Shooting Society	1st Sun	Simms, MT	Hardtack Henry	406-727-7455
Honorable Road Agents Shooting Society	2nd Sat	Ennis, MT	Mt. 2 Steppn	406-682-7857
Rocky Mountain Rangers	2nd Wknd	Noxon, MT	Jocko	406-847-0745
Bigfork Buscaderos	3rd Sat	Bigfork, MT	Skalkaho Slim	406-857-3622
Last Chance Handgunners	3rd Sat	Boulder, MT	Montana Packer	406-443-0583
Rosebud Drygulchers	4th Sat	Forsyth, MT	Sgt. Blue	406-356-7885
Yellowstone Regulators	4th Sat	West Yellowstone, MT	Lonesome Lamar	406-646-4742
Greasy Grass Scouts	2nd Sun	Garryowen, MT	Prairie Annie	406-638-2438
Greasy Grass Scouts Mounted	As Sched	Garryowen, MT	Prairie Annie	406-638-2438

NEBRASKA

Club Name	When They Meet	Where They Meet	Contact	Phone Number
Alliance Rifle Club	1st Sun	Alliance, NE	Panhandle Slim Miles	308-762-7086

NEBRASKA (cont.)

Club Name	When They Meet	Where They Meet	Contact	Phone Number
Oregon Trail Regulators	2nd Sat	Scottsbluff, NE	Doc Viper	308-623-1797
Eastern Nebraska Gun Club	2nd Sun	Louisville, NE	Cherokee Gambler	402-639-4889
Flat Water Shootists	3rd Sun	Grand Island, NE	Scorpion Blain	308-226-2567
Turkey Creek Regulators Mounted	2nd & 4th Sat	Ohiowa, NE	Ira Shooter	402-629-4324

NEVADA

Club Name	When They Meet	Where They Meet	Contact	Phone Number
High Plains Drifters	1st Sun	Fernley, NV	Fernley	775-575-3131
Pahrump Cowboy Shooters Association	1st Sun	Amargosa, NV	Lash Latigo	775-727-8790
Eldorado Cowboys	1st Wknd	Boulder City, NV	Charming	702-565-3736
Nevada Rangers Cowboy Action Shooting Society	2nd Sun	Jean, NV	English Andy	702-648-6434
Roop County Cowboy Shooters Assn.	2nd Sun	Sparks, NV	Russ T. Chambers	775-747-1426
Desert Desperados	3rd Sun	Las Vegas, NV	Buffalo Sam	702-459-6454
Silver City Shooters Society	4th Sun	Indian Springs, NV	Oklahoma	702-657-8822
Silver State Shootists Club	4th Sun	Dayton, NV	Bull Moose	775-841-1928

NEW HAMPSHIRE

Club Name	When They Meet	Where They Meet	Contact	Phone Number
The Dalton Gang Shooting Club, of NH LLC	3rd Wknd	Dalton, NH	Littleton Sidecar Dalton	603-444-6876
Monadnock Mountain Regulators	Last Sun	Keene, NH	La Bouche	603-352-3290
Pemi Valley Peacemakers	As Scheduled	Holderness, NH	Captain Side Burns	603-539-4584
White Mountain Regulators	As Scheduled	Derry, NH	Callous Clyde	603-434-6026
Merrimack Valley Marauders	As Scheduled	Pelham, NH	Sheriff Rusty P. Bucket	603-881-3656
New Hampshire Mounted Shooters	As Scheduled	Holderness, NH	Richard Moody	603-487-3379

NEW JERSEY

Club Name	When They Meet	Where They Meet	Contact	Phone Number
Thumbusters	2nd Sun	Monmouth, NJ	Ol' Sea Dog	732-892-7272
Jackson Hole Gang	4th Sun	Jackson, NJ	Emberado	609-466-2277

NEW MEXICO

Club Name	When They Meet	Where They Meet	Contact	Phone Number
Magdalena Trail Drivers	1st Sat, 2nd Wed, 3rd Sat	Magdalena, NM	Slippery Steve	505-835-8664
Otero Practical Shooting Association	1st Sat	La Luz, NM	Alamo Rose	505-437-6405
Magdalena Trail Drivers Mounted	1st Sun	Magdalena, NM	Rimrock Mike	505-835-2623

NEW MEXICO (cont.)

Photos courtesy Gila Rangers

Club Name	When They Meet	Where They Meet	Contact	Phone Number
Gila Rangers	2nd Sat	Silver City, NM	Captain Eli McDaniel	505-388-4060
Seven Rivers Regulators	3rd Sat	Carlsbad, NM	Drop M'Dead Ted	505-885-2975
Lost Almost Posse	3rd Sat	Los Alamos, NM	Buncle Steve	505-662-6034
Rio Vaqueros	3rd Sun	Truth or Consequences, NM	More Or Les	505-744-5670
Rio Grande Renegades	3rd Sat & 4th Sun	Albuquerque, NM	Rancid Roy	505-898-4894
Tres Rios Bandidos	4th Sun	Farmington, NM	Long Step	505-325-4493
NRA Whittington Center Gun Club	As Scheduled	Raton, NM	Range Boss	505-445-4846

NEW YORK

Club Name	When They Meet	Where They Meet	Contact	Phone Number
Pathfinder Pistoleros	1st Sun	Fulton, NY	Sonny	315-695-7032
Bar-20 Straight Shooters	2nd Sat	Chittenango, NY	Renegade Ralph	315-363-5342
Boot Hill Regulators	2nd Sun	Chester, NY	Colonel Bill	845-354-4980

Photos courtesy Border Rangers

Club Name	When They Meet	Where They Meet	Contact	Phone Number
Border Rangers	2nd Sun	Greene, NY	Colesville Bob	607-693-2286
Hole In The Wall Gang	2nd Sun	Calverton Range, NY	Patchogue Mike	631-289-8749

NEW YORK (cont.)

Club Name	When They Meet	Where They Meet	Contact	Phone Number
Diamond Four	3rd Sat	Odessa, NY	Kayutah Kid	607-796-0573
Circle K Regulators	3rd Sun	Ballston Lake, NY	Annabelle Bransford	518-877-7834
D Bar D Wranglers	4th Sat	Wappingers Fall, NY	Jerimiha Bass	845-266-5722
The Long Riders	4th Sun	Shortsville, NY	Scruffy	585-787-0942
East End Regulators	Last Sun	West Hampton, NY	Diamond Rio	631-585-1936
The Shadow Riders	As Scheduled	West Hampton Beach, NY	Snake River Cowboy	631-477-1090

NORTH CAROLINA

Club Name	When They Meet	Where They Meet	Contact	Phone Number
Walnut Grove Rangers	1st Sat	Bostic, NC	Ross Rutherford	828-287-4519
Old Hickory Regulators	1st Sat	Rocky Mount, NC	Father Time	252-291-3184
Old North State Posse	1st Sat	Salisbury, NC	Buck Shot Bowers	704-278-1283
Carolina Rough Riders	1st Sun	Charlotte, NC	Pecos Pete	704-996-0756
Carolina Cattlemen's Shooting and Social Society	2nd Sat	Raleigh/Creedmore, NC	Reverend Will U. Sinmore	919-693-1644
Carolina Single Action Shooting Society	2nd Sun	Eden, NC	Carolina Kid	336-498-6449
Cross Creek Cowboys	3rd Sat	Fayetteville, NC	Grizzly Greg	910-424-3376
Gunpowder Creek Regulators	3rd Sat	Lenoir, NC	Horsetrader	828-754-1884
Piedmont Handgunners Assn.	3rd Sat	Lexington, NC	Tosco	336-249-0011
Bostic Vigilantes	4th Sat	Bostic, NC	Bostic Kid	704-434-2174
Iredell Regulators	4th Sat	Statesville, NC	Roy Rugers	803-927-4196

NORTH DAKOTA

Club Name	When They Meet	Where They Meet	Contact	Phone Number
Dakota Rough Riders	As Scheduled	Bismarck, ND	Yellowstone Vic	701-530-9227
Dakota Peacemakers	As Scheduled	Center, ND	Mark Montgomery	701-794-3391
Sheyenne Valley Peacekeepers	As Scheduled	Kindred, ND	Doc Neilson	701-588-4331

OHIO

Club Name	When They Meet	Where They Meet	Contact	Phone Number
Firelands Peacemakers	1st Wed, 3rd Sat	Rochester, OH	Johnny Shiloh	440-984-4551
Middletown Sportsmens Club, Inc.	1st Sat	Middletown, OH	Deadwood Stan	513-894-3500
Tusco Long Riders	1st Sat	Midvale, OH	Ol Smokeless	330-756-1004
Big Irons	2nd Sat	Middletown, OH	Deadwood Stan	513-894-3500
Sandusky Co. Regulators	2nd Sat	Gibsonburg, OH	Cat-Claw Shaw	419-862-2861
Ohio Valley Vigilantes	2nd Sat	Mt. Vernon, OH	Rowdy K	419-529-0887
Miami Valley Cowboys	2nd Sun	Piqua, OH	Buckshot Jones	937-615-2062
Scioto Territory Desperado's	3rd & 5th Sun	Chillicothe, OH	Lucky Levi Loving	740-745-1220
AuGlaize Rough Riders	3rd Sun	Defiance, OH	Bear River Smith	419-258-6483

OHIO (cont.)

Club Name	When They Meet	Where They Meet	Contact	Phone Number
Briar Rabbit Rangers	4th Sat	Zanesville, OH	Grizzly Killer	330-204-4606
1st Ohio Cowboy Mounted Shooting Association	As Scheduled	Middletown, OH	Tatonka Dan	513-932-1021

OKLAHOMA

Club Name	When They Meet	Where They Meet	Contact	Phone Number
Tater Hill Regulators	1st Sat	Tulsa, OK	Taos Willie	918-355-2849
Shortgrass Rangers	1st Sat & 3rd Sun	Grandfield, OK	Captain Allyn Capron	580-357-5870
Cherokee Strip Shootists	1st Sun	Stillwater, OK	Querida Kate	405-372-0208
Indian Territory Single Action Shooting Society	2nd Sun, 3rd Sat, 4th Wed & 5th Sun	Coweta, OK	Montana Dan	918-224-6292
Oklahoma Territorial Marshals	4th Sun	Oklahoma City, OK	Prospector	405-485-3406

OREGON

Club Name	When They Meet	Where They Meet	Contact	Phone Number
Orygun Cowboys & Cowgirls	1st Mon, 2nd Sun, & 3rd Sat	Portland, OR	Bart Star	503-391-8917
Merlin Marauders	1st Sat	Grants Pass, OR	Ten Sleep Good Guy	541-472-5123

Photos courtesy Dry Gulch Desperados

Club Name	When They Meet	Where They Meet	Contact	Phone Number
Dry Gulch Desperados	1st Sat	Milton Freewater, OR	G.D. Rimrock Goldvein	509-394-2418
Horse Ridge Pistoleros	1st Sun	Bend, OR	Big Casino	541-389-2342
Yamhill County Mounted Shooters	1st Sun	Yamhill, OR	Spotted Pony	503-662-3046

OREGON (cont.)

Club Name	When They Meet	Where They Meet	Contact	Phone Number
Siuslaw River Rangers	1st Sun	Florence, OR	Johnny Jingos	541-997-6313
Klamath Cowboys	2nd Sun	Klamath Falls, OR	Wimpy Hank Yoho	541-545-3120
Jefferson State Regulators	3rd Sat	Ashland, OR	Sourdough Smitty	541-826-2933
Oregon Trail Regulators	3rd Sat	La Grande, OR	Road Agent	541-963-2237
Oregon Old West Shooting Society	3rd Sun & 4th Sat	Albany, OR	Grizzly Wulff	503-390-1714
Fort Dalles Defenders	4th Sun	The Dalles, OR	Bad Eye Lefty	541-298-1457
Umpqua Regulators	4th Sun	Roseburg, OR	Big Lou	541-484-5900

PENNSYLVANIA

Club Name	When They Meet	Where They Meet	Contact	Phone Number
Hollidaysburg Sportsmen Club	1st Sat	Hollidaysburg, PA	Hidesman 'The'	814-535-1999
Perry County Regulators	1st Sat	Ickesburg, PA	Dutch P. Coaltrain	717-789-3893
Boothill Gang of Topton	1st Sun	Topton, PA	Lester Moore	610-821-8215
Whispering Pines Cowboy Committee	1st Sun	Wellsboro, PA	Mac Traven	570-723-8885
Logans Ferry Regulators	2nd Sat	Pittsburgh, PA	Mariah Kid	412-793-1496
Westshore Posse	2nd Sun	New Cumberland, PA	Doc Hornaday	717-432-1352
Mainville Marauders	2nd Sun	Mainville, PA	Gettysburg	570-387-1795
Dakota Badlanders	3rd Sat	Allentown, PA	Dakota Jack Gunfighter	610-837-8020
Jefferson Rifle Club, Inc.	3rd Sat	Jefferson, PA	Vermin	717-225-4119

Photos courtesy River Junction Shootist Society

River Junction Shootist Society	3rd Sat	Donegal, PA	Mattie Hays	724-593-6602
Blue Mountain Rangers	3rd Sun	Hamburg, PA	Diamond Rose	610-562-0314
Silver Lake Bounty Hunters	3rd Sun	Montrose, PA	Buckshot Blackman	570-663-3045
Purgatory	3rd Wknd	Titusville, PA	Dry Gulch Geezer	814-827-2120
El Posse Grande	4th Sun	Muncy Valley, PA	Black Hills Barb	570-538-9163
Elstonville Hombres	4th Sun	Manheim, PA	Basket Lady	717-949-3970
Stewart's Regulators	4th Sun	Shelocta, PA	Ellie Sodbuster	724-479-8838
Conestoga Wagoneers	As Scheduled	South Ampton, PA	Loose Change	215-497-9560
Cheyenne Mounted Shooting Group	As Scheduled	Douglas, PA	Hub Cell	215-538-1251

RHODE ISLAND

Club Name	When They Meet	Where They Meet	Contact	Phone Number
Lincoln County Lawmen	4th Sun	Manville, RI	Bill English	401-736-3400

SOUTH CAROLINA

Club Name	When They Meet	Where They Meet	Contact	Phone Number
Piedmont Regulators	2nd Sat	Anderson, SC	Montana Brown	864-233-1980
Hurricane Riders	3rd Sat	Aynor, SC	Chicora Kid	843-497-8560
Savannah River Rangers	3rd Sun	Jackson, SC	Creede Kid	706-860-0549
Geechee Gunfighters	4th Sat	Givhans, SC	Beau Knight	843-556-8737

SOUTH DAKOTA

Club Name	When They Meet	Where They Meet	Contact	Phone Number
Deadwood Seven Down Regulators	1st Sun	Spearfish, SD	Smallbore	605-578-2797
Cottonwood Cowboy Association	2nd Sat	Watertown, SD	J.D. Henry	605-886-7929
Black Hills Shootist Association	3rd Sun	Pringle, SD	Hawkbill Smith	605-342-8946
Bald Mountain Renegades	4th Sun	Faulkton, SD	Grease Cup	605-598-6744

TENNESSEE

Club Name	When They Meet	Where They Meet	Contact	Phone Number
Wartrace Regulators	1st Sat	Wartrace, TN	Sassy Lora	615-896-8450
Memphis Gunslingers	2nd Sat	Arlington, TN	Sagebrush Jim	901-380-5591
Smoky Mountain Shootist Society	2nd Sat	Knoxville, TN	Tennessee Tombstone	N/A
Greene County Regulators	3rd Sat	Greeneville, TN	Tennessee Deadeye	423-349-4924
Tennessee Mountain Marauders	3rd Sat	Dayton, TN	Big River Hondo	423-554-4485
Tennessee Trail Bums	3rd Sun	Manchester	Wiley Fish	931-728-5327
Ocoee Rangers	4th Sat	Cleveland, TN	Ocoee Red	423-476-5303

TEXAS

Club Name	When They Meet	Where They Meet	Contact	Phone Number
Comanche Trail Shootists	1st Sat	Midland, TX	John Larn	915-689-3444
South Texas Pistolaros	1st Sat	San Antonio, TX	Lady BJ	830-334-2546
Texas Rivera Pistoleros	1st Sat	Corpus Christi, TX	Sofilthy Odell Mcmeaness	361-991-7215
Texas Troublemakers	1st Sat	Brownsboro, TX	Lefty Tex Larue	903-849-2655
Orange County Regulators	1st Sat	Orange, TX	Huxley Strong	409-886-1692
El Vaqueros	1st Sun	Breckenridge, TX	Tom Donovan	254-559-9896
Texas Peacemaker	1st Wknd	Tyler, TX	Sundown Jim	936-564-1180
Old Fort Parker Patriots	1st Wknd	Groesbeck, TX	Slowaz Molasses	(254) 412-0904
Canadian River Regulators	2nd Sat	Clarendon, TX	Capshaw	806-335-1660
Texican Rangers	2nd Sat	Fredericksburg, TX	Lassiter Thunder	210-657-6538

TEXAS (cont.)

Club Name	When They Meet	Where They Meet	Contact	Phone Number
Travis County Regulators	2nd Sat	Smithville, TX	Shotgun Sally	512-694-6803
Bounty Hunters	2nd Sat	Levelland, TX	Cable Lockhart	806-299-1192
Texas Tenhorns Shooting Club	2nd Sun & Last Sat	Greenville, TX	Cole Bluesteele	817-577-1854
Lone Star Frontier Shooting Club	2nd Wknd	Ormsby Ranch, TX	Shadrack	817-297-9148
Oakwood Outlaws	2nd Wknd	Oakwood, TX	Texas Alline	903-545-2252
Big Thicket Outlaws	3rd Sat	Beaumont, TX	Shynee Graves	409-860-5526
Tejas Caballeros	3rd Sat	Austin, TX	Big Hext Finnigan	512-894-0897
Red River Regulators	3rd Sun	Texarkana, TX	Mr. Buffalo Dung	903-585-2873
Texas Historical Shootist Society	3rd Sun	Columbus, TX	Pepper Russell	713-723-0854
Comanche Valley Vigilantes	3rd Wknd	Glen Rose, TX	Nueces Outlaw	817-508-0774
Alamo Area Moderators	4th Sat	San Antonio, TX	Dusty Lone Star	210-680-8840
Butterfield Trail Regulators	4th Sat	Abilene, TX	Cob-Eye Zack	915-698-0685
Badlands Bar 3	4th Wknd	English, TX	T-Bone Dooley	903-628-5512
Tejas Pistoleros, Inc.	4th Wknd	Eagle Lake, TX	Texas Paladin	713-690-5313
Texas Regulators	4th Wknd	Magnolia, TX	Alsey Miller	281-391-2495
Jersey Lilly Shooting and Social Club	As Scheduled	Del Rio, TX	Ed Mcgivern	830-775-1983

UTAH

Club Name	When They Meet	Where They Meet	Contact	Phone Number
Big Hollow Bandits	1st Sat	Heber, UT	Marshal Diablo	435-654-3986
Copenhagen Valley Regulators	1st Sat	Mantua, UT	Sure Costalot	435-723-1947
Crow Seeps Cattle Company L.L.C.	1st Sat	Mayfield, UT	Blue John	435-528-3942
North Rim Regulators	1st Sat	Kanab, UT	Autum Rose	435-644-5053
Hobble Creek Wranglers	2nd Sat	Springville, UT	Utah Rifleman	801-489-5267
Rio Verde Rangers	2nd Sat	Green River, UT	Doc Nelson	435-564-8210
Dixie Desperados	2nd & 4th Sat	St. George, UT	Buzzard's Brat	435-986-9759
Diamond Mountain Rustlers	3rd Sat	Vernal, UT	Cinch	435-722-5118
Deseret Historical Shootist Society	3rd Sat	Layton, UT	Porter Rockwell	801-782-3049
Mesa Marauders Gun Club	3rd Sat	Lake Powell, UT	Happy Jack	435-979-4665
Roller Mill Hill Gunslingers	3rd Sat	Panquitch, UT	Widtsoe Kid	435-676-8382
Wasatch Summit Regulators	3rd Sun	Park City, UT	Chaos Kelly	801-255-7732
Castle Gate Posse	4th Sat	Price, UT	Cowboy Murder'n Maude	435-637-8209
Wahsatch Desperados	4th Sat	Kaysville, UT	Dally	801-967-5542
Utah War	5th Sat	Park City, UT	Jubal O. Sackett	801-944-3444

VERMONT

Club Name	When They Meet	Where They Meet	Contact	Phone Number
Verdant Mountain Vigilantes	1st Sat	Circle D Ranch Marshfield, VT	Slippery Slim	802-426-3824

VIRGINIA

Club Name	When They Meet	Where They Meet	Contact	Phone Number
Cavalier Rifle and Pistol Club	1st Sun	Richmond, VA	Kuba Kid	804-270-9054
Virginia City Marshals	1st Tues	Fairfax, VA	Virginia Vixen	703-455-4795
Hogtown Wild Bunch	1st Wknd	Lynchburg, VA	Curley Butch	434-528-8543
Blue Ridge Regulators	2nd Sun	Lexington, VA	Bad Company	540-886-3374
K.C.'s Corral	3rd Sat	Mechanicsville, VA	Virginia Jake	804-730-6341
Mattaponi Sundowners	3rd Sun	West Point, VA	Flatboat Bob	804-785-2575
Pepper Mill Creek Gang	4th Sun	King George, VA	Slip Hammer Spiv	540-775-4561
Roanoke Rifle and Revolver Club, Inc.	As Scheduled	Roanoke, VA	Beer Slinger	540-776-0057

WASHINGTON

Club Name	When They Meet	Where They Meet	Contact	Phone Number
Mica Peak Marshals	1st Sat & 3rd Sat	Spokane Valley, WA	Old Lead Spreader	509-926-3665
Renton United Cowboy Action Shooters	1st Sat & 1st Sun	Renton, WA	Jess Ducky	425-271-9286
North East Washington Regulators	1st Wknd	Colville, WA	B. B. Wolfe	509-722-4110
Black Rock Bunch	2nd Sat	Yakima, WA	Pataha	509-452-1181
Smokey Point Desperados	2nd Sun	Marysville, WA	Mudflat Mike	425-335-5176
Apple Valley Marshals	3rd Sat	East Wenatchee, WA	Silent Sam	509-884-3875
Ghost Riders-Snoqualmie Valley Rifle Club	3rd Sun	Snoqualmie, WA	Kwicksdraw Cuervo	425-222-6058
Black River Regulators	4th Sat	Littlerock, WA	Montana Slim	360-754-4328
Custer Renegades	4th Sun	Custer, WA	Fleetwood	360-318-9758
Webfoot Buckaroos	4th Sun	Poulsbo, WA	Alzada Slim	360-308-8384
Rattlesnake Gulch Rangers	Last Sat	Benton City, WA	Crisco	509-628-0889
Beazley Gulch Rangers	Last Sun	Quincy, WA	Caliche Jack	509-785-4503
Old West Cowboys & Guns Shooting Society	As Scheduled	Mill Creek, WA	Bear Britches	800-735-1348

WEST VIRGINIA

Club Name	When They Meet	Where They Meet	Contact	Phone Number
Shady Spring Shootist Society	1st Sat	Ghent, WV	Rat Killer	304-763-3951

Photos courtesy Kanawha Valley Regulators

Club Name	When They Meet	Where They Meet	Contact	Phone Number
Kanawha Valley Regulators	3rd Wknd	Elanor, WV	Shanghi Mike	304-925-3544
Cowboy Action Shooting Sports, Inc.	4th Sun	Berkeley Springs, WV	Last Word	304-289-6098
The Railtown Rowdys	As Scheduled	Bluefield, WV	Miss Print	304-589-6162

WISCONSIN

Club Name	When They Meet	Where They Meet	Contact	Phone Number
Rock River Regulators	1st Sat	Beloit, WI	Col. McKeever	608-756-5142
Cheyenne Regulators Mounted	1st Sat	Cheyenne, WI	Bruce Gorkowski	307-635-2332
Western Wisconsin Wild Bunch	2nd Sat	Holmen, WI	Sierra Jack Cassidy	608-788-6966
Bristol Plains Pistoleros	2nd Sun	Bristol, WI	Chicago Steely Bob	847-322-2647
Liberty Prairie Regulators	3rd Sat	Ripon, WI	Dirty Deeds	920-748-4833
Blue Hills Bandits	3rd Sun	Rice Lake, WI	Lone Lady	715-458-4841
Oconomowoc Cattlemen's Association	4th Sat	Oconomowoc, WI	Deuce Bisley	262-549-5828
Wisconsin Old West Shootist, Inc.	4th Sat	Boyceville, WI	Mississippi Traveler	715-262-4000
Twin Lakes Sportmans Club	4th Sun	Twin Lakes, WI	Lonny Ray	773-775-5261
The Pioneers	As Scheduled	Sharon, WI	Snapshot	262-882-5251
Good Guys Posse	As Scheduled	Sharon, WI	Longtooth	847-927-0664

WYOMING

Club Name	When They Meet	Where They Meet	Contact	Phone Number
Cheyenne Regulators, Inc.	1st Sat	Cheyenne, WY	Wolfer Charlie	307-635-9944
Cheyenne Regulators Mounted	1st Sat	Cheyenne, WY	Wolfer Charlie	307-635-9944
Colter's Hell Justice Committee WSAS	1st Sat	Cody, WY	Caprock	307-527-4213
Bessemer Vigilance Committee WSAS	1st Sun	Casper, WY	M.R. Fearnot	307-473-1013
Southfork Vigilance Committee WSAS	2nd Sun	Lander, WY	Sweetwater John	307-332-9203
Powder River Justice Committee WSAS	3rd Sun	Buffalo, WY	Red Angus	307-684-9473

INTERNATIONAL CLUBS

AUSTRALIA

Club Name	When They Meet	Where They Meet	Contact	Phone Number
Mount Rowan Rangers AUS	Sat	Ballarat	Brent Squires	613-5342-8400
The Wiski Mountain Rangers AUS	1st Sun	Melton	Brian J. Hare	039-772-4944
Bullet Spittin Sons O' Thunder NZ	2nd Sat	Palmerston North	The Hangman/Will Lynch	64-6-357-3109
Wass Of Nz NZ	2nd Sat	Palmerston North	Brian Pickett	61-6-356-9830
Wairarapa Pistol Club NZ	2nd Sun	Gladstone	Southern Cross	64-6379-8062
SSAA Western Action Australia AUS	2nd Sun	Mareeba	Virgil Earp	61-7-4093-9056
Adelaide Pistol & Shooting Club AUS	3rd Sun	Korunye	Bill Harding	61-8-8528-2268
Cowboy Action Shooters Australia AUS	3rd Sun	Beacon Hill	Mister Skye	02-9975-7983
Golden Downs Rangers NZ	3rd Sun	Wakefield	Byn Lawless	64-3541-8421
Tararua Rangers	3rd Sun	Carterton	J.E.B. Stuart	64-6-3797575
Fort Bridger Western Action Shooting Club AUS	4th Sun	Seymour	Duke York	61-3-9551-2902

CANADA

Club Name	When They Meet	Where They Meet	Contact	Phone Number
Waterloo County Revolver Association	1st Sat	Kitchener, Ontario	Ranger Pappy Cooper	519-863-3742
Mission Frontier Shootists	1st Sun	Mission, British Columbia	Gifford Gringo	604-855-4231
Wentworth Shooting Sports Club ONT	2nd Sun	Hamilton	Stoney Creek	1-905-560-8939
Otter Valley Rod & Gun Inc. ONT	4th Sun	Staffordville	Glen Foster	519-842-2142
Ottawa Valley Marauders	As Scheduled	Ottawa, ONT	Reverend Damon Fire	613-825-8060
Alberta Frontier Shootists	As Scheduled	Kelsey Alberta	Mustang Heart	780-464-4600
Western Canadian Frontier Shootists Society BC	As Scheduled	Victoria	Grey Fox	250-474-3244
Western Canadian Frontier Shootists Society BC	As Scheduled	Kamloops	Caribou Lefty	250-372-0416
Islington Sportmen's Club ONT	As Scheduled	Palgrave	Walter Yovdoshuk	905-936-6746

EUROPE

Club Name	When They Meet	Where They Meet	Contact	Phone Number
Western Shooting Club Stone Valley	Last Sat	Limburg, Netherlands	Pete Cody	31-4-6433-1075
Czech Cowboy Action Shooting Society	As Scheduled	South Bohemia, Czech Republic	George Roscoe	20-7-772-2024
Old West Shooting Society Switzerland	As Scheduled	Zurich, CH	Hondo Janssen	01-271-9947
SASS-Finaland	As Scheduled	Lahti, FN	Quincannon	35-8-400-470300
British Western Shooting Society	As Scheduled	Redcar, UK	Bob Dunkley	16-422-53-3333
Club Hipico Del Maresme	As Scheduled	Barcelona, Spain	Martin Rosell	34-3-759-1887
SASS Germany	As Scheduled	Regensburg, Germany	Santa Klaus	0049-941-24924
Sweetwater Gunslingers Austria	As Scheduled	Vienna, AT	Wyatt H. Ristl	+4312721278